A HISTORY OF ENGLISH LITERATURE
By Emile Legouis & L. Cazamian
In Two Volumes

A HISTORY OF
ENGLISH LITERATURE
THE MIDDLE AGES
AND THE RENASCENCE
(650–1660)

EMILE LEGOUIS

PROFESSEUR À LA FACULTÉ DES LETTRES DE PARIS, LL.D. (OXON.), LL.D. (GLASGOW).

Author of *Le Général Michel Beaupuy; La Jeunesse de Wordsworth; Chaucer; Spenser; Défense de la Poésie française; Wordsworth and Annette Vallon; Dans les Sentiers de la Renaissance anglaise*, etc.

LOUIS CAZAMIAN

PROFESSEUR À LA FACULTÉ DES LETTRES DE PARIS, LL.D. (ST. ANDREWS).

Author of *Le Roman social en Angleterre; Modern England; Carlyle; Etudes de Psychologie Littéraire; L'Evolution psychologique et la littérature en Angleterre*, etc.

A HISTORY OF
ENGLISH LITERATURE

BY

EMILE LEGOUIS & LOUIS CAZAMIAN

IN TWO VOLUMES

VOLUME ONE

THE MIDDLE AGES & THE RENASCENCE
(650–1660)

BY

EMILE LEGOUIS

Translated from the French by
Helen Douglas Irvine

New York

THE MACMILLAN COMPANY
1926

PRINTED IN GREAT BRITAIN

INTRODUCTION

THE literature of the English language, one of the literatures richest in original beauty, is the most extensive ever known to the world. Literary production in the past and the present, taken together, has attained to a greater mass in English than in any other tongue, ancient or modern. Long though this work be, it does not attempt to cover the whole field. It has confined itself to the English literature of the British Islands, leaving to others both the literature of the United States and the literature of the various British dominions, a vast subject which is growing with prodigious rapidity. Only by forgoing any picture of literary expression overseas, has it been possible to trace the history of English literature not too superficially, and to show its development coherently and harmoniously, because with unity of place.

This history was first written for the students of English who, year by year, are becoming more numerous in the universities of France. Its appeal was also to all those Frenchmen who have a curiosity regarding England and things English, who desire to reduce the results of scattered reading to order, to grasp the dominating features of succeeding periods and follow the reflection in books of the development of a great people. The authors had not the ambition to reach the English public, which was, they already knew, richly provided with histories of literature, both erudite and brilliant, ample or condensed, the productions of one or of several minds.

The expectation of the authors was therefore exceeded when their work was so favourably received in Great Britain that its translation into English was deemed desirable. It may be that their enterprise was thus fortunate partly because of the character they intentionally gave it. Their experience as university professors had warned them that, if they were to prepare their own students for knowledge of a foreign literature, they must take into account certain demands proper to the mentality of their nation: they must satisfy that need for connected composition, for the presentment of a chain of facts and ideas, without which the French do not easily assimilate the matter they study. The unforeseen result of the method they therefore pursued was that the English critics found in their book a certain novelty; they considered that even in English it would not overlap with any other work, but would be attractive and useful, Moreover, the authors' view of English

v

literature is that of outsiders, who are indeed fervent admirers of its strength and splendour, but yet have an independence of mind due to their foreign training, to the fact that they have not inherited nor been nurtured on this literature, but have approached it consciously and of deliberate choice, as men rather than as children, and their judgments may in consequence have an added impartiality, their praise more weight. In these ways there is compensation for the inevitable inferiority of a foreign historian, his lack of the instinctive, almost innate love, which immediately affects the subconscious mind and may inspire the critic of his own nation's work with some such moving, profound epithet as reveals the race. Duly conscious as they are of this original taint, the authors were the more pleased when they found their conception of English literature to be far from unacceptable to British minds. The agreement seems to them proof that the friendly effort they have made to penetrate the mysteries of an intellectual nationality, and to share it in so far as outsiders may, has not been entirely in vain.

It is true that the generous reception accorded to this book does not stand in isolation. French study of English literature has had no more valuable encouragement than the benevolent interest with which it has been followed in England during the last half-century and especially during the last thirty years. It is encouragement justly bestowed considering, merit apart, the lack of prejudice and the fervour, even enthusiasm, with which English is now studied in France.

Although the production of theses for the doctorate was naturally hindered for a time by the war, those existing already deal with all the various periods of English literature from the beginning to the present day. Among those of which the subjects are general, we find *The Feeling for Nature in Anglo-Saxon Poetry, The English Masques of the Renascence, The English Public and English Men of Letters in the Eighteenth Century, The Social and Literary History of the Town of Bath, English Poets and the French Revolution, The Sociological Novel in England in the Middle Nineteenth Century, The Influence of Science on the English Novel and on English Thought, Socialism and the Evolution of Contemporary England.*

More numerous are the monographs which have for subject Renascence writers, for instance John Lyly, Ben Jonson, Milton or Herrick, or writers of the classical period, such as Locke, Defoe, Swift, James Thomson, Edward Young, Horace Walpole, Wesley or Sterne, or Pre-Romantics like Cowper, Crabbe and Burns, or Romantics properly so called—Wordsworth, Shelley, Keats, Charles Lamb, or the so different Jane Austen and Sidney Smith, or again the moderns—Ruskin, Meredith, Thomas Hardy.

To these works, which go deep, cover their whole subject, derive from sources directly and often reveal new evidence or a new interpretation, which are erudite and yet aspire to a public beyond the initiate, English criticism has not been niggardly of approval. It has immediately admitted several of them to rank in their own sphere as classics, if the term may so be used, and has demanded and insisted that they be translated into English.

Our list has dealt only with the theses, the immediate fruits of academic labour. It might well have included the works which the same authors have written freely, and also those individual books of wider reputation to which the British public have finely rendered homage, Taine's work in a former day and now those of J. J. Jusserand and André Chevrillon.

The work now presented to the British public was thus born in a propitious atmosphere. It is no summary of the studies enumerated above, for it aspires to more than the mere noting of results obtained in France. It cannot therefore be said merely to focus the conclusions of earlier monographs. In its defects and its qualities it claims entire independence. Undoubtedly, however, its birth was encouraged by the ardent curiosity and sympathy which its subject aroused in France, and also, to a high degree, by the feeling that England herself looked favourably on French efforts to understand her mentality and interpret her literature.

E. L.   L. C.

The division of the book into two parts, the first dealing with origins, the Middle Ages and the Renascence, the second with the modern and contemporary periods, entails obvious differences of presentment and even of method. It would be vain to deny that they are partly due to the different habits of thought of the two authors. Yet even had the whole book been written by one man, he would have been led, almost inevitably, to pursue a different method in treating of the past and of the present.

The past has been for many years the material of scholars. Its literary monuments follow each other less closely and are less overwhelming in their bulk, but they are weighed down by commentaries, surrounded by exegetic works, which sometimes, especially in the case of the giants—Chaucer, Shakespeare, Milton—attain to truly formidable proportions. There is here no question of breaking new ground. The historian's task is to hew a way through all the barriers of earlier criticism, which yet must not be neglected, and attain to contact with the original works. It behoves him to use the best conclusions of his predecessors without repeating their accomplishment, for the publication of a new book is justified only if it make a new contribution to knowledge.

This, to particularise, is to say that every new French history of English literature must take into account two works, variously remarkable, among those which have in France been devoted to this subject. Taine's famous book, published in 1864, remains one of the most characteristic productions of this philosopher whose ideas left a profound imprint on the second half of the nineteenth century. The doctrine expressed in it, its brilliancy and vigour, and the author's reputation, will always find it readers, whatever progress time and the researches of scholars may bring to new histories of literature. It is desirable that Taine's luminous and enthralling book continue to introduce the English to French criticism, and there is no danger that oblivion will overtake this, one of the master achievements of an exceptional mind.

More recently Monsieur Jusserand returned to the same subject in his *Histoire littéraire du peuple anglais*, of which the first volume appeared in 1896 and the second in 1904. His work is conceived on quite other lines than Taine's. An historian first of all, whose scholarship is such that he has made numerous discoveries and closely discussed many special problems, he has painted with the greatest accuracy and picturesqueness England as she is revealed by her writers. To attempt to do over again what he has accomplished to such perfection would be no less vain than presumptuous. That he may be able to bring his solid and brilliant history down to the present day is much to be desired.

These two works have, the one of them mainly and the other exclusively, the same subject as the first part of the present book. Taine, writing sixty years ago, could not know the history which is contemporary for the men of our day. Moreover his picture, full enough for the earlier periods, leaves gaps with increasing boldness from the eighteenth century onwards. Thenceforward he supplies rather a series of brilliant articles than a complete, closely written and continuous story. As for Monsieur Jusserand, his history stops, so far, before Milton, about 1625.

The duty of him who travels the country crossed by these pioneers is surely not to follow in their footsteps, but to seek, as much as possible, the paths they have explored least willingly, the points of view which have most seldom been theirs. There is no occasion to attempt, after Taine, to rear an imposing determinist construction, to deduce, from categorical assertions on race, conditions and time, both the general characteristics of English literature and the special marks of the writers who made it. Against Taine's seductive and imperious theory strong objections have been raised, principally in the introduction to Auguste Angellier's *Robert Burns* (*Les Œuvres*, vol. ii.). To restate it in its entirety is no longer possible, and to revise it would change what is and should be a calm and free exposition of known facts into a long controversy. On the other hand, all who seek mainly to conjure up for themselves the manners, the institutions, and the life of the past, may be referred to the learned and vivid pages of Monsieur Jusserand's work, simply because it exists and admirably fulfils its author's purpose.

What seems not indeed to have been omitted, but to have been given a secondary place in both these histories, is the æsthetic aspect of their subject, and by divergence from them in this respect an essential task may be accomplished. It can be neither idle nor ill-timed to endeavour before all else in a history of literature to show the earliest signs, the early gropings, the progress and retrogression and the triumphs of the artistic sense. To this end the study of form is quite as important as that of thought or even feeling. The evolution of language, now slow, now quickened by a catastrophe of history, the formation or deformation of metre, the hardly won advances of prose, passing from its original aim of mere intelligibility to that of measure and beauty: these are subjects worthy of the leading place in a work on literature. It will be seen that the first part of the present book does not disregard ideas or, on occasion, historical considerations, but it does not make them its chief object. It does not seek them nor suffer itself to be detained by them for long, and it reserves the space, thus left free, for the direct presentment of significant works, describing their matter and their manner. Thus it is hoped that a useful complement to earlier histories of value has been supplied. These remarks apply to the first volume. The second, which follows its own method, has a separate introduction.

The translator deserves all thanks for the accomplishment of her difficult task. No less than her wide knowledge of English Literature and most patient industry was required to find out all the hints and allusions to the original writings scattered without any direct reference throughout the French text.

E. L.

LIST OF WORKS FOR GENERAL REFERENCE

THE history of English literature from the beginning to 1660 is traced in certain authoritative works, either entirely or almost entirely. To refer to them at the opening of each chapter would be wearisome. It has seemed better to give here a list of works which will not again be separately noticed unless they develop a particular point in a way not found elsewhere.

The Cambridge History of English Literature, 14 volumes (1907–16). The first seven volumes go down to 1660. Each volume contains excellent bibliographies.

Henry Morley, *English Writers*, 11 volumes (1887–95). This work ends about 1616, at Shakespeare's death.

W. J. Courthope, *A History of English Poetry*. The four first volumes, published from 1895 to 1903, go down to the end of the seventeenth century.

Chambers's Cyclopædia of English Literature, 1903 edition in 3 volumes. This is less a consecutive history than a collection of extracts. The first volume goes down to 1700.

B. Ten Brink, *Geschichte der Englischen Literatur* (1st part 1877, 2nd part 1893). English translation in Bohn's Standard Library in 3 volumes (1895–6). This incomplete work goes down to about 1550.

H. Taine, *Histoire de la Littérature anglaise*, 4 vols. (1864). The two first volumes go down to the Restoration, 1660.

J. Jusserand, *Histoire Littéraire du Peuple anglais* (1st vol. 1896, 2nd vol. 1904). At present this work stops at the end of the reign of James I., 1625.

The development of the language and literature cannot be better followed than in the texts published by the Clarendon Press:

Sweet, *An Anglo-Saxon Reader in Prose and Verse*.

Morris and Skeat, *Specimens of Early English*. Vol. i., 1150–1300; vol. ii., 1298–1393.

W. W. Skeat, *Specimens of English Literature*, 1394–1578.

Biographies of authors will be found in the *Dictionary of National Biography*.

CONTENTS

BOOK I

ORIGINS

BOOK II

THE FOURTEENTH AND FIFTEENTH CENTURIES (1350–1516)— FROM CHAUCER TO THE RENASCENCE

BOOK III

THE PREPARATION FOR THE RENASCENCE (1516–78)

BOOK IV

THE FLOWERING OF THE RENASCENCE (1578–1625)

CONTENTS

BOOK V

THE END OF THE RENASCENCE (1625–60)

HISTORY OF ENGLISH LITERATURE

BOOK I

ORIGINS (650–1350)

CHAPTER I

ANGLO-SAXON LITERATURE (650–1066)

1. That Anglo-Saxon Literature is distinct from English Literature.—Until recently the English looked upon Chaucer as the father of their poetry. They discovered the earliest source of their literature in that fourteenth century in which, on British soil, the fusion of the Anglo-Saxons and the Franco-Normans was consummated. To-day they trace their literary origins back to the seventh century. They give out that Cædmon and the unknown author of *Beowulf* were their first poets, and would go beyond these were it not that they lack older monuments. The stages and the motives of this recession in conquest of the past are curious.

From the time of the battle of Hastings in 1066 until the religious reformation of the sixteenth century, works prior to the Norman Conquest lay forgotten in cloisters where they were deciphered only by a few monks among whom knowledge of the former language was traditional. The dissolution of religious houses resulted in the loss of a large number of these documents, but, in compensation, it brought to light others to which a few scholars turned their attention. At first, especially for polemical reasons, they were concerned only with the religious and historical origins of the nation, or else with the characters of the language in which the documents were written, but gradually, after the charters and the books of devotion, old works of literature were explored, and some sort of collection of poets was made. The idea arose that a real national literature had flourished before the Norman invasion. There was, in the beginning, no thought of identifying it with English literature, properly so called, and it was known as Saxon or Anglo-Saxon, words which marked it as separate and distinct. But during the last sixty years or so, the correctness of these very words has been disputed; they have been criticised as cutting what was an indivisible whole into two parts, and many scholars of the present day speak instead of old or primitive English literature. To the question—When does English literature begin?—they answer unhesitatingly that it begins with the first verse sung, the first line written in a Germanic tongue in the country now called England.

It may be that, unknown to themselves, this answer has been dictated as much by sentiment as by history. Until Germany had given evidence of her power in the world of intellect, England seems to have been at little pains to discover the expression of her national genius in the works which the Anglo-Saxons have left behind them. It was Germany, in her desire to prove her near kinship with the people who had produced Shakespeare and Milton, who made all the advances. Afterwards, the glory won by the Germans at the end of the eighteenth century in the fields of letters and philosophy, together with hostility to the France of Voltaire and Napoleon, inclined the English to strengthen those distant ties of intellectual kinship which bound them to the Germans, a new tendency first noticeable in the works of Coleridge, De Quincey and Carlyle. The political prosperity and growing military power of Germany ensued in the second half of the nineteenth century, and they had an influence which was decisive. It was at the very moment at which defeated France was submitting to the Treaty of Frankfort that German and English philologists began to suspect the legitimacy of the word Anglo-Saxon, and extended the word English to cover all the language spoken and all the literature written in Great Britain from the time of the Germanic invasion, thus implying that linguistic and literary progress had suffered no interruption important enough to make the use of distinct terms necessary.

This tendency met with an unconscious ally in democratic sentiment, then in vigorous and umbrageous growth, which made in England a rough distinction between two castes, the caste of the Franco-Normans which was the aristocracy, and that of the Saxons with which the whole remainder of the people were identified. Every loss of prestige to the former class, every doctrine which tended to give it an adventitious and foreign character, could not fail to please the majority.

At the same time the love, even infatuation, for the "gothic," with which romanticism slowly infused all Europe, had exalted the most mutilated products of the Middle Ages at the expense of the so-called classical literatures, and had even gone so far as to surround the works of the barbarous ages with prestige. Works hitherto unknown or despised had been revealed as real treasures, glorious to appropriate. What Addison rather contemptuously called the "Gothic manner in writing" (*Spectator*, No. 70) had come to be admired by artists. It was a new enticement to the English to annex the most copious mediæval vernacular literature which had been preserved before those of Scandinavia or France.

Philology countenanced the annexation with its high authority. It placed beyond dispute the essentially German character of the English language. It proved, with the help of rediscovered texts, that the absorption into the old Germanic framework of foreign words, whether French or Latin, was progressive although considerable, that here and there the frames were perhaps strained or broken, but that they nevertheless subsisted. Philology, with its attentive lens, caught the slight successive modifications of speech, found nowhere a break in continuity, and concluded that there was a hidden unity behind the slow changes.

The transition from philology to literature seemed easy, and for many critics of the present day the distinction, formerly admitted, between Anglo-Saxon and English literature has ceased to exist. If terminology alone were in question, to waste time on assent or contradiction would be puerile. But the new doctrine obscures fundamental truths. For it is the property of the scientific study of languages to show that every seeming revolution in speech derives from an unnoticed gradual process. Philology succeeds unfailingly, where there is not a lack of texts, in proving that no sudden break exists anywhere in language. If supplied with texts, it will trace language back to Adam. But reflection shows that it would be as wrong, on this account, to give different names to Latin and the Romance languages, and to the literature of ancient Rome and the literatures of the nations now called Latin, as to Anglo-Saxon and English. Whither might not such a conception lead? To broaden meaning until all necessary distinctions are lost, is, in this instance, to forget that variations of language, however gradual, have finally such a cumulative effect that they render one age incomprehensible to another, although the two be undeniably connected by a progressive linguistic evolution. However it may be with the English language, there is no other literature which has lived and developed in as much ignorance of its indigenous past as English literature. Italian and French were never quite weaned of their maternal Latin, but Anglo-Saxon literature, when the first great literary works of the fourteenth century appeared, was not only dead, but also unknown; its documents had been buried deep; they were written in a language which had become unintelligible, and could therefore exert no possible influence. The true unity of a literature is constituted by the persistence of a language which remains fairly intelligible from one age to another, and by the succeeding and more or less active influences, sometimes manifest and sometimes hidden, but none the less continuous, of the works which are literary landmarks. If this be so, Anglo-Saxon literature cannot be an integral part of English literature. It has rightly no other relation to English literature than the life of his father or mother has to the life of the hero of a biography.

It is the prologue rather than the first chapter of the book. Yet this prologue happens here to be indispensable. For if the Latin antecedents of Romance literatures are deposited in Latin literature, Anglo-Saxon literature is too slender and too special to have, at least for Frenchmen, its special place. Its most natural place is at the approach to English literature, its mere descendant, yet a descendant having certain derived characteristics and certain deep feelings which cannot be well understood until their germ has been descried in Anglo-Saxon works. Thus the right of Anglo-Saxon literature to open a history of English literature is again established, together with the justice of the term Anglo-Saxon.

2. Anglo-Saxon Literature is not a direct expression of the Pagan Age.— The Anglo-Saxon literature which has reached us is, on the whole, the work of clerks who lived from the seventh to the eleventh century. If they did not create all of it, they preserved it all. It is therefore an essentially Christian literature. The editors allowed nothing to survive which seemed to them to conflict formally with their religion. Hence came a vast elimination of which we cannot even conjecture the importance. Hence also arose modifications and amplifications of such of the old legends as were not sacrificed, changes which gave them an edifying turn certainly not theirs originally.

It is among these clerks that we must first place ourselves to understand not only the pages which emanated from them directly, but also the character and tone of the older fragments which they spared.

Let us go back to the end of the seventh century. The conquest had reached its term. Driven forward by the Huns, the Germanic tribes dwelling between the Elbe and the Oder and along the Danish coast, had invaded the eastern territory of Great Britain and held it for 200 years. The Angles were masters of the land north of the Humber, the Jutes of the land of Kent, and the Saxons of all the remaining country south of the Thames. Pagans at their arrival, these peoples had undergone mass-conversion at the end of the sixth century, and the first dated writings appeared at the end of the seventh.

The oldest collections of laws show a civilisation which was already considerable and was permeated by the spirit of Christianity. The Anglo-Saxons were already a settled people, tillers of the soil, enjoying protection against theft and plunder, and an organised justice which deprived the individual of the right to vengeance and, as much as possible, substituted fines for corporal punishment. In each state a hierarchical society, in which centralisation and democratic institutions were happily balanced, had been established.

Nothing is therefore more illusory than to take the extant Anglo-Saxon literature for a primitive product, and to seek in it the reflection of Germanic barbarism. To blend the romantic picture Tacitus gives us of the first-century Germans with the picture of England in the eighth century is equivalent to placing on one plane the *Hymn of the Fratres Arvales* and the Æneid. In the pages of the Latin historian the remote germs of English political institutions or family customs may be discerned, but we must relegate to a dead past his descriptions of savages who went half-naked or clothed in the skins of wild animals, whose sole occupations were war and hunting, those nomads incapable of prolonged labour who lived in sordid huts and caves, whose indolence kept them cowering by their hearths for days together, who knew nothing of agriculture and despised it. There is no relevance in what Tacitus tells of the religion of these tribes, their gods who corresponded to Mercury, Mars and Hercules, their cult of Ertha, the Earth Mother, the forests of their superstition in which their atrocious human sacrifices were consummated. These particulars are such as characterise any people not yet civilised. They are doubtless interesting to know, but they belong to conditions of an earlier society which linger only vaguely in the memory of the age of civilisation. Between the time of which Tacitus speaks and the period of the Venerable Bede, the Angles and Saxons underwent transformations compared to which all the revolutions of their later history, even the Norman Conquest, were trifling. They experienced migration and contact with a population of another race, the partially Romanised Celts, they relinquished a half-nomadic life for a life concentrated in fixed places, they exchanged war, misery and famine for a state of relative peace and prosperity, and finally they underwent a deep and fervent mass conversion to Christianity, which disorganised the system of morals while it reformed it, which brought the clerks into communion with Latinity, and which severed most bonds with the still pagan Teutonic world.

During these convulsions, nearly every possible survival of primitive poetry was uprooted, together with the mythology on which it rested. The mythology of which Tacitus speaks, the gods Tuisco and Mannus, can and even should be forgotten by whoever wishes to understand *Beowulf*. The names of the deities had ceased, when *Beowulf* was written, to have interest for anyone but a philologist, who might note the traces they had left in language, particularly in the names of the days of the week. The ancient rites had been totally submerged, save for some local practices or magic formulas or charms, which often had an alloy of Christian words, such survivals as folklore discovers to this day in the remote countrysides of Europe. Only traces of savage customs were to be observed, or such sporadic revivals of barbarism as the reigning code condemned. Everything derived from the barbaric past had been purified and ennobled, and also enervated, in an atmosphere of Christianity which already was almost one of chivalry.

It is no less dangerous to merge in a single whole Anglo-Saxon poetry and the poetry of the Scandinavians, or continental Germanic poetry where it was still pagan. The *Niebelungenlieder*, although compiled at a later date, give, at least in the Hagen epic, a powerful picture of the warlike furies and the atrocious vengeances of the earliest ages. Nothing like or approximating to them is to be found in the whole body of Anglo-Saxon verse. Scandinavia and Iceland preserved in the *Edda* and in their prose sagas abundant characteristics belonging to primitive beliefs and customs. In spite of manifest likenesses of form and versification, sometimes amounting to identity, the content of their legends is in extreme contrast with Anglo-Saxon literature. In the *Edda* there is perfect harmony between the fabulous, immense, strange subject-matter and the vehement style. In Anglo-Saxon poems the excessiveness for the themes of the traditional form, the disparity of dulcified subjects and verbal violence, is immediately striking. The *Edda* is full of allusions to a mythology of extravagant proportions, to legends which may not be preserved in their original integrity, but of which the spirit at least is kept, and seems, indeed, to be strengthened rather than softened. The *Edda* presents, in abbreviated form, powerful dramatic pictures of fights between barbarous men, and of struggles between gods yet more barbarous and unbridled than the men. No wish to edify seems to have dominated or restrained the poet. At one time he gives full rein to his imagination, at another his realism is intense. He shows barbarism by turns in its acts and in its visions. But Anglo-Saxon poetry, taken as a whole, is a continuous piece of edification, elegiac in its dominant tone. It is a long Christian lamentation breathed by ingenuous and fervent men.

3. **The Anglo-Saxon Latinist Clerks : Aldhelm, Bede and Alcuin.**[1]— Before dealing with the Anglo-Saxon poetical texts which seem most ancient, it is necessary to recall the Christian Latinists, about whom alone we have precise data. To them and to those like them we owe the preservation of the traces of primitive poetry. They spoke the native language and often themselves wrote verses in the vernacular, and in their Latin writings customs are indicated and scenes are sketched which reveal the life of their times more clearly than does Anglo-Saxon poetry. Sometimes, moreover, through their Latin, the imaginative background of their race makes itself felt with singular force, so that the characteristics of the national literature can thus be better understood.

The migration of the Germanic peoples into Great Britain was still in process when Christianity was first introduced among them. As early as 597, the monk Augustine came from Rome to convert them and founded in Kent, where the Jutes had established themselves, the church of Canterbury.

At much the same time, Christian Ireland was sending missionaries to the Angles, and was building the monasteries which were the earliest civilising influences in Northumbria. From these two centres Christianity spread among the Saxons who were occupying the south and west of the island, that is from centres diverse as the mother-churches whence they sprang. Their differences led to a struggle for supremacy which lasted until in 664 the Synod of Whitby gave Rome the victory over Ireland. The distinction between the two disciplines subsisted, however, for a much longer time, and two distinct spirits are revealed in Christian writings, according to whether they emanate from the north or from the south, and are apparent through the Latin which was the invariable medium of the clerks.

Aldhelm (650?–709) was a product of the school of Canterbury. He was the pupil there of Abbot Hadrian, an African monk, and of Theodore, the Greek monk of Tarsus. A Saxon of noble birth, Aldhelm is said to have been a successful poet in the vernacular, but only his Latin works are extant. As abbot of Malmesbury, and afterwards as bishop of Sherborne, he was at once a saintly prelate and a humanist. He was as conversant with the Latin poets of the classical and of later periods as with the Scriptures and the writings of the Fathers. He was a seventh-century stylist, an artist who was at once a Barbarian and a refined scholar. It is strange to find the expedients of Anglo-Saxon rhetoric intruding themselves into his Latin works, which abound, to an amusing degree, with alliterations and in which he indulges all his Anglo-Saxon taste for imagery and periphrasis. As a rule, he addresses himself to ladies, that is to nuns, and there is a curious coquetry in his discourses to them. It is the praises of virginity which he indites in prose, the praises of virgins in hexameters. His Latin is grammatically correct to a point which is rare at the end of the seventh century, but his origin is revealed by his too heavily decorated style, by his violent and numerous metaphors and by his habit of materialising the abstract. He alludes, for instance, to

---

[1] The works of Aldhelm, Bede and Alcuin are included in Migne's *Patrology.*

the golden necklace of the virtues, the white jewels of merit, the purple flowers of modesty, the swanlike whiteness of old age, and he speaks of "the opening of the gates of dumb silence," "the shining lamps of chastity in which the oil of modesty burns," "the unclean sink of impurity in which the vessels of the soul are miserably engulfed," "the bastion of the Catholic faith shaken by the war-machines of secular arguments and overthrown by the battering-rams of atrocious ingenuity." These images are the very web and woof of his prose. The same characteristics reappear, with less startling effect, in his verse. His riddles, which have a place between the riddles of Symposius and the Anglo-Saxon riddles of which we shall speak later, are ingenious and sometimes graceful. In his taste for riddles, as in his passion for metaphors, the Latinist Aldhelm betrays his origin.

The great Latinist of Northumbria, the Venerable Bede, affords a striking contrast to Aldhelm. Whatever may be thought of his taste, Aldhelm was first of all an artist with whom manner has precedence over matter. But of Bede (672–735) the reverse is true. This Angle, who was brought up in Wearmouth Abbey, and spent his whole adult life in the monastery of Jarrow, was the most learned theologian and the best historian of Christianity of his time. He absorbed and he summed up in himself the culture of an age which had lost its continental inheritance. The variety of his knowledge and his interests appears in the subjects of his princi-pal works—a treatise on metre, a natural history, a universal chronology of the Christian era, based on serious astronomical studies, a martyrology, lives of the abbots of Wearmouth and Jarrow, a life of Saint Cuthbert, above all, the *Ecclesiastical History of the Angles*.

The historical and biographical works are the most interesting for us. They are distinguished by an honest love of truth and by diligent documentary research. Bede's conceptions and style are impersonal, clear, simple, much above the level of his time. His pre-eminence is one of intelligence. He informs on points of fact and he interprets manners and customs. His *Ecclesiastical History* is still the chief authority for the early period of which it traces the history from a religious point of view, the years between Julius Cæsar's conquest and 731, that is four years before the author's death. The conversion and the struggle between the Roman and the Irish Church and final triumph of the former, are its principal themes. Yet Bede, the historian and learned man, has been too exclusively praised. His extreme simplicity, which is in so great contrast to the artificiality of Aldhelm, and the weakness of his surviving Latin verses, have done harm to his literary reputation. In Bede, more than in any other Anglo-Saxon Latinist or any vernacular poet, the poetry, the charm and the meaning of this age of early Christian fervour are to be found. The spirit of his lives of saints and abbots and his *Ecclesiastical History* is more intimate and penetrating than any which breathes in other works. His direct narration of facts, and the marvels of an artless faith in which he clothes them, are far more eloquent than all the effusions and the paraphrases of the poets. Moreover, Bede, like Aldhelm, was a student of vernacular verse of which his lucid reason enabled him to interpret the genius. The whole of the so-called Cæd-monian epic could better be spared than those few bald pages in which Bede tells us how the poor peasant Cædmon received his inspiration. All the verses of Cyne-wulf taken together would be poor compensation for the ensuing scene, which has been quoted over and over again and can never be quoted too often. It occurs in the account of the conversion of Northumbria in 633. When Ædwin and his nobles had been asked to embrace Christianity, one noble spoke as follows:

"So, O king, does the present life of man on earth seem to me, in comparison with the time which is unknown to us, as though a sparrow flew swiftly through the hall, coming in by one door and going out by the other, and you, the while, sat at meat with your captains and liegemen, in wintry weather, with a fire burning in your midst and heating the room, the storm raging out of doors and driving snow and rain before it. For the time for which he is within, the bird is sheltered from the storm, but after this short while of calm he flies out again into the cold and is seen no more. Thus the life of man is visible for a moment, but we know not what comes before it or follows after it. If, then, this new doctrine brings something more of certainty, it deserves to be followed."

Nowhere else is there anything at once so exact and so ample. The image is as great as it is intimate, precise although mysterious. Shakespeare never produced one which was more striking or which better conveyed the feeling of life's strangeness. Nothing equal to it is to be found in the whole of Anglo-Saxon poetry.

It is true and characteristic, if a fact of undetermined importance, that Bede was the disciple of the Irish monks settled in Wearmouth and Jarrow. The pious simplicity of the way of life in these monasteries, a simplicity they created, remained dear to him. Although he rallied to allegiance to the Church of Rome, he never stifled regret for the pleasant days of his youth, and the Celts or Gaels who were his masters can hardly be denied an important share in the training of his fine mind. To acknowledge this is to touch the insoluble problem of what influence the Celtic spirit secretly exercised on extant Anglo-Saxon poetry.

The illustrious Alcuin (730?–804), Charlemagne's collaborator from 790 onwards, also came out of Northumbria. He was brought up in York. Northumbria gave this great clerk to a France which had relapsed to barbarism. Alcuin left his country when the earliest civilisation of the Angles was about to be extinguished, for the terrible Danish invasions, which ruined monasteries and centres of learning, were beginning. Although as much of Alcuin's life as is historical was spent among the Franks, he stayed in his own country until he was sixty years old, and is therefore a representative, and a brilliant one, of the culture and the mentality of the Angles. His Latin poetry is less correct but more personal than Aldhelm's and sometimes has a fine ring. He finds moving distichs in which to bid farewell to his monastic cell before he leaves it for the court, and that cell, giving on to a blossoming orchard and green lawns, beside a stream, seems indeed to have been a place to regret. He sighs as he reflects that another will occupy it, that he will no longer be able to meditate verses in it, yet he recollects that all in this world is fleeting, that such is the common lot.

Many lines of his work are addressed to Charlemagne, whom he celebrates under the name of David, or compares to Homer, himself assuming the name of Flaccus (Horace). It is, however, his prose which is of special interest to us. Alcuin, writing prose, is an educationist who resumes all branches of knowledge in manuals. He treats grammar, rhetoric, dialectics and the rest in the form of dialogues or catechisms, having questions and answers. Sometimes the conversation is between a young Saxon and the young Frank whom he teaches, sometimes between Alcuin and Charlemagne himself, sometimes between Alcuin and his pupil Pepin, the emperor's son. Often the questions are very like riddles, a proof of the strong Anglo-Saxon taste for those ingenious exercises. The answers are nearly always periphrases or metaphors. There is no better introduction to an intelligent reading of Anglo-Saxon poetry than any extract from the dialogues in which the pupil is the questioner:

" What is the body ? The spirit's lodging.
" What is hair ? The clothing of the head.
" What is the beard ? The distinction between the sexes, the mark of age.
" What are the eyes ? The guides of the body, the vessels of light, the index to thought.

Sometimes fancy becomes rich and beautiful as well as curious.

"What is the sun? The splendour of the world, the beauty of the sky, the grace of nature, the honour of the day, the distributor of the hours.

"What is the sea? The path of boldness, the earth's bourne, the divider of regions, the receiver of streams, the spring of showers. . . ."

If the vulgar tongue be substituted for Latin, there is no difference in style between these didactic definitions and Anglo-Saxon poetry. Like Aldhelm, Alcuin carried into his Latin the turns of thought and the imaginative and slightly childish mentality of his fellow-countrymen. If the great clerks whom we have enumerated have left us no verses in the vernacular—such as they wrote have been almost all lost—they are yet hardly less representative of the Anglo-Saxon spirit than are the writers in the vulgar tongue. It was among these men, perhaps by them, perhaps by anonymous clerks like them, that the poems which have reached us were compiled or were, at least, edited and expurgated.

The characters of Roman writing seem to have been imported with Christianity, and to have taken the place of the runes, which the Germanic peoples engraved on monuments and used for brief correspondence, but in which they do not appear to have recorded the verses of their poets, the gleemen or scops. It follows that memories of the pagan epoch have invariably been transmitted to us through the medium of the clerks, and that what we call Anglo-Saxon literature has therefore been inevitably subject to the influence of Latin, and to no other foreign influence. It is a literature in which the direct and realistic expression of the national genius, unmodified by Christianity, is rarely found and dangerous to seek.

It is a literature compiled by clerks, but by clerks whose fathers were warriors and vikings, and who were very near the surviving memories of the warlike age. The word battle, the thought of prowess, awoke irrepressible ardours in them. It cost them little effort to call up the manners and the scenes of so recent a past. The terms of an unaltered language, the accents of unchanged prosody, the recurring combinations of words and images inevitable to alliteration: all these often took them back to the days of adventures by land and sea and led them to preserve such fragments as oral tradition had handed down to them. Thus their poetry, even when it is entirely Christian, is full of reminiscences and echoes of paganism. Less dominated by Latin than their prose, it deforms and reforms Holy Writ, in accordance with its own traditions, even while it reproduces it. It thinks Scripture anew and interprets it in national terms. It crowns biblical warriors with the helmet and shields them with the lime-wood buckler, and sends the saints of the Mediterranean to voyage over grey and ice-cold seas, while the low, rainy sky of the north broods over Palestine, wolves roam the Holy Land, and crows and wild swans fly above it. Thus this poetry presents a continual contradiction, yet constantly, by changes of scenery and of actors, creates anew while it claims to translate, so that its very inaccuracies are alive and partly original.

Such is the general character of this literature, which, although fundamentally Christian, is here and there still pagan in feeling and everywhere national in form.

4. Anglo-Saxon Poetry: Its Manuscript Sources, its General Character.[1]— The way in which the texts of Anglo-Saxon literature have reached us is significant.

---

[1] The Anglo-Saxon poems have all been collected by C. W. M. Green in his *Bibliothek der angelsächsischen Poesie*, 4 vols. (1857–64). The two first volumes contain the texts, the others a glossary. Revised by R. P. Wilkes in 1894 (Leipzig).

Among the very numerous studies of this poetry, we would cite, in addition to the general histories by Ten Brink, Courthope, Taine and Jusserand and the first volume of the *Cambridge History of English Literature*, Stopford Brooke's *History of Early English Literature to the Accession of King Alfred* (1892) and *English Literature from the Beginning to the Norman Conquest* (1898), two works which contain excellent translations into English verse; J. Earle's

Leaving on one side documentary and practical works, whether historical or religious, and also the chronicles, texts of laws and homilies and the various translations, we find almost the whole exclusively poetical literature in four manuscripts attributed to the eleventh century. The first of these, the so-called *Junius* manuscript, named after the scholar, Milton's friend, who bequeathed it to the Bodleian Library, contains the paraphrases from the Bible known as the Cædmonian Poems. The second is the *Codex Exoniensis*, which was given to Exeter Cathedral by Bishop Leofric in the eleventh century and was almost forgotten until 1826. Its contents are a curious medley of pious poems, of half-pagan lyrical and elegiac compositions, and of riddles and sententious verses. Thirdly, *Beowulf* and the Biblical fragment *Judith*, unknown until the end of the eighteenth century, are strangely associated in the British Museum manuscript. And lastly, in the manuscript which was discovered in 1832 in the capitular library of Vercelli in North Italy, there are entirely religious poems and, especially, metrical lives of the saints. To these must be added two short fragments of verse from some still more recently recovered pages of parchment, the one on the battle of Finnesburh and the other on an episode of the life of Waldhere, otherwise Walter of Aquitaine, and also the important fragment, the *Death of Byrhtnoth* or *Battle of Maldon*, published in 1726 from a manuscript which is lost. Such is almost the whole of the known poetry of the Anglo-Saxons, and it is on these texts that the attempt must be based to establish the dominant features of this poetry, which is at once strongly characterised and very uniform.

At the time when the extant texts were compiled, its form was already fixed. This primitive metrical literature had been subject, before it assumed its present guise, to a process of ossification. The most ancient works are posterior to the date at which versification and rhetoric assumed definite shape, and every subject, whether Christian or pagan, epic or personal, great or small, whether the story of the Creation or a riddle on a rake, is clothed in the same dress. Literary decoration and the turn that is given to a theme are always identical. The singer's voice has unchanging volume. The effect on the senses and the imagination hardly varies.

1. The most profound and also the most general element in all poetry is to be sought in language. The qualities and deficiencies of a language predetermine the field of poetry and its successes and failures, almost independently of the personal genius of the poets who use it. The chief task of a poet is to take skilful advantage of the resources a language offers to him. Words have a particular expressive value which is outside or beyond their meaning, and although the force of association of ideas may supply a grace or an energy, a lucidity or a mystery other than that which belongs to a word at its simplest, the fact remains true that the maximum of suggestion is reached when sound and meaning are in harmony. Thus it might be said, of the essence of the English language, that in its Teutonic elements it surpasses French by its vigorous strokes, but that it speaks with a less melodious voice. What the French weakly call *force*, has an English name, *strength*, from the Anglo-Saxon *strengtho*, in which seven muscular consonants strangle a single vowel, but in the French word *oiseau*, a solitary consonant hums among soft vowels and diphthongs, with such effect that it makes the English *bird* (A.S. *bridd*) seem to have little power of suggestion.

The primary character of the Anglo-Saxon language derives from the predominance of its consonants. Not only are syllables introduced by a consonant

Anglo-Saxon Literature (1884), and W. P. Ker's *The Dark Ages* (1904) and *Epic and Romance* (1897). In French there are Hubert Pierquin's *Les Lettres, les Sciences, la Philosophie et la Religion des Anglo-Saxons* (Paris, 1914), and Emile Pons' *Le thème et le sentiment de la nature dans la Poésie anglo-saxonne* (1925); and, for the language, the first volume of René Huchon's *Histoire de la Langue anglaise* (1923).

or group of consonants (*h, sp, st, str, hr, thr,* etc.), but these consonants form the vital part of syllables. They are explosive, not quiescent, and their noise drowns the neighbouring vowels, a characteristic of which the persistence is proved whenever any French word passes through an English throat, as when *donne* becomes *ddonne* or *plaine, pplaine*. The value given to the initial consonant, together with the tonic accent, which throws the root syllable into relief, and with the emphasis on the essential word of a sentence, make up the law of Anglo-Saxon versification. The comparative insignificance of vowels is shown in the rule that vowel sounds, which may be substituted for alliterations or repetitions of initial consonants, need not be identical. For here it is not the sound of the vowel but the absence of the consonant which is important. The effect is produced by the momentary softening of the line.

The normal line is made up of an undetermined number of syllables divided into two sections, in each of which there should be two rhythmic accents. The recurrence of the same consonant or group of consonants, to introduce the two accentuated syllables of the first section, and that of the first accentuated syllable of the second section, give the alliteration, as follows:

> *st*eap *st*anlitho—*st*ige nearwe (*Beowulf*, II. line 159).
> Steep stone slopes, paths narrow.

There is often only one alliteration in the first section.

2. While the line is thus based on accent combined with alliteration, and while both of these depend on the predominating value of consonants, the style and the construction of the poetic phrase derive from another characteristic of the language.

Unlike modern English, which is one of the most analytical and least inflected of languages, Anglo-Saxon expresses changes of tense, number and persons either by modifications of the root vowels or by differences of termination. It is a language nearly as synthetic as Latin, endowed with four cases for either number, several declensions of the noun, two declensions of the adjective, and numerous conjugations of the verb. Its syntax, that of an inflected language, shows a very complex use of cases and great freedom in the arrangement of words. This freedom of construction is to-day one of the points in the old language which astonish an Englishman. Its effect in poetry is to cause the place of words to be strictly governed by the needs of the alliterative line or the exigencies of emphasis. There is an abundance of separate, disconnected words in apposition, with something of the effect of superimposed interjections.

It is impossible, even in the most literal translation into an analytical language like English or French, to reproduce the staccato of these phrases without either introducing connecting links or becoming unintelligible. There is in the original a greater abruptness, a more interrupted sequence than that of which modern syntax allows.

3. Probably, however, no potentiality of the language had more influence on the rhetoric of the Anglo-Saxon poets than the ease with which it allowed them to make composites. This primitive tongue is poor in the grammatical suffixes and prefixes which transfer a word from one class to another, which make an adjective of a noun or a noun of a verb, or make two nouns into a new one, their separate meanings being lost in the process. The constituent elements of derivatives and composite words often remain clearly discernible and keep their distinct sense. Thus to crucify is to fasten to the cross, *rod-fæstnen*; a butcher is a slaughterer of cattle, *hrith-heawere*; the third finger is the ring finger, *hring-finger*; a literate man is one learned in letters, *stæf-cræftig*. The passage from words in current use

and employed in prose to the words which poets invent for a particular effect is unmarked, so that it is often difficult to determine which terms are strictly poetic. Alfred's prose gives us *æfter-genga,* or after-comer, for successor; *ærend-gewrit,* or written message, for letter; *cynestol,* or king's seat, for throne; all words much like those composites which are found only among the poets—for instance, *eard-stapa,* or earth-walker, for traveller; *breost-nett,* or breast-net, for corselet; *death-reced,* or death-chamber, for grave; *ban-hring,* or bone ring, for vertebra.

From language this process passed to thinking. Even when they were writing Latin, the Anglo-Saxons developed their ideas by means of accumulated periphrases. Their poets make an extensive use of this possibility of the language, and the peculiarity of their composite words is that they are used not of necessity, for lack of a simple equivalent, but as ornaments, to show a quality of the subject-matter and throw it into relief, or, more frequently, for pure love of these terms, or again, for the sake of alliteration. The body becomes the bone-chamber; the heart, the treasure-chamber; thought, the treasure of the breast; the breast, the close of the heart; the warrior is the man with the corselet, the lance-bearer or the swordsman; the sailor is the traveller on the waters; armour, the warrior's garb or the shirt of battle; and man, the earth's inhabitant or the word-carrier.

Many primitive customs and beliefs are revealed by these poetic synonyms. The chief or king is the *beag*-giver—*beags* being rings which served at once as ornaments and as money—or he is the gold or treasure giver; the banqueting hall is the mead or wine hall, or else the roofed hall; and warriors are lime-bearers, that is, bearers of limewood shields.

Numerous composite words bear witness to the Anglo-Saxon enthusiasm for war: battle is the game of blades, the conflict of lances or the cracking of banners, and the sword is battle lightning, while blood is the sweat of war or the flow of carnage.

The elements and natural phenomena supply as many composite terms as war. The sea is the path of sails, the whale's road or the swan's pathway; the flood is the waves' journey; fog, the helmet of the air; and darkness, the helmet of night.

These composites are sometimes heaped upon a simple word, like heavy, barbaric jewellery. Cædmon has quite thirty synonyms to denote Noah's Ark. The more of them a poet collects, the more pleased he seems to be, and the poems often so closely recall the Litany to the Virgin—"Mystical Rose, Tower of David, Tower of Ivory, House of Gold, Ark of the Covenant, Gate of Heaven, Morning Star"—as almost to suggest an attribution of this prayer to an Anglo-Saxon clerk.

A poet will not say "when night came," but "when the noble gleam its setting sought, darkened the northern firmament, dusk amid clouds, o'erveil'd the world with mist, with darkness cover'd, when night clos'd over the cultured land's adornments." [1]

Often an object is designated only by composite words or periphrases, and its identity must therefore be guessed. Thus the eyes must be understood by "jewels of the head," the body by "fleshly clothing," armour by "the eorl's raiment." It was a sport of the poets to cause an object to be divined by one of its attributes, an amusement known as "kenning" which led to the riddle, so that collections of riddles are naturally among the most interesting of these poetical productions.

Almost the whole rhetoric of the Anglo-Saxons is made up of such perpetual periphrases. These poets abound in abrupt metaphors, condensed in single composite words, but they hardly ever make the consecutive and extensive comparisons which are born both of imagination and of reason. Only the artist who is

---

[1] B. Thorpe's translation of the *Legend of St. Guthlac,* line 1212.

master of himself and at peace can note the resemblances of different objects and study them side by side. He rarely does it if he feel passion, never if he be without culture. It would be hard to find in Anglo-Saxon poetry a metaphor which is not swift and violent, or of which the lines are amplified or merged in a harmonious picture.

The character of the language, of the metres and of the style is so marked that there is among all the poems a likeness which does not escape monotony. These poets modulate their voices very slightly and lack the alternatives of solemnity and lightness. Their joy weighs as heavy as their sorrow, their irony is brutal as a blow from a sledge-hammer. The traditional form and the single line give an air of grandeur to particular poems, but imprison and restrict individual initiative. Throughout the three centuries for which Anglo-Saxon literature is known, hardly an approach can be perceived to that differentiation of genres which is the sign of vitality and progress. The epic unity of form and tone is at first impressive, but its continued tension grows wearisome, and the periphrastic accompaniment enriches but overweights and obscures the style. None the less, this is a strong and an impressive poetic form. It remains to examine the value of the themes which it clothes.

5. **The Poems which refer to the Pre-Christian Epoch : "Widsith," "Deor," "Beowulf."**—The Anglo-Saxon poems in which the traditions of the pagan epoch have been preserved are both the most beautiful in themselves and the most interesting to us. It has been seen that we cannot expect ever to find in them a direct picture of pre-Christian times, since they were compiled or edited some time between the eighth and tenth centuries by clerks who knew Latin, whose minds were coloured by Christian morality, and who had access to some models from Græco-Roman literature. Yet the authors of these poems had kept the old passion for adventure, together with the memory of the wild life of their ancestors and the ancestral legends and verses. There is a certain analogy between their state of mind and that which the nineteenth century called romanticism. From a distance, through the medium of their purified feelings, they caressed with their melancholy their dream of the past. They were civilised men who returned to barbarism in spirit and impregnated it with their moral sense. They were a little like Virgil, nobly retracing the history of Rome's infancy, or Tennyson expurgating the perverse Arthurian legend. They often recast the poems which a tradition, doubtless oral, had handed down to them, suppressing whatever shocked their consciences, and intercalating new passages or adding edifying conclusions.

The short poems *Widsith* and *Deor* lift a corner of the veil which hides the past. They purport to be the songs of two scops or poets living on the continent in an age already fabulous. Widsith or "Great Traveller" has wandered much from tribe to tribe, and he gives a list of the princes who have made him presents. Among these are Eormenric, King of the Goths, Attila, King of the Huns, and Albouin, King of the Lombards, whose date is more than two centuries later than Attila's, the second third of the sixth century instead of the middle of the fourth, so that Widsith is plainly no historical figure but a typical scop who is an excuse for bringing together names famous in history and legend. The enumeration of Germanic tribes is valuable to historical geography, and the literary attraction consists almost entirely in the lustre of the proper names and their suggestions. Both Hrothgar, who recurs in *Beowulf*, and Hagen, celebrated in the *Niebelungenlieder*, figure in *Widsith*. The poem gives an idea of the wandering minstrels who went from court to court, singing the praises of the princes from whom they received or expected largesse. It concludes as follows:

> Say in song their need, speak aloud their thankword!
> Always South or Northward someone they encounter,
> Who,—for he is learned in lays, lavish in his giving—
> Would before his men of might magnify his sway,
> Manifest his earlship.
>   Till all flits away—
> Life and light together—land who getteth so
> Hath beneath the heaven high established power.[1]

The *Lament of Deor* is the effusion of a more sedentary and less happy *scop* than Widsith, one disgraced by his lord who has preferred his rival, but consoled for his ill luck by recollection of the normal inconstancy of fortune. He recalls heroes and gods who were not spared tribulations, and concludes every strophe—this is the only Anglo-Saxon poem which has this strophic form—with a sort of refrain:

> *That* he overwent; *this* also may I.[2]

But the only poem which attempts a picture of the primitive age on a large scale is the *Lay of Beowulf*.[3] The date of the compilation of this work makes it the most ancient epic of the Teutonic world, and historically its subject takes us back to the first half of the sixth century. It speaks of the Frankish defeat of the Goths under Hygelac (the Cochilaicus of Gregory of Tours), which occurred about 512–520, a fight in which the young warrior Beowulf is said to have distinguished himself by strength and valour.

Neither the subject nor the characters are in any way peculiarly Anglo-Saxon. Not only is there no question of the island of Great Britain, where the Anglo-Saxons were established as early as the fifth century, but there is also no mention of the lands near the Elbe which they inhabited previously. The scene is, by turns, the Danish island Seeland and the country of the *Geats* or Goths in the south of present Sweden, and Beowulf, the hero, is a Geat. This is thus no national epic; even if the common origin of the tribes be taken into account, it is remarkable that almost at the moment at which an unknown Anglo-Saxon poet was commemorating his forebears of Scandinavia, the still pagan people of that country were beginning their redoubtable descents upon the shores of Great Britain, visiting upon the Anglo-Saxons the very ills which these had once inflicted on the Britons. The question arises, therefore, whether *Beowulf* be not an adaptation into Anglo-Saxon of a Scandinavian legend, a hypothesis supported by the fact that the chief incidents of the story of Beowulf, the slayer of monsters, recur in the Icelandic saga *Grettir*. It is, however, plain to anyone who has read the prose and metrical sagas of the north, that *Beowulf* has a markedly different tone and turn of narrative from these works, that in it their wildness has been tamed, and that it has a predominating moral tendency, and lacks the violent strangeness of Norse literature. On the other hand, by feeling and imagination, as well as by language, *Beowulf* comes very near the rest of the extant Anglo-Saxon poems. It is, in fact, a mixed and slightly artificial production, which has a foreign basis but is national in form.

The constituent elements of the poem are likewise a medley. Certain episodes and, above all, a sustained noble gravity of tone, would make *Beowulf* an historical poem, but the incidents of the plot are romantic and supernatural. It is like an Iliad which should have Hercules instead of Achilles for hero, his triumphs over monsters for theme, and about whom purely historical beings and scenes should form a frame for the story. There is a striking incongruity between the realism of

---

[1] Stopford Brooke's translation.   [2] Stopford Brooke's translation.
[3] Heyne's edition of the old text (Paderborn, 1863) has often been reprinted. Translations into modern English have been published by J. Earle (Oxford, 1892), J. M. Garnett (verse translation, 1883), W. Morris and A. J. Wyatt (Boston, 1898).

some pictures—the descriptions of banquets and still pagan funeral rites—and the obstinate idealism which gradually turns the strong-armed fighter into a sort of saint, and depicts a king's court in which nothing is heard but noble sentiments and counsels of modesty and wisdom. The later chivalrous and adventurous romances are foreshadowed in *Beowulf*, although the poet never abandons the noble epic tone and seems to feel it beneath him to minister to mere curiosity.

Every incongruity which analysis can discover disappears in the movement and the style of the poem. In spite of grave structural faults, the use not of one but of three successive stories, in spite of a monotonous and slightly childish theme, the work is that of an artist. Its sustained dignity and regular, rather restricted march is such that some critics, comparing it with the poems of Scandinavia, have been impelled to see in it the influence of classical antiquity.

Beowulf, with some valiant Geats, comes to the help of Hrothgar, King of the Danes, whose palace of Heorot is wasted by the nightly attacks of Grendel, a monster of the race of the *eotens*, or giant ogres, the issue of Cain. Every night Grendel emerges from his lair in the marshes beneath the cliffs, in order to seize and devour one of the king's companions. In a terrible hand-to-hand struggle, Beowulf tears off an arm of this monster, who is mortally wounded and flees to his den to die, whereupon all is joy in victory and deliverance.

But Grendel's mother avenges her son. She renews the attacks on Heorot, and Beowulf resolves to go forth to fight her in her home. Diving after her into the waters of a sinister lake, he meets her in combat in the cave in which she dwells beneath the waters. When he is all but worsted he seizes a magic sword which hangs on the wall, and plunges it in the body of the fearful beast, and then, when the Danes believe that he has already fallen a victim to his daring, he returns to Heorot in triumph, bearing Grendel's gigantic head.

He becomes king of the Geats and reigns over them gloriously for fifty years. But some jewels are stolen from an ancient treasure guarded by a dragon, who thereupon sets out in fury to devastate the king's realm, burning with his flaming and pestilential breath all that lies in his path. Beowulf slays the dragon and saves his people, but he is himself mortally wounded during the encounter by the monster's venomous tooth, and he dies nobly, consoled by the thought that he has sacrificed himself for his subjects, and that he is bequeathing to them the incomparable treasure which has been in the dragon's keeping. He has, however, been forsaken during the fight by all his thegns but one, and great evils are prophesied for the Geats bereft of their king.

It is seen that the labours of Beowulf are far from attaining to the ingenious variety of those of Hercules. All the monsters he meets in combat are equally fearful and vague; the horror is produced by their mysterious outline, the night which surrounds them and the sinister places they inhabit. The descriptions of the marshes in which Grendel's mother dwells is perhaps the most famous passage in the poem. A sombre imagination and the sadness of a northern landscape have united to paint this powerful picture. But the sadness is not confined to the references to nature. It is diffused throughout the poem, never absent from it. It recurs in elegiac form in the episode of the origin of the treasure, which was buried by the last survivor of a proud family, and came into the dragon's possession. Even in the intoxication of fierce battle and of the hero's victory, sadness is perceptible. There are constant allusions to the nothingness of life, of courage and of glory, and although Beowulf is in every point a hero, the ideal of an active force serving good and triumphing over evil, the poem does not convey that effect of fortifying energy which might be expected of it. This poem which is a glorification of bold enterprise leaves a bitter taste, or at least an impression of universal melancholy.

It makes life seem sad, effort vain. The reason for this must be sought in its atmosphere. It takes one into a dark place whither the sun's clear light does not penetrate, where fogs and unwholesome vapours are never quite dissipated by the sun's rays. A certain joy in life is needed to make a work of imagination healthy, but Beowulf, or rather the poet who narrates his adventures, has introduced the Christian idea of earthly life among his gloomy scenery, has plumbed the emptiness of mortality, and found it of little worth at the very moment at which he celebrates mortal glory. This is indeed a poem which has come out of a cold cell in a Northumbrian cloister. It breathes the air of the tomb.

6. **Lyrical and Elegiac Poems : the " Ruined Burg," the "Lover's Message," the " Maiden's Complaint," " The Wanderer," " The Seafarer."** —The melancholy which weighs upon *Beowulf*, especially on its latter part, often recurs in several undated short poems, which are distinguished from those already mentioned by a complete severance of ties with the continent and a break with pagan tradition. All the same, these poems are not distinctively Christian; rather they are Christian only in some of their details and in their conclusion. They are laments, usually desolate. Their voice is something like that heard in the so-called "Songs of Ossian," with which Macpherson conquered Europe at a moment in the eighteenth century when men were avid of the vague and the melancholy. These Anglo-Saxon verses strike, perhaps more truly than the authentic fragments of Celtic poetry, that note of lamentation, at once personal and human, to which the name of Ossianic has since been given.

There is, for instance, a complaint written on the ruins of an old town which might be Bath, the watering-place which was so magnificent in Roman times, before the Saxon invaders destroyed it. A poet comes to visit the remains of this splendid town, long after the days of its splendour, and is grieved by the sight of the "ruined burg."

> Many were the mead-halls, full of mirth of men,
> Till the strong-willed Wyrd whirled that all to change.[1]

The poem is a series of monotonous laments in which the word ruin recurs incessantly like an inevitable refrain.

There is also a series of lyrical poems, or rather elegies, which are more intimate and have reached us in the guise of personal effusions, but which are so obscure that the question has arisen whether they be not detached parts of longer romantic compositions. The habitual melancholy is missing only in one of them, the *Lover's Message*, in which an exile sends a message to his love by means of runes carved on a wooden tablet. By a fiction in harmony with the enigmatic style affected by this poetry, the wood itself is made to speak, to relate its origin in a forest and its voyage on a ship, and to marvel that man has been able to give it a tongue. This wood is employed by the lover to ask the maiden to join him in his place of exile where he has become powerful and prosperous and will surely make her happy.

> Soon as ever thou shalt listen on the edges of the cliff
> To the cuckoo in the copse-wood chanting of his sorrow,
> Then begin to seek the sea, where the sea-mew is at home.[1]

More obscure, but richer in feeling, is the elegy which might be called the *Wife's* or *Maiden's Complaint*, were it certainly the utterance of a slandered woman who laments that she is banished from the neighbourhood of her love. Equally well, however, it may be the complaint of a young thegn kept from joining his dear and exiled lord. The singer's suffering is caused by her faithfulness. She has been condemned to dwell in a cave "in a grove amid this wood," and thence, "in the

---

[1] Stopford Brooke's translation.

early dawning" she comes alone to spend a whole summer day mourning her griefs beneath the shelter of an oak. She dreams of her beloved, who also is consumed by sorrow and who is often compelled to assume an air of gladness. She imagines him sitting "under the o'erhanging cliff, overfrosted by the storm," where he endures

> Anguish mickle of the mind, far too oft remembers him
> Of a happier home! [1]

The elegy *The Wanderer*, of fuller scope, is certainly a song of friendship. A young thegn has been obliged, after the death of his beloved lord, to seek another protector beyond the seas. His dreams on the path which leads to exile are sad.

> And it seemeth to him in spirit, that he seeth his man-lord,
> Clippeth him and kisseth him, on his knee he layeth
> Hands and head alike, as when he from hour to hour,
> Erewhile, in the older days, did enjoy the gift-stool.
> Then the friendless man forthwith doth awaken,
> And he sees before him only fallow waves,
> And sea-birds a-bathing, broadening out their plumes;
> Falling sleet and snow sifted through with hail—
> Then the wounds of heart all the heavier are.[1]

As however he considers that vicissitudes of fortune overtake even chiefs and that misery is common to all men, he understands that his grief is but a part of the universal order of change:

> Doom of weirds is changing all the world below the skies.[1]

He is like the old warrior who fights over again the battles of his younger days and who cries with Ossian:

> Whither went the horse, whither went the man? Whither went the Treasure-giver?
> What befel the seats of feasting? Whither fled the joys in hall? [1]

The Seafarer, the most original of the Anglo-Saxon lyrical poems, may be taken as representative of this poetry, with its defects and qualities. Its capital defect is its obscurity which reaches an extreme point, and is such that the subject of the poem has been interpreted in many ways. Is it a composition of a regulation type, in which the irresistible attraction of the sea for a seafaring man, well though he know its evils and dangers, leads to the thought that as the sailor despises well-being on dry land, so man ought to reject earthly pleasures for the happiness which awaits him beyond death? Or is it a poem which has been inspired from two distinct sources, a description of a seaman's rough life to which a pious Christian conclusion has been added?

Is it the monologue of a sailor who, with little order and more than one repetition, descants on his conflicting feelings for the sea, his love and hate, fear and desire? Or is it, as some ingenious critics maintain, a dialogue between an old seaman, who recounts the misery of his life, and a youth who answers every warning with the voice of his irrepressible vocation?

Such ambiguity is enough to prove that this short poem is imperfect in form. It is striking, none the less, by the sombre and violent picture it gives of northern seas in which suffering from cold mingles with the pains of water and wind. The extreme redundancy at least has as nucleus a powerful and realistic impression. Even although the ending is blurred and lost among pious effusions, the opening lines are full of energy:

> With a bitter breast-care I have been abiding:
> Many seats of sorrow in my ship have known!
> Frightful was the whirl of waves when it was my part
> Narrow watch at night to keep on my vessel's prow

> [1] Stopford Brooke's translation.

> When it rushed the rocks along. By the rigid cold
> Fast my feet were pinched, fettered by the frost,
> By the chains of cold. Care was sighing then
> Hot my heart around; hunger rent to shreds within
> Courage in me, me sea-wearied! This the man knows not,
> He to whom it happens happiest on earth,
> How I, carked with care, in the ice-cold sea,
> Overwent the winter on my wander-ways,
> All forlorn of happiness, all bereft of loving kinsmen,
> Hung about with icicles; flew the hail in showers.
> Nothing heard I there save the howling of the sea,
> And the ice-chilled billow, 'whiles the crying of the swan!
> All the glee I got me was the gannet's scream,
> And the swoughing of the seal, 'stead of mirth of men;
> 'Stead of the mead-drinking, moaning of the sea-mew.[1]

Swiftly these memories are obliterated. The sailor soon wearies of the facile pleasures of towns. Spring brings back to his heart the passion for adventure:

> Trees rebloom with blossoms, burghs are fair again,
> Winsome are the wide plains, and the world is gay—
> All doth only challenge the impassioned heart
> Of his courage to the voyage, whosoever thus bethinks him,
> O'er the ocean billows, far away to go.

And here the poet finds a strange and beautiful image to express this lure:

> For behold, my thought hovers now above my heart;
> O'er the surging flood of sea now my spirit flies,
> O'er the homeland of the whale—hovers then afar
> O'er the foldings of the earth! Now again it flies to me,
> Full of yearning, greedy! Yells that lonely flier;
> Whets upon the whale-way irresistibly my heart;
> O'er the storming of the seas.[1]

If it be impossible to follow all the truncated argument of *The Seafarer*, at least, through its mists, a powerful vision of polar seas and the fascination of their perils can be discerned. And this is something which persists in literature. This very passion for the sea and for adventure recurs in some great modern English poets—Byron, Swinburne and Kipling—whether or not they have known the old Anglo-Saxon song.[2]

7. The Songs of War: "Brunanburh," the "Battle of Maldon."[3]—As might be expected, it was in their war songs that the Anglo-Saxons best retained the vestiges of their wild, primitive mood, especially in those which celebrated their own battles. This fact is independent of chronology. Nothing perhaps reflects their past better than the sort of ode which is inserted in the prose chronicles, compiled by some monk, to glorify the great victory which Athelstan, King of Wessex and Mercia, and his brother, Edward, won at Brunanburh in 937 over the Scots under Constantine and the Northmen whom Anlaf led out of Ireland. The fierce enthusiasm of victory breaks out in savage irony addressed to the defeated or fleeing invaders. The swiftness, even lucidity, of the ode allows the hypothesis that it was one of those popular *cantilenas* which were known to have flourished among the Anglo-Saxons. While the narrative and elegiac poetry is often so obscure that we can hardly believe it to have been meant for the people and understood by them, we have here a song which it is easy to imagine intoned, and caught up by all the soldiers of the victorious army. The fact that it contains no original detail, that all its circumstances are general, and that it ends with the oldest of Anglo-Saxon commonplaces on slaughter, strengthens the impression that this is

---

[1] Stopford Brooke's translation.
[2] Donady, *La mer et les poètes anglais* (1912).
[3] Translated into modern English by C. L. Crow (Boston, 1897), J. M. Garnett (Boston, 1882), etc.

I—C

a work which connects with a long tradition of songs of war. The story, which in the epic fragments is continuous, is here cut up into a series of short, irregular stanzas. We can imagine it sung to the accompaniment of the harp.

The history of the battle is resumed in a sequence of short, enthusiastic stanzas, in which, in turn, the West Saxons and the Mercians are extolled, the Scots and the Northmen held up to ignominy. The poet's massive irony expends itself on Constantine who came to attack Athelstan after he had sworn fealty to him:

> To his home in the North, Constantinus.
> The hoar war-hero was unable to boast
> Of attendance of men; he was robbed of his kinsmen,
> Bereaved of his friends on the battle-field,
> Conquered in fight, and he left his son
> On the place of slaughter, wasted with wounds,
> The boy in the battle. He durst not boast,
> The grey-haired warrior, of the clash of swords,
> The aged enemy . . .[1]

And the poem ends with the customary description of the field covered with the dead:

> Behind them they let the corpses share
> The dark-feathered fowl, the raven black,
> The crooked-beaked, and the ashy-feathered,
> White-tailed eagle enjoy the prey,
> The greedy war-hawk, and the grey-clad beast,
> The wolf in the wood.[1]

Some sixty years after the ode on the victory of Brunanburh, an unknown poet told the story of a national defeat, that of Maldon, in which, in 993, Byrhtnoth, the old chief of the East Saxons, met his death, as he strove to drive back a band of Northmen whose ships were coming up the Penta, a little to the north of the Thames. We have only a fragment of 325 lines of this poem, which seems, since it does not name a single one of the enemy, to have been written soon after the fight. It is not a lyrical song, but a detailed epic narrative which, by its rhythm and its general shape, recalls the battles of the Iliad more than does any other Anglo-Saxon poem. In spite of the extreme simplicity and the wholly national character of the poem, it provokes the question whether it be modelled on the classical epics. That poetry native to the country should, by mere chance, have attained to such a likeness to the classics seems incredible, and the surmise of imitation is tenable, since all Anglo-Saxon literature had been impregnated with Latin by the time this poem was written. But it must also be admitted that the copy, if such it be, is a very general one, and is drawn from a distance. *The Battle of Maldon* is no paraphrase of an ancient model. Its historical subject is local and quite recent. It is, in fact, the only extant fragment of a national epic in Anglo-Saxon.

The Saxons are Christians, repelling pagans, but all the noble sentiments in the poem refer to martial valour, love of battle, a leader's sacrifice of himself for his men, the loyalty of soldiers to their leader. Already the chivalrous point of honour is much to the fore. Out of his eagerness for battle, Byrhtnoth allows the Northmen to pass over the Penta in order that the fight may engage. When the Saxon chief is wounded to death, he rejoices and breaks into laughter, and he dies thanking God that he has been suffered to strike great blows before his end, and that many joys have been vouchsafed to him on earth. His death is the signal for the flight of the cowards, led by the traitor Godrich, but it redoubles the ardour of the brave to avenge their fallen chief, and they die about his body. Their

---

[1] Translation by J. M. Garnett.

heroism is summed up in words spoken by the old chief, Byrthwold, as he brandishes his ashwood lance:

> The braver shall thought be, the bolder the heart,
> The more the mood, as lessens our might.
> Here lieth our lord, all hewn to pieces,
> The good on the ground: ever may grieve
> Who now from this war-play thinketh to wend.
> I am old in years: hence will I not,
> But here beside mine own dear lord,
> So loved a man, I purpose to lie.[1]

This *Battle of Maldon* is like some embryonic *Roland*, a Song of Roland earlier than the legend. As in the French epic, there is a glorious defeat and an heroic death. It was long thought probable that about the beginning of the eleventh century, near the date of the *Battle of Maldon*, a first sketch, in the form of a lay, existed for the *Song of Roland*, and the question arises whether there were not, in this period, a close resemblance between the two poems. Probably not, for *Maldon* is a strictly historical poem, which does not magnify its subject and which neither introduces the marvellous nor leaves room for its introduction by an editor. It is not the germ of something greater than itself but the fragment of a completed whole. The sentiment of the two works is indeed almost identical. Byrhtnoth makes it a point of honour to allow the Northmen to ford the river unhindered, exactly as Roland refuses to sound his trumpet in order to summon Charlemagne. Both heroes, out of chivalrous pride, prepare disaster. Byrhtnoth's attachment to his king, Æthelred, and that of his brothers-in-arms to himself, their leader, are matched by the tie of duty and love which binds Roland to Charlemagne and all the Frankish warriors to Roland. The coward Godrich is a pendant to the traitor Ganelon. And Byrhtnoth, like Roland, is a Christian slain by the pagans, whose last words are for God, the supreme leader of warriors, and who, because he is valiant and dies in battle, is sure of God's love.

In spite, however, of all these points of resemblance, *Byrhtnoth* is markedly distinct from *Roland*. It has the bare severity of history, while *Roland* has the prestige of legend. Heroic as they are, the exploits of the *Battle of Maldon* are not superhuman. They are more solid and less poetical than those of *Roland*, not deeds of impossible prowess but the actions of men who do no more than fight to the death. Disaster in *Byrhtnoth* is not transformed by imagination, and, in spite of the proud words of the dying chief, the noble harangues of his friends, the blows they finely deal, and all the delirium of danger and death, this poem is sad, as *Roland* cannot be sad, with its hope and triumph enduring even in defeat, its unfailing confidence in the divine mission of the Franks, and its radiance of light and colour beneath so much blue sky.

Byrhtnoth has a unique place in pre-Conquest poetical literature. Its apparently strict adherence to the actual course of events was unmatched until the advent of the Anglo-Norman *trouvères*, in particular Wace who sang the battle of Hastings. But while this poem does not use legend to transfigure facts, it yet dignifies them by the truly epical march of its story and the nobility of its alliterative verse, elements of greatness which are lacking in Wace's octosyllabic lines. It has a rough simplicity which is disconcerting at a time when Anglo-Saxon poetry was exaggerating its rhetorical character. This poem is like a sign of vigour, a promise of renewal, at a moment when the literature to which it belongs is overweighted with periphrases to the point of exhaustion. *Byrhtnoth* stands in such isolation that no theory can be founded on it, yet it poses the question whether native poetry were not capable, without foreign help, of a new development, an unexpected renascence.

---

[1] Translation by J. M. Garnett.

8. The Riddles.[1]—It may seem strange to include among the most interesting of the poetical works of the Anglo-Saxons an extant collection of riddles, attributed by several critics to Cynewulf, although on unconvincing evidence. But that riddles are thus dignified ceases to surprise when the enigmatic turn always affected by Anglo-Saxon poetry is remembered, its way of denoting an object by qualities rather than an exact name, its cult of periphrasis and its search for verbal subtleties, all tendencies which give a special tone to maxims and which whet curiosity. That the *scops* used to put riddles, to test the sagacity of the guests at banquets before whom they displayed their talents, may be admitted. But the riddles which have come down to us are not original and are all Christian. Most of them are founded on the Latin riddles of the clerk Aldhelm, who had himself taken the riddles of Symposius as models, and others derive from the Latin of Tatwine, Archbishop of Canterbury. The Anglo-Saxon riddle is, however, a very free copy. It became poetical when, so to speak, it ceased to be utilitarian. From a mere ingenious definition, intended only to arouse attention and sharpen the wits, it grew into a description, often copious, and not only personified its subject, but also animated it and gave it life. The narrow frame of the Latin riddle had been broken. Thus did Phædrus and, above all, La Fontaine, deal with the dry Æsopic fable. The Anglo-Saxon riddles are usually true poems, of varying and sometimes considerable length. They violate all the laws of the riddle at once, lack its curt precision and are too often diffuse and vague. As riddles, they must be allowed to be failures, but they make up for technical defects when the poet, led away by his subject, forgets to appeal to reason and speaks to the imagination. Anglo-Saxon prolixity, which wearies when it confuses and deforms the severe lines of the Bible, is easily excused when the translation of a riddle is in question.

The Anglo-Saxon riddles constitute a sort of encyclopædia, in which figure the animals, especially the domestic animals, the celestial bodies and phenomena, contemporary products of art and useful objects, arms, tools, musical instruments and articles of clothing. Several of them add to our picture of the customary life and implements of the Anglo-Saxons. If some are so obscure that they cannot be certainly solved, and some so marvellously gross that their presence in a pious compilation like the *Codex Exoniensis* is astonishing, others belong of right to literature, for instance the riddle on a shield:

> I am a recluse, with iron wounded,
> With faulchion scar'd, sated with works of war,
> Of edges weary; oft I battle see,
> Perilous fight; for comfort hope not,
> Or that safety to me shall come from martial strife,
> Ere I with generations shall all have perished;
> But they me shall strike with sword:
> The hard of edge, intensely sharp, hand-work of smiths,
> Shall bite among people: I must await
> The hostile meeting: never the healing tribe,
> In the battle-place, might I find,
> Who with plants my wounds would heal,
> But to me the edges' sores become increas'd,
> Through deadly stroke, by day and night.[2]

The riddle on a bull's horn, which can be both a trumpet and a cup, is rich and brilliant. There is first an armed warrior who is the bull, then a maiden "with rings adorned" who "fills my bosom," says the horn, and then warriors

> On horseback bear me; then with wind I must,
> Resplendent, swell from some one's bosom.

---

[1] A. J. Wyatt, *Old English Riddles* (Boston, 1912)—a good edition. Translations into modern English by Stopford Brooke, *Early English Literature* (1892), and B. Thorpe, *Codex Exoniensis* (1842).
[2] B. Thorpe's translation of Riddle VI.

When the riddle describes the elemental forces of nature it becomes really lyrical. The riddle on the *Wind* or the *Storm* (Riddle IV.) is one of the most original and most modern of short Anglo-Saxon poems. It has been compared, without hyperbole, to Shelley's *Ode to the West Wind*, or rather to his *Cloud*, for in it the storm in exaltation chants its deeds and the changes it works. The storm is first represented as held, by the will of the Creator, chained and captive beneath the earth, powerless within its dungeon. Set free, it stirs up the waters of the sea:

> Foamy strives wave against wall,
> Dusk rises mountain o'er deep;
> Dark on its track, in ocean,
> Another goes so that they meet,
> The land's limit near, the high shores.
> There the wood is loud, the ocean-guests' noise;
> Still remain the rocky cliffs
> From the watery strife, the crew's outcry.
> When the towering mass on the cliffs presses,
> There shall be hope for the vessel, in the fierce contest,
> If it the sea shall bear, at that terrific time,
> Of guests full, so that it shall forthwith
> Be borne away, though vitally assail'd,
> Yet foamy ride on the waves' backs
> There shall be some terror to men display'd.[1]

The clatter of the tempest on land, as it pursues its destructive path over cities and the dwellings of men, is painted on as grand a scale, although the drawing is more confused and obscure.

Here the subject—the terror of the hurricane—and the necessary repetition of identical violent effects, combine to veil the habitual weaknesses of Anglo-Saxon poetry. Its qualities are thrown into relief, its defects momentarily hidden. The poem is powerful and arresting.

9. Christian Poetry: The Cædmonian Poems and "Judith." [2]—In all the poems hitherto examined there is some revelation of Christianity, or at least a certain attenuation of pagan characteristics, but they are not decidedly religious poems either in subject or in immediate intention. We have still to deal with the Christian poetry, properly so called, which is by far the larger, if the less original and, with few exceptions, the less formally beautiful part of this poetry. Whether because a greater volume of it was written, or because it was naturally more carefully preserved by the clerks, it fills almost all the extant collections of Anglo-Saxon verse.

This poetry is proof of the fervour with which, immediately upon their conversion, these Germanic pirates embraced the religion of Christ. At the end of the seventh and throughout the eighth century they made the great island they had conquered in an age of darkness into the most ardent and most radiant home of Christianity. Alliterative verse came to the aid of clerkly Latin to express their faith, spread it among the laity and made it really popular.

The origin of this Christian poetry in the vulgar tongue must be sought in the pages of Bede. He relates that in the monastery of Streoneshalh, now Whitby, in Northumbria, there was a brother whom God had honoured with his gifts and who excelled in glorifying piety and virtue in song. "Everything the clerks taught him out of Holy Writ, he soon afterwards reproduced in the English language, in poetic words and most melodiously." This man had reached old age without taking

---

[1] B. Thorpe's translation.
[2] B. Thorpe, *Cædmon's Metrical Paraphrase of Parts of the Holy Scriptures, with an English Translation* (Society of Antiquaries, 1832); H. Balg, *Der Dichter Cædmon und seine Werke* (Bonn, 1882); F. A. Blackburn, *Exodus and Daniel* (Boston, 1907).

orders or learning any skill in poetry. "Wherefore being sometimes at feasts, when all agreed for glee's sake to sing in turn, he no sooner saw the harp come towards him than he rose from the board and turned homewards. Once, when he had done thus, and gone from the feast to the stable where he had that night charge of the cattle, there appeared to him in his sleep One who said, greeting him by name, 'Sing, Cædmon, some song to me.' 'I cannot sing,' he answered, 'for this cause left I the feast and came hither.' He who talked to him answered, 'However that be, you shall sing to Me.' 'What shall I sing?' rejoined Cædmon. 'The beginning of created things,' replied He." [1] Then Cædmon sang verses he had never heard to the glory of the Creator:

> Now must we praise the Guardian of heaven's kingdom,
> The Creator's might, and his mind's thought;
> Glorious Father of men! as of every wonder He,
> Lord eternal, formed the beginning.
> He first framed for the children of earth
> The heaven as a roof; holy Creator!
> Then mid-earth, the Guardian of mankind,
> The eternal Lord, afterwards produced;
> The earth for men, Lord Almighty. [2]

Cædmon awoke, remembered the words of the song he had composed in sleep, and added to it many others, all to the glory of God. Then he went to the reeve of his village and told him of the gift he had received from Heaven, and the reeve took him before the abbess, who assembled all the clerks and bade Cædmon sing to them. All were agreed "that a heavenly grace had been conferred on him by the Lord. They translated for Cædmon a passage in Holy Writ, bidding him, if he could, put the same into verse. The next morning he gave it them, composed in excellent verse, whereon the abbess, understanding the divine grace in the man, bade him quit the secular habit and take on him the monastic life. . . . He kept in mind everything that was taught to him, and as beasts of the field ruminate, so he turned it into melodious song, so sweet to the ear that his teachers became his hearers. He sang of the Creation of the world, of the origin of man, and of all the history of Israel, of their departure from Egypt and entering into the Promised Land, and other passages of Holy Scripture, the Incarnation, Passion and Resurrection of Christ, and His ascension to Heaven, the coming of the Holy Ghost, and the teaching of the Apostles. He sang also of the terror of future judgment, the horrors of hell-pangs and the joys of heaven."

There is nothing in the Christian poems to approach the charm of Bede's artless story, as appears if his few, very representative quotations of verse be compared to his Latin prose, with its wealth of precise circumstance which gives everything a character. In the verse there are no facts. Their place is taken by ejaculations, repetitions and periphrases. Scholarship no longer admits the extant poems, written on the subjects Bede enumerates, to be the direct work of Cædmon, the old singer. They are paraphrases from other sources, at most later and altered versions of Cædmon's original. But their character has been little changed. The poems of the so-called Junius manuscript, which are not by Cædmon but are called Cædmonian in memory of him, are essentially biblical paraphrases. Some are on passages in the books of Genesis, Exodus and Daniel, and other fragments, not biblical in the strict sense, have for subject the fall of the rebel angels, Christ's descent into Hell and his temptation by Satan. To these it is natural to add the fragment of a poem on Judith, although it is of later date and, strangely enough, not included in the Junius manuscript, but in the same manuscript as *Beowulf*.

What has been said of the origins of this biblical poetry makes the intention of

---

[1] J. R. Green's translation.   [2] B. Thorpe's translation.

the Anglo-Saxon poets sufficiently clear. They would not and could not invent. Their aim was to popularise Holy Writ. If sometimes they added to the Bible, their additions were based on pious commentaries or earlier Christian poems which they regarded as equally authentic, for instance on the poem in which Avitus of Vienne relates the Fall of the Angels.

What, then, is the original element which can be proved to exist in their poems? It is first and especially an originality of form. They recast the Bible in the mould of their national poetry, transposing it into alliterative verse, and giving it that half-epical, half-lyrical turn which characterises all their poetry, and which made their rendering of several passages of the Hebrew poem a happy one.

Secondly, they transcribed not only with all the fervour of recent converts, but also with all the artlessness of an ignorant people, who imagined the Jews like themselves, who saw God in Heaven with his angels like their own king surrounded by his thegns, who could not escape from themselves, their own customs and their own climate, and who instinctively put their own feelings into Jewish history, and pictured a Judæa washed by the sullen and icy waters of the North Sea.

This transposition is especially noticeable in the sea pictures, which testify to the nautical experience of the vikings, and in the battle stories, which rekindled the ardour of the scops, so that they drew on their pagan tradition for conventional details—the clash of spears, the helmeted warriors, the war-cries, the black crows cawing over carrion.

The misunderstanding has curious and picturesque effects, and the too complete assimilation of the Bible makes for life and vehemence, but there is monotony in these poets' imagination, which unfailingly reduces the whole of the world's contents to two or three sentiments and two or three unvarying descriptions.

If, for a moment, these Anglo-Saxon poems are not read indulgently, if we cease to make allowances for them, but, like some critics, overpraise them, the heavy pompousness of the paraphrases at once becomes evident, in contrast to the sober and sublime vigour of the Bible; and Ten Brink is seen to be guilty of flattery when he says that "the originality of the Anglo-Saxon poet of *Genesis* is revealed only in detail and execution. The simple, terse expression of the Scriptural narrative is exchanged for a broad, often impassioned, epic style." Very often, the Anglo-Saxon has overlaid beauties not apparent to him with the weight of his words:

The Bible	The Paraphrase
And the earth was without form and void; and darkness was upon the face of the deep. And the Spirit of God moved upon the face of the waters. And God said, Let there be light: and there was light.	The earth as yet was not green with grass; Ocean cover'd, swart in eternal night, Far and wide, the dusky ways. Then was the glory-bright Spirit of heaven's guardian Borne over the deep, with utmost speed: The Creator of angels bade, the Lord of life, Light to come forth over the spacious deep.[1]

Indisputably, the Anglo-Saxon diverges from his model; he is himself. But the sum of his originality is his promiscuous piling-up of words, which hides, rather than reveals, the great outline of the primitive chaos. Above all, it drags out the act of creation, which showed the might of God by its very swiftness. The God of the Anglo-Saxon fumbles awkwardly before he lights up the world. There could be no better lesson on the difference between grandiose verbosity and the true sublime.

The effect is not accidental. It recurs in almost every passage of this para-

---

[1] B. Thorpe's translation.

phrase, which partial critics quote with approval. *Exodus* has the same defect, that of detailed description which aims at grandeur and misses sublimity. The Bible says:

"And Moses stretched out his hand over the sea; and the Lord caused the sea to go back by a strong east wind all that night, and made the sea dry land, and the waters were divided."

Mr. Stopford Brooke praises what he calls the "vivid realistic way" of the Anglo-Saxon poet in the paraphrase, but it is a very childish realism, which consists in making Moses describe the phenomenon to his people as he accomplishes it.

> Lo! ye now with your eyes behold,
> Most beloved of people, a stupendous wonder;
> How I myself have struck, and this right hand,
> With a green sign, the ocean's deep:
> The wave ascends; rapidly worketh
> The water a wall-fastness, the ways are dry,
> Rugged army-roads; the sea hath left
> Its old stations; where I before have never heard,
> Over mid-earth, men to journey,
> Are variegated fields, which from this time,
> Through eternity, the waves have covered.[1]

Thus the great wizard, whose silent gesture had worked the miracle, is changed into an artless gossip whom the miracle seems to amaze as much as it does his people.

Although the later poet who paraphrased *Judith*,[2] and who deserves gratitude for his choice of this admirable book of the Apocrypha, is more vigorous, a comparison of his Anglo-Saxon text with the original shows that he also has not recognised true sublimity, and stumbles beneath the enormous weight of his poetic ornament and conventions. It should perhaps also be said that to the confused intelligence of the Anglo-Saxon poet, that quality of keen, steely decision which constitutes the character of the heroine was inconceivable. The biblical Judith never says a word which does not lead straight to action; the Saxon Judith wraps her thought in periphrases, so that the feeling of action is lost. She repeats herself interminably. Her gestures, like her thoughts, reach us through a fog of words. Compare her words in the two texts—for instance, when she beseeches the Lord for help before she strikes Holofernes, or when, returning to Bethulia with the Assyrian general's head, she summons the Jews to battle: always a showy, awkward verbosity is substituted for the cutting precision of lucid words. The woman of action has been changed into a sort of prophetess, drunk with excitement, exalted, vague and frenzied.

There remains that part of the Anglo-Saxon biblical epic which treats of the *Fall of the Angels*,[3] and the machinations of the prince of the fallen angels to avenge himself on God, who has cast him into Hell, by causing Adam and Eve to commit the first sin. It is the very subject of Milton's *Paradise Lost*, and this identity of theme, together with certain likenesses of emphasis and language, have given rise to a surmise that Milton, who was Junius's friend, was inspired by the old poem. The presumed imitation has even shed a sort of reflected glory on the Anglo-Saxon work. The paraphrase is here not of the Bible, but of a Latin poem by Avitus, and there is a freedom of imagination not found in the other Cædmonian poems, and an attempt at a psychological explanation of the first sin. The versification, the style and even the vocabulary also have special characteristics which

---

[1] B. Thorpe's translation.
[2] A. S. Cook, *Judith* (with English translation, Boston, 1904).
[3] E. Sievens, *Der Heliand und die angelsachsische Genesis* (Halle, 1875).

make it resemble the continental Saxon poem, *Heliand*, or *The Saviour*, and critics incline to think that it is a translation or imitation of a lost poem of similar origin.

However this may be, the *Fall of the Angels* is interesting by its study of motives —those of Satan, jealous and ambitious but courageous and great; of Eve, seduced but not perverse; of Adam who yields to Eve because he knows her for lost and would share her fall. The lines spoken by Satan have outstanding energy. The conception of some of his monologues is worthy of Milton, as when he dreams of emancipating himself from the divine supremacy, or when, in the depths of Hell, he plots his vengeance. Unfortunately, it was in the form of the poem that the author, since he had not invented the subject, had most scope, and his style is extraordinarily redundant and wordy. Without many cuts the poem can hardly bear translation. If Milton knew it, he may have owed to it some vigorous strokes of his brush, but he cleared away its terrible prolixities and repetitions, and reclothed their sentiment in the majesty of his close, strong language. Milton might be a Cædmon whom the lessons of classical antiquity and a better understanding of the Bible had taught to compose, to select and to direct.

10. **Cynewulf : "Christ" and the Lives of the Saints.**[1] — While the critics, robbing Cædmon like another Homer, have bereft him of the biblical poems, they have brought out of the void a poet whose very name was previously unknown. It was noticed that two poems in the *Codex Exoniensis*, the *Christ* and the *Life of Saint Julian*, and two in the Vercelli manuscript, *Saint Helen* and the *Fate of the Apostles*, included runic characters which, when deciphered, gave the same name, *Cynewulf*. The conclusion was that this must be the name of the author, especially as the passages containing the runes had a personal and almost autobiographical character which distinguished them from others. Starting from this discovery, the critics were for a time so daring as to claim for this poet the authorship of most of the other verses included in the same two manuscripts. On the basis of a dubious solution of the first riddle, all the riddles were attributed to Cynewulf. Doubtful resemblances of form and subject were a pretext for assigning to him other lives of the saints, those of Saint Andreas and Saint Guthlac, and other pious poems, the *Phœnix* and the *Dream of the Rood*. Almost, he was erected into the single author of all the Christian Anglo-Saxon poetry extant. Finally, a search was made in history for this Cynewulf, and after much conjecture he was identified, not certainly but probably, with a Cynewulf who was bishop of Lindisfarne and lived in the middle of the eighth century. Every trace of a personal confession contained in these poems was then collected, and a portrait and biography of Cynewulf was constructed. He was a wandering singer or poet who lived a gay and secular life. The accuracy of some of his battle-scenes and seascapes showed that he had fought on land and sailed the seas. Finally, after a dream in which he had a vision of the Holy Rood, he changed his life, became a religious poet, sang of Christ, the apostles and the saints.

The structure is ingenious but it is frail, and it was no sooner conceived than gaps were made in it, so that to take up a stand on it is to risk perpetual falls into the unknown. The fact is that nothing is known either to show which works are properly ascribed to Cynewulf, or the century in which he lived or his place of birth. While he seems to have been born in Northumbria, his verses, like all those of his fellow-countrymen, have reached us in the dialect of the West Saxons.

It can hardly be disputed that Cynewulf's reputation with critics has gained by

---

[1] A. S. Cook, *The Christ of Cynewulf* (Boston, 1900), *The Dream of the Rood* (Oxford, 1905); I. Gollancz, *Cynewulf's Christ*, (1892, with translation). Translation into modern English by J. M. Garnett (Boston, 1901); translation of *Elene* by L. H. Holt (Yale Studies in English, 1904), and of *Andreas* by R. K. Root (ibid., 1899).

the pleasures of discovery. It is not uncommon in these days to hear him compared to William Cowper or even Dante. His *Christ*, which seemed to its first editor a tissue of obscurely tangled threads, is to-day translated, annotated and published like a classic. The severity with which Cynewulf's work must be estimated is made indispensable by the extravagance of the praise given to it.

Of the probable writings of Cynewulf, that is of those which contain his runic signature, the *Christ* alone is original, at least in part. Its seventeen hundred lines have been disentangled by scholarship to show a composition in three parts, a sort of triptych which celebrates the Advent of Christ, that is his birth, his going-away or Ascension, and his second coming at the Last Judgment. Even after patient study has marked such distribution of the poem into parts, it is difficult to read it without losing the thread on every page, so profound is the obscurity of the thought and so hesitating the march of the narrative. The obscurity is a little due to the loss of the beginning of the poem, but much more to the radical weakness of a befogged intelligence, led away by words rather than guided by ideas. Cynewulf's verses are vague effusions, based on anthems, homilies and hymns, and they suffer by a comparison with their frequently sublime originals, even more than do the Cædmonian paraphrases when these are put side by side with the words of the Bible.

This is proved if the third *passus* of the *Christ*, the fullest and most imposing of the three, be examined. Its basis is the admirable hymn, *De Die Judicii*, formerly ascribed to Saint Gregory, which is itself no more than a metrical version of one of the most beautiful chapters of the Gospels, the twenty-fifth of Saint Matthew. Out of its twenty-three distichs Cynewulf makes eight hundred lines, and the sole effect of his vast additions is to draw a thick veil over the sober grandeur of the images, to obliterate the sublime unity of thought and sentiment, and to surround with darkness the central idea so brilliantly clear in Christ's dialogue with the righteous and the wicked—"Inasmuch as ye have done it unto one of the least of these my brethren, ye have done it unto me."

It is hardly credible that although Cynewulf has kept this thought, he does not seem to have perceived its grandeur, to such a point has he smothered it with trite and commonplace developments. It is possible to read the third *passus* without noticing it.

Even those of Cynewulf's images which have been most praised by his commentators are often no more than weak embroideries on the severe and strong outline of his original. It takes him ten lines to render the first distich, "Suddenly the great day of the Lord will come, Like a thief in the dark night falling upon unwitting sleepers," and he adds to it only words, not a single exact circumstance. Or else, with thick, prosaic commentary, he drags out a phrase which impresses by its brevity. "The glorious King will sit upon his heavenly throne, Surrounded by the trembling (*tremebunda*) ranks of his angels," is rendered by Cynewulf as follows:

> Heaven's angels' King holy shall shine,
> Glorious o'er the hosts, the powerful God;
> And around him chiefs most excellent,
> Holy martial bands shall brightly shine,
> A train of blessed angels: they inwardly
> Tremble with fear, for terror of the Father.
> Therefore 'tis not any wonder, how of worldly men
> The impure race, sadly sorrowing,
> Shall sorely dread, when the holy race,
> White and heaven-bright, the archangel-host,
> Before that countenance is with dread affrighted.

[1] B. Thorpe's translation.

Even where he depicts the catastrophe of the Last Day, winning high praise from the critics for poetic power, and giving himself free rein, it is hard to discern anything in his work but unending, wearisome repetition of the words which express the idea of ruin and conflagration.

It is not suggested that Cynewulf is insincere, but it is maintained that all the many sighs and incoherent complaints of his gloomy spirit are not worthy to be compared with the high exaltation of a clear-eyed Christian. Exuberance of language and prolix facility of versification: these are the sum of Cynewulf's qualities. He has written some of the most fluent and melodious verses in Anglo-Saxon poetry, but he has done it by the sacrifice of all precision, and the accomplishment is not worth its price.

The runic signature of the same Cynewulf occurs in a *Saint Julian* and a *Saint Helen*, poems which are pleasantly differentiated from the *Christ* by their continuous story and the respite they afford from vague effusiveness. Two other lives of saints, Saint Andreas and Saint Guthlac, once also attributed to Cynewulf by some critics, are now denied to him. The absolute decision of this question of authorship, when the author concerned is so hypothetical a person, has little importance. It is more interesting to establish the distinguishing characteristics of hagiography in Anglo-Saxon verse.

Saint Julian, Saint Helen and Saint Andreas are exotic saints, whose legends, doubtless transcribed from Greek to Latin, have been, on the whole, faithfully followed by the Anglo-Saxon poets. All of them have an oriental element of the marvellous, evidently seductive to the Anglo-Saxon imagination, a taste which was to affect profane literature also, and to make the English the first translators of the complicated romance of *Apollonius of Tyre*, whence Shakespeare drew the incidents of his *Pericles*. Since invention had hardly any part in the writing of these lives of saints, their principal value, beyond the few modifications of the stories, is to show what were the themes which appealed to the imagination of their authors.

The life of Saint Juliana, a Christian maiden of Nicomedia, victorious over the demon Belial, who tries vainly to tempt her, and a martyr to her faith, is distinguished by the clearness and swiftness of the story. But the pace involves dryness and an absence of poetry and emotion.

The life of Saint Elene or Saint Helen is told more expansively. The story is that of the Invention of the True Cross by the mother of the Emperor Constantine after his victory over the Huns (*sic*). Constantine's warlike expedition, the battle and Helen's voyage over the sea to Judæa give scope for the traditional descriptive effects, so that the native verse is in its element and easily falls into the epic mood.

Saint Andreas is the most crowded and the most Byzantine of these legends. Long analysis would be necessary to exhaust the list of the saint's miracles on his way to deliver the apostle, Saint Matthew, held captive by the cannibal Myrmidons. He crosses a raging sea, Christ being, without his knowledge, the pilot of his boat; in invisible form, he enters the dungeon in which Saint Matthew lies; the cannibals are infuriated when their prisoner is set free; Saint Andreas is tortured but remains invulnerable; he avenges himself by a flood which he lets loose upon the town by an order to one of the columns of his prison to scatter torrents of water; his wrath is appeased by the prayers of the terrified people; he commands the mountain to be riven, and the waters, into which the people had been plunged up to their armpits, are cast into its breach; the astounded Myrmidons undergo mass conversion.

These are only some of the incidents which swarm in the seventeen hundred lines of the poem. The exuberant wealth of happenings saves *Saint Andreas* from the diffuse wordiness of most Anglo-Saxon Christian poems. It is less diluted than most of them. The unknown author is nevertheless to be suspected of a rhetoric not so innocent as that of his predecessors. As Stopford Brooke has well said, he is a "sensationalist." So, truth to tell, is Cynewulf, when in *Saint Helen* he piles up in cold blood the periphrases he loves too well. "I was stained with crimes," he says when he is confessing his sins, "till the Lord, my . . . bone-house unbound, breast-lock unwound, song-craft unlocked."

They are strange, these poems. The web of the Byzantine romances is studded with heavy Anglo-Saxon jewellery.

Besides the lives of these exotic saints, there is one of a native saint, Saint Guthlac. It is, unfortunately, the most imperfect of the four, made of two badly joined parts of which the first is confused and mediocre. Yet this poem deserves a brief attention, for it confirms and completes certain observations suggested by the Christian paraphrases.

It is founded on a story told in Latin prose by Felix, a monk of Crowland in Mercia. Saint Guthlac's life, as related by Felix, is worthy of a place beside the life of another saint which is told by Bede, that of Saint Cuthbert. It is rich in legends which are of the soil of Great Britain, redolent of artless popular beliefs. To read it is to feel oneself at the very source of the religious feeling of the past. Guthlac, the son of a Mercian noble and born near the end of the seventh century, has become a hermit, and has built himself a hut in a lonely island in the midst of wide marshlands to the north of Granta. There he is tormented by hideous demons, "who speak the British tongue"—perhaps none others than the first owners of the land the Mercians had engrossed. He makes every kind of humble divination, showing his simple shrewdness, and accomplishes numerous unambitious cures which pass for miracles. But what especially endears him is a fondness for animals worthy of Saint Francis of Assisi. The birds tamed by his kindness are all about him. He loves the beasts, knows their ways, talks to them, is really saddened if they are guilty of an unjust or malicious action.

His life in prose is full of true charm and fragrance. Together with the stories by Bede which have been mentioned, it gives an idea of the rich material which the ingenuous faith of this country and these ages offered to religious poetry. But the metrical life of Saint Guthlac makes a painful impression of emptiness. All that was concrete and picturesque in the Latin prose has given place, in these verses, to an exalted treatment of the subject which makes it unintelligible to a reader without other knowledge of it. The story has no thread; there are no outlines; everything is confused. The struggle with the demons has become an abstract argument. Even the second part of the poem, which deals with the death of the saint and has moments of beauty, cannot still the regret for the exactness of the prose original. Here again is evidence of the sins of this oppressive rhetoric, which so rarely allows the Anglo-Saxon poets to express themselves simply.

11. Other Christian Poems: the "Dream of the Rood," the "Bestiary," the "Phœnix." Didactic Poems.—The Christian poetry of the Anglo-Saxons is not all comprised in the Biblical paraphrases and the lives of the saints. It also includes some noteworthy poems of a different kind.

It has been seen that Cynewulf was led by his devotion to the Cross to choose the legend of Saint Helen as a subject, and it is tempting to see in him the author of the *Dream of the Rood*, since such a dream is said to have determined his conversion. To personify the Holy Cross was a natural tendency of faith, more than once manifest in the Latin verses of the clerks. Thus in Saint Fortunatus's admirable and impassioned hymn, *Vexilla Regis prodeunt*, the poet's love is moved by the wood of the Cross which the cruel lance has stricken and which flows with blood and water. "Beautiful and shining tree . . . chosen the holy limbs to touch, blessed Cross from whose arms hung the Ransom of the World. . . . Hail, Cross, sole hope! . . ."

The same sentiment and the same image have inspired the Anglo-Saxon poet. Incapable of the concentrated and poignant forcefulness of Saint Fortunatus, he has at least an ingenious dream of his own, not so diffuse as to be without outline. In it he sees the miraculous tree, by turns shining with jewels and bathed in blood. It speaks to him and relates to him its life from the day when it was struck down on the verge of the forest, to that on which "the young Hero, brave and strong," was lifted on to it, and it trembled as it received the kiss of God in Man. It is now honoured by men, their beacon-light and the cure for all their ills.

At an early date Christian literature gave symbolic meaning to natural phenomena, and particularly to animals which were especially fabulous. It followed, in so doing, both the parables of the Bible and Greek fables. Hence the *Bestiaries* of the Middles Ages, called *Physiologi* in Latin. Anglo-Saxon is the first vernacular language in which a *Bestiary* occurs, a mere fragment embracing the Panther, the Whale and part of a passage on the Partridge. Anglo-Saxon verse lends itself to this poetic form much as it does to the riddle. The same stretch of imagination is needed. The description of the Whale—Fastitocalon, who is as large as an island, so that confiding ships anchor on his sides and sailors land on his back, to kindle a fire and feast—is on a scale which Milton repeats. Naturally, the enormous beast chooses the very instant at which pleasure reaches its height to plunge into the sea, taking ship and sailors with him. Even so the devil plays with the souls of men, duping them with his false lures that he may the better carry them off to Hell.

The *Phœnix* is an independent poem, but it is very like these others in character. The fourth-century poet Lactantius, taking his subject from Ovid and Claudian, had transformed the mythological phœnix, which burnt itself to be reborn of its own ashes, into a symbol of Christ and the Christian soul. His short Latin poem, *Phœnix*, is a work of eighty-five distichs, conventional in style, a mosaic of the classical poets which is spoilt by its dryness and its too enigmatic turn.

This time the Anglo-Saxon poet, who has expanded the theme to seven hundred lines, has the advantage over his model. Anglo-Saxon plenty here relieves happily the effects of a Latin drought. The poet brings new moving warmth into his treatment of a subject which mythological memories and terms had frozen to lifelessness. Instead of getting further away from nature, as he diverges from his model, he sometimes seems to put the fresh life of his own impressions into an entirely artificial composition. He thus more than compensates for his inevitable inferiority in lucidity and terseness. His endearing if diffuse description of the paradise in which the Phœnix dwells is preferable to the cold brevity of the Latin. It is true that either northern impotence or Anglo-Saxon rhetoric has made the poet unequal to painting a flowery and sunny place of delights, and that he is most at ease when he is paraphrasing the list of the scourges which this Eden is spared. But even in this too negative description there is more charm than the poets of his country were wont to put into their pictures. His smooth and ample verses succeed better than those of Lactantius in suggesting the marvellous harmony of the songs of the Phœnix. The ardent homily with which the poem ends is a commentary on Lactantius's last line—"Aeternam vitam mortis adepta bono"—which has a strong precision beyond the later poet. But the homily has an unction and a melody which finally make this poem probably the most attractive of all those written in alliterative verse.

This survey of the Christian poetry must include several short didactic pieces, the *Gifts of Men*, the *Weirds of Men* and *Ten Instructions of a Father to his Son.* In these, Anglo-Saxon poetry is sententious. The *Dialogues between Solomon and Saturn*, in which the fantastic varies the didactic, are more curious. They are imitations of a lost Latin original, itself taken from a vanished Greek source, and are the prototypes of the dialogues between Solomon and Marcolf which were so popular in the Middle Ages. Saturn, who has nothing in common with the god of mythology, is a Chaldean prince sprung from a family of demons. He is acquainted with all books but not with the magic of the *Pater Noster* which he makes Solomon explain to him.

It is not always in such amusing fictions that Christian morality finds expression. It loves to bring before men lugubrious images of death and decomposition, to humiliate the body which constantly leads the soul to stray from the path of salvation. Hence the struggles between body and soul which held so large a place in the imagination of this age of faith. Anglo-Saxon poetry soon took possession of this theme, of which the cruelty was aggravated by the habitual heaviness of alliterative verse. Thus it is with the *Discourse of the Soul to its Body*. The soul inveighs against the body, already corrupt and the prey of the voracious worm with jaws sharper than the needle, which once tempted to the sins for which it now suffers the pains of Hell. The soul, in revenge, describes with savage joy the decomposition of the fatal body.

The grave is similarly evoked at the end of a volume of homilies, but this time it is Death who speaks and with sombre realism calls up the picture of man's last abode.

It is true that these images cannot be taken as peculiar to the Anglo-Saxon imagination. They are essentially Christian and also, it may be said, representative of the gloomiest of the Christian centuries. It is, however, impossible not to notice how aptly the rude verse and violent rhetoric of the Anglo-Saxons render their dismay and emphasise their horror.

12. **Anglo-Saxon Prose. Alfred, Ælfric, Wulfstan.**[1]—The breach between Anglo-Saxon and English poetry is everywhere apparent, and to pass from Cynewulf to Chaucer is to bridge a deep gulf. The poetry of the Anglo-Saxons is deliberately archaic. In order to produce a desired emotional state in its hearers, it reverts to traditional turns of expression, to words almost consecrated, as religion works its effects by the constantly recurring use of an ancient liturgy. This poetry is modelled on an earlier age of which the remoteness cannot now be determined. It retains many periphrases and locutions already obsolete, imitates and systematises the disorder of primitive lyrical construction. The poetic form tends towards the past.

On the other hand, the tendency of the prose is towards observance of the rules of ordinary speech, unless it copy the Latin prose of the clerks. Its object is to instruct and inform, not to move, and since it thus educates the understanding, it necessarily turns to the future. There is therefore nothing surprising in the fact that the prose writings of the Anglo-Saxons, which are much less curious than their poetry, are also much nearer ourselves. No revolution seems to separate Alfred's pages from those of Caxton, Ælfric's from Wycliff's. There is a change but no break. National and linguistic continuity is felt to exist; there almost seems to be a continuity in the thought moulding the phrases which are very like each other. While an Englishman has to make a quite considerable effort in order to read the verse of the Anglo-Saxons, he finds it comparatively easy to understand their prose.

If such facility be not marked in the oldest prose literature, this is because it

[1] *The Whole Works of King Alfred the Great*, ed. J. A. Giles, 3 vols. (Oxford and Cambridge, 1858); Stopford Brooke, *King Alfred as Educator of His People and Man of Letters* (1901); H. Sweet, *Selections from Ælfric's Homilies* (Oxford, 1896); A. Napier, *Wulfstan's Homilies* (Berlin, 1883); B. Thorpe, *Homilies of the Anglo-Saxon Church*, 2 vols. (Ælfric Society, 1844–6); C. L. White *Ælfric, a New Study of His Life and Writings* (Yale Studies in English, 1898).

is either of earlier compilation than any of the poetry extant—like the laws of Ina, King of the West Saxons, which were promulgated at the end of the seventh century although our transcription dates only from the time of Alfred—or because some of this prose is more than half poetry and seems to be fragments of old epic tales. This character belongs to many passages of the chronicle usually attributed to the influence of King Alfred, of which we have distinct versions written by the religious of different monasteries, those of Winchester, Canterbury, Abingdon, Worcester and Peterborough, the last-named having continued their narrative to the middle of the twelfth century. In this chronicle several references to early times, brief but impressively vehement, are pagan in feeling and emphasis and seem to date from the pre-Christian period. Even in the references to the eighth century there is a suddenness and a roughness in the narrative which betray that mental and grammatical habits were still empirical. It is continually necessary to complete the ellipses and to relate the pronouns to their proper subjects, as with a story told by a small child. For instance, the chronicler relates, as follows, the beginning of the struggle between Cynewulf and Sigeberht in 755:

> This year Cynewulf took from Sebright his kingdom, and the councillors of the West Saxons [did as much], for unrighteous deeds, except Hamptonshire, and he [that is Sebright] reigned there [that is in Hampshire] until he slew the alderman who stayed longest with him. Then Cynewulf drove him to the forest of Andred, where he remained until a swain stabbed him at Privett, and he [that is the swain] revenged the alderman, Cumbra.

The alderman is not named until he is mentioned for the second time.

This formless prose was succeeded at the end of the ninth century by a regular prose, possessed of nearly all its essential parts. Since it is modelled on Latin texts, which are almost literally translated, it is very near English prose, as that was fixed, and also near French prose which was formed under the same masters.

Alfred, the glorious king of Wessex, was the pioneer of the prose-writers. The exclusively poetic or Latin literature which had hitherto flourished had emanated principally from the north-east, the country of the Angles, or from Central Mercia. About 800, the supremacy was passing to the south-west, and the king of Wessex was tending towards the sovereignty of all the Germanic groups settled in the island. But the Danish invasions supervened, and with them the destruction of the centres of religion and letters. In the year 878 it seemed as though nothing would escape the invaders. It was then that the young King Alfred withdrew to Athelney in Somerset, formed there a nucleus of resistance, defeated the Danes, and won from them a treaty which left him the south of England while they remained masters of the old country of the Angles and Northern Mercia.

After his victory, Alfred set himself to retrieve his country from the barbarism to which it had relapsed. A decadent and demoralised clergy had sunk into depths of ignorance. Alfred did for Wessex what Charlemagne, a hundred years earlier, had done for the country of the Franks: he endeavoured to teach the people, and to re-establish Christian discipline and culture, and for this end he brought foreign monks into his kingdom and reformed education. It was under his influence that the earlier poetic works, which had almost all been written in the Northumbrian dialect, were transcribed into the language of the West Saxons.

The part which the king himself took in this literary movement was considerable. His early education had been much neglected, and he had to learn before he could teach. He surrounded himself with scholars and learned men, learnt Latin after he was grown up, for Saxon had been the only language of his childhood, and had no sooner learnt it than he began to translate the works which seemed to him most apt to civilise his people. It was thus that he became the father of English prose-writers.

Whether in the works he inspired or in those he himself produced, an effort is apparent to regularise the old elliptical, abrupt style, with its obscurity and lack of continuity. Thus the Annals or Chronicles of Winchester, Alfred's capital town, were amplified and given smoothness until they are almost a continuous story, in which, for instance, the history of the king's war against the Danes can be read without any irritating difficulty in following the text.

Alfred himself is credited with a translation of the *Universal History* of Orosius, the compilation which made antiquity known to the Middle Ages. The task was difficult, for Orosius, a Spanish historian and theologian of the fifth century, writes an obscure, tortured Latin. Sometimes Alfred, as he himself says, translates "word by word, sometimes meaning of meaning." Although the literal translation had the most formative influence on prose, it is naturally the free version which most attracts us. Its very weaknesses are characteristic. Alfred, who does not know Latin very well and who has acquired no historical sense, aims at producing a work of pedagogy. The result is that he is often very inexact, and that, as he diverges from his author, he attains to a certain originality. While he deletes what seems to him of little use to his subjects, he also makes additions, especially in the geographical section. One of the stories he adds, that of Ottar's sail along the shores of Scandinavia, is so simple and elementary in style that its vocabulary differs only slightly from modern English. The conclusion is that the spoken language was almost fixed.

Of Alfred's other translations—Bede's *Ecclesiastical History of the Angles*, the *Pastoral Rule* of Gregory the Great and the *Consolation* of Boethius [1]—it is the Boethius which is the most interesting. His choice of this book, which was again translated by Chaucer, is characteristic. Boethius has reproduced the Platonic and Stoic doctrines, coloured by Christianity and at their highest moral level—the distinction between true and false happiness, the lofty discussions on the existence of evil, on human liberty and on divine prescience. He gives these abstractions a dramatic frame. Philosophy herself appears to him in his prison, and drives away the Muses, those prostitutes who were vainly seeking to console him. Thus he makes use of allegory, and although his style is not always pure and is often mannered, it is full of life and movement. His book could not but suffer gravely when it was translated by Alfred, who mistakes the meaning fairly frequently and is incapable of conveying the fine shades. When he renders the metrical passages, which have a classic elegance, his limitations obtrude themselves. But in nobility of sentiment he is the equal of the Latin author. He explains, as follows, his reasons for undertaking this arduous task:

I have desired material for the exercise of my faculties that my talents and my power might not be forgotten and hidden away, for every good gift and every power soon groweth old and is no more heard of, if wisdom be not in them. Without wisdom no faculty can be fully brought out, for whatsoever is done unwisely can never be accounted as skill. To be brief, I may say that it has ever been my desire to live honourably while I was alive, and after my death to leave to them that should come after me my memory in good works.

This king's literary work was, like his political work, interrupted for almost a century after his death in 901. The sketchy civilisation of Wessex was once more scattered to the winds, and the clerks relapsed to ignorance and inertia. They were gradually redeemed thence, during the tenth century, by a reform of the monas-

---

[1] King Alfred, *Old English Version of Boethius*, ed. Sedgefield (Oxford, 1899).

teries which was inspired by the similar movement accomplished in France under the influence of the Benedictines. Religious houses were founded and organised in England, on the model of the abbeys of Cluny and Fleury, in which a strict rule enjoined intellectual work. This innovation was led by Dunstan, Archbishop of Canterbury, and his friend Æthelwold, "the father of the monks." Secular priests, not bound to celibacy, then abounded in the monasteries. They retained something of the patriarchal constitution which the church of Ireland had originally given to their communities, and therewith very disorderly morals, much laziness and gross superstition. The fact is proved by the so-called *Blickling's Homilies*, a medley of canonical and uncanonical legends which swarm with strange arguments and allusions. It is to works of this kind that Ælfric alludes when he says, "I have seen and heard many heresies in many an English book which unlearned men, in their simplicity, took for great wisdom." Stories of the saints, replete with the marvellous, and the obsession that the end of the world was at hand, take up most space in this collection.

It was at this time that the strict rule of St. Benedict was introduced. Morals once more became austere. The lives of the saints did indeed remain the principal subject of study and the marvellous continued to fill a large place in them, but the stories, as compared with their predecessors, were pure and even reasonable. Two men who with Alfred are the best writers of Anglo-Saxon prose are connected with this reform, Ælfric and Wulfstan.

Ælfric was a pupil of the monastic school which Æthelwold founded at Abingdon, and he wrote in the first years of the eleventh century. We owe to him a *Colloquium* for teaching Latin by conversation, and a vocabulary which was the first Latin–English dictionary. But he made his name by his *Homilies*, that is, his compilations and translations from the Fathers of the Church which form two series of forty sermons each, and commemorate the various saints venerated by the Anglo-Saxon church.

Ælfric's prose, unlike that of Alfred, is written not to be read but to be spoken to the people, in the conventional tone of a priest delivering a sermon. It has therefore a rhythm which brings it near to verse: its sentences are divided into sections, more or less equivalent to the metrical line, and it is frequently alliterative. For this reason scholars were long uncertain whether to classify it as verse or prose. It celebrates the saints, as the scops once sang the deeds of warriors. This poetic prose marks a great advance on that of Alfred. It aims at beauty, measure and harmony. It is remarkably clear and finished. There is much less awkwardness and effort in the connection of phrases than in Alfred's writings. In fact, the author is consciously literate, even when he is using the vulgar tongue, and he excuses himself, with some shame, for the popular character of his translation of the Latin homilies, pleading the ignorance of his fellow-countrymen.

Wulfstan, who was Archbishop of York from 1002 to 1023, was first of all a preacher. The most remarkable of his homilies dates from 1012, the time when the English were suffering the ills of the Danish invasions. With deep feeling, the homilist deplores the irreligion and immorality of his people, to which he attributes their misfortunes, and he proclaims the near advent of the great chastiser, the Antichrist. Wulfstan is less of a finished artist than Ælfric, but the popular emphasis of his language gives it rich colour and lively tones.

After Wulfstan all was over: the Antichrist came indeed. The Danes became masters of the country, and then, after a short interval of independence, the Anglo-Saxons were brought under the Norman yoke. Such prose writings as we have prove, however, that, even without the Norman Conquest, Anglo-Saxon prose would have taken shape, modelling itself on Latin, and, with the exception of part of its vocabulary, would have become much what it was when in the fourteenth century it regained a place in literature.

It was poetry which was principally affected by the Conquest. The poetic form had outlived its time and had little life left in it. It was conventional and was getting farther and farther away from the real language of the people. It was fated to be abolished and superseded. The aesthetic ideal was to undergo a change, or rather a revolution. England was to learn to love verse of another kind, other cadences and new subjects. All the rich ornament which profusely decorated verse with a pomp still half barbaric was to go out of fashion. Poets were to shed their periphrases and ejaculations, and gradually to learn sobriety of style and an art almost unknown to them, that of stating facts clearly, grouping them, and inventing stories.

CHAPTER II

1. General Character of Old French Literature.—The literary ideal changed at the Norman Conquest of 1066. The conquerors were, it is true, of the race of the pagan Danes whose incursions had for so long afflicted Great Britain, but from the time they had become masters of the French province which has been called Normandy, they had been gallicised with a rapidity which was prodigious, and had forgotten their paganism with the country of their origin and its language and traditions. At the time of their conquest of the great island they were real Frenchmen, in language and civilisation, nor had they failed to draw into their expedition many an adventurer from neighbouring French provinces.

It was therefore the French literary ideal which they imported into Great Britain together with their laws and administration. Before their supremacy, the native language receded, was degraded so that it was kept alive only by the lower strata of the population. Anglo-Saxon literature disappeared entirely, was not only silent for a century, but severed nearly all its ties with its past. The only literature other than Latin which was known to whomsoever had any knowledge of letters was the literature of France. It was in its infancy at the time of the Battle of Hastings, but a rapid growth made it the first of European literatures in the twelfth and thirteenth centuries, and spread its glory and influence far beyond the confines of France. One of its chief developments took place in Great Britain. Slowly, little by little, it permeated the conquered people, so that, when the English were ready once more to put their own language to literary uses, they took both matter and manner from French works, basing and forming their own productions upon them. Complete ignorance of Anglo-Saxon poetry is no barrier to understanding Chaucer, but to be ignorant of French mediæval poetry is to be entirely unacquainted with Chaucer's literary origins.

There are thus two necessary prefaces to English literature, and the French is more indispensable than the Anglo-Saxon to comprehension of its final form. It is therefore important to discover which of the most general characteristics of established French literature were such as by their novelty to impress English writers, and by their beauty to persuade them to imitation.[1]

(1) The one of these characteristics which is most widely found, and which is most thrown into relief by a study of Anglo-Saxon, is undoubtedly clarity. To turn from *Beowulf*, or even the *Battle of Maldon*, to the *Chanson de Roland* is to come out of darkness into light. The impression is received from all sides at once. It is an outcome of the subject, the way of telling the story, its spirit and the mind behind it, but above all and always it results from the difference between the two languages. That the old French authors wrote clearly is generally recognised, but it has been too much the fashion to see this gift as merely consequent on the analytical tendencies and logical aptitudes of their thought, and to make it a pretext for

---

[1] The analysis of these characteristics is taken from E. Legouis, *Défense de la poésie française à l'usage des lecteurs anglais* (London, 1912).

35

assigning prose to them as their province, and denying them the poetic faculty. Their clarity is not, however, purely abstract. It is a veritable light, shining in the dominant vowels, illuminating the best and only noteworthy verses of the troubadours. Some examples must be cited of the success often achieved by any poet who took happy advantage of the genius of the language.

In the old romances we read that,

> Bele Erembors a la fenestre au jor
> Sor ses genolz tient paile de color

or that,

> Bele Yolanz en chambre koie
> Sor ses genoux pailes desploie
> Coût un fil d'or, l'autre de soie.

In the *Chanson de Roland* there is the following description of sunlight streaming upon an army·

> Esclangiz est li vespres et li jurs;
> Contre l'soleil reluisent cil adub (arms)
> Osbert e helme i getent grand flambur,
> E cil escut ki bien sunt peint a flurs,
> E cil espiet, cil oret gonfanun.

and this one of Durandal, Roland's sword:

> E Durandal, cum ies clere et blanche
> Cuntre soleil si reluis et reflambes.

Chrestien de Troyes has dazzling passages, and there are the following two lines from Marie de France:

> Fils d'or ne gette tel luur
> Cum si chevel cuntre li jur.

There is lively, splendid colour in these lines. After the Anglo-Saxon verses it is almost blinding. Yet itself pales if it be compared with more southern poetry, where profusion of sonorous vowels makes a red and yellow vividness. For the Englishmen who knew them, the verses of such as Bernard de Ventadour had even more colour than those in the *langue d'oïl*:

> Tant ai mon cor plan de joja
> Tot mes denatura;
> Flors blanca, vermelh e bloja
> Me sembla la froidura.

The peculiarity of the *langue d'oïl* was less colour than sheer light, white light or the transparency of water flowing over rock, or of a pure fountain playing on a bed of fine sand. It is a question whether any language has ever been as well endowed as French with native sounds to suggest this clarity that has neither fire nor colour. Perhaps it is the surprising dominance of the *é* over the *a* and the *o*, those more obtrusive vowels of the south. The word *cler* (*clear*), which expresses the sensation, is itself an admirable achievement, and its worth was so well understood by the old French poets that they made it the favourite of their vocabulary, and it gives atmosphere to their poems. The predilection was shared by Roland's singer, in whose epic it would be interesting to count the lines in which the word occurs, always placed so happily that it makes a picture:

> *Clere* est la lune, les esteiles flambient.
> Trestat (passe) la noit, e apert la *clere* albe.
> Contre le ciel en salt (saute) li fous (feu) tuz *clers*.
> Parmi la bouche en salt forts li *clers* sancs.

This whiteness is everywhere in the verses of Chrestien de Troyes, as well as in the old romances and pastorals:

> En un vergier, lez une fontenelle
> Dont clere est l'onde et blanche la gravele
> Siet fille a roi, sa main à sa maxele;
> En sospirant son doux ami rapele.

It was from the perception of this light and the effort to reproduce it that the most beautiful verses of the English language, as renewed in the fourteenth century, were born. It is not only curious, but also highly significant, that the English poets adopted the word *clere* anew, and used it hardly less than their French predecessors and for like effects. Thus Chaucer, in his delicious address to the Virgin:

> Continue on us thy pitous eyen *clere.*

And he begins his most lyrical song with the line:

> Hyd, Absolon, thy gilte tresses *clere.*

He says of the bells hanging on the monk's bridle that they "ginglen clere," and everywhere, with this word and many others having the same effect, he gives the impression of a changed atmosphere, one which is more luminous and happier, which, in a word, is French.

(2) It would certainly be wrong to attribute this omnipresent clarity to language only. The aptitude of the writers to seize a luminous detail is as manifest as that of the language to express it and give it value. Something in their taste for well-lit pictures was the outcome of their joy in life, their pleasure in blue sky and sunlight. They never missed an opportunity to shed light upon a picture. *Roland,* which is a song of disaster, is a series of brilliant touches. Clear light falls from the heavens by day and by night. It streams over armies ready to commit slaughter. Colour bursts upon the "banners, white, blue and vermilion" (*gonfanons blancs et blois et vermeils*). Nothing is more luminous than Roland's portrait: with clear and laughing face (*le vis cler et riant*), ready for the fight, mounted on Veillantif and with his arms in good state, he whirls the handle of his lance which points skywards, and has streaming from its end a pure white pennon, with a golden fringe which strikes the hero's hands. There is no bright spot so small that the poet does not notice and acclaim it. He sees a warrior's "spurs of fine gold," another's "golden and beflowered shield," the gems "flashing" upon the helmet of the emir, whose white beard is like "blossom," "blossom in April," or "the blossom of a thorn." He has picked up the point of light which the teeth of the Ethiopians make in their black faces:

> Ne n'unt de blanc ne mais que sul les denz.

He admires the sparkle of the beaten metal of armour. Even horrors take on a sort of beauty for him. The mounted warriors wade, up to their bodies, in "vermilion blood" (*en sanc vermeil*). When a hard blow had been dealt, "vermilion blood gushes forth up to the arms" (*li sancs vermeilz en volat jusqu'as braz*). The "clear" blood (*tout cler*) of the dying Oliver is radiant (*raiet*) on his body. Thus dazzling pictures are made of the most terrible wounds. The iron of a lance, transfixing a body, hangs it with brilliant pennons:

> El cors li met tote l'enseigne bloie.

And we pass continually from this exterior luminosity to the sunshine of the heart which gives light from within. There is close association between the ideas of shadow and of evil. The devils inhabit the land of Valnaire (Black Valley), where all the stones are black and the sun never shines. A gloomy and sad countenance is an index of crime, as in the Saracen Abisme:

> Plus fel (cruel) de lui n'ont en sa cumpaignie. . . .
> Unkes nul hume ne l'vit juer ni rire.

On the other hand, every one of the righteous has gaiety for his sign, and turns, like Charles, his face to the rising sun:

> Turnet sun vis vers le soleil levant.

The games of the French are gay and played in the open air, "beneath a pine, beside an eglantine." They sit on "white silk stuffs." There is noisy, frivolous merriment among them. Ganelon says of Roland that "for a single hare he winds his horn all day":

> Pur un sul lievre vait tut le jur cornant.

Archbishop Turpin's exuberant merriment and his contempt for the monk who spends his time praying rule out every idea of a lugubrious, forbidding religion. Even the love of fighting is no gloomy appetite for slaughter. It is love of movement, noise, colour and glory. At the end of their life of warfare the fighters have a glimpse of the paradise where they will rest "among holy flowers" (*en saintes fleurs*), "crowned and decked with flowers" (*couronnés et fleuris*).

It is true that these men know sorrow:

> Mult ad apris ki bien conoist ahan (pain).

These French shed tears easily. They weep and they swoon as Beowulf did not. Just because they get so much joy out of life, they have cause to regret it. They complain, too, of exile from their country:

> Tere de France, mult estes dulz païs.

Friend mourns friend. Roland mourns Oliver with impassioned tenderness. Words fail the Beautiful Aude when she learns the death of Roland, and she can but die also. Generally, however, the men are men of action. Never, like the Anglo-Saxon heroes, do they give the impression that the spring of life, which is love thereof, is broken. Soon they leave their mourning and make another beginning, once more "brush forward on their coursing steeds":

> Brochant avant sur leurs destriers courants.

Such was the great revelation of early French literature to the Anglo-Saxons. It was the contribution which a race in love with light and life, believing itself God's people, made to a race languishing not indeed for lack of heroism, but for lack of clear light overhead and of faith in itself and the future. Beowulf, a victor, spoke as he left the earth words full of the Christian consciousness of the nothingness of earthly things. The conquered Byrhtnoth died proudly, but without a hope for his country.

The poets of Anglia had called sinister landscapes and lugubrious scenes into being with a strength of characterisation and atmospheric truth before which the corresponding passages of the French *trouvères* sink to insignificance, for instance the attempts of the author of *Roland* to describe the fearful portents which announce the death of his hero. In his cold and unimpressive catalogue of horrors, he uses words too slight for the images they would convey. But when, at Hastings, a primitive fragment of verse rings out in Taillefer's song, movement, gaiety and light enter English literature. Half the gifts and aptitudes of English poetry have then their beginning. Taine's theory that all English poetry derives from Anglo-Saxon and all English prose from Franco-Norman is therefore inaccurate. Taine sees in old French poetry only the elements which degenerate to "gossip and platitude." It is made up, for him, of dull stories, mere statements of fact which "never wait for poetry and painting." He even says of the poet of *Roland* that there is "no splendour and no colour" in his story. It is a strange opinion for one who had read *Beowulf* immediately before *Roland*, a poem truly all of gloom before one woven of clarity. Taine's estimate can only be explained by supposing that he was unconsciously under a romantic influence which caused him to confuse poetry with sadness and murkiness, prose with clarity and lightness of heart. He reserves the word poetic too exclusively for happenings during a dark night in which nothing is heard distinctly, only the tramping of feet and cries of rage or pain. To follow him closely would be to reject all the poetry of southern countries, that of Italy and even that of Greece, as no more than measured prose in comparison with the sombre and often formless effusions of the Germanic and Scandinavian tribes.

(3) Taine is, however, right when he adds that the style of *Roland* is "bare, without images." This bareness is one of the most marked features of old French poetry. To turn to it from the poems of the Anglo-Saxons is to receive, among other general impressions, that of having left violence for calm. To an ear still a little deafened by the Anglo-Saxon clamour, the voice which speaks quietly or sings in a gentle undertone at first seems weak. Some time is needed before the charm of softer, more modulated tones can be savoured. The surcharged, ejaculatory rhetoric of Anglo-Saxon poetry gives an appearance of singular poverty to a language which is really new, in which words have as yet no past and figures and periphrases have still to be born.

From the time at which it is first known, Anglo-Saxon is a traditional language with a style already inclining to decadence. It possesses the accumulated wealth of a long life. Its remoteness from the object or idea it expresses is seen in the very sumptuosity of the decoration. The literary ornaments are so many veils, which prevent contact with things rarely denoted by their simple name. The French of the eleventh century, on the other hand, starts naked as it was born, without heirlooms or the pomp of inherited rhetoric. It may be said to have created its splendour out of nothing, only by its own radiance. It is slight as a river at its source, transparent as the water which gushes from a rock, but vital as that which has space and the future before it. It takes its words straight from the vulgar tongue, uses only the same terms as everyone else. It has no solemn or strange periphrases with which to make its effects. All it can do is exactly to choose the best of the common words, and to combine them in harmonious and varied groups. To move and captivate, it must have facts, the interest of a story, or else, for more lyrical compositions, the naked beauty of feeling and idea. It is by these signs that the infancy is recognised of a literature which may one day have great fortunes and make a tradition, but which has as yet no heritage to help or hamper it.

The same is true of the fixed poetic language of England. It made hay of all its former opulence. But after the long winter which ensued on the Norman Conquest, it had a season of renewal. It sprang again to life, bereft, stripped naked, prosaic, pedestrian, glued to facts, careful only for the accuracy after which it long tried vainly, yet with honest concentration on this modest aim. And when, at the advent of Chaucer, the language of English poetry had completed its initiation, the fine slightness and bareness of its framework were still distinctly perceptible beneath the poet's graceful images and his movement, his sprightliness, and his varied colours. Poetic language had begun again at the very beginning in order to make itself what it was, and what it still is.

(4) A merit of old French poetry from which the English reaped abundant advantage has still to be noticed. The French *trouvères* have, not without reason, been reproached for monotony and long-windedness. But to turn to them from the scops is to be struck, perhaps equally, by the almost endless variety of their themes and their moods and by the large number of the works in which they have resisted the temptation to gossip, and successfully found for their conceptions an artistic frame, sometimes bare and severe, at others prettily decorated, but proportionate to their matter, so that subject and form are happily balanced.

After reading the chief Anglo-Saxon works, it is easy to imagine the surprise with which some Englishmen gradually learnt to know the fertile and artistic literary productions of their conquerors. One has but to take the omnipresent, uniform alliterative line, which magnified all subjects alike, whether great or small, gave them all the same lyrical and epic tone, and to place it beside these varied French verses, ranging from the alexandrine to the monosyllabic line, beside their endless combinations of assonances and rhymes, which between the two extremes of the long *laisses* of the *chansons de geste* and the short, sparkling stanzas of the songs, run through the whole gamut of strophes, and are able, with their odd and even rhythms, to reproduce every step and gait, to translate the finest shades of feeling, from heroism to impertinent frivolity.

There are, for instance, French Lives of the saints, primitive poems of which the *Life of Saint Alexis* is the noblest that remains. To whomsoever has read some of the amorphous, tormented hagiology sung by the Anglo-Saxons, it is a surprise to come upon the calm stanzas on one assonance of *Saint Alexis*. From the first, they give the impression that a new world has been entered, in which grave and deep religious feeling is so allied to the simplest and surest art that the result can only be called perfection. Every part of the story, every corner of the picture, is, without effort, enclosed in a stanza. The story proceeds without hurry or jar. Emotion seems to be evoked not by the words, but by the details, that is the facts, which are presented without emphasis, in an order so luminous that it has the effect of the inevitable.

In *Roland* it is the dash which is admirable. The long *laisses*, the chained assonances of decasyllables, succeed each other, as do the charges of the Frankish and Saracen knights in the interminable fight. If after each there is a pause, the next starts with the same gait and covers another stage. The assonance constitutes the uniformity in the lines of the *laisse*, so much alike that they are a distinct and coherent group, but the association is freer than that effected by rhyme, and each line retains an undefinable but sufficient individuality. Nothing could be more alert and ongoing than these disciplined masses which "brush forward on their coursing steeds," moved by one impulse, lit up, here and there, by the sonorous clarity of the syllables—"Halte-clère, Joyeuse"—as by the brandished swords of galloping horsemen.

The heroic age and the great *chansons de geste*, in which the *laisses*, the chained assonances, lend themselves to grandiose expression, as in the description of the fight between Roland and Oliver (Gérard de Vieme), or to metrical eloquence, as in Charlemagne's apostrophe of his barons (Aimeri de Narbonne), was succeeded by the age of romances, which was neither free from convention nor innocent of diffuseness and platitudes, but which made its own contribution of new graces. After the decasyllabic or alexandrine line came the line of eight syllables, and the distich superseded the *laisse*, or stanza. Everything speaks of smaller ambitions, less width and space. It is a decline to the petty, to a prettiness, sometimes exquisite, which attains to a perfection of its own in many passages of Chrestien de Troyes' considerable works, in the short lays of Marie de France and in the first half of the *Roman de la Rose*. But the same verse-form lent itself well to satire, to the fable and the *fabliau*, and with its serried rhymes was a good medium for Renart's ironies, for the highly flavoured stories of conjugal misadventure, and for Jean de Meung's encyclopædic satire.

Always there were, not indeed below, but round about these different works, countless songs, romances and *pastourelles*, at first and at their most beautiful in free verse and varied rhythms, but passing, gradually, to a formal lyricism, increasingly stereotyped in metre and sentiment. Although the surviving examples of these old romances are all too few, there are enough of them to show that they had the very qualities which have been denied or too grudgingly allowed to the old French poets. A strangeness, together with the vagueness of the refrains, refutes the charge of lack of mystery, excess of dry light and exaggerated regularity. Sometimes there is the charm of delicious, fanciful unreason (*Volez vos que je vous chante ?*), or, in a few stanzas, an emotional drama of inexhaustible melancholy (*Gaiète et Orior*). More often, in the *Reverdis*, the *jeu-partis*, the tensons, the rondels, the *ballettes*, there are rhythms light as a bird, so winged and so singing that as one reads them one hears a tune:

> Por coi me bat mes maris
> Laisette!

Every verse-form, every arrangement of rhymes and every stanza afterwards used in English poetry is to be found here in seed or in flower. Henceforth English, like French, poetry had a variety of forms proportionate to its variety of subjects.

It should be added that the change in the verse was not merely exterior. Its inner character was from this time modified. The principal accent came to fall where it fell in French, before the cesura and on the rhyme. The culminating points became the end of the line and the end of the hemistitch. The line rose towards its rhyme, instead of falling, as formerly, from the initial alliterations. The pleasure of echoing and recalling sounds gave to vowels an importance in the line at least equal to that of consonants. Words, even Germanic words, were for long severely constrained in order that they might be bent to the exigencies of a foreign rhythm not made and hardly fitted for them. Even to-day the traces of this struggle have barely disappeared. French poetry captivated the Anglo-Saxons to such a point that it changed their ear, and obliged them to return to accents at fixed intervals and similar and echoing terminations—to syllabism, measure and rhyme.

2. **Anglo-Norman Literature.**[1]—It was essential to recall the chief characteristics of French mediæval literature, in general, without limitations of time or province, because the whole of this literature was, as long as it lasted, known and loved by the Normans, and much of it was gradually translated or imitated by the English. Three centuries after the Conquest, the æsthetic character which we have noticed in this literature reappeared, almost in its entirety and with hardly any admixture, in Chaucer's English works. It behoves us now, however, exactly to determine the special contribution of the Normans to old French literature. To have confined ourselves to what they alone produced would have been manifest error, for the works which had most influence on early English poetry—the larger part of the chivalrous romances, the great allegories, the *Roman de Renart*, the *fabliaux*, the free and the formal lyrics—are of continental origin. Their particular contribution, and especially that of the Anglo-Normans, must, none the less, be distinguished and characterised, in order to understand the minds of the Conquerors, that is of the people whose literary tastes and needs were to make the most direct impression on the unified nation which sprang of their fusion with the vanquished.

The Norman element is, before the Conquest, difficult to unravel from the mass of French literature. What is certain is that the Normans had already severed every tie with the language and poetry of the Scandia whence they emanated. They may have kept the adventurous and warlike character of their Scandinavian

---

[1] G. Lanson, *Histoire de la Littérature française*, Parts I. and II.; Gaston Paris, *Littérature française au Moyen âge, La poésie du Moyen âge* (2 series), *Poèmes et Légendes du Moyen âge*; J. Jusserand, *Hist. Litt.*, op. cit. Book II. chaps. ii. and iii.; W. H. Schofield, *English Literature from the Norman Conquest to Chaucer*, chap. iii. (excellent bibliography).

ancestors, but marriages, the influence of their new surroundings and their conversion to Christianity had gallicised them swiftly and fundamentally. From the eleventh century onwards, Normandy had a high repute for clerical science and piety, solid orthodoxy, and the beauty of her religious buildings which are intermediate between the romanesque and the gothic. Rouen was a lettered, artistic and religious capital city in which mystery-plays were already being performed. The Normans did more than any other people to propagate the cult of the Virgin, and to introduce the feast of the Immaculate Conception which was long forbidden by the Church. In spite of this, their ties with Rome were very close; their clergy were, on the whole, orthodox and rational. In the matter of poetry, they found the epic readymade when they settled in France. "They hardly seem," says Gaston Paris, "to have taken a personal part in the epic movement which was going on around them." But they had a passion for this kind of poetry, for instance for the *Chanson de Roland*, which is not theirs but which they preserved, and whence some primitive fragment is said to have been sung by Taillefer before the army at Hastings. Their highest claim to be poets would be found in the *Vie de Saint Alexis* by Tedbald de Vernon, if the origin of this work were certain.

They landed on English soil, and for more than a century their language showed no essential difference from French. The Norman and Angevin kings remained intellectually continental and French until they lost Normandy and Anjou in 1204. Many of the best French writers of the time lived at their court; many of the principal works of the twelfth century were composed there. The reign of Henry II. (1154–99) marks the zenith of this literary glory.

Already, however, it is possible to see that the *trouvères* born in Great Britain, or called thither from the continent, were under a special influence. Public taste dictated the matter and the form of their writings unless these had a political inspiration. They are nearly all chroniclers, by their subjects and their style. This is true of Gaimar with his *Lestoire des Engles*, Wace with his *Roman de Brut* (Brutus) and *Roman de Rou* (Rollo), Benoît de Sainte-More with his *Lestoire e la généalogie des dux qui unt esté par ordre en Normendie*, his *Roman de Troie*, and his romance of *Æneas*, Eustace or Thomas de Kent with his *Alexander*, Garnier de Pont Saint Maxence with his *Vie Saint Thomas le Martir*.

Many of Taine's reproaches, which are too general because he extended them to all French poetry, would be well founded if he had limited their application to the Anglo-Normans. On the whole, Anglo-Norman verse does not deserve to be called very poetic. Almost all the verse certainly known to have been written by an Anglo-Norman poet, or a French poet at the Anglo-Norman court, has an indisputably prosaic character. It falls short in sensibility, in enthusiasm, in the search for beauty. It is made up, for the most part, of versified chronicles and didactic treatises. The Anglo-Normans were dominated either by intellectual curiosity or by utilitarianism. The epical and lyrical metres of their predecessors were almost exclusively succeeded by an octosyllabic line, which uses rhythm and rhyme only to aid memory, and since to the constraint of verse it adds none of its rightful pleasures, it often awakens regret for prose.

The conquest of England inspired the *trouvères* not with epics after the style of *Roland*, but with metrical chronicles. The Battle of Hastings in the *Roman de Rou* has an almost equally surprising effect if it be read after the description of the fight at Maldon, in which Byrhtnoth died, or after that of the Battle of Roncevalles where Roland met his death. The legendary glory of Roland and the epic heroism of Byrhtnoth alike are gone. Wace's very long story is copious and well-informed history and nothing more. It states the happenings in the camp from hour to hour, from the eve to the morrow, reproduces the very words of the combatants, records the tactics of the two leaders, and describes the details of their armour, and the most trifling incidents of the battle. There is certainly no lack of heroic motifs, for instance the successive refusal of Raoul de Conches and of Walter Giffart to bear the duke's standard, because they wish to fight themselves. There is lively presentment of the tumult of the battle—"Moult oïssiez graisles sonner." But there is little poetry. The narrator may love fine sword-play and the din of the *mêlée*, but he no more loses his head than Froissart in the story of Crecy. He knows how to classify the enormous mass of information he has collected and to sift evidence. Throughout, his octosyllabic couplet trots forward at an even pace, and he holds the reins with the steadiest hand.

Wace's characteristics recur, more or less, in all the Anglo-Norman poems of the great period. There is a less contrast, but one still striking, between the purely French romances of Chrestien de Troyes and those of Benoît de Sainte-More who lived at the court of Henry II. Chrestien turns to romantic and picturesque use all the historical remains in the legends which are his material. His aim is to please by strangeness of adventures and graces of style. But Benoît, who is first of all a chronicler, gives a pseudo-historical air even to his inventions. He is spirited but not poetic.

Many of these Anglo-Norman writings are, for that matter, real history, and even such of them as are fabulous or legendary pretend to truth. The aim of several is to satisfy the ingenuous curiosity of readers who wished to know foreign nations and the present and the past. Other poems, of yet more positive design, attempt to weld together the legends scattered throughout the land of Great Britain, and thus to facilitate the fusion of its conflicting races. Their authors would have rallied, on English soil, divergent hostile patriotisms, united Britons, Angles and Normans in the praises of the country they all inhabited, in which all that was and had been was equally dear. The great island had never received such homage as was tendered it in the *Brut* (Munich MS.). Praise, practical as its author, runs through these verses in which the country is reviewed as by a conscientious geographer: its orography and hydography, its mineral and agricultural wealth, the history of its population—all pass, in good order, before one whose admiration never modifies his cool judgment. And nothing is more striking than the smiling aspect, the plenty, this alert observer discovers in the country which Anglo-Saxon poetry had wrapped in fog and horror. It is almost comfortable already. The surrounding sea is no longer "the path of the storm," but the wide, convenient high-road of an easy foreign trade.

Anglo-Norman is thus distinguished from French literature by a more marked didactic and utilitarian tendency, and by a weakened æsthetic character. This is not surprising if it be remembered that its first mission, on entering a country which had relapsed to ignorance and was populated by enemy races, was to instruct and to unify. Inevitably the native purity of the French language was very soon adulterated in an island in which it was cut off from its roots among the people. The mother-tongue of the settlers in a foreign land is always thus corrupted or stiffened. It becomes a written, bookish language, preserved with effort and artificially, or, as a spoken tongue, it is contaminated by contact with speech which differs from it profoundly, and suffers from the outset an accretion of many words disfigured by their passage through foreign lips. Thus foreign geographical terms, and expressions referring to local customs which survived the Conquest, adhered to Norman-French. The momentary brilliance of Anglo-Norman letters was, therefore, mainly due to the continental writers attracted to the court of the kings of England, and literature was kept alive among the Anglo-Normans, properly so called, only in so far as it was useful. As for the English who practised writing in the language of the Conquerors, they could not but aggravate the artificial or incorrect character of this literature in a tongue which was not their own.

The consciousness of these inevitable lapses inclined the more intelligent of Anglo-Norman writers in the twelfth and thirteenth centuries to turn to Latin.[1] It is true that Latin was then attracting a large number of clerks and literates throughout Europe, who were thus lost to the cause of progress in the vulgar tongue. But this loss was felt in Great Britain more than anywhere else, and literature there may be said to have been beheaded—it lost its leaders—for the sake of Latin, the only common language in a country where babel reigned. It was not only the clerks who wrote Latin, nor did they confine its use to religious treatises. It was employed in this age in works of every kind, serious and frivolous, learned and popular, many of which greatly surpassed the writings in the English of the conquered or the French of the conquerors. William de Jumièges' *History of William I.*, Ordericus Vitalis' *Ecclesiastical History*, William of Malmesbury's *Chronicle of the Kings of England*, and Henry of Huntingdon's *Annals*, are the principal monuments of the serious part of this literature in Latin,[2] and of the fantastic, mystifying works, the best known is Geoffrey of Monmouth's *History of the Britons*. The best examples of the works apparently more frivolous, but also more truly literature, are the letters and stories of Girardus Cambriensis, the Latin jests and miscellaneous profanities of Walter Map, and Nigel Wireker's *Speculum Stultorum* or Comic Adventures of the Ass Brunellus.

From what has been said, it follows that the study of literary monuments of the time should extend from French to Latin, if all and the highest intellectual activity of the inhabitants of Britain after the Norman invasion is to be understood. If the aesthetic elements which were to fashion renascent English literature are to be analysed, it is necessary to go further, to study not only the Latin of England, but also all the Latin, whatever its origin, of the religious offices which sounded week by week in the ears of the faithful, and had plainly an influence on the English verse-form in process of evolution.[3] When mediæval Latin poets finally gave up attempting to reproduce the prosody of antiquity, when they wrote Latin verses with a purely accentual rhythm, and took advantage of the numerous similar endings of words in Latin to enrich their productions with sonorous rhymes, they provided the vernacular poets with models of versification. It was, in fact, they who first fully realised the resources of the new versification, and fully exploited its potentialities for the solemn and the comic. In no language was there for a long time anything to match the perfection of the hymns of the Church which were repeated throughout Christendom, Jacopone's *Stabat Mater* or Celano's *Dies irae*. Nor was there anything to equal, for comic effect, the sonorous, single-rhymed quatrains of the *Goliards*, or unfrocked clerks, attributed to Walter Map:

> Meum est propositum in taberna mori:
> Vinum sit appositum morientis ori,
> Ut dicant, cum venerint, angelorum chori:
> Deus sit propitius huic potatori.

The Latin verses, which the faithful conned in church or drinkers trolled in the taverns, could exercise a considerable influence on English poetry from the time when the Anglo-Saxon line was finally abandoned, and new paths were explored for a metre which should be at once accentual and rhymed. The Anglo-Saxons had been able to translate much Latin quantitative verse without

---

[1] J. Jusserand, *Histoire Littéraire*, op. cit. Book II. chap. iii.; W. H. Schofield, *English Literature from the Norman Conquest to Chaucer*, chap. ii.

[2] J. Gairdner, *Early Chroniclers of Europe* (1879); H. Morley, *English Writers*, vol. iii. op. cit.

[3] G. Saintsbury, *History of English Prosody*, vol. i.; *Cambridge History of English Literature*, vol. i. chap. xviii.

modifying their own prosody, for there was no common measure between the two verse-forms. But from this time Latin rhymed verse was allied with French verse to undermine and overthrow the Anglo-Saxon form. English poetry was to aim henceforth, although vainly for many generations, at analogous effects of high lyricism, jollity and swing.

Before dealing with poetry in English, another force which had important and lasting influence on it, and reached it first through the French and Latin of the conquerors, must be mentioned. There is in Anglo-Norman literature, on the whole so practical and prosaic, one region in which sentiment and the marvellous are paramount. They exist, it is true, only in the subjects, and do not affect the even calm of the writers' tones. Yet they are there whenever a chronicler, pursuing his curious search for stories, has heard and wishes to repeat some Celtic legend.[1] It must continually have happened that the Normans became aware of the tales which had been traditional among the Britons around them since their glorious days and were the depository of their hope of revenge, and also of the fair dreams of adventure and love by which their imaginations were charmed. If some of these poems reached England from Armorica, through the medium of continental French poetry, there were others which passed straight from the Britons in Wales to the Anglo-Normans.

Was this Celtic influence, which is always a little mysterious and indeterminate, now exercised for the first time? Probably not. In Anglo-Saxon times the neighbourhood of the vanquished Britons had already had its effect. History no longer admits that the Britons suffered mass extermination at the hands of their Germanic conquerors, but teaches that as well as the Irish, untouched within their island, and the still independent Britons of the western and northern mountains, there were many survivors of this race in the centre and the south who were merged in the conquering people. We have seen that the conversion of the Angles to Christianity was the work of the Church of Ireland, and that Bede emanated from a monastery founded by Celts and animated by their spirit. Anglo-Saxon hagiography is partly of Celtic inspiration, and there is a great resemblance between the lives of the Irish Saint Brandan and those of the Anglo-Saxon saints Cuthbert and Guthlac. Even the half-pagan poetry of the Anglo-Saxons is often much akin to what is nowadays called Celtic mystery and strangeness. The romance of *Beowulf* opens with a prologue on the mysterious origin of the hero which is singularly like the story in the British cycle of the appearance of Arthur. However, on the one hand, the defeat of the Church of Ireland by the Church of Rome, and, on the other, the exclusive, little inquisitive character of the Anglo-Saxons, seem to have put very strict limits to their poetic debt to the Britons.

All this was changed at the coming of the Normans. For the first time, the proscribed Saxons felt themselves the brothers of the Welsh whom they had formerly despised and persecuted. The Normans, meanwhile, were the first to effect a fusion between these races, and they did it by violence. In the reign of Henry I. they made a cruel and bloodthirsty conquest of Wales, hitherto independent. For two centuries this subjugation was nothing like final, but the contact, so early established by measures of force, made the Anglo-Normans curious about their adversaries. Hence works were written which at first were hardly literary in themselves, but which were important for the echo which they found in French, and even more in English, literature.

The first of these works in date, and the one most fruitful of consequences, was the Latin *History of the Britons* which Geoffrey of Monmouth wrote before 1147, and dedicated to the son of Henry I. The author had been brought up in a

---

[1] G. Saintsbury, *Flourishing of Romance and Rise of Allegory* (1897).

Benedictine monastery near Monmouth in Wales, of which place he was arch-deacon when he wrote his book. He poses as a truthful chronicler, and claims to translate an old and unknown British book. He had, in fact, no precursors, save Gildas (sixth century), who does not mention Arthur, and Nennius (tenth century), who says very little about him. Moreover, exploration of the Celtic literatures has yielded nothing except what is later than Geoffrey and imitated from him.

Thus Geoffrey is, in large part, the creator of the Arthurian legend. His book is a work of imagination in disguise, and it is impossible to say to what extent tradition helped him. But it was certainly with an historian's gravity that he wrote out his fables.

Following Nennius so far, he makes Brutus, the father of the Britons, into the great grandson of Æneas, who came to Britain and there founded Troynovant, or New Troy, afterwards called London.

But the most curious parts of his story are those which concern Arthur, repre-sented as the heroic defender of the Britons, and Merlin, whose prophecies he collects. Arthur appears as the conqueror of the Anglo-Saxons, the Picts and the Scots. He brings Ireland, Iceland, Scandinavia and Gaul under his imperial rule, enters into conflict with the Roman emperor, triumphs over him, and makes the Romans his slaves. Ever victorious, he lives until the end of the seventh century.

In spite of the protests of several clerks, Gerald de Barri among others, Geoffrey's fables were accepted. They were assimilated first by the Normans and then by the Anglo-Saxons. Both peoples were presently enthusiastic for the British hero, their racial enemy, and adopted him as a glorious ancestor. The illusion was singular, but it had its part in weakening racial hatred and giving birth to English patriotism.

Geoffrey Gaimar, a mediocre Norman troubadour, was the first to turn this story into French verse. He shows Arthur, after his victories, summoning a meeting of the kings at Caerleon—the City of the Legions—and there crowned in splendour, and thus he gives the first suggestion for the legend of the Round Table. Other Celtic legends gathered about the early nucleus. Marie de France contributed to them in lays written at the court of Henry II. Allowing for the part of Chrestien de Troyes, the conclusion is that the British cycle was evolved princi-pally by the Anglo-Normans, and that Walter Map, who was half-Norman and half-Welsh, presumably welded together the Arthurian legend and the legend of the Holy Grail. He is credited with giving the cycle its religious and moral character, in that he represented Guinevere, Arthur's wife, as an adulteress, and her lover, Lancelot, as unworthy, by his sin, to accomplish the quest of the Holy Grail, which was reserved for his son, Galahad. The *Queste del Saint Graal, Lancelot du lac* and *Mort d'Arthur* are attributed to Walter Map.

The powerful imaginative leaven of this story, the most beautiful and varied of all those in the minds of the English when they again began to write, must not be forgotten. It was a story all the more stimulating to them because it was set in their own country, and they believed it to be national.

3. **English Literature from 1066 to 1350.**[1] **Changes in the Language.**—Small though the æsthetic value of Anglo-Norman literature may be, it is great in comparison with that of the contemporary literature in English, labouring, as this did, under the disadvantages of a despised language, loss of tradition and lack of culture. It was a literature written by half-literate men for an ignorant people.

---

[1] J. Jusserand, *Hist. Litt.*, op. cit. Book II. chap. iv.; W. H. Schofield, *English Literature from the Norman Conquest to Chaucer*, op. cit.; John Edwin Wells, *Manual of the Writings in Middle English*.

The three centuries after the Norman Conquest produced writings which show the gradual transformations undergone by the old language, and are therefore full of interest for the philologist, but which offer hardly anything to the amateur of literature. He may be touched by the very awkwardness of these attempts at literary composition, but he esteems them merely as rude translations, inharmonious verses which hesitate between alliterative rhythm and the cadence of the rhymed line, and alternately obey and ignore the laws of syllabism. All this licence would have horrified the scops and it gave the *trouvères* good matter for ridicule.

The reconstruction was slow, but the ruin of Anglo-Saxon rhetoric was prompt, almost, indeed, instantaneous. It had two principal causes, the repeated efforts of English writers to translate the works of French poets, often to translate them literally, and the wide and deep changes swiftly wrought in the speech of the vanquished people by their lack of culture and by the contaminating influence of the language of the conquerors.

Several modifying processes affected Anglo-Saxon.[1] The vocabulary suffered the rapid and final loss of a considerable number of words, of nearly all those proper to the old poetic style, and it received, in exchange, French words which penetrated it slowly and gradually. By degrees English came to borrow the words which denoted the customs and ideas imported from Normandy—the learned terms of warfare, hunting and falconry, words which referred to chivalry, scientific and legal language, courtly speech, abstract and technical terms and those connected with art and luxury. Thus was constituted the modern English language, in which words of French origin or words based, in imitation of French, on Latin or Greek, are much more numerous than Germanic words, although these, in current speech and frequency of use, are to the others in the average ratio of ten to one.

At the same time, there was a modification of the form and the pronunciation of such Anglo-Saxon words as subsisted. Most often they were contracted: unprotected by any culture and assailed by deforming foreign attempts to pronounce them, they tended to keep only their essential, that is their accentuated, syllable. They were like a besieged fort, holding only the central tower, abandoning the outer works. There resulted an increase of the monosyllables which are so numerous in modern English.

Degradation overtook, in particular, the terminations in use among the Anglo-Saxons. The Norman Conquest affected them in two ways: first, it suppressed or weakened many of them, and thus accelerated the progress of the English language to its present analytical state, in which relations previously indicated by inflections are shown by distinct words; secondly, certain particular inflections were chosen for survival out of the number of those customary among the several peoples of Anglia, Mercia and Wessex, whose differences were reproduced in the chief Middle English dialects, those of the north, the centre and the south. While endings of words were indeterminate and at rivalry, the language of the conquerors sometimes had the additional weight which made it the arbiter of victory among them. This is the best explanation of the extension to all declensions of the plural in *es* or *s*, at first used only in one of the declensions of the noun.

French grammar contributed several of its uses. Anglo-Saxon formed the comparative and superlative of adjectives by inflection, but French introduced the use of the adverb also, so that, while the Germanic form was retained for monosyllables, mostly of Saxon root, the analytical form came to prevail for polysyllables, which were mainly derived from the French. Similarly, possession,

---

[1] *Cambridge History of English Literature*, vol. i. chap iii. by Henry Bradley ("Changes in the Language to the Days of Chaucer"); H. Bradley, *The Making of English* (1904); O. Jespersen, *Growth and Structure of the English Language* (1906).

formerly expressed by the genitive case, was expressed henceforth either by the genitive ending or by a preposition.

Anglo-Saxon, as a whole, was gradually simplified to modern English, a language of singularly few grammatical complications. Genders, arising out of the form of words or obscure and forgotten traditions, needed too delicate treatment to allow them to remain intact in a country of mixed population, and they were logically distributed according to sex, the neuter being reserved for all words in which there is no idea of sex. Only vestiges of the old grammar were left—the few present irregularities of the verb and the noun, and the genitive case, the only one which has survived. The article and the adjective became invariable. Pronouns and auxiliaries were introduced to mark in the verb persons and tenses which had been expressed by inflections.

Thus a regular syntax, in which inversion and ellipses were only exceptionally allowable, was introduced. The poetic language lost closeness, freedom, and some elements of the picturesque, but the language as a whole gained lucidity and precision.

The final result of these transformations was not felt until the sixteenth century. In the meanwhile inflections kept a semblance of life, the varied, sonorous vowels first giving place to a uniform *e*, often arbitrarily used, which was perceptible to the ear at the beginning of the period in question, but was swiftly tending to purely orthographic existence. Philologists give the name of Middle English to the language of this long period of transition.

We are not here concerned to describe the slow and deep-reaching evolution in detail, and must be content with a mere sketch, instead of a complete picture. At first, French and English naturally kept separate. The conquerors spoke French, the vanquished Anglo-Saxon, which lost the dignity of an official and of a literary language. French became the language of the court, the schools and the law-courts, and, alternately with Latin, of the Church and of science. Knowledge spread among the burghers and among the landed gentry, who were largely Norman. It was only when they found themselves confined to Great Britain, after the loss of Normandy by John Lackland in 1204, that the conquerors began to pay any attention to the native language. Then it was that insular patriotism was born in the Norman, now cut off from the continent, and as his preoccupation with the people among whom he lived increased, he learnt their speech. The simplifications of English of which we have spoken, the sort of compromise effected between the two languages, made it possible for the two races to understand each other, more or less. The words which the Normans found most difficult, in meaning or pronunciation, were gradually dropped and replaced by their words. The whole of the thirteenth century is filled with these changes, which were accomplished in silence and by degrees, and which were hallowed by the custom of the fourteenth century. The Normans had, by this time, in great part abandoned French, and the native people had brought their language to a point at which it had lost the crabbed visage of its birthplace. Henceforth English reigned alone: in 1350 it took the place of French as the language of the schools; in 1362 it became that of the law-courts; and in 1399 it was used in parliament for the first time by Henry IV. In the same period prosody, which for long had wavered between one and the other of the two traditions, attained to perfect balance with Chaucer, who combined respect for the native tones of his fellow-countrymen with obedience to the essential laws of French versification. Whatever be the individual merits of the poets who preceded Chaucer, they do no more than mark the steps to that honourable place where he is enthroned as the first great metrical writer of his country.

4. Literature in English. The Religious Writers.—A hundred years of complete silence followed the Norman Conquest, and when a few writings in the native language reappeared towards the end of the twelfth century, they were mainly works of piety. To a disinherited people, no longer able to read, the essential Word, which helps man to work out his salvation, had to be carried first. Homilies, sermons in prose and in verse, translations of the Psalms or parts of the Bible, rules for a devout life, lives of the saints and prayers—these fill the pages which form the mass of what may be called English literature until about the middle of the fourteenth century. They are at first almost the whole of this literature, and they are its predominant part until this period ends. Inevitably, their only local element is language. As regards their matter, they are transcriptions, often literal, from Latin or French. If the passage of generations somewhat modified their religious sentiment, these were changes which affected all Europe, and sprang not from conditions in England, but from the widespread fluctuations of piety in the Middle Ages. The asceticism of cloisters, the growing tenderness which mingled with the devotion to the Virgin Mary, and the exaltation which was imbued with chivalry and mysticism, were reflected, in turn, in these English works.

Whenever they are specifically English, they owe it to the very popular character of their public. The problem was to gain the ear of an oppressed, poor and ignorant people, and more than elsewhere it was therefore necessary to use a very simple language and to multiply explanations and concrete details. Sometimes, also, the choice of the subject and the mood of the story were determined by a gentle pity for the miserable state of the faithful. Again and again, an author excuses himself for using a language so much despised as English, saying that he has wished to write for men who know no French and have no edifying books. He knows that his style is bad, that his rhymes are weak, but he believes himself justified by his aim. It is chiefly the progress in form which to-day has interest for those who go through this starved period of English literature.

The earliest in date of these religious writings, the *Poema Morale*,[1] which in its original form goes back to about 1170, is a grave exhortation to Christians to turn aside from the paths of this world and to enter those of devoutness and salvation. The preacher begins with self-accusation—he has reached old age without giving enough of his thoughts to God. He begs men to remember the Day of Judgment, to keep the thought of Hell and Paradise ever before them. Let them leave the broad road which leads to Hell and take the strait path to Heaven.

The feeling animating the poem is sincere and sometimes ardent, but severe and sad. While the conception of Paradise is mainly spiritual, Hell is depicted with all its arsenal of material terrors. Souls are tortured by fire and cold in turn: burning, they think that to freeze is felicity; freezing, they sigh for the flames. Although the Old and New Law are said in one passage to be comprised in love for one's neighbour, charity is not preached except as the means of salvation. The asceticism of the cloister is predominant, and the individualism of the Christian who must esteem himself above his kin. "Nor let wife hope in husband, nor husband in wife. Let each man live for himself throughout his days."

The novelty of this poem is not doctrinal but formal. In style and versification, these four hundred lines of seven accents, in sections of four and three, are an innovation, and the form had a high destiny, for it was adopted by most of the popular ballads. Since the rhythm is iambic, the line is, at the same time, regularly syllabic. Almost every one of these lines, which are rhymed in couplets, contains a maxim, sometimes well turned and in the nature of an antithesis, so that it is easy to remember. The sententious style contrasts with the epical manner of the Anglo-Saxons. The old phraseology has gone, and has been replaced by a simple

---

[1] Text in Morris's *Specimens*, vol. i. op. cit. English translation by Gasquet (1905).

I—E

language, without images and bare and precise, but animated by some homely comparisons, at once exact and prosaic:

> Each man with what he hath may buy him heaven,
> Both he that hath more and he that hath less,
> This one with his penny, the other with his pound,
> 'Tis the most wondrous bargain that any man found.

We feel ourselves not far removed from the couplets of a Defoe, blunt and practical. There is the same lack of poetry and the same skill in speaking straight to simple people.

There is no originality of matter in *Ormulum*,[1] a mere translation and paraphrase of some forty of the Gospels read at Mass, which was written about 1200 by the monk Orme, a native of North-east Mercia. This author's most salient characteristic probably is the respect for ancient tradition which made the commentaries of the Venerable Bede his inspiration. But the form of his work is entirely new, and remained an isolated phenomenon of literature. The seven-accented line with a fixed cesura (4+3) is used as in the *Poema Morale*, but is unrhymed, is made on the pattern of the quantitative Church verses, ends with a redundant feminine syllable, and is completely regular as regards the place of its accents and the number of its syllables. It is like a first essay in blank verse. Regularity is its only merit. The author is afflicted with pedantry and purism to a singular degree. He invents a new spelling, best illustrated in his redoubling of the consonant after every short vowel. Deliberate and diligent, spending all his energy on manner, Orm marks the beginning of the desire to subject the universal indiscipline of the language to rules.

There is more poetry in some of the contemporary prayers.[2] The *Prayer to Our Lady* has warmth and emphasis, although its rhythm is uncertain; and in a few effusions of the early thirteenth century there is the tender mysticism of a Hugh of Saint Victor, for instance in the *Luve Ron* of Thomas of Hales, which contains the first truly artistic and poetic stanzas in the new language. It is with Villon's accent and in verses as cadenced as his, that the poet speaks of the transitory nature of earthly joys, and with an emotion already romantic that he enumerates the illustrious heroes and ladies of the past:

> Hwer is Paris and Heleyne,
> That weren so bryht and feyre on bleo,
> Amadas, Tristram and Dideyne,
> Yseude and alle theo,
> Ector with his scharpe meyne,
> And Cesar riche of worldes feo,
> Heo beoth iglyden ut of the reyne,
> So the schaft is of the cleo.[3]

The *Ancren Rewle*,[4] the best specimen of the prose of this time, is equally suave. It consists of rules for the ascetic life given by a prelate to three anchorites, women who have decided to live not in a convent, but in a solitary dwelling near

---

[1] Holt edition (Oxford, 1878). Extracts in Morris's *Specimens*, vol. i. op. cit.

[2] F. Furnivall, *Early English Poems and Lives of the Saints* (1862).

[3] Where is Paris and Helen,
That were so bright and fair of face,
Amadis, Tristram and Dido,
Isoud and all they,
Hector with his sharp strength,
And Cæsar rich of world's wealth,
They both glide out of the realm,
So the shaft is off the cliff.

[4] S. Morton (Camden Society, 1853). Modern English translation by Gasquet (1905).

a church. There is a new sweetness in these artless and minute instructions. The atmosphere is that of a period in which devotion to the Virgin is supreme, and the consciousness of feminine nature has entered even asceticism. This rule also exists in Latin and in French, but the English does not seem to be a translation.

The pious writings of the early fourteenth century are more alert in style, and can be vivacious, gay and charming. The *Life of St. Brandan*,[1] a translation from the French, introduced the English to the enchantments and marvels and the optimism of the beautiful Celtic legend. The *Life of St. Dunstan*, which is attributed to Robert of Gloucester, is full of homely touches and cordial light-heartedness. These rude and artless verses have a comic liveliness which compensates for their unrelieved prosaic character, for instance, in the scene in which the saint, busy at his little forge, receives a visit from the devil in the guise of a pretty woman who smilingly talks nonsense to him. The saint is not taken in, but puts his pincers in the fire while she is speaking; then suddenly, when they are red hot, pinches the devil by the nose, so that he flees, writhing and howling:

> As well for the Devil to have been at home, and wiped his nose,
> He never hied him thither more, to heal his cold.

At about the same time, in 1303, a Gilbertine monk, Robert Mannyng of Brunne, in Lincoln, undertook to translate, under the title of *Handlyng Sinne*,[2] the *Manuel des Péchés* which one of his fellow-countrymen of the previous century, William of Wadington, had written in the French of England, the debased language for which he excused himself by pleading his birth:

> De le françois ni del rimer
> Ne me doit nul homme blâmer,
> Car en Angleterre fus né
> Et nourri, ordiné et élevé.

Wadington, in forty-four stories, had shown the paths of sin. Mannyng by turns follows, neglects and adds to this model, showing more independence than was customary. Although he uses the octosyllabic line with great licence, his verse is much more rhythmic, alive and vigorous than that of his Anglo-Norman prototype. He has, moreover, sacrificed a fair number of dull, theological dissertations to the forcefulness of his narratives. He adds a dozen stories of mainly local origin. His object is amusement as much as edification. He is an observer of the customs of his time and paints them in lively colours. He inclines to satire, and he makes frank attacks on the landlords, anticipating *Piers Plowman*, and does not spare the clergy, whom he blames for laxity, luxury and frivolity. A true monk, he has little indulgence for women, and makes them responsible for the sins of men.

But his real merit is that he can tell a story well, clearly, with go, and with a certain agility hitherto unknown in England. To invent was not his part. When he does not copy Wadington, who himself had said of his book, "Rien del mien ni metrai," he draws on the common treasure. His stories are always interesting, in spite of their childishness and strange moral standpoint. They are very like the stories peddled by the Franciscan friars, to stimulate curiosity as much as devoutness and popular charity.

The demand for pious stories was abundantly supplied by a collection of twenty-four thousand lines of verse, the *Cursor Mundi*,[3] which dates from about 1320. It is an embellished version of the New Testament, in the Northumbrian

---

[1] *The Early English Legendary or Lives of the Saints*, ed. C. Hortsmann (Early English Text Society), vol. lxxxvii.
[2] Edited by Furnivall (Roxburghe Club Publications, 1862, and Early English Text Society), vol. cxix.
[3] Edited by R. Morris (Early English Text Society), lvii., lix.–lxii., lxvi., lxviii., xcix., ci.

dialect, and an octosyllabic metre more regular than Mannyng's. Its aim is to interest the people in the Bible stories, thus providing a counter-attraction to the romances. "Mast es it wroght for frankis man," says the author, and declares that he speaks to Englishmen. His poem may be described as the matter of the dramatic mysteries in narrative form. The Bible is not its only source, for its unknown author has recourse also to the *Historia Scolastica* of Peter Comestor, and does not hesitate to draw on many other French and Latin writers of the previous age. His copious verses are often picturesque, and are full of humanity, and that they enjoyed a great popularity is proved by the number of manuscript copies in which they have reached us.

A work of more local significance is that of the hermit Richard Rolle of Hampole.[1] For one thing, this writer is the only one of his time whose life is known to us in some detail. His reputation for sanctity was well established when he died, for the Cistercian sisters, whose convent was near his hermitage, expected his canonisation so confidently that they had an office written in his honour, together with his life in Latin.

He was born in Yorkshire about 1290, studied theology at Oxford, and at the age of nineteen fled, in fear of temptation, first from the university and then from his family, who thought him mad. He became a hermit. The fame of his sanctity spread through the neighbourhood and men came to visit him, but even while he was answering questions, he went on writing his meditations, and "what he said differed from what he wrote." He is the most diligent religious writer of his time. Such was his absorption in contemplation, that his friends could divest him of worn clothes, mend them and put them on him again without attracting his notice. Enthusiastic and visionary, mystical and fervent, he is a connecting-link between the orthodox saints, of whom he is the last, and the Protestant visionaries—Fox, Bunyan, Wesley and their like—whom he resembles in certain particularities of his life. He is tempted by the devil in the semblance of a girl he had once loved. He is haunted by fear of death and Hell. He has moments of tenderness so exalted that his prose halts, for instance in his *Nominis Jesu Encomion*:

> Therefore Jhesu es thy name. A! A! that wondyrful name! A! that delittabyll name! This es the name that is abown all names. . . . I gede abowte be covatyse of reches and I fande noghte Jhesu. I rane be the wantonnes of flesche and I fand noghte Jhesu. I satt in companyes of worldly myrthe and I fand noghte Jhesu. . . . Therefore I turnede by anothir waye, and I rane abowte be poverte, and I fande Jhesu, pure borne in the worlde, laid in a crybe and lappid in clathis.

Unfortunately his verse does not fulfil the promise of fervour which this mood contains. It is wordy and mediocre, never without the taint of the scholastic and the puerile. Although a layman, never in orders, whose conduct and enthusiasm were ruled by intimate inspirations, Richard Rolle nevertheless represents the most rigid orthodoxy of his time. About 1340, when Wyclif was already sixteen years old and about to drive a breach in the system of strict Roman discipline, he extols it in his *Pricke of Conscience*. He becomes its defender a generation before the clergy were indignantly denounced by Langland for their abuses and stung by Chaucer's wit.

Rolle's aim is to give an impulse to devoutness, by first showing forth the miseries and vicissitudes of this world, and then depicting the after-life, of which his presentment is as concrete and grossly material as was usual among the preachers of the day. Diseases are among the pains of Rolle's Purgatory—dropsy, gout, ulcers, boils, paralysis, quinsy, leprosy—and so is a fire of which the heat

---

[1] *English Prose Treatises of Richard Rolle of Hampole*, ed. G. G. Perry (Early English Text Society, 1866); *Pricke of Conscience*, ed. R. Morris (Philological Society, 1863).

is graduated according to the gravity of sins. Great sins burn like wood, small sins like straw, those of middling import like hay. He emphasises the value of prayer, almsgiving, fasting and Masses as means of relieving the souls in Purgatory. At this moment of history, it is curious to come upon his unhesitating declaration of the efficacy of pardons bought from the pope or the bishops, who hold the keys of this treasure of the Church, purchased for her by her doctors, saints and martyrs. The pains of Rolle's Hell are heat, cold, dirt, evil smells, hunger and thirst—the damned drink fire and suck vipers' heads to quench their thirst—and also darkness, the sight of devils, vermin, the blows of red-hot hammers wielded by demons, tears of fire, shame, red-hot chains and despair.

No idle tale overtaxes this author's credulity. One could wish, for his own sake, that many of his grave explanations had been written in jest. There is, for instance, his prescription for discovering the sex of a child in the act of birth: if its first cry be *A* it is a boy, if *E* a girl; for was not Adam's initial *A* and Eve's *E*?

The good hermit was a little too credulous, behind even his own generation. He awakes a longing for the rough good sense of Langland and Chaucer's merry scepticism. And he makes us sigh also for Chaucer's art, as we read the ten thousand octosyllabic lines which versify his visions and display the childishness of his matter, unrelieved by any merit of form. These are poor verses. He himself confesses that he had no regard for the beautiful:

> For I rek noght, thogh the ryme be rude,
> If the maters thar-of be gude.

He marks the decline of religious poetry in the first half of the fourteenth century.

5. **Secular Poetry from 1200 to 1350.**—A little later than religious poetry, yet side by side with it and growing rapidly from age to age, a secular literature developed which was founded exclusively on French works. It was, as was natural, predominantly chivalrous, and was inspired by French romantic poems. It has therefore very little originality of matter, but it betrays national instincts in a preference for subjects and heroes connected with the land of Britain. Large parts of every one of the romantic cycles of chivalry were turned into English in order that junglers might tell them to the people, but from the beginning the British stories were most valued, and gave the native poets matter for their most popular, and here and there also for their most original, songs.

In the first years of the thirteenth century Layamon, a priest of Ernley, on the Severn and near the Welsh border, put Wace's *Brut* into English verse for the benefit of his fellow-countrymen.[1] Wace, with the curious mind and the detachment of an Anglo-Norman *trouvère*, had followed Geoffrey of Monmouth's fabulous history of the Britons, and had therefore glorified that people at the expense of their Saxon adversaries. And Layamon, or Laweman, a pure German by race and tongue, faithfully repeated this story, as though he were ignorant of his own origin. His sympathies are all with the Britons; the Saxons are for him barbarians whose victories grieve him sorely and whose defeats delight him. It is not astonishing that he has scandalised modern English historians, almost to the point of being dubbed traitor. Freeman, the historian of the Norman Conquest, cannot enough despise this Anglo-Saxon who betrays his race, whose national heroes are not Alfred and Hengist, but Brutus, the descendant of Æneas, and the famous King Arthur. None the less, Layamon's patriotism is as ardent as it is mistaken. His error draws attention to the fact that the two races who had been enemies were already inextricably fused. They constituted a new unity which was already the English nation, and had England for its place and symbol. It is because he sees

---

[1] *Layamon's Brut*, ed. F. Madden (1847). Extracts in Morris's *Specimens*, vol. i. op. cit.

the Britons as legitimate owners of England that Layamon makes common cause with them against the Saxons, whom he regards as invaders, and there is not a doubt that when he speaks of the Saxons he is secretly thinking of the Normans, the oppressors of his fellow-countrymen.

Layamon is, on the whole, a faithful translator. He contributes nothing new except certain passages of the Arthurian legend. These principally reflect the developments of this legend in the half-century which separated him from Wace, yet he deserves honour for first revealing some of the most poetic touches in the story. Living, as he did, on the Welsh March, he may have had direct access to traditions of which his forerunners were unaware. Most of his additions are, however, accepted nowadays as either based on a text of Wace other than that printed, or borrowed from the lost *Chronique rimée* of Geoffrey Gaimar.

Nevertheless, Layamon is no mere translator. He cannot be classed among the *trouvères*, with their curiosity and the simple amusement they found in their own fine tales. He is a scop, and has kept something of the epic mood and the wild, impassioned note of Anglo-Saxon poetry, together with part of its vocabulary, a rhythm which still hesitates between rhyme and alliteration, and certain traces of the ancient mythology and the sombre, ancestral enthusiasm for war. He is, moreover, the first writer to weave about King Arthur a fairy lore of which there is hardly a word in Geoffrey of Monmouth or in Wace. He is more at his ease than they in the realm of the marvellous. When he tells the story of the passing of the king we seem to be listening to Malory:

> When these words were spoken,
> There came thither wending,
> A little boat moving,
> On the waters it floated,
> And two women in it,
> Wondrously formed;
> And lo! they took Arthur,
> And swiftly they bare him,
> And softly him down laid,
> And forth 'gan their sailing.
> Then was it accomplished
> What Merlin said whilom,
> That great woe would follow
> On Arthur's forthfaring.
> Still think the Britons
> That Arthur yet liveth
> And dwelleth in Avalon
> With the fairest of all elves;
> Still wait the Britons
> For Arthur's returning.

Very far from attaining to Wace's easy fluency, correctness and courtliness, Layamon, awkward and blunt, yet has a plebeian way which is not unpleasing. He recurs to the massive ironies of the Anglo-Saxon epic. Thus he tells how the British King Uther, with Arthur's help, defeated his brother Pascent, who together with Gillomar, the savage Irish invader, attempted to dethrone him. At the moment when Uther has wounded Gillomar to death and Arthur has slain Pascent, the poet's voice has the very tones of the *Ode of Brunanburh*:

> On the head he smote him
> So that he down fell,
> In his mouth his sword thrust—
> Uncouth his dinner—
> So went the sword's point
> In the earth beneath him.
> And then spake Uther,
> "Pascent, now lie there,
> Now hast thou Britain,

> To thy hand hast won it.
> So is now hap to thee;
> Therein death hath come to thee;
> Dwell shalt thou therein
> With thy fellow Gillomar,
> And well enjoy Britain.
> To you I deliver it;
> Ye twain may presently
> Dwell in the land with us;
> Nor dread ye ever
> Who food will give ye."

Such passages, occurring in a chivalrous romance, show the transitional character of Layamon's curious version of the Arthurian story. He was at once the last of the scops and the first of the English *trouvères*.

The works which came after his were principally rhymed chronicles, translations which include nearly all the cycles and are interesting mainly when they have a national character. Popular sympathy was to gather later about Robin Hood, the outlaw and unmatched bowman, a Saxon, proscribed by the Normans, who lived in Sherwood Forest with Maid Marian, his love. Meanwhile the English people were beguiled by the prowess of Beves of Hampton, or they followed in amazement the improbable adventures of Sir Guy of Warwick, who left his wife, the fair Felice, that he might deserve her by his exploits, and who went to Palestine, slew the giant Colbrant and died as a pious hermit.

These romances were hardly more than copies of French or Latin books. There is more originality of plot, manner and spirit in the romances of *Havelock* and *Horn*, which were inspired by Scandinavian legends. Both had already been told in French by the indefatigable *trouvères*, but the versions of the two unknown English poets are independent, attractive, and in some ways superior. They have a distinct manner due to a different public. For there was something rough and popular about the audiences of the English junglers. They would have wearied of long traditional descriptions of magnificent ceremonies and sumptuous halls, of unending analyses of courtly love. They wanted a quicker-moving story, a franker sentiment, and homelier realism in descriptions.

These two romances appeared in their English form towards the end of the thirteenth century. French chivalrous poetry was beginning to exhaust itself with repetition, and to give place to prose as a medium for reaching a public which had almost ceased to seek anything in literature except the element of the curious in adventures. But the romances had only just reached the people of England, whose minds were less cultivated, simpler, and more susceptible to the charm of rudimentary poetry.

After his *Lestorie des Engles* Gaimar had written the *Lai de Havelock*, the title being a corruption of the name of the Dane Anlaf Cuaran, who fought at Brunanburh. The English poet,[1] while seemingly unaware of Gaimar, yet does not derive immediately from the original legend, for the usual outline of the French romances has plainly influenced his style. Its beginning recalls the popular story which was to be crystallised in the famous ballad of the *Babes in the Wood*.

Goldburh, daughter of Athelwold, the good king of England, is left an orphan and the ward of her uncle Godrich, Earl of Cornwall, who has promised to marry her to the best man in the kingdom, but who really is envious of her throne and thinks of ridding himself of her. As for Havelock, son of the Danish king Birkabeyn, he is in the power of the wretch Godard, his guardian, who delivers him to the poor fisherman Grim to be put to death. Grim spares the boy, who reaches England, where he is long a wanderer but is at last hired as scullion by Princess

---

[1] *Havelock the Dane*, ed. W. W. Skeat (Oxford, 1902).

Goldburh's cook. Thus humbly placed, he amazes the countryside by his strength and his exploits, and Goldburh's uncle ironically marries her to him, as the best man he knows. But Goldburh recognises the youth's royal birth by the light which issues from his mouth and by a sign, the red cross he bears on his shoulder. With the help of a vassal who has remained faithful, Havelock reconquers Denmark, then wrests England from Godrich. Godard is dragged over stony soil by an old mare and then hanged, and Godrich is burnt alive. Thus all ends for the best.

Love plays an insignificant part in this romance in which adventure dominates. But the simple and artless narrative throws the element of the pathetic into full relief. In the beginning, when Godard's atrocities are related, we are a little reminded of Ugolino's tower, or of the prison in which Hubert makes ready to burn out little Arthur's eyes at the order of King John. Godard goes to visit his nephew Havelock and his two nieces in the dungeon in which he has cast them to die of cold and hunger. He kills the two little girls there, but his heart fails him so that he cannot finish the business. The miserable hut of the fisherman Grim, his dialogue with his wife Dame Leve, the fisherman's revulsion of feeling when he sees that the boy is of royal race, the mixture of pity, reverence and self-interest which decides him to spare and even to serve the child whom he had sworn to kill— these scenes and others are so vigorously realistic as to appeal to every class of reader, and interest the simplest of them.

Havelock is a narrative in octosyllabic couplets, approximately correct. *Horn*,[1] with its very short lines, not syllabic but accentuated, has the form of a lay intended to be sung. Love, which is hardly mentioned in *Havelock*, is dominant in *Horn*. Thus *Horn* is particularly interesting as being transitional between the romances of the twelfth and thirteenth centuries and the romantic ballads of the later period.

According to the *trouvère* Thomas, who wrote *Horn et Rimenhild* in the twelfth century, Horn was the son of Havelock and Goldburh, the hero and heroine of the preceding romance. The two stories have in common their Scandinavian origin, but the later of them has much the larger share of the marvellous and the exotic.

There is a great difference between Thomas's version, with its five thousand alexandrine lines and long single-rhymed stanzas, and the lively English poem, which has fifteen hundred brief lines of two accents, so that it is about seven times shorter than the other. Its adventures are hardly less numerous, but the descriptions introduced on the slightest pretext have disappeared. Thomas never loses an opportunity to describe, whether holidays, feasts, ceremonies, fights, persons or clothes, and he fully analyses sentimental feelings. But his pictures and his analyses are alike conventional in type, and it is only because of the courtliness and refinement which he shares with all his school that the English poem awakens any regret for their tedium. There is much more go and energy in the English *Horn*. When we hear it, we do not feel that we are listening to a *trouvère* with his poetical recipes and his readymade developments of a situation. In spite of its improbabilities, the balder story comes nearer to the frank, manly tone of the epic.

Horn, the son of the king of Suddene, is a child when his father is slain by the Saracens, who land on the coast and waste the country. But Horn is so handsome that the Saracens cannot make up their minds to kill him, and with twelve other noble boys they put him on board a ship without sails or oars. The current bears these children, safe and sound, to the land of Ailmar, King of Westernesse. Under this king's care Horn is well treated and taught, and wins love from everyone, but especially from Rymenhilde, the king's daughter, who gives herself to him. When their love is discovered, Horn is banished from the kingdom by Ailmar. He asks the girl to wait seven years for him, after which time she may, if he has

[1] Morris and Skeat, *Specimens*, vol. i. op. cit.

not returned to her, marry another. She gives him a ring which is to remind him of his love and endow him with strength to withstand every trial. The seven years are filled with adventures and prowess. At their expiry, Ailmar compels his daughter to accept the hand of Madi, King of Reynes. Horn, whom she warns, hastens to the palace and reaches it on the wedding-day. He enters, disguised as a pilgrim, and his face smeared with black, so that he is not recognised, but is taken by everyone for a beggar. The bride is beside herself with grief and disfigured by tears, but she goes through the rites of a wedding-day. The scene of her recognition of her lover gives an idea of the swiftness and simple pathos of this poem. When she omits to pour out wine or ale for the supposed pilgrim, he asks her for a drink, because " beggars are thirsty," and while she is serving him he alludes obscurely to the past, turning her heart to ice since she fancies him a messenger sent to announce her lover's death to her. For some time he encourages her in this mistake, even giving her, as a last memorial of him she had loved, the gold ring which had been her own present. Thereupon she exclaims:

> " Heart, now thou burst,
> For Horn hast thou no more
> That thee hath pained so sore."
> She fell on her bed,
> There her knife is hid,
> To slay therewith her loathed king
> And herself, both,
> On that same night,
> If Horn come not might.
> To heart knife she set,
> But Horn anon her let,
> His shirt-lap he can take,
> And wiped away that black,
> That was on his neck,
> And said, "Queen, so dear,
> I am Horn, thine own.
> Nor canst thou me not know.
> I am Horn of Westernesse,
> In arms thou me kiss."

There are no subtle analyses in *Horn*, but it has what is better, the undisguised voice of passion.

Havelock, and even more *Horn*, show how much borrowing from French chivalrous poetry went on at this time, and how original English poetry was beginning to be, even when it borrowed. There is the same mixture of imitation and independence in the other poetic forms acclimatised in the same period. As early as the middle of the thirteenth century, a curious poem was written in eighteen hundred octosyllabic lines, *The Owl and Nightingale*.[1] It is one of the *disputoisons* or tensons, held in so much honour by the poets of Provence and France, an allegorical debate between an owl and a nightingale who discuss the rival merits of their song. Finally they decide to submit the dispute to "Maister Nicole of Guldeforde. . . . He wuneth at Porteshom, at one tune in Dorsete. . . ." The solution is proposed by the nightingale and accepted by the owl, who knows that if, in his youth, Master Nicole loved the nightingale and "other wighte gente an smale" overmuch, he has grown older and wiser. Master Nicole has often been cited as author of the poem, but since it praises him he was more probably the author's friend.

This poem is older than *Havelock* and *Horn* by half a century. It is the first work in English which is written correctly and under French influence, and which

---

[1] *The Owl and Nightingale*, ed. Stevenson (Roxburghe Society, 1838), Thomas Wright (Percy Society, 1843), F. H. Stratman (Krefeld, 1868), and J. E. Wells (The Belles Lettres Series, Boston). Extracts in Morris and Skeat, op. cit. vol. i.

therefore shows that the foreign form had been so assimilated as to allow native words to be fitted to it pleasantly as well as exactly. It is true that it does not attain to beauty: it has a stiffness, as of a language not yet supple, and it is weighted by many tedious passages and repetitions. But the style is lucid, there are lively touches, and an attempt is made to use rhyme for emphasising points and outline.

The scene is well set: the picture of the flowery hedge in which the nightingale sings, and of the ancient, ivy-grown trunk on which sits the owl, is clear. The opponents are made to join issue cleverly. Later the fable does indeed unmask itself rather too completely. The adversaries evince a litigious acrimony, more appropriate to the law-courts than the woods. They are veritable litigants and forget too easily that they are birds. It is soon evident that the nightingale, with his voice "of harpe and pipe," stands for careless youth, the owl, with his mournful cry, for the wisdom of old age. Both are pious, but while the nightingale hymns a rapturous piety, thinking to win heaven with songs, the owl insists on the need for gravity, self-examination and good works. The poet is inclined to side with the owl, but on the whole his dramatic impartiality is sufficiently indicated, and Maister Nicole's verdict is left doubtful.

Although it has less lightness and charm, is harsher and heavier and more carefully moral, *The Owl and Nightingale* is very like some pages of old French poetry. But this time it seems that we are concerned with an original work. The markedly iambic line, much accentuated and made up almost entirely of mono-syllables, tends to diverge from the French while it imitates it. The metrical line is more robust and less fluent than its French models, more beset with consonants and poorer in vowels.

This poem, in the middle of the thirteenth century, was isolated, but in the early years of the next century the various forms of a poetry no longer exclusively religious or chivalrous were multiplied. With the fourteenth century the satirical spirit entered English in adaptations of the *fabliaux*, some of them so lively that they herald Chaucer. Such is the fable of *Dame Siriz or the Weeping Bitch*,[1] in which a self-styled witch, a true *Macette*, favours a clerk's love-suit to a merchant's wife. The burgher woman is unmoved until the witch appears before her, leading a little bitch to whom she has given pepper and mustard to make it weep, and whom she declares to be her own daughter, metamorphosed for having rejected the advances of a clerk. Clerks are, she says, redoubtable persons. And the frightened burgher's wife thereupon lets her lover have his will of her.

Here disrespect for morals knows no restraint. Nor does it in the *Roman de Renart*; and it is with the same mocking spirit and pleasure in beholding the tricks of the unscrupulous that a poet relates, in *The Fox and the Wolf*,[2] the amusing cunning of a fox who falls carelessly into a well, and induces the wolf, after due confession and sermon, to pull him out and take his place there. Here, indeed, only language shows that poet and public are not French.

We have the same impression when we read the few extant songs of the period. Some, dating from the reign of Edward I. (1272-1307),[3] far surpass in lyrical charm the verses we have examined, and their inspiration and form are entirely French. They have the French way of evoking pictures of spring and flowering gardens, and these *clichés* take the place of the sombre, northern suggestions of the Anglo-Saxons. But the literary novelty of the language can lend to this poetry a sincerity

---

[1] *Middle English Humorous Tales in Verse* (Boston, 1913).
[2] *The Fox and the Wolf*, ed. T. Wright and J. O. Halliwell in *Reliquæ Antiquæ* (1845); Mätzner in *Altenglische Sprachproben* (1867), and G. H. McKnight in *Middle English Humorous Tales in Verse* (1913).
[3] Wright, *Specimens of Lyric Poetry* (Percy Society, 1842). Extracts in Morris and Skeat, *Specimens*, vol. ii. op. cit.

and pathos which are absent from the outworn and conventional French verses of the same age. Thus, in the graceful song *Alison*, a refrain on the French model supports a stanza of mixed three- and four-accented lines, which has skilfully arranged rhymes, some of them repeated as often as five times:

> A pleasant hap I have y-hent,
> I wot from Heaven it is me sent,
> From all women my love is lent,
> And lights on Alison.

In the song *Springtime* the misery of passion is portrayed. The lover sees joy everywhere around him, in the sky, among the birds, among the very worms —"worms woo under clods"—among lovers who secretly whisper, and among women "who wax wonder proud, so well it will them seem." But for lack of the only love he desires, he "this joy-weal will forgo, and in the wood be banished." Elsewhere freer and more native rhythms give out a yet more spontaneous note:

> Summer is y-comen in!
> Loud sing cuckoo!
> Groweth seed and bloweth mead,
> And springeth the wood new.
> Sing cuckoo! cuckoo!
>
> Ewe bleateth after lamb,
> Loweth after calfe cow;
> Bullock starteth, buck verteth
> Merry sing cuckoo!
>   Cuckoo! cuckoo!
> Nor cease thou ever now.
> Sing cuckoo now!
>   Sing cuckoo!

We quote also the simple refrain of a poem of courtly love which has otherwise nothing of the popular:

> Blow, northern wind,
> Send thou me my sweeting,
> Blow northern wind, blow, blow, blow!

Folk-songs of this type reappear only at the end of the sixteenth century, for they were long overlaid by a more formalist poetry. But at this time the numerous and exact descriptive touches bear witness to a more marked feeling for nature than is perceptible in most of the contemporary French songs.

But it is perhaps in the political songs,[1] made from the middle of the thirteenth century onwards, that the native genius shows itself most unmistakably. Elsewhere imitation is the rule and themes are borrowed wholesale from foreign sources. But the political songs are inspired by events within the country; they express aspirations, anger, loves and hates which are specially English. At first, it is true, they were written in Latin or French: they originated with the clerks and were meant for the ruling class. But very soon the junglers began to compose them for the people, and therefore in English. It is noteworthy that the earliest of these satires appeared during the Barons' War, when the nobles ranged themselves about Simon de Montfort to give royalty check. The whole English people were moved by this great quarrel, and the support of the popular or Anglo-Saxon element was indispensable to the audacious campaign of the rebel peers. In 1264 a song on the Battle of Lewes ridiculed Richard of Cornwall, the brother of King Henry III:

> Richard that thou be ever trichard,
> Trichen shalt thou never more.

[1] T. Wright, *Political Songs of England from the Reign of John to Edward II.* (Camden Society, 1839).

Presently the voice of social satire was heard in the land. In tones that are harsh and often coarse, which must have been echoed by common men up and down the country, the vices of the nobles, the state and the clergy were denounced. Song sided with the people against their governors, for instance in the *Song of the Husbandman*, which complains of the burden of taxes and the oppression of bailiff and woodward. Song rose even against the king when he was tyrannous and, like Edward II., dissolved his parliament to save his favourite. The repetition of rhymes at short intervals crystallised in the memory some rough truths which served as rallying cries to the multitude:

> For might is right,
> Light is night,
> And fight is flight.
> For might is right, the land is lawless,
> For night is light, the land is loreless,
> For fight is flight, the land is nameless.

Another poet anticipated Langland in his denunciation of all the vices of society: the law, the Church, the priests, the friars mendicant—all had been alike corrupted by love of money:

> And if the rich man die that was of any might,
> Then will the Friars for the corpse fight,
> It is not all for the calf that cow loweth,
> But it is for the green grass that in the meadow groweth,
> So good.

The Knights Hospitallers were no better, nor were the nobles, the physicians, the traders, the bakers. The honest and pious poet is indignant against every kind of fraud.

It was easy for this entirely national poetry to become patriotic. The English attentively followed foreign events. France was now their enemy, and there was great rejoicing when the news came, in 1302, of the defeat of the French chivalry by the burghers of Flanders:

> Listen, lordings, both young and old,
> Of the Frenchmen that were so proud and bold,
> How the Flemish men bought them and sold,
> Upon a Wednesday,
> Better them were at home in their land,
> Than for to seek Flemings by the sea strand,
> Where through many a French wife wringeth her hand,
> And singeth, Welladay!

When the English were drawn into the struggle directly, patriotism became exalted, and burst, in the first and victorious period of the reign of Edward III., into songs of triumph. A northerner, Laurence Minot,[1] came forward as official bard to the king, to sing his victories in Scotland, Flanders and France. Thus he celebrated, soon after the events, Halidon Hill, the naval battle of Sluys, the siege of Calais and other royal exploits.

The heavy and pitiless irony heaped on the vanquished in these war-songs recalls the Anglo-Saxon verses. Yet with the triumph there is a certain gaiety which, although in doubtful taste, moderates that fierceness which belonged to the old poetry.

Edward and his soldiers are incomparable heroes; all their enemies are braggarts and cowards, false and perjured traitors. But justice is surely not to be expected in poetry of this kind, to which it is unessential and of which it might diminish the effect. Such religious sentiment as mingles, here and there, with the insults, has a purely conventional air, and, if it be sincere, its sincerity is superficial.

---

[1] J. Hall, *The Poems of Lawrence Minot* (Clarendon Press).

In the absence of depth, we might hope to come upon the exact or picturesque details about the various fights which would give substance to the poems without hampering their lyrical swing. But there are none such. There is hardly place for narrative in these songs: they do little more than chant the praises of the victors and cover the vanquished with insults.

All the same, they are interesting. They bear witness to the national unity and to the high self-esteem which the English nation had acquired. These trumpet-calls are a prelude to the rich literature of the next generation. We see the English at Bannockburn avenging themselves on the Scots. We see the lilies trampled underfoot, France humiliated, who had been so proud, so sure of herself, so disdainful.

It is the metrical form of Minot's songs which gives them their special value. They are written in the Northumbrian dialect and combine popular and artistic elements. Alliteration reigns everywhere, vigorously holding together verses which, none the less, are always rhymed. Sometimes the line seems to be the direct product of the old alliterative line, its rhyme being superadded. The rhyme and the very regular stanza, with its fixed form, derive from France. As often as not, moreover, the line is not purely accentual, but also as syllabic as the most correct specimens of the time. Conscious artistry is also shown in the frequency with which the most important word in the first line of a stanza echoes that in the last line of the preceding one.

All this makes of each poem a whole which owes much to deliberate arrangement, and, incontestably, the combined effect of these artifices of rhythm and structure is that Minot's poems have an impetus, a beguiling lyrical movement, not due to their thought. Nor does it proceed from their language, which is conventional, without images, and frequently prosaic, and which abounds with padding and platitudes.

The great victories of Edward III. were being sung in London, and Minot's poems were current in the countryside, when Chaucer was born and when his mind received its first impressions. Glory in the field of battle was followed by literary achievement as brilliant. The long period of dependence was about to end. The English language, which had hitherto conned what others said, often stammering the while, now had faith in its destiny. Nothing is more striking than the number, the originality and the worth of the works which made the latter half of the fourteenth century a flowering season in English literature.

This brilliant efflorescence was the result of the progress made in the two previous centuries. Their arduous and obscure task was gradually to merge the so disparate elements of the new language in a harmonious whole. Whoever listens to the poetry attentively at first perceives discords and then becomes aware of the progress realised. So far, it is only by flashes that beauty is reached, but already the principles which should regulate style and verse have been discovered. The place of the old epic verse-form is not yet filled, for it has not found a fit successor either in the too slender octosyllabic line, or in the line of fourteen syllables, which is only seemingly long, since it is divided into sections (8+6), but which is, for this reason, too staccato in its movement. Some poets, however, have already been able to tell their tales fluently or to sing with some grace or warmth of feeling in short-lined verse. This English, with its popular tendencies, is still deficient in courtliness and art, but nothing remains to prevent it from acquiring these qualities as well as others, for it is on the eve of becoming the language of the court as well as that of the countryman and the burgher. As yet nothing is finished, but everything is ready.

BOOK II

THE FOURTEENTH AND FIFTEENTH CENTURIES
(1350–1516)—FROM CHAUCER TO THE RENASCENCE

CHAPTER I

THE FOURTEENTH CENTURY (1350–1400)—ROUND ABOUT CHAUCER

1. **England in the Second Half of the Fourteenth Century. Political and Social Conditions.**—The victories of Edward III. made England conscious of her strength and unity, but, with the exception of Minot's mediocre songs, they did not inspire the nascent literature. It is remarkable that almost all the works which are the glory of the second half of the fourteenth century appeared in the unhappy years between 1360 and 1400 which followed on the triumphant period.

It was in these years, after the Treaty of Brétigny, that the political wisdom of Charles V. won back for France almost all the English conquests, that the king, grown senile and luxurious, caused men to forget his exploits, and that his heir, the Black Prince, met with an early death. In these years, also, the child Richard II. began his reign, which was one of the most unfortunate England has known, whether during the period of the regency, with its miserable rivalries, or during that of the king's personal rule, capricious, arbitrary, disorderly and spendthrift. The Black Death wasted the people; the Kentish peasants made their formidable rising under Wat Tyler; French descents insulted English land; and Wyclif incited the religious schism which divided the population into the two parties of the Lollards and the orthodox. Yet it was during these seemingly calamitous years that the poetry which is truly English had its first season of flowering. Lamentations, satire and denunciation fill the works which treat of politics or religion. Clergy and rulers are represented as equally corrupt and incapable, immoral and undisciplined.

Nevertheless this poetry, as a whole, has such an air of energy and youth as throws doubt on the importance to daily life of the apparent realities of history. It has to be acknowledged that, disasters and visitations notwithstanding, everyday life pursued its course confidently, eagerly, even merrily. In spite of them, the country became more and more prosperous, the burgher class grew wealthy, and the people enjoyed a measure of independence as the Norman and English races came to be almost completely fused. In spite of everything Merry England was born. There were inevitable miseries, but they left ample room for joy and hope. The light of heart loved frank feasting, mirth and holidays; the austere sighed over the world's sins, yet did not lose courage, but set themselves strenuously to reform abuses. Social conditions were unstable, and the news of a passionate revolt could make men tremble, but the rebels were individuals who had ceased to bend beneath the yoke, and had thrown off oppression and inertia. They were judging, blaming, criticising, jeering, growing angry. They had attained to free thought and free speech.

62

2. Prose from 1350 to 1400. Trevisa, Mandeville, Chaucer, Wyclif.—
The state of society is better understood after a glance at the prose literature
of this time. Its bulk is so small and its literary quality so slight that it is hardly
of value except as giving information about the period. English prose took form
with a slowness which is striking in comparison with the activity of France and
Italy and the value of their productions in this sphere. Villehardouin and Joinville
were writing even in the thirteenth century, and France now boasted of Froissart,
Chaucer's contemporary, while Italy had Boccacio. Meanwhile in England, where
there was no dearth of talented men, the rivals of the continental chroniclers still
used Latin as their medium. Thus the learned and intelligent Higden wrote his
Polychronicon in Latin before 1363, and Walsingham of St. Albans, towards the
end of the century, compiled in Latin chronicles which match the pages of Froissart
in their spirited descriptions of scenes.

English was still a disinherited tongue, used for translations. A Gloucestershire
parish-priest, John of Trevisa, undertook to translate Higden's *Polychronicon*,
and completed this enterprise in 1387.[1] He does not always understand the easy
Latin of his original, and his awkward prose, in the archaic dialect of the south-
west, is to-day chiefly interesting because his own additions show the changes
which had come to England in the quarter of a century between himself and Higden.

Higden had given a striking picture of the variety of the languages and dialects
spoken in England. He had deplored that southern and northern Englishmen were
hardly comprehensible to each other. He had attributed the corruption of the
English language to the circumstance that French alone was taught in the schools
and used in translating Latin, so that the sons of nobles were trained in French
from their cradles, and men of lowlier birth turned, from snobbish motives, all
their energy to learning French.

But Trevisa assures us that all this, which was true in Higden's day, had been
altered in 1385. For some eight years English had replaced French in the schools:

Here avauntage is [he adds characteristically] in oon side and disavauntage in
another side; here avauntage is that they lerneth her gramer in lasse tyme than children
were i-woned to doo; disavauntage is that now children of gramer scole conneth na
more French than can hir lift heele, and that is harme for hem and they schulle passe
the see and travaille in straunge landes and in many other places. Also gentil men
haveth now moche i-left for to teche here children Frensche.

This abandonment of French, which was necessary to the growth of the
language, showed its effects on prose literature only at a later time. For the
moment English was used for nothing more venturesome than translations,
either from French or from Latin.

The prose differs very much according to which of these two languages is that
of the translator's original. As a rule, the style of the translations from French
is markedly the more lucid and fluent, because of the great degree of identity
which had come to exist between the syntax and construction of French and
of English.

This is apparent if Trevisa's work be compared to the *Travels of Sir John
Mandeville*,[2] which was believed, until recently, to be an original work, and of
which the authenticity and the authorship have successively given rise to long
controversies.

It is now established that this pretended narrative of journeys to Palestine
and China is a fiction of the type produced by Defoe and Swift at the beginning
of the eighteenth century.

---

[1] See Higden's *Polychronicon* in the Rolls Series (French and Latin versions).
[2] *The Buke of John Mandeville*, ed. by Warner with the French text (Roxburghe Club, 1889);
The Travels of Sir John Mandeville, modernised version, ed. Pollard (1900).

It relates that in 1322 Sir John Mandeville, an English knight of St. Albans, left his country to travel in the East, whence he returned after thirty-four years, in 1356. Then, as an old, melancholy and gouty man, he told the tale of the extraordinary things he had seen on his road. In fact, this Sir John had never existed, but was the creature of the imagination of a French physician, Jean de Bourgogne, who amused himself by recounting these adventures in French, and was able, thanks to the credulity of the age and his own apparent artlessness, to pass them off as more genuine than the matter of Marco Polo. It is curious that this literature based on a hoax, which was to root itself so deeply in England, first appeared in France.

The book, with its imaginary English hero, was naturally well received in England. Translated in 1377, it had a great success, and the manuscripts of the translation are very numerous. It was a work which evoked countless fantastic scenes—countries where men were fed only on serpents and hissed like them, countries of dog-headed men, or of men with feet so large that they held them over their heads as sunshades. The author himself confesses that had such things been told him he would not have believed them. He goes on his way, heaping together, pell-mell, true travellers' tales, bestiaries, the scientific anecdotes of Pliny the Elder. The true and the false are closely intermingled.

Owing to his simple, effortless and slightly childish style, his English translation had a happy effect on the development of prose literature.

Chaucer's prose writings are, in point of bulk, an important part of his work.[1] But they have little of the originality shown in his verses. He too is no more than a translator when he writes prose. He translated from Latin to English, about the year 1381, the *Consolation* of Boethius, which, together with the *Roman de la Rose*, was his habitual reading. Of the two prose stories in his *Canterbury Tales*, one "The Tale of Melibeus," which purports to be told by himself, is borrowed from Jean de Meung, who had translated it from the *Liber Consolationis et Consilii* of the judge Albertano de Brescia (1246), while the other, the Good Parson's Tale, is in part translated from the famous French sermon of Friar Laurence, *La Somme des Vices et des Vertus*. Chaucer also brought together several Latin treatises in his *Astrolabe*, a work intended to teach astrology to his son Lewis, then ten years old.

On the whole, Chaucer's prose conforms to the rule already stated: it is the more English for being translated from French, the stiffer for being translated from Latin. Everywhere, however, it has the qualities which mark a good writer. It would be easy to quote pages in which it attains to loftiness, as when Philosophy appears to Boethius in his prison, or passages showing precision and swiftness, like those which enumerate the misfortunes of poor Melibeus.

Except for his Boethius, in which he happily followed Alfred, Chaucer's choice of originals is regrettable. Their scholastic character hides the beauties of form which distinguish his style from that of his contemporaries. Chaucer was not, however, so much under the influence of the schoolmen that he failed to see where they were ridiculous. He would have us read his prose tales, especially "Melibeus," with a smile which makes them less dry and stiff.

All these are prose-writers who were translators. We have still to speak of a man who was by turns a translator and an original writer in prose, an author of mediocre prose who gave to English prose literature an impulse and an efficacy which were decisive. This was John Wyclif, called the first Protestant, the adversary of the papacy and the assailant of Catholic dogma.[2]

---

[1] *The Student's Chaucer*, ed. Skeat (Oxford).
[2] *Select English Works of John Wyclif*, 3 vols. ed. Arnold (Oxford, 1869–71); *English Works of Wyclif hitherto Unprinted*, ed. Matthew (Early English Text Society, 1880); R. L. Poole, *Wyclif and Movements for Reform* (1889).

He was born about 1324, was a professor at Oxford and chaplain to Edward III., and was very learned in theology and in Roman and English law. He was drawn into that struggle between the king of England and the pope which was at once political and religious and which broke out in 1365.

The prestige of the papacy had suffered by its defeat at the hands of Philip the Fair at the beginning of the century, and by the removal to Avignon. France had set the example of revolt against the financial claims of the Church of Rome. England followed, when Urban V. demanded of Edward III. arrears for thirty years of the tribute which John Lackland had promised to pay to his predecessor. An anonymous pamphlet defended Urban's claim, and Wyclif was charged or took upon himself to answer it. He had already the spirit of independence and the confidence in individual logic, as applied to the Scriptural text, which characterise Protestantism. But he began with moderation, claiming merely to echo the national hostility to Urban's demands. Gradually the quarrel grew heated and enlarged its scope. Wyclif attacked the ecclesiastical hierarchy and the papal supremacy, and since the court supported him weakly, he appealed to the people. Hitherto, down to 1380, he had written in Latin, but he now wrote in English. With the help of others he translated the Bible, and at the same time he popularised his ideas by means of the preachers who were called "poor priests," and were soon to be known as Lollards. Educated but poor men, clothed in coarse woollen garments, they went from parish to parish, opposing the friars against whom Wyclif had declared war. Their severe and practical sermons were in contrast to the scholastic grandiloquence of the friars.

From 1380 onwards Wyclif's ideas, hardly different till then from those later enunciated by Langland or hinted by Chaucer, had a new direction. They became an attack on dogma, for he renounced belief in the Eucharist except as a symbol, and attacked devotion to the saints and the use of indulgences.

He was forsaken by all his former friends. The Peasants' Revolt of 1381 had frightened the nobles and the burghers and brought traditional and conservative ideas back to favour, and Wyclif's doctrines were condemned by the Archbishop of Canterbury and by Oxford University. He was not, however, personally molested, and he ended his life in peace in 1384, in his cure of Lutterworth in Leicestershire.

There is no disputing his social importance in the latter half of the fourteenth century. As a writer of prose he also, in two ways, played a considerable part.

He was, to begin with, the first translator of the Bible into the vulgar tongue. He translated the New Testament, while Hereford, his coadjutor, translated the Old. Undoubtedly his translation is very faulty, for his aim was to be literal, and he had a long habit of writing Latin and found it difficult to attain, late in life, to true English prose. He abounds in Latin constructions, makes too much use of relative clauses. Nevertheless he supplied the first elements of that biblical language which was to be an integral part of English and to be used for the famous Authorised Version of 1611.

Secondly, Wyclif first appealed directly to the nation by such leaflets and pamphlets as were to swarm in the days of the real Reformation. If Wyclif in these writings shows himself destitute of every artistic quality, he yet deserves recognition for the logic and the vigour with which he posed in them certain formulas.

The agitation which his doctrine and writings stirred into being must always be kept in mind when the literature of the end of the fifteenth century is studied.

3. **The Dialects. The Reappearance in the West of Alliterative Verse.—** It is poetry and not prose which is the glory of this age. The pith of the matter was there, rich and vital. But there was an obstacle to the birth of a literary era which should be harmonious and complete. For if classes were beginning to draw

closer together and races to intermingle, the language of the country could not yet be said to have reached unity. The period is perhaps that in which the diversity of the dialects of England can best be perceived. Leaving on one side the small differences of speech which distinguished almost every county from another, there were at least four dialects which were struggling for supremacy, so equally matched that it was impossible in 1380 to say which of them would have the greatest future —the Northern, Southern, East Midland and West Midland dialects. Each had its own literature, and the awakening in the fourteenth century had at first the effect of enriching all four together, so that confusion did not lessen but was intensified. The study of the literature of this century is therefore necessarily fragmentary. The critic first perceives that progress in the north, and more especially in the west, was far slower than in the rest of the country. It is plain, even if vocabulary and grammar be left out of account, that these districts remained attached to the forms of the past. They kept their taste for alliteration, and at least one of them retained, surprisingly, the alliterative verse-form, almost pure and still vital, able to make a final struggle for life.

Since the Norman Conquest, alliterative verse had led a subterranean existence, showing itself, here and there, even in the south, at the beginning of the thirteenth century, then lost to sight, to reappear, abundant and flourishing, in the west of England about the middle of the fourteenth century. On the Welsh border and farther north, in Lancashire and Cumberland, it prospered especially, as was natural since the Welsh March was the part of England least accessible to French influence. This district was also the most backward, the last to be settled by the Saxons and by the Normans, and that in which artistic culture had been most retarded by the unceasing warfare with the Welsh. The author of *William and the Werwolf* pleads his lack of art and genius to excuse his use of the alliterative rather than the octosyllabic line.

The provincialism of a backward district does not, however, by itself explain the return to this old verse-form. It was due also to the failure of the new versification to fill the place of the old epic verse. Chaucer had not yet imported from France the decasyllabic or heroic line which was to take precedence of all others. The prevalent short and slight rhythms could not satisfy men in whose ears the last echoes of the epic verse of their ancestors were still ringing.

Moreover, the versification derived from France lacked an assured prosody. Accent hovered, doubtfully, over the different syllables of words of French origin, and even Germanic words were infected by the uncertainty. The relation between rhythm and tonic accent was, in consequence, not clearly perceived. There were thus various reasons why the old verse-form should come back to life at the moment when the spirit of the nation was reborn.

The consequences of the return to the old form were that the poetry of the west regained an epic swing, resumed the use of the epithets and synonyms necessary to alliteration, revived many archaisms, and, finally, restored the Teutonic elements of the language to the first place. This archaism, which was also provincialism, was to consign poems of this date, many of them remarkable, to a long oblivion. As examples of the difficulty of this local poetry, verses can be quoted which are to-day as strange to read and as hard to understand as a line of *Beowulf*:

> Schon schene upon schaft schelkene blode.
> (Shone sheen upon the shaft the warriors' blood.)

Nevertheless these alliterative poets do not, like some nineteenth-century poets, submit their vocabulary to the criterion of the exclusively Germanic. None of them makes it a rule to banish words of foreign derivation. The new language had so penetrated the people, even of remote districts, that statisticians find almost as many French and Latin words in the alliterative poems as in Chaucer. But these words have been more anglicised: their spelling has grown English for the reason that the alliterative poets are generally less literate than the others, and use words not as they read them but as they hear them. Accent, in particular, gives an English character to the words of foreign root, for the initial tonic accent necessary to alliteration is imposed on them, instead of the final accent which was theirs originally and which rhyme emphasises and preserves.

It must not be thought that versification in these districts was unaffected by continental influences. If much verse was written, with even artificial correctness, on the Anglo-Saxon model, rejecting rhyme and excluding the stanza, there are also poems, like those of Laurence Minot, which are both rhymed and alliterative, and in which the lines are grouped either in irregular stanzas not unlike the *laisses* of the Early French *trouvères*, sometimes followed by a short-lined refrain, or in completely regular stanzas which observe the most minute rules of the fixed form of French poetry.

There is also a curious contrast between the form and the subject of these verses. The Cædmonian line is revived for poems of chivalry, or allegories inspired by the *Roman de la Rose*, or descriptions of customs which are plainly of a younger age. But this form, even when it is an imitation, has the advantage of giving the English poets an independence they often lack when they have recourse to a metre copied from the French. The originality is chiefly perceptible in details of style. Moreover, these alliterative poems, being really provincial, often have a roughness which is of the people, a harsh flavour of the soil, so that, for good or for evil, they are very distinct from the poetry of the court.

The earliest in date of the alliterative poems is a fragment of a romance of the Holy Grail called *Joseph of Arimathia*.[1] It is based on a French story in prose which it condenses. It acquires a certain originality from its vigour of language, particularly noticeable, as in Anglo-Saxon poems, in the narratives of war and battle. Two fragments have been preserved of a romance called *Alexander*,[2] which is connected with the romances of the ancient cycle.

The romance of *Guillaume de Palerne or William and the Werwolf*[3] has reached us in a complete state and its exact date is known. This translation of the French romance of the same name appeared in 1355. It is a real fairy-tale, its hero a prince of Spain changed into a wolf by his stepmother, but retaining, in this fierce shape, his kindly nature. The translator follows the story faithfully but not slavishly, for he makes cuts and additions, adding chiefly some pretty descriptions of nature and some artless homely details which redeem the rusticity of the language and the awkwardness of the construction. The alliterative verse is of very correct structure, and keeps its native vigour although neither the beauty nor the harmony of the best of the old models. Here, more than elsewhere, the general defect of this verse-form in the fourteenth century is perceptible. The lack of rhyme is felt in the strongly rhythmic line. It is as though a hammer fell heavily on an anvil not of iron, but of wood, and gave out a dull and disappointing sound.

4. "Sir Gawayn and the Grene Knyght." "Pearl."—The four alliterative poems contained in a single manuscript and entitled *Pearl, Purity, Patience* and *Sir Gawayn and the Grene Knyght* are much superior to those we have examined. In spite of their profound differences of subject and form, these poems have analogies of language and feeling which cause them usually to be attributed to

---

[1] Ed. by Skeat for the Early English Text Society (xliv.).
[2] Ed. by Skeat for the Early English Text Society (Extra Series, xxxi.).
[3] Ed. by Skeat for the Early English Text Society (Extra Series, i.). Extracts in Morris and Skeat, *Specimens*, vol. ii. op. cit.

the same poet. The dialect is that of Lancashire, the probable date round 1360–70. The author is unknown, and attempts to identify him with the Scottish poet Huchown of the Awle Ryale, who wrote a *Morte Arthure* and the *Pistil of Susan*,[1] or with the philosopher Strode, Chaucer's enigmatic friend, are no more than conjectural. If, however, it be admitted that there is question only of one poet, his works give some indications of the probable course of his life and cast of his mind. He was well versed both in the Bible and in profane poetry. He was familiar with castles, banquetings, hunts and tournaments. He knew courtly society and he knew the country, even the wild and solitary country of the western hills. His life had periods of worldliness and periods of devout religious observance, but he was never careless of moral edification. The praise of purity and chastity is the dominant note of each of his poems.

His only secular work is *Sir Gawayne and the Grene Knyght*,[2] which owes much to all the earlier Arthurian romances, and especially to the *Perceval* of Chrestien de Troyes. But its special subject, the singular adventure which is its theme, are known only through this author. There is no reason why the "stiff and strong" work to which he alludes as his source should not have existed. Anyhow, by his choice of incidents, his pictures and descriptions and the grouping and proportioning of the parts which make a whole, he proves himself an experienced artist.

Strange is the entry of the Green Knight, a giant on a giant horse, into the great hall of Camelot, where King Arthur is keeping Christmas among the Knights of the Round Table. He has come to try Arthur's knights. He will allow his head to be stricken by the great axe he holds in his hand, if the striker will swear to come in a twelvemonth and a day and receive a like stroke from him. As they all are hesitating, and Arthur, for the honour of the Round Table, is about to take up the challenge, Gawain claims the axe and severs the head of the unknown knight from his body. Unmoved, the giant picks up his head, calls upon Gawain to keep his word, and departs at a gallop, leaving all amazed.

When the year has passed, Gawain sets out, according to his promise, to find the Green Knight. Long is his quest through rugged, mountainous country. At last, on Christmas Eve, he finds himself before the comeliest castle he has ever beheld, and is very honourably received there. For three days he is the guest of a noble old man, who is master of the house, and of his wife, who is fairer even than Guinevere. Every morning the old man goes off hunting, and every morning the lady visits Gawain's chamber to tempt him with the offer of her love. The courtly but pure Gawain resists temptation, yet accepts from the amorous lady a girdle of green silk "with gold schabed," which shall preserve him from being slain. And when, thereafter, Gawain comes to his ordeal, the axe, falling on his head, does no more than cut his skin, in expiation of his fault in taking the girdle. Eventually his host proves to be the Green Knight, and his temptress Morgayn la Fay, who had undertaken to humiliate Arthur and his knights. Gawain returns to Camelot, and Arthur causes a band of bright green to be worn by each of the lords and ladies of his court for Gawain's sake.

This very well written poem is remarkable for the liveliness and variety of its scenes. There is delicate psychology in the scenes of the temptation, and the theme, the triumph of chastity, is lightened by a smile. The poet gracefully delineates the feelings of the gallant knight, mirror of courtesy, caught between his politeness and his desire to remain pure, all of whose virtue is preserved to him without a slur upon his gentleness. The story has many analogies with the tale

---

[1] G. Neilson, *Huchown of the Awle Ryale* (1902).
[2] Ed. by Morris for the Early English Text Society (Extra Series, 1897); translation into modern English by J. L. Weston (1898). See G. Paris, *Histoire littéraire de la France*, vol. xxx.

of the second book of the *Faërie Queene*, but both in human and in dramatic interest it is superior to Spenser. Gawain is really tempted, whereas Sir Guyon is temperance incarnate, and passes, bloodless and abstract, through the voluptuousness of the Bower of Bliss. The author of *Gawayne* draws a man where Spenser draws insensate virtue.

There is also realistic vigour in the description of the three successive hunts. The details are taken from life, and nothing is left out of the stag-hunt, not even the making of the quarry and breaking of the deer. Love of the open air and a feeling for nature are perhaps the most distinctive characteristics of this poem. It has two stanzas which, before Tennyson, describe the year's cycle. The seasons succeed each other, and for Gawain their flight brings ever nearer the hour of his redoubtable tryst: the cold and gloomy winter gives place to the fructifying showers of spring; the birds sing and the flowers blow; then summer ripens the crops and hardens the grain, and finally the leaves fall and the grass is grey.

The poet is never more at his ease or more original than when he is describing rough weather and a rugged landscape. Here instinct leads him to join hands with the scops. It is the mournful scenery of *Beowulf* which rises all around Gawain as he makes his way to the green chapel. He has marvellous fights with beasts and men, but they are as nothing to the assaults of winter:

> For werre [1] wrathed [2] hym not so much, that wynter was wors,
> When the colde cler water fro the cloudes schadden, [3]
> Ner [4] slayn wyth the slete he sleped in his yrnes, [5]
> Mo nygtes then in-noghe [6] in naked rokkes,
> Ther as claterande fro the crest the colde borne [7] rennes,
> And henged hege [8] over his hede in hard ẏsse-ikkles. [9]

Elsewhere he passes through a mountain forest, with enormous oaks, whitened by the snow:

> With roge raged mosse rayled ay-where,
> With mony bryddes unblythe upon bare twyges,
> That pitosly ther piped for pyne of the colde.

He has a striking vision of a misty morning in the hills—"each hill had a hat and a mist-cloak huge."

Thus the Anglo-Saxon mist enwraps this poem of Celtic origin, a poem of chivalry and courtesy which has for hero, not the Gawain whom a tradition, followed by Tennyson, made into the type of a quarrelsome, frivolous and volatile knight, but Gawain of the unstained shield, who rivalled the valour of Lancelot and the chastity of Perceval and Galahad.

Pearl [10] is a poem entirely different in origin, structure and atmosphere. It is an allegory which connects not with the Arthurian cycle, but with the *Roman de la Rose*. The author is not unacquainted with this poem, although, since he speaks of the "pure rose of Clopinel," that is of Jean de Meung, his knowledge of its conclusion seems to be faulty. The allegorical element of his work is combined with a symbolism directly derived from the Apocalypse, whence he borrows his concluding vision of the New Jerusalem. This mixture constitutes the originality of the poem, and saves it from the dry formula of the prevailing type of allegory, with its too conventional frame. It acquires singular greatness and religious fervour from its biblical inspiration. There is nothing in English poetry of this period which better recalls Dante's mystic visions and the refinements of feeling in Petrarch's sonnets.

The poet has lost his pearl, by which he means his daughter, a child two years old who was doubtless called Margaret, for such plays on words, originating in

---

[1] war. [2] irked. [3] shed. [4] nor. [5] armour. [6] enough. [7] burn. [8] high. [9] icicles.
[10] I. Gollancz, *Pearl*, edition with modern English rendering (1907).

the Gospels, were frequent among mediæval theologians. He has lost her in a garden; she has passed through the grass into the ground, which means that she lies in the churchyard in her grave. Ever since, mourning and weeping, he has often gone to the place where she disappeared, and his grief has thus been somewhat allayed.

On an August day he goes to this garden, and in spite of the flowers and scents which make it delightful, he groans and wrings his hands, then lies down on the flowery ground and sinks into a dream which transports his soul into the realm of the marvellous.

He is carried to a glorious country bathed in unimaginable light, where the rocks are of crystal, the woods have leaves which shine like burnished silver and pearls of the orient are the gravel. He advances, to the sound of the joyous songs of birds with flaming plumage, until he comes to a river with beryl banks and a bed of pebbles which are precious stones:

> As glint through glass they glimmer'd and glow'd,
> As streamin stars, when dalesmen sleep,
> In the welkin shine, on a winter night.

It seems to him that Paradise must be on the farther side, but he seeks in vain for a bridge or ford by which he can cross. Then he perceives, on the other bank, a child "full debonair" and robed in glistening white. He recognises that he has seen her already, and of a sudden his heart is filled with ineffable happiness. He can neither speak nor move, and fears that his least gesture may cause the vision to fade away. But the child herself rises and comes towards him, "so smooth, so small, so sweetly slight." Her white garments are bordered with precious stones; on her head there is a crown of white pearls; and a marvellous and flawless stone is fastened in the centre of her bosom. He understands that this is the pearl he has lost for so long. The child reproaches him gently for calling his pearl lost when she is in the beatitude of Paradise. He would rejoice, were he a "gentle jeweller." He must not seek to reach her; the river between them is crossed only through death. But she tells him of her celestial life, her bliss as the spouse of the Lord. Is not the Kingdom of Heaven of little children? Her innocence has ensured eternal life to him. She is of the hundred and forty and four thousand virgins whom Saint John saw on the mount in New Jerusalem, clothed in their wedding garments.

The child cannot lead her father to the city of the blessed, but the Lamb has vouchsafed her the right to give him a sight thereof. She guides him towards the source of the river, while they walk on opposite banks, and he sees the city as the Apocalypse describes it, the white-robed procession of singing virgins, clothed in pearls, the Lamb in their midst, and the angels round about them. Then in the radiant host he perceives his little queen and would run to her, but the effort awakens him, and he finds himself once more in the churchyard, his head upon the grave-mound, dismayed and sighing but resigned to God's will. He cries that it is better thus, that he cannot wish to see his Pearl again, for she is better where she is.

The extent to which the poem borrows from the Apocalypse lessens its originality, the desire to edify overweights it, here and there, with didactic and theological passages, and the descriptions might be called too flamboyant. None the less, there is no other allegory of the time which unites so much fervour with such beauty. When compared with *Pearl*, the most charming of the contemporary allegories, the story of the daisy, who is Chaucer's Queen Alcestis, is frivolous, for all its refinement and delicious roguery, and the most powerful of them, *Piers Plowman*, is chaotic and formless. In *Pearl* everything is harmonised to glorify purity, and at the same time a human emotion, the father's grief, in turn rebellious and resigned, gives dramatic movement to the whole poem. Through all that is imitation and through the burdensome weight of doctrine, there shines a rare refinement of feeling. Something exquisite in the poet's senses makes him susceptible to nature even in his moments of most devout mysticism.

Nothing less than this sincere pathos, this wealth of imagination, could have put life into the difficult and complicated stanza which the poet adopts. His highly alliterative line has four accents in a very marked iambic rhythm. The stanza has twelve lines, as rigorously disposed as the lines of a sonnet. It is indeed a sonnet which concludes with two couplets instead of two tercets. Further, the hundred stanzas of the poem are in groups of five, associated because the last line of the first of them recurs in the others like a refrain, so that the final rhyme of the first stanza is repeated five times. And the last word of each stanza recurs at the beginning of the next.

These rules are both strict and puerile, and the fact deserves to be noted because it throws the greater simplicity of Chaucer's versification into relief. Moreover, it is indicative of the tendency to over-refinement which afflicted the author of *Pearl*, in his remote district and with his out-of-date vocabulary.

The two other poems, which are in the same manuscript and are therefore attributed to the same unknown author, *Purity* and *Patience*,[1] are both in alliterative verse and without rhyme or stanzas. *Purity* is an epic narrative of the Fall of the Angels, the Flood, the Angels' Visit to Abraham, the Feast of Balthazar and the Fall of Nebuchadnezzar. *Patience* recounts the life of Jonah. In both, purity and submission to the divine will are, as in *Pearl*, the principal themes. Although didactic they give much space to pictures, and the ample rhythm and style are in harmony with the grandiose descriptions, such as that of the Flood and that of the raging sea. A suspicion of humour sometimes finds its way into these poems, as when the poet describes Jonah's sojourn in the whale's belly, but on the whole he is both serious and fervent. His epic manner recalls *Cynewulf*, but has less verbal exuberance and a less fluid melody, a more concrete outline and more weightiness.

5. William Langland and his " Piers Plowman."—William Langland's *Piers Plowman*, the most popular, if the least artistic, poem, of the fourteenth century, also belongs to the west. It emanates, however, not from Lancashire but from the west midlands, and certain elements of its vocabulary are taken from the dialect of the south. But although the language is more difficult than Chaucer's, it is less outlandish than that of *Gawain*. The verse is purely alliterative: it is quite uncontaminated by French versification and makes no concession to rhyme. On the other hand, the general form of the poem, a vision framing moral allegories, is borrowed from the continent, so that this work is in the succession of the *Roman de la Rose*.

Yet how much it differs in spirit from the French poem! How national it is! How near the people! Its importance to the historian of morals and religion is such that it has called forth, even from literary critics, an admiration which is excessive in view of the lack in this work of the most elementary art.

That it appeared in three successive versions adds to the difficulty of studying it. There are three texts of very unequal length.[2] The first, the shortest and least

---

[1] R. Morris, *Early English Alliterative Poems* (Early English Text Society, 1869). Extracts in Morris and Skeat, *Specimens* ("The Deluge," "The Destruction of Sodom").

[2] They have been published in 2 vols. by W. Skeat (Oxford, 1886). Extracts of Text B in *The Vision of William concerning Piers the Ploughman*, ed. W. Skeat (Oxford); J. Jusserand, *Les Anglais au Moyen âge: l'épopée mystique de William Langland* (Paris, 1893); J. M. Manly, "Piers the Ploughman and its Sequence," in *Cambridge History of English Literature*, vol. 2, chap. i.

formless, dates from 1362, so that it followed close on the Treaty of Brétigny and the great plague of 1361. The date of the second text is 1377, the last year of the reign of Edward III., when the Black Prince was dead and the child Richard heir to the throne. The third and considerably enlarged version belongs to the end of the century, between 1395 and 1398, when Richard II. had grown unpopular and was arousing the discontent of his subjects, particularly the London burghers, by his senseless prodigality.

Are these three texts the work of one or of three succeeding authors? Critics have posed the problem and it is still unsolved. The data given by the several texts certainly do not make it easy to construct a consistent life of the poet.

It appears that he was called William Langland, or Langley, and was born in Shropshire about 1330, that is six years after Wyclif and ten before Chaucer. He lived for some time in the Malvern Hills, then, tonsured but only in minor orders, he settled in London, in Cornhill, with his wife Kitte and his daughter Calote, and followed the craft of a public scribe. Certainly he knew the law courts and legal language. We have the picture of a tall, gaunt man with shaven crown, who passed haughtily along the streets, neither greeting the serjeants nor doing reverence to lords and ladies, and whom many took for a madman. Yet he also represents himself, not without irony, as a sort of beggar, going from door to door and pleading his tonsure to excuse himself from working with his hands, earning a livelihood by singing a *Placebo* or a *Dirige* for those who gave him alms.

Whatever his life may have been, his work is that of a man of profoundly religious mind, who is indignant at the vices of a society Christian only in name. He gives first a satirical picture of the actual world, then a vision of the world as it would be if the teaching of the Gospel were truly practised. His poem may be summed up as a work of edification, never artistic in intention and very rarely so in fact.

We have seen that from the middle of the thirteenth century England had the habit of these social satires. The novelty of *Piers Plowman* consists in its ample scale, the relief into. which certain realistic scenes are thrown in the course of the allegory, and the author's fervour and energy. His rare comprehension of the political and religious necessities of his time is also new. No less than Wyclif is he convinced of the need for a reform of the secular and regular clergy, although he does not follow Wyclif in dogmatic innovations. He recommends a parliamentary system in which the king, supported by the Commons, would govern for the public weal. The boldness and novelty of his thought are, in this century, often astonishing.

The qualities of mind and heart which we feel that he possessed could not but make his poem by turns vigorous and lofty. He had too such rude vital force and hearty irony that the scenes which animate his preaching are most intensely alive and full of movement.

He was, however, entirely without the art of construction or arrangement. He loses himself, and us with him, in his labyrinthine allegories and pictures. Confused even in the earliest version, his plan becomes more complicated and incoherent every time it is retouched, and to sketch the outline of the whole poem is almost impossible. Even to indicate the subject of each of its different parts is difficult.

Disguised as a shepherd, the poet falls asleep one May morning in the Malvern Hills, and has a vision of a vast field full of folk—poor and rich, workers and idlers, nobles and burghers, bad clerks and jesters. The crowd swarms as in a thronged market-place, a contrast to Chaucer's peaceful picture of his pilgrims. It seems to the dreamer that Lady Holychurch appears to him amid this disorder, and tells him that the crowd is busied with things of the earth rather than things of heaven, that man's chief duty is to seek Truth, that Faith without works is nothing worth, that only love, otherwise Charity, leads to heaven.

When the crowd of sinners, now repentant, wish to set out for the sanctuary of Truth, no one knows the road, not even the palmer who has lately visited the most famous shrines. Was there ever a pilgrim who cared about Holy Truth? Then appears the person who names the poem, Piers Plowman. For fifty years he has served Truth by working, and from Conscience and Good Sense he has learnt the road. He offers to lead the pilgrims, first describing the allegorical country through which the way lies. The difficulties cause the most corrupt and cowardly to turn back. Then Piers announces that before he starts he must plough half an acre of land, and while he does this he gives advice to the "loveli ladies, with oure [1] longe fyngres, that habbeth selk and sendel," and obliges everyone to follow his example. Those who seek to escape their task are reduced to obedience by Hunger's rough handling. In its first form the poem ends here with the poet's awakening, closing with a peroration on the small value of papal pardons and the greater efficacy, at the Last Judgment, of an upright life.

Within this frame there are, however, two almost detached episodes which are longer than itself and unconnected with each other. They are moralities in narrative form, each possessed of independent and real dramatic merit, and they are proof of close relations with the theatre of the time. They might be called two comedies, the Marriage of Lady Meed and the Confession of the Seven Deadly Sins.

Lady Meed is "wonderliche clothed," wearing rings "of the preciousest perre" on all her fingers, and on her head a crown richer than the king's. She is a powerful but dubious personage whose name has been perverted by the evil times to a bad sense. She has a whole retinue of courtiers and flatterers who persuade her to evil. They prepare to wed her to False, and her marriage contract has been drawn up duly, when the opposition of Theology causes the business to be carried to London, to the king's court, where the righteous, by their own courage and the advice of Conscience and Reason, prevail upon the king to break off the marriage, and wreak justice upon the guilty, in spite of the devices of the wicked and their bribery of royal officers. There follows a lively description of the flight of False and his company, who take refuge with the Pardoners, the Merchants, the Minstrels and the Friars, in turn, and are gladly harboured by all of them.

The Confession of the Seven Deadly Sins is the sequel to a sermon by Reason, who also invites all sinners to seek "seint Truth." It is only the homely realism of his descriptions of the Seven Deadly Sins which is personal to Langland—for these seven are everywhere in mediæval literature. Langland, however, makes them not abstractions but living beings, vitalised by the force of comedy and by many details taken from life. Of Covetousness and Gluttony he speaks with peculiar gusto. Abominable though the Sins may be, they yet are all capable of remorse. Repentance prays to God for all the kneeling sinners.

> And have reuthe on thise Ribaudes that repente hem here sore,
> That evere thei wratthed the in this worlde in worde, thougte or dedes.

The poem, which was already crowded, was more than doubled in length when it was rewritten for the last time, and acquired a sequel in the shape of a number of visions, grouped by the poet under three titles, graduated so that they hold out the hope of a clear arrangement. Having shown the ills and vices of actual life, he produces a triple vision, *Do Well*, *Do Bet*, and *Do Best*. Unfortunately the benefit of the implied classification does not go beyond the titles. Elsewhere all is disorder, incoherence, chaos. Moreover, the sequel lacks the lively scenes which form

[1] Over.

the attraction of the first part. The last version of the poem, the only one extending to the end, is a preacher's amplification of the earlier text, the work of a Langland grown old, if not of a second or third author. The thought is as vigorous as
ever, the tone has loftiness, often a new nobility, but the confusion is such that
the work cannot be read continuously, and only a few fine passages stand out from
the rest.

As the beginning of the poem recalls the morality-plays, so the sequel, which
still has a dramatic turn, is often reminiscent of the mysteries. There is an imaginative effort to revivify the great scenes of the religious life. Passus XXI. in the
third text is a dramatic narrative of the mysteries of the Passion and the Resurrection which gives much space to dialogue, a play with magnified stage directions.

The scene is laid, as in the Mysteries, betwixt Heaven, earth and Hell. Jews,
soldiers, thieves, the multitude who acclaimed Jesus at his entry into Jerusalem:
these stand for earth.

Heaven is a dramatisation of a verse of the Vulgate: "Mercy and Truth are
met together; Justice and Peace have kissed each other." These abstractions have
become angels, of whom some, severe and implacable, debate with others who are
indulgent to human weaknesses, and all finally embrace, signifying thereby that
Mercy will triumph over strict Justice.

Finally, a loud voice is heard to cry upon Hell to open its gates, and Christ,
resplendent with light, enters thither in spite of Satan.

These are the loftiest and most lyrical passages of the whole work. Like gems,
they would gain by extraction from their matrix.

In this conclusion of the poem Piers Plowman is not forgotten. He reappears,
from time to time, but transfigured, changed to a symbol. Sometimes he seems to
be confused with Christ Himself, who also was poor and worked with His hands;
sometimes he represents the mass of the faithful. From pilgrim he has become
the object of the pilgrimage. Conscience, awakening from long sleep, finally sets
forth in quest of him.

Such, in brief, is this powerful and formless work. Whoever considers its ideas
only, must give it high praise. Indignant at the degenerate Christianity of his century, Langland opposed to the practices of his time the essential and neglected
virtues, especially work and charity. His attacks on the vices of the clergy are
such as were common and current in the Middle Ages. There were precedents for
them in the *Roman de la Rose* with Jean de Meung's *Faux Semblant*, not to go any
farther. It should, however, be noted that the vice against which Langland's
satire is especially directed is not Hypocrisy. Sloth and Avarice or Covetousness
are rather the objects of his hatred. His satire, at its liveliest, is accompanied and
directed by an intense religious fervour, unknown to de Meung and not found in
Chaucer. He does not destroy but seeks sincerely to cleanse and rebuild. He is
impelled not by the need to free his reason, but by the desire to strengthen and
purify the moral life of himself and those about him, and at the same time to rid
political and social life of their worst iniquities. This aspiration, together with his
choice of a ploughman for his hero, gives him the appearance of a rebel against the
aristocratic system and social inequalities. But his real preoccupation is with the
Christian life: the poor are nearer to Christ than others, less removed from Him
by the vices to which idleness leads. Piers, who is a ploughman, is also the Christian;
if he be not Christ Himself, he is at least one of the lowly of mankind, in whom
Christ became incarnate and of whom He made His apostles.

As regards the form of this poem, Langland shows himself powerless to build
up a harmonious whole, but able to create animated scenes, either comic or deeply
pious. The vigorous and frank quality of his verses is striking. But partly because

of his archaic versification and partly because of his real lack of art, his verses never thrill the sensibilities as poetry should. He is neither an artist nor a musician. These two deficiencies must modify his reputation, and while his work is of first-rate value to social historians, his literary merit is barely second-rate. In spite of the immense immediate popularity of his poem, he has almost no descendants. He is the last noteworthy writer of alliterative verse. A few imitations in the beginning of the fifteenth century, and, down to the sixteenth, a few sporadic essays which do not seem to derive from him: there was nothing more. English verse acquired fixed forms within his lifetime, not however from him but from Chaucer.

6. **Scotland. Barbour's "Bruce."** [1]—Meanwhile a change which had occurred in the north-east was fruitful of consequences. Northumbria had long been distinguished by the literature of the Angles, and, after a prolonged silence, had successively produced, in the first half of the fourteenth century, the *Cursor Mundi* and *Pricke of Conscience* of Richard Rolle of Hampole, and Laurence Minot's war-songs. The dialect spoken south of the Tweed was debased, but between the Tweed and the Firth of Forth it became more than a dialect, the rich and productive national language which was Scots. From the tenth century onwards Scotland constituted a nation made of mixed elements: in the north Scots who had come from Ireland and Picts, Gaelic-speaking peoples without part in literature in English; between the Clyde and the Solway Britons and Saxons whose dialect was akin to that of Lancashire; in the Lothians English-speaking Northumbrians with an infusion of Scandinavians.

It was in the Lothians and the east of Scotland that that variety of literature in English which is Scottish literature developed and flourished, the literature of a people who for long were as much England's enemy as ever the French could be. The Scottish War of Independence from 1286 to 1342 made the Scots conscious of their nationality, and united the men north of the Tweed and the Esk in a hatred of England, which, as Minot's songs prove, the English were not slow to reciprocate.

Scotland had in her recent history heroes to celebrate—Sir William Wallace, the Douglas, Robert the Bruce—and their half-historical, half-legendary exploits seemed to force poetry into existence.

About the middle of the fourteenth century the language of Scotland was hardly distinguishable from the Northumbrian dialect. Its most special characteristic was the effect of a French influence due to the alliance between Edinburgh and Paris which, from the thirteenth century onwards, drew some French courtiers to Scotland and many Scots to France. As words taken directly from France, without passage through England, were adopted into the language, so the spirit of the French versifying chroniclers penetrated the literature more than in England.

The octosyllabic line was most held in honour in Scotland, and the general character of the poems shows that historical and practical sense which the Normans brought into literature in English. In its tone and form, Barbour's work is in the succession of all the tribe of rhymed chroniclers since Gaimar and Wace. But it was Barbour's fortune to find a national subject of powerful interest. His frank simplicity and ardent patriotism lead us to overlook the almost consistently prosaic character of the thirteen thousand lines of his *Bruce*.

John Barbour, archdeacon of Aberdeen, of whom nothing is known save that he made two journeys to England and two to France, composed a *Siege of Troy* and some lives of the saints, but it is by his *Bruce*,[1] written between 1375 and 1378, that he has earned his place in literature. This poem is to Scotland what the *Chanson*

---

[1] Ed. by W. Skeat for the Early English Text Society. Extracts in Morris and Skeat, *Specimens*, vol. ii. op. cit.

de Roland is to France, the surpassing national poem. The difference of the two in date is, however, such that the *Bruce* lacks the epical character of *Roland* and its element of the marvellous, and is a chronicle in verse, very nearly a history, its facts no more transformed than they would be by a patriot historian. It is not an epic but history, and recent history, hardly three-quarters of a century old when it was written, so that the author could get information from living witnesses. It is the work of a man who has investigated happenings and wishes to tell the truth. It was, as he states at the opening of his poem, his opinion that,

> Storys to rede are delitabill,
> Suppos that thai be nocht but fabill;
> Than suld storys that suthfast wer,
> Hawe doubill plesance in heryng.
> The fyrst plesance is the carpyng,[1]
> And the tothir the suthfastnes
> That schawys the thing rycht as it wes;
> And suth thyngis that ar likand
> Tyll mannis heryng are plesand.
> Tharfor I wald fayne set my will,
> Giff [2] my wyt mycht suffice thartill,
> To put in wryt a suthfast story,
> That it lest ay and with in memory,
> Swa that na lenth of time it let,
> Na ger [3] it haly be ferget.

And Barbour's verses have indeed, by a singular and merited good fortune, become a source for all historians.

At the same time, Barbour is a moralist, and also an artist in so far that he is careful of the general unity of his work. Numerous as are the events about which he rhymes, he has only one hero, Robert the Bruce, the centre of the whole poem, and he intends that one moral idea shall reign over his whole work. The Bruce began his glorious career by a criminal act, by slaying a traitor at the foot of the altar in a place of sanctuary. This is Barbour's opening. The Bruce's heart will therefore not rest in the Holy Land according to his desire: this is the conclusion of the poem.

There is a greater amplitude in the ideas of freedom, patriotism and independence which animate all these verses.

But the work is one of those in which matter is infinitely more important than manner. The subject in its naked simplicity is more arresting and wonderful than the most romantic imaginings of the Middle Ages. Nothing is more moving than this story of a struggle for independence maintained by a people fewer in number than their oppressors, whose yoke they had already felt, and who had seized their strong places and overrun their country with soldiers.

Deliverance sprang from the lowest depth of misery, when the Bruce took to the open country and for years led the life of a hunted beast, hidden in the mountains and perpetually in danger of capture, escaping by killing his assailants with his own hands, by climbing barefoot over sharp cliffs, by the cunning with which he divined and forestalled the traps laid for him. At last, he fled to the small island of Rachin, and thence returned at the head of a growing company, which finally, in 1314, won the great victory of Bannockburn over Edward II. and secured the independence of Scotland.

Step by step, Barbour follows his hero through the struggle. He does not obtrude himself but leaves facts, which he knows to be more moving than all the rhetoric of poets, to speak for themselves. If he interrupts his narrative, it is to draw from the past lessons useful to the present. He wrote at a time when the glory of Bannockburn had been tarnished by sanguinary defeats. The misfortunes of

---

[1] Telling.   [2] If.   [3] Make.

his country in the first years of the Bruce's career had come of dissensions and of a foolish appeal to the king of England to decide the disputed succession to the Scottish throne, and Barbour would have his countrymen remember this:

> And wys men sayis he is happy,
> That be othir will him chasty.
> For unfayr thingis may fall, perfay,
> Als weill tomorn as yhisterday.

He would have Scotland keep for ever the freedom that is of greater worth "than all the gold in world that is":

> A! fredome is a noble thing!
> Fredome mays man to haiff liking;
> Fredome all solace to man giffis:
> He levys at es that frely levys.

7. The Dialect of the East Midlands or King's English. John Gower.— However important literary production, in the dialects we have reviewed, may have been, no one of them triumphed over the others. Victory fell to the speech of the east midlands, the district of London and the two universities of Oxford and Cambridge, and that in which the king had his residence. For this reason this language has been called the King's English. Its pre-eminence was established once for all in the end of the fourteenth century.

Although to-day this victory seems quite natural, since social forces were already making London the political and social centre, the universities the intellectual centre of the nation, the dialect of the east midlands was perhaps, when it was on the very eve of becoming English like none other, the poorest, the most completely disinherited of literature. Since Anglo-Saxon times, almost all English poetry had been produced apart from it. It could boast of hardly a poem besides the romance of *Havelock* and Robert Manning's *Handlyng Sinne*. Reflection shows that the fact is not astonishing, for it was in the neighbourhood of the court and the universities that the English language was most degraded and existed most precariously, that it was always subordinate either to Latin or to French or rather Anglo-Norman. King, nobles and clerks despised it. French, long the only tongue of any outside the vulgar herd, had its natural stronghold in this district, and was more tenacious of life here than elsewhere. Men better endowed than their fellows avoided the common language or had recourse to it only for practical ends. Their literary ambitions did not find scope in a tongue which was so meanly prized.

The case of John Gower [1] is very representative of prevalent conditions. He used Latin and French in turn, and reached the point of writing in English only late, probably under the influence of Chaucer's success. The date of his birth is unknown. Was he, as was long believed, some ten years older than Chaucer, or was he his junior? He died eight years after him, in 1408, and was probably his exact contemporary. The work of the two poets grew side by side, and, although Gower is not without merit of his own, he is chiefly valuable because he serves to measure the greatness of his rival.

He was a Kentishman, but this origin had only a slight effect on his language, which is hardly at all different from that of London and the court. He was a gentleman, possibly a clerk who did not take major orders. He was well read, and his library, if the word may be used, seems to have contained much the same French and Latin books as Chaucer's.

Undoubtedly he was once young, for he wrote love ballades in English-French,

---

[1] Complete edition in four volumes of his works, ed. by G. C. Macaulay (Clarendon Press, 1899-1902); *Confessio Amantis*, ed. by Henry Morley (1899).

ballades which lack fire but are not without a certain grace. This was a lover on the courtly model, seeking in vain to touch an unfeeling heart:

> En le douls temps ma fortune est amière,
> Le mois de Maij sest en yvern mué;
> Lurtie truis si jeo la Rose quière,
> Vous êtes franche et jeo suis fort lié
> *(Ballade* xxxvii.)

The third line at least needs translation—

> I find the nettle when I look for the rose—

for its language is not Parisian. He is aware of the fact and excuses himself for it:

> Et si je n'ai du français la faconde,
> Pardonnez-moi que je de ce fors voie (I go astray),
> Je suis Anglais; si quiers par telle voie (and therefore I beg)
> Etre excusé . . .

The very rhythm of his French verse tends to be anglicised, to beat time to the iambic measure. In spite of his effort after correctness, Gower proves better than anyone else how artificial was this uprooted language, at once learned and corrupt. He reminds us of Chaucer's Prioress:

> And Frensch sche spak ful faire and fetysly,
> After the scole of Stratford attĕ Bowe,
> For Frensch of Paris was to hire unknowe.

Gower is the last in date of the Anglo-Norman poets. He deserves to rank among them less by a few little love-pieces than by his long poem, or rather his long sermon in verse, which is called *Speculum Meditantis,* or *Miroir de l'Homme,* and has recently been rediscovered. It is a sermon against the immorality of the age, and it justifies Chaucer's epithet of "moral Gower" which was to cling to his friend's name for ever. This clerk, concerned especially to note and display the vices of his generation, was indeed much more a moralist than a poet. He is without a trace of that joy in life and pleasure in observing it which are so vivid in Chaucer. He compares what he sees with his ideal, that of a pious clerk and a student, finds all abominable, and condemns unreservedly.

Thus it was with his most remarkable work, *Vox Clamantis,* which was inspired by the Peasants' Rising of 1381 and which he elected to write in Latin. It is a very substantial poem which has real historic value, a pendant to *Piers Plowman* written by a member of the wealthy class, by a frightened landlord whose misfortune it was to live in Kent, the county in which the formidable rebellion broke out. Gower's terror gives these verses a strength and emphasis which are lacking in his other work.

This rising under Wat Tyler and Jack Straw began near Gower's land, and more than one of his tenants was doubtless among the rebels. It was during the first years of the minority of Richard II. The impoverishment of the Treasury, the levy of new subsidies for an unfortunate war and the insolence of the farmers of the taxes had provoked popular anger and rebellion. Several tax-collectors were put to death, and after them lawyers, courtiers, and partisans of the real regent, John of Gaunt, Duke of Lancaster. The number of the rebels increased. One hundred thousand men marched on London, demanding the abolition of serfdom and the reduction of rents. A true social revolution had been let loose in the country, and for a moment the insurgents were masters of London, where they sacked the palaces of the Archbishop of Canterbury and John of Gaunt. They destroyed but they did not steal: they even hanged a man in their own ranks for theft. Then the king rode out to meet them, and Wat Tyler, while in parley with him, was slain by the mayor. The king procured the dispersal of the rebels by promising redress of their grievances, then revoked his promise, and the rising was ended by cruel repressive measures.

Gower, now in his fifties, was haunted by this rebellion as by a nightmare. His interests were all on the side of the landlords. He had no sympathy with the popular cause, yet considered the ills of society to be the outcome of social vices which were ruining the state. His alarms and his grievances are voiced in the Latin distichs of *Vox Clamantis*.

The poet first has a vision of a crowd of members of the populace changed into wild beasts and uncurbed by reason—asses, fierce as lions, who will bear no more burdens, oxen who refuse to draw the plough, dogs who bark at huntsmen, cats who have reverted to wildness. A jay, who stands for Wat Tyler, harangues them, to the sound of shouts of "Down with honour! Perish the law!" and at the tail of their company John Ball, an excommunicate priest, preaches on the text:

> When Adam delved and Eve span,
> Who was then a gentleman?

The swarming mass of people lays Troynovant, or London, waste. Their strength is broken by the death of the jay, but the ship of the state is still adrift and puts in at the island of Disorder. Then a voice from heaven advises Gower to write down what he has seen in his nightmare.

The rest of his poem contains his waking thoughts and is entirely didactic. The misfortunes of the age spring from the general corruption. There are three classes of society, the clerks, the warriors, otherwise knights and nobles, and the third estate, namely the villeins and labourers, the traders and the lawyers. All are riddled with vice. The court is a meeting-place for everything abominable.

The poem ends with a prayer to the young king, Richard II., to bring virtue back to the court, and with an appeal to all men to mend their ways, remembering how short is earthly life. Gower declares his love for his country: he has wished, he says, that men should hear not only what he himself feels to be true, but also the voice of the people, which is often the voice of God.

It is a great pity that this work, into which Gower has put the best of himself, his utmost sincerity of thought, vehemence of satire and depths of narrow but coherent morality, should have received the dress of a dead language, while on the one occasion when he used the speech of his country he worked against the grain of his temperament and talent, and wrote an entirely artificial poem.

For he did finally make up his mind to write in English, perhaps incited by the growing reputation of Chaucer, who had already produced most of his works and was soon to begin the *Canterbury Tales*. It was about 1383 or 1384 that Gower composed his single English poem, his *Confessio Amantis*, an immense compilation of stories extending to forty thousand octosyllabic lines. He tells us he did it at the bidding of King Richard, who charged him that "some newë thing I shuldë boke," and thus he excuses his use of the vulgar tongue:

> And for that fewë men endite
> In oure Englisshe, I thenkë make
> A bok for King Richardës sake.

He has the credit of having sought, a little before Chaucer, a thread on which to string some hundred stories. The idea was not quite new: it had been exemplified in the *Speculum Historiale* of Vincent de Beauvais, the *Gesta Romanorum* and the *Sept Sages*, to which the *Decameron* would have to be added, were it not clearly unknown to Gower as to Chaucer. The idea was a happy one, but how awkwardly Gower executed it!

He tells us with a sigh that he is going to sing of love, rather than follow his

own taste and write a moral book. Love is the last subject he would choose for
himself, but something must be conceded to the reader who prefers amusement
to wisdom:

> For thilkē cause, if that ye rede,
> I woldē go the middel wey
> And write a boke betwene the twey,
> Somwhat of lust, somwhat of lore.

It happens that Venus, who has little fondness for him, advises him one day
in May to make his confession to her priest Genius. The obedient poet goes to the
confessional and asks Genius to question him, point by point, thus sounding his
conscience in the article of love. Genius consents, but declares that, in order that
the confession may be complete, he will be obliged, in the course of the examination, to speak of the different vices. He will explain each of them by means of a
story, so that the lover may know whether or no he have the same guilt on his
conscience. When the confession has ended, Venus mocks this superannuated lover,
who decides to withdraw.

The device allows the seven deadly sins, subdivided into many secondary
sins, to defile through seven books. Genius has received a complete scholastic
education, but he ceases to excel when he endeavours to adapt his examples to
his precepts. To illustrate hypocrisy he tells the tale of the deceiving Trojan Horse.
To show that murder, an effect of anger, is to be condemned, he relates the story
of Pyramus and Thisbe: Pyramus kills himself out of despair, which is anger, when
he believes that Thisbe has been the lion's victim, and the moral is that nothing
should be done in a hurry. The proof that carelessness is injurious to love is found
in the story of Phaeton, who drove his father's chariot carelessly, freezing and
burning the earth by turns, so that Phœbus caused him, as a punishment, to fall
from the chariot and be drowned.

The connection of these stories with the morality of love is so absurd that, after
praising Gower for attempting a unified plan, we are tempted to regret that he did
not write his little stories haphazard, without trying to give them a frame. For
as a narrator he is abundant and clear, and since he has read much, he has had no
difficulty in finding curious and sometimes attractive stories among his books.
Several of his tales recur in Chaucer, who sometimes preceded and sometimes
followed him in selecting them. Once or twice Gower was inspired by a better
original than Chaucer, as when he took the story of the Knight Florent which
corresponds to the tale of the Wife of Bath.

This is as much as can be claimed for Gower. An almost immeasurable distance
separates him from Chaucer. He is doing penance when he obliges himself to
treat of love, undertaking a task so ungrateful and so contrary to his nature that
he could have discharged it well only with the help of the sense of humour he lacked
deplorably. Like him, Chaucer posed as despised by Venus and ill-used by Cupid,
but—not to speak of his unrivalled and unfailing power to awaken sympathy for
lovers—his confession of impotence is delightful because it is wrapped in humour.
In Gower, there are, or seem to be, velleities of humour, but they are invariably
abortive. There is too much reality in the awkwardness with which this poet resigns himself to his distasteful subject. Once and again, a sigh escapes him because
he cannot return to the moral teaching natural to him, and these regrets are the
sincerest part of his poem. He is indeed, as Chaucer said, "moral Gower," and it
is unfortunate that he ever forsook his rôle. Venus was right when she told him:

> And tarie thou mi Court nomore
> But go ther vertu moral dwelleth,
> Where ben thi bokes, as men telleth,
> Whiche of long time thou hast write.

And we are grateful to Gower for having made the goddess own Chaucer for her true disciple and poet:

> Of ditēs and of songēs glad
> The whiche he for my sakē made
> The land fulfilled is over al.

Gower, learned, industrious and copious, is the typical average poet of his century. His writings are what Chaucer's might have been without Chaucer's genius.

CHAPTER II

1. **Chaucer best expresses his Century.**—All the writers of this time reveal some aspect of contemporary life and of prevailing feeling and thought. The author of *Pearl* shows us the mysticism of refined minds, Langland the anger which was threatening the abuses of governments and the vices of the clergy, Wyclif the ardour for religious reform which already could amount to Protestantism, Gower the fear aroused in the wealthier class by the Peasant Rising, Barbour the break between the literature of Scotland and of England and the advent of patriotic Scottish poetry. Each had his own plan, his dominant and, on the whole, narrow passion, a character which was local and of his time. Each was enclosed within the limits of a restricted experience, if not within those of a dialect incapable of expansion and without a future.

It is Chaucer's distinction that he turned impartial, eager and clear-sighted eyes not only on the past, which his books discovered to him, but also on all the society of his time, on foreign countries and on every class in his own country. His work reflects his century not in fragments but completely. More than this, he is often able to discern permanent features beneath the garments of a day, to penetrate to the everlasting springs of human action. His truthful pictures of his age and country contain a truth which is of all time and all countries.

He was born in London about 1340, the son of a city wine-merchant, and therefore by birth a member of the burgher class. At seventeen, however, he was a court page, for whom a pair of red and black breeches was provided. Two years later he became a soldier, took part in the campaigns of Artois and Picardy, was captured by the enemy and remained a prisoner until the king paid his ransom. After his return to England he was attached to the king's person, first as valet and then as squire, but his great patron was John of Gaunt, Duke of Lancaster and son of Edward III. From the age of about thirty he was charged with diplomatic missions to France, Flanders and Italy, in succession. He was granted a pension and also, in 1374, the office of comptroller of the duties and aids on wools, hides and wine in the port of London. In this way, as a courtier, he was again brought into touch with the London burghers among whom he had been born. In 1385 he was released from his office of comptroller, and in the next year he was returned to Parliament as a knight of the shire of Kent.

Lancaster's disgrace supervened, and Chaucer fell on evil days. He lost his

---

[1] *Complete Works*, ed. W. Skeat, 6 vols. (Oxford 1896), and supplementary vol. (1897); *The Student's Chaucer*, ed. Skeat, complete in 1 vol. (Oxford, 1895); Globe Edition, ed. A. W. Pollard (1903). Many works on Chaucer. Works of the Chaucer Society from 1868 (1st series, 99 volumes; 2nd series, 54 volumes, in 1922); J. R. Lowell, paper in *My Study Windows* (1871); A. W. Pollard, *A Primer of Chaucer* (1893); R. K. Root, *The Poetry of Chaucer* (1906) (revised ed., 1922); E. Legouis, *Chaucer* (Grands Ecrivains Etrangers, 1910); G. L. Kittredge, *Chaucer and his Poetry* (1915), etc. See works on English Literature of Taine, Jusserand, Ten Brink, etc. For Chaucer's sources, see E. G. Sandras, *Etude sur Chaucer considéré comme imitateur des Trouvères* (Paris, 1859). For Chaucer's influence, C. Spurgeon, *Chaucer devant la critique en Angleterre et en France depuis son temps jusqu'à nos jours* (Paris, 1911), and *Five Hundred Years of Chaucer Criticism and Allusion* (Chaucer Society, Second Series, 1918–22).

place and part of his pension, but was accorded other favours when the duke returned to power. For a time he was Clerk of the King's Works at Windsor, and by Edmund Mortimer, Earl of March, he was made forester. He relapsed to poverty, but his fortunes recovered just before his death in 1400, when the son of John of Gaunt usurped the throne as Henry IV.

Thus his life was active and his employments diverse. He was page, squire, diplomat and official in turns. He mingled with courtiers, soldiers and city burghers and merchants. He had dealings with foreigners in Flanders, France and Italy. And throughout he remained, for such part of his days as his official duties left free, an impassioned student and untiring reader.

What is most striking in Chaucer is the interest he took in every one of the different worlds through which he passed and all his heterogeneous occupations. He was at his ease at court, among traders, among clerks, with the people. To observe was as much his joy as to read. It is inconceivable that there was an hour of his life whence he did not extract pleasure. He could bear a heavy burden of work easily, with the air of an idler whose life is all pleasure. The literary work he accomplished is considerable in extent, but far more remarkable for the radiance of his sympathy and the length and breadth of his clear vision.

2. His part in the Formation of English Poetry.—We know nothing of the work of artistic preparation which is to be presumed from Chaucer's success in poetry, but it was indubitably intense and long. Genius doubtless accounts for the lengths by which his poetry outdistanced Gower's, but something is due to the persevering will of an artist who gave himself unstintingly to the acquisition of necessary technique. Alone among his contemporaries, Chaucer put art first. He did not seek to direct men, to judge events, to reform morals or to present a philosophy. Poetry was his only object. Up to the very end, the task he set himself was to write verses which should have charm and life. To realise the immense effort which this involved it is only necessary to remember the state in which he found the versification and the poetic language of his dialect.

It is hardly possible to exaggerate the part he played as creator of English versification. Save the frail octosyllabic line already in use, he had himself to forge all his instruments. He imported the decasyllabic line from France and, under Italian influence, made it pliable. It became the heroic line which was the surpassing vehicle of the great poetry of England. We have seen that the progress of this poetry was barred by the lack of a verse-form at once ample, ductile, noble and sonorous. Chaucer used the new line alternately in stanzas and in couplets, the stanza for songs and the couplet for narratives. He cast it in moulds unknown to his country—the roundel, the virelay, the ballade. Out of all his essays two came to dominate: the seven-lined stanza (*ababbcc*), to which his name has since attached, and the couplet. But what fashioning and refashioning, what experiments and doubts, this presupposes! All his youth and part of his maturity must have been mainly dedicated to this labour which, since nearly all his earliest works are lost, cannot be traced.

His immediate choice of his own dialect as the vehicle of his poetry is proof of his decision and of his sure judgment. He did not, like Gower, allow himself to be tempted either by Latin or by French. He risked his whole literary fortune on London English, the King's English, of which it has been said how poor it was. He found it a thing of nought and left it so rich that English poetry had but to add blank verse to it in order to be fully equipped.

Chaucer's first act of faith in the only tongue which was to him a living language, notwithstanding he clearly saw its defects, was to inculcate in it all the delicacy and refinement he perceived in the poetry of France. He disregarded the debased, artificial and prosaic Anglo-Norman, and went straight to the continent to seek masters and models.

To wed the vocabulary of his native land to the courtliness of France was his first and essential task. He recast English words—that is, surviving words of Teutonic origin and acclimatised words of French origin—in the moulds of the French poets. He expressed in English all the graces and refinements he found in the poetry of France.

Unlike the authors of the *Grene Knyght* and *Piers Plowman*, he definitely broke with the Anglo-Saxon literary tradition. His face was turned to the south, and he took the whole of his ideal from the continent.

He might be thought unlucky in his time. There never was a period in which French poetry was apparently more frail and destitute than that which intervenes between Rutebeuf and Villon or between the *Roman de la Rose* and Charles d'Orléans. In this poor, meagre and pretentious garden there was little but artificial flowers to cull. And, because of the accident of date, it was from one of the most debilitated of the French poets, Guillaume de Machaut, that Chaucer took his first lessons. He could learn from him neither animation nor vigour, nor frankness of style, nor strength of feeling and thought. But Machaut was refined, as much a musician as a poet. Although not a great artist he was yet pure artist, and well fitted to give the young Englishman the teaching he needed in the rules of his craft. In France, it was Machaut who chiefly propagated the poems made in fixed forms, the ballades, roundels, *chansons royales*, and it was from him that Chaucer learned to use these forms for his lyrical verses. For his narratives and descriptions he is no less in debt to Machaut's lays. He often also emulates those French pupils of Machaut who were his contemporaries, Eustache Deschamps, Froissart, Otto de Granson. His work is full of details borrowed here and there. He followed with slightly ironic curiosity a tenson on the comparative merits of the Leaf and the Flower. He took part in the symbolic cult of the Marguerite or daisy, which in the second half of this century, out of deference to some great ladies named after that flower, superseded that of the Rose.

Nevertheless, it was above all to the *Roman de la Rose* that he owed his initiation as a poet. At some unknown moment of his life, probably as his youth was ending, he translated the famous *Roman* into English verse. It is not unlikely that he produced the version of which we possess a part, and which is most faithfully and exactly translated. This was excellent practice, calculated to bring discipline into the versification and style of a young poet. If he does not always attain to such fresh colours and sonorous rhymes as Guillaume de Lorris, it is that he was hindered by his interpreter's task and by a language as yet unformed. He is conscious of the fact. He complains that "ryme in Englisch hath such skarseté," and meanwhile he practised to such good purpose that he brought nearer the day when this difficulty disappeared.

The *Roman de la Rose* did more for him than discipline his style. It was the work which had the most comprehensive and constant hold on him. Its double character, due to the difference, amounting to contrast, between the two poets who composed it, did not shock Chaucer as an interruption of unity, but made this work—this Bible of poetry—doubly attractive to him. According to his mood, he was inspired by Guillaume de Lorris or by Jean de Meung. Guillaume, with his delicate grace and the clarity of his atmosphere of love, caught him first, in his youth. Later it came to pass that the flood of ideas, satire and classical reminiscences, which rolls through the work of Jean de Meung, was better suited to his need of more solid and humorous nourishment, and this poet began and continued to charm him more than any other, so that he borrowed from him again and again, even for his final masterpiece.

The first effect of the *Roman* was, however, in one sense to pervert his genius while it helped to fashion his style. It led him into the sphere of the allegorical and kept him there for many years. Chaucer's reverence for this poem was such that it delayed the flowering of his dramatic genius, which he neglected until after his journey to Italy. Such prolonged restraint would be more regrettable had he not produced some entirely charming works in the form of allegories, and had his art not gained by the slow process of cultivation and ripening to which it was subject when, as it were, he put himself to school. Only after these trials did he risk the hard enterprise, often so dangerous to formal beauty, of representing life directly.

IIis debt to France goes beyond the many imitations which can be discovered in his work, the reminiscences of the *trouvères* in lines, reflections, descriptive touches, opinions or quips. He owes another debt to France which is vaster, more diffused through his poetry, less easy to apprehend but not less certain. He is no mere recipient of her largess. She has bequeathed to him a whole heritage, not isolated possessions but his very nature. His mind is as French as his name, which is a form of *chaussier*. He is the lineal descendant of the French *trouvères*, one of them in all but language.

It was not that he gallicised his grammar or vocabulary more than his contemporaries. But this first great literary artist of his country attempted to express in his own language the poetic beauty which he felt in the best French verses and which answered to his urgent instinctive need. This ideal, to which he attained, was the very inverse of that of the scops.

As the reader passes from their works to his, he has again, in striking degree, the impression of dawning clarity which he received when he left Anglo-Saxon for old French poetry. The rarefied, white light shed over Chaucer's work, hardly ever touching the violent colours of more southern poetry, is exactly the same in tone as that which shone for the poets of the Île-de-France. A Frenchman may enter Chaucer's country and be conscious of no change of sky or climate.

Like the French *trouvères*, Chaucer has a lightness of heart which is not tumultuous but diffused. It is born of his pleasure in life and is revealed by his taste for the well-lit pictures which call up spring, the month of May, flowers, birds and music. One line, in which he resumes the youth of his Squire, might be the device of all his poetry:

> He was as fressh as is the moneth of May.

This line is entirely French, the essence of the earliest French poetry.

The same may be said of his pitch, neither too high nor too low. His voice, too, has a pure, slightly frail quality. He never forces his tone; rather, he sometimes uses a mute. It is an even voice, made to tell a long story without weariness or jar, perhaps not rich or full enough for the highest lyricism, but wont to keep to the middle tones in which meaning is conveyed to the mind most clearly and exactly.

There is the charm of fluent simplicity, complete correspondence of words and thoughts. Chaucer's best verses merely note facts, external details or characteristics of feeling.

There is constant restraint, alike in expressing emotion and satire. When he touches the pathetic, he stops short of cries and weeping; he tempers his irony with wit, and he provokes smiles rather than unchecked laughter. Everywhere there is undefinable sobriety and good manners which imply that the poet is ruled by intelligence, rather than carried away by passion. In other words, his temperamental and intellectual powers are perfectly balanced.

All these qualities belong, in the same measure, to the old French poets and to Chaucer. His French extraction is proved by his possession of all of them, and by the fact that he goes beyond them only at those rare moments when, under an Italian influence, he rises above both his own nature and French nature. When Chaucer forsakes France he is a little denaturalised.

It should be added that with the virtues of the French *trouvères* he has the faults from which the best of them are not exempt. Like them, he too often does not condense, is garrulous, often charmingly but yet indisputably. There are times when he lacks the sinew and the pace which an occasion demands, when he dawdles instead of hastening his steps, walks instead of flying. His discreet poetry is near the border-line of prose; it has its awkward, slow and platitudinous moments. There is padding at which we smile, but which we must recognise for what it is. Again like the old French poets, Chaucer has, however, a good-humoured, artless way with him, which makes all these manifest defects into an additional attraction. Sometimes he even uses them to point his sharpest quip.

These characteristics do not belong only to his youth, but are permanent in him. Chaucer cannot be said to have had a French period. He is always French, although he sometimes gathered riches abroad, as he marvelled at antiquity or at Italy. Fundamentally unchanged, he acquired from the Italians and Latins a certain adventitious diversity, and ended by using his French manner to paint the society of England.

3. **His Lyrical and Allegorical Poems.**—Chaucer seems to have begun his work by composing love lyrics, but nothing remains of his earliest poetry. There are, however, enough of his roundels and ballades, written at a later date in moments spared from his more ambitious poems, to prove the virtuosity of which he was capable in this field. He was certainly the equal of the most skilled of his fellows in France, and often he imported a characteristic of his own into these conventional forms—his pity, always moved by the sufferings of a woman, in the *Compleynt of Anelida*, the savour of his homeliness, or his humour which makes jests against himself. In his *Ballade of Griselidis*, which is his triumph in the field of lyricism, he mingles the extreme artifice of a learned craftsman with the most comic sportiveness. But in these works he merely gives, as in play, some proofs of his mastery of their style. He turns from them to that domain of narrative in verse which is properly his and in which he did almost all his work.

It took him a long time to decide on direct narrative. He could not at first rid himself of the poetic artifices of the age. From the time of the *Roman de la Rose* every poem begins with a dream which leads to an allegory, and for many years Chaucer let himself be carried along by this current. He accepted the received formula almost as though it were a necessity, submitted to such restraint without apparent effort, merely inserting, from time to time, an episode or a detail which expressed his nature or is the medium of his comments.

The first of his poems which can be dated is the *Boke of the Duchesse*, written on the death, in 1369, of Blanche of Lancaster, the wife of John of Gaunt, in order to sing her praises and depict the grief of her husband. This voluminous and composite funeral monument, astonishing to-day by the artificial rather than ingenious complexity of its plan, yet reveals, here and there, the poet's nature. Flowers which are fair, fresh and delicate grow abundantly between the stones of this flamboyant architecture. In the poem Chaucer represents himself as a lover racked by sleeplessness, reading from the *Metamorphoses* the touching story of Ceyx and Alcyone. When finally he does fall asleep, he dreams that he is present at a hunt of the Emperor Octavian, and that while endeavouring to follow it he discovers in a wood a handsome knight, all clothed in black, who is mourning and who describes to him the charms of his lost and well-beloved wife, and the ineffable joy he knew during his too brief union with her.

As though to assert its origin, the poem abounds with imitations of the *Roman de la Rose* and Machaut's *Dits*. It is, moreover, an occasional poem, inspired by the desire to please the Duke of Lancaster by transfiguring his grief. It suffers from prolixity and makes, at a first reading, an impression of some confusion. Nevertheless, whoever reads it, remembering its date, and compares it with the existing English verse, is struck by the progress it marks. It is the first poem in this language to contain fully artistic passages. The lines which are the farewell of the phantom Ceyx and relate the death of Alcyone are the perfection of simple pathos. Nothing could surpass their harmonious tenderness, their exquisite restraint and the grace and justice of their divisions and their rhymes:

> "And farewel, swete, my worldes blisse!
> I praye God your sorwe lisse:
> To litel whyl our blisse lasteth."
> With that hir eyen up she casteth
> And saw nought: "Ah," quod she for sorwe
> And deyd within the thridde morwe.

Over and over again the allegory gives place to realism. A conversation, on the whole both probable and lively, is held between the poet and the unknown knight, and if this partly dramatic character of the poem be given full value, it will be seen to modify its defects, and even to excuse them by giving them probability. The mourner's prolixity and repetitions and his confused enumeration of his lady's virtues are in place in this sudden outpouring of his feelings. They make the picture appear less circumscribed and didactic. There is a pathetic element in the very exuberance and incoherence of this overflowing sorrow. Already, too, there is a hint of humour in the appearance of the questioner, the poet himself, who figures, on this his first coming into his own poetry, as a man "of little wit," slow of understanding, amazed by the spectacle of a strong passion of which the lyricism is beyond him.

Chaucer was again to have recourse to allegory in 1382, when he wished to celebrate the betrothal of Richard II. and Anne of Bohemia, this being the probable subject of his *Parlement of Foules*. The frame is even more heavily laden than is that of the *Boke of the Duchesse*, for Chaucer had read much between the dates of the two poems, and had added Latin and Italian models to those he found in France, for instance, Cicero's *Somnium Scipionis* and Boccaccio's *Teseide*. He again represents himself as falling asleep after reading. This time his book is the *Somnium Scipionis*, and it is Scipio in person who appears to him in his dream to lead him to marvellous gardens where Venus has her temple, but where Nature is "the vicaire of thalmightye lorde." It is the fourteenth of February, St. Valentine's Day, and Nature enjoins the male birds to choose their mates. She holds in her own hand a female eagle of great beauty who shall, with its own consent, go to the worthiest.

The interest of the poem lies in its variety of moods, its transitions from the lofty to the homely. Nature holds a full parliament: there are the lords, namely, the eagles and other birds of prey, who express the most delicate sentiments ever heard in courts of love, and there are the commons of winged society, the water-fowls, feeding on worms and grain, who are deaf to chivalrous eloquence and voice coarse and selfish good sense. This diversity of tone gives unexpected dramatic liveliness to the narrative. The comic is allied with the purely romantic, so that in the *Parlement of Foules* there is the germ of that antithesis between the ideal and the real which is the special glory of the *Canterbury Tales*. We are already confronted with a scene in the human comedy, and with the impartiality of this narrator, who has, doubtless, a preference for noble sentiments, but makes it his duty to leave room for other feelings beside them. Even while he chides the materialists, he is plainly aware of their good sense, and uses them to denounce the slightly forced element in the refinements of courtly love.

The same quality saves and redeems Chaucer's most ambitious effort in the field of allegorical poetry, his *Hous of Fame*, in which he seems to have wished to compete with the *Roman de la Rose*, raising as ample a symbolical structure. His avowed object is to tell of the capricious nature of glory, and the strange fashion in which rumour and news are fabricated and spread in the world. To shed light on this theme, he has recourse to all the customary machinery. The action of the poem is introduced with extreme slowness. There is a discussion on the origin and truth of dreams. The god of sleep is duly invoked. At last comes the dream itself; the poet finds himself in the temple of Venus where he sees the whole story of Æneas painted on the walls. A golden eagle carries him aloft in a giddy flight to the House of Fame, which is reared in the heavens and accessible to all the sounds of the earth. He meets there all the authors he has read and admired. He sees the goddess herself and is witness of the strange way in which she distributes her favours. Thence he passes to the House of Rumour in order to discover how news is manufactured. From every side he sees bearers of false and true messages arriving, and his ears are deafened by the din. At this point the poem breaks off suddenly.

Chaucer did not care to finish it, a sure proof that the fiction was not entirely to his taste. He found, as he wrote, that he was incapable of sustaining his part, of persevering in artifice as a good allegory requires. The real made too frequent an appeal to him. He could not maintain his own illusion uninterruptedly. The best passages of the poems are those in which his sense of humour bursts, with a quip, the bubble he has blown in the air. When the *Hous of Fame* arrests our attention to-day, it is that Chaucer is speaking familiarly of himself, of his life "as an hermyte," absorbed in reading, who goes home from his work to abstract himself from the world and lose himself in his beloved books, "tyl fully dasewyd ys [his] looke."

The passage in which the golden eagle bears him through the air is very characteristic. It is possible that this bird was born of that by which Dante was rapt to the fiery sphere, and that Chaucer had read the *Divina Commedia* immediately before he wrote his poem. He wishes to make it clear that he is not of the race of Dante. The way in which the London burgher follows the great Florentine on his voyage through space is curious. The justice of his self-characterisation is delicious: he is, he says, not apt for sublime flights, but he consoles himself with the light scepticism which is of his nature, stating his preference for walking with his feet on the solid earth. He is much afraid that Jupiter intends to "stellifye" him. For a moment he admires his near view of the Signs of the Zodiac and of the Galaxy or Milky Way, but soon he declares that he is too old to learn the secret of these marvels, and fears to burn his eyes by looking at the stars from so near. Flying is not for him: give him feet, not wings. From the height of the empyrean he is thinking regretfully of the good muddy tracks which plough the road from London to Canterbury.

In this imperfect and characteristic poem, Chaucer, with his intelligent, bantering spirit, strolls through the "highest heaven of invention." He refuses, once for all, to give himself wholly to the sublime or to believe profoundly in purely spiritual conceptions.

For analogous reasons, Chaucer did not finish his *Legende of Goode Women* which he wrote about 1385. This indeed has nothing of the allegorical except the prologue, and the prologue is charming. It is Chaucer, the conventional poet, at his most graceful and most personal. He has an unstudied expansiveness, tells us again how much he loves the books which hold all the stories, which he leaves only in the month of May to go to the meadows and pay duty to Nature personified in the daisy. It is when he has spent a whole fine day admiring the little flower he so loves, that he dreams at night in his arbour where he "bad men sholdë me my couchë make." He sees

> The God of Love, and in his hande a quene
> And she was clad in reäl habit grene.

Her head is crowned with a garland of daisies,

> For al the world ryght as a dayësye
> Ycorouned ys with whitë leves lyte,
> So were the flourons of hire coroune white.

Behind the royal couple walk nineteen most noble ladies,

> And trewe of love thise wemen were echoon.

The god finally perceives the poet on his knees before a daisy, and chides him for daring, all unworthy, to approach love's flower. Is he not love's heretic, since he has translated the *Romaunt of the Rose*? Has he not, by depicting Criseyde's unfaithfulness, thrown suspicion on all women? The good queen intercedes for the poet, who has also, she says, written books of pure love and devotion. She asks leave to choose his penance, and decrees that he shall compose a glorious legend of virtuous women, virgins and wives, who were loyal in their lives, and tell also of the knaves who betrayed them. It appears during the course of the prologue that the good queen is Alcestis, that incomparable wife who sacrificed herself in order to give back life to Admetus. We are thus led to see a glorified Anne of Bohemia in this Alcestis, and her young husband, Richard II., in the handsome and irritable god of love. As for the nineteen fair ladies in the train of Alcestis, they are those whose virtue the poet is commanded to celebrate.

Chaucer begins by throwing himself into his task. He always excels at depicting the self-denial and suffering of women in love, and he makes use of ancient sources, especially Ovid's *Heroides*, to write several most pure and touching legends, those of Thisbe, Lucretia, Philomela and Ariadne, among others. But the same mocking good sense, which prevented him from finishing the *Hous of Fame*, came to whisper irreverently in his ear as he was writing out his legends, to grumble that he should have to enhance the beauty of these deserted women and vilify their seducers. It seemed to him that this was not reality, and even his books revealed to him certain faults in some of the heroines who were the set objects of his praises— Cleopatra, for instance, and Medea. The outcome was that this poem also was not finished. The task imposed by a queen became an intolerable penance, and there is not a doubt that Chaucer was right to leave it for the *Canterbury Tales*. Yet the legends, incomplete as they are, contain exquisite passages, and moreover they did Chaucer the service of taking him away from allegory—only the prologue of this poem is allegorical—and inducing him to tell, after the ancient masters, some imperishable tales of love and grief. Now translating and now adapting, Chaucer was able to give a personal turn to these famous themes. He has not Ovid's brilliant rhetoric, but there is an advantage in the artlessness of his style. He is both less witty and more feeling than his model. This poem is the last he wrote before the *Tales* and it leads to them directly. It is, further, in this poem that Chaucer first used the ten-syllabled rhyming couplet to which he returned in his masterpiece.

4. Chaucer under Italian Influence. The Knightes Tale. "Troylus and Criseyde."—Taken as a whole, all the poems which have been mentioned are in the French succession. But the three last, written after Chaucer's first journey to Italy in 1372, show numerous traces of the influence of Italian poetry. He was immediately sensitive to the genius of the great Italians whose works he knew at least in part—Dante, Petrarch and Boccaccio. From them, better than from the too distant poets of antiquity, he learnt to enrich his line which was still a little slight, to find more glowing images and more impassioned themes. The influence which these three poets had on him was however very unequal. He was, without doubt, fully conscious of the greatness of Dante, whom he calls the "gret poet of Itaile," but he was no less aware of the difference between his own genius and that of the sublime visionary. As we have seen, he banteringly refuses to follow Dante to the regions of the air, and he borrows from him only very sparingly. It is when, in the Monk's Tale, he tells the story of Ugolino, that he comes nearest to emulating him, and then he transforms the terror of the scene so that it becomes touching. Fear does not render Chaucer's Ugolino speechless or leave him dry-eyed when he knows himself condemned to die by starvation, but the poet compensates by the moving, homely complaints he puts into the mouth of the youngest child who weeps for a little bread. Chaucer was not made, like Dante, to plunge into Hell or rise to Paradise.

He probably knew Petrarch personally, saw him at Padua and heard him read his story of Griselda in Latin. He retained respect for this poet:

> Fraunces Petrark, the laureat poete,
> Highte this clerk, whose rethorique swete
> Enlumynd al Ytail of poetrie.

But Chaucer could not follow in the footsteps of the great humanist, so near to the ancients, so cognisant of philology, so much ahead of his contemporaries on the road of the Renascence. As for Petrarch the sonneteer, his excessive subtlety and his idealism refined to a quintessence, could not appeal to a nature as normal as Chaucer's, whose tenderness was never far removed from joviality.

It is significant that Chaucer's only important borrowing from Petrarch is the story of Griselda, a Latin translation of the last of Boccaccio's tales. Boccaccio was assuredly the Italian to have most influence on Chaucer, who, none the less, never mentions his name. Boccaccio provided him with some of his most remarkable stories, and also, almost invariably, with a model for the most splendidly decorated and warmly passionate of his verses. It was, however, only Boccaccio the poet and the compiler of De Casibus Virorum Illustrium and De Claris Mulieribus whom Chaucer knew. He does not seem ever to have read the Decameron, for all that he was to figure to posterity principally as the storyteller who rivalled Boccaccio.

Chaucer's debt to the poems of Boccaccio's youth is especially considerable. He condensed and abridged the Teseide to make his Knighte's Tale, retelling the story of the rivalry of Palamon and Arcite, two youths who were as brothers, their affection heightened by a shared captivity, until the day when love for the same maiden brought them to face each other as enemies, armed for a fight. Chaucer, adapting freely, was able to extract from the exuberant Teseide the romance of sentiment which is buried in those pseudo-epical ten thousand lines. He kept the best of Boccaccio's descriptions, yet introduced homely scenes of his own, and made Theseus into a humorous personage after his own mind.

The most memorable result of his contact with Boccaccio's poetry was, however, Troylus and Criseyde, a poem half translated and half adapted from Il Filostrato. In this Boccaccio uses a frame borrowed from the Roman de Troie of Benoît de

Sainte-More to express all his feelings as a lover "laid low by love" (*filostrato*). In the person of the knight Troilo, he is loved and then betrayed by Cressida, and his love is served by his mistress's young cousin, the sceptical yet disinterested Pandaro, who abounds with worldly wisdom and considers that to aid a passion is a fine and virtuous action.

This burning, harmonious and swiftly moving poem was retold by Chaucer, who took as many liberties with it as he had done with the story of Palamon and Arcite, but this time enlarged and lengthened his original instead of condensing it. The changes involved are due to a different conception of characters and sentiments. Boccaccio's first object had been to depict passion and voluptuousness, but Chaucer was drawn especially to the study of character. In his poem, the ardent, breathless tale of love is accompanied by a comedy of which Pandarus is the central character, and a very different Pandarus from Boccaccio's Pandaro. Pandarus is not the cousin but the uncle of Criseyde, a man in middle life, familiar in his ways, fond of chaff and inclined to gossip, such a great quoter of proverbs and maxims that he sometimes reminds us of Polonius and sometimes of Sancho Panza, playing, the while, the part of Macette. It is his interminable chatter which constitutes Chaucer's addition of two or three thousand lines to the Italian poem. In consequence, the action of Chaucer's poem is markedly slower than Boccaccio's, but its added element of comedy relaxes that strain of the pathetic which is felt in *Il Filostrato*. Instead of expressing the sentimental, like Boccaccio, Chaucer's aspiration is to reflect life. He lets a livelier air, as from an open window, into the heavy and perfumed atmosphere of the boudoir in which Boccaccio confines us. The most poetic passages of the poem are literal translations from the Italian, for instance the description of the despair of Troylus after the departure of his mistress (Book V. st. 29–99), but all the drollery has been invented by Chaucer. It is strange that Chaucer, faced with a Latin author, deals with him exactly as an English dramatist of the Renascence would have done. He does what Shakespeare was to do again and again. He accepts and preserves, almost intact, the tragic elements of his theme and the sentimental beauty of the youthful leading characters, but everywhere he rearranges, transforms or creates anew the character-studies. Even thus Shakespeare faithfully retells the love of Romeo and Juliet, but develops the characters of the nurse and old Capulet on original lines and creates Mercutio. Whatever force the tragic and sentimental scenes of the English dramatists may have, they are rarely the element in their plays which is most personal to them. It is with the comic that they are especially concerned. Chaucer, by instinct, made a precedent for the great national dramatist who wrote more than two hundred years after him.

Although his *Troylus and Criseyde* does not quite conceal his efforts to reconcile originality and imitation, although it has lost the just and certain proportions of its model, and makes exotic Neapolitan flowers to bloom beneath unquiet Kentish skies, it is yet an admirable work, astonishing if its date be remembered, far superior in point of style and versification to anything in contemporary English literature. And from the fact that he felt himself hampered while he wrote it, Chaucer learnt a fruitful lesson. Instead of pursuing further these imitative exercises which left him only half his freedom, he sought a subject which should be truly his own. In his *Troylus* he was half Italian and half English. In his master-piece he was to be all English.

5. The "Canterbury Tales."—Up to this time Chaucer's work, although he sought inspiration in France and Italy, or rather because he was the too docile pupil of foreign masters, is interesting mainly to the English. He deserves admiration for having civilised his country poetically, but he had spent his strength almost entirely on translating and adapting. He was still no more than the "great translator" praised by Eustache Deschamps, the word being taken in its wide sense. His part was that of interpreter between the continent and his country. Who could have hoped that, as he neared his fiftieth year, he would suddenly be revealed as himself a master, the painter of English society, and the creator of a work which in this fourteenth century would leave the contemporary poetry of France far behind it, and even, in some respects, that of Italy also?

The genius which was to flower had been his from the beginning. He did not suddenly become an observer. He had already seen and retained much, although hitherto he had not found among his models a mould in which to cast his observations. Without doubt, there was already that rich diversity in his nature which made him curious of the beautiful and the ugly alike, which was compounded of poetry and prose, piety and scepticism, grace and humour. When, however, he wished to house this complexity, he found only literary forms apt to isolate one or other of its aspects. He had been held by allegory or lyrical narrative when his genius was impelling him, irresistibly, towards dramatic and realistic storytelling, the weaving of a web in which the threads would be both comic and sentimental.

So far, he had brought only two considerable poems to completion, the one a mere translation of the *Roman de la Rose*, the other his adaptation of *Il Filostrato*, a poem whose original harmony he disturbed by his efforts to introduce into it matter of his own. He had begun two other important poems, but had been unable or unwilling to finish them. The *Hous of Fame* discouraged him by the factitiousness of its allegorical machinery and the use, or rather abuse, of personified abstractions which its plan entailed; he wearied of the *Legende of Goode Women* because it imposed on him a partisanship, obliged him, by its preliminary conditions, to be unfailingly sentimental and partial, and therefore necessarily monotonous. Did he wonder whether he would ever find a more pliable and wider frame, in which he could fit stories as varied as life and mobile as his changing moods, stories in which he could be lyrical and epical, by turns, which he could tell tenderly, swiftly, poetically, feelingly, humorously or merrily?

It was at this moment that he bethought him of the collections of stories of which several had been made in the Middle Ages, on the plan so awkwardly reproduced by his friend Gower in the *Confessio Amantis*. The *Decameron* would undoubtedly have stimulated him further had he not been, to the best of our knowledge, unaware of it. Yet Boccaccio's example was not such as to fulfil his aim of variety. That society of elegant young gentlemen and ladies, hardly distinct from each other, telling tales while the plague raged in Florence, was not the band of storytellers he wanted. It was strongly individualised narrators, taken from the most diverse classes, whom he wished to interpose between himself and his readers. And at last he had the very simple and yet quite novel idea of a pilgrimage which would unite people of every condition. Since the spring of 1385 he had been living at Greenwich, on the road of pilgrims from every county in England who were constantly drawn to the shrine of Saint Thomas à Becket at Canterbury. Often and often he had watched the progress of their variegated cavalcades, men and women, knights and burghers, handicraftsmen and clerks, mingled in momentary fellowship. One fine day, moved by devoutness or mere curiosity, he may himself have joined one of these troops. No sooner had he got his idea than the work went of itself. He had but to describe his pilgrims, give each of them his individual characteristics as well as the marks of his rank, then put an appropriate tale into his mouth.

Thus the first requisite was to present a band of storytellers clearly. No enterprise could be more difficult at any time, difficult to-day and more difficult at a date when nothing of the sort had yet been attempted. The simplicity of Chaucer's method, its complete lack of any artifice, the sure hand with which he traced portraits to form the prologue of his *Tales*, are surprising. He made his group of pilgrims into a picture of the society of his time of which the like is not to be found elsewhere. Except for royalty and the nobles on the one hand, and the dregs of the people on the other, two classes whom probability excluded from sharing a pilgrimage, he painted, in brief, almost the whole English nation.

There are thirty of the pilgrims, following the most diverse trades. The Knight with his son, the Squire, and the Yeoman who bore the Squire's arms, represent the fighting class. A Doctor of Physic, a Man of Law, a Clerk of Oxford and the poet himself give a glimpse of the liberal professions. The land is represented by a Ploughman, a Miller, a Reeve and a Franklin, trade by a Merchant and a Shipman, the crafts by a Wife of Bath, a Haberdasher, a Carpenter, a Webbe or Weaver, a Dyer and a Tapicer, the victuallers by a Maunciple, a Cook and the Host of the Tabard. The secular clergy provide the Good Parson and the odious Sompnour or summoner of an ecclesiastical court, who are joined on the road by a Canon addicted to alchemy. The monastic orders supply a full contingent—a rich Benedictine Monk, a Prioress with her chaplain Nun, a mendicant Friar, and not far from these religious, a doubtfully accredited Pardoner wends his way.

Chaucer, desiring distinct outlines, first used the easiest and clearest method of differentiation, which is to contrast various callings. This results—especially in those days did it result—in a whimsical medley of colours and costumes which at once catches the eye, and it allows a whole series of habits and tendencies to be suggested by half a word. Only the generic features, the average characteristics of each calling, have to be marked, in order to give a sufficiently definite picture which has its own identity. Thereafter all that is left to do is to make each person talk as befits his station and nature.

The idea looks so simple that all the noise it has made in the world might be thought exaggerated. It was, however, a novelty. It had no precedent outside obscure corners of a rudimentary drama, and it was to mark a turning-point in European thought. It was more than a literary innovation. It was a change of mental attitude. Poetry turned, with tolerant curiosity, to the study of man and manners. For the first time, the relation between individuals and ideas was clearly realised. Ideas ceased to be an end in themselves, and became interesting as revealing him who expressed them, who believed in them, or who was pleased by them. And they acquired therewith an unforeseen value. The ideas which Chaucer had hitherto given to the world could not be called very original. They were less novel and perhaps less powerful than those, for instance, of Jean de Meung. It would be easier to extract some sort of philosophy from Jean de Meung's works than from Chaucer's. When, however, Chaucer's ideas emanate from a man of a given temperament, represent the prejudices of a class or the routine of a trade, they immediately take on youth or fun, become penetrating and sometimes profound, although they themselves are unchanged. It is that dramatic use is made of them. Their value in isolation or abstraction matters as little as ever, but they are richly significant because they fall from the lips of a definite person who reveals or betrays himself by their means.

For such an end it is necessary that the author efface himself voluntarily. Chaucer is fully conscious of the realism to which he obliges himself. He assumes the part of mere interpreter, a chronicler and no more, who relates without altering a word or a tone stories he has heard told. By his grouping of representatives of the different callings, and by his impartiality which allows individuals to speak and never dictates their thoughts or words, he has painted, with minute exactness, the body and soul of the society of his time. He is as truly the social chronicler of England in the late fourteenth century as Froissart is the political and military chronicler of the same period.

Chaucer has collected the descriptions of the pilgrims in his general prologue, which is a true picture-gallery. His twenty-nine travelling companions make almost as many portraits, hung from its walls. They face us, in equidistant frames, on the same plane, all hanging on the line. Chaucer is a primitive, aiming at exactness of feature and correctness of emblem. He is a primitive also by a certain honest awkwardness, the unskilled stiffness of some of his outlines, and such an insistence on minute points as at first provokes a smile. He seems to amass details haphazard, alternates the particulars of a costume with the points of a character, drops the one for the other, picks either up again. Sometimes he interrupts the painting of a pilgrim's character to put colour on his face or his tunic. It is an endearing carelessness, which hides his art and heightens the impression he makes of veracity:

> Ses nonchalances sont ses plus grands artifices.

Who enters this gallery is first struck by some patches of brilliant colour, dominating one or other of the portraits, the squire's gown,

> Embrowded was he, as it were a mede,
> Al ful of fresshë floures, white and reede,

and near him the yeoman who serves him "in coote and hood of grene." How the Prioress's rosary "of smal coral," its decades, "gauded al with grene," and its hanging brooch "of gold ful schene," stands out against her dress! There are faces as strongly coloured as any of the fabrics or accessories—the pustulous countenance of the Sompnour, "a fyr-reed cherubynes face,"

> With skalled browes blak, and piled berd,

and the Miller, whose beard "as any sowe or fox was reed," with his wart whence sprouts a tuft of red hairs, his wide and black nostrils and his mouth "as wyde as was a gret forneys." There are also duller colours to rest the sight, and to make the cruder hues more brilliant by contrast. The pious and modest Knight was "nought gay,"

> Of fustyan he werede a gepoun,
> Al bysmotered with his habergeoun.

The poor Clerk was "ful threadbare," the Man of Law "rood but hoomly in a medled coote," the Reeve wore a "long surcote of pers," or blue, and the Good Parson is drawn without line or colour, so that we are free to imagine him lit only by the light of the Gospel shining from his eyes.

Essential moral characteristics are thrown into relief with the same apparent simplicity and the same real command of means as the colours and the significant articles of clothing. Mere statements of fact, suggestive anecdotes, particulars relating to calling and individual traits, lines resuming a character—all these make up a whole which stands out upon its canvas. The outline is strong and clear although sometimes a little stiff, in the steady light which is shed on it, and it is unforgettable.

Chaucer was not content to make his pilgrims typical only of their several callings. Sometimes a classification of another kind crosses with that by trades and enriches it. Thus the Squire stands for youth and the Ploughman for the perfect charity of the humble, while in the Wife of Bath there is the essence of satire against women. Nor is this all. Chaucer, by details he has observed for himself, puts life into conventional descriptions and generalisations made by others. He adds individual to generic features; even when he paints a type he gives the impression that he is painting some one person whom he happens to have met. He mixes these two elements in varying proportions and with great although imperceptible skill. His figures, a little more generalised, would be frozen into symbolism, mere cold abstractions, while a few more purely individual features would cause confusion, destroying landmarks and leading attention astray.

Thus English society, which to the visionary Langland seemed a swarming and confused mass, a mob of men stumbling against each other in the semi-darkness of a nightmare, was distributed by Chaucer among a group which is clearly seen restricted in size and representative. Its members pause before us long enough for us to identify each one. Each has his own life and an identity which is for all time, yet together they resume a society.

Chaucer does not only draw frank or delicately traced portraits which give to his characters the immobility of permanence. He also makes each pilgrim step out of the frame in which he first placed him. The artist does not pass straight from portrait to tale. He does not let us forget, on the road to Canterbury, that each storyteller is a living being who has his own gestures and tones. As the cavalcade pursues its course, the pilgrims talk among themselves. The poet shows them calling to each other, approving each other, above all squabbling. They criticise each other's stories, and so betray their preoccupations, feelings and interests. In this way a comedy of action goes through the whole poem, connects its different parts, a comedy which is no more than sketched, yet is adequate, in its incompleteness, to reveal the author's intentions and his dramatic vigour. The persons he has painted are again discovered by their own acts and words. As always happens when an analytical portrait gives place to a direct presentment, some of the pilgrims are found to be more complex, their limitations less discernible, their characteristics more numerous and their outline less definite than had appeared. This is certainly true of the famous Wife of Bath, indubitably the most vigorous of Chaucer's creations, who lives less by her tale than by the immense monologue in which she gives outlet to her feelings as she rides along the road. As she speaks, she seems to be magnified before our eyes, to overflow the exact boundaries which the portraitist set to her personality, and to acquire pantagruelian dimensions. Not until Panurge and Falstaff arrived was there her like in literature. The same is true of the Host of the Tabard, the pilgrims' jovial guide, who is barely sketched in the prologue, but who, little by little and by successive touches, by his various remarks as they journey, is made to tell us much of his temper, his tastes, his dislikes and his private life. He is all the more real and living for never being analysed.

The tales gave Chaucer one means of finishing the portraits of his pilgrims. He found them in every corner of mediæval literature, as diverse and unequal as he could wish. The poet used their lack of originality to impart an added probability to his poem, for his pilgrims are supposed not to invent but to retell stories. Above all, he used the tales to characterise the tellers. He chose for each of them a story suited to his class and character, or, at least, he did this admirably where he had time. His first plan was immense, each of the thirty pilgrims undertaking to tell two tales on the way to Canterbury and two on the way back, so that there would have been one hundred and twenty tales altogether. In fact, Chaucer was not able to allot even one story to each of his travellers, nor, still more regrettably, had he time in every case to adjust story to teller. He was still hesitating about the assignment of certain tales when death surprised him. Enough was, however, accomplished to allow us to appreciate his design and his executive talent.

In a certain number of cases, the tale is so subordinate to the vast comedy in which it has place that its original form has a little suffered. More often, it is its meaning which is changed. It is possible to consider a story by itself to judge whether the writer has succeeded in his aim of producing the strongest possible impression by his distribution of the parts, his manipulation and unravelling of the plot, and his arrangement of details in view of the surprise of the conclusion. The excellence of a tale then depends simply on the skill with which its thread is followed, and on the grace or liveliness of its writing. But the same story may be told to reveal an alleged narrator. It then behoves the author to conceal himself, to sacrifice his own literary talent and sense of proportion and give place to another, who may be ignorant, garrulous, clumsy, foolish or coarse, or moved by enthusiasms and prejudices unshared by his creator. Chaucer follows this principle to most of its consequences in that part of his work to which he was able to put the finishing touches. He very carefully allows more than one of his pilgrims to reveal themselves by introducing into their stories irrelevances, digressions which break the even course of a tale but which give an opening for the information, the discursiveness or the fads of the speaker. We notice this as we read the tales of the Wife of Bath, the Pardoner and the Yeoman of the alchemist Canon.

Elsewhere, the very fact that a story is assigned to a particular person is enough without any digressions, as when the tale of Griselda, fount of abnegation, is told by the good idealist Clerk, or when the graceful and mincing Prioress tells the story of the little cleric, devotee of Mary, who was slain by the Jews, or the Nun relates the tale of the miracle of Saint Cecilia, with its conventual atmosphere.

Chaucer goes so far as to give us stories which he invites us to think repellent or ridiculous. The Monk recites a litany of lugubrious and monotonous "tragedies," which sadden the Knight's good heart and make the Innkeeper yawn. He is not allowed to tell his funereal beads to the end, and when interrupted relapses into silence. The poet is prevented from finishing the tale of Sir Thopas which he allots to himself. The Host of the Tabard chides him for singing a chivalrous ballad, with rhyme but without reason. In such instances as these, the reader is expected to find his pleasure not in the excellence, but in the very extravagance or tediousness of the stories.

These tales are deliberately exceptional. In general, the poet's gift of life is revealed within the stories as in the frame of the poem. Chaucer's own contribution is of varying importance. In the serious, strictly poetic part of the *Canterbury Tales*, his original work is very slight: he makes only insignificant additions, restrained in detail, to his borrowed material, and his merit is mainly in his style, which is often admirable for simple pathos and gentle humanity. The comic and realistic stories, which have analogies with the French *fabliaux*, are in very different case. These he has so much enriched that he might be called their creator. He deserves this title, at least in part, even when he is compared to the author of the *Decameron*, who put so much heat and red blood into a literary form usually of the driest. While, however, Boccaccio observed the conciseness proper to this form and did no more than paint manners, Chaucer, less condensed and less passionate, addressed himself more and more to the study of character. He repeats within several of his stories that effort to capture individuality which is the glory of his prologue. Boccaccio is on the road to picaresque fiction, but Chaucer is pointing the way for Molière and Fielding. As we read the *Tales*, especially those of them which are humorous, we have constantly the impression that a birth is in progress. A leaven of observation and truth is fermenting within these established literary forms, which once had a perfection of their own, but which are narrow and about to be discarded. In this travail, modern drama and the modern novel are showing their first signs of life.

6. **Conclusion.**—If all this poet's work be regarded together, he is clearly seen constantly to have advanced nearer truth. He found poetry remote from

nature, its essence being fiction in the accepted belief, while its task was the ingenious transposition of reality in accordance with artificial rules. In the beginning Chaucer submitted to the received code, dreamt with his contemporaries, like them had visions of allegorical figures and combined imaginary incidents. Or he sought the matter of his poems in books, borrowing his subjects and characters. Then, by degrees, he reached the point of deeming nothing as interesting and as diverse as Nature herself. Relegating his books to a secondary plane, ridding himself entirely of the allegory and the dream, he looked face to face at the spectacle of men and set himself to reproduce it directly. He made himself the painter of life.

It is well known how dry, morose and bitter such reproduction of reality can be. It may breed disgust with life and men. Chaucer, without flattering his model, placed it in an atmosphere which is good to breathe. No one can read him and not be glad to be in the world. Whoever enters through the door he opens feels a healthy air blow on him from all sides. This is partly because Chaucer writes in a dialect still new, uses words which he was the first to put to real literary use. The language breathes a freshness, as when earth is turned in April, such vernal youth as it could never have at another time. Usually this novelty of language coincides with crudity of thought and puerility of art. But Chaucer, who begins English poetry, ends the Middle Ages. It happened that he inherited all the literature of France, rich by three centuries of generous effort, free of speech and fertile of thought, already a little weary because it had produced too much. For Chaucer, a literature in its autumn and a language in its spring combined as they have rarely, if ever, done before or since. He is at once very young and very mature; he unites the charm of a beginning to the experience of a long life. When he repeats a description or an idea which has become a little jaded in its native language, he often gives back to it the grace of novelty by the artlessness of his expression. In his highly skilled verses, English words, frozen by a long winter of waiting, first gave forth their fragrance.

To this advantage, due to exceptional circumstances, Chaucer added natural gifts, the first of them the wide sympathy which is otherwise called indulgence. To this especially his poetry owes the soft, lovable and smiling light which is shed on it. For some of his fellow-men he feels affection or respect; about all the others he has so much curiosity that they interest him. No one is excluded. He is not easily repelled. He loves the world's variety, is grateful to defects for their difference from virtues. He looks at himself without illusions, judges himself without bitterness, is carried away by no desire to excel. He places himself on the average level, and finds all the multitude of men beside him. It is the consciousness of shared failings which makes fellowship among men. Of all writers of genius, Chaucer is the one with whom it is easiest to have a sense of comradeship.

Sympathy of this kind, founded on clear self-knowledge, is a form of intelligence. If it were absolutely necessary to define in a word the novelty of Chaucer's masterpiece, it might be said to show, most of all, the progress of intelligence. It evinces a weakening of the passion which leads to lyricism or satire and is supported by self-confidence and by the energy of desires, hopes, loves and hates; a weakening also of the imagination which transforms and magnifies reality, projecting it on to another more or less arbitrarily chosen plane, and which produces epical, romantic or allegorical poems. In the *Canterbury Tales* the element of the poet's personality has been subdued, superseded by pleasure in observing and understanding. Hitherto this degree of peaceful, honourable spectatorship had never been reached by poets. More noble and more essentially poetic works had indeed been written: we have but to name two with different claims to greatness, the *Chanson de Roland* and the *Divina Commedia*. Some of the line of French song-makers, stretching

I—H

from the twelfth-century romancers to Rutebeuf, and past him to reach its apotheosis, a hundred years after Chaucer, in Villon, were more exquisite than the English poet and sounded more thrilling notes than he, nor did he ever attain to the refinements of feeling and language which Petrarch put into his sonnets. But where, before the *Canterbury Tales*, can we find a poem of which the first object is to show men, neither exalted nor demeaned, to display the truthful spectacle of life at its average? Chaucer sees what is and paints it as he sees it. He effaces himself in order to look at it better.

He is the pioneer of that group of spectators who regard with amused indulgence, without seeking to redip it in dye of one colour, the web and woof of variously coloured threads which is the chequered stuff of a society. Doubtless he has judged certain colours to be more beautiful than the others, but it is on the contrasts they afford that he has founded both his philosophy of life and the laws of his art.

CHAPTER III

1. **Chaucer's Imitators and Disciples in England.**—England took two centuries to produce a poet worthy to rank with Chaucer. Nothing better proves his genius than the powerlessness of the succeeding generations to equal or even to understand him, a fact the more striking because all the poets knew him and rendered him homage. When, however, they believe themselves to be imitating him they do no more than follow his inferior work, in which he does not surpass the average level of his time. They leave on one side the poems in which he rose above his contemporaries. Most of them barely reach the plane of Gower. Criticism in the fifteenth and even in the sixteenth century was so incompetent that it constantly placed Chaucer and Gower together, and Lydgate, that retrograde and prolix disciple of Chaucer, beside the two of them.

The years from 1400 to the Renascence were a period disinherited of literature. Several causes of this destitution may be discovered, but none which is satisfying save the fact that no writer of genius was born during these long years. The only excuse for the poverty applies to poetry alone. It is that, in the transition to the analytical modern English which was in course, the last inflections were disappearing. The result was that Chaucer's accurate and sure versification ceased to be understood soon after his death. When the final *e* had become entirely mute, Chaucer's line, badly read and transcribed, and later badly printed, seemed to be variable and irregular, to contain a differing number of syllables and irregularly distributed accents. His successors, whose ear was imperfect, were not offended by this lack of rhythm, but felt that it authorised them to licence in their own verse-making. The English verse-form was thrown off its balance, and definitely recovered a sure rhythm only with Spenser.

This cause of decline was one which an harmonious poet would have charmed away, as indeed the poets of Scotland did exorcise it. Other causes of decadence, drawn from history, might be revealed by diligent search. The fatal effects on art of the Wars of the Roses (1454–83) might, for instance, be exaggerated, although this terrible civil conflict covered only a fourth of the vast desert space of time. Before this war, England under Henry V. experienced a time of military glory which recalled and exceeded the victories of Edward III., and the finest works of the fourteenth century had appeared during the deplorable and humiliating reign of Richard II. But it came to pass that neither triumphs nor disasters could inspire literature. Miserly Nature created only imitators and reiterators of outworn themes. The sense of the beautiful seems to have died with the sense of life and of reality. Contact with the continent, once so fruitful, could not revive the flagging literary impulse. Contact hardly existed except with France, herself disabled. Italy, which Chaucer had revealed, remained forgotten for a whole century.

England suffered not only checked progress, but also retrogression. Literature resumed its course as though the *Canterbury Tales* had never been written. The decline was immediate. Its signs appeared even in those who knew Chaucer, were near him and called him master, in Occleve and Lydgate.

99

Both were aware of his superiority. It is touching to see how Occleve represents himself as the stupid scholar of an excellent master:

> My derĕ maister,—God his soulĕ quyte,—
> And fader, Chaucer, fayne wold have me taught,
> But I was dulle, and lerned lyte or naught.

Occleve, dull indeed, saw in Chaucer only an all-wise philosopher, a pious poet, almost a saint. Chaucer's humour escaped him. Lydgate is more discriminating, for while he agrees with Occleve that no poet was left "that worthy was his ynkehorne for to holde," he was conscious of Chaucer's wit, and shows his indulgence, not unmixed with scepticism, for verses submitted to him by his youthful disciples. But neither Lydgate nor Occleve was capable of continuing Chaucer's work.

Thomas Occleve[1] (1370?–1454?) is the author of a *Letter of Cupid* long ascribed to Chaucer. It is a translation of the *Epistre du Dieu d'amours* of Christine de Pisan, which was a reply to Jean de Meung's sarcasms against women. It recalls the *Legende of Goode Women* in theme, but it substitutes reasonings for imagination, humour and life.

In his *La Male Règle de T. Occleve,* which is a sort of confession, the poet informs us that he led a debauched youth, and that none was better known than he to the keepers of taverns and cook-shops in Westminster. The story of his irregularities entails some descriptions of London which are historically interesting although they have no value as poetry.

His principal work is the *De Regimine Principum,* written in 1411–12 to win the favour of the Prince of Wales, afterwards Henry V. It is a series of lessons on conduct, imitated from the Latin work of the same name which the Roman Ægidius wrote for Philip the Fair. Dissertations, historical examples and tales are used to inculcate the lessons. The whole is clear, fluent and sufficiently correctly versified, but the intellectual and artistic weakness is reminiscent rather of the didactic Gower than of Chaucer.

John Lydgate[2] (1373?–1450?) has the distinction of being the most voluminous poet of the fourteenth century and even of all the Middle Ages in England. About 140,000 lines of verse, authentically his, are extant. This Benedictine monk of Bury St. Edmunds was principally an indefatigable translator and compiler. His longest poems are the *Storie of Thebes* and *Troye-Book,* which retell the famous romances, the *Falls of Princes,* adapted from the Latin of Boccaccio, the *Temple of Glas,* a heavy allegory of love, the *Pilgrimage of the Life of Man,* translated from Guillaume de Deguileville, and some lives of saints, those of Saint Edmund, Saint Margaret, Our Lady and others.

Lydgate's retrograde tendency is striking. He reverts in his *Troye-Book* to the original story, whence Boccaccio and Chaucer, in *Il Filostrato* and *Troylus and Criseyde,* had extracted the dramatic essence. He has forgotten that Chaucer took the best of his *Falls of Princes* for his Monk's Tale, and ironically ignored the rest, that Chaucer caused a Nun to relate the life of a saint with all its marvels, and thus disclaimed responsibility for it, and that he wearied of the allegory of his *Hous of Fame,* much as it exceeded the *Temple of Glas* in animation and picturesqueness. But no example could stay Lydgate's flow of words.

With Lydgate decomposition overtook English verse. He admits that he "toke

---

[1] Works ed. by Furnivall (Early English Text Society, i. and ii).

[2] There is no complete edition of Lydgate's works, but there are several good editions of his principal poems. *The Pilgrimage of the Life of Man,* ed. Furnivall and Miss Locock (Early English Text Society, 1889, 1901, 1904); *Temple of Glass,* ed. J. Schick (ibid., 1891); *Troy-Book,* ed. H. Bergsen (ibid., 1906, et seq.).

none hede nouther of shorte nor longe," that is of accentuated and unaccentuated syllables, a candid confession which excludes the possibility of blaming copyists for the irregularities of his verse.

Much read and much admired by his contemporaries, who were grateful to him for telling so many stories, and telling them with a certain briskness, it is long since Lydgate has been disturbed except by courageous specialists. The small number of his verses which are still read are those extracted, as in an anthology, by Warton from his *Lyf of Our Lady*, or a few short pieces, religious and secular, a few fables, and, especially, *London Lickpenny*, which hymns with some liveliness the griefs of a countryman suing for justice in London. Unfortunately Lydgate's authorship of this, the most popular of the poems ascribed to him, is uncertain.

Here and there, especially in the most Chaucerian of his poems, the *Complaint of the Black Knight*, there are pleasant descriptions, but in spite of them we ask whether this Benedictine ever had time to lift his eyes from his books and papers and look at nature. It is certainly from books that he seems to have taken all his verses which speak of nature.

Much more attractive than the works of Occleve and Lydgate are certain short poems of which the authors are unknown or uncertainly known, and which were long attributed to Chaucer, so that they are included in many editions of his works.[1] A study of their versification and language has, however, proved that they belong to the fifteenth, a few of them even to the sixteenth, century.

A translation of Alain Chartier's *Belle Dame sans Merci*, made by Sir Richard Ros about 1450, is negligible. It dilutes the French octosyllabic lines into the heroic metre, filling them out with expletives and padding, and the result has no merit but correctness of rhythm. *The Cuckoo and the Nightingale* (1403), now restored to Sir Thomas Clanvowe, who knew Chaucer, is, however, an agreeable poem, gracefully relating an argument between the two birds. Its rhythm is light and rapid, and its well-turned and pure language recalls both the *Parlement of Foules* and the prologue to the *Legende of Goode Women*. It is true that the charm of these three hundred lines is in the detail, for the conception—the debate between love and chastened experience—is not new. It goes back to the thirteenth-century debate between the *Owl and the Nightingale*.

The prologue of the *Legende of Goode Women* also inspired a charming allegory, the *Flower and the Leaf*, which was modernised by Dryden, who took it for Chaucer's. But Chaucer certainly did not write these disjointed verses, and they are now admitted to be the probable work of an unknown lady of the middle fifteenth century. The author reproduces the debate between the flower and the leaf to which Chaucer made only passing allusion.

The Leaf symbolises work and the serious and useful life, the Flower frivolous leisure. It is, however, possible to disregard the moral of this poem, and be charmed by the delicious opening descriptions of spring and nature, richer and less restrained than those of Chaucer. There are pretty effects of light and shade in the oak-wood to which the lady who cannot sleep resorts one spring day. There she sees appear, first the ladies and knights of the Leaf, dazzling in their pearls and ornaments or clad in gilded armour, and all crowned with laurel chaplets, who seat themselves beneath an oak. From another side there enter an equally sumptuous company of knights and ladies wearing flowery chaplets, who engage in a merry dance. It is all artificial, but the colour and brilliancy are delightful. A storm supervenes, and the followers of the Flower are drenched, their adornments spoilt. The queen gives them shelter and restores their beauty, and then all disappear.

This poem, like the one noticed before it, marks if not an advance on Chaucer's

---

[1] In the seventh volume of Skeat's edition of Chaucer (Oxford, 1897).

work, yet a difference from it. It is less substantial, real and humorous, but it has some added lightness, agility and airiness, and a new dewy quality. Although the fiction of a dream has been abandoned, the poem is more purely dreamy than its predecessors. This is, assuredly, the most exquisite product of the fifteenth century.

The *Court of Love* is a less freshly coloured poem, but one which is more mischievously witty, shows greater power of characterisation and has a surer rhythm. It is the one of these poems which might best be claimed for Chaucer, had it not the "gilded" style which hints at "rhetoriqueurs." It is, in point of fact, the furthest removed from him in date, recent criticism having ascribed it to the first half of the sixteenth century. The author, who calls himself "Philogenet, of Cambridge Clerk," loses his way in the palace of Cytherea, where Admetus and Alcestis are vice-regents. Philabone, a lady of the court, informs him of the rules of the place, and shows him the persons who have obeyed or broken the laws of love. Among the latter are such as have deliberately refused to love and are now tormented by regrets. The poet enters the service of the fair Lady Rosial, who at first treats him harshly, but becomes gracious at the entreaty of Pity. The poem is concluded by a choir of birds, of whom each one intones a beautiful hymn of the Church.

Were this poem not too imitative, and did not "Philogenet" rather preserve acquired qualities than add to them or transform them, the fifteen hundred lines of his *Court of Love* would redeem the sterility of this impoverished time.

To imitate was then the rule. Langland's imitators matched Chaucer's. As early as the extreme end of the fourteenth century, an unknown author wrote the *Crede of Piers Plowman*,[1] a vigorous satire against friars of all orders. At an unknown date the Ploughman's Tale,[2] which Chaucer had not time to write, was annexed to the *Canterbury Tales*, serving as a vehicle for the grievances of some Lollard. There is a whole series of fairly mediocre poems, alliterative or other, which are evidence of the continued popularity, well into the sixteenth century, of the great fourteenth-century satire.

They occur both before and after the Wars of the Roses. When, after this long period of sanguinary civil conflict which suspended all literary activity, poetry reappeared in the reign of the first Tudor sovereign, Henry VII., its languor and weariness and its unrhythmic verse are strangely reminiscent of Occleve and Langland. Yet, when the nausea produced by the repetition of so many old characteristics and old faults has been overcome, it is possible to discern in it vague signs of the coming Renascence.

The mediocre poet Stephen Hawes [3] (1475–1530) illustrates this point. He is yet another of the allegorists, but, while he is too much an echo of the past, he also feebly heralds Spenser. When the Wars of the Roses destroyed almost the whole of English chivalry, they relegated the old chivalrous poetry to a dreamlike past. The attempts to revive it which were made at court did no more than reconstruct an empty show, for the soul of this poetry had gone. It had become imaginative material, almost as unreal as allegorical scenes and personages. In compensation, however, chivalry had acquired the prestige which belongs to the remote, and the melancholy which attaches to regret, both elements of romanticism. It is only this vaguely romantic atmosphere which gives some interest to the languishing platitudes and uncadenced verses of Hawes. He complains that

---

[1] Inserted in W. Skeat's edition of *Piers Plowman* (Oxford, 1906).
[2] In vol. vii. of W. Skeat's edition of Chaucer (Oxford, 1897).
[3] *The Pastime of Pleasure*, ed. T. Wright (Percy Society, 1845); *The Example of Vertue* (original edition 1512, reprinted 1530).

no one but himself in his generation cultivated true English poetry. So neglected was it that his king, Henry VII., reverted to an old precedent, and made a Frenchman, Bernard André of Toulouse, his poet laureate. Hawes, who acknowledged as his masters the trinity of Gower, Chaucer and Lydgate, and especially Lydgate, is like a ghost from the past. He writes allegories according to the formula of the *Roman de la Rose*, and, like Spenser, complicates it by the addition of chivalrous elements. Learned and didactic, he rejects all poetry which does not enclose a lesson.

He anticipates Spenser in that the subject of his principal works is the fashioning of man, by discipline, to an ideal of virtue. In his *Example of Vertu* (1503-4), he relates the allegory of a youth led by Discretion or Reason who finally marries fair Purity, the daughter of the King of Love. So long is the road he travels, so many his obstacles and so fearful the monsters he must slay, that he is sixty years old when he reaches his goal, and there is nothing better left for him to do than to ascend straight to heaven with his beloved.

Hawes's chief work, the *Pastime of Pleasure*, or *Historie of Graunde Amoure and La Belle Pucel* (1505-6), has a like plan. His aim in it is to exemplify a transcendent education, to show by what degrees of study and prowess perfection can be reached.

Graunde Amoure, the hero of the poem who tells his own story, relates that after falling asleep in a flowery valley he sees the Lady Fame appear to him. She tells that La Belle Pucel dwells in the magic tower of Music, but that giants bar the way thither. After serving a long apprenticeship to Ladies Grammar, Logic and Rhetoric, who constitute the Trivium, and Arithmetic, Music, Geometry and Astronomy, who are the Quadrivium, and after having slain the giants with his sword Clara Prudence, Graunde Amoure finally attains to La Belle Pucel, marries her, grows old and dies. Time writes his epitaph in the only lines of Hawes which still live in men's memory:

> For though the daye be never so long,
> At last the belle ringeth to evensong.

In general, Hawes's style, sometimes aggrandised by Latinised words, sometimes entangled by awkward constructions, is among the worst known to English poetry. Never did poetry in English sink to lower depths of the prosaic than when Lady Grammar explained the nature of a noun to her pupil. The verses on the garden of Greek roots and on cooking recipes are much better than these.

Barclay and Skelton, the two last writers of verse who are in the mediæval tradition, at least show some novelty of subject or manner.

Alexander Barclay [1] (1474–1552), a Dominican, careful of doctrine, morals and orthodoxy, and a good Latinist, is hardly more than a translator, yet a free translator who adds matter of his own to his original. He is also the first of his nation to have come across a subject of German origin. His *Ship of Fools* is a translation made in 1509 from the Swabian poet Sebastian Brant, not directly but through the medium of a Latin and a French translation. This fiction of a ship in which all fools are invited to embark, so that the author is able to review every kind of folly and insanity provided by mankind, had a great success in England as on the continent. Barclay did not miss his opportunity of adding some peculiarly English types to the crew.

He was also the first to introduce the eclogue to his fellow-countrymen. In his

---

[1] *The Ship of Fools*, ed. T. H. Jamieson, 2 vols. (1874); *Certain Eglogues of A. B.* and *The Mirour of Good Manners* (Spenser Society, 1885); C. H. Herford, *Studies in the Literary Relations of England and Germany in the Sixteenth Century* (1886); *The English Versions of The Ship of Fools*, by A. Pomper (Longmans, 1925).

youth he had written five eclogues, which he published in 1514, two of them imitations of Mantuanus, who was to be one of the classic Latin authors of the Renascence. They have nothing of the idyll, but are moral satires, discussions between a townsman and a countryman, between a poor poet and a rich miser, an exposition of the miseries of a courtier's life.

Barclay chose his models well, and he has the merits of sincerity of speech and a realism sometimes racy, but his style lacks ductility, his language is rude, and his verse suffers from the general lack of rhythm.

John Skelton (1460?–1529) [1] is a fantastic personage, hard to classify or define. As a learned humanist who won praise from Erasmus, an Oxford laureate famous for his Latin verses and known as a grammarian, he belongs to the Renascence. He is very well acquainted with ancient poets and mindful of the mythology of antiquity. His occupations were serious, for he was tutor to the future Henry VIII. and rector of Diss in Norfolk. But he writes verses like a buffoon, in many respects like a man behind his times. He is faithful to satirical allegory, and sets fine order and classic nobility and elegance at naught. He found heroic verse debased, and, instead of attempting to reform it, most often abandoned it in favour of a short irregular line and rhymes multiplied until a dozen of them sometimes follow each other. His verses might have been improvised by some untiring tavern poet. He deliberately turns his back on beauty, is fully aware of what he is about, and acknowledges that his only aim is to strike hard and straight:

> Though my rime be ragged,
> Tatter'd and jagged,
> Rudely raine-beaten,
> Rusty and moth-eaten;
> If ye take wel therewith,
> It hath in it some pith.

The pith is mostly satire. In this age of dull repetitions Skelton pleases because he is brutal and coarse. No one has handled prelates more roughly, not even the Protestants among whom he is not numbered. Of his numerous poems, many of which are lost, the most interesting are the *Bowge of Court*, the *Boke of Colin Clout* and *Why Come ye not to Court ?*

The first of these (1509?) is an allegory which recalls the *Ship of Fools*. The poet is on board a magnificent ship which is to take him to the land of Favour, and his voyage is troubled by the intolerable company of Fortune's friends, Favell or Flattery, Suspecte or Suspicion, Disdain and Dissimulation. They conspire against him, and he is about to throw himself into the sea in order to escape them, when he awakes—all has been a dream. How familiar is every one of these allegorical figures! Yet never, perhaps, have they been as living and as busy as in this poem. Exceptionally it is written in the stanza of seven heroic lines called Chaucerian.

Colin Clout (1519) is a peasant, another Piers Plowman, who like him chastises the vices of the clergy. With disorderly energy Skelton poses as the mouthpiece of popular wrath.

The last of these three poems, written in 1522, is a violent indictment of Cardinal Wolsey, the all-powerful minister of Henry VIII. It includes a stinging description of the terror in which he was held by the noblest of the kingdom.

Although Skelton's habitual tone is satirical, and he uses complacently the coarsest insults and worst indecencies, he yet showed himself capable, on occasion, of feeling and even of a certain grace, as in his *Boke of Philipp Sparowe* (1503-7), an elegy on the death of a sparrow who belonged to fair Jane Scroupe. It echoes the little poem of Catullus, with the difference that the Latin poet's eighteen

---

[1] *The Poetical Works of John Skelton*, ed. Dyce, 2 vols. (1843).

lines have become 1382 lines of Skeltonic verse. It is a hotch-potch of reminiscences and buffoonery, alternating with passages full of freshness and charm. There is something of everything in John Skelton, that first rough sketch for Rabelais. Taken all together, however, his poetry represents rather the last stirrings of the dying Middle Ages than the first signs of life of the Renascence.

2. **Scottish Poetry from 1400 to 1516.**—There is pleasure in passing from the English to the Scottish poetry of the fifteenth century. It is not that the matter of poetry had been renewed in Scotland. North as south of the Tweed, the allegorical school was dominant and Chaucer's personal influence reigned. The Scots had, however, kept the artistic sense and a line which had an assured rhythm, and they had a vitality which contrasted happily with English languor. This is the most glorious period of all their old poetry.

The patriotic impulse which had caused Barbour to write his *Bruce* in the previous century had almost ceased to be felt. The only poem which matches *Bruce* is *Wallace*,[1] written about 1461 by the minstrel called Blind Harry. He differed from Barbour, who related the comparatively recent exploits of the Bruce, for he went back to an earlier hero whose date was a hundred and fifty years before his own. The fabulous element looms much larger in *Wallace* than in *Bruce*. Wallace's exploits are magnified and multiplied. But the two poems tell their tale with the same naked simplicity. Barbour's prosaic quality is even intensified in Blind Harry, who is platitudinous. He is devoid of poetry, merely amasses detail, and his substitution of decasyllabic couplets for Barbour's eight-syllable verses only protracts the line awkwardly and increases its monotony.

This poem is isolated, and it heightens, by contrast, the ornate, even exaggeratedly brilliant, character of other Scottish verse in this century.

The first in date of the poets of Scotland who were influenced by Chaucer is King James I. (1394–1436). Doubts have been thrown on his literary claims, but they have not seriously shaken the beautiful and touching tradition that the *Kingis Quair*[2] expresses in verse a romantic incident of his life which he himself commemorated.

At eleven years of age he was taken captive by the English, together with the ship which was carrying him to France, and, in spite of the truce between Scotland and England, was kept a prisoner for nineteen years, but honourably treated and carefully educated.

During this captivity he fell in love with Lady Jane Beaufort, niece to Henry IV., whom he married in 1424.

His poem describes his love, and is a graceful medley of allegory and reality. Chaucer's work must have been much read by the young prisoner, for the *Kingis Quair* is full of Chaucerian reminiscences. Especially James remembers the charming passage of the Knightes Tale in which Palamon and Arcite see, from the window of their dungeon, the fair Emely walking in the garden, and at once fall in love with her. He had read and re-read Chaucer's translation of the *Roman de la Rose* and the love-scenes in *Troylus and Criseyde*, particularly that in which the lovers first meet, and his head was filled with the poems in which a dream leads to a marvellous allegorical vision. His poem is inspired from all these known sources, but because he himself had partly lived through the traditional fictions, there is a freshness in his imitations which is quite personal, and more than once his stanzas surpass their models in emotion.

His complaint on his long captivity, his contemplation of the "gardyn faire"

---

[1] Ed. by J. Moir for the Scottish Text Society, 1884–9.
[2] Ed. by Skeat for the Scottish Text Society. Extracts in Skeat's *Specimens*, op. cit. See J. J. Jusserand, *Le Roman d'un roi*, in *Revue de Paris* (Feb. 1884), and *Jacques Ier d'Ecosse ut-il poète?* (Paris, 1897).

"fast by the touris wall" of his prison, the birds' song, "so loud and clere," which stirs him to love—all this is the most natural prelude to the appearance of the girl:

> For quhich sodayn abate, anone astert
> The blude of all my body to my hert.

The sight of her is such that—

> My hert, my will, my nature and my mynd,
> Was changit clene ryght in another kind.

He recovers enough to gaze at the fair vision, to note her features and ornaments, and especially the heart-shaped ruby:

> That, as a spark of lowe,[1] so wantonely
> Semyt burnyng upon her quhytĕ throte.

There was in her—

> Beautee eneuch to mak a world to dote.

This prelude has so much charm and emotion that we willingly follow the poet through the dream which leads him from the palace of Venus to those of Minerva and of Fortune. Others have taken us thither before, but James can often point out a graceful or brilliant detail. And throughout the fantastic journey suspense reigns as to the outcome of a passion we know to be sincere:

> O besy goste![2] ay flikering to and fro,
> That never art in quiet nor in rest.

It is easy for us to share his joy when he wins to the "presence suete and delitable" of his mistress:

> And thankit be the fair castell wall,
>   Quhare as I quhilom lukit forth and lent,
> Thankit mot be the sanctis marcial,[3]
> That me first causit hath this accident.
> Thankit mot be the grenĕ bewis[4] bent,
> Throu quom, and under, first fortunyt me
> My hertis hele,[5] and my comfort to be.

This royal pupil, who commends his book to Gower and Chaucer, his "maistiris dere," is a correct and harmonious versifier. His dialect is tempered by his assiduous reading of English models, and exempt from the difficulty increasingly felt in the poetry of his successors.

These, on the other hand, have more raciness, for they had not spent their youth in the English court. One of the most interesting of them is the Dunfermline schoolmaster, Robert Henryson (1425–1500),[6] who evinces a real independence even when he is imitating Chaucer.

He had read and admired *Troylus and Criseyde,* but his moral sense was shocked by the conclusion of the story. How could the faithful Troylus be killed and the fickle Criseyde be happy with Diomede thereafter?

> Quha wait[7] gif all that Chaucer wrait was trew?

Henryson, one cold day in Lent, set himself to recast the conclusion of the story and write the *Testament of Cresseid.*

His Diomede soon deserts Cresseid, who becomes a light-of-love among the Greeks, and in punishment is afflicted by Heaven with leprosy. Then "with cop and clapper" she goes begging from door to door. One day Troylus, who is not

---

[1] Flame.   [2] Restless spirit.   [3] Saints of March.   [4] Boughs.   [5] Healing.
[6] Complete works edited by A. Laing (1865), and by Gregory Smith (Scottish Text Society, 1906 et seq.); *The Testament of Cresseid,* by Skeat, in vol. vii. of his full edition of Chaucer's works (1897).
[7] Knows.

dead, is returning from a glorious expedition and passes near the place where she sits. Not recognising her, yet reminded by her "of fair Cresseid, sumtyme his awin darling," he gives her a generous alms:

> For knichtlie pietie and memoriale
> Of fair Cresseid.

When he has gone, and she learns from the other leper folk who he is, she falls to the ground. Before dying, she writes her testament, bequeathing her body to the worms and toads, and all her goods to the lepers, save a ring, set with a ruby, which is to be carried to Troilus after her death. When he receives it and hears her story—

> For greit sorrow his hart to birst was bown.

He causes "ane tomb of merbell gray" to be raised above her grave.

Henryson seems to have been guided by his sense of reality at least as much as by a moral aim. He thinks this miserable end the most probable for the Cresseids of this world. Chaucer, in pity, had drawn a veil over the life of his heroine after her fall. Henryson is no less pitiful: his heart aches for Cresseid even while he is describing her horrible chastisement. His morality is penetrated with sympathy and humanity. His *Testament of Cresseid* has been accepted as the natural sequel to the romance. It is written in the same stanza as Chaucer's poem and is as correct and harmonious.

Henryson was no mere sentimental moralist. His moral fables show him in more homely guise, capable of mischievous energy. He tells us that he has had a vision of an old man,

> The fairest man that ever befoir I saw,

who declares that he is a Roman and named Æsop. This Roman Æsop without a hump—how remote we still are from the Renascence!—can tell a good story, with a mischievous smile, and the thirteen fables he dictates to Henryson—*The Cock and the Jasp, The Uplandis Mous and the Burges Mous, Schir Chantecleir and the Fox, The Lyoun and the Mous, The Wolf and the Lamb,* and the others—are among the best fables ever told. The matter is commonplace and everything is in the manner. They are not epical fables, such as Chaucer wrote, when jestingly and in heroic tones he sang the adventures of the cock and the fox, but they are copious, crowded with detail and with notes of customs or characteristics, abundantly picturesque, much more extensive than those of La Fontaine. What life and go there is in the most celebrated of them, which is imitated from Horace, *The Uplandis Mous and the Burges Mous*! How amusing the contrast between the rural mouse in her "sillie scheill" (poor hut),

> Withouten fyre or candill birnand bricht,

and her sister, the burgess mouse, whose dwelling is a larder in a rich man's house, and who says to the other:

> My Gude Fryday is better nor your Pace! [1]

All this is told with a swing and with fine humour, in the seven-lined Chaucerian stanza, and with sympathy for the animals brought on the scene. Happily the moral is placed by itself, so that nothing spoils or hinders the pleasure of the story.

Other qualities are revealed in Henryson's other short poems. *Orpheus and Eurydice*, founded on Boethius, has a pathetic lyricism, and *Robene and Makyne*, which is half-way between a *pastourelle* and a pastoral, is ingeniously constructed. Makyne has vainly sighed for Robene for "yeris two or thre," but he cares nothing

[1] Easter.

for her, thinks only of his sheep, and repels her harshly. Hardly has she left him than he regrets her, and it is then his turn to beg and implore. But she reminds him of his hardness, laughs at his sighs, and bids him adieu:

> Makyne went hame blythe anewche [1]
> Attour the holtis hair. [2]
> Robene murnit, and Makyne lewche; [3]
> Scho sang, he sichit sair: [4]
> And so left him bayth wo and wrench,
> In dolour and in cair,
> Kepand his hird under a huche [5]
> Among the holtis hair.

The *estrif* or *disputoison* is recalled, save for the fresh country air that blows through the poem. Of all the Scottish poets of this time, Henryson has most rustic realism and savours most of the soil.

The one of this remarkable group who is justly reputed the greatest is, however, William Dunbar (1460?–1520?). [6] This churchman, first in Franciscan habit, then unfrocked, at one time a wandering preacher, at others sent by James IV. on embassies to London and Paris, became in some sort the poet laureate of Scotland. Some hundred of his poems are extant. Nearly all of them are short, but their variety of subject and versification is surprising. Dunbar's prolificity has nothing in common with the flat long-windedness of a Lydgate. He is an artist, even, in some respects, a great artist. It is true that there is nothing new in his thought or feeling. He does not abandon the mediæval frames; both his allegories and his satires keep to the traditional grooves. Nor does he ever, like Villon whose verses he knew, thrill with a personal and vibratingly emotional note. He is without Chaucer's and Henryson's fine gifts of observation. But he has to a rare degree— one never reached before him and seldom since—virtuosity of style and versification. No one hitherto had put so much colour in pictures; no one, above all, had given such a swing to lines and stanza. It matters little that Dunbar has not much to say which touches the heart or the mind. He dazzles the eyes and ravishes the ears.

It is brilliancy which is especially remarkable in his official allegories, for instance *The Thrissil and the Rois* [7] in which he symbolises the marriage in 1503 of James IV. to Margaret Tudor, daughter of Henry VII., that union of Scotland and England. Dunbar has recourse to the convention of a vision during sleep, but what a wealth of coloured words he uses, how rapidly the allegories, usually so slow, unfold themselves in his hands! His flamboyant style can doubtless be criticised, yet artifice is in place in such occasional verse. Poetry of this kind, in which conventionalised and highly coloured heraldic figures are substituted for real beings— the lion, the eagle, the thistle, the rose—is surely suited to the celebration of a marriage between two countries. The very violences of the style are those of an artist whose effects are new, as when he speaks of birds singing—

> Amang the tendir odouris reid and quhyt.

He goes farther in his *Goldyn Targe*, in which he uses unremittingly a nine-line stanza having two rhymes. Nothing in this allegory shows an advance on the *Roman de la Rose*. There is yet another dream and description of a day in May; the white sail appears of a ship from which seven ladies "in kirtillis grene" are landed. The poet is accused by Dame Beauty and defended by Reason, who shields him with a golden targe or shield, so that his enemies are powerless against him

---

[1] Enough.   [2] Over the grey hills.   [3] Laughed.   [4] Sighed sore.   [5] Cliff.
[6] Complete edition of his works in 3 vols, by Small, Mackay and Gregor (Scottish Text Society, 1884–93).
[7] See W. Skeat, *Specimens*, op. cit.

until Presence blinds Reason by casting a powder in his eyes. The poet is then held prisoner until he awakes.

Certainly Dunbar does not wish to be taken seriously, but he gives the reader the pleasure of dazzling decoration and of a freedom of movement which, for once, keeps at bay the tedium which threatens all allegories. Can this rainbow-hued country, in which all the colours of precious stones—rubies, beryls, emeralds, sapphires—radiate together, be grey Scotland? It would be easier to believe ourselves transported to the kingdom of a Haroun al Raschid. The oriental imagination of this northerner is astonishing.

The natural must not be expected of this great decorator, nor mystical and fervent piety of this Franciscan. It occurred to him, one day, to bring the seven deadly sins on to his stage, but for no graver purpose than to set them spinning in a wild, macabre dance. We have enough edifying pictures of these sins to allow us to thank Dunbar for treating them as no more than the pretext for a mad whirligig. His *Dance of the Sevin Deidly Synnis*, written in lyrical twelve-lined stanzas, is perhaps the most characteristic of his poems. We do not seek in it either justice of detail or religious horror of vice. It has instead the marks of a strange coarseness, and is fuller of buffoonery than of edification. It ends with a rough jest against the Highlanders whom Dunbar held in derision. But the verbal swing and the giddy liveliness of these ten stanzas are marvellous.

Dunbar was a master of satire, especially of the jovial invective and repeated and unbridled insults which Scots call "flyting." Rabelais himself could hardly have held his own with him in this field, in which his vocabulary positively seems to be drunk, so dizzy is the play of rhymes and alliterations.

It should be added that Dunbar was ingenious in his choice of themes for his satires and framework for his mocking invective. Now he sees in a dream a demon in the guise of St. Francis who brings him the habit of his order, and to whom he explains why it does not please him to resume it (*How Dunbar was desired to be be one freir*). Now he makes a pretended apology to the corporation of tailors who have complained of his ridicule, which he is thus enabled to repeat with more sting than ever (*The Tournament*). Or again, in order to mock a charlatan who has tried to fly on wings of his own making and has fallen and broken his leg, Dunbar pictures him attacked by all the fowls of the air when he takes his flight (*The Fenyeit Freir of Tungland*).

In every verse-form he excels. He uses Langland's alliterative line with as much success as the Chaucerian metre. He unites the metres of both masters when, with extraordinary cynicism, he relates the fable of *The Two Mariit Wemen and the Wedo*, whose scabrous conversation he overhears, as they sit in their garden after some hearty drinking. The remarks on the obligations of matrimony which, in alliterative verse, he puts in their mouths would have brought blushes to the cheek even of the Wife of Bath.

On occasion, however, he is capable of a higher lyricism. There is a note of melancholy in his *Lament for the Makaris*, in which he names the poets of his country and of England who have died. It recalls Villon's enumeration of the illustrious ones whom death has ravished. The Latin refrain, "Timor mortis conturbat me," sounds in these short stanzas the knell of the departed. But they have not Villon's sober exactness nor his intimate thrill. The effect produced is more external, and is due, above all, as it always is in Dunbar, to astonishingly skilful rhythm.

The fact that Dunbar's merits may, in the last analysis, be summed up as mastery of form, does not impugn his right to a place of honour. For with him there is no question of inert perfection, but of intense life such as belonged to none of the *rhétoriqueurs* whose contemporary he was. Far from bending beneath the load of his rich vocabulary, he carries it easily. He has dash, and this is to say that he is half-way to lyricism.

Very different from this frequently coarse Bohemian was the high-born Gavin Douglas (1475?–1522?),[1] a churchman who became a bishop, and whose personal history mingled with that of Scotland when, after the disaster of Flodden in 1513, he was drawn into politics. While he hardly corresponds to the usual idea of a prelate, he was yet a man of heart and of honour, and also a man of letters who first gained distinction in the field of traditional poetry, and ended by showing himself almost a precursor of the humanism of the Renaissance.

In his youth he began with allegory. At twenty-six he wrote the *Palice of Honour* (1501) in which he imitates Chaucer's *Hous of Fame*. The difference between the subjects of the two poems is reflected in their titles. It is the House of Honour which this poet enters in his dream, where dwell illustrious men who in their lives have followed the laws of truth and loyalty. Douglas modestly declares that he can find no place there for himself. In the course of the dream he mixes the sacred and the profane, moral allegory and mythology. The nymph Calliope explains the redemption of man to him, at his desire. There is a scholar as well as a moralist behind these puppets.

Later Douglas wrote *King Hart*,[2] in which he shows much maturer psychological power. His great model is still the *Roman de la Rose*, but he also knows the *Séjour d'Honneur* of Octavien de Gelais whom he had already imitated in his earlier poems, and he has felt the influence of the morality plays which were then supreme in the theatre.

There is a constant mingling of humour and melancholy in this allegory. King Hart, or Heart, is made captive by Dame Pleasance, and delivered by Dame Pietie, then marries the charming enemy who has overcome him. But, after seven years, Age knocks at the gate of the palace of Pleasure, and all the young and flighty courtiers, who once had surrounded her, flee, and are at last followed by the dame herself. Reason and Wit then warn the king to return to his own castle, where he is ere long assailed by the hideous army of Decrepitude. Before he dies he makes an ironic testament.

The scene of the arrival of Age, most unwelcome of visitors, is full of life, and there is much graceful melancholy in the king's farewell to Youth:

> Sen thou man pas, fair Youth heid, wa is me!

In spite of their merits, these poems have too little novelty to have ensured Douglas's renown by themselves. He has another claim to fame in that, first in Great Britain, he translated Virgil into verse (1512–13). Before him, only Chaucer had rendered a few fragments of the Latin poet, and in such reedlike tones that he seemed to be writing a parody. Caxton, the first printer, had published a prose version made from a pretended French translation which was really a mediæval romance and of which Douglas says that, although Caxton had called it "Virgill in Eneados,"

> It has na thing ado tharwith, God wait,
> Ne na mair lyke than the devill and Sanct Austyne.

Douglas aimed at translating exactly, word for word, but need for comprehension and the imperfection of his language often led him to render one word or one line by several. He retains something of the Middle Ages and travesties characters, as when he makes a nun of the Sibyl or a gentle lord of Æneas.

He translates into heroic couplets in which he uses more licence than in his other poems. Altogether this is an interesting work, energetic and sometimes brilliant.

[1] Complete edition of his works by John Small (Edinburgh, 1874).
[2] Extracts in Gregory Smith—*Specimens of Middle Scots*.

Its most curious part is the prologues which precede each book. These contain the most original and most Scottish verses of the poet. In them Douglas writes as his fancy bids him, of himself or of the season. In a description of winter which begins the seventh book, and one of spring which opens the twelfth, he may be said to have anticipated by two centuries his fellow-countryman Thomson, of *The Seasons*, for he is as faithful to nature and prodigal of detail. His exuberance is especially striking, his abundant colours, scents and sounds. He is like a Dunbar striving for realism. But in the long run his scene is felt to be crowded: mind wearies and eyes ache. His language is moreover the most difficult of the period because of the number of the learned and popular sources whence it derives. An Englishman is unable and a Scot hardly able to read Douglas without a glossary.

In his prologues he allows himself full rein, for he writes them only for his own pleasure. In that to Book XII.[1] he would merely have us know how the singing of the birds woke him at four in the morning and he resumed his translating. Sometimes his readers share the diversions of a humanist, as when he adds to Virgil a thirteenth book translated from the Italian Maffeo Vegio. Its prologue informs us that in a dream the writer is charged by Vegio to make this translation. He at first refuses, pleading unfitness, but Vegio insists that he who has translated the poem of a pagan is far more bound to do this service to a Christian, and finally the Italian poet prevails by the argument of twenty blows with a cudgel.

These particularities of his Virgil show, almost as much as his earlier allegories, that Douglas was not in the full stream of the Renascence. He stood on its brink, marking the transition from one age to another.

We have still to speak of his countryman Sir David Lyndsay, who poetically was even more attached than he to the past. Lyndsay's life was, however, a long battle which coincided with the Reformation, and he definitely belongs to the sixteenth century.

3. The Old Ballads.[2]—The works we have reviewed constitute, in Scotland as in England, the official poetry of the fifteenth century. This is far from being all the poetry of the period. There were also anonymous popular verses, both ruder and more truly alive, which often cannot be localised or dated with any precision. They cannot all be claimed for the fifteenth century, for poems of the sort must have had an earlier beginning and certainly were produced until a later time, but the impulse to make them seems to have been particularly active in this century, to which, moreover, the oldest extant specimens belong.

The word ballad, vague as it is, denotes them best. But they must be in no way identified with the courtly ballade, which was fixed in form and peculiarly learned and artificial. The two words doubtless share a derivation from *baller*, to dance, and the ballad and ballade both originated in the poetry which accompanied dancing and implied musical declamation with a collective refrain. But hardly more than the traces of this prototype remain. When the popular ballad of Great Britain emerges from the shadows it retains no more of its primary form than warrants a presumption, more complete than for other kinds of poetry, of co-operation between the poet and his audience. It has even been supposed that a ballad is the spontaneous and joint composition of a group of people. Reflection shows, however, that this theory has little plausibility. There could be agreement for the purposes of poetry among a number of people only in the sharing of a passion, and the work of an artist or several successive artists has to be recognised

---

[1] Printed by W. Skeat in *Specimens*, op. cit.

[2] F. J. Child, *The English and Scottish Popular Ballads*, 5 vols. (1882–98), critical edition; Edition in 1 vol., with introduction by G. Kittredge (Boston, 1904); F. G. Gunmere, *Introduction to Old English Ballads* (Boston, 1894); D. Laing, *Early Popular Poetry of Scotland and the Border*, ed. Hazlitt, 2 vols. (1895).

in a ballad of any length. It was artists, however primitive, who interpreted the multitude. Once a ballad existed, the public did in some sort collaborate in its making, for memory altered, modified or suppressed, and new circumstances suggested opportune additions. Oral tradition changed the form of the poem. Like money in circulation, it lost, little by little, its imprint; its salient curves were blunted; and long use gave it a polish it did not have originally. The exact fact to which it owed its birth grew misty in retrospect, and from being, in a humble way, historical, the ballad became romantic and acquired the prestige of the remote.

Perhaps, therefore, it is time rather than the mode of their making which gives ballads their special character. They differ from other poems because we never, or hardly ever, hear them as they were originally. At some moment of its life, already, it may be, a long one, a ballad becomes public knowledge, and the subtle effect of the human emotions excited while it has been endlessly repeated may indeed have given it the value of a collective work.

It may be said that this is equally true of the old songs which were not written down for many years. But a ballad is not a song. Usually it holds a story: it is the fragment of an epic; sometimes it is plainly the summary of old chivalrous poems of which only the essence has been kept for the purposes of a short recitation and to make a rapid impression on simple minds. Or else the ballad relates for a district a glorious or ill-omened incident which is known to all and has familiar heroes, so that, however allusively the poet expresses himself, he is sure of being understood even by the most ignorant.

The ballad exists everywhere in Europe, but is most copious and lively in the outlying regions, in Spain in the south and in Scandinavia in the north. Great Britain, insular and isolated, produced many ballads, especially on the Border, the scene in old days of so many sanguinary encounters of Scots and English.

We have spoken of the popular rhymes, dating from the fourteenth century, on Robin Hood, bowman and outlaw, but the ballads, a whole cycle of them, which are consecrated to his exploits do not go back further than the sixteenth century. While the existence of numerous ballads in the fourteenth and fifteenth centuries may be conjectured, there are only two which can certainly be placed before the Renascence: *Chevy Chase* and *The Nut-brown Maid.*

Chevy Chase[1] is the oldest and the finest of the epical ballads. In theme and sentiment it is akin to *Roland* or *Byrhtnoth*. It is at least half-historical, its subject the struggle between Percy of Northumberland and the Douglas of Scotland at the beginning of the fifteenth century. The manners it reveals are at once violent and chivalrous, a love of battle combining with generosity to enemies. But that which in *Byrhtnoth* has an epic swing is here lyrical. This ballad is a sung recitation, a sort of melopœia. Already it has the metre which was to be pre-eminently that of the ballads, the seven-accented line in two divisions (4+3) and the rhymes in couples. The division is so fixed that the couplet can be considered as a quatrain:

> The Persé owt off Northombarlonde
> An avowe to God mayd he
> That he wold hunt in the mountayns
> Off Chyviat within days three.

The division often leads to the rhyming of the first and third sections, giving quatrains with cross-rhymes (*abab*). The tendency to regularise rhythm also has the effect in the later ballads of making the lines syllabic, that is to say alternately of eight and six syllables. In *Chevy Chase* the verse is primitive in its rudeness and has the minimum of ornament.

---

[1] Text in W. Skeat, *Specimens*, op. cit.

There is in this ballad a manifest basis of realism. It tells an incident all too truly characteristic of life on the Border, where there was little distinction between warfare and brigandage. Percy wishes to hunt in enemy country, less for love of the deer than to provoke his adversary. He rejoices greatly when, after the hunt, the Douglas arrives and the battle begins. Yet these wild opponents have the spirit of chivalry: the Douglas, in order to spare "guiltless men," proposes to Percy to meet him in single combat. But the ardour of Percy's followers, who would think it shame to leave all the danger to their chief, cannot be restrained, and the fight is general. When the Douglas is slain, Percy, who a minute before had been drunk with battle, gives rein, before the body of his enemy, to artless grief and sincere admiration:

> The Persé leanyde on his brande, and sawe the Duglas de;
> He tooke the dede man be the hande, and sayd, Wo ys me for the!
> To have savyde thy lyffe I wold have partyd with my landes for years thre,
> For a better man of hart, nare of hand, was not in all the north countrè.

The minstrel who so vigorously sings the fine sword-play is mindful of the evils to which such violence will give rise:

> The chyld may rue that ys un-borne, it was the more pittè.

Sincere emotion is betrayed by these very contradictions. The poem wins us by the truthfulness of its feeling as of its restrained decoration and its details. Whether or not the details be strictly historical, we follow the vicissitudes of the conflict, the part played by the English bowmen, the tactics of the Douglas when he caused his men to advance in scattered formation, the hand-to-hand struggle.

There is a sort of Homeric impartiality in this war ballad. The Percy and the Douglas show equal heroism, although their virtues are opposed like those of an Achilles and a Hector. The poet's English patriotism is clearly discovered only at the end. When he hears that the Douglas is slain, the king of Scotland is in despair, but Henry IV., learning Percy's death, is undismayed in his pride:

> God have merci on his soll, sayd kyng Harry, Good Lord, yf thy will it be!
> I have a hondrith captayns in Ynglonde, he sayd, as good as ever was hee:
> But Persè, and I brook my lyffe, thy deth well quyte [1] shall be.

He then despatches an army which wins the victory of Humbledon.

It is almost impossible to exaggerate the importance of this short literary epic. Its success was not confined to the people, but extended to men of letters and poets. Sir Philip Sidney wrote of it about 1581:

> I never heard the old song of Piercy and Douglas, that I found not my heart more moved than with a trumpet; and yet it is sung but by some blind crowder with no rougher voice than rude stile; which being so evil apparelled in the dust and cobweb of that uncivil age, what would it work trimmed in the gorgeous elegance of Pindar?

As though to obey Sidney's wish, a poet of the first years of the seventeenth century gave to the ballad, without deforming it overmuch, a correct form, modernised language and regular rhythm. Addison, in the full stream of the classical period, read it in this version, which yet seemed to him ancient, and praised it discriminatingly in the *Spectator*. He realised the ballad's Homeric qualities, and used it as a text to preach that the beautiful is the simple. He loved it as Molière loved the "old song of Henry IV. of France" and for the same qualities, just style and natural feeling. Finally Bishop Percy (1765) inserted the oldest text in his *Reliques*, and *Chevy Chase* was one of the mediæval poems which induced romanticism. Soon the very irregularity of its verses was found to have a special charm, and this rudeness inspired Coleridge to give a new harmony to his *Ancient*

---

[1] Requited.

I—I

Mariner and, above all, to his *Christabel*. It is sincerity of tone, like that of *Chevy Chase*, which, down the ages and among extravagances and artifices, brings back to natural truth the poetry which has left nature too far behind.

Such fine romantic ballads as *Sir Patrick Spens, Clerk Saunders* and *Child Waters* cannot be certainly ascribed to the fifteenth century, for the versions of them which have reached us are all of later date. But a poem of a special kind, which encloses the elements of a simple ballad in the framework of a courtly *disputoison*, may be claimed for this century.

A lady is represented as using the story of *The Nut-brown Maid* [1] to free women of the reproach of inconstancy constantly levied at them by men. The dark maid, who is a baron's daughter, is visited by her lover whom she believes to be a squire of low degree, and who comes to bid her farewell because he has killed a man and must hide in the woods as an outlaw. But neither his picture of a life of pains and peril, nor even his avowal that he has another mistress, can bend her from her will to follow him for love's sake. He has but proved her, as Griselda was proved, and, sure of her heart, he reveals himself as an earl's son who will make her lady of his heritage in Westmorland.

There cannot here be question of a popular composition. Nothing could be more artistic than these thirty six-lined stanzas with their alternating refrains. Each stanza has lines of seven accents, divided in $2+2+3$, and a system of multiplied rhymes puts very severe constraint upon the poet. Yet the simplicity of style and sincerity of tone do not at all suffer. While the lady, who may be supposed to be the author, plays the part of the Nut-brown Maid, the other speaker takes that of the outlaw. There is a dialogue, each of them in turn speaking a stanza with its refrain. The dramatic interest and liveliness thus given to the little poem cause its thesis to be forgotten in its story. The unadorned stylistic fabric, which admirably renders emotion, does not lack broad images, such as those in the first answer of the enamoured lady when her beloved announces his crime and banishment to her:

> O lord, what is this worldys blysse that changeth as the mone!
> My somers day in lusty may is derked before the none.
> I here you say, farewell: Nay, nay, we départ nat so sone.
> Why say ye so? wheder wyll ye go? Alas! what have ye done?
> All my welfàre to sorrowe and care sholde chaunge, yf ye were gone;
> For in my mynde, of all mankynde I love but you alone.

If this poem be not a popular ballad but the work of a courtly poet, it does but show the degree to which even the learned poetry of the time could absorb popular songs and be inspired by them. In this echo of some humble love-ballad there is not one false note. Whoever can bring himself to read the lamentable imitation of it which Matthew Prior made in the beginning of the eighteenth century, and in which everything is falsified, both style and sentiment, will recognise that the essence of poetry existed in this disinherited fifteenth century as it did not in the classical period. The *Nut-brown Maid*, which was printed in 1502, belongs incontestably to the reign of Henry VII.

4. The Drama of the Middle Ages.[2]—It is with the drama as with the

---

[1] Text in Skeat's *Specimens*, op. cit.

[2] For the history of the English theatre in the Middle Ages, see E. K. Chambers, *The Mediæval Stage*, 2 vols. (Oxford, 1903); J. J. Jusserand, *Le Théâtre en Angleterre jusqu'aux prédécesseurs immédiats de Shakespeare*, 2nd ed. (Paris, 1881); A. W. Ward, *History of English Dramatic Literature to the Death of Queen Anne*, 2nd ed., 3 vols. (1899); C. M. Gayley, *Plays of Our Forefathers and some of the Traditions upon which they were Founded* (New York, 1909). For texts, see A. W. Pollard, *English Miracle Plays, Moralities and Interludes* (Oxford, 1890 et seq.) The plays of the different towns—Chester, Coventry, Towneley, York, etc.—have been published separately. Pieces excellently selected as representative of the development of the drama are given by J. M. Manly in vol. i. of his *Specimens of the Pre-Shakespearian Drama*, 2 vols. (Boston, 1900–3).

ballad. It cannot be said to have been either created or fully developed in the fifteenth century. But this was the period in which most of the cycles of the Christian theatre were compiled and in which the miracle plays, not yet subject to competition from dramatic performances of a more modern kind, reached their apotheosis. It is therefore fitting to determine the characteristics of the mediæval dramatic art of England in this rather than in another century.

Such characteristics are, in point of fact, few in number.

The religious theatre is an institution of Christianity which had the same origin and a like evolution in all the Christian countries of Europe, so much so that it is seen wrongly or out of perspective if it be studied in one country alone. In that great common fatherland which was Christendom in the Middle Ages, nations were, from the spiritual point of view, hardly more than are to-day the provinces of a centralised state. Therefore to relate the history of the Christian drama of England is, in many respects, little more than to repeat what is known of that of France. It is thus possible to deal with the subject allusively and rapidly.

Everyone knows that this drama was an offshoot of the liturgy, which, with its solemn staging, lent itself well to dramatic development. The germs of the drama were in the offices of the Church, in the chants alternating between the priest and the congregation or the choir which represented it, the recitative passages, the plastic decoration, the processions, the ritual of movement and gesture. It was in the form of " tropes," or declamation in dialogues, that drama made its first appearance. Two tropes of the Easter office, which were declaimed in England in the tenth and eleventh centuries, before as well as after the Norman Conquest, have been preserved, and make it almost certain that, with or without the Conquest, religious drama would have evolved in England as in every Christian country.

First given within the church and declaimed in Latin, these dialogues developed into small dramas when they left the church and were played in the porch and when they exchanged Latin for the vernacular, two conditions essential to the needed liberty. The best-known example of a transitional play of this kind is *Adam*, which was written in French, but by a Norman or Anglo-Norman of the twelfth century, and which seems to have been performed not in France, but in England. Very interesting because of its place at the origin of two great dramatic literatures, it is so also intrinsically. Restrained, even a little bare, but grave in thought, its sentiments just, decided and precise, and its language vigorous, it has a real value. It comprises three parts—the fall of Adam and Eve, the death of Abel, and a procession of the prophets who announce the coming of the Redeemer. The scene of Eve's temptation by the devil shows a certain refinement and some poetic grace. Almost all and the best characters of the religious drama are to be found in this old Anglo-Norman play.

But it was necessary for this drama to emancipate itself completely from the Church. It had to leave the church precincts for the highways, to take up its station in the market-place or the streets. Moreover, before the plays could be popular, they had to abandon not only Latin, as in France, but French also. It was essential that their language should be English.

Dramatic progress is connected with the development of the fairs, the increase of wealth, the rise of the burgher class, the prosperity of corporations, and finally the emancipation of the vulgar tongue. Little by little drama severed its connection not only with the Church, but also with the clergy, who at first provided all the actors. Not without resistance from the clerks, the mendicant friars and the Franciscans, who lost their monopoly, the actors came to be laymen. As a rule, henceforth, the clergy were no more than the playwrights. This change became marked and was accelerated from the second half of the thirteenth century onwards.

The first plays in English were performed under Henry III., and at the same time a certain realism was introduced upon the stage.

In this reign also the great cyclical representations had their beginning, those in which the sacred history relating to an annual feast was depicted in successive scenes on the holiday. The Easter and Christmas cycles were the first in date, but the institution in 1264 of the feast of Corpus Christi and its generalisation early in the next century gave this day pre-eminence. The Easter and Nativity cycles, hitherto distinct, were united and were performed together on Corpus Christi day, which was less crowded with other events than Christmas and Easter day and which fell in the summer. All Holy Writ was thus staged at the same time and place, all the great facts of religious history reproduced in sight of the people. In some places, as in Chester, the performance was on Whit-Sunday rather than on Corpus Christi day.

Some towns, because of the fame of their fairs or the powerful organisation of their gilds, became celebrated for these representations, and the English miracle-plays we now possess are named after the places in which they were given. The cycle, embracing the whole of sacred history, is always the same, but differs locally in detail, mood, language and versification, its tone being more dignified or homelier in one place than in another. The plays of Chester and Coventry—Shakespeare may, as a child, have seen these last—those of Woodkirk Abbey, near Wakefield, called the Towneley Plays, and those of York have been preserved, as well as fragments of the Digby, Newcastle and Dublin plays. Other towns had cycles which have been lost.

The cycles were first compiled in the fourteenth century, but we possess them only as they were rearranged in the fifteenth, or even the sixteenth, for some were played until the theatre of the Renascence was nearing its apotheosis.

The popularity of the miracle-plays in the fourteenth century is attested by Chaucer, who relates in his Miller's Tale of Absolon, the merry clerk, that

> Sometyme to shewe his lightnesse and maistyre
> He playeth Heródes on a scaffold hye;

and who, in the play of the Flood, shows the Miller himself to be well informed about Noah's quarrels with his wife. Langland gives a yet more significant proof of the influence of the theatre, for he has cast more than one scene of *Piers Plowman* in the mould of the miracle-plays.

We can picture one of these immense representations, for instance that at York on Corpus Christi day.[1] Every gild in the town contributed to it, and the festivities included forty-eight plays which comprised the whole of Scripture. We know not only the order of the plays, but also the gild responsible for each of them, appropriately chosen as far as possible. To the Armourers fell the expulsion from Paradise (the flaming sword), to the Shipwrights the building of the Ark, to the Fishermen and Mariners the Flood, to the Chandlers the shepherds following the star, to the Goldsmiths the adoration of the Magi, to the Bakers the Last Supper, to the Pinners and Painters the Crucifixion, to the Butchers the Mortification of Christ, to the Scriveners Doubting Thomas, and so forth.

An idea of the staging can be had if the meaning of pageant, a word of uncertain etymology, be understood. It sometimes referred to the platform on which a play was given, sometimes to the representation itself. Some platforms were fixed in a particular place, and the audience went from one to another of them, following the series of the plays. But elsewhere the pageant was mounted on wheels and movable, and the spectators stayed in one spot while these stages on wheels successively paused before them, gave their performance, and passed on to another

[1] See H. Morley, *English Writers*, vol. iv., op. cit.

point where the performance was repeated. Most of the gilds had their own pageant. Sometimes the action made several pageants necessary for one play, for instance one for Paradise, one for the earth and one for Hell. Each included, beneath the stage, a room in which actors spent the intervals between their appearances and properties were kept.

The duration of the performances varied with the number of the plays, but was always several days. In Chester, where the series included only twenty-four plays, it took three days. The nine first were given on Whit-Monday, nine more on Whit-Tuesday and the six last on the Wednesday.

What we know of the English theatre in the fifteenth century shows that it was very powerfully organised, that the gilds took an important part in its development, and that there was long local resistance to the engrossing of the plays by professional actors. In fact, its vitality and popularity were such as were surpassed nowhere. The number and diversity of the provincial centres, particularly in the north and the west, prove how widespread was the passion for the theatre.

Two points in which the English differed from the French drama must be noted. In England, although all the plays of the period are generally called miracle-plays, there are hardly any traces of what the French call *miracles*, that is plays concerned especially with the Virgin and the saints, as distinguished from the *mystères* which were founded on Holy Writ. All the cycles preserved in England are of scenes from the Bible. Secondly, the growth of the religious theatre was less disturbed in England than in France, and its development checked less early. It continued to flourish when the Renascence was in full swing, so firmly was it established in local custom and popular favour.

The extant English cycles offer another advantage to modern students. While the French mysteries in the collection compiled by the Brothers Greban are, on the whole, mediocre and monotonous, there is in the very various English plays a dignified emotion or a homely swing which sometimes makes itself felt through the awkwardness and rudeness of the style. It may be said that these plays, in the form in which they have reached us, prove that great artistic effort, no less real where it was mistaken, went to their making. They are almost all written in complicated and difficult stanzas, which have the fault that they are apt to sacrifice dramatic quality to lyricism. There are stanzas which multiply their rhymes and unite lines different in measure—as *aaabab* or *aaabaaab* or *aaaabcccb*, *b* standing for a short two-accented line among others usually of four accents. But while the stanza is learned, the rhythm is, as a rule, unformed and metrical padding abounds. The principal defect is due to the unfitness of such stanzas to render dramatic movement or easygoing dialogue. The difficulty of finding a metre appropriate to drama was the great obstacle to dramatic progress until nearly the end of the sixteenth century. The unknown authors of the miracle-plays are not poets enough to animate their awkward stanzas. Yet they are, at moments, capable of pathos, and more frequently there is full-flavoured comedy in their scenes.

As elsewhere, the religious drama had a value due to the simple grandeur of the total conception, and the artlessness of the means used to call up the whole of Scripture before the people is disarming. The poets effaced themselves before their subjects. They had no freedom of invention, hardly of composition, were debarred from discovering motives for action except within strict limits. Since the stories were known to everyone, the principal interest was in the spectacles. Only here and there and accidentally does the author himself intervene, analysing passions or sentiments.

This happens in the play *Abraham and Isaac*,[1] which was written in the fifteenth

---

[1] See, for text, E. Smith and Le Toulmin, *Anglia*, vol. vii. (1884).

century and belongs to an unknown cycle. It has one scene of two hundred lines, than which nothing could be more pathetic. It is that which depicts the conflicting sentiments of the father who has the will to obey God, but is stayed by love for his child, and of the son divided between submission to his father and fear of death. Little Isaac trembles before the gleaming sword, thinks of his mother in grief, asks for the fatal stroke yet would avert it. The *Iphigenia* of Euripides has not more feeling, nor Shakespeare's *King John* when little Prince Arthur implores his executioner. We are irresistibly moved to tears; moral emotion and physical suffering are mingled. The only defect of this touching scene is its slowness, which has a slightly monotonous effect. The succeeding scene, in which Isaac, saved from death, expresses his childish joy and tenderly thanks the ram sacrificed in his stead, is very charmingly artless.

It is, however, in comic passages that the English playwrights show most go and originality. Comedy in the Middle Ages often mingled, in varying proportions, with solemn themes, in concession to a public condemned to listen to many an edifying declamation. Comedy of this sort has never been more developed than in certain English cycles. We have spoken of the fortunes of the *fabliau* in Great Britain, its progress in the hands of Chaucer, and the part it assigned to nature and observation. It has also an important place in some of the English plays, especially the Towneley Plays, which are more rustic than the others. In these, the *fabliau* is not in the unfinished state of a rough sketch, but has been retouched, again and again, and betrays a long experience of scenic effects. The complicated stanza which contains it, to which we have already alluded, is proof of real artistic labour.

It was only in the comic parts of the plays that their authors were fully independent, in the passages which owed nothing to Holy Writ saving the scenes in which they could safely be introduced. Sometimes the playwright enlivened secondary biblical characters; sometimes he entirely invented characters in order to provide comic relief where the gloom was heaviest. Thus a dramatist cheered the first human tragedy by the gift of a servant named Garcio to Cain, while others gave realistic vigour to the detractors of the Blessed Virgin, to the soldiers sent to kill the Innocents, to the Pharisees who brought before Christ the woman taken in adultery, to the beadle of Pontius Pilate, to the workmen who set up the Cross, to the soldiers who watched by Christ's sepulchre. There was nothing to prevent them from lending the manners and speech of the common people they knew to these supernumeraries. Shakespeare and his rivals did exactly the same thing, kept the tragic central pattern of their source often intact, and added to it a comic border of their own.

Of the English comic scenes, two took up more space than others in the Towneley Plays,[1] those concerned respectively with Noah's wife and with the shepherds who followed the star.

Noah's quarrels with his wife, when he has to make her enter the ark, are very lively. He is most respectful of the divine injunction, but cowed by his mate, who is the typical scold of the *fabliaux*, shrewish, contradictious, stormy, giving blow for blow. Frightened as she is of the Flood, the arrangements of the ark do not please her, and she has barely entered it when she takes herself off to spin alone in a corner. Her husband and her sons and daughters implore her vainly: she will not budge. But no sooner does Noah tell her to do just as she likes than she changes her mind and comes on board. She is still, however, in a bad temper, and Noah has to beat her soundly before things are in train. From the moment of her beating Mrs. Noah is appeased and becomes a charming travelling-companion,

[1] *Towneley Plays* (Early English Text Society, Extra Series, lxxi., 1897).

helping to navigate the ark and send forth the birds, all her talk good sense and kindliness.

The broad comedy of this character in no way lessens the piety of the play, and occurs amid such artless simplicity that it is hardly discordant. Goodman Noah conversing with the Lord, monologuing as he builds the Ark, describing what he does as he goes along and complaining of his stiff back, and the concluding ingenious dialogue which suggests the various incidents of the voyage: all this makes a homely, cheerful whole, in which the buffoonery is not out of place.

The same mingling of simple piety and farce goes to make the nativity-play, but here the farce is more developed and almost constitutes an independent comedy in rustic northern dialect.

With the honest shepherds, who appear telling the troubles of their life—hard winters, the oppression of gentlemen—or who complain of the cantankerousness of their wives, there mingles a certain Mak, a cunning scamp, almost a precursor of the Shakespearian Autolycus. The action of the farce is that he steals a sheep from the others and conceals it, and that his theft is discovered. The sheep is put in a cradle, and Mak's wife, on her bed, groans as though she were just delivered of a child. When one of the good shepherds wants to give the baby a sixpence, the trick is exposed. And no sooner has Mak been tossed in punishment than the angel begins to sing "Gloria in Excelsis," and the good shepherds, led by the star, set out for the Crib, discoursing on the angel's beautiful song and on the prophecies. Before the Crib their demeanour is the same as before the cradle of the sham baby. They are touched by the infant's charm; they bring him simple presents, one a bird, another cherries—at Christmastime!—the third a ball to play at tennis. Their words of adoration alternate with their pity for the frailty and tininess and the poverty of the Divine Child.

It is very remarkable that in these two plays, *Noah* and the *Nativity*, the very brisk and copious comic element does not clash with the religious sentiment. This is due to the heartiness of the comedy, which has neither reservations nor irony. It does not imperil the dignity of the play to which it belongs. It is not destructive. It can be reconciled with faith and tender emotion. It is at once bold and artless. We shall see that, for like reasons, the comic blends easily with romantic or tragic elements in the best of the Renascence dramas. On the other hand, the cynical realism of *Maître Patelin*, also a fifteenth century work, would be hard to imagine in a religious frame. *Maître Patelin*, with a theme somewhat analogous to the Mak episode, is markedly superior to the artless Towneley Play in refinement of analysis and pointed wit, but has a fundamental harshness, a certain dryness and cruelty. Nor is the French play in any sense rustic: it does not breathe the healthy country air which surrounds the shepherds of the *Nativity* and good-for-nothing, sheep-stealing Mak. In differences of this kind, rather than in a diversity of theory, the profound causes are to be discerned for the eventual triumph in English drama and rejection by French drama of the mingling of the tragic and the comic.

The earliest moralities preserved in England also belong to the fifteenth century. Later born than the mysteries, which are linked up with the epical period of the Middle Ages, the moralities are a product of the allegorical period. To the plays taken from the Bible, they are as is the *Roman de la Rose* to the old epics. For the characters of sacred history they substitute abstractions, vices or virtues. They are at their origin as much penetrated as the miracle-plays with Christian teaching, but they have a more intellectual character. While a miracle-play is essentially a spectacle, appealing primarily to the sight, a morality demands greater attention to the spoken word. Its text is more important than its scenery.

Although generally, as we pass from the miracle-plays to the moralities, we seem to go from the greater to the less great, to what is less alive and more coldly and artificially constructed, the morality must none the less be recognised to mark a necessary stage and, in a sense, a considerable advance in the progress towards the modern drama. The author of a morality can arrange his subject freely, attempt construction and unity. He is led to analyse human qualities and defects, to emphasise psychological characteristics. Miserliness, for instance, cannot be presented without study of the character of a miser. In this way the morality, even the religious morality, prepared drama for emancipation from religion. Its theme is the struggle of the forces of good and evil which contest for the human soul. This problem continued to confront the poet who was no longer inspired by the Christian faith. The permanent basis of every dramatic work had been discovered.

The material conditions of the theatre were transformed. Instead of multiplied, often movable pageants, the morality used a single, unchanging stage. In the earliest extant English morality, the *Castell of Perseverance* [1] (middle fifteenth century), the unchanging scene showed a castle in its centre, and in its corners scaffolds for the World, the Flesh, the Devil, and God. As the miracle-plays led to the numerous and changing scenes of historical drama, so the moralities prepared the way for tragedies restricted to one plot.

The exact date at which the morality had its rise is unknown. It was doubtless not later than the middle of the fourteenth century, not far removed in time from Langland's great religious satire which was so filled with animated, almost scenic moral allegories. Allegories were early introduced into the miracle-plays. In the Coventry cycle there are such characters as Contemplation, Calumny, Detraction, Truth, Justice, Peace, Death, and, in the Digby Mysteries, especially in the play on Mary Magdalene, the World, Luxury and Curiosity figure, as well as the Seven Deadly Sins.

In the *Castell of Perseverance*, the oldest and longest of the moralities, the reign of allegory is undisputed. "Humanum genus," placed between his good and his bad angel and long the slave of Pleasure and Folly, takes refuge in the Castle of Perseverance with the Christian virtues. He is seduced by Covetousness, who makes his way into the castle and prevails on him to leave it. But before his death, as his soul is about to be carried to hell, he is saved by the intervention of Peace and Mercy.

An analogous conception recurs in the shorter moralities, *Mankind*, approximately of the same date, and *Mundus et Infans* and *Hyckescorner*,[2] which belong to the early sixteenth century. These plays are, however, less tensely grave and have comic passages. In *Mankind* it is the demon Tityvillus whose jokes give the comic relief, while in *Hyckescorner* the scamp who names the piece plays malicious tricks with his companions in debauchery, Free Will and Imagination.

These moralities, by turns cold and scholastic or comic in a very mediocre degree, have little merit. But another of the same period is really impressive and might well be called the masterpiece of its kind, the play of *Everyman*.[3] For long it was believed to have originated in Holland, having been printed in Dutch as early as 1495 and before any edition of the English text. To-day, however, the dominant opinion is that the play was born in England, where certainly it seems to have been very popular down to the Reformation.

The tragedy is that of Christian death, and it is staged with poignant restraint

[1] Partly printed by A. W. Pollard in *English Miracle Plays*, op. cit.
[2] These three moralities are printed by J. M. Manly in *Specimens of the Pre-Shakespearian Drama*, op. cit.
[3] Printed by F. Sidgwick (1902), by Pollard, in *Fifteenth Century Prose and Verse* (1903), and by Farmer, Early English Drama Publications (1906).

and force. God sends Death to summon Everyman, and he, in anguish, implores a respite, and obtains only a few hours to gather together the friends who shall go with him on his supreme journey. Everyman appeals vainly to Fellowship, his boon companion, to Kindred and to Goods. None of them will hearken to him. Then he remembers Good Deeds, whom he has long abandoned, who is lying on the ground, weak and miserable, but who hears his prayer, helps him, and recommends to him her sister, Knowledge. Knowledge sends him to Confession, and Everyman, shriven of sin, is ready to meet God. At the moment at which he reaches the grave, Beauty, Strength, Discretion and Five-Wits depart, in spite of their promise to follow him. Knowledge would go with him but cannot. Only Good Deeds is left; she alone is not vain and will plead for him. Everyman dies pure of sin and forgiven.

The conception is simple and enthralling. There is here no classical influence, and yet nothing could be more classically constructed. The beauty of the work is its sincerity. There is an inevitability in the subject. In a sense, every dramatic work, whether ancient or modern, seems frivolous by the side of this essential tragedy. It has recently been revived in Great Britain and the United States and has made a profound impression on its audiences. All the moralities, all controversial works which followed *Everyman,* have something small and ephemeral as compared with it. It would be a complete masterpiece were its form less naked, less dull, less devoid of brilliancy. The artistic impulse seems wholly to have exhausted itself on the construction, which is itself no more than a severe staging of the transcendent message of Christianity.

After the fifteenth century the miracle-plays were still performed, but their form had been fixed and was not changed henceforth. The morality, on the other hand, had an active life, and was used by the dramatists of the Renascence and the Reformation as a means to their ends.

5. **Prose in the Fifteenth Century.**[1]—English prose of the fifteenth century amounts to little if the name be reserved for writings which have originality and some artistic value. There was the same reason for inferiority as in the preceding period: Latin still attracted writers whose purpose was not strictly utilitarian or who were more than mere translators. The bold movement of Wyclif and his partisans had, moreover, been checked. The first half of the fifteenth century was a period of narrow orthodoxy in which the cruelly persecuted Lollards were reduced to silence. Only in the second half of this century did a few rare works which deserve notice appear in English prose. It would, however, be wrong to conclude from this dearth that the spread of reading and learning had been arrested. Education made its way in spite of foreign and civil wars and was diffused. The number of persons able to read and write increased and the first epistolary collections were made. The lateness of English as compared to continental prose is principally due to the fact that it was still poorly provided, and was too easily able to enrich itself by translations of numerous foreign and especially French books which continued completely to satisfy the reading public. In this century men had not yet abandoned the paths of the Middle Ages. Literary sentiment was still not national, which is to say that there was as yet no artistic ideal.

It was the desire to bring the last Lollards back to orthodoxy which decided the learned Reginald Pecock (1395?—1460?) to write in English. This Welshman, who had taken orders and become bishop, first of St. Asaph and then of Chichester, was, as early as 1447, disquieting the clergy by the arguments he used to defend them, and he put the finishing touch to their indignation in 1455 by his *Repression*

---

[1] For extracts from prose-writers of the fifteenth century see **A. W. Pollard**, *Fifteenth Century Prose and Verse* (1903), and W. Skeat, *Specimens*, op. cit.

of Overmuch Blaming the Clergy,[1] in which he defends images, pilgrimages, the temporal goods of the Church, the hierarchy, the papacy, the friars and the monks, but founds his argument only on reason. He puts natural law above Scripture and the sacraments. He has recourse only to logic and does not defer to the principle of authority.

To Wyclif and his disciples, who founded all their faith on Holy Writ, he retorted by invoking, as superior to the Scriptures, "the boke of lawe of kinde writen in mennis soulis with the finger of God." The words of Scripture ought, he says, to be "interpretid and brought forto accorde with the doom of resoun in thilk mater; and the doom of resoun oughte not forto be expowned, glosid, interpretid and broughte forto accorde with the seid outward writing in Holi Scripture."

To establish these principles in the vulgar tongue was in those days to create a scandal among the orthodox, the very class whom Pecock professed to champion. It was criminal to reason about religion with so much independence, to argue with heretics, to bring the people into these disputes by speaking to them in their own language.

Summoned to disown his book or go to the stake, Pecock chose disavowal, and not he, but his book, was burnt.

This logician, as intrepid as indiscreet, stands in isolation, and was afterwards mistaken by the Protestants for an adherent. He was understood neither by his own nor by the following century.

His prose shows a marked advance on that of his predecessors. He had clarity, the gift of choosing homely examples, and a wealth of words. His vocabulary was even excessive: drawing on its double source, English and French, he is tautological and redundant.

Sir John Fortescue [2] (1394?–1476?) was a lawyer who wrote mainly in Latin. Like Pecock, he based his arguments on the law of nature, for instance in his *De Natura Legis Naturæ*, but his object is to establish the right to the throne of Henry VI., the grandson of the Lancastrian usurper. He premises that there are three kinds of government—absolute and monarchical, republican, constitutional and monarchical. The Lancastrians are legitimate kings because of the English constitution. Fortescue was the first to admire the constitution of his country, which he praises in his *De Laudibus Legum Angliæ* (1468–70).

When the Lancastrian cause was lost, Fortescue went over to the Yorkists and wrote, this time in English, his little treatise of forty pages on the *Gouvernance of England*. He had stayed in France with Henry VI. when this king was a fugitive, and he takes France as the type of an absolute, England as that of a limited, monarchy. This writer affords the first example of national political pride. He admires his own country, as compared with France, for its greater liberty and more abundant riches, his patriotism leading him so far that he celebrates the outstanding valour of his compatriot highwaymen. The French, he says, are, like the Scots, too cowardly to steal. "Ther is no man hanged in Scotland in vii yere to gedur ffor robbery. . . . But the Englysh man is off another corage. Ffor yff he be pouere, and see another man havynge rychesse, wich mey be taken ffrom hym be myghte, he will not spare to do so."

The *Paston Letters*,[3] the correspondence of the Paston family, are interesting rather to the historian than to the student of literature. While scholars, clerks and nobles still wrote in Latin, the middle class was taking to English. The letters

---

[1] Ed. C. Babington for Rolls Series, 2 vols. (1860).
[2] *Sir John Fortescue, his Life and Works*, ed. Lord Clermont, 2 vols. (1869); *On the Governance of England*, ed. C. Plummer (Oxford, 1885).
[3] Ed. J. Gairdner, 4 vols. (1901).

have been preserved of three generations of the Pastons, a well-to-do Norfolk family, and they give much intimate and curious information about English life from 1422 to 1509. Passages are not lacking which suggest the barbarism of the period, but the picture as a whole is of a very modern middle-class society, much engrossed by money matters, leases and the letting of land, the management of property, lawsuits, home comforts, domestic cleanliness. We learn what men read in those days and how severely they brought up their children. Dame Agnes inquires if her son Clement be working well at the Inns of Court, and begs his tutor that otherwise "he wyll trewly belassch hym, tyl he wyll amend, and so ded the last maystr, and the best thet ever he had, att Caumbrege." There is a sure and serious affection between husband and wife and they work together to establish the family fortunes. The wife shows great courage when the house is attacked by a band of enemies during her husband's absence.

There is nothing literary in these letters about business, all of them utilitarian, and they cannot be said to show that their writers used the English language easily and fluently. They managed to understand each other, nothing more.

English prose was still formless and indefinite, distributed among numerous local ways of speech, when in 1474 the first English printer began his work. William Caxton [1] (1421–91) has himself told how hampered he at first was by the anarchical state of his language. The unity constituted by the King's English in the fourteenth century had as yet been realised only in poetry. Evolution was, moreover, still in course, so that in his sixtieth year Caxton found the language very different from that spoken in his childhood. He asked himself how he could please everyone. To make himself more certain of being understood he sometimes places the French beside the English word, as *chasse* and *hunt*. He wrote as he habitually spoke, avoiding too rustic terms, aiming at the comprehension of clerks and gentlemen, having his books revised by Master John Skelton, poet laureate of Oxford University. He thus succeeded in being intelligible, and he hardly went beyond this modest ideal. He is a mediocre translator and the best of his prose occurs in his explanatory prefaces, in which he shows himself a good fellow and a man of cheerful disposition.

It is usual to number the discovery of printing among the causes of the Renascence. By helping the spread of knowledge it certainly favoured the great literary revolution which was at hand. But it is possible, at least in England, to ask whether its first effects were not to fortify and prolong the Middle Ages. To draw up a list of the books issued from the English printing presses during almost fifty years is to cast up the balance-sheet of the past. It is barely possible to discern, here and there in such a list, a book which heralds the new age.

Caxton himself had nothing of the humanist. He was a Kentishman, a member of the Mercers' Company, who at twenty years old left England for the Low Countries. He settled in Bruges and there acted as a consul responsible for the trading interests of his fellow-countrymen. His stay in Flanders acquainted him with the most civilised court in Western Europe, that of the Dukes of Burgundy, to whose dominions Flanders belonged. In this court, although a great appetite for art and learning was manifest, letters were still confined in the mediæval frames. It was with French literature that Caxton came to be impregnated, and to its propagation that he devoted his energies as translator and printer. Bruges was one of the first towns to take advantage of Gutenberg's invention, and Caxton, having been initiated by the printer Colard Mansion, finished an incomplete translation of the *Receuil des Histoires de Troye* by Raoul Lefèvre, chaplain to

---

[1] His prefaces and epilogues have been partly reprinted by W. Pollard in *Fifteenth Century Prose and Verse*, op. cit. See E. G. Duff, *William Cxton* (Chicago, 1905).

the Duke of Burgundy, and published it at Bruges in 1474. It was the first printed English book. The second was the translation of another French work, a moral and allegorical treatise on the game of chess.

When more than fifty years old Caxton returned to England, in 1476, and established the first English printing-press near Westminster Abbey. Amid much encouragement and protected by Earl Rivers and by the Duke of Gloucester, afterwards Richard III., he worked there until his death in 1491.

What is interesting is his choice of books for printing. He has right neither to the glory of having discovered printing, which belongs to Gutenberg and Schoeffer, nor to the glory of erudition won by the Aldi of Venice and the Etiennes of France, nor even to that of producing beautiful volumes. He was essentially a practical man, on the look-out for books likely to please, and also a man whose personal tastes were determined by his long sojourn on the continent and by his age. But although his title to represent his nation has been questioned, it is impossible not to be struck by the fact that the library he formed is very like that of the Paston family. It contains the same mixture of poetry, chivalrous romances, moral allegories and books of devotion.

He was a great admirer of Chaucer and printed the *Canterbury Tales* (1478) and *Troylus and Criseyde*, but he also found room for Lydgate and Gower.

He preferred prose, however, as a medium for the translations of French chivalrous romances which he made or had made—the *Recuyell of the Historyes of Troye*, the *Boke of Histories of Jason*, the *Lyf of Charles the Grete*, the *Morte d'Arthur*, the *Foure Sonnes of Aymon*. It was also into prose that he translated the *Historye of Reynart the Foxe* from the Dutch.

Among works of piety issued from his press were the Hours of the Church, a life of Christ, and a translation of the *Golden Legend* which had the largest circulation of all his publications.

Nothing shows the mediæval character of his reading and his mind better than the Æneid he published in 1490, which is translate dnot from Virgil but from a baroque romance of the Middle Ages.

If it be remembered that Caxton's immediate successors, Wynkyn de Worde, Richard Pinson and the others, did not notably deviate from his lead in their choice of publications up to 1530, it becomes clear that the English Renascence began amid a considerable body of books which were penetrated by the mediæval spirit. It might even be thought, so nearly complete is the absence of the books properly called classical, that the country remained outside the current along which Europe was being swept towards Greek and Roman antiquity. But in justice it should be said that the English found it more convenient to procure books of the newer kind from continental publishers, and to keep their own presses, still few in number, for popular books written in their own language.

What is most remarkable, from the literary point of view, is the development of English prose for which Caxton, a mediocre writer, was responsible. French prose, of which he definitely perceived the qualities, was his ideal. He admired "the fair language of French, which was in prose so well and compendiously set and written, which methought I understood the sentence and substance of every matter" (*Recuyell of the Historyes of Troye*). He himself aimed at a like clarity and like ease.

In producing prose renderings of the mediæval romances he followed the example of the French of the fifteenth century. He thus ensured a longer survival and wider popularity to these romances, which he made accessible to all men. In English, verse had hardly ever embellished them, and, had it not been for the minstrels, they would have fallen into neglect. Prose secured that the stories they enclosed became known. In more or less shortened form, these romances passed from hand to hand, the principal one of the wares the pedlar bore in his pack. In the chap-books of the Elizabethan period, they kept romance alive in the minds of simple people, awoke those dreams of extraordinary adventure to which many dramatists of the Renascence appealed and which others of them mocked. By means of these compilations, the Middle Ages were kept from dying altogether, and sank, instead, to deeper and deeper strata of consciousness. Whatever may have been the value of the new works which sprang of the Renascence, the old stories still made the first and the favourite appeal to popular imagination. They shared the rôle with the ballads, which were multiplied in the same period as they, and which often epitomised in a few verses stories like theirs.

Among the prose versions of old romances published by Caxton there was, however, one which was to be not only food for the people but also a feast for the fastidious. Caxton was well inspired on the day he printed Sir Thomas Malory's *Morte d'Arthur*.[1] He tells us that when he had published the noble feats of Hector, Charlemagne and Godfrey of Bouillon, he was "instantly required" by "many noble and divers gentlemen" also to imprint those of Arthur who belonged to the realm of England. In reply, he pleaded that "divers men hold opinion that there was no such Arthur," yet allowed himself to be persuaded. The translation he used was ready to hand, having been made by Thomas Malory, knight, member of parliament and Lancastrian, who shared the misfortunes of his party and died in 1471. His translation was complete in 1469 and published in 1484.

Malory represents himself as translating a French book. In truth he seems to have had recourse to many books, so that his *Morte d'Arthur* is a compilation. He has brought together scattered romances and co-ordinated them, without eliminating the traces of disparity. In spite, however, of the immense parentheses which recount the separate adventures of Sir Balin, Sir Pelleas, Sir Palomides, Sir Bors, the history of Tristram and Isoud, we can distinguish in his work the lines of a dominant story, that of Arthur, which is logically followed by the tale of the Sangreal. Malory tells of Arthur's triumphant reign, the unfaithfulness of his wife Guenever who takes Launcelot for her lover, Launcelot's punishment by the failure of his quest of the Sangreal, the finding of which is reserved for the purer Galahad. He shows the knights disaffected to the king because of Guenever's sin, and relates Mordred's revolt and Arthur's death. The book ends religiously, for Guenever becomes a nun and Launcelot a hermit. Romantic though it be, we feel that it bears a relation to actualities. The painter of the evils of civil war in this legendary kingdom was a victim of the Wars of the Roses, and the fact sometimes brings a moving gravity and melancholy into his pages.

But both this application to the author's own time and the moral lesson which unites the adventures are uncertain, vague and hesitating in Malory's work. Even the moral is inconsistent, for Launcelot and Guenever in their sin are cited as an example to true lovers. Hence the Puritan reproach, formulated by Roger Ascham: "the whole pleasure of whiche booke standeth in two speciall poyntes, in open mans slaughter and bold bawdrye." In fact, this over-loose compilation lacks unity both of thought and of plot.

It has, however, another unity, that of manner, tone and atmosphere. Malory transports us to a strange country in a distant world, unreal, impossible and yet imaginatively coherent—a country where all is tourneys and battles, where the only dwellings reared are castles, a country without agricultural life or trade, a

---

[1] The original edition has been reprinted with notes and a commentary by H. O. Sommer, 3 vols. (1889–91). See also Globe Edition, E. Strachey (1893); and Kittredge, *Who was Sir Thomas Malory?* (Harvard Studies and Notes in Philology and Literature, vol. v.)

region of mirage in which the marvellous is at home and fantastic personages are plausible.

It is the evocation of a vanished epoch, of a sort of golden age, a story of the Round Table written during atrocious civil conflict. It is a refuge, beneath hovering and all-diffused melancholy, from the hardships and crudities of the present.

The narrator of these fanciful tales found a style which fits them well—simple, even childish, monotonous, but harmonious and having poetic cadences. A clear, transparent and smooth style which does not date. It breathes a soft archaic odour. It betrays neither labour nor culture. The charm of this prose is that it is made up of poetic reminiscences inherited from a long line of earlier poems. The style is that of the fairy-tales which are told to little children, and makes a Frenchman think of Perrault's stories, but it is the product of a period which was less wise than Perrault's and of a narrator less self-conscious than he. It is delicious prose of a particular kind, although unfit for other than its own purpose, as is apparent when the author attempts to reason. But when he relates he reaches excellence. An artist like Tennyson could do no better than translate almost literally Malory's story of Arthur's death and of the colloquy between him and Sir Bedivere. There are even good judges who prefer Malory's simple prose to the too elaborate verses of the Victorian poet.

The literary importance and influence of this collection cannot be exaggerated. It is England's first book in poetic prose, and also the storehouse of those legends of the past which have most haunted English imaginations. It is the work which kept the chivalrous spirit alive among the literate, the poets and the gentry, while the people were fed by the chap-books. Whether such a book would have met with a like fortune in France is doubtful. The author does not sufficiently dominate his material for a French audience. He is incapable of making an explanation or giving a sign of self-consciousness. He repeats his tale like a marvelling child trying to tell faithfully what it has heard and not entirely understood. He gives a wide field to the imagination and does not trouble himself about the intelligence.

The second important prose work that appeared after Malory's was another translation from the French. It was Froissart's *Chronicles*, translated by John Bourchier, Lord Berners (1467–1533)[1] and published in 1523–5. Lord Berners's excellent prose, as animated, lively and highly coloured as his original, yet represents a return to the fourteenth century, as does also his other book, *Huon of Bordeaux*,[2] which contains the story of the dwarf Auberon. These books appeared when the humanist movement had begun, and the first troubles of the Reformation were manifesting themselves. Without abandoning French, writers were about to add to it the direct study of Latin or even Greek, and on occasion to prefer to it the southern languages. The same Lord Berners was a pioneer of the new prose and a precursor of the Euphuists in his translation of the *Golden Book of Marcus Aurelius* from the Spanish of Antonio de Guevara. He is the connecting-link between the two ages in prose, as Skelton and Douglas, on very different grounds, are in poetry.

[1] Reprinted by W. P. Ker in *Tudor Translations* (1901–3).
[2] Reprinted by the Early English Text Society, Extra Series, xl., xli., xliii. and l. (1882–7).

BOOK III

THE PREPARATION FOR THE RENASCENCE (1516–1578)

CHAPTER I

THE PART OF THE HUMANISTS

1. Special Characteristics of the English Renascence.—The Renascence showed in England almost all the characteristics which it had throughout Europe: thought was liberated and broadened so that it broke its scholastic framework; destiny and morals ceased to be the matter only of dogma and became problematical; a rebellion against the spiritual authority was first incited by the Reformation, which was soon afterwards the enemy of this ally, the Renascence; men looked with a new wonder at the heavens and the earth as they were revealed by the discoveries of the navigators and astronomy; superior beauty was perceived in the literature of classical antiquity, particularly in the recently recovered works of ancient Greece.

At the same time, the Renascence had in England certain additional characteristics which were so special that they gave rise to a truly national literature. The difference was mainly in the time of flowering and in the quantitative mixture of elements, but it was also an outcome of the power each nation simultaneously acquired, when once it was enfranchised from the unifying Catholic discipline, of revealing its own character and of standing in opposition to other nations instead of blending with them. It was from the time of the Renascence that the various European nations began to follow the divergent paths which ended in the contrasts they now present.

The chief peculiarities of the English Renascence, as compared with the same movement in Italy and France, may be stated as follows.

The renewal affected literature later and more slowly in England than in those countries. Not because humanism was tardily introduced, for England's initiation into humanism was, if subsequent to that of Italy, yet quite as early as that of France. But humanism in England had for a long time no decided effect on poetry and prose. The national language was still immature. Prose lacked a strong tradition and glorious precedents, and the best humanists still made use of Latin. It is significant that the two books which appeared in England in this period and attained to European fame—Sir Thomas More's *Utopia* (1516) and Bacon's *Instauratio Magna* (1620)—were both written in Latin. As for verse, it had, since Chaucer, been irregularised, and it did not definitely regain equilibrium and measure until Spenser's work began in 1579: all the preceding years of the sixteenth century show no more than a series of incomplete experiments, ground which was won and then lost. In consequence, English literature had its flowering season when the magnificent Italian literature had already entered on its decadence, when France had produced Rabelais and Ronsard and his Pleiad, and

Montaigne's essays were appearing. Malherbe was nine years old when Shakespeare was born. It was therefore in a generation enriched by all the substance of France and Italy that England realised for the first time her high literary ambitions.

Secondly, the Renascence held more aloof from the plastic arts in England than in Italy or even in France. The English Renascence occurred in a country which had no pictures or statues except those bought abroad, and in which the most determined Reformers were zealously protesting against images. It had therefore a more inward and moral effect than the similar movements on the continent. It reached its triumph not before, but after, the Reformation, when the Anglican religion had spread throughout the country and was beginning, here and there, to be tinged with Calvinism. In so far as the Renascence was an aspiration to every form of beauty and the cult of every kind of energy, it was not quite at ease in the already Puritan atmosphere breathed in this country. There were doubtless free spirits in England, but they were rebels and notorious. A morality which was sincere and natural in the majority had, on pain of obloquy, to be assumed by the others. The total result was increased seriousness, increasing pangs of conscience, less serenity, and intensified passion in the matter of faith and conduct.

On the other hand, although the spread of Protestantism all over England caused her to break with the Middle Ages more decidedly than France and Italy, her literature remained more nearly mediæval than that of either of those countries. The fact is the more striking because literature in the preceding centuries had been a less direct expression of national sentiments in England than elsewhere. English literature had been almost all imported from France, had mainly consisted of translations and adaptations. It had not assumed a truly national shape. The greatest poet, Chaucer, had been essentially French. None the less, the truth remains that, although the Renascence and the Reformation beckoned to new paths, England was faithful to the cult of the past longer than the continent. The fact is explained by the continuance of popular influences. While in France the Renascence was eminently aristocratic, in England it was always regardful of the masses. It preserved and increased the vogue of the ballads. The theatre, the home of the most magnificent product of the period, was accessible to all men, appealed to the humble as to the great. For the people follow in literature fashions derived from former days, hold to them tenaciously and do not abandon them.

A patriotism more and more intense and passionate, even aggressive and disdainful, favoured this continuity by glorifying the annals of the nation, its history, legends, traditions and antiquities. While this patriotism gave rise to an ambition to rival the masterpieces of Greece and Rome as well as those of Italy and France, it inspired at the same time antagonism to the foreign influences which seemed to threaten the national genius. It was an obstacle to Italianism, that most potent of the infatuations of the Renascence. It is impossible to say whether in England, in this century, Italy were more the object of wonder or of scandal, of admiration or of disapproval. Increasingly England felt and wished herself to be different from the rest of Christendom.

2. **The Beginnings of Humanism (1490-1578).**[1] — During some thirty years, from 1490 until about 1520, when the religious quarrels began, there was in England an efflorescence of humanism which was accomplished only by a few elect spirits, but was pure, serene and full of hope. Some young Englishmen were attracted to Italy by the desire to learn Greek, knowledge of which had been

---

[1] For this chapter see the general histories of literature cited at the beginning: *Cambridge History of English Literature*, vol. iii. chap. i.; Courthope, *History of English Poetry*, vol. i. chap. v. and vol. ii. chap. i.; Morley, *English Writers*, vol. vii.; Jusserand, *Histoire littéraire du Peuple anglais*, livre iv. chap. i. See also Green, *A Short History of the English People*, and G. Saintsbury, *A History of Elizabethan Literature* (1890).

carried thither by refugees after the fall of Constantinople to the Turks in 1493. They were eager to see the manuscripts of the masterpieces these fugitive Greeks had saved and brought with them, and in quest of this revelation they journeyed to Florence, Bologna, Padua, Venice and Rome. Thomas Linacre (1460–1524), grammarian, physician and translator of Galen, should be named among them, and William Grocyn (1446–1519), both of whom returned to Oxford about 1490 and there established the teaching of Greek on sound principles. John Colet (1467–1519) found in Italy, perhaps while he listened to Savonarola, Ficino and Pico di Mirandola, the inspiration of that enlightened and purified Christianity which he preached in London and Oxford, and founded on renewed study of the text of the New Testament and an historical examination of Saint Paul's mission. By the foundation of St. Paul's School in 1504, Colet also provided the first model for a reformed secondary school of which the teaching should be based on Latin and Greek. For this school he caused William Lily (1468–1522) to write and Erasmus to revise a Latin grammar which was to reign supreme in schools until our own day, and to become in the eighteenth century, after some rearrangement, the Latin grammar of Eton.

Such prestige did the New Learning acquire from these three masters, that Erasmus, when he resolved upon a profound study of Greek, and was too poor to go to Italy and dissatisfied with Paris and the college of Montaigu, made several visits to England, from 1499 onwards, as much to complete his own education as in search of an easier life. Under Colet's influence his studies took a more religious turn, and he devoted himself for a time to the reform of Christianity, which both he and Colet would have wished to see accomplished by persuasion, knowledge and the purification of morals, without a break in unity.

(a) THOMAS MORE.—The other side of the nature of Erasmus, his admiration for antique thought and form shown in his *Adages* (1500), his wit, his mockery which had free play in his *Praise of Folly* (1509), was better echoed by another of his English friends, Thomas More (1478–1535).[1] It was under More's roof that he wrote the *Praise of Folly*, and of him that he said, "When did Nature mould a temper more gentle, endearing and happy than the temper of Thomas More?" It was with Erasmus in his mind that More wrote his *Utopia*, the masterpiece of English humanism.

More was the pupil of the Oxford Hellenists and the friend of John Colet and William Lily. He was associated with Erasmus in the translation from Latin of some excerpts from Lucian. But he did not live only with books. He was a well-known lawyer and at one time a member of parliament. In 1515 he was sent to the continent to negotiate a commercial treaty with the Low Countries, and it was while on this mission that he began his famous book, which reveals a sagacious observer of his own times as well as the adventurous dreamer who was Plato's disciple. The other English humanists of his day were scholars and educationists. Only he of them all had the creative gift, and had he written his *Utopia* in his mother-tongue instead of Latin, although European glory would doubtless have come to him less speedily, he would to-day be one of the leading figures in English literature. Instead he has strictly no place in it, except in right of some controversial treatises and a history of doubtful authorship.

His *Utopia*, which was not translated into English until 1551, cannot, however, be neglected because of the language which clothed it, for it is the true prologue

---

[1] The English works of Sir Thomas More, published in 1557. His poems reprinted in 1906. His *Utopia* translated into English by R. Robynson in 1551; by Richards in 1923 (Oxford). Edition of Latin and English texts published in 1895. Studies on More by H. Morley, *English Writers* (1891); W. H. Hutton (1895); H. Brémond (1904); and J. Delcourt, *Essai sur la langue de Sir T. More* (1913).

of the Renascence. With most vigorous emphasis it opposes all the conceptions of the past. Better than any book it marks the new turning in the paths of thought.

Its inspiration is twofold. Its frame is furnished by the recent maritime discoveries of the Portuguese and Spaniards, more particularly by the stories of Amerigo Vespucci. But fundamentally the book is derived from Plato's *Republic*, that Greek philosopher's dream of an ideal state, and from the impulse to react against the stiff, inert conception of society which had reigned for centuries.

More is in opposition to established ideas in almost every particular. He makes fun of scholasticism which barred the way to thought with dialectical forms. He establishes that Greek is superior to Latin philosophy, which he considers insignificant save for some writings of Seneca and Cicero. His hero Hythloday earns a right to the gratitude of the Utopians by introducing them to the works of Plato, Aristotle and Plutarch.

More is in revolt against the spirit of chivalry. As much a humanitarian as a humanist, his hatred and contempt for war are like Swift's. Soldiers are to him "men-slayers," and he makes little of the point of honour and of military glory, of all that made up the atmosphere of the admired romances which Caxton had lately broadcast through the land. War was, according to More, justifiable only in the last resort, and should be waged in a purely utilitarian spirit, using the tricks of espionage and treachery. Unwittingly he was taking up the same ground as Machiavelli, who at this moment was writing *Il Principe*.

He extols communism, forbids the acquisition of property, and, reverting to the ideas of Lycurgus, discredits gold, which he would put to the meanest uses. He would make work compulsory for all men, but only for nine hours a day. Thus theft would disappear from Utopia and there would be no occasion to apply the hard penal laws of England.

In More's mind there is an ideal of a life which would be easy for the whole community. He is not of those whose consolation for the miseries of this present life is a picture of the life to come, for he cites happiness as the end of existence. He protests against asceticism and the contempt of wellbeing and honourable pleasure. It is from him that Rabelais borrowed the doctrine of his abbey of Thélème.

Like all Utopians, More bases himself on faith in the goodness of human nature. He believes in it as did Rousseau. His disapproval of asceticism causes him to glorify the senses which reveal natural marvels and God who made nature. He is regardful of everything which pertains to the body, of bodily health, necessary to the health of the soul, and of the comfort of dwellings. The Utopians do not suffer a man to be either cruel to himself or "unkind to nature."

In Utopia all religions are authorised and toleration is the law. Even the Christian religion, which has been introduced thither, enjoys no privileges. No religion has anything to recommend it beyond the examples it provides.

This book should be read as the exercise of a mind giving itself free play and unconcerned with the practical application of its own theories. More wrote in Latin, not for the people but for the learned. We are brought to ask, in astonishment, whether he did not, more than once, write against his own deep convictions. For the creator of this Utopia was a fervent Christian, a submissive Catholic, and an ascetic who wore a hair shirt. This apostle of toleration was, as chancellor, a persecutor of the first Protestants and ended by dying a martyr to his faith. The contrast between his Utopia and his own life betrays a principle of unreality. The ideas of his book were on a level with his intelligence rather than deeply rooted in his conscience.

Yet this book cannot be called the unstable product of a youthful imagination. More was thirty-eight years old when he wrote it, and more than one of its pages contain reflections suggested by his practical experience as a lawyer and a member of parliament. When he sees in the existing society "a conspiracy of the rich against the poor," he is not guilty of mere rhetoric. He supports his assertion by facts which are contemporary and English, the enclosures of land which were depopulating the countryside, especially in the south-east, the eviction of small tenants because rich landlords found that grazing farms were more profitable than their holdings. The lessened demand for workers on the land was causing great misery, so that "even a beast's life seems enviable" as compared with that of a labourer. When More attacks the barbarous penal laws he is aiming a blow at the executions with which, as a lawyer, he was too familiar in a country where twenty criminals could be seen hanging from a gallows in a row. He is the very antithesis of the judge Fortescue, who was proud of the bravery of English robbers. When he recommends houses of "a gorgeous and gallant sort," well lit by glazed windows, he is thinking of the healthy and pleasant dwellings he had seen in Holland and comparing them with the dark, inconvenient and miserable homes of the London and England of his day.

This book is partly the work of a dreamer led by his fancy and a logician who systematises his ideas. But it is also written by a satirist who attacks the errors and evils bequeathed by the Middle Ages. It is unlikely that More thought his conception could be realised in its entirety, but he very heartily wished to awaken the desire for certain necessary changes.

His *Utopia* stands alone as representing England's literary contribution to pure humanism. Ten years after he wrote it More himself was drawn into the religious controversy, and obliged, whether he would or no, to abandon the sphere of intellectual exercises for that of narrow ecclesiastical quarrels in which he is next found.

It is a great pity that he did not write a work of such general interest as *Utopia* in English. His humanist's culture is not evinced only by his Latin writings. He left behind him certain pages in English which show, no less than *Utopia*, the degree to which this admirer of Plato was impregnated with Socratic dialectics. The dialogue between the old prisoner Anthony and his nephew Vincent, which More wrote in his prison, to prove that he was neither more unfortunate nor more of a prisoner than the rest of mankind, is so admirable that Socrates might have approved it or envied him its authorship. And if he be indeed the author of the historical fragment on Richard III. attributed to him, he must be recognised as a rival of Tacitus, so vivid is the portrait he paints, so strong his colours, so intense his attack. It is to this fragment that the atrocious, implacable figure which has remained in men's memory is due, the character on which Shakespeare founded his famous tragedy. Whether the picture conform to reality is doubtful, but artistically it is an astonishing success. It has unity of structure and effect far beyond anything hitherto achieved by an English chronicler.

The pages which prove More's solid classical culture represent only a part of his rich and complex personality, curious of everything in life and nature, conscious of the variety in the souls of various men. His favourite pastime was to observe the habits and instincts of animals. He had a spontaneous and most lively dramatic talent, and although he never wrote for the stage, he dramatised, in the driest controversial treatises, living and comic characters, who speak their own language or even their native dialect. His English prose abounds with such humorous passages as his predecessors lacked. It contains also many turns of familiar talk, sayings and popular expressions which he seems to have been the first to coin or circulate. One wonders if he took them from current speech, or invented them entirely. His natural gaiety, "the kind and friendly cheerfulness with a little air of raillery" which was, Erasmus tells us, expressed on his face, seasons his prose, as it showed itself in his speech throughout his life and on the very scaffold. We do not know whether to praise him most for his humour or his wit.

Nevertheless, we cannot follow those who have called him the earliest of the modern English prose-writers. This humanist seems, if the doubtful case of *Richard III.* be excepted, to have done all his artistic work in Latin. His English prose is all improvisation, and he lets loose in it, without rule or measure, his extraordinary lawyer's flow of language. His latest critic calculates that some of his sentences are as much as four yards long, measured line by line in the original edition. He never sought to mould English prose, which then, above all things, needed to be made lighter and more definite. He left this task entirely to men who were much his inferiors in genius, open-mindedness and liveliness of observation, men who recognised their duty of giving, on the model of the ancients, firmness and regularity to the structure of English sentences. Yet to More belongs the honour of having provoked one of the best prose works of his time, his biography by his son-in-law, William Roper, which was written about 1535 but did not appear until 1626, in Paris. This is an admirable book from every point of view. Nothing could be simpler, clearer or more pathetic than its story of More's last moments, and it makes an impressive advance in clarity and construction on More's own writings.

(*b*) THE EDUCATIONISTS: ELYOT, CHEKE, WILSON, ASCHAM.—The men who were inspired by classical antiquity after More were educationists rather than imaginative writers. They have more in common with More's masters than with More himself. But they have over him the advantage that they wrote their best work in English and have not only a marginal place in English literature.

It is thus with Sir Thomas Elyot (1490–1546)[1] whose *Governor* appeared in 1531. This treatise on moral philosophy and education, written for those who would be called to govern their country, was founded on the Italian works of Pontano and Patrizzi and is full of the spirit of antiquity. It abounds with Greek and Latin reminiscences.

The influence of the civic morals of Rome is very evident in it, although Elyot was a convinced Christian. He adapts the manner of Plutarch to English history, for instance in the scene in which he shows the prince, afterwards Henry V., obeying the judge who sends him to prison, and the king congratulating himself on a fearless magistrate and a son submissive to justice. By this scene, of which the historical truth is most doubtful, Elyot inculcates the Roman respect for law. His prose is less of the people and less spontaneous than More's, but, on the other hand, more restrained and classical.

The humanism of a man brought up on antiquity is also the most salient characteristic of a book written against the seditious, the *Heart of Sedition, how grievous it is to a Commonwealth*,[2] by Sir John Cheke (1514–57), teacher of Greek at Cambridge. This good Hellenist, noted for the love of Greek which he spread around him, gave in 1549 forcible expression to English conservatism in his *Heart of Sedition*. It is directed against the Norfolk rebels who were led by the tanner Ket. Already we have that hostile picture of popular risings which recurs half a century later in Shakespeare's *Henry VI.* and *Coriolanus*. Cheke shows himself vigorous in argument, eloquent and occasionally homely and humorous. He has both the tone and the arguments which are heard again from the Shakespearean Menenius Agrippa.

Form was almost as important to Cheke as matter, and he made attempts

[1] Edited by Croft (1889).
[2] 1st edition 1549. Reprinted by G. Langbaine (Oxford, 1641), and in Holinshed's *Chronicle*.

to reform the English language. Sir Thomas Wilson (1525-81)[1] was concerned solely with style in his *Arte of Rhetorique,* published in 1553, in which this so-called English Quintilian recommends purity and simplicity of language. He reviews and derides all the verbal affectations of his time, and proscribes "inkhorn terms," "outlandish English," the barbarous legal language made up of deformed Anglo-Norman words, and the abuse of archaism by the "fine courtier" who "wil talke nothing but Chaucer."

These men are good masters, sensible and sure, fashioning both mind and style by their precepts and example. But their personalities are too restrained to have made a deep imprint on their prose. Roger Ascham (1515-68)[2] had qualities which threw him more into relief. He was the most popular of the educationists of his time, and the most pungent of the group of writers—Cheke, Wilson, Sir Thomas Smith and Watson—who about the middle of this century transferred from Oxford to Cambridge the honour of guiding England along the paths of the Renascence. Ascham was Cheke's friend, and in some degree his pupil, tutor to Elizabeth in his sixteenth year, a good Protestant, even tinged with Puritanism, yet prudent enough to be Mary Tudor's Latin secretary. He left behind him two books of which one was devoted to the physical education of the young and the other to their intellectual instruction.

The first of them, *Toxophilus* (1545), is intended to revive the love of archery for which Ascham felt an almost romantic passion. He even considers the bow to be a superior weapon to the cannon, and believes that the physical and moral health of his country is bound up with the practice of this obsolete sport.

His other book, *The Scholemaster,* was published in 1570, two years after his death, and contains his advice to masters on the teaching of Latin.

Ascham puts life into these treatises by his personal presentment of his ideas. He brings forward his own practice and experience, his memories, and interesting anecdotes related firsthand. His parentheses stimulate flagging attention. His preoccupation with Latinity does not debar him from a moral point of view. He admires the great writers of ancient Rome, but abominates, as papistical and corrupt, the Rome of his own time. He vigorously attacks the Italianism of the English nobility, especially the dangerous sojourns in the country of licence which rich young men of wealth and fashion were wont to make. He cares less for literary beauty and refinement than for solid and healthy education.

He also has the merit of having worked assiduously to advance the progress of the English language. He is aware, he says in his preface to *Toxophilus,* that to write in Latin would have been "more honest for my name," but he decides to use English both to further "the pleasure or commoditie of the gentlemen and yeomen of Englande," and because everything has been written in English "in a maner so meanly, bothe for the matter and handelynge, that no man can do worse." Indisputably he helped to perfect the language by his use of it. His style is much laboured, penetrated with Latin turns of phrase and Latin elegancies. Numerous symmetrical, balanced, antithetical sentences, sometimes marked by alliteration, occur in his work, all that is best in the prose of the Euphuists without their eccentricity and false ornament. It is true that Ascham in his Romanised dress is a little stiff and hampered. But his faults are trifling as compared with the benefit prose derived from submitting to the discipline of the ancients, especially Cicero and Seneca, whose periodic style and nervous conciseness Ascham

---

[1] 1st edition 1553. Reprinted (Oxford, 1908).
[2] *Toxophilus,* 1st edition 1545; reprinted by Arber (1861). *The Scholemaster,* 1st edition 1570; reprinted by Arber (1870), by Aldis Wright (1904), and in *Elizabethan Critical Essays* by Gregory Smith. Complete works, ed. Giles, 4 vols. (1864-5). German life by Dr. Katterfeld (1879).

imitates by turns. The training which he imposed on himself and which he recommended for schoolboys had a salutary effect. He desired that a pupil should first translate a passage from Latin into English, and then, after a sufficient interval, be required to put his own English version back into Latin. By repeated use of this exercise Ascham himself acquired a relative facility of expression. The too heavy clothing of his thoughts finally became so pliable that the man, sincere, sensible and good-humoured, can be descried beneath it. He is one of the earliest writers of classical English prose.

These were the chief of the educationists, such of them as left a name behind them. The work which was being accomplished at this time cannot, however, be understood unless we add to their number all the nameless makers of the Renascence, all the unknown masters who were training their English pupils in the universities and the schools to admire and imitate the masterpieces of antiquity.

CHAPTER II

HUMANISM did not long remain without other admixture. Hardly had it affected literature than its influence was crossed and opposed by that of the religious Reformation. Most of the men of whom we have just spoken had to choose between the Pope and Luther or Calvin. The free development of their culture was interrupted and they were drawn into the religious struggle. In the year after that in which *Utopia* appeared Luther published his famous thesis at Wittenberg. More's career was thereby transformed: the rest of his life was devoted to the defence of Catholic unity. Sir John Cheke died at forty-three years old of remorse for having abjured Protestantism under Mary Tudor. Ascham in his writings mingles Puritan ideas and pedagogic counsels. For others, controversy constituted all their life and the whole of their work.

Matter for controversy was from the outset mainly provided by the questions of the translation of the Bible into English and of the dissolution of religious houses, both destined to influence language and literature importantly.

1. Tindale. Translation of the Bible and the Book of Common Prayer.— It was the question of translating the Bible which brought Sir Thomas More and William Tindale into conflict.

William Tindale (1484–1536) [1] was the first to be inspired by Luther's example, and as early as 1522 he began to translate the New Testament into English. As he was prevented from pursuing this work in England, where the king was still at this date a determined defender of orthodoxy, he took refuge on the continent, and finally had his translation printed at Cologne in 1525. In spite of the measures taken by Henry VIII., it was introduced into England, where the ground had been prepared by Wyclif and where there were some local survivals of the spirit of the Lollards. Tindale's version of the New Testament, which was founded both on Luther's translation and on editions of the Greek and Latin texts elucidated by the commentaries of Erasmus, was a basis for the famous Authorised Version of 1611.

Tindale, who had been a pioneer during the dangerous years in which the Government of England was the champion of the papacy, maintained an active controversial defence of the Reformation. A good humanist, who had enjoyed a solid university education and knew the ancient and several modern languages, Tindale is a talented controversialist, especially in his treatise *The Obedience of a Christen man and how Christen rulers ought to governe,* which was printed in 1528. The advantage to the formation of vigorous, clear and swift-moving English prose which arose out of the reformers' need to speak to the people is apparent in his work. In order to justify the translation of the Bible into the vulgar tongue, he not only uses the arguments based on good sense which appealed to the many, but also defends English against the orthodox allegation that it was incapable of rendering the original text adequately. He lays down that, on the contrary,

[1] Complete works with preface by Foxe, published 1573. See R. Demaus, *William Tyndall, a Biography* (1871).

"the Greek tongue agreeth more with the English than with the Latin." He discovers a deep-rooted affinity between English and Hebrew, thus first perceiving a truth of which the application had presently to be extended to the very spirit of the two peoples. Like the humanists, he makes mock of the scholastics who applied Aristotelian logic to the interpretation of Scripture, and he is again in agreement with them in condemning the mediæval romances, the stories of Robin Hood and Bevis of Hampton, Hector and Troilus. But it is for reasons of morals that he rejects these tales, as licentious and ribald fables, not because he wishes another æsthetic ideal to be adopted. It is neither Homer nor Virgil which he would substitute for them, but only the Bible. From the first, he marks the agreement and the disagreement of humanism and the Reformation.

It was Thomas More, the most lettered and skilful of the Catholics, who replied to Tindale, particularly on the question of translating the Bible. In this controversy More does not appear to advantage. He himself had recommended the translation of Scripture and he was obliged to contradict his own proposition. He liked, moreover, to write in Latin, and it was incumbent on him in this dispute to use English. His position was the difficult one of a quiet scholar who is compelled to take part in a public meeting and to speak against liberty. He equivocates, hints that the Church was not absolutely opposed to the translation of the Bible, but only to unfaithful versions falsified by heresy. But his acuteness showed him from the beginning how unfitting it would be to deliver up Holy Writ to the interpretation of the ignorant man in the street, "suche blynd bayardis as wyll whan they rede the byble in englysch be more bysy than wyll bycum them." He foresaw the swarming of the sects and the eccentricities of the Independents, and proposed a middle way. Let each bishop decide to whom in his diocese a copy of the translation might be entrusted and from whom it should be withheld or withdrawn.

But the public demand had already gone beyond such partial toleration. Tindale was persecuted and put to death in the Low Countries in 1536. Yet Henry VIII. had broken with the papacy and had sent Thomas More to the scaffold in the previous year (1535). The Reformation was officially established in England, and Tindale's translation of the Bible, completed by Miles Coverdale in 1535,[1] was broadcast over the country. Four other translations were added to it during the next thirty years. The sacred texts of the Hebrews and the early Christians were in all men's hands, to be from this time a check or counterweight to the reading of Græco-Roman classics, and to introduce into prose the biblical dialect which was to tinge so much of English literature. What is noticeable in these successive translations, and what was preserved by the Authorised Version of 1611, is the traditional prose which was adopted, one removed from pedantry and triviality, simple and yet a little quaint, to which the beauty of the original texts and a certain magic of style, especially perceptible in Coverdale, clings in varying degree. This prose, thus created, had incomparable influence. It appealed to all classes, penetrated by way of religious feeling to all minds, and gave a certain beauty to the speech even of the most ignorant and uncultivated, while it militated against the tendency to pedantry of the most learned. Its effects were especially conspicuous in the seventeenth century.

To the translation of the Bible, the Book of Common Prayer, drawn up under Edward VI. in 1549,[2] was added. It is an anonymous compilation from the Latin missal, published under the direction of Archbishop Cranmer, and its cadences

---

[1] *Writings of Coverdale*, ed. Pearson (Cambridge, 1844).
[2] J. Dowden, *The Workmanship of the Prayer-Book in its Literary and Liturgical Aspect* (1899), and *Further Studies in the Prayer-Book* (1908.)

are such as to lift up the hearts of the faithful like poetry and to awaken the admiration of purely æsthetic critics. In this prayer-book Latin sonority has passed into a tongue which seemed hardly able to contain it. The mingling of the Saxon and French elements of the language is perfect. The disjointed and jarring character of pure Saxon has been eliminated. Everything connects, blends, harmonises, for instance in the General Confession: "Almighty and most merciful Father, We have erred and strayed from thy ways like lost sheep, We have followed too much the devices and desires of our own hearts . . ."

These chosen sounds must be imagined rolling from the lips of a clergyman who is a skilled reader and who gives the rhythm to the congregation. It must be remembered that these sonorous and melodious phrases were repeated every Sunday in every church in England. Only thus can the impulse be understood which such a model could give to a language as yet indefinite and in search of paths.

2. The Dissolution of Religious Houses.—The other great change in the reign of Henry VIII. which reacted on letters was the suppression of the religious houses from 1535 to 1539.[1] To-day it is still difficult to say whether the measure was to the detriment or advantage of learning. There was an enormous destruction of books, deplored by the Protestants themselves, for instance by Bishop John Bale, one of the most determined enemies of the papacy. The Benedictine monasteries, which had been asylums for studious clerks, disappeared, and no like places of refuge arose in their stead. The numerous schools attached to many religious houses vanished also, and it was a long time before they were all replaced. Such of the Oxford and Cambridge colleges as were reserved for the religious became empty. The two great universities lost a considerable number of students. Higher education suffered: Greek, which had been brilliantly taught since the end of the fifteenth century, almost ceased, for a long period, to be studied. It was many years before the reformed foundations of schools and colleges compensated for the losses.

On the other hand, the end of the monasteries hastened the abandonment of scholastic philosophy which they had principally maintained, and this was favourable to a bolder spirit of intellectual enterprise. For the relations of the religious houses in England with sister houses on the continent, relations established by the Reformers with their brothers in Germany, the Low Countries and Geneva were substituted. Finally, the books which escaped the plunderers did not remain secreted and immobilised on the shelves of monastic libraries, but were henceforth read and studied. The great ardour of antiquaries dates from this time. The earliest of them was John Leland (1506?–1552), who was commissioned in 1533 to examine all the ancient monuments of the country, especially the archives of cathedrals, colleges, priories and abbeys. He aspired to enrich the royal library with all the precious documents which had been delivered to the riflers, and was distressed to see young scholars sent from Germany to extract from them pages which went back with them to their own country, to rank there as national monuments. Leland spent six years travelling about England, exploring all the libraries, and he published a formidable list of the wealth he discovered. This was the limit of his capacity: his ambition to use his over-copious material was not realised. His *Itinerary*[2] served, however, to open a road, and at the end of the century it furnished Harrison[3] and Camden[4] and their like with material.

The same patriotic impulse is accountable for the many chronicles, Protestant

---

[1] See *Cambridge History of English Literature*, vol. iii. chap. iii., and F. A. Gasquet, *Henry VIII. and the English Monasteries*, 2 vols. (1888).
[2] *Itinerary*, first published by T. Hearne in 1710–12. Modern edition by L. T. Smith (1906–7).
[3] W. Harrison, *Description of England*, published in 1578 in Holinshed's *Chronicle*.
[4] W. Camden, *Britannia* (in Latin, 1586. English translation by P. Holland, *Britain*, 1610).

in spirit, which appeared in the latter half of the sixteenth and the early seventeenth century. Edward Hall's *Chronicle*, published in 1548, traced the struggles of Lancaster and York and those of the first two Tudor reigns. Raphael Holinshed's *Chronicles*, which go back to remote origins, were written in collaboration with others, published in 1578 and continued to 1586, and were for long the great repertory of national history, used by Spenser and Shakespeare, among others. John Stow, between 1561 and 1604, issued eleven editions of his *Summarie of English Cronicles*. John Speed's *Historie of Great Britaine* was published in 1611; and William Camden's history of the reign of Elizabeth was written in Latin in 1615 and translated into French, and from French to English in 1625.

None of these authors is either a writer of great talent or a veritable historian. Almost all of them collect evidence uncritically and filch from their predecessors. They have a mediocre talent for composition and cannot resist puerile anecdotes. But they are all equally animated by the desire to glorify the part played by England in the past as in the present.

3. Latimer and John Foxe.—Besides these almost impersonal productions, the Reformation provoked in the middle of the sixteenth century the very living work of a preacher, Hugh Latimer (1485–1555),[1] whose energy and good sense produced some of the most pungent pages of English prose of the period. At a time when religion wavered, when the country abruptly passed from one form of observance to another at the will of the governors, Latimer, in spite of one or two politic retractions, showed almost continuous zeal and courage in preaching as he believed, against Catholicism during Wolsey's ministry, against the bastard reform of Henry VIII., and against the laxity of the Protestant clergy under Edward VI. He ended at the stake, having refused, under Mary Tudor, to repudiate his heresy. His last words to Bishop Ridley, the companion of his martyrdom, are famous. "Play the man, Master Ridley; we shall this day light such a candle, by God's grace, in England as I trust shall never be put out."

These words have the accent of Thomas More, whom Latimer resembles in his homely, almost jocular manner of presenting his thought. He is like More, but has not his underlying refinement or his frequent moments of detached observation and reflection. Latimer's sermons are characterised by an absence of theology and dogmatic discussion. Born of the people, a farmer's son, his mind had a popular cast. His subject was morals, and he illustrates it by countless allusions to the most familiar things, proverbial turns of speech, apologues and conceptions which were striking in their simplicity.

He believed in the power of sermons and preached especially against the clergy who did not preach. In his most celebrated sermon, that of 1549, "Of the Plough," he attacks the laziness of the Protestant clergy. His wit is broad and he scoffs at silent prelates with a comic use of alliteration: they are "pampering of their paunches," "mounching in their mangers." He relates, with much go, how he went to carry the gospel to a village grown unaccustomed to sermons, and found the church empty, because it was Robin Hood's day:

> It is no laughing matter, my friends, it is a weeping matter, a heavy matter, a heavy matter, under the pretence for gathering for Robin Hood, a traitor and a thief, to put out a preacher. . . . If the bishops had been preachers, there should never have been any such thing.

A famous passage has its natural place in his argument:

> I would ask you a strange question. Who is the most diligentest bishop and prelate

---

[1] G. E. Corrie, *Latimer's Sermons* (Parker Society, Cambridge, 1844), and *Sermons and Remains* (1845); R. Demans, *Hugh Latimer, a Bibliography* (1881); R. W. and A. J. Carlyle, *Hugh Latimer* ("Leaders of Religion," 1900).

in all England, that passeth all the rest in doing his office? . . . I will tell you. It is the devil. . . . He is never out of his diocese. . . . He is ever at his plough.

And the devil will bring back popery:

Away with Bibles and up with beads! Away with the light of the gospel and up with the light of candles, yea at noon-days.

There are two pages on this theme, and their energy and redundancy are equally astonishing. The good Latimer's phrases have the very same turn as those of the stump-orators in London to-day. He keeps his audience breathless by his mixture of mother-wit and feeling and his sudden apostrophes. His great desire to be understood by the most ignorant makes him a pioneer among prose-writers. He simplifies and clarifies. By instinct and for his immediate purposes he accomplishes a work analogous to that of a pedagogue like Ascham. He often formulates his phrases briefly and balances them symmetrically. Yet, preoccupied as he is solely with religion, he is consistently careless of style. Although literate himself, he never gives a thought to literature, which has given but little thought to him.

Beside Latimer, another and very different writer may be ranged, the recorders of his last words on the stake and of the deeds and sayings of all the English martyrs who suffered for the Protestant faith and were the victims of Roman prelates "from the yeare of oure Lord a thousande" onwards. It may be claimed for John Foxe (1516–87) that he wrote the book of this century which, after the Bible, made most noise. His martyrology, *Actes and Monuments of these Latter and Perilous Dayes* (1563),[1] is inevitably the work not of an historian but of a partisan, but if the author be often credulous and partial, he is also sincere. Each martyrdom is related with the simplicity of an official report. There are no flowers of style, but the wood-cuts in the original edition depict the tragic scenes, the instruments of torture, the stake. Nothing did more than this work to spread hatred of the papacy in England and to maintain the spirit of heroism which was to appear again in the days of the Puritans. The book was known outside England, served the Huguenots as a breviary, and gave d'Aubigné material for " Feux," one of the books of his *Tragiques*. It was first written by Foxe in Latin, but was translated by him into an unadorned English, without literary form, minute and dramatic when it relates interrogatories and tortures. To-day it astonishes by the fury which animates it, and which can still hold a reader's attention, enormous though the volume be and terrible its monotony.

4. Scotland. Lyndsay, Buchanan and Knox.—In Scotland the religious Reformation provoked a contemporary literary movement, evinced in the verses of Sir David Lyndsay, in the Latin works, both verse and prose, of Robert Buchanan and in the treatises of John Knox.

Sir David Lyndsay (1490–1555)[2] is the last of the line of the Scottish poets of the fifteenth century. By the form of his poetry he connects with the Middle Ages, but his ardent Protestantism distinguishes him from his predecessors. His work consists of a series of virulent satires which herald d'Aubigné's *Tragiques*. Hence there is a certain contradiction between his matter and his manner. His denunciations of Rome are contained by the traditional frames. He is a Jean de Meung who writes a *Roman de la Rose* after Luther. There is the same discrepancy in his life as in his writings, for this fervent democrat, this associate of John Knox, was also the companion of James V. from whom he received the high heraldic office of Lyon King at Arms.

Besides his *Satyre of the Thrie Estaitis*, of which we shall speak presently, he

---

[1] Ed. Cattley, 8 vols. (1836–41), and Pratt, 8 vols. (1877).
[2] Works edited by David Laing, 3 vols. (Edinburgh, 1879).

wrote *The Dreme* (1528), *The Complaynt* (1529), *The Testament of the Papyngo* (1530), *The Historie of ane nobill and vailyeand squyer, William Meldrum* (about 1550), and *The Monarchie, or Ane Dialog of the Miserable Estait of this World* (1552).

With prolix energy, without discrimination or beauty, but with a certain biting force, he denounces in these poems kings and prelates and their abuses and impostures. In his *Dreme* he descends into Hell, where he sees popes, emperors, kings, cardinals and archbishops chastised for the ambition which kept them from succouring and instructing the poor. His vision brings him back to Scotland, and there he meets a poor lean man, in rags, "with scrip on hip and pyikstaff in his hand," who is preparing to leave the country. It is John the Common Weal, who will not return until Scotland have a good king.

Lyndsay's satires were at first predominantly social, but with years they became more and more Protestant. His last and most considerable poem, *The Monarchie*, is a history of the most famous kingdoms of the earth, beginning with Daniel's vision of the four beasts which became the empires of Babylon, Persia, Greece and Rome. The author's basis is one of Knox's sermons. His octosyllabic lines are so virulent as to recall Skelton, whose verses they surpass in regularity, but also in an inexorable prosaic quality. Lyndsay has nothing of the poet except metre, but his brutal satire strikes hard and multiplies blows without flinching. Often coarse, he owed his immunity from persecution to his licentiousness. For Lyndsay as for Rabelais, ribaldry was a passport for daring.

The celebrated humanist George Buchanan (1506–82)[1] wrote almost wholly in Latin, and he therefore has here no place except as a witness to the classical culture of a Scot, and to the alliance between the Renascence and the Reformation which he represented. He had close relations with France, where he studied and taught, by turns in Paris and in Bordeaux where Montaigne was among his pupils. Reputed the first Latinist of his time, he was famous for his Latin verses and for his tragedies on the classic model, *Jeptha* and *Saint John the Baptist*. He had already distinguished himself by his satires against the Franciscans, the guardians of scholasticism, when, about 1560, he became one of the champions of Protestantism in his own country. It was at the moment when Scotland, impelled by Knox, was effecting her religious Reformation. Buchanan, who until 1567 was Mary Stewart's tutor, became her determined enemy after the murder of Darnley, and wrote against her his *Detectio Mariæ Reginæ*. He ended as the stern school-master of James VI., the pedant king, and wrote his *De Jure Regni apud Scotos* (1579) and his *Rerum Scoticarum Historia*. This was the last and most notable of a series of histories of Scotland which were written by Catholics and Protestants in the course of the sixteenth century and bear witness to the ardent Scottish patriotism. Buchanan has left behind him only two short treatises in Scots, but they are remarkable. His career shows what disturbance humanism suffered by the Reformation; party spirit is violently manifested by this man whose tastes first led him to pursue intellectual culture and learning for its own sake.

Buchanan left the glory of being the first great Scottish prose-writer to John Knox.[2] Knox (1505–72) was the reformer, the Calvin of Scotland. However much before him Lyndsay and Buchanan may have espoused the cause of reform, he was the Reformation itself. It was when he had taken refuge in Geneva with Calvin that he wrote, in 1558, his pamphlet against the two queens who were barring the spread of Protestantism in Scotland and England, *The First Blast of the Trumpet*

---

[1] Complete works published by the Scottish Text Society (1892). Study by P. Hume Brown Edinburgh, 1890).

[2] Complete works edited by D. Laing, 6 vols. (Edinburgh, 1846–64). Life by Hume Brown, 2 vols. (1895). See also Andrew Lang, *John Knox and the Reformation* (1905).

against the Monstrous Regiment of Women. In 1559, back in Scotland and all-powerful there, he tormented and terrified Mary Stewart by his bold preaching, and until his death he pursued his ardent Calvinistic apostolate.

Knox, who wished for immediate effect, wrote in the language of his country. His *History of the Reformation of Religioun within the Realme of Scotland* is not the work of a professional writer, but of a man of action who relates history in which he played a great rôle. His composition is not good, but his book is full of matter, of vigorous and picturesque passages in which humour and satire mingle. His stories of the murder by the men of the reformed religion of their persecutor, Cardinal Beaton, and of his own interviews with Queen Mary, have been found worthy to be compared with the more expressive pages of Saint Simon. Knox, who wishes to appeal to England as to Scotland, avoids the dialectal peculiarities of his mother-tongue, and writes so as to be understood on both sides of the Tweed.

In all these men, and especially the Scots, there is something which presages a new era, social as well as religious, an age of democracy as well as of Protestantism. There are signs of a progress towards the triumph of the Presbyterians and the Puritans. In the meanwhile, the reformers' need to speak to the people frequently led them to use the vulgar tongue rather than Latin, and it is undeniable that they largely contributed to the advance of English prose, that medium which the humanists had too often disdained.

CHAPTER III

POETRY owes less to the Reformers. They kept aloof from it as secular and frivolous. It was humanism which provoked the renewal of poetry, and especially the influence of the Italian Renascence. The task involved was considerable, for verse had to be saved both from the languor which had overtaken it with such as Stephen Hawes and from the artistic disarray which such as Skelton had brought upon it. Everything had to be done over again. Under Henry VIII. two poets of the court undertook the task, and it was in Italy that they found both models and stimulus. These pioneers, whose labours were ended by premature death, were Wyatt and Surrey.

1. **Wyatt.**—Sir Thomas Wyatt (1503–42),[1] who made sojourns in France and Italy, brought back from the latter country, in 1527, the admiration for lyrical poetry which he found there, and a desire to fashion English verse on the model of the Italians, or of the Ancients seen through an Italian medium.

His first object was to restore to English verse the nobility, grace and harmony it had lost. But as he groped after this ideal he showed how difficult was his enterprise. He seems at first to have perceived only the law of syllabism, and it is possible to find, doubtless in his earliest work, verses in which there is no discoverable regularity in the use of accents. So uncertain is his prosody, that we are driven to ask whether he were unaware of the iambic rhythm, or whether he pronounced such words as *bannèr, suffèr,* [*dis*]*pleasùre, fearèth,* as iambuses, throwing the accent on to the last syllable. His rhymes manifestly fall on unaccented syllables.

Gradually, however, he attained to comparative regularity. He went further than this. He borrowed from the Italians poetic forms which were unknown to his fellow-countrymen. Sometimes he uses Dante's *terza rima,* sometimes Serafino's *strambotti,* octaves rhyming as *ababccc,* and sometimes he imitates the Petrarchian sonnet. It was this last importation, effected in France at much the same time by Marot and Melin de Saint-Gelais, which had by far the largest consequences. This was due not only to the beauty of the form, but also to the fact that the sonnet was then the principal vehicle for the direct expression of personal feeling, without recourse to fiction or allegory.

It was by the sonnet that lyricism again entered English poetry. Whether it were translated or imitated mattered little. It rendered the music of feeling or passion. It called forth the rare word, the metaphor, subtlety and condensation. Its very brevity necessitated artistic labour.

Wyatt wrote no memorable sonnets, but he blazed the track. His imitations of Petrarch brought bold and new images into English. He speaks of love who—

> Into my face presseth with bold pretence,
> And there campeth displaying his banner.

[1] *Tottel's Miscellany,* reprinted by Arber (1903). Wyatt's poetic works were edited by R. Bell in 1854. See also, for Wyatt and Surrey, Edmond Bapst, *Deux gentilshommes et Poètes de la Cour de Henri VIII.* (Paris, 1891); L. Einstein, *The Italian Renaissance in England* (1892); W. C. Simmonds, *Sir Thomas Wyatt and his Poems* (Strasburg, 1889).

and tells that, upon rejection,

> . . . to heart's forest he fleeth,
> Leaving his enterprise with pain and cry.

This impassioned language was current and normal fifty years later, but before Wyatt it was entirely unknown.

Wyatt's sighs and supplications are Petrarchian. He is himself in other sonnets in which he pulls himself together and tells his mistress hard truths. His nature was frank and manly, like the proud portrait which Holbein made of him. The groans of humility suited him ill:

> My heart I gave thee, not to do it pain,

he says; and again:

> For he that doth believe bearing in hand,
> Plougheth in the water and soweth in the sand.

He bids farewell not to his mistress only, but to love also:

> Farewell, Love, and all thy laws for ever;
> Thy baited hooks shall tangle me no more:
> Senec and Plato call me from thy lore
> To perfect wealth, my wit for to endeavour.

And he bids love:

> With idle youth go use thy property.

He does indeed renounce love poems for satire. And his satires, imitated from Horace and Alamanni, are among his happiest innovations, reflecting his energetic and bold character. The courtier, withdrawn from the court, relates the vice and wretchedness he has seen. He mocks the gallants who advance their fortunes by marrying old rich widows. He tells, after Horace and Henryson, the fable of the fieldish mouse and the townish mouse, perhaps less happily than those predecessors, but with a proud accent to point his moral reflections.

The cavalier tone of his personal sonnets and his satires recurs in a few poems which are true songs, for instance, that beginning, "Madam, withouten many words," in which he calls upon his mistress to answer him yea or nay, and that last summons to his love which has kept its place in most anthologies:

> My lute, awake! perform the last
> Labour that thou and I shall waste;
> And end that I have now begun:
> And when this song is sung and past,
> My lute! be still for I have done.

2. **Surrey.**—Although he speaks of his vanished youth, Wyatt died young, at thirty-nine years old, so that he gave no measure of his powers. Still less did Surrey do so, for he was sent to the scaffold by Henry VIII. when he was only thirty.

The names of these poets are permanently linked in literary history. Born fourteen years after Wyatt, Surrey seems to have been the disciple of the older man whose name he celebrates in fine verses. The Earl of Surrey (1517–47) [1] was thus not obliged, like Wyatt, painfully to discover the rhythm of verse. Almost all the verses he left behind him are regular and harmonious. His nature was less energetic than Wyatt's, but he was a better artist. The accomplishment of his short life is remarkable. His personality, that of a great gentleman and a poet, is like a first sketch for Sidney's.

Much more dominated than Wyatt by the Petrarchian convention, Surrey sang in sonnets his entirely imaginative love for Geraldine or Lady Elizabeth Fitzgerald. The elegiac tone is natural to him. His special note is that of love for

---

[1] *Tottel's Miscellany*, op. cit. *The Poems of Surrey*, ed. Bell (1854).

nature, and with happy effect he mingles descriptions of nature with his love plaints.

But it is perhaps in some impersonal sonnets that his merit as an artist shows itself best. There may be a satirical allusion to a contemporary personage in his sonnet on Sardanapalus, but it should be read for its absolute value, its dignified swing, its structural force, and its effort to condense thought:

> Thassyrian king in peace, with foule desire,
> And filthy lustes, that staynd his regall hart,
> In war that should set princely hartes on fire:
> Did yeld, vanquished for want of marciall art.
> The dint of swordes from kisses seemed strange:
> And harder, than his ladies syde, his targe:
> From glutton feastes to souldiars fare, a change:
> His helmet, farre above a garlands charge.
> Who scarce the name of manhode did retayn,
> Drenched in slouth and womanish delight,
> Feble of spirte, impacient of pain:
> When he had lost his honor, and his right:
> Proud, time of wealth, in stormes appalled with drede,
> Murthered himself to shewe some manful dede.

A like grandeur distinguishes the sonnet which praises Wyatt for his translation of some of the Psalms of David. The humanist is betrayed in an allusion to Alexander preserving Homer's poems in an ark of gold, and is revealed elsewhere also, even in the love effusions, for instance in that curious lyrical piece, "When raging love," in which the poet consoles himself for his heartaches by thinking of the countless ills endured by the Greeks before they became masters of Ilion.

Nature and the poets of antiquity alternately console Surrey for his lover's griefs and his sadness when he is in prison. His most intimate poem is that in which, "prisoned in Windsor he recounteth his pleasure there passed":

> Where I in lust and joy
> With a king's son, my childish years did pass,

the allusion being to his close friendship with the Duke of Richmond, natural son to Henry VIII. The elegy depicts his early joys—games, hunting, the "secret groves" and the "wild forest," above all the pleasures of friendship:

> The secret thoughts, imparted with such trust,
> The wanton talk.

No other poem gives in so short a compass a richer description of the luxurious and chivalrous life of a young nobleman:

> The palme-play [1] where, despoiled for the game,
> With dazed eyes oft we by gleams of love
> Have missed the ball, and got sight of our dame,
> To bait our eyes, which kept the leads above.

Remembering that nearly all Surrey's verses have a just and sure harmony, it is impossible to exaggerate the loss which English poetry suffered by his premature death. Less directly influenced by the Italians than Wyatt, he had a perfectly just sense of what befitted the poetry of his nation. For the sonnet on the Italian model cultivated by his friend—two quatrains followed by two tercets—he substituted the less elaborate and easier English form which Shakespeare afterwards adopted, three quatrains with different rhymes ending with a couplet. But his chief title to glory is that he introduced blank verse into English when, probably in the prison which he left only to go to his death, he translated the second and fourth books of the Æneid. He may have been induced to make this translation by the example of Cardinal Ippolito de Medici (1541). The innovation is in the pure

[1] Tennis.

spirit of the Renascence. It was to be attempted in all modern languages, with unequal results. How indeed was it possible not to blush for rhyme which none of the ancients authorised by their example, and not to try to dispense with it when translating their hexameters? Surrey's blank verse is simply the decasyllabic or heroic metre shorn of its rhymes. Of classical origin, it is learned verse, in no way popular. That Surrey was able immediately to give it almost all its distinctive characteristics is remarkable. It had to be saved from too close resemblance to rhymed decasyllabic verse; it was necessary that the sense of the words should not be complete at the end of each line, for this would have caused the lack of rhyme to be felt and produced wearisome monotony. To avoid this defect, Surrey decided to imitate Virgil in dividing lines, letting the sense run on from one line to another. But he did this too little, and without the sure touch and facility which his imitators acquired long after him. His line is stiff and lacks ductility. But it catches the epic tone, and shows itself much more apt to render Virgil's poetry than a rhymed line. This partial translation, which was little removed in date from that of the Scottish Douglas, proves that a revolution had been accomplished between 1520 and 1540. If Surrey's verses are far from attaining to the smooth Virgilian beauty, he has dignity and often strength. Thanks to him, English poetry acquired a magnificent instrument which, once perfected, became the metre of the drama and of the epic.

Wyatt and Surrey published nothing in their lifetimes. It was not until ten years after Surrey had been legally murdered that Richard Tottel, the printer, brought their verses out, together with those of some inferior authors, in the famous collection of songs and sonnets commonly known as *Tottel's Miscellany*. The influence of the two poets could not therefore be felt immediately, nor did it take effect as soon as the *Miscellany* appeared, numerous though the readers of this collection were. A whole generation passed before the lead of Wyatt and Surrey was followed. The very form of the sonnet was almost forgotten, and the name was used to designate short poems of very varying structure, often mere songs. These two poets must be admitted to have been much in advance of their time, English poetry to have been unripe for their ingenious essay. Yet they were in no way in revolt against the national tradition. Wyatt was a great admirer of Chaucer, had read the old poet assiduously. Nor did he reject the French models traditional in his country, for he made translations of Melin de Saint-Gelais. But this Italianism did not take root in English poetry or bear fruit there until forty years after his death. Almost all the work of the French Pleiad was produced before England had made a step in advance. She did not even keep the position which these two young courtly writers had won for her.

3. **Sackville.**—Thomas Sackville (1536–1608),[1] the only poet after Wyatt and Surrey and before Spenser who left memorable verses behind him, reverted to the mediæval tradition. He was, none the less, a humanist who gave England her first classical tragedy. But chance willed that his only contribution to poetry, other than drama, was the *Induction*, which was followed by the *Complaint of the Duke of Buckingham*, written in 1563 for the *Mirror for Magistrates*. This *Mirror* was a series of stories concerning the misfortunes of the great figures in English history, and was written by several poets. Sackville conceived the idea of the collection, and his verses constitute its only merit.

The conception is in itself evidence of the patriotism which was impelling Englishmen to explore their annals. This enormous poem is founded on Lydgate's *Falls of Princes*, which was an adaptation of Boccaccio's *De Casibus Virorum Illustrium*, previously imitated by Chaucer in his Monk's Tale. The authors of

---

[1] *The Mirror for Magistrates*, ed. J. Haslewood, 3 vols. (1815). Sackville's complete works were edited by R. W. Sackville-West (1859).

I—L

the *Mirror for Magistrates* cull their examples not from universal but solely from English history, but this effect of recrudescent patriotism cannot be called a literary innovation.

Sackville's *Induction*, written in the seven-line stanzas (*ababbcc*) beloved of Chaucer, takes us back to the vision and allegories of the *Roman de la Rose*. As a dark winter night is coming on, and the poet is mournfully reflecting on the miserable end of the great ones of the kingdom, and wishing he could describe them in order "to warn the rest whom fortune left alive," he sees approaching the sad shape of Sorrow, who offers to guide him to the realms of the dead, where he will hear their complaints. Led by her, he sees at the gate Remorse, Dread, Revenge, Misery, Care, Sleep, Old Age, Malady, Famine and War. He crosses the Acheron, passes near Cerberus, and enters the kingdom of Pluto, where, first of the fallen princes, the Duke of Buckingham comes to relate to him his woes.

It is difficult to imagine a gloomier series of stanzas. The darkness is uninterrupted, and it is this very excess of misery which constitutes the novelty of the poem. Never, since Dante's *Inferno*, had the Middle Ages conceived a vision so tensely and implacably sinister. A stronger brush was needed, a palette richer in sombre hues, a more solemn tone, than any which belonged to the *trouvères*. The best of those old verses, even Chaucer's, had a certain frailty. The language was too slight, the rhythm not sufficiently marked. But Sackville used an English which had contracted its grammar and dropped its terminations, and he re-established alternating accents more regularly than even Wyatt and Surrey. Just because he wrote at a time when the accentual rhythm of verse was in process of being reconstituted, he exaggerated his scansion with a powerfully monotonous effect, which he further emphasised by repeated alliterations.

The men of the Renascence who re-established rhythm were preoccupied by ancient metres. It was they who first used the words *iambus, trochee* and *spondee* to denote the combinations of accentuated and unaccentuated syllables in their lines. Chaucer gave no thought to anything of the sort, but was guided by ear alone, and escaped the more rigid laws observed by the earlier poets of the sixteenth century, or rather such few of them as wished to restore metre. Versification wavered for some time between anarchy and excessive regularity before it reached equilibrium. Sackville belongs to the small number faithful to scansion, and he hammers out his syllables with striking emphasis but monotonous persistence. He has, however, undeniable artistic sense, and he uses this very ding-dong to reinforce the energy of his gloomy pictures. Spenser was inspired by him when he painted the most lugubrious scenes of the *Faerie Queene*, for instance the Cave of Despair, and even more when he wrote the melancholy stanzas of his *Complaints*, especially the *Ruins of Time* and the *Tears of the Muses*. Sackville really deserves to be called the connecting-link between Chaucer and Spenser. He lacked the variety of both these great poets perhaps because he soon left poetry for politics, ending as Lord Buckhurst and Lord High Treasurer. We have to judge his lyrical powers from a single lyric. His verses were isolated in a generation of which the poetic faculty was mediocre, hardly existent. He deserves the glory of having helped to renew English poetry.

4. Various Poets. Gascoigne.—Nothing could be emptier than this period. A bare mention suffices for the "tragedy" of *Jane Shore*, which was inserted by Thomas Churchyard in the *Mirror for Magistrates*, and was correctly versified but no more; for the *Eclogues* of Barnaby Googe (1563), poor in rhythm, Protestant rather than poetical; for the epitaphs, epigrams, songs and sonnets in which George Turberville modestly imitated Wyatt and Surrey; and for Thomas Tusser's advice to farmers and their wives, swelling in bulk from 1557 to 1573, *Hundreth Good*

*Pointes of Husbandrie, A Hundreth Good Poynts of Huswifery, Five Hundreth
Pointes of good Husbandrie.* Tusser's collection of practical counsels are completely
prosaic, yet have some go and wit, and they are written in popular four-accented
lines which seem to move at a gallop.

Verse continued for the most part to appear in collections or miscellanies,
issued by a bookseller and induced by the success of *Tottel's Miscellany*. They
were of diminishing interest. They included the *Paradyse of Daynty Devises* (1576),
by Richard Edwards, choirmaster of the Chapel Royal, and the *Gorgeous Gallery
of Gallant Inventions* (1578), collected by Thomas Proctor.

Only one writer deserves less cursory notice, George Gascoigne (1525?–77),[1]
who essayed to grope his way along all the new paths opened by the Renascence,
although he made no great advance on any of them. A soldier and a poet, he was
an amateur of poetry. Besides drama, he wrote in his youth love poems and slightly
scandalous confessions, his *Hundreth Sundrie Flowers*, "bounde up in one small
Poesie: Gathered partely by Translation in the fyne outlandish Gardins of Euripides, Ovid, Petrarke, Ariosto, and others, and partly by invention out of our owne
fruitefull orchardes in England." These *Flowers* only appeared in 1573. Meanwhile
the ageing author had become pious and moral. It was then that he wrote the *Glass
of Government*, in 1575, his satire in blank verse, the *Steel Glass*, in 1576, and the
Droome of Doomesday. To these should be added the short metrical treatise called
Certayne Notes of Instruction concerning the making of verse or ryme in English.
Whatever form he chose, Gascoigne was almost always first in the field, and he
is renowned for having written the first prose story taken from real life, the first
prose comedy, the first tragedy translated from Italian, the first masque, the first
regular satire and the first treatise on English prosody. But this versatility proves
him prolific rather than artistic. He writes easily, without brilliancy or distinction.
His blank verse is correct, but flat and dull; it reminds us of a hammer striking on
a wooden anvil. He has, however, a curious mind, he is discreet, and there is go in
his verses. His few innovations were so soon exceeded that hardly a trace is left
of them. At one time a disciple of Italianism, he afterwards repudiated this fashion.
His *Steel Glass*, which is his best-known work, compares the truthful metal mirror
of older days with the too flattering glass, doubtless of Venetian crystal, used by
the gallants and ladies of the poet's time. Here Gascoigne denounces the pro-
fanity and luxury of modern manners. He would revert to ancestral customs,
and in his *Notes* he analogously advocates the reduction of the vocabulary to
monosyllables, to the only words which were, in his opinion, of truly English
origin. It is curious to notice how nationalism awoke in all these men, who at
one time were humanists or Italianate, and with nationalism the desire to bar
out foreign importations.

---

[1] Complete works ed. by W. C. Hazlitt, 2 vols. (1869–70), and by J. W. Cunliffe in 1907, and
for the Cambridge University Press in 1910. See also the study on Gascoigne by F. E. Schelling
(Boston, 1893).

CHAPTER IV

1. **Humanism in the Theatre.**—English dramatic writing produced no masterpiece in this period, yet felt its way along the most various paths, and acquired an experience without which the Elizabethan drama would have been impossible. It partook both of the past which had survived, and of the future for which it was preparing.

The miracle-plays were performed almost till the end, although, since the Protestants looked askance at them, they gradually lost ground, and the cycles of the different towns disappeared, one after the other, as the Reformation advanced. In any case, these plays did no more than prolong their existence. They no longer changed: they merely persisted in the form which they had assumed in the fifteenth century. The interesting point is that they still had a large public, and that dramatic innovations did not supplant them, but were introduced side by side with them.

Moralities, on the other hand, did not only continue to be much appreciated, but were also modified and renewed in accordance with circumstances. Those produced until about 1520 were Christian and no more. They may be said to have had neither place nor date. But the moralities came to be impregnated with the spirit of the Renascence or the Reformation. Two distinct groups of them appeared, which voiced respectively humanist and Protestant tendencies.

Tedious though was the morality *Magnificence*,[1] written by John Skelton about 1516, it yet showed a new standpoint. It did not merely, like its predecessors, represent the struggle between Heaven and Hell. Skelton, who seems to have aimed at warning Henry VIII. against mad extravagance, does not deal with the great problem of Christianity, but enforces a particular moral lesson. His hero, Magnificence, is brought to ruin by a succession of bad counsellors, and would kill himself were he not saved by the intervention of Good Hope, Circumspection, Perseverance and others. This is the first specimen of a laicised morality.

In its two successors the spirit of the Renascence is much more clearly marked. They are inspired neither by the usual moral lesson nor by religious faith, but by the love of knowledge. Manifestly they were born in academic circles in which knowledge is the ideal goal and in which the devil is named Ignorance.

The morality of the *Four Elements*,[2] which was printed in 1519, and of which fragments are extant, is very curious. It is contemporary with More's *Utopia*. Like More, the author is under the influence of the tales of Amerigo Vespucci. He teaches geography, cosmography, almost all the sciences known to his time. The Messenger, who speaks the prologue, discourses gravely on science and deplores the lack of learned books in England and English. Only frivolous books, he says, are written in English, and only the rich man is esteemed wise in England. Yet true wisdom is in knowledge, in knowledge of God who can be known only by His works, and therefore in the study of nature. The play leaves theology on one side. The

---

[1] Edited by A. Dyce, *Skelton's Works* (1843), and by R. L. Ramsay (1906).
[2] Edited by W. C. Hazlitt in Dodsley's *Old English Plays*, vol. i. (1874).

subject is the instruction of the child Humanity, son of "Natura Naturata." He is entrusted to Studious Desire, but his progress is interrupted by the temptations of Sensual Appetite, who takes him to the tavern. The child has interpreted ill the words of Nature, who bade him use his senses. Only at the end of the play does he again show a taste for knowledge.

Sensual Appetite here plays the part of clown, as does his friend Ignorance, who detests philosophers and astronomers and boasts of his own power, saying that he is mightier than the king of England or France, that he is the greatest lord alive, and has more than five hundred thousand servants in England. He addresses the audience directly:

> For all that they be now in this hall,
> They be the most part my servants all,
> And love principally
> Disports, as dancing, singing,
> Toys, trifling, laughing, jesting;
> For cunning they set not by.

A geography lesson produces a burst of patriotism. Studious Desire instructs Humanity that the earth is round; Experience displays a globe, enumerates the countries she has visited, dwelling on America, and deplores that Spaniards, Portuguese and Frenchmen have gone farther than Englishmen:

> O, what a thing had be then,
> If that they that be Englishmen
> Might have been the first of all
> That there should have taken possession.

She would have wished all these countries to have been civilised and converted to religion by the English.

A like ardour to instruct fills John Redford's pedagogic morality, the *Play of Wyt and Science*,[1] which dates from the end of the reign of Henry VIII. Reason, after the manner of a high-born father, wishes to marry his daughter Science to Human Wit, the son of Nature. It matters not that Wit is neither well born nor rich:

> Wherefore, syns they both be so meet matches
> To love each other, strawe for the patches
> Of worldly mucke! syence hath inowghe
> For them both to lyve.

But Wit for long lacks wisdom. In his youthful eagerness to know, he imprudently attacks Tediousness and is saved only just in time by Honest Recreation. She, unfortunately, does not satisfy him, and he leaves her and falls asleep in the lap of Idleness. Without knowing it he has become a fool when, at last, he reaches the presence of Science, who repels him for an ignorant suitor. But in a mirror he sees himself as he is and is disgusted. After a term of chastisement and hard labour, he again attacks Tediousness, this time with a good sword, and slays him. Science, who has watched the encounter from the summit of Mount Parnassus, now accepts her destined spouse, first warning him:

> But yf ye use me not well, then dowt me,
> For, sure, ye were better then wythout me!

This is an ingenious and well-arranged morality, which is pervaded by strong rationalist conviction. It resumes the spirit of the Renascence well, and bears witness to the appetite for knowledge which caused schools and colleges to be born in the land. The comic element is supplied by an episode in which Ignorance is heard blundering through a lesson in the alphabet given him by his mother,

---

[1] In *Specimens of the Pre-Shakespearian Drama*, ed. J. M. Manly, vol. i. (1897).

Idleness. The mistress, who represents the old somnolent methods of teaching, is no less ridiculous than her idiot pupil.

2. **The Reformation on the Stage. Lyndsay. John Bale.**—Very early, the Reformation attempted to take possession of the morality and use it for its own ends. Passion, inevitably unjust and sometimes brutal, gave life to more than one Protestant morality-play. They appeared in the north and in the south. The first in date was written by the Scot Sir David Lyndsay whose reforming zeal we have already seen.

His *Satire of the Thrie Estaitis* [1] was played in 1540 at Linlithgow before the king of Scotland, the bishops and the people. It is as political as it is religious. The three estates are the nobles, the clergy and the merchants, and all three are pilloried together, censured for giving too much ear to Sensuality, Wantonness and Deceit. The grievances which John the Common Weal, the man of the people, has against them are just enough, and it is pleasant to see him obtain the needed reforms with the help of Good Counsel and Correction.

Lyndsay's special attack is against the Church. Dame Veritie, who desires access to the king, finds her way barred by the lords spiritual, scared at her advent. An abbot wishes to cast her into prison, and a parson recommends that she be put to death, under cover of the king's momentary subjection to Dame Sensuality. The same priest summons Veritie to declare by what right she is addicted to preaching. He threatens her with the stake, and when she refuses to retract, Flattery, a monk, exclaims:

> Quat buik is that, harlot, into thy hand?
> Out, walloway! this is the New Test'ment,
> In Englisch toung and printit in England:
> Herisie, herisie! fire, fire! incontinent.

In a comic interlude the social satire is dominant. Pauper recounts his misadventures. He used to keep his old father and mother by his labour and owned a mare and three cows. When his parents died the landlord took the mare as a heriot; the vicar seized the best cow at his father's, and the second best at his mother's, death. The third cow went the same way when his wife died of grief, when also the vicar's clerk bore off the uppermost clothes of the family. There is nothing left for Pauper to do but to beg. The parish-priest has refused him Easter communion because he no longer pays tithes. He has only one farthing in his pocket with which to plead for justice. A Pardoner arrives, boasting of his relics and insulting the New Testament, which sells to the injury of his trade. With his last farthing Pauper buys a thousand years' indulgence, but when he asks to see his purchase a fight ensues and the relics fall into the gutter.

These passages give an idea of the violence of the attack and of the life it imparted to the morality.

The Protestants of England were no less ferocious. Their most famous dramatic champion was Bishop John Bale (1495–1563), who even attempted to turn the fixed and traditional miracle-plays to Protestant uses. Under the name of tragedies, comedies and interludes, he wrote scenes in harmony with the reformed faith, taking them from sacred history and principally from the life of Christ. But he gave the chief of his efforts to morality-plays, combined with history which was sometimes contemporary, as in his *Proditiones Papistarum* and *Super utroque Regis Coniugio*. The most interesting of his dramatic essays is, however, his allegory *King Jehan* [2] in which he recasts history to his liking. He makes of the deplorable

---

[1] In David Laing's edition of Lyndsay's complete works (1879).
[2] Edited by W. J. Manly in *Specimens of the Pre-Shakespearian Drama*, op. cit., vol. i.

John a great king, hated and calumniated by the clergy. For John had been bold enough to rebel against Rome, and all his faults, crimes and cowardice are therefore wiped out. He is represented as a man misunderstood, a noble victim, the first Protestant. This play merits a particular place in the history of the theatre. It is the half-open chrysalis, the morality-play whence the historical drama is about to emerge. Real and allegorical characters are mingled in it. John is betrayed by Dissimulation and threatened by Sedition. Moreover, abstractions are changed in the course of the play into living beings. Sedition, for instance, becomes Cardinal Stephen Langton, Usurped Power the pope. This is a travesty of history and yet history, and, through the medium of another and Elizabethan work on the same reign, it was to leave its mark on Shakespeare's *King John*.

3. **Heywood's "Interludes." "Calisto and Meliboea."**—John Heywood's (1497?–1580)[1] interludes or farces, written under Henry VIII., cannot be called Catholic answers to Protestant attacks since they preceded the offensive of the Reformers. Two of them were printed as early as 1533. Heywood, a good Catholic and the friend of Thomas More, wrote in the mediæval tradition, in the spirit of the *fabliaux* which certainly did not spare churchmen. He was original in avoiding morality-plays and in having no purpose but to amuse. He has no notion of ecclesiastical or theological controversy. His *Interludes* are mere comic dialogues, scenes from *fabliaux* sometimes modelled on the French. But he is of his own nation almost the only representative of this school of dramatic writing. The four interludes which he certainly wrote are controversies in burlesque. In *Witty and Witless*, James and John discuss whether it be better to be a fool or a wise man: they are echoing the *Dyalogue du fol et du sage* performed at the court of Louis XII. In *Love*, an unloved lover and his unloving mistress seek, each of them, to prove himself the more miserable, while another couple, a lover beloved and a man who is neither loved nor a lover, dispute the right to be called the happier. In the *Play of Weather*, ten characters demand of Jupiter that he send them weather suited to their needs or desires, and the god finally decides that each of them shall be satisfied in turn. In the *Four P's*, four characters, a Palmer, a Pardoner, a Potycary and a Pedlar, discuss which of them shall tell the biggest lie. The pilgrim declares that in all his travels he has never seen a woman lose patience, and the others themselves allow that he has won the prize.

These plays are, it is seen, without plot, but Heywood puts life into his characters and expresses himself with a drollery which recalls Chaucer. There is a grotesque description of Hell equal to the Sompnour's in the prologue to his Tale. Good humour reigns everywhere. Yet these writings are hardly dramas. If, as is probable, Heywood also wrote the *Pardoner and the Friar* and *Johan Johan*, the story of a husband deceived by his wife, Tyb, and Sir Johan, the parish-priest, he came much nearer to farce in them. Their characters and incidents conform excellently to the old comic tradition, and their dramatisation could not be more vigorous. In these two pieces Heywood was inspired by French originals, *Farce nouvelle d'un pardonneur, d'un triacleur et d'une tavernière* and *Farce de Pernet qui va au vin*. Although he wrote under Henry VIII. he never even suggests the Renascence.

Not, that is, unless the comic monologue *Thersites*, played about 1537, may be ascribed to him on the evidence of style. Its subject and its allusions are loaded with classical reminiscences. The play is a free adaptation from the Latin of Ravisius Textor, or Jean Tixier de Ravisé, professor of rhetoric in Navarre College in Paris. Antiquity supplied the material for this farce, which had many analogies

---

[1] *The Dramatic Writings of John Heywood* (Early English Drama Publications, 1905); A. W. Pollard, *John Heywood, a Critical Essay* (Gayley's "Representative Comedies," vol. i., 1903).

with the *Franc Archer de Bagnolet*, and which brought the braggart on to the English stage for the first time.

Another novelty isolated in the reign of Henry VIII. was the adaptation of the famous Spanish play *Celestina* which was printed in 1530 as *Calisto and Melibœa*.[1] The English playwright has kept only the four first of the sixteen acts of his original. He has changed the long crowded drama with its tragic conclusion to a romantic comedy having a moral and cheerful ending. The character of the procuress Celestina, the descendant of Dame Siriz and the prototype of Macette, is indeed the same in the English as in the original version, but before she throws Melibœa into the arms of Calisto, the girl's father intervenes to save her on the brink of the abyss. Thus the didactic instinct cuts short a romantic drama.

4. **Progress of the Theatre after 1550.**—There was no further change in the first half of the century, but from 1550 onwards innovations came thick and fast.

It is about the middle of the century that the formation of troops of professional players, in addition to the amateurs who performed in the miracle-plays, can be clearly traced. In more than one school and more than one college of the universities there were performances especially of classical pieces, but usually they were written by the masters and acted by the pupils. But the people of the provinces as well as those of the capital wished to be amused, and they were no longer satisfied with the miracle-plays and moralities. Interludes, otherwise farces, were in great demand and were provided by professional actors. These were at first poor wretches, always under suspicion, who were harried by the authorities as rogues and vagabonds. Before they could be left in peace they had to obtain the patronage of a magnate, a baron at the least. There was no lack of such willing protectors who appreciated their services. The first company to obtain letters patent was Leicester's, in 1574, but it was not the first to stroll about the country. In London the players were at the mercy of the civic authorities, who made their life hard, less perhaps from Puritan prejudice, than because the highly popular dramatic performances constantly gave occasion for disorder, and by attracting a great concourse of spectators might spread the plague, during these years in which it was endemic.

Against the persecuting Lord Mayor the actors invoked the help of the queen and the magnates. Their chief plea was that they contributed to the queen's pleasure and had need of practice in order to be worthy to play before her. The Privy Council supported them against the City. They first played in London in the courtyards of certain inns. Then, to escape constant annoyance and prohibitions, some of them built, in 1576, their first theatre, outside the city but on its confines, on waste land in Shoreditch.

London meanwhile enjoyed more select performances. The Inns of Court were a home for the drama of classical tendencies, and a connecting-link between the stage of the universities and that of the popular theatres.

That the queen might be ensured a supply of worthy actors, the choristers or children of the Chapel Royal were trained to perform plays, both those specially written for them by the master of the Chapel Royal and others. These boys, both singers and actors, performed for the public as well as for the court, and were for some fifty years the dreaded competitors of adult and professional actors. Their example was followed by other London schools—St. Paul's, Westminster, and Merchant Taylor's—where the most gifted pupils were trained to act and were proud to contribute to the royal diversions. Nothing, not Puritan disapproval nor civic alarms, could stem the growing passion for the theatre which was felt by the whole nation —nobles, burghers and people.

[1] Hazlitt's *Dodsley*, op. cit., vol. i. *Six Anonymous Plays* (Series I., ed. Farmer, 1905).

(*a*) THE CLASSICAL INFLUENCE. COMEDY.—The first English comedy of the classical school was *Ralph Roister Doister*,[1] written about 1533 by Nicholas Udall (1506–56), headmaster successively of Eton and Westminster. Instead of making the Westminster boys act Plautus, Udall wrote for them, according to the laws of the classical drama, a comedy in five acts, inspired by Latin comic plays. He borrowed some characters from the ancients, but took others straight from English life. The hero Ralph recalls the Pyrgopolinices and Therapontigone of Plautus, is swaggering, stupid and fatuous as they. Since the play is intended for school-boys, Udall does not make him a libertine as in the Latin original, but a man really in love, even sentimentally and tearfully amorous. As he endows him also with avarice, so that he keeps an eye on his lady's dowry, the character is confused and lacks verisimilitude. Side by side with Ralph appears Merrygreek, a parasite from ancient comedy, but one who plays his part for fun rather than self-interest. It is the parasite about to be changed into Mascarille or Scapin.

Besides these imitated characters, there is the heroine, Dame Constance, who is courted by Ralph, a worthy and chaste matron annoyed by an impudent fool. When she knows that she has been slandered to the merchant Goodrich, whom she loves honourably, she sends up to heaven a fine prayer for protection. About her are her maids, one young and the other old, real English servants painted with merry realism. In fact, Udall accepts aid from Plautus, but has no superstitious veneration for him. His aim, like that of his contemporary Rabelais, is to amuse, "for mirth," he says, "prolongeth life and causes health." The principal scenes are that in which Merrygreek reads to Constance a love-letter from Ralph and makes it insulting by revising the punctuation, and that in which the roisterer besieges his mistress's house and, in spite of a warlike disguise—Merrygreek has put a hen-coop on his head for a helmet—is routed by the dame and her maids.

Udall may have had a moral purpose—he may have desired to satirise glory—but his chief aim was to cause innocent laughter. He has not only produced a farce on the classical model, but has also constructed a plot without expelling gaiety. His verse is stiff and stilted, but his language has a savour.

There is even more go in a farce performed about the same time in Christ's College, Cambridge. This takes nothing from antiquity except its distribution in acts and its regular construction. Subject and characters are completely English and completely rustic. *Gammer Gurton's Needle*,[2] which was printed in 1575, was written by a Master of Arts of the university, reputedly by a certain William Stevenson. Gammer Gurton loses the needle with which she sews breeches for her servant Hodge. The good-for-nothing Diccon persuades her that it has been stolen by her neighbour, Mother Chatte, and quarrels and recriminations follow. The whole village is turned upside down. The parson intervenes, and Diccon takes advantage of the confusion to steal a ham. Finally Hodge utters a scream and the needle is found sticking in his breeches, and all is thereupon discovered. This story is not refined, but the dialogue has go; the rhymed verse, nimbler than Udall's, lends itself to comic effects; the realism is not adulterated by borrowings from antiquity; and there is an unsurpassable drinking-song, "Back and side go bare."

(*b*) THE CLASSICAL INFLUENCE. TRAGEDY.—But farces, even when they were divided into acts in the ancient manner, could not lead to dramatic progress. They had had a place in the miracle-plays. The novelty was all in the isolation of the comic element. It was in tragedy that the national theatre and the theatre of antiquity came together most significantly.

Like the Italians and the French, the English were far more inspired by Seneca

---

[1] Reprinted by E. Arber (1868). See also Manly's *Specimens*, op. cit., vol. ii.
[2] In Manly's *Specimens*, op. cit., vol. ii.

than by the Greek theatre.[1] He was a somewhat dangerous model, for his were oratorical tragedies, and it is a moot point whether they were written to be staged or to be declaimed. He used again the mythological themes of the Greeks, but used them, like a romantic, neither for their national sentiment nor because he believed in their legends, but for their brilliancy. He knew nothing of dramatic movement, and there is no action in his tragedies. His characters rarely voice real sentiments: their speeches abound with maxims; their language is emphatic and lyrical, full of choice metaphors which show great force of oratory and real subtlety in analysis. Long monologues alternate with passages made up of short questions and answers, each crowded into a single line. Seneca's political allusions are frequent and he often attacks tyrants. Most of these characteristics recur in the work of his imitators, but what they have taken from him by preference is certain of his expedients, sometimes his choruses and more often the phantom who has the duty of explanation. Above all, they have been impressed by the atrocity of his subjects, and have learnt from him to associate the idea of tragedy with that of crime, nearly always monstrous crime. *Agamemnon* and the horrors of the Atrides, *Œdipus*, *Medea*, *Phædra*, and, above all, *Thyestes* and the horrible banquet of Atreus, led to tragedies of atrocious vengeance like *Titus Andronicus* and the *Duchess of Malfi*.

Five of Seneca's plays were separately translated and perhaps performed between 1559 and 1566, before the translation, published in 1581, of his *Ten Tragedies*. As early as 1562 Thomas Sackville and Thomas Norton produced the tragedy of *Gorboduc, or Ferrex and Porrex*,[2] which was imitated from him although it had an independence. Sackville was the author of the *Induction* to the *Mirror of Magistrates* and the best poet of his day, and both playwrights were lawyers and politicians. Their tragedy was given in one of the Inns of Court.

Seneca's influence is apparent in the uninterrupted seriousness of the play, in the sustained nobility of the style, in the almost abstract character of the scenes, where all the action falls to messengers and to confidantes, male and female, in the abundant speechifying and also in the sanguinary plot. King Gorboduc abdicates in favour of his two sons, Ferrex and Porrex, who, like another Eteocles and Polynices, at once take up arms against each other. Ferrex is slain, and their mother, whose favourite son he is, kills her other son, Porrex, the slayer. The people are angered, rise in rebellion, and put father and mother to death. Anarchy, usurpation and the death of the usurper ensue.

In spite of these piled-up crimes, the play is cold and lacks movement and drama. Its authors were better fitted to express ideas than to put life into characters. They had a didactic aim, for they wished to depict the misfortunes of a kingdom to which the succession is uncertain—a constant preoccupation of Elizabethan politicians—and the horrors which accompany civil war and result from anarchy. Their tragedy would assuredly have interested Corneille had he known it. It is Seneca after the style of lawyers and members of parliament. The authors have a certain originality because of the didactic sense which, in spite of everything, connects Gorboduc with the moralities, and because of the patriotic feeling which made these young humanists choose their subject from the annals of England, as the subject of *King Lear*, with which it has analogies, was thence taken. They stand less apart from the national tradition than at first appears from their superficial resemblance to Seneca, that is, from their use of choruses, and their cult of gloomy effects combined with their rejection of the spectacular. But the symmetrical plan of their scenes—Ferrex and Porrex consulting their good and their

---

[1] *Cambridge History of English Literature*, vol. v. chap. iv.; J. W. Cunliffe, *The Influence of Seneca on Elizabethan Tragedy* (1893); F. L. Lucas, *Seneca and the Elizabethan Tragedy* (1922).
[2] In Manly's *Specimens*, op. cit., vol. ii.

bad adviser in turn, advisers who are almost as much abstractions as vice and virtue—betrays an artless simplification inspired by morality-plays rather than by Seneca. That the moral of the play may be the more distinct, and perhaps also that spectators unused to such heights of seriousness may be diverted, each act opens with a pantomime in which the lesson it conveys is illustrated.

This is therefore no mere academic tragedy. It is a work which stands first in a line of succession, the first unrelieved English tragedy and therefore the play which led to Kyd's *Spanish Tragedie*. It brought the idea of fatality on to the English stage. In spite of its great defects it established a high artistic level. Finally, it was the first play in which the blank verse formed under the influence of antiquity was used. The metre which Surrey had invented for his translation of Virgil served Sackville and Norton when they emulated Seneca. They handled it forcibly and with dignity, but were incapable of giving it the ductility necessary to the stage. Twenty-five years were to pass before their initiative was followed triumphantly. Their merit is that, though they did not reach success, they attempted.

(*c*) VARIOUS INFLUENCES.—*Gorboduc* was significant, but appeared in isolation. Round about this play there were many tentative efforts and importations from abroad, all of them pointing English drama along different paths. It has been possible to group several plays under the title "Prodigal Son Series." [1] This time the prototype was a work by a Neo-Latinist, the Dutchman Gnaphœus whose *Acolastus* had been translated by John Palsgrave in 1540. He was imitated with great talent and with original additions in *Misogonus*, performed about 1560. The author, uncertainly identified as Thomas Richardes, wrote a strongly constructed and well-arranged play, enlivened by frankly comic scenes. The morality *Nice Wanton*, which appeared about 1560, connects with the same series and is a commentary on the adage "Spare the rod and spoil the child." In 1575 George Gascoigne produced his *Glass of Government* imitated both from *Acolastus* and from the *Rebels* of Macropodius.

George Gascoigne, ever in quest of novelty, is the best witness to the diversity of the influences operative at this time and of the sources whence plays derived. Besides the *Glass of Government* he wrote *The Supposes*, a prose translation of a comedy by Ariosto, and *Jocasta*, a tragedy which purports to be a translation from the *Phœnissæ* of Euripides, but is in truth a rearrangement of the Greek tragedy by the Italian Lodovico Dolce.

Italian influence is yet more apparent in a free adaptation by an unknown author of the Florentine Grazzini's *La Spiritata*, under the title *The Bugbears* (1561), in which a son obtains three thousand crowns from a miserly father by frightening him at night with noises attributed to ghosts, and is thus enabled to marry his mistress. Other plays inspired by Italian comedies also appeared, but only their names have been preserved.

(*d*) FORMATION OF THE NATIONAL DRAMA.—Each of these classical, neo-classical and Italian influences had its part in blazing the track to the English national drama, which absorbed the most diverse elements. But the plays of this period which belong to one group were not adaptations but truly English, and although they have weaknesses and an element of the ridiculous, they reveal the national drama as already almost a reality. They conform to that broad type which was finally adopted for drama and was followed by Shakespeare and his contemporaries.

Dramas of this type still partook of the morality-plays, at least in right of certain characters, but they tended more and more to stage the scenes of an episode of history or a romance, and they were wont to relieve tragedy or romance

---

[1] See for this group *Cambridge History of English Literature*, vol. v. chap. v.

by scenes of broad comedy, more or less skilfully related to the principal plot, thus observing the great tradition of the miracle-plays.

The most striking of these plays are *Appius and Virginia* (1551?), *Damon and Pythias* (1564), *Horestes* (1567), *Gismond of Salerno* (1567), *Cambyses* (1569) and *Promos and Cassandra* (1578).[1]

Three are obviously connected with the moralities. Like Bale's *King John*, they mingle abstractions and real characters. *Horestes* is entitled "A Newe Enterlude of Vice Conteyninge the Historye of Horestes" (Orestes). *Appius and Virginia*, of which the ridiculously emphatic language remained dear to Shakespeare's Pistol—"The furies fell of Limbo lake"—dramatises the well-known story of Virginius, who slew his daughter to save her from the wicked judge Appius. Appius is impelled by the vice called Haphazard, and Conscience and Justice appear to him. Homely and comic scenes alternate with tragedy. There is a curious mingling of all the earlier dramatic elements with a classic theme.

Cambyses is yet more significant. The author is usually identified as Thomas Preston, Master of Arts of King's College, Cambridge, a learned man who became master of Trinity Hall. The marked and yet artless bad taste of the style has thrown doubt on this authorship, yet the play shows signs of having been written by a humanist, for Herodotus is followed step by step, and there are many mythological reminiscences. The full title, as printed, is very characteristic, *A Lamentable Tragedie mixed full of plesant mirth containing the Life of Cambises, King of Persia, from the beginning of his kingdome unto his Death, his one good deede of execution, after that, many wicked deedes and tyrannous murders committed by and through him, and last of all, his odious death by Gods Justice appointed.*

Preston's method is that of the authors of the miracle-plays. He cuts up the story from Herodotus into scenes as they did the Scriptures. Not the whole of the story is in his play, but nearly all of it. He makes no attempt to weave a plot or by simplification to give unity to characters. Cambyses is represented in all the diversity and chronological incoherence of his actions. He begins well by ordering the execution of a prevaricating delegate, then, impulsive under the influence of wine, commits a series of atrocious crimes, almost all of them instantaneously, and passes immediately from the exaltation of love at first sight to passionate and murderous fury against his new-made bride. The playwright, by refusing to make any selection among the deeds of his hero, has rendered him lifelike and complex enough, has shown his double physical and moral nature and given him a temperament. There is here a character which ought already to be called Shakespearean.

Cambyses is not always on the stage, but gives place to buffoons. We can discern, in the raw, the expedients of a playwright who, chiefly by varying his scenes, appeals to a heterogeneous public, caters for coarse as for other tastes in order to reach all his audience.

Allegorical mingle with historical characters, the better to bring out the moral, the most important abstraction being the vice called Ambidexter, whose part it is both to impel to evil and to ensure the punishment of the guilty. Ambidexter is a cynic who takes pleasure in discovering and encouraging human perversity, and revels in the sight of foolishness. In his chuckle we seem already to hear Iago, even more Gloucester (Richard III.) winning Queen Anne's heart by false protestations of love. This is the sardonic, diabolical and sharp-sighted sinner, bad all through, without a trace of conscience, snapping his fingers at prejudices, his philosophy a fundamental atheism.

---

[1] *Appius and Virginia* and *Damon and Pythias* are printed in Hazlitt's *Dodsley*, vol. iv.; *Promos and Cassandra* in Hazlitt, *Shakespeare's Library* (1875), vol. vi.; *Cambyses* in Manly's *Specimens*, op. cit., vol. ii.

The connection of the buffoonery with the tragedy is weak, yet exists and is already a little Shakespearean. Thus, Cambyses has just decided to make war on Egypt when three soldiers enter, rejoicing in the prospective expedition, counting on slaughter and plunder. The truth, as undoubted in the days of Cambyses as in the sixteenth century, is illustrated that war is not the exclusive concern of princes and generals, but is as much the common soldier's business as the king's. Similarly Shakespeare, when he deals with Falstaff's enrolments, shows the seamy side of the glorious profession of arms, adopting the point of view he keeps in all his popular scenes, whether English or Roman. It is the tradition of the miracle-plays combined with that of the morality-plays.

In *Cambyses* all the elucidation of the plot is spectacular. The murders are not recounted, as in *Gorboduc*, but the playwright carefully stages them in full. He reproduces the execution of Sisamnes who is beheaded and scalped—the artless stage directions stipulate for a false skin—his scalp being afterwards pulled down over his ears. On the stage, Cambyses, to prove that he is not drunk, pierces the son of Praxaspe full in the heart with an arrow.

At the same time, this author carries pathos to the highest point. He puts into the mouth of the dying child of Praxaspe touching complaints which bring tears perforce. The scene recalls little Isaac ready to go to the stake in the mystery of *Abraham,* and anticipates the child Arthur in Shakespeare's *King John* seeking to move Hubert who has been ordered to burn out his eyes. But Preston reaches a yet higher degree of pathos. He sends a mother to mourn over the body of her son, and causes Cambyses to have the child's heart cut out that the father may know it was wounded in the very centre. After this, how could an audience be satisfied with only hearsay of butchery, messengers' tales?

To compensate for these episodes, Preston gives his public an open-air scene, a garden in which a fair lady and a lord stroll along the paths while the lord supplies the absence of scenery by describing the landscape and the flowers. Thus a breath of fresh air blows through the horrors of the melodrama.

This play reveals on examination all the characteristics of English drama of the great period. It lacks only two things, genius and style, or rather, perhaps, only one, genius made manifest in style.

The awkwardness of Preston's writing was so complete and his bombast so ridiculous that his play, after a long term of popularity, became the laughing-stock of succeeding dramatists. Shakespeare amused himself by parodying it in Falstaff, who says, when he wishes to use fine language, "I will do it in King Cambyses' vein." Preston's rhetoric is in the highest degree both frantic and artless. Some of his metaphorical epithets have the most ludicrous effect, as when a character speaks of her "christall eyes," or the mother of little Praxaspe of her "velvet paps." Moreover, the playwright is so little at his ease with the fourteen-syllabled rhymed lines which he uses for tragic passages, that he mutilates grammar by the suppression of articles or by most astonishing inversions in the very places in which he aims at simple statements of fact.

Undoubtedly the great lack was of a metre fitted to drama, a ductile line which would leave freedom of movement to the playwright. Failing this, verse might have been relinquished for prose. In verse, the attempt made in *Gorboduc* had not yet been pursued, and prose had been tried only by Gascoigne in his *Supposes.* English drama made decided progress when a flexible metre had been adopted, more or less generally, and when prose was used with increasing frequency. As for the remaining and too prominent traces of the morality-play, it was not difficult to get rid of them. Even in *Cambyses* they appeared only in the names of characters. To eliminate them from that play it would have been necessary only to rebaptise a few supernumeraries, including Ambidexter, who were still called after abstractions. Richard Edwards, the author of *Damon and Pythias*, a far better if a possibly less significant play than *Cambyses*, contrived to do without abstractions altogether. He produced a tragi-comedy which, save for its versification, would not have seemed out of place had it appeared among a number of others of the great period. The same praise could be given to Whetstone, who wrote *Promos and Cassandra* in 1578, and from whom Shakespeare derived *Measure for Measure*, that gloomy comedy. Hitherto all had been experiment, but the advent of the works undeniably great was very near.

BOOK IV

THE FLOWERING OF THE RENASCENCE (1578–1625)

CHAPTER I

GENERAL CHARACTERISTICS OF THE GREAT PERIOD

1. The Translations. Their Number and their Influence.[1]—Although the great Renascence period, often somewhat inexactly called the Elizabethan age, came to be markedly original, its literature had its rise among a multitude of ancient and foreign influences. The rich soil was fertilised by a deep layer of translations. By 1579 many of the great works of ancient and modern times had been translated into English, almost all of them by 1603, the end of Elizabeth's reign. Some of these translations formed current reading and some became as popular as the best writings of English authors. There were certain of them which had an influence equal to that of the masterpieces of the age.

It is easier to notice the rare exceptions constituted by the few important works which were omitted than to enumerate the Greek and Latin authors done into English during the century. It is surprising that, at a time when Platonism awakened so much enthusiasm and inspired so many poets, Plato was, save for some fragments, neglected by the translators, and that, while the English theatre was enjoying an unmatched flowering season, the Greek tragedians were forgotten. Æschylus and Sophocles were not touched. Nor was Euripides, save for his *Phœnissæ*, of which Gascoigne, in 1559, produced a version entitled *Jocasta*, but one which he borrowed from the Italian. Of the Latins, Plautus was overlooked except for *Menœchmi*, which was translated by Warner in 1595, although English comedy more than once followed in the footsteps of Plautus.

Among the moderns, no translation was made of Machiavelli's *Il Principe*, although this book was a veritable guide to many statesmen, and was commented on and, above all, attacked by many writers. Nor was there any translation of Rabelais—the first appeared in 1653—although he was known to several authors and imitated by them.

Of famous books, few besides these escaped. Practically all the others, of the past and of the present, were brought under contribution. It is true that all the translators were not able to use their originals directly, as was Philemon Holland, that good humanist and general translator of his century, who gave his country Livy (1600), Pliny the Elder (1601) and Suetonius (1609), not to mention Plutarch's moral writings (1603). But most used Italian and, in particular, French versions as intermediaries. Thomas North retranslated Plutarch's Lives, basing himself on Amyot's text (1579).[2] Thomas Nicolls, citizen of London, borrowed his Thucydides (1550) from the French of Claude de Seyssel, whose own translation of the Greek historian had been based on the Latin of Laurentius Valla. Adlington's

---

[1] *Cambridge History of English Literature*, vol. iv. chap i. Many of these translations have been reprinted in the *Tudor Translations*.
[2] In *Tudor Translations* (1895).

version (1566) of the *Golden Ass* of Apuleius was taken from Guillaume Michel's translation, his *Ethics* of Aristotle (1547) from the Italian, and his *Politics* (1597) from Leroy's translation. Sometimes French was an intermediary even between Italian and English, as for Bandello, who reached England by way of Belleforest's version.

These indirect translations were often not the least remarkable for their literary merit and their influence. The instance of Thomas North is typical. He improved on Amyot's homely style, and by the quality of his idiomatic English produced a really national book. So lucid are his narratives, with such ease and precision does he tell his stories, that he does not suggest a translation. With a less sure and a more fanciful touch, but with a style which is full of go, John Florio, in 1603, gave Montaigne's essays[1] to England. Like Plutarch's Lives, they became the everyday reading of many. Next to the Bible, they were the most widely known of foreign productions.

The translations in verse are more unequal. Some are deplorable, like Stany-hurst's *Æneid* (1582), in which the impossible hexameter is used, together with a most baroque vocabulary, interspersed with contemporary slang and trivialities. This is an involuntary caricature of the most harmonious of poets. Phaer's *Virgil* (1562), while without such absurdities, lacks any positive merit, as do the translations by Golding of the *Metamorphoses* of Ovid (1565-7), by Sir John Harrington of *Orlando Furioso* (1591), and by Carew (1594) and Fairfax (1604) of *Gerusalemme Liberata*.

Du Bartas, who was admired as a Huguenot no less than as a poet, who was called the "treasure of humanism and jewel of theology," was happier than Ariosto or Tasso, for Sylvester, between 1590 and 1606, produced a vigorous translation of his *Semaine*, as bombastic and fantastic in style as the original, abounding in the composite epithets which the French soon rejected, but which found a home in English poetry, the English language being more adapted and propitious to their use than the French. This translation met with a considerable and a prolonged success.

But the masterpiece of verse translation was incontestably Chapman's *Homer*. Thanks to Chapman, the Iliad (1598-1609)[2] became a great Elizabethan poem, vehement, rich in verbal audacities. It was doubtless far removed from the serene Greek simplicity, but its energy and brilliancy were such as to impassion, two centuries later, the young Keats, who had no access to the original sources of Hellenism.

These translations from du Bartas and Homer really became part of the treasure of Elizabethan verse, as the versions of Plutarch and Montaigne belong to the great prose. The same might be said of the passages from Ovid and Lucan, reproduced by a poet like Marlowe, or of du Bellay's *Visions* and *Ruines de Rome*, as rendered by a master of rhythm like Spenser. Side by side with these patent and frankly avowed translations, dissimulated borrowing and plagiarising were frequent in this period in which literary copyright was disregarded. It will be seen that the sonneteers were the most considerable of the borrowers. English style and prosody were formed by these countless translations. They profited the great, the writers who were not robbers, but who found their language waxing rich and pliable by the schoolboy exercises to which it was subjected.

2. Italianism.—Among the foreign influences one was incontestably dominant, that of Italy.[3] Elizabethan literature, which came to be the expression of the

[1] In *Tudor Translations* (1892-3).
[2] Reprinted in Morley's *Universal Library*.
[3] Einstein, *The Italian Renaissance in England* (1892); M. A. Scott, *Elizabethan Translations from the Italian* (Modern Language Association of America, 1895-9).

national genius, had its birth in Italianism. The word may seem too narrow when the large number of French works then circulating in England are considered, and also the influence exercised by Spain, especially through the medium of the chivalrous romances—*Palmerin, Amadis* and Montemayor's famous *Diana* were all done into English by Anthony Munday before the end of the century—and through the picaresque romance *Lazarillo de Tormes*, which was translated in 1576. Since, however, France and Spain were themselves impregnated with Italian culture, the English were apt to find Italy even in what these other countries produced. And in these years Italian books, like the journey to Italy, were the great matter in England. As well as the works already cited, Castiglione's *Cortegiano*, translated by Thomas Hoby in 1561, should be mentioned, the book whence the Elizabethan gallants derived the principles of courtliness. Of more consequence to the development of drama and the novel in English were the tales of the *novellieri*, the short stories told so dramatically, vivaciously and skilfully by Boccaccio, Cinthio, Bandello, Straparola and their like. It is not easy to imagine how English drama would have been nourished without these comic or tragic and often licentious stories, these tales of pleasure, love, violence, blood and tears. No complete translation of them was made at this time, but many of them appeared scattered among successive collections, such as those of Fenton and Painter in 1567, Whetstone in 1582, Turberville in 1587.

The meeting between the English and the Italian spirit which had already enriched Chaucer's poetry brought a wealth of splendour to sixteenth-century England. The English character was, however, already at this time too definite and too insular merely to reflect a foreign country. The Reformation had not yet penetrated the nation deeply, nor absorbed it wholly, but it had made so distinct an impression that there was necessarily a reaction against the prestige of the country which was the seat of Catholicism, and in which the Renascence had flowered with a sensual ardour reminiscent of paganism. By the second half of the century there were two opinions about Italianism; the new dangers to which Italy exposed her admirers were cited in opposition to her artistic attractions. We have seen that Roger Ascham, good humanist and good Protestant, gave up to this dispute half his *Scholemaster*, a book professedly about a method of translating Latin. It is true that the very violence of his attack throws into relief the fascination by which his contemporaries were held. He complains of the translations through which the products of Italian licence were steadily flowing into England, and his invective did not stem this stream. But Ascham's disapproval and that of the Puritans forced even the "devils incarnate," as they named those who returned from the peninsula, to depreciate the country which had at once dazzled and corrupted them. Usually the Italianate Englishmen criticised the books they themselves had imported, the morals which had corrupted theirs, the decadent civilisation which had given them a taste for forbidden pleasures. Though depraved, they felt that they still were not as the Italians. Italy, which excited the licentious imagination of the English, came little by little to be for them a land of unspeakable debauchery, the country of Machiavelism, crime and poison. It was their Utopia of irregularity. Thus both action and reaction must be discerned in the undeniable Italianism of the period. From being the stimulus and the model of England, Italy came to stand for the antithesis to the national character, which it defined by force of contrast. The literature of England was enriched by an immense looting of Italian treasures, and the spoils carried back to the island were there exhibited, not only as marvellous works of art, but also as objects of reprobation.

3. **Patriotic Exaltation.**[1]—More than three-quarters of the sixteenth century

[1] See Jusserand, *Histoire Littéraire du Peuple anglais*, op. cit., vol. ii. book v. chaps. i. and ii.

I—M

passed before English literature did more than grope its way. Elizabeth, who was to name the great period, had been twenty years on the throne before a definitive step had been taken. By two successive advances, the one made in 1578, while Drake was sailing round the world, the other in 1589, on the morrow of the Armada, England caught up with her continental rivals, if indeed she did not outpace them.

About the year 1578 appeared John Lyly's *Euphues* and Spenser's *Shepheard's Calendar*, and all Sidney's work, in verse and prose, was written at about the same time, although it was not published until after his death. The impulse for this production was derived from patriotism. It sprang from England's growing consciousness of strength, her pride of prosperity, the spirit of adventure which animated her sons and caused them always to aspire to the first place, and her faith in her own destiny.

Everything, even religion, combined to stimulate and reinforce this patriotism. For very many, Protestantism, now triumphant, was no more than deliverance from foreign supremacy. It was summed up in the rejection of the papacy. It broke the bonds which had for centuries connected England with the continent by subjecting her to Rome. If the English still conceived of union with Europe, they dreamt, with Sidney, of a confederation of all the Protestant states with England at their head, an association of the powers of good which should be ready to affront the powers of evil personified in Philip II., the Catholic monarch. The majority favoured an entirely insular Christianity, monopolising divinity for national ends. The Hebraic spirit was beginning to be substituted for the properly Christian spirit. The extreme formula of this overweening religious egoism was expressed by Lyly, who, in 1580, declared of God that he always had a tender care "of England, as of a new Israel, his chosen and peculier people," and who ended by announcing that "the living God is only the English God."

For most men, the exactions of God did not go beyond those of patriotism. Except for the still limited group to whom their faith was all in all, the Puritans who made it their first business to seek salvation, the people turned from such austere cares and gave themselves up to enjoying life. These were still the days of Merry England. The ardour of the first Reformers, their vehement preaching and the heroism of the martyrs under Mary Tudor, might give another impression, but in truth the country was still indifferent, if not sceptical, eager not for religion but for games and pleasure, ambitious of the free development which is the very spirit of the Renascence. The intellectual paganism of humanism rested on the broad basis of an instinctive paganism scattered wide among the people.

The manner of the official Reformation in England excluded edification. Several times over, the English in the sixteenth century passed from one form of religion to another, as a herd might change masters, without enthusiasm or revolt. Kept in the beginning of the Reformation within the bounds of orthodoxy by Henry VIII., the champion of the papacy, they allowed him, on the occasion of his divorce, to implicate them in the schism, and then accepted a sort of Anglican Catholicism, with a new pope in a king who was the slayer of women and the most hypocritical and bigoted of bloodthirsty princes. Under Edward VI. they became real Protestants, and followed the services of their church in a Lutheranised prayer-book. Mary Tudor easily re-established Roman Catholicism among them, and might perhaps have reunited England to the papacy permanently, had not the prevalent indifferent and conciliatory spirit been alarmed by the burning of the Protestant martyrs, and had not the queen's marriage to Philip II. irritated and disquieted patriotism. When Elizabeth restored Protestantism she did it amid general rejoicing, but as pope she was political, not devout, well fitted to govern men who desired independence of Rome, but were in no wise inclined to profound conviction or to proselytism. Public opinion supported the queen when she restrained the Puritans as when she opposed the Catholics.

4. The High Conception of Poetry.[1]—It was this tepid religious feeling which allowed literature to spring to vigorous life and the Renascence to flower. To the tardiness of the Reformation in closing its grip on the country England owes the glory of her drama, her most magnificent literary achievement, and also a large part of the glory of her other poetry under Elizabeth and James I.

This love of letters had its beginning in the patriotic pride which was impelling England to claim a pre-eminent place in every field of activity. She was nearly a whole century behindhand in maritime discovery and seafaring. With one bound she caught up with her rivals, Spain, Portugal and France, and insisted on outdistancing and ousting them. For the first time she was actuated by the spirit of imperialism. It gave birth to a swarm of tales of distant exploration and ensured their success, stories which do not exactly belong to literature, but were an element of literary animation and fertility. While Englishmen like Richard Eden, about the middle of the century, were translating and reproducing foreign stories of adventure, they were also becoming adventurers themselves and celebrating their own discoveries. In 1589 Richard Hakluyt published his great work *The Principall Navigations, Voiages and Discoveries of the English Nation made by sea or over land . . . at any time within the compass of these* 1500 *yeares*, and in 1598 issued a much augmented edition thereof. His task was continued by Samuel Purchas, who, in 1625, brought the chronicle up to date in *Hakluytus Posthumus*.

Literature was swept onwards by this spirit of conquest and self-glorification. England balanced her literary accounts and was ashamed to realise her poverty as compared to France, her indigence by the side of Italy, and her virtual destitution in comparison with antiquity. The latest in the field, she decided, arrogantly, to become the first. She had faith in her own genius and language, and also in her prosody if she could but reduce it to order. Hitherto she had been paralysed by timidity or by a certain languor, but she was now ready to be bold. She was prepared to venture on the various genres in which the ancients and the moderns had won distinction—pastorals, epics, comedies and tragedies, lyrics of every form, every kind of prose, romance, criticism, history and philosophy.

A magnet to draw her into each of these paths was the faith in the greatness of letters, and particularly of poetry, with which the Renascence had gradually inspired her. This faith made the poet the first of men. It was in 1579 that the Puritan Stephen Gosson, who had stigmatised poetry as a school of immorality, provoked Sidney's eloquent retort, his *Apologie for Poetrie*, written at the same time and in the same spirit as Spenser's lost treatise—the *English Poet*. Sidney recalls that to the Romans the poet was the *Vates*, the diviner or prophet, and establishes his superiority over the historian and the philosopher. "Of all Sciences," he says, " . . . is our Poet the Monarch." This gallant champion of jousts and battlefields esteemed that the poet deserved the laurel-wreath as much as the soldiers.

Spenser proclaims that heroes and famous poets are born together. He shows that civilisation and poetry advance side by side. In particular, he insists that poetry is "a divine gift and heavenly instinct not to be gotten by labour and learning, but adorned with both; and poured into the witte by a certain enthousiasmos and celestiall inspiration." It is true that this platonic doctrine was common to the men of the Renascence, but it seems especially to have penetrated English poetry,

---

[1] *Elizabethan Critical Essays*, ed. Gregory Smith, 2 vols. (1904); G. Saintsbury, *History of Criticism*, vol. ii., book iv., chap. v. (1902); J. E. Spingarn, *A History of Literary Criticism in the Renaissance* (1899).

which had almost its sole theoretical basis in a belief in the necessity of poetic enthusiasm. The Greek word recurs in English poetry in various vernacular forms, all of them proof of the assimilation of this article of faith. It is this enthusiasm which Shakespeare calls a "fine frenzy," which Drayton calls a "fine madness" when he is praising Marlowe or a "clear rage" when he is praising Shakespeare. None are poets who are not possessed of this demon. Drayton expects the poet to see "brave translunary things." The classical Daniel, a writer of pure and noble verse, is criticised by Spenser because—

> Yet doth his trembling Muse but lowly flie,
> As daring not too rashly mount on hight.

And Drayton disdainfully considers Daniel's "manner better fitted to prose."

There was insistence that the candidate for poetic glory should have exaltation, and this quality therefore became a current one, genuine in the great, simulated in others. The object of their transports was beauty, to which Spenser addressed a magnificent hymn, and which Marlowe, in a famous passage and with poignant melancholy, declared to be beyond complete expression:

> If all the pens that ever poets held
> Had fed the feeling of their masters' thoughts,
> And every sweetness that inspired their hearts,
> Their minds, and muses on admirèd themes;
> If all the heavenly quintessence they still
> From their immortal flowers of poesy,
> Wherein, as in a mirror, we perceive
> The highest reaches of a human wit;
> If these had made one poem's period,
> And all combined in beauty's worthiness,
> Yet should there hover in their restless heads
> One thought, one grace, one wonder, at the least,
> Which into words no virtue can digest.

The generation lived in this fever. Poetry was then neither the privilege of a caste nor the apanage of a few. It was widely disseminated, heated men's brains, and sometimes turned their heads, gave a lyrical turn to the whole of literature, beflowered and falsified the prose which was all poetic. To the poets whose names are known those many anonymous writers must be added whom a set of verses or a song, sometimes exquisite, proves to have had at least their hour of illumination. Everyone felt the breath that was passing—the passion for artifices of language, the perception that words hold something beyond their meaning, the pleasure in savouring words, the pleasure in the beautiful or at least in the fantastic. The courtier was surprised to find the man of the people as ingenious as himself. "The age is grown so picked that the toe of the peasant comes so near the heel of the courtier, he galls his kibe," says Hamlet, as he listens to the gravedigger's punning. The awakening of mind and imagination was sudden, lively and general. It occurred first at court, but soon spread throughout the nation.

5. **The Spirit of Independence. The Rejection of Strict Rules.**—For all the extensive borrowing from abroad and avowed respect for ancient precedents and traditional rules of conduct, and in spite of the passing fashions which temporarily made a law of the strange or the eccentric, the general impression conveyed is one of frank and free boldness. A wide initiative was left to individuals. This is apparent if the language and versification, the common instruments of poets, be studied. There was no established grammar to fix and stereotype syntax. The first English grammar, Ben Jonson's, was written under James I., but it perished when the author's house was burnt, and appeared in fragments only after his death. There was more than one *Art of Poetry* compiled, but none of them had acknowledged authority.

In the matter of grammar, the critics of to-day are surprised to discover that the separation of the parts of speech was not yet recognised. A dictum on Shakespearean grammar may be extended to the whole language:

> Any irregularities whatever, whether in the formation of words or in the combination of words into sentences, are allowable . . . almost any part of speech can be used as any other part of speech. An adverb can be used as a verb, . . . as a noun, . . . or as an adjective. . . . Any noun, adjective or neuter verb can be used as an active verb.[1]

The restriction was to the intelligible, and must be acknowledged not always to have been respected. On the other hand, writers were incessant creators, perpetual innovators. Words were not labelled and immobilised. There was something improvised and energetic in the mode of their use which became impossible in periods of fully constituted grammar.

Prosody also retained a mobility and pliability which had the happiest effect on true artists, although it misled the others to such licence that in the end verse relapsed to prose. It cannot be said that a fixed prosody existed at this time, that the value of each word had been established once for all and independently of its use. While in lyrics and solemn poetry words had their full and constant phonetic value, in dramatic verse they were increasingly governed by circumstances, and suffered contractions and extensions entailed by the need of speed or emphasis. One word might be taken to contain a varying number of syllables. Words were elastic, could shrink or expand. The astonishing blank verse of the theatre, especially of Shakespeare's plays, provides inexhaustible material for the study of these varying inflections which almost always are found to conform to one law, to follow nature, that is true passion or feeling.

Versification was not reduced to a single principle, but sometimes acknowledged the syllabic and sometimes the accentual law. Some verses are governed by no rule except that of the recurring *ictus*, or beats. They disregard both number of syllables and number of regular feet.

The great mass of the verse is at once syllabic and accentual. The heroic or decasyllabic line, either blank or rhymed, has precedence, and is found on analysis to contain, as a rule, five iambic feet. But it remains syllabic only in virtue of the elastic prosody. And it allows of very great diversity in the placing of accents and the character of feet. It is a much varied, sometimes a very subtle, subject of study. The line differs, moreover, with different poets. Spenser's rhymed line is very different from Donne's; Marlowe's, Dekker's, Fletcher's and Massinger's blank verse are of widely diverse types; and such a metrical evolution can be discovered in the course of the poetical career of Shakespeare, considered by himself, that it has been possible to found on it the chronology of his dramatic works.

Analogous remarks apply to the combinations of rhymes and stanzas. The couplet or rhymed distich, which was to be adopted almost exclusively by the classical school, was already used frequently, but in its structure there was a freedom which subsequently disappeared. Its rhythm is varied because the place of the pause is shifted and because the sense is often continued from one line to another. The line is rarely self-contained, as it came to be later, and it keeps, if it does not enlarge, the freedom of movement which Chaucer had given it.

English poets were curious of every happening in continental literature, and were aware of the rules for the use of masculine and feminine rhymes introduced by the Pleiad. In France, the principle of the alternation of the two kinds of rhyme was established when Sidney and Spenser began to write. Sidney was enough awake

---

[1] E. A. Abbott, *A Shakespearian Grammar*, p. 5.

to the law to observe it, with very happy effects, in some of his songs. But no one in England seems to have had the idea of making it absolute. Its establishment in France may be regretted. When alternation became the rule, the artistic, that is the free use of the two kinds of rhyme, had to be suppressed, and alternation gradually became a mnemo-technic device. It did not leave to the poet the decision of whether he would write a particular poem in masculine or in feminine rhymes, or a duly proportioned mixture of both, nor did it allow him to fortify ideas or feeling by suitable rhyme. Where choice should have been, or remained, free, a police regulation was introduced, and was accepted with surprising unanimity, not only for songs, but also for the longest narratives. At one blow, some harmonious combinations were ruled out, for instance the tercets of the sonnet, which was debarred from the *abc abc* disposition of lines. English poetry did without such rules. In the classical period it almost reached the point of abandoning the feminine rhyme altogether, or relegating it to the domain of humorous verse. But Elizabethan poetry proscribed nothing, and used feminine rhymes abundantly, never, however, in obedience to a mechanical external law, but always to produce an effect of sweetness and melody. This small point shows the divergence of form between the poetry of France and of England at the Renascence. In consequence, it was more possible in England than in France to refine on the varieties of the stanzas for which France had supplied the model and to multiply their types.

CHAPTER II

THE habitual distinction between prose and verse must be momentarily suspended in order to present together the three men who, about 1578, simultaneously, although with very unequal resources, were initiators of the literature dedicated to beauty. It is a distinction which loses importance at this time, because poetry penetrated everywhere. The prose of such romances as *Euphues* and *Arcadia* is entirely poetic. Only the drama really needs separate study. Lyly, except for his dramatic work, Sidney and Spenser are rightly presented side by side.

1. **John Lyly.**[1]—John Lyly (1554–1606) is the first in date of the writers who consciously and persistently used an artistic style and whose chief aspiration it manifestly was to say a thing well. It is even possible to ask if Lyly had any other clearly determined aim. But that his art was mainly artifice is a matter of little importance. He fulfilled the expectations of his fellow-countrymen so opportunely that his studied and strange way of writing set the fashion for a long period. For a good dozen years the "euphuistic" manner which he inaugurated reigned at court and spread thence through almost all literature.

The father of euphuism was born of a family of grammarians. He was the grandson of the William Lyly who was the friend of Erasmus and More. After studying at Oxford, "where I tyred at a drie breast three yeares," he went to London, and there, with the help and patronage of Lord Burleigh, was able to live by his wits, at first in the guise of a moralist. In 1578, at the age of twenty-four, he published his famous *Euphues, or the Anatomy of Wit,* a book filled with wise lessons and bristling with attacks on irreligion and immorality. The hero, Euphues, or the Well-Endowed, is a young Athenian—a disguise for an Oxford man— noble, handsome, quick-witted and with a passion for travelling, but also presumptuous, apt to misuse his gifts, and too little disciplined by education. He goes to Naples—which is to say London, or rather the Italianate society of the capital— a city which is a proverb for licence. He is deaf to the counsels of a wise old man who enumerates to him the vices of the town, and enjoys himself very much there, frequenting parties and festivities and succumbing to the charms of a siren. He loses all his virtue, even to his loyalty in friendship, and forsakes his evil courses only after he has himself been the victim of the perversity which surrounds him.

When a friend introduces him to his mistress, Lucilla, he falls in love with her, supplants this friend in her favour, and is about to marry her when the fickle lady transfers her preference to a third and unworthy suitor. Euphues thereupon leaves Naples in disgust and returns to Athens, the city of philosophers, to dwell there among his books.

This brief story, which seems to reproduce an actual experience of the author, ends with moral and religious dissertations. In turn, Euphues preaches caution against every woman, the reform of education—he translates Plutarch's treatise— and belief in God.

[1] *Euphues* reprinted by Arber (1868). *Complete Works of Lyly,* ed. Bond, 3 vols. (1902); A. Feuillerat, *John Lyly* (1910—a biographical and literary study).

The book had an undoubted success, proved by the four editions into which it ran in eighteen months, but it aroused anger in some quarters. Oxford complained of having been travestied, some smart thrusts had been made at ladies, and England protested against the rough handling she had received.

Of such things Lyly recked little. He was tenacious of his style but not of his ideas, and in 1580 he published *Euphues and his England*, in which he is prodigal of flattery to his country, its queen, its universities and, above all, its ladies. It is for them he writes. "*Euphues* had rather lye shut in a Ladyes casket than open in a Schollers studie." All the satire of the earlier book has gone. English beauty is declared unsurpassed. "There is no beautie but in England." Englishwomen are the most chaste of their sex, at whose altar Lyly sacrifices the women of Italy. Peace and religion reign under Elizabeth. "The living God is only the English God."

The slight narrative contained in this second book shows off the national virtues. The heroines are models of constancy and virtue. Iffida dies of grief because she has lost her Thyrsis and repels all the lovers who would console her. Camilla remains faithful to her Surius in spite of the suit of the inflammable Philautus. The story varies these perfections by witty and realistic scenes which faithfully portray London society, graceful analyses of feminine sentiment, and even an original character—Lady Flavia, the matron who has passed the age of passion, but likes to be surrounded by loving young couples, helping them while she mischievously reveals their manœuvres. Euphues is reduced in this book to a spectator whose business it is to express his admiration for England and the English.

Lyly, although he was preceded by the translators of the *novellieri*, Painter, Fenton and Pettie, has been justifiably called the first English novelist, that is the first storyteller who made it his business to paint society unromantically. But the matter of his *Euphues* did not, by a long way, delight his contemporaries as did the mannered graces of the style he affected.

There are in euphuism two distinct elements. There is first a principle of counterpoise and symmetry in sentences, a way of balancing clauses. The tendency in this direction was widespread in this century. Ascham, for instance, attained to symmetry by imitating Seneca's antitheses. Even the alliterations which Lyly used to emphasise balance had been employed by more than one of his predecessors, among others by Pettie in *A Petite Pallace of Pettie his Pleasure*. But Lyly does constantly and methodically what his forerunners did spasmodically. He makes a rule of the accidental. Moreover, he refines on their accomplishment. He doubles their simple alliterations, making his either direct or crossed (as in "The *h*ot *l*iver of a *h*eedlesse *l*over," or "Let my *r*ude *b*irth excuse my *b*old *r*equest"). A prose thus constituted is almost as regulated and measured as verse. Manifestly it suffers from excesses, and these are to-day more conspicuous than its other qualities. Yet the innovation it represented was of service at a time when there was need to cast the formless in a mould, to impart art to the inartistic.

The second element of euphuism is more peculiar to Lyly. He wished to decorate his style and knew not how to do it except by images and similes. It was necessary to render the abstract concrete. Unfortunately Lyly knew books well and nature very ill. He therefore had the idea of finding ornaments for his prose in ancient mythology and history and in fantastic notions of natural history borrowed from Pliny the Elder through the medium of the bestiaries, herbaries and lapidaries dear to the Middle Ages. These compilations contained a fabulous fauna and flora of great decorative value to old tapestries, which seemed to Lyly marvellously adapted to illuminating his pages as he desired. He was not himself a believer in the unnatural nature he describes, but then his search was not for truth, only for decoration.

It thus came about that he makes current use of these fantastic fictions as terms of comparison, adding to them yet more singular inventions of his own. In spite of their extravagance and complete unreality, they serve to prove his statements. The discord between form and substance is the more striking because he poses as a moralist. Yet what shocks us to-day then gave pure enjoyment. Lyly's ingenuity was admired, and his followers were pleased that they could imitate him without much difficulty, so plain was the recipe for this style of mechanical graces. Subsequently, it is true that the word euphuism lost its exact meaning and became synonymous with every kind of affectation and preciosity. The epithet was stretched to include the various artifices of Sidney, Shakespeare and Donne. Yet we have but to open *Euphues* and read a single page in order to discover the distinctive characteristics of this special disease of language. It recurred, in a slightly milder form, in Lyly's plays, where it was sometimes a virtue, giving point to retorts and balance to dialogue.

2. **Sir Philip Sidney (1554 – 86).** [1]—Lyly is a curiosity of literary history; Sidney and Spenser, his contemporaries, are great figures whose glory is still resplendent.

In his own generation Sidney successively enjoyed a personal and a literary prestige. Nothing he wrote was printed in his lifetime, all being published posthumously, and he first constituted the complete type of a gentleman of culture. He realised the chivalrous ideal retouched and perfected by the Renascence. In him the qualities of antique valour were combined with the new virtues for which humanism had created the need. He was not only the perfect knight, but also the lettered courtier, such as Castiglione would have him be. But until some years after his death men did not learn that this Bayard had also been a Petrarch.

Of very high birth, a grandson of the Duke of Northumberland and nephew of the Earl of Leicester, brave, always ready to lay down his life, an accomplished horseman who had won distinction in the lists, sensitive on the point of honour and unfailing in extreme courtesy even to the humblest, Sidney had adapted the virtues of chivalry to the needs of a new age. He was a politician and a diplomat, who dreamt of grouping the Protestant nations against the pope and the king of Spain under the leadership of England. He had a passion for letters and art. He knew the ancients well, and was conversant with modern languages, French, Italian and Spanish. He was saturated with Mediterranean culture, with knowledge not only of literature but also of the plastic arts of Italy, in which country he had stayed.

All these gifts and accomplishments enriched a nature which was serious, intense and tinged with melancholy. Before Sidney could realise the type of a gentleman he had to control the violent impulses to which he was subject. Gallantry did not satisfy the deepest needs of a soul capable of a great passion.

(*a*) THE "ARCADIA."—He revealed in his *Apologie for Poetrie* his ideal of noble and classical beauty in writing. But his spontaneous taste did not always agree with his reason. Losing his way in his quest of beauty, he sought it long in ornament and preciosity and in the vagaries of the most capricious fancy. His *Arcadia* was written about 1580 to beguile a momentary exile from court and to please his sister, the Countess of Pembroke. It is a romance in which he gives rein to his fantastic invention and lets his pen trace the strangest arabesques. From the time it was published, in 1590, it inculcated in a whole generation a taste for literary jewellery, both real and false.

---

[1] Complete works ed. by A. Feuillerat (Cambridge English Classics, 3 vols., 1914 et seq.). Lives of Sidney by Fulke Greville, Lord Brooke (1652, modern ed. by Nowell Smith, 1907) and J. A. Symonds ("English Men of Letters," 1886).

In this work Sidney mingles the pastoral and the chivalrous, a fusion already effected by Montemayor, the Spaniard, in *Diana*, and he brings together all the fantasies belonging to these two genres in stories hopelessly romantic.

The whole is a pastoral, since its action takes place almost entirely in the ideal Arcadia, whither King Basileus has retired and where he brings up his daughters as shepherdesses. The country is the most delightful in the world, its people the earth's happiest inhabitants. "Here a shepherd's boy piping, as though he should never be old; there a young shepherdess knitting, and withal singing, and it seemed that her voice comforted her hands to work and her hands kept time to her voice-music."

But this is above all a story of love and chivalry. Arcadia figures only as a background, and the peace of the beautiful country is disturbed by bloodthirsty wars. Passion, which Basileus would have kept remote from his daughters, is introduced by two strange princes, Musidorus and Pyrocles, who, disguised respectively as a peasant and a woman, make their court to the most virtuous Pamela and to radiant Philoclea. The king is smitten with Pyrocles, whose woman's guise deceives him, and the queen, who discovers the fraud, is consumed with guilty love for the same prince. The redoubtable Amphialus is enamoured of Philoclea, and with the help of his mother, black-hearted Cecropia, he for long keeps the maidens captive and repels with the strength of his arms all attempts to set them free. But all Cecropia's sophistry fails before their purity of heart. Vainly she whispers cynical counsels to Philoclea, threatens her with death, has her whipped and her sister also, shows her a false vision of the beheading of Pamela that she may know her lot should she reject Amphialus. Love and virtue save the persecuted damsels. Finally, when Amphialus has been vanquished and slain, the beautiful loves of Musidorus and Pamela and of Pyrocles and Philoclea end in a double marriage.

This is the principal plot, but it is crossed by many episodes, more numerous in every one of Sidney's successive versions of his romance. The result has the air of a thing of pure caprice, the unbridled imaginings of a young man, a fiction staged outside time and in a land of chimera. Yet these extravagances, which would have delighted Don Quixote's heart and are in the tradition of the chivalrous romances, have a freshness because of Sidney's pleasure in telling a story and his sincere love for everything that is of valour and courtesy, because of his spontaneous passion for all beauty, whether of the body or the soul. His fictions are a convenient frame for his ideas on morals and politics and his observations of life. For there is reason in this unreason, even realism in all this extravagance. Here and there the chivalrous and the sentimental are interrupted by the comic. The rustics Dametas, Miso and Mopsa play in the romance the part of clowns in the theatre. It is, however, by his attempts at character-study that Sidney especially marks a progress. He contrasts his virtuous with his vicious characters, and his painting of vice has considerable boldness, as when he depicts the perversity of Queen Gynecia, in love with Pyrocles, or the cruelty of the wretched and godless Cecropia, apt for every crime, as she inflicts horrible physical and moral tortures on her prisoners. Even more Sidney enriched the descriptive art of his time, particularly where the painting of love is concerned, by his search for detail in his portraits, by his analyses of expression and gestures, and by his observation of the correspondence between attitude and feeling.

The value of *Arcadia* is thus in its manner, in the style which clothes it, and in which merits and striking defects mingle very strangely. Artifice is as much present as in euphuism, but is of a quite different kind. Sidney refines upon the refined; he is not content with purely verbal conceits although he perpetrates a few of them—"Zelmane, exceedingly sorry for Pamela, but exceedingly exceeding that exceedingness in feare for Philoclea." Generally it is on thought or feeling that he refines, following his constant quest of the fair and the exquisite. A learned embroidery enriches the slightest details and heightens the most insignificant incidents, so that not a line of the story is left quite unadorned. But the decoration is not of the mechanical euphuistic kind, but is the result of the constantly active and constantly renewed play of fancy. Both the euphuists and Sidney aimed at imagery, but Lyly's images are like the flowers and birds on painted papers and printed stuffs. Sidney's images are woven into the very web of his fabric. They may be in doubtful taste, but they are creations.

It was essentially this quality which the French classicists were to stigmatise as preciosity and modern English critics as the pathetic fallacy. Sidney lends life, feeling and will to the inanimate and the abstract. Cool wine, when he writes of it, seems "to laugh for joy" as it nears a lady's lips, bloodstained armour to "blush that it had defended his master no better." Hail is blown against a face by "the pride of the wind." When women, disporting themselves in a river, beat the water with their hands, "the water, making lines in his face, seemed to smile at such a beating, and with twenty bubbles not to be content to have the picture of their face in large upon him, but he would in each of these bubbles set forth the miniature of them." As these ladies came out of the water "with some drops [it] seemed to weep, that it should pass from their bodies."

Such prettinesses recur in Shakespeare, scattered throughout his work, whether voiced by little Prince Arthur or Miranda or Antony. They have sometimes a charming effect of gallantry. When Sidney's princesses dressed they "covered their dainty beauties with the glad clothes"; when they undressed, they "impoverished their clothes to enrich their bed." Thus Romeo will ask:

> What lady's that, which doth enrich the hand
> Of yonder knight?

The language of the most sugared courtesy is reached. The name a lady speaks is perfumed by her mouth. "Plangus whose name was sweetened by your breath" is Sidney's rendering of "Plangus whose name you have spoken."

Pearls, with and without flaws, might be endlessly fished from this sea of preciosity. There is a general agreement of good taste that they are many too many, and that they are heaped poll mell, true and false together. Yet each of them implies a refining effort and a love of the beautiful which is interesting even when it goes astray among the fantastic and the excessive.

All is not, however, vain ornament. Sidney, working at language, often by bold and new combinations of words reaches close and vigorous expression. He is the first Englishman who was conscious of all the resources his language held for the impassioned style. His metaphors are sudden and elliptical. All the energy as well as the preciousness of the Shakespearean style exists in germ in his *Arcadia*. Of two brothers about to die of their wounds he says that each was "more dying in the other than in himself"; of Pamela that "she could no longer keep love from looking out through her eyes and going forth in her words." When a girl is in extremity of woe he speaks of "her eyes wherein sorrow swam." A lover pities his ears because "you shall never hear the music of music in her voice." Such passages, thrown into relief by a vigour of style hitherto unknown, are numerous.

But Sidney's real innovation was due, like Spenser's but independently of him, to senses sharpened by the contemplation of plastic works of art. In his romance, which he wrote when the *Faerie Queene* was no more than planned, he shows a sense of line and colour and of effects of light and shade hitherto unknown to the English. No one can appreciate him without reading the pages in which he describes

Kalander's Italian garden and, above all, the works of art in the pavilion at the end of that garden. He must be watched as he takes pleasure in analysing and commenting on the intentions of the sculptor or the painter. Better still, he should be observed when he portrays his characters, describing them as though they figured on a master's canvas, for instance when he reproduces the studied and symbolical dress donned by Amphialus to visit Philoclea, his prisoner and the object of his unrequited love, and when he paints the attitude of that fair captive plunged in bitter thought in her solitary chamber. This sense of the externally picturesque is supported by an equal power of interpreting feeling which enables Sidney to attain to some charming new effects, both graceful and penetrating, as in the passage which shows the married bliss of Argalus and Parthenia, that ideally matched pair, before Argalus was summoned to the presence of King Basileus and the two were separated:

> The messenger made speed and found Argalus at a castle of his own, sitting in a parlour with the fair Parthenia, he reading in a book the stories of Hercules, she by him, as to hear him read: but while his eyes looked on the book, she looked on his eyes, and sometimes staying him with some pretty question, not so much to be resolved of the doubt, as to give him occasion to look upon her: a happy couple, he joying in her, she joying in herself, but in herself because she enjoyed him: both increased their riches by giving to each other.

To these merits Sidney sometimes joins that of eloquence, as when he causes Queen Helen to give vent to her grief over the body of Amphialus, or the tortured Pamela to lift up a noble prayer to Heaven, or the same pure heroine to reply to Cecropia's cynical counsels.

The work is densely crowded, and with a medley of matter. On the whole the style deserves to be strongly condemned. It is the most poetic prose imaginable and therefore that most remote from prose. Nor has it the advantage of Lyly's artificial style, which at least provided a model of regular, symmetrical and well-balanced sentences. But Sidney let his pen run into sentences almost as interminable as those of Thomas More, weighed down with incidents and complicated by parentheses. It was especially the poets whom he influenced. A whole century of writers, including Shakespeare, the amorists of the Renascence and the so-called metaphysical poets of the seventeenth century, were full of the refinements and strange subtleties of which Sidney had brought the dangerous and dazzling model from Italy and to which he had given the strength of his youthful ardour.

(b) "ASTROPHEL AND STELLA."[1]—Sidney needed the constraint of a restricted form to discipline his exuberant fancy, and needed also the magnet of a strong passion to draw him away from the complicated prettinesses of a style too agreeable to him. Passion came when Penelope Devereux, daughter of the Earl of Essex, to whom he might have been betrothed in her childhood, was the wife of Lord Rich and he became aware of his love for her. Bitter regret for lost happiness, the irresistible desire to possess his beloved, despair at her first coldness, the sweetness of feeling himself loved by her even when she fled him, the struggle in his truly virtuous heart between duty and passion, reason and desire: such is the theme of *Astrophel and Stella*. To express feelings which had some analogy with Petrarch's, Sidney had recourse to the sonnet, which had been neglected in England since Surrey's day. Within the narrow bounds of its fourteen lines he enshrined each movement of his heart, each incident of his love. She is Stella, his star; he Astrophel, enamoured of the star.

He had already paid court to the muse, following prevailing poetic fashions,

---

[1] 1st ed. 1591. Modern ed. by A. W. Pollard (1891), and Flügel (Halle, 1889). Reprinted from the 1st ed. by Sir Sidney Lee in *Elizabethan Sonnets*.

but he now rejected such foppery. He listened now only to his heart—"Look into thy heart and write." Doubtless he found in himself the feelings of lovers of all time, and often his real sincerity has a traditional turn and voice. Doubtless also he refined to a quintessence and was subtle in order to make his sonnets beautiful and worthy of his beloved. A sonneteer's truth cannot be simple and naked. In Sidney's verses there are many figures and metaphors; there are even antitheses and ingenious verbal elaboration. The closeness of the form often leads to obscurity. They cannot be cursorily read. A whole allegory is sometimes condensed into a single line or even a single word. A thought is clothed in a figure which is often brilliant and rare, but which needs interpretation. In the sonnets there are constantly such energetic and new expressions as have already been noticed in the prose of *Arcadia*. "My truant wit," "Great with child to speak," "my sunburnt brain," "the blackest face of woe": all of these occur in the first sonnet.

Through the sonnets the figure of the high-born young man appears more and more clearly revealed. The quality of his soul gives them a particular ring. It is not the peculiarly spiritual exaltation of the mystical and religious Petrarch, nor the sensual ardour of a half-pagan artist like Ronsard, and his is not and could not be such frank and troubled love as Spenser felt for his betrothed. His is a knightly passion, breathing an atmosphere of chivalry in a region whence the lists of tourneys are not hard to reach. We have glimpses, too, of the courtier and diplomat whom love snatches from his habitual thoughts. He is silent and melancholy at festivities and in the noble company he keeps; he is accused of pride because he seeks solitude, because he finds sympathy only in the moon's wan countenance, which seems to him to be the face of a lover scorned as he is, rejected like him.

Beautiful and poignant although the best sonnets of *Astrophel and Stella* are, they are surpassed in emotion by the songs and lyrical pieces which follow them in the same collections. The fourth song is a strange and plaintive serenade. The eighth is neither more nor less than the most passionate personal poem in all Elizabethan literature. The two lovers, who at last find themselves together in Maytime "in a grove most rich of shade," are in a delirium of grief and joy. Astrophel lifts up to Stella a love-cry in which amorous Nature, all about them, has part. In answer, she declares in a voice such "as not ears, but heart did touch," that her passion is equal to his, but begs him to guard the honour of both of them. Nowhere in literature is there a refusal which is more like yielding; nowhere a more generous bestowal of the heart such as makes the refusal of the body seem of no account. Nothing else in the lyricism of the English Renascence is at once so ardent, so true, so direct and so noble.

It will be seen that the author of *Arcadia* and *Astrophel* was both the champion of poetry and the first of the literary critics of his time, in merit as in date. It is important to remember, with his verses, his eloquent defence of letters written in a beautiful prose, free of the affectations of his romance. Only thus can the loss be understood which English literature suffered when Philip Sidney fell heroically at Zutphen fight, at the age of thirty-two.

3. **Edmund Spenser.**[1]—Since Sidney's works did not appear until after his

[1] Spenser was born in London about 1552, of a family in modest circumstances, went to Cambridge as a bursar, was at first inclined to take orders, in 1578 became secretary to the bishop of Rochester, then a courtier, entered the service of the Earl of Leicester in 1579, was appointed secretary to the governor of Ireland in 1580, spent the rest of his life in Ireland except for two visits to London in 1589–91 and in 1596. The estate of Kilcolman, which was granted to him, was pillaged by the Irish rebels in 1598. He died in London in January 1599.

His *Shepheard's Calendar* appeared in 1579; the three first books of the *Faerie Queene* in 1590, the six last in 1596; his *Complaintes* in 1591; *Colin Clouts Come Home Againe* in 1595; the *Amoretti* and the *Epithalamion* in 1595; the *Four Hymnes* in 1596; the *View of the Present State of Ireland* was written in 1598 and appeared in 1633.

Complete works, ed. by R. Morris (Globe Edition); A. B. Grosart, 9 vols. (1882–4); E. de death, it was Spenser who first revealed poetic beauty to his generation. For the England of 1579, lagging behind the continent, seeing the Renascence flower there while she remained almost sterile, the appearance of the *Shepheard's Calendar* inaugurated a period of self-confidence and vast hopes. Spenser was the master of the language whose "numbers flowe as fast as spring doth ryse." He seemed able to tune English verse, which had been so long rebellious, to the natural tones of his voice. For him the language ceased to be refractory.

From the beginning he had, like the French Pleiad, a patriotic literary programme. He was a translator and admirer of du Bellay, and he aspired to awakening the national muse from her languor and making her rival her most illustrious sisters. But, unlike the Pleiad, he founded his faith on admiration for the old poets of his country. Over and over again he calls Chaucer his revered master, "well of English undefyled." He says that when he himself began to write verse he modelled himself on Chaucer, and if their temperaments were too much contrasted to allow of other resemblance, at least he saturated himself with the old poet's language. It was his intention not to break with the past, but to sink his roots deep into it. Hence he had, as compared with the poets of France, an originality which prepares us to understand the distinct character of his *Faerie Queene*.

(a) THE "SHEPHEARD'S CALENDAR."—It is true that he began by clothing with his archaism a poetic genre which is in the spirit of the Renascence. He was first archaic in a pastoral. In his *Shepheard's Calendar* his humanist's tastes combine with his love for the soil. He nationalises his eclogues by pungent words borrowed from the old poets of his country and from provincial vocabularies. Thus he makes free imitations of Theocritus, Bion and Virgil, especially of Mantuanus and of Marot, yet is never the mere reflection of an ancient or foreign writer.

The merits of the poem are properly those of style and are, in view of their date, astonishing. At last a poet had arrived who wrote neither carelessly nor laboriously. Quite unlike the "ragged rymers" of the period, "so pained and travailed in their remembrance, as it were a woman in childbirth, or as that same Pythia, when the traunce came upon her," Spenser has an unfailing and truly admirable ease. The quiet, sure flow of his sentences is sheer enjoyment. He was even archaic with a very precise artistic intention, seeking effects analogous to those of the painters who

blaze and portrait not onlie the daintie lineaments of beautie, but also round about it to shadowe the rude thickets and craggy cliffs, that, by the baseness of such parts, more excellencie may accrew to the principall: for oftentimes we find ourselves, I know not how, singularly delighted with the shew of such naturall rudenesse, and take great pleasure in that disorderly order. Even so doo those rough and harsh tearmes enlumine, and make more clearly to appeare, the brightness of brave and glorious wordes. So oftentimes a discorde in musicke maketh a comely concordance.

This is the first note of conscious artistry sounded by an English poet, and the first time that so close a parallel was made between poetry, music and painting. The impression of artistry is doubled when the versification of the collection is studied. Spenser's virtuosity at the outset of his career is surprising. Never yet had English poetry held, and never would it hold again, a poem in which the combinations of lines and rhymes were both as variously rich and as novel. In the *Calendar* there are as many as five different forms of stanzas in heroic or ten-

Selincourt (Oxford), 1 vol. Good annotated editions of Books I. and II. of the *Faerie Queene* by Kitchen (Clarendon Press); of the *Shepheard's Calendar* by Herford (1895); of the *Four Hymnes* by L. Winstanley (1907).

Biographies by R. W. Church ("English Men of Letters," 1879); A. B. Grosart, in 1st vol. of complete ed. of Spenser (1882-4); and in French by E. Legouis, *Edmund Spenser* (1923). Many detailed studies, especially in the United States.

syllabled lines. Elsewhere, in the songs, lines of unequal length are combined in small, quite novel strophes. Spenser's song on Elizabeth (Eclogue IV.) has the light-hearted rhythm of the most graceful songs of the Pleiad. Certainly, matter is of less importance to him than form. To mourn the death of an unknown woman (*Dido*, Eclogue IX.), he translates Marot's fine elegy on Queen Louise of Savoy, but he transfigures the French poem, of which all the lines are of the same length, by inventing a learned and varied stanza, closed by a refrain which rings like a knell. He really gives wings to a touching plaint which, in the original, clings to the earth.

These songs are the gems of the *Calendar*. But his musicianly efforts went further. The metres of which we have just spoken constitute only half of those used in his eclogues. They form its regular, lofty portion, which is based on syllabism. Another portion is rudely designed, in popular metres which follow no law save that of the four accentual beats. In the last analysis this part of the poem derives, by way of Chaucer disfigured by the changes in the language, from the alliterative verse of the Anglo-Saxons.

To these stylistic and metrical innovations Spenser added the art of composition. The reader of to-day may think that the thread which connects his twelve eclogues and makes them into a single poem is thin and factitious. But Spenser was proud to have found, first among ancients or moderns, a way of forming eclogues into a harmonious whole, each of them corresponding to a month in the year and having a certain more or less apparent fitness to its appropriate atmosphere and season. Some of the shepherds change, but others reappear, especially Colin Clout, about whom they centre, in whom the poet paints himself, and who returns at regular intervals to utter his amorous sighs. The principles of unity and of variety are skilfully blended, the rude eclogues alternating with those loftier in tone. The alternation is more deliberate than that of dignified and homely scenes on the stage, but it obeys the same law. We may smile at the meticulous symmetry of the *Calendar* even in minute details. The excessive number of its calculated consonances and discords astonishes rather than charms us to-day, but these artistic exaggerations were greeted with transports of joy at a time when the still formless state of poetry made the demand for artistry urgent.

As compared with these external innovations, the matter of the eclogues is less important. They are found to include three principal themes, for which Spenser was unashamedly inspired by his predecessors—love, poetry and religion. He owes so much to his forerunners, especially Virgil and Marot, that there is a temptation to overlook the personal and even autobiographical element which does nevertheless exist in his imitations.

The love which Colin Clout, Spenser's pastoral name for himself, bears to the scornful Rosalind, the poet's indignation when the muse is neglected and the singer reduced to misery, his Puritanic velleities, leading him to condemn the idle and proud prelates, the Anglican shepherds who had turned to secular pleasures— all this has relation to Spenser's cares of the moment and to the trend of public opinion.

With its many allusions, some of them still clear, many others plain to contemporaries, the *Shepheard's Calendar* united, at the time of its appearance, the interest of its matter to the charm of its manner. For the first time an English poet seemed to triumph over his European rivals, and in the very genre which was generally attractive in the sixteenth century, in pastoral poetry. Spenser marked the first score in the game of parallelism between England and antiquity or modern Italy, which the English critics were to pursue, all ready to acclaim the victory of their national champions. The merit of the poem is great; its date and circumstances turned it into a triumph. From the moment of its publication Spenser was the acknowledged national poet.

(b) THE HYMNS. "MOTHER HUBBERD'S TALE."—At the same time his ambition grew. Like Virgil, he began with eclogues; like him he afterwards attempted the glorious enterprise of an epic. From pastoral he passed to chivalrous poetry. His *Calendar* was hardly finished when he was faced with a prospect of a courtier's life. He entered the household of the powerful Earl of Leicester, Elizabeth's favourite, and was admitted to the society of Philip Sidney, the earl's nephew. From this moment dates his first idea for the *Faerie Queene*, the great work of his life to which his other verses were no more than marginal scribblings.

But even in 1580, before the beginning of that sojourn in Ireland which he felt as a weary exile and which lasted until the end of his life, he had completed some characteristic verses which did not appear until later, when they had been more or less retouched. The essence of his philosophy is expressed in his hymns to Love and Beauty, composed, he tells us, "in the greener times of my youth." With his sensuous artist's nature, enamoured of beauty and continually in love, he was the true Pamphilus his friend Harvey called him, yet was tormented by a need for truth, tossed between paganism and Christianity, the Renascence and the Re- formation; and he thought to reconcile his senses and his conscience by following Plato, who identified supreme beauty with good. He found that this reconciliation of his dream had been effected, even better than in *Phædrus* and the *Banquet*, by the Italian Marsilio Ficino, who christianised the spirit of Platonism. It was therefore with an ardent eloquence that he put into magnificent verse the sublime dreams of the Greek philosopher as interpreted by this modern disciple. Pure Love is the civiliser of the world which himself drew from chaos and ever since has maintained in harmony.

Spenser saw earthly beauty, and especially the beauty of woman, which inspires love, as the reflection and index of divine beauty, virtue rendered visible, the beam from on high lodged in a body and fashioning its fleshly habitation into a marvellous palace:

> Therefore where-ever that thou doest behold
> A comely corpse, with beautie faire endewed,
> Know this for certaine, that the same doth hold
> A beauteous soule, with faire conditions thewed;
> Fit to receive the seede of vertue strewed;
> For all that faire is, is by nature good;
> That is a sign to know the gentle blood.

This exquisite belief reconciles contraries, makes the pleasures of the eye into a school of perfection and love into a moral law. By virtue of this faith Spenser ennobled all his loves, gave his brush full leave to paint in fullest detail the bodily charms of his heroines, and saw all the stirrings of his own passion as impulses heavenwards. He became aware of the danger of this doctrine only towards the end of his life, when nearly all his verses had been written.

At about the same time as these exalted hymns, Spenser wrote a poem of quite another kind, a harsh satire in the form of a fable, to which he gave the name of *Mother Hubberd's Tale*. The reverse side of idealism is contempt for reality or discontent with it. Throughout his life Spenser was a morose judge of the society of his time, viewing it pessimistically. Dithyrambic eulogies of the incomparable Elizabeth are a screen for continuous denunciation of the mean intrigues of the court, the debased morals, the political corruption, the simony and inertia of the clergy, the decadence of the spirit of chivalry, and above all the neglect of letters and art. Spenser has a sort of artless faith in the golden age which he sees far behind him in an abolished past. The personal disappointments which this nervous and irritable poet suffered certainly contributed much to the blackness of his outlook. He was convinced that a poet has a right to one of the first places in a well-ordered society, that a sort of Prytaneum in which he would dwell remote from all material cares ought to exist for him, but he did not find great men and ministers disposed to satisfy his ambitions. His rancour gathered against Lord Burleigh, the great treasurer, the counsellor who more than any other had the queen's ear and who economically dispensed her favours and the powers she delegated.

Burleigh is hidden in the form of the Fox in the fable of the Ape and the Fox which constitutes *Mother Hubberd's Tale*, while the Ape is, at least sometimes, the Duke of Anjou, brother to Henry III. of France and a candidate for the queen's hand. The poem was written when Elizabeth seemed to incline to this Catholic suitor, who was hated in her kingdom as a foreigner and a member of the royal family responsible for the massacre of St. Bartholomew. The Ape and the Fox, two brazen adventurers, are shown passing through Elizabethan society, having luck now with the clergy, now with the court. They take advantage of a day when the Lion—that is the monarch, Queen Elizabeth—sleeps to steal his crown. The Ape thereupon becomes king and the Fox prime minister, and their shameless tyranny prospers until the Lion awakes. Except gaiety and humour, the fable has all the merits of its genre. It reveals the poet's powers of observation and his vigour. The metre, which is deliberately rude, suits the satirical intention, and its harshness has that easy amplitude which Spenser evinces in his properly poetic work.

(*c*) THE "COMPLAINTS."—The same condemnation of the age recurs copiously in the *Complaints, containing sundrie small Poems of the World's Vanitie*, published in 1591. *Mother Hubberd's Tale*, doubtless enlarged and retouched, figures here, but does not strike the dominant note of the collection, which is especially one of indignant or sorrowful eloquence. It is the "discours fatal des choses mondaines," which du Bellay recommended as essentially proper to lyricism. The total result is, to tell truth, lugubrious, in the spirit of the Middle Ages rather than of the Renascence, so monotonously sombre in colour as to recall the *Mirror for Magistrates*. The work is not wholly original. It includes translations—of Petrarch's *Visiones*, of du Bellay's *Visions* and *Ruines de Rome*, of the *Culex* attributed to Virgil. In all the original poems there is pessimism, founded on the disappearance of great souls and triumph of mean natures and a reference must be understood both to the death of Sidney and Leicester, followed in 1590 by that of Walsingham, the Mæcenas of the century, and to the growing power of Burleigh. This is the theme of the *Ruines of Rome*, the first poem of the *Complaints*, a long lamentation over the ruins of Verulam, cradle of the race of Dudley (Leicester). It is the subject also of the *Teares of the Muses*, in which each of the nine sisters sighs out her despair in turn and declares barbarism to have returned and knowledge to be scorned not only by the people, but also by the great, who should be its patrons. In this degenerate age the Muses find nothing to praise. They have no lofty subjects; Clio has nothing to write. Singers have not quite vanished from the land, but the rare favours are granted to parasites and sycophants. Luxury reigns, and the love which is sung with success is that which is impure. The singers of chaste and divine love must give place to vile rhymesters with "dunghill thoughts." As the favour of the great is withdrawn from the Muses, they are adopted by the vulgar, who debase them to their own level. Melpomene and Thalia are miserable, especially Thalia, who complains that, where once there were the delights of comedy,

> In stead thereof scoffing Scurrilitie,
> And scornful Follie with contempt is crept,
> Rolling in rymes of shameless ribaudrie
> Without regard, or due Decorum kept.

I—N

Here it becomes apparent that Spenser was out of tune with the spirit of his time, especially as it found its strongest and liveliest expression in the drama, which was embarking on its astonishing career at the moment when the *Complaints* were published. After nearly ten years Spenser repeated Sidney's attacks, and they had come to lack their earlier justification. Spenser's ideal of nobility was offended and scandalised by the troubled, tumultuous life of the popular theatre.

The *Complaints* include, however, a more personal poem, an elegy less strained in its vehemence which begins in a mocking spirit. This is the graceful fable called *Muiopotmos, or the Fate of the Butterflie*. The poet uses it to express his voluptuous nature; then shows his brilliant butterfly caught in the web of the horrible spider, fatal enemy to all poetry and love in this world. Intoxicated with beauty, Clarion, the butterfly, flies into the garden of Nature to make his booty of delights. Light and joyous, he flits confidently from flower to flower, ignorant of malice and perfidy until the day when he becomes the victim of Aragnol, who sucks his blood. Spenser wrote nothing livelier or more charming than this mock-heroic fable, and its plaint, more intimate and sincere than the sombre rhetoric of the poems which accompany it, moves our pity more than they.

(*d*) "ASTROPHEL." "COLIN CLOUTS COME HOME AGAINE."—Spenser wrote other elegies as well as the *Complaints*: his *Daphnaïda*, which voices, in a fiction imitated from Chaucer's *Boke of the Duchesse*, Arthur Gorges' mourning over the death of his wife, and especially his *Astrophel*, an allegory of the life and death of Sir Philip Sidney. In both these poems he resorts to the pastoral form in order to decorate and transform reality. Sidney, the valiant knight, becomes a shepherd of Arcady wounded to death by an enraged boar, and the hero of Zutphen cannot be said to gain by the change. Spenser, in spite of years and the alteration of public taste, is still faithful to his first and bucolic love. In the *Teares of the Muses* he shows Euterpe weeping over her deserted groves, but he himself still frequented them.

Another pastoral, *Colin Clouts Come Home Againe*, was the vehicle of his impressions of a visit to London in 1589–90, during which he published the three first books of the *Faerie Queene* and experienced the recognition and smiles of his sovereign, but also vexation, disillusionment and neglect. *Colin Clouts Come Home Againe* is the most autobiographical of his poems, and his contribution to the pastoral genre which has most novelty. Colin Clout (Spenser), the shepherd, is visited by the Shepherd of the Ocean (Sir Walter Raleigh), who is charmed by his music and takes him to the court of Cynthia (Elizabeth), the great shepherdess. The meeting with the brilliant adventurer who, on the morrow of the Armada, pointed England towards her future on the sea and in her colonies brings the spirit of the new age into Spenser's poetry. When the Shepherd of the Ocean is thus introduced into an eclogue, it is as though an eagre of the tide unexpectedly flooded the meadows on which flocks had pastured for centuries. Spenser takes pleasure in describing how the herdsmen are scared by their visitor, who "came far from the main-sea deepe." In their stupefaction, their landsmen's fear before tales of the unknown waters, the sudden transformation of a mainly agricultural into a maritime country, one destined to be mistress of the seas, is figured.

Colin's stay at the court is no less interesting: we are shown his adoration of the queen, his marvelling at the songsters and the ladies who form Elizabeth's magnificent train, his joy at the enthusiastic hearing given to his rustic lays, and then his sudden awakening from his fair dream, his discovery of the base intrigues, jealousies, false promises and luxury hidden beneath the seeming decorum, and of the malignity masked by courtesy. Angered and disgusted, Colin escapes and returns to his humble and simple shepherd's life and its constant and virtuous loves.

(e) THE "AMORETTI" AND THE "EPITHALAMION."—Soon after his return to Ireland, in 1591, Spenser began his suit to Elizabeth Boyle, to whom are addressed the *Amoretti* sonnets and the superb *Epithalamion* which concludes them. These poems have a place to themselves among the works of Spenser. Only in them does he voice his feelings without recourse to allegory. The innovation illustrates the importance of the part played by the sonnet in this period. It was almost the sole medium of direct effusion and personal expression. Spenser, whose eyes were on the past, began by overlooking the sonnet. Sidney, with the glorious *Astrophel and Stella* series, was the first to use it, long after Wyatt and Surrey, and much more powerfully than they. It was the publication of *Astrophel and Stella* in 1591 which really gave rise to the passion for the sonnet, and which prepared the way for the *Amoretti* and several other collections. In the first rank of the works of the English Renascence, Spenser's sonnets come between those of Sidney and Shakespeare, from which they are distinct in form as in sentiment. His three quatrains, linked by an artistic arrangement of rhymes and followed by a couplet, make a harmonious whole (*abab, bcbc, cdcd, ee*). Exceptionally at this time, these sonnets depart from Petrarch's precedent and are those of a betrothed lover. There is not here the unquiet of Sidney in love with Lord Rich's wife, or of Shakespeare whose mistress deceived him with his friend. Spenser's sonnets are unique by their purity. They tell a story of love without sin or remorse, its varying fortunes, the lover's sighs until the day on which he is accepted, and his final joy. In default of ardent passion, the *Amoretti* have the charm of a harmonious and pure atmosphere; they are bathed by a white light. They show better than anything else the quality in Spenser which Coleridge excellently named "maidenliness," his love of the virginal in woman.

Undoubtedly they have much that is borrowed or reminiscent. The sighs which Spenser breathes often echo those of Petrarch and the Petrarchians; his indifferent and scornful fair, whose pity he long implores in vain, recalls the cruel ladies of tradition. But the poet's distinctive voice is heard in sonnets like the sixth, in which he rejoices in the maiden's prolonged resistance, as the index of her untouched heart never troubled by desire, and as the pledge of a chaste ardour which, once lit, will not be quenched. The same voice sounds in the sixty-seventh sonnet, in which he tells, in charmed surprise, of the sudden moving of this virginal heart which has been so timid and which, at the very moment when he deems it lost for ever, gives itself unreservedly to him and is happy to be captured.

The chastity of these sonnets is neither shyness nor reticence. In many of them the poet extols his mistress's beauty with a great sensual wealth of detail and colour, and does not conceal the ardour of his desires, even while he restrains their impatience (Sonnet 83).

Charming though they be, the *Amoretti* are equalled, if not surpassed, by others of the illustrious sonnet series of the Renascence. But the *Epithalamion* which is their conclusion has no equal. In amplitude and splendour it excels all other compositions of the same kind. Even antiquity produced no such poem, none which was unswelled by legends and yet carried so much sail. Its twenty-three stanzas, of from seventeen to nineteen lines, merely describe enthusiastically the whole of the poet's wedding-day, from the dawn of the sun which lit its glorious hours to the night which left the bride in her husband's arms. Each stanza frames a rite of the festival, and beneath the rich, ennobling mythological decoration, simple, homely circumstances are revealed of this wedding celebrated in a small Irish town on the 11th of June, 1594. This song of joy finds matter in abundant and melodious realism. The poet's genius does not need the rare and the subtle in order to reach beauty, for he knows that beauty has an inexhaustible spring in the common incidents which seem vulgar to other eyes. Never did his genius show its sovereign power as in the *Epithalamion*. The breath which fills each ample strophe and passes unabated through them all to the end, the clear light which floods each successive picture, and the fine classical structure of the whole poem, simple, luminous and inevitable, make this ode Spenser's most perfect production and the lyrical triumph of the English Renaissance. All his gifts are united in it and seem to be raised by happiness to a higher power.

He celebrated the marriage of another almost as successfully as his own in *Prothalamion* (1596), which is filled with smooth images and harmonious lines. Before he died he wrote two more hymns to celestial Love and Beauty, as an antidote to the terrestrial hymns of his youth. With years came regret for his early exaltation, that of an artist too much enamoured of women's bodily splendours, and also disgust with a world in which all beauty is ephemeral, a prey to the unceasing assaults of mutability. His thoughts were turning to religion and God, to longing for the great rest which knows no change, when death took him in 1599, at the age of forty-seven.

(*b*) THE "FAERIE QUEENE."—Even without the *Faerie Queene*, the beauty and the bulk of Spenser's work would have assured him the first place among Elizabethans other than playwrights. Yet it was the *Faerie Queene* which was his masterpiece. He worked at it for twenty years and left it unfinished at his death. It was his own soaring ambition and the supreme pride of England, which confidently pitted this poem, as soon as its first books appeared, against the most famous epics of ancient and modern times.

It is true that it has not been wholly translated into any language. The insularity of its renown cannot be explained by the fact that it is consecrated to the enhancement of the glory of England and her sovereign, for epics are strictly national by custom. It is the external complexity and the allegorical dress of this poem which have turned readers away from it, even English readers, who give it a formal admiration but hardly glance at it. Its real beauty is screened by its preface, in which the poet explains his virtuous design to make it at once an edifying treatise and a sort of creed in cipher, intelligible only to the initiate. Spenser himself innocently misled the public. He did not acknowledge to himself that his poem was one of the world's most magnificent picture-books. He assumed the grave airs of a preacher, yet could not sustain the part unflinchingly. This admirable painter and enchanting musician posed as a professor of morals. Therefore he has given little satisfaction, except to a few unexacting souls, among those who seek doctrine in a book, and he has alienated those who read verse for pure pleasure.

He would have escaped this neglect had he kept to the first title he had in mind, one much better fitted to indicate the character of his work—*Pageants*, that is decorative pictures, such rhythmic processions and rich spectacles as the Elizabethans loved passionately. His book is indeed nothing else than this, or rather all that makes its beauty consists of nothing else. But the men of his time thought themselves obliged to bring a moral lesson to the forefront. Already this tendency was more marked in the English than in continental nations. The English were beginning to take a national pride in their seriousness, as a quality which distinguished them from the southern peoples whom they considered more frivolous and dissolute than themselves. Spenser was the more inclined to this attitude because he wished to emulate Ariosto and counted on superior virtue to enable him to surpass *Orlando Furioso*. He therefore abandoned his *Pageants* and wrote a vast allegory in order "to fashion a gentleman or noble person in virtuous and gentle discipline." Like Ariosto, he created a fairylike chivalry, but he intended each of his knights to represent one of " the xii. private moral virtues as Aristotle hath devised." The poet does indeed admit that it would have been better if his message had been " delivered plainly in way of precepts," but he makes concession to " the use of these days, seeing all things accounted by their showes, and nothing esteemed of, that is not delightfull and pleasing to commune sence."

It must be acknowledged that in his two first books his aim of edification is sufficiently fulfilled. The allegory is continuous and the moral constantly to the fore. But in the later books both are obscured and the romance is dominant. Spenser is no longer on a higher plane than Ariosto, but walks beside him. Neither as an allegorist nor as a writer of romance does he excel, but as the showman of pageants he is incomparable.

He lacks, first, the simple restrained line of a good allegorist. He has not the central idea, the ardent passion or the unity of design which are essential conditions of a powerful and effective allegory. Instead of unity he has complication. His characters are created for more than one purpose, are both moral and historical personages. His King Arthur, in love with the Fairy Queen, is Magnificence—the supreme virtue which, according to Aristotle, includes all others—and he is also the symbol for divine grace; moreover, he suggests Leicester, Elizabeth's favourite. Artegal is Justice incarnate and stands at the same time for the severe Lord Grey of Wilton to whom Spenser was secretary in Ireland. The allegorical story is thus both moral and political. In the first book the adventures of the Red Cross Knight represent, in turn or simultaneously, the Christian soul in quest of truth, the alternatives offered by Protestantism and Catholicism, and the advances and lapses of faith in the sixteenth century. At times the reader in search of absolute comprehension and interpretation is bewildered and feels lost. He is reassured only when he tells himself that to understand is not necessary, to gaze is enough.

Sometimes the allegories are obscure even in detail, and reveal themselves as puerile when they are too well sounded. The masque of Cupid, played in the palace of the enchanter Busirane, is very beautiful to the eye. Yet it owes its place to an inconsistency, for while it is intended to show the ills which Cupid inflicts on his victims, in the plot it occurs at the order of a lewd magician who wishes to win the love of a fair captive. The poet is interested not by the significant, but by the picturesque, and often, when his didacticism is most in evidence, he seems himself to nod. He declaims platitudes in sonorous tones; he is sententious, sometimes frankly tautological.

It certainly is not that his mind is weak, but that his energy is usually reserved for pictures. Here and there, inspired by the occasion, his intellectual vigour breaks forth, as though to vindicate itself. He evinces a penetrating sense of the mystery of memory in his picture of the old archivist crouching in a back chamber in the house of Alma (the temperate soul). With poignant force he represents the tragedy of despair leading to suicide in his famous allegory of the Cave of Despair.

But such passages are exceptional in the poem and cannot be said to give it its character. The same may be said of the romantic element, which charms intermittently and attains to the exquisite only here and there. Spenser, when he wished to create characters, even in a romance, was impeded by his allegory, which asked not for living beings, but for bodiless abstractions. To write a romance was not to fulfil his engagements. He is conscious of this fact and weakened and constrained thereby. Yet he enjoys recounting the strange adventures of his heroes, and, even more, those of his heroines, although most of his women pass through his cantos leaving behind them only a memory of their wondrous beauty. Belphebe and Amoret are, however, more substantially present. Spenser has invented an ingenious fable, worthy of Greek mythology, to account for the birth of these twin sisters, one of them a huntress-maid brought up by Diana, the other educated by Venus and vowed to love and marriage. From this premise he derives two contrasted portraits, two distinct lives, almost two characters. But it is Britomart who, alone among Spenserian heroines, really has the dimensions of a romantic creation. Her adventures are traced through three books of the poem. She is a new Bradamante and she certainly owes many characteristics to Ariosto's heroine. She is the chaste and indomitable warrior-maid whose lance makes the most valiant champions bite the dust, and also the passionate woman in love who struggles not to lay bare her heart, who knows the tortures of jealousy, and who at last yields, happy in her defeat, to the emotion which possesses her. Spenser concentrates on the portrait of this enamoured heroine all the power of subtle analysis of which he is capable. It is mainly she who changes the allegory into a romance.

But even this character is too largely imitated to account for the glory of the poem. The *Faerie Queene* is essentially a picture-gallery. Spenser is a great painter who never held a brush. It was his fate to be born in a country in which the plastic arts did not flourish until two centuries after his time. Had he been born in Italy, he might have been another Titian, a second Veronese; born in Flanders, he would have forestalled Rubens and Rembrandt. Fortune made him a painter in verse, perhaps the most wonderful who has ever lived.

Since he seems never to have been on the continent, his initiation took place in the England which had for a hundred years been enriched by works of art imported from abroad. He visited the fine collections of his patron Leicester, and knew masterpieces through engravings or through the tapestries of Flanders and Arras. Sidney had spoken to him of the Venetians, of Veronese who had painted his portrait and of the art critics he had met. The ambition to rival painting was born in English poetry through Spenser and Sidney simultaneously. It exists in the *Faerie Queene* as in *Arcadia*.

Many stanzas of the *Faerie Queene* are descriptions of tapestries and pictures, and the line and colour of words competes in them with that on the canvases of the masters. When Spenser purports to draw a person or a scene from nature, he is still inspired by the painter's method. He is unendingly enthralled by the human body, especially woman's body; no one of its details wearies his patience or escapes his observation. His grotesque and monstrous descriptions are not inferior to those in which he aims at absolute beauty. The grotesque is but the reverse of the beautiful: the horrible Dragon who slays the Red Cross Knight is as much a masterpiece of painting as the nymph Belphebe.

With marvellous success he seeks *chiaro oscuro* effects. He enjoys painting the nude, and he excels at reproducing the rippling surface or changing colour of stuffs.

A great allegorical composition tempts him as much as a portrait. His Wedding of the Thames and the Medway is on the scale of a fresco which would cover a ceiling or a wall in an imperial palace.

But a picture in which everything was in a state of arrested motion was not his sole model. His art was often ruled by the pageants, the processions of costumed characters with expressive gestures whose attitudes revealed the abstractions they represented. Such is his description of the Seven Deadly Sins or his procession of the Seasons and the Months. In these he almost exceeds the limits of poetry in his desire to reproduce in detail, necessarily by successive presentations, those feasts of the eye in which innumerable participants allowed the spectators simultaneously to enjoy every part. Nothing is too long for him. His joy in painting never flags.

He was also influenced by the pantomimes dear to his contemporaries, and in order to eliminate abstractions from his poem, to give a body and a countenance to everything, he staged the moral principles he wished to inculcate. He seems sometimes to be using verse to reproduce the acting of mimes who are taking part in a morality-play, for instance in the episode of the fight between Sir Guyon and Furor and Occasion (II. iv. 4-16). So much is he carried away by his pleasure in a picture that he often half forgets its symbolical and moral meaning. His verses are like all the great allegorical canvases of the Renascence: we contemplate them not for edification, not always even for the meaning we hope to discover in them, but for their perfection of form and brilliancy of colouring. Such is, among others, his allegory of the House of Care, by which he wishes to show the tortures of a heart torn by jealousy. He imagines a lover who believes himself betrayed passing a night in a forge, where the terrible noise of the hammers prevents him from sleeping. The whole scene is pantomimic, thrown into relief with incomparable vigour, and it produces the effect of a nightmare, but it does not suggest jealousy with any precision. It might apply to insomnia induced by any cause—fever, nightmare or toothache. The wonder is in the vision itself and the strength with which it is impressed on the reader's imagination.

The whole of the *Faerie Queene* is full of these suggestions. Where usually a poet would throw a passing hint, adopt a traditional way of speech or merely a metaphor, Spenser insists so that he tends to produce reality. He does not, like others, like Ronsard, content himself with declaring that he is the nurseling of the Muses, or saying that it has been granted him to see, in the wood beside the spring, the daughters of Memory and the Graces. He tells us the exact spot at which he has been allowed to contemplate them, and shows them dancing, substantial as a painter could make them. In his verses they exist as substantially as the poet who has the vision (VI. x. 5-30).

He borrows the idea or subject of his pictures from everywhere, from books as from paintings and pageants and the scenes on the stage of his time. He rejects no poetic source. We find in him reminiscences of Homer, Lucretius, Virgil and Ovid, Guillaume de Lorris, Chaucer, Langland, Lydgate and Malory, Stephen Hawes and Sackville, Ariosto and Tasso—to cite only the chief of his creditors. Hence the rich diversity of his illuminations, a whole which has elements so disparate that we are driven to ask how his poem could blend them and attain to a sort of unity. Happily the fusion had already been made, and had produced the richest and most complex spectacle of the time, the masque, which was the father of the ballet dear to Louis XIV. and the ancestor of the opera, which combined mythology, allegory and fairy-tale and was accompanied by symbolical dances and music. Much honoured in Spenser's day, it reached its climax after his death, under James I. Spenser occupies a transitional place in the history of the masque. His poem was inspired by the masques he had seen, but itself supplied one of the richest models and, above all, one of the strongest imaginative stimulants to the magnificent masques which came after him.

The *Faerie Queene* may be said to have fixed in a descriptive poem the masques of the English Renascence, thus reviving and perpetuating the ephemeral enchantment of those spectacles. Spenser keeps the sumptuous and changing scenery of the masque, the scene-shifting, the composition of groups, the gestures and pantomime of the actors. He also reproduces the alternation of masque and anti-masque, that is of the lofty and the grotesque. Finally, the music of the stage is matched by that of his verses.

Thus he found readymade the framework of his imaginings. As spectator of some masque, he had seen the fairyland in which his strange stories happen, which is the home of his countless visions. It is essentially the country of the Arthurian romances, of Malory's *Morte d'Arthur*, but it has acquired more substance; it is the country of *Orlando Furioso*, presented not by a mocking fancy, but with a seriousness which carries conviction. A country of a thousand enchantments, a wild, desert, indeterminate region of immense forests, Spenser drew it largely from the "savage land" of Ireland, where his dreams could all but grow real and observation could revive his fancy.

It is a world in which surprise is habitual and strangeness the rule. In the end we become acclimatised to it and believe in it, as we accept the impossibilities of dreams and nightmares. As in a dream, a thin thread unites the fantastic discords. The passage from place to place and scene to scene is easy: as in a theatre, a mere lowering of the lights allows scenery to be swiftly changed.

Thus it is that this great poem, so artificially constructed, its disparate elements fused neither by heat of passion nor by fire of intellect, has another unity communicated to it by imaginative force. It has its harmony of atmosphere. Everything is bathed in the same strange, fantastic moonlight in which the contrast between whites and shadows is heightened and wonders are expected as native to the place.

For this dream-world to which Spenser's poem introduces us, and which had a certain operatic charm, it was necessary that the long unfolding visions should be constantly accompanied by music which would suspend the activity of the logical faculties and help to give credence to the chimeras. The illusion is effected by means of the powerful monotony of the nine-lined stanza, the stanza of the courtly ballade with decasyllabic lines to which a final alexandrine is added.[1]

Had Spenser been less painter than narrator, he would not have substituted this stanza for the *ottava rima* of his Italian masters, for he would have feared to make his story fragmentary by this alexandrine line, of which the majestic length always suggests a conclusion, marking the end of each stanza and isolating it. But he liked the architectural effect of the long *finale* in his descriptions, and the expanded stanza corresponded to his wonted phrasing, to the long periods habitual to him, as to his contemporaries, even in prose. His stanza was the mould natural to his syntax and his thought. Although it was used by many poets after him, and by some of the greatest—Thomson, Byron, Shelley, Keats—it never seems to adapt itself as well to their tones as to his, for the moderns have a mode of thought and expression which is briefer, more analytical and more disjointed than Spenser's. The poet of to-day is shorter in the wind. His breath fills less easily and less constantly the broad interior of this harmoniously proportioned urn.

Spenser's metre, deliberately lengthened and weighted, is so ample and so slow that its majesty, like that of a deep, evenly flowing river, compensates for the qualities it has lost. The very fact that the poem is written in stanzas and all in this measure has important consequences. We hear music which has slowed down, music with a perpetually recurring measure which lulls our intellect and little by little leads us away from the real world into another, a world of order and harmony where this stanza seems to be the natural rhythm. It keeps time in this fairyland. It measures the hours in this region of nowhere, this kingdom of illusion. It has a hypnotic effect, induces a slumber in which the things of life are remote and we are in communion only with the poet's pictures. Every movement is regulated by it and obeys its law, as though it were a metronome by which all the characters timed their acts and words. Never hurried, eternally reborn, its empire is that of a continuous sound in nature, as of the winds or the sea. No single stanza read

---

[1] The formula of the line is *a b a b b c b c c*. It is a true stanza, a perfect stanza of which the rhymes are so interlaced that it cannot be broken.

separately can give an idea of the immense part which the stanza plays in this poem, in which each one inherits the cumulative force of all its predecessors. From his perception that they are on one pattern, the reader is brought to feel every individual stanza to be essential to the general order, and this unconscious recognition of an inevitability of form gives added value to the contents of the verses.

It is here and in his pictures that Spenser is marvellous. His glory must not be established on the less solid elements of the *Faerie Queene*. To let it rest on the moral value or the thought of the poem or on the feeling it conceals would be mistaken. Nor do we diminish his glory when we are thus careful of its security. It is enough for the renown of this great poem that, to music of unfailing harmony, it unrolls before our eyes innumerable dazzling visions. It is enough for Spenser's name that he was one of the master musicians, and perhaps the greatest of the picture-makers, of this world.

4. Other Court Poets. Raleigh, Oxford, Fulke, Greville. — Sir Walter Raleigh (1552?-1618)[1] was near Lyly, Sidney and Spenser in age and Spenser's friend, and was, like them all, connected with the court. He was occasionally a poet. He is the type of the fine courtier, high-spirited, proud and bold, who writes some striking verses, like marginal scribblings to the page on which his wonderfully active career is set forth. Of his long poem to Cynthia, otherwise Elizabeth, nothing is left but a fragment in which the former favourite of the queen flogs himself into a pretence of devouring love and despairing regrets. Of far more worth are his few sonnets, of which one magnificently welcomes Spenser's masterpiece, and some short lyrical pieces in which this adventurer condemns the emptiness of the courtly life which had fascinated him (*The Lie, The Pilgrimage*).

Raleigh gave more time to prose than poetry. With attractive simplicity he relates his expedition to Guiana in search of the fabulous Manoa. In the prison he left only for the scaffold he wrote an eloquent *History of the World*, in which his shortcomings as an historian are redeemed by superb pages. About 1593 he had been suspected of sympathy for Marlowe's atheism, although he was, in point of fact, a deist with his own philosophy who ended his life absorbed in grave religious thought. In the work of this amateur there is something at once strange and passionate which compels attention.

Among the men of the court, Edward de Vere, Earl of Oxford (1550-1604),[2] was distinguished as much by his cult of poetry as by the extravagance of his life. The typical great Italianate lord, he resumed in himself several of the vices and some of the artistic and literary qualities of the Transalpine peninsula. His lyrical verse is scattered among such collections of the period as the *Paradise of Dainty Devices* (1576) and does not lack grace and facility. He exemplifies the taste for letters which reigned in the court circle and which might be found in a dissolute fop like himself as well as in a daring adventurer like Raleigh, or in Sidney, the mirror of perfect chivalry. Beside the court poets, professional men of letters were ranged— Lyly who dedicated his *Euphues* to Oxford, Spenser who headed his *Calendar* with Sidney's name and addressed the preface of his *Faerie Queene* to Raleigh. The court and its neighbourhood were the first home of the Renascence.

Oxford was Sidney's enemy. Sir Edward Dyer, famous in his own time for his lost elegies, and Fulke Greville, Lord Brooke (1554-1628),[3] were his most intimate

---

[1] Life by William Oldys (1736, reprinted 1829), by E. Gosse (1886), by H. de Selincourt, *Great Raleigh* (1908), etc. Collected poems published by J. Hannah (1886). *The Discovery of Guiana* (1st ed. 1596, reprinted in Hakluyt's *Voyages*, vol. iii., 1598). *The History of the World* (1st ed., 1614).

[2] His poems were collected by Grosart in *Miscellanies of the Fuller Worthies Library* (1872).

[3] *Certain Learned and Elegant Works Written in his Youth and Familiar Exercise with Sir Philip Sidney* (1633); *Life of Sidney* (published 1652); *Remains* (poems on the monarchy and on religion: 1670); *Complete Works*, published by Grosart, 4 vols. (1870).

and constant friends. Fulke Greville wrote his verses in his youth although most of them did not appear until after his death. He was Sidney's first biographer. Thoughtful and sententious, a great admirer of Elizabeth, whose royal greatness he celebrated and whose personal praises he sang in his *Cælica*, Fulke Greville's work includes beautiful imaginative lines and others which have a noble but slightly standard and superannuated grace. The cast of his mind made him a man of the period of *Euphues* and *Arcadia*. His Myra, who bathed,

> Washing the waters with her beauty's white,

is the sister of Sidney's Philoclea.

CHAPTER III

POETRY FROM 1590 TO 1625

1. Elizabethan Poetry from 1590 to 1603.—Outside the theatre, almost all the literature of the Elizabethan period properly so called, that is down to 1603, derived from Lyly, Sidney and Spenser. Romances bore the imprint of *Euphues* and *Arcadia* in turn or simultaneously. Pastorals imitated from Spenser or Sidney abounded. *Astrophel and Stella*, from the moment of its publication, provoked a whole flowering season of sonnets. The successive appearance, about 1590, of Sidney's sonnets and *Arcadia*, and of the first books of the *Faerie Queene*, was the signal for an intense literary activity. It was then that a whole generation born some ten years after Spenser entered the arena of letters. The poetry alone shows such a literary ferment as makes very difficult the task of presenting the new works methodically. Doubtless drama attracted the writers who were most vital and energetic, but the majority of them turned from time to time to pure poetry as a relaxation, and wrote verses in the fashionable poetic genres. We are thus led to follow genres rather than individuals. First, however, we must deal with the voluminous works of two poets whose contribution to the drama was slight and unimportant. Their production continued into the next century, but the date of their birth and the atmosphere in which their talent was formed make them two Elizabethans. They are Daniel and Drayton.

Each of them produced one of the longest poems of the period, the *Faerie Queene* excepted. The American critic Lowell could call Daniel's *Civil Wars* and Drayton's *Polyolbion* the megalosaurus and plesiosaurus of the Renascence. These poets express, more directly than Spenser, their patriotic feeling, which is less troubled than his by the dream of a golden age or by hostility to the present. They survive only in a few pages of verse and a few short poems, but their figures are distinct and can be traced in every part of the considerable body of their works.

(*a*) SAMUEL DANIEL.—Samuel Daniel (1562–1619)[1] was born in Somerset, and the son of a music-master. After having passed through Oxford and visited Italy, he was tutor first to William Herbert, son of the Earl of Pembroke and of Sidney's sister, and then to a daughter of the virtuous Countess of Cumberland. After Spenser's death he became a sort of voluntary poet-laureate. Under James I. he was dramatic censor and groom of the chamber to the queen. His tastes were sober and moderate; he lived quietly in his London house cultivating the Muses; then retired to a Somersetshire farm. By the even march of his existence he contrasted with most of his contemporary poets. His poetry, well behaved as he, is the most tranquil and classical of the period. Nearly everything in the English Renascence which shocked French taste when this had been purified by the seventeenth century is missing from Daniel's work, and so is the "fine frenzy" beloved of the Elizabethans. He was a moralist and historian first of all; he wrote the poetry of reflection, not of passion. His calm voice could, in that tumultuous time, hardly

---

[1] Complete poetical works in *Chalmers's British Poets*, vol. iii.; complete works in prose and verse published by Grosart, 5 vols. (1885). His *Delia* reprinted by Arber in *An English Garner*, vol. iii.

make itself heard. A correct and pure writer, he brought the qualities of prose into verse. Imagination is rare in his subjects and never disturbs his style.

He made trial of the theatre, but since he lacked the impetuous vigour of his dramatic rivals, since he was in love with nobility and serenity, he turned from the popular stage and wrote tragedies, classical in form, modelled on Seneca and the French poet Garnier—*Cleopatra* in 1594 and *Philotas* in 1611. These academic dramas could have no more than a *succès d'estime*. He succeeded better with his masques, which contain very attractive passages: *The Vision of the Twelve Goddesses* (1604), *The Queen's Arcadia, a Pastoral Tragi-comedy* (1606) and *Hymen's Triumph*.

Round about his chief work, *Civil Wars*, are grouped a fair number of miscellaneous poems, sonnets to Delia, epistles, dedications, panegyrics, funeral eulogies, pastoral songs. The even quality of his verses is surprising for his day. He translates with charm the suave eulogy of the golden age in Tasso's *Aminta*. There is real feeling in his *Letter from Octavia to Antony* (1599), and even more in his *Complaint of Rosamond* (1592), in which the unhappy mistress of Henry II. mingles her regret for her transgressions and her sighs for her lost beauty. She draws the moral from her story herself, and it is softened as it passes through her lips.

But a mood of serious reflection was more habitual to Daniel than fancy or tenderness. It is not only by accident that the lines from his work which are most often quoted are the lyrical dialogue between Ulysses and the Siren, standing for honour and pleasure, labour and rest, and the *Epistle to the Countess of Cumberland*, in which he defines, in fine, strong and calm stanzas, the sage who inhabits the serene temples of wisdom and is raised above private passion or political agitation.

Apt as he is to discourse and discuss in verse, his talent is happily displayed in a didactic poem in the form of a dialogue, *Musophilus* (1599), which contains a general defence of letters. Musophilus constitutes himself champion of letters against Philocosmus, who recommends an active life and rules out all poetry which does not impel to heroic action. Like Spenser in the *Teares of the Muses*, but with less vehement rhetoric, Musophilus deplores that so little patronage should be given to literature. He sees poetry and eloquence as the guardians of lofty morals and the forces which cleanse a nation. He has a deep faith in the strength and destiny of his mother-tongue. What a great thing it would be if England, first of the nations in worth, became first in poetry also! Daniel has a vision of an English literature which should be read over the whole world. It should supplant Italian literature, now decadent:

> When all that ever hotter spir'ts express'd,
> Comes better'd by the patience of the north.

Patriotism was Daniel's dominant feeling and it led him to devote his capital effort to the history of his country. He recounts no such dream of the past as Spenser, nor such a long, mainly legendary chronicle as William Warner, in rude and awkward fourteen-syllabled lines, told in *Albion's England* (1586), a miscellany of ill-arranged stories which was so successful that it was republished in successive and enlarged editions until the author's death in 1609. Daniel did not share Warner's desire to begin his book at the Flood and bring it down to the execution of Mary Stewart. He was impressed by the effects of civil war and uneasy lest, since the succession to Elizabeth was entirely uncertain, it should be renewed. He therefore chose no period of glory for his theme, but told in narrative the story which was at this moment being dramatised, which Shakespeare was taking for the subject of his plays, the history of the bloodthirsty struggle between the houses of Lancaster and York. The eight cantos of Daniel's *Civil Wars*, published from 1595 to 1609, treat of the misfortunes of England from the reign of Richard II. until the break between Warwick and Edward IV., and in spite of their seven to eight thousand lines they leave the tale unfinished. It corresponds exactly to the Shakespearean "histories," *Richard II., Henry IV., Henry V.* and the two first parts of *Henry VI.*, sometimes following them and sometimes going ahead of them. Daniel's exposition is more accurate, cool and dignified than the plays, which bring on to the stage a succession of animated pictures by turns chivalrous and comic, arbitrary alike in their omissions and additions. It is strange to read Daniel's calm stanzas, and to remember the tumultuous dramas in which the same stories are told, or Spenser's romantic transfiguration of the national annals. Daniel's clear and expressed intention is to transfigure nothing:

> I versify the truth, not poetize.

Unfortunately he poetises all too little. Conscientiously he keeps pace with facts, adding fictions only very rarely. It is remarkable that his fictions have the same turn as in the pseudo-classical epics. They are inserted deliberately as ornaments, intellectual relaxations, for instance the mythological origin he fabricates for printing and artillery, two ill-omened inventions which Nemesis orders Pandora to supply.

This element of the marvellous is exceptional in Daniel's work. If his facts are dull, so much the worse; if dramatic, so much the better. Nor does he seek to interest by penetrating or lively portrayal of character. His calm narrative does scant justice to such outstanding personalities as the wild Margaret of Anjou, or to scenes of violence like Jack Cade's rebellion. If there is fairly lifelike psychology in his story of the first interviews between Edward IV. and Lady Elizabeth Gray, it probably is that the author is inspired by the staging of this incident in *Henry VI.* The best part of his poem is, besides a few vigorous stories, the moral reflections arising out of his patriotism as it is wounded by his own story of atrocious intestine conflict.

On the whole this long poem is a mistake. The careful and correct Daniel, treating the most tragic of subjects, is tedious. It is his misfortune to have misused his gifts. It would have taken a d'Aubigné to do justice to material as sombre and as bloodstained.

With his qualities and defects, Daniel was the writer of that day whose work was most justly estimated when it appeared. Spenser, who knew him at the outset of his career, praised his harmony and the pathos of his *Complaint of Rosamond*, but blamed him for flying too timidly and near the ground, exhorting him:

> Then rouze thy feathers quickly, Daniell.

Ben Jonson more bluntly says that he was "a good honest man, but no poet." Drayton considered that he was "too much historian in verse" and that "his manner better fitted prose." He was indeed, as will be seen, one of the best prose-writers of his time. William Browne, on the other hand, admired the purity of his poetic style and called him "well-languaged."

This purity, then so rare, won him a recrudescence of favour in the nineteenth century. Writers like Wordsworth and Coleridge who were working for the simplification of the language praise Daniel for having banished eccentricities and arbitrary inventions from his style. Southey is struck by his discreet use of the pathetic and says that he writes "always in a strain of tender feeling, and in language as easy and natural as it is pure."

His contemporaries, who loved ardour, missed in his work the passionate qualities and the movement, brilliancy and variety which they prized more than aught else. For us, the very absence of the merits which the Elizabethans often carried to excess makes pleasantly restful reading of his verses. It is as though we sailed for a day on smooth waters after passing through a storm. Moreover, if his reflections are not strikingly new, they are, as a rule, full of good sense and reason and are lit by a serene philosophy: he is dignified and proud as well as wise. He is, moreover, never harsh and constantly self-controlled.

(b) MICHAEL DRAYTON.[1]—Drayton's career ran parallel to that of Daniel and his poetry belongs to much the same genres. Yet it is the antithesis of Daniel's poetry. Instead of even, rather timid purity, it has warmth and dash, flights and falls.

He was born in 1563, one year after Daniel and one year before Shakespeare, in Shakespeare's Warwickshire, which lies at the heart of England. He was brought up on the borders of the Forest of Arden, on the banks of the Ankor:

> Fair Arden, thou my Tempe art alone,
> And thou, sweet Ankor, art my Helicon.

He cherished poetic ambitions in his first youth, for he tells us that at ten years old he implored his guardian, "clasping my slender arms about his thigh," to make him a poet, and the guardian smilingly set him to read Mantuanus and Virgil, while a minstrel of Polesworth Castle, where he was page, introduced him to popular songs and ballads. It is not known whether he were ever at a university, and his poetic production began late. He made his real beginning with *Idea, the Shepherd's Garland* (1593), which was inspired by Spenser, but is neither archaic nor moralising. Disguised as Roland, Drayton sings the praises of Beta, or Queen Elizabeth, and bewails, in turn, the vanished heroes of England and the rejection of his suit by his hard-hearted mistress, Idea. In 1594 he published his first sonnets with the title *Ideas Mirrour*. His eclogues and his sonnets reappeared in several successive editions, always with corrections and additions, a fate shared by most of his verses, for he was perpetually in quest of change.

In 1596 he had turned to historical poetry and he wrote his *Mortimeriados*, which he retouched and republished in 1603 under the title of *The Barons' War*. In moments snatched from this history he wrote the *Heroical Epistles of England* (1597).

Upon the death of Elizabeth he acclaimed the advent of James I., the lettered king, of whom, after the reign of the parsimonious queen, writers expected a sort of age of gold. Drayton was soon disappointed, and abandoning the court, he wrote two obscure and mediocre satires, *The Owl* (1604) and the *Man in the Moon* (1605), then certain odes far superior to his satires (1606).

Thereafter he concentrated on his immense *Polyolbion*, which he planned before 1598 and of which the first eighteen cantos appeared in 1613, the twelve others in 1622. In 1627, when he was growing old, he produced a collection which is full of freshness and includes his *Nymphidia* and his *Quest of Cynthia*, and in 1631 he published the *Muses Elizium*. He died in this year at the age of sixty-eight.

The whole of his very diverse work shows an abundant fancy, active and animated, but not subtle. He versifies with extreme facility. Reading certain of his poems, for instance the ode on the Battle of Agincourt, we are carried away by the martial rhythm, although the substance is thin and the thought as banal as in Laurence Minot's songs. Drayton's style has vigour and colour without correctness. He cares for colour more than for line. His amorphous sentences, and his periods connected by relatives at once vague and heavy, are stumbling-blocks to

---

[1] Complete works in *Chalmers's British Poets*, vol. vi. Selection of poems ed. by Bullen (1883). *The Barons' Wars, Nymphidia and other Poems*, ed. Morley (1887). Selections from the poems of Daniel and Drayton ed. by Beeching (1899). For criticism see O. Elton, *Michael Drayton*, (2nd ed., 1905.)

the reader, who follows him with some difficulty. There are striking, energetic words, but hardly a stanza has its rightful balance. This poet does not err from lack of industry or because he improvises hastily, for never were verses more courageously retouched than his. He went so far as to rewrite the whole of his *Mortimeriados*, substituting the *ottava rima* for its original seven-lined stanza. The benefit of such alterations is not invariably evident, but he always accounted for them to himself by particular reasons.

It pleased him to be independent, an innovator in such matters. He wrote his immense *Polyolbion* in alexandrines, contrary to the custom which favoured lines of ten or fourteen syllables. On the whole the choice was not happy. Against the four rhythmic accents of the French alexandrine, the English contains six, and is thus longer, slower and heavier. The monotony caused by the median cæsura is the more wearisome. Drayton's example was not followed. Mr. Elton, the most sympathetic of his critics, quaintly defines the effect produced: "it has a kind of heavy dignity, like a Lord Mayor's coach."

Drayton was better inspired when he used the decasyllabic couplet in many of his poems, for instance in his *Heroical Epistles*, where the couplet has a pliability and a variety of division which characterised it too little when it was handled by the later classicists. His epistle to Henry Reynolds (1627), which is in this form, contains, if not his *ars poetica*, at least his opinions on the poets of his time, and it shows his romantic tastes very clearly.

His work has more than one analogy with that of William Dunbar—poverty of thought and commonplace feeling, but swing and go and a rhythm which carries the reader along. All that survives of Drayton in anthologies is some short poems —the martial ballad to the glory of Agincourt and the ardent stanzas on the voyage to Virginia—and *Nymphidia*, that amusing fantasia in which he relates the great quarrel which brought Oberon and the knight Pigwiggen to blows for love of Queen Mab. Here he acknowledges a debt to Chaucer, who sang of Sir Thopas, and to Rabelais, who celebrated Pantagruel, but forgets Shakespeare, who in *Midsummer Night's Dream* celebrated the fairy queen and called lilliputian elves to life. He derives his tone and his form from Chaucer. He repeats the very stanza of *Sir Thopas*—aaabcccb, eight-syllabled separated by six-syllabled (*b*) lines, these last with feminine rhymes. He parodies the chivalry and tournaments which Spenser sang in the *Faerie Queene*, and he remembers Orlando's fury in the madness of his Oberon. But these literary reminiscences are easily carried by a fantasia which has no aim but to provoke laughter. Drayton's search is for the comic rather than the graceful, the grotesque rather than the poetic. He shows Oberon mad with jealousy, flying at everyone he meets, armed with an acorn which he brandishes by the stalk, mistaking a wasp for Pigwiggen and a luminous worm for a devil. He hurls himself at a hive, smears himself with honey and wax, rides an ant who throws him into the mud and climbs on to a molehill, whence he tumbles into a lake and is somewhat calmed by the water. Finally he makes a boat of his acorn and escapes. The episode is typical of the tone and character of this tiny children's epic.

Laughter dominates it, but in some other little poems Drayton's fancy, although never exquisite, is yet graceful and almost dreamy, for instance in his *Quest of Cynthia*, in which he represents himself as following the goddess through the country, where her divine steps have left charming vestiges, for many little flowers have opened beneath her feet. He reaches her at last, and the two decide to live together in love and innocence. Here Cynthia symbolises nature. The theme might be that of a Lake poet, but it is clothed in Elizabethan fancy.

Drayton's long poems have the same qualities of energy and imagination as the short, but are clogged and petrified by his rebellious material. Where, to sustain his more ambitious work, he needed intellectual force and deliberate reflection, he disposed only of vivacity and fancy. This is true of his *Barons' Wars*, a pendant to Daniel's *Civil Wars*. Like Daniel, Drayton wished to paint one of the tragic periods of the national history and to construct in epical form what was being presented on the public stage. But instead of the Wars of the Roses which Shakespeare dramatised, he chose the reign of Edward II. and the Barons' struggle against Queen Isabella's favourite, Mortimer, a theme which Marlowe had staged in *Edward II*. Less of a purist than Daniel, addicted to conceits, capable of more grandiose images, but afflicted with a confused syntax, Drayton is less inclined than he to moral reflection, but, having more fire, succeeds better in producing vigorous and brilliant pictures. He has some fine martial stanzas, and others, to describe the murder of Edward II., which are powerful, while those which paint the amours of the queen and Mortimer, and show the young Edward about to break in on them to avenge his father's death, are coloured and voluptuous, Italian in the manner of *Venus and Adonis* or *Hero and Leander*. The poem has over Daniel's the further advantage that it confines itself to a subject which has unity. But its defect arises out of the poet's moral indecision. He is drawn to the different characters of his story in turn when they love or suffer, and distributes his sympathy with that of the reader.

He seems to have no preferences and to aim at no conclusions, and the interest of his narrative suffers.

His *Heroical Epistles* (1597) may have been partly inspired by the success of Daniel's *Complaint of Rosamond*. But his chief model was the letters exchanged between the famous lovers of mythology in Ovid's *Heroides*. Drayton's patriotism led him similarly to present the famous characters of English history. He gives us, with the answers, Rosamond's letter to her lover, Henry II.; King John's letter to Matilda Fitzwalter; those of Queen Isabella to Mortimer; the Black Prince to the Countess of Salisbury; Isabella to Richard II.; Queen Katherine, widow of Henry V., to Owen Tudor; Eleanor Cobham to her husband, Gloucester; Suffolk to Queen Margaret, wife of Henry VI.; Edward IV. to his mistress, Jane Shore; Mary, Queen of France and daughter of Henry VIII., to Suffolk; Surrey to Lady Geraldine; Dudley to Lady Jane Grey. As a means of bringing life back to history, dramatically as on the stage, the idea is ingenious, and it is proof of the appetite of the nation for everything taken from their annals. The psychological essay was also a happy one. Drayton is not without sense of character, although it is not strong and penetrating enough in him to throw his personages into the relief which would have saved them from confusion and preserved this interesting poem against the assaults of time. More clearly than elsewhere we have here the impression that Drayton just misses success, that he all but has the talent necessary to a masterpiece, but that something lacking in his intellectual and artistic equipment holds him back on the brink of triumph.

We come to the one of his works which by its size and the number of years he spent on it is chief, his *Polyolbion*, in which his ardent patriotism finds vent better than anywhere else. Here he forsakes history for geography. He celebrates in fifteen thousand alexandrines the isle "of many blessings" (Polyolbion), conducting the reader through all the counties of England, by means not of such a rapid catalogue of resources as that made by the author of *Brut*, but by numerous detailed descriptions enriched by all the local legends.

The work is imposing because it is so greatly ambitious, and touching because through all difficulties and the inevitable monotony of his plan the poet is upheld by love for his native land. From Cornwall and Devon to Hampshire and the Isle of Wight, thence, by way of Salisbury and Bristol, to Wales and to the Midlands,

Warwickshire, the poet's birthplace, then Oxford, London, Surrey, Sussex, Kent, through Suffolk and Norfolk, and through every county to the north, to Yorkshire in the east and to the Lake Country in the west, he pursues his way.

The erudite character of the poem is emphasised by the notes appended to its eighteen first cantos by the learned John Selden, heir to the glory of Camden the antiquary. But accuracy formed only half of Drayton's plan. He wished also to poetise. Hence the dualism curiously emphasised by Selden's initial note:

> To gentlewomen and their loves is consecrated all the wooing language, allusions to love passions and sweet embracements feigned by the Muse amongst hills and rivers. Whatsoever tastes of description, battle, story, abstruse antiquity, and (which my particular study caused me sometime remember) law of the kingdom, to the more severe reader.

It must be acknowledged that a puerile mythology decorates the poem. Every hill, every valley is personified. Every river, in particular, is endowed with life, turned into a genius or a nymph. The process is easy and unvaried; it is as though Boileau's Rhine "à la barbe limoneuse" were multiplied a hundredfold. There are no descriptions, in the modern sense, of natural features. Each stream and slope has a surprising memory replete with history or legend, and reproducing, as well as a passage of real history, the past of Brut's country, Albion.

What is astonishing is the untiring zest with which Drayton pursues a theme at once flat and extravagant, multiple and monotonous. In the districts which he knows more intimately, like his own county of Warwickshire, he stays to paint pictures which are both lively and fresh. His deer-hunt in the forest of Arden is often quoted. And even in the dullest passages he has some lines, written from the heart and frankly worded and turned, which awake nodding attention and interrupt the increasing impression of bad taste and the ridiculous.

Nothing but the analysis of a canto can give an idea of this astonishing work. In the sixteenth the poet leads us from stream to stream to London, following the Coln as it flows, by way of St. Albans and Uxbridge, into the Thames a little below Windsor.

The poem begins with the Ver, a small tributary of the Coln, which passes Watling Street on its course. The Roman road and the stream engage in conversation, Watling Street asking the Ver the reason of the great changes which have occurred on its banks and made a fertile corn-growing country into a sandy waste:

> At which the silent brook shrunk in his silver bed,
> And feign'd as he away would instantly have fled;
> Suspecting present speech might passèd grief renew. ,

But the road persists, inquiring why Verulam, the cradle of the race of Dudley already sung by Spenser, is in ruins. Finally Ver answers that Verulam was ruined by the destruction of the monasteries, whereat the Catholic stream cannot contain its indignation. To pacify it, Watling Street offers to relate its own history from the days of Malmutius, together with that of its sisters, the three other great Roman roads. Accordingly it describes the course of each and the villages through which they have passed. When it pauses, Ver urges it to continue, and

> With these persuasive words, smooth Ver the Watling wan,
> Stroking her dusty face.

At last the story is told, and

> This said, the aged street sagg'd sadly on alone.

The canto goes on to eulogise the situation of London and the wealth and activity of the great river port. It ends with a diatribe against the gentry, declaring them

I—O

to be lazy and devoted to luxury and to be impoverishing their country by importing from abroad, at great cost, the articles necessary to their extravagant and epicurean tastes.

This canto, neither worse nor better than the average, may be taken as typical. More than once it might provoke laughter and ridicule, for the humanised rivers, roads and hills cut very strange figures, and there is something childish, fitted to childish minds, about the whole conception. But the spirit of the Renascence was, after all, youthful in the extreme. The whole period is not exempt from a suspicion of puerility, mingled with all that it had of the great and the sublime.

Drayton's was a mad enterprise. The game was lost before it was begun. Yet his ardour, his fancy, his eccentricity, his flatness, his very bad taste, make his *Polyolbion* a characteristic product of his time.

(c) THE COLLECTIONS OF LYRICAL VERSE. THE SONGS.—Besides Daniel and Drayton, there were in the Elizabethan age dramatic authors who wrote a little verse as secondary to their plays, and also minor poets who followed one of the literary fashions of the moment. Certain genres were particularly in favour, and to note their characteristics will repay us better than to deal with each individual by himself.

In those days the works of single authors were less read than the collections in which some publisher arbitrarily brought together sets of verses, often of uncertain authorship. Here and there these books include the signature of a great lord or a famous poet, but usually the poems are signed only by initials and sometimes nothing indicates their authorship. Tottel's famous *Miscellany* had been followed by the *Paradyse of Dainty Devises* in 1576, *A Gorgious Gallery of Gallant Inventions* in 1578 and *A Handefull of Pleasant Delites* in 1584, and now came the *Phœnix Nest* in 1593, the *Passionate Pilgrim* in 1599, *England's Helicon, England's Parnassus* and *Belvedere* in 1600, *Poetical Rapsody* in 1602, and others. In almost all these collections exquisite poems are elbowed by others which are mediocre or even deplorable; the worst rhymesters are associated with the true poets.

It was in these collections that some poets placed their best work, like the prolific Nicholas Breton (1545?-1626), whose engaging pastoral vein was never better displayed than in the *Helicon*, and Richard Barnfield (1564-1627), whose most charming little odes appeared in the *Passionate Pilgrim* and were long attributed to Shakespeare.

The shortest pieces, and especially the songs, are what is best in these collections.[1] The Elizabethan age cannot claim the song exclusively, for songs were made throughout the English Renascence. Songs are of all time and all countries. Yet they were perhaps never so copious, so various and so winged as in this period. They best accomplished the blending of the genius of the people and the artistic sense awakened by humanism. The fusion was attempted in all genres but with very unequal success. In most of the long poems taste is shocked by frequent disparities. The reader of to-day is offended by the excess of disorder and of pedantry in turn. But in numerous songs and slight lyrical pieces artifice is so well wedded to nature that the two are hardly distinguishable. The rudeness or clumsiness of the popular muse has been penetrated by graceful refinements of vocabulary and a pliability of versification once unknown to it. The best examples have a perfection which is never recaptured.

And the song was everywhere, sung in halls and parlours, trolled along the

---

[1] *Elizabethan Lyrics*, ed. Bullen (1885); *England's Helicon*, 1st ed. (1600), reprinted by Bullen (1887); *English Garner*, ed. Arber, 7 vols. (1877-83); *Seventeenth Century Lyrics*, ed. Saintsbury (Rivingtons); *English Madrigal Verse* (1588-1632), ed. Fellowes (Oxford University Press, 1920). Criticism: J. Erskine, *The Elizabethan Lyric* (1903); Saintsbury, *A History of Elizabethan Literature*; *Cambridge History of English Literature*, op. cit. vol. iv., chap. vi.

roads. It was in towns and in the country, on the stage and in romances. It filled whole collections; some poets specialised in it, but here and there an excellent ditty was born on the lips of a fine lord or lady who never made another. England, destitute of the plastic arts, became the impassioned lover of song. She had her traditional airs, and she listened eagerly to those which reached her from abroad, especially from Italy. She translated foreign songs and took them to herself, transforming them and inspired by them to new endeavour. Most were love-songs, some very free and profane. But others were religious, and many purely fantastic. They were in every mood—grave, mocking, sentimental, cynical. They were sung to the accompaniment of virginals, the spinet of that day, or of flageolots or of the viola da gamba or the guitar. They were written by the greatest and by unknown poets. England, Merry England, was a nest of singing-birds.

Spenser inserted very beautiful slightly elaborated songs in his *Shepheard's Calendar*. His natural richness and loftiness led him to make of the song a little ode, if not such a magnificent ode as *Epithalamion*. Sidney kept nearer to the song properly so-called, of which some specimens, very full of life, follow his sonnets, the first with the refrain, "To you, to you, all song of praise is due," and his nocturns, "Only joy! Now here you are," and "Who is it that this dark night?" He is less happy in the large number of songs scattered through his *Arcadia*. The most popular of his songs is the *Dirge of Love*, "Ring out your bells!" Many are bold, passionate songs, not without a fantastic element which is sometimes exquisite, and nearly always they have a catching refrain.

The author of *Tamburlaine* and *Dr. Faustus* laid his sonorous trumpet aside one day to play a pastoral air on a reed-pipe. He sang the shepherd's call to the shepherdess, "Come, live with me and be my love," and Raleigh answered for the girl with a refusal, "If all the world and love were young."

These are true and charming songs. But the period was not satisfied with a few scattered airs, and there were whole collections which included verse and music. One of the first in date was made by William Byrd, gentleman of the Chapel Royal, who in 1587–8 published his *Psalms, Sonnets and Songs of Sadness and Piety*, a simple, lucid and pleasant miscellany although one without much poetry. Its light songs are imitated or translated from the Italian.

Much warmer in tone, richer in imagery and more effeminate and languorous is the collection of Nicholas Yonge, *Musica Transalpina* (1588), in which the Italian note sounds yet more clearly. Yonge was a merchant whose trade brought him into touch with Italy. He or the nameless gentleman who supplied him with his translations was so much under Italian influence that he imitated even the terminations of metrical lines in that language and ended almost all his own with feminine rhymes. Here and there something turgid or banal or a richness which is slightly common spoils this curious collection.

Something fundamentally commonplace and a commonplace formal correctness also mar John Dowland's three *Books of Songs or Airs* which appeared in 1597, 1600 and 1603. A musician of repute, John Dowland, about 1580, visited France, "a nation furnished with great variety of music." Then, having acquired, he says, a surer judgment, he made a stay in Germany and in Italy, where he was much appreciated, and afterwards in Denmark. In 1597 he returned to England and gave lessons on the lute. The airs in his books are, except for a few well-turned pieces, better than their verses.

Thomas Campion's four *Books of Airs*, published from 1601 to 1613, are of far greater value. This doctor of medicine, whose distraction was music, was a true poet. He turned critic and attacked rhymed verse, at which he excelled, in order to defend measured metres modelled on antiquity. In his *Books of Airs*, where he fortunately follows the national tradition, he protests against the earlier collections. He will have nothing to do with Italian or French airs. His intention is to publish English airs, and he states that he will endeavour to couple words and notes harmoniously. His songs are by turns simple and strange, ancient and modern, sensual and passionate, bacchic and pious, worldly and rustic. Their form and matter are of every kind, but in all the rhythm is excellent and the language pleasant.

Some of Campion's most graceful songs occur not in his collections, but in his masques. The most exquisite songs of all were to be heard on the stage, and in order to cull them nearly every comedy and romantic play of the age must be searched.

Some on mythological themes, pretty but a little mincing, are in John Lyly's comedies, but appeared only in the posthumous edition of 1632, and are attributed by the most recent critics not to him but to the period after his—"Cupid and my Campaspe played," "O yes, O yes, if any maid." Many very pleasing songs occur in George Peele's *Judgement of Paris*. The best of the songs of Robert Greene and of Lodge are, however, in their romances, that lovely cradle-song "Weepe not, my wanton" in Greene's *Menaphon*, and the charming madrigal "Love in my bosom like a bee" in Lodge's *Rosalinde*.

The songs with which Shakespeare has sown his work are the most original and spontaneous of all and the richest in impressions of nature. A fresh and rustic realism runs through more than one of them—the contrasted notes of the cuckoo and the owl in "When daisies pied" in *Love's Labour's Lost*, the song of Amiens on ingratitude in *As You Like It*, with its evocation of the keen-toothed winter wind and the waters warped by frost, or, in the same play, the page's song, its anacreontic moral the fresher for being trilled among green cornfields and English acres of rye, or again the vagrant's song which Autolycus sings full-throatedly in *Winter's Tale* as he tramps the long English roads—"when daffodils begin to peer," and the white sheet is "bleaching on the hedge" and "the sweet birds, O how they sing!"

There are also the purely fantastic songs which still borrow much from nature, the cradle-song in *Midsummer Night's Dream*, sending the "spotted snakes with double tongue," "the thorny hedgehogs" and the "newts and blind-worms" from the bank where Titania sleeps; Ariel's, who lies "in a cowslip's bell" and flies "on the bat's back," his call to the fairies:

> Come unto these yellow sands,
> And then take hands,

and his wonderful song of the sea-change suffered by Ferdinand's father, "full fathom five" beneath the waters.

There are the short, light songs of feeling, that which tells of the birth of love, "Tell me where is fancy bred" while Bassanio in the *Merchant of Venice* chooses the casket; Balthazar's song on the inconstancy of men in *Much Ado About Nothing*, "Sigh no more, ladies," and the song to which poor, forsaken Marianne listens in *Measure for Measure*, "Take, O, take those lips away."

A few are more ambitious, like the dirge in *Cymbeline* over Imogen's body, with its resignation to death which comes to all, and finishes "joy and moan."

But the list is inexhaustible. Shakespeare's many songs cannot even be classified. Most of them were born of a particular occasion and are implanted in a scene whence they cannot be taken without injury—Desdemona's willow song, Ophelia's mad song, Iago's drinking song, the ironical snatches sung by the fool in *King Lear*, and the incantations of the witches in *Macbeth*, not to mention Falstaff's hummings and those of the gravedigger in *Hamlet*, or the sprightly airs of Pandarus with their evil reek.

These songs have been collected, even translated with some success, in a single volume,[1] but as a rule they are not intended to be separated from the scene in which they take flight. By themselves, they lose their atmosphere with their occasion. Many are frail as butterflies' wings, and at a touch the gold dust which is their sparkle falls away from them.

Their rhythm is as various as their meaning. Some are all rhythm, made, it would seem, for their air and refrain. They vanish at the attempt to wring sense from them, for instance "When that I was and a little tiny boy," the epilogue to *Twelfth Night*. The nimble versification is unfailingly marvellous. Every resource and variety of form is used—the eight- and six-syllabled iambic line, the seven-syllabled trochaic line, the anapæstic line, combinations of these metres, refrains which do not scan but which delight the ear, simple and double rhymes, the most various arrangements of echoing words. The law governing them cannot be specified, for almost each one has its distinct form, line or stanza. They are made for music, and their only rule is to fit the air with which, or for which, they have been created.

Shakespeare's contemporaries had not his varied wealth or his realism, but they decorated their plays with songs as sweet and melodious as his, especially Thomas Dekker, the author of "Cold's the wind" and "Art thou poor," Beaumont and Fletcher with their "Lay a garland on my hearse," "Hence all you vain delights," and "Drink to-day and drown all sorrow," and Webster with his "Call for the Robin." Ben Jonson has many songs, a little classical in turn, scattered through his masques and comedies—"Queen and huntress," "Still to be neat," "Come, my Celia"—and the well known "Drink to me only with thine eyes," which occurs not in a play, but in his collection *Under-Woods*.

The use of songs persisted on the stage until the last in date of the great dramatists, Shirley, who provides a magnificent specimen, "The glories of our birth." The Restoration did not break the tradition, and charming songs echo through Dryden's plays.

This rich age produced a lyricism which approximated to the popular ballad, as in Drayton's ode on Agincourt, and also little delicate poems worthy to figure in the Anthology. The transition from the one to the other was insensible. The total result was very English owing to the mastery acquired over words and sounds and owing to an indefinable valiancy of turn and expression. The aroma of antiquity and the scent of modernity were blended. Nothing else in all this wealth of literature is as essentially poetic. This is its delicate, swaying crest, its exquisite and supreme flower.

(d) THE SONNETEERS.[2]—The vogue of the sonnet in the Elizabethan age was as brief as it was intense. With few exceptions it was confined to the six years from 1591 to 1597, during which some twenty collections appeared one after the other under the impulse given by Sidney's *Astrophel and Stella*. All these were of love sonnets, and some which are complimentary and dedicatory and are scattered through the books of the period should be added to them.

Nothing better shows in miniature the general characteristics of Elizabethan poetry, the mingling of the conventional and the independent, the imitated and the original, of which it is constituted. So great is the influence plainly exercised on the sonnets by Italy and France that recently, when the distinction between the work of masters and pupils was overlooked, they were characterised as an artificial product. Undoubtedly to write a love sonnet after Petrarch is to Petrarchise, and all who wrote them subsequently to the great Italian are in some sort his disciples. But as much is true of any poet who casts his poetry, even a line

---

[1] Into French, by Maurice Bouchor (1896).
[2] *Elizabethan Sonnets*, ed. Sidney Lee, 2 vols. (1904); Sidney Lee, *The French Renaissance in England* (1910).

thereof, in a mould already in use, yet no one refuses to acknowledge his originality if he produce a personal impression in the form which another has invented.

In spite of the sonnets of Wyatt and Surrey, the English had neglected this genre and had even forgotten the exact meaning of the word sonnet, applying it to lyrical effusions very various in form. Such was the current designation of the *Hecatompathia: or Passionate Centurie of Love*, which Thomas Watson brought out in 1582 and which is in reality made up of little poems of eighteen lines divided into three sestets. The young poet himself introduces them ingenuously as exercises in style having no correspondence with his own sentiments. They are paraphrases of the foreign Petrarchians without value beyond harmony of style. Watson penetrated the highly susceptible language with the images and the subtle turns of thought brought into favour by the continental sonneteers.

Many later writers of regular sonnets, or at least of poems of fourteen lines, did no more than Watson. The search for sources, so active in the last half-century, has discovered in Ronsard and Desportes and the minor and major Petrarchians of Italy the origin of many sonnets found in Henry Constable's *Diana*, Samuel Daniel's *Delia*, Thomas Lodge's *Phillis* and the like. These poets made many liberal translations; they are chiefly to be valued for their style, which sometimes, as with Daniel, is highly distinguished.

Daniel, the calmest and most temperate of the Elizabethans, the poet of rest, may be taken to typify the men who wrote sonnets to be in the fashion, without conviction and probably without a real mistress to sing. She whom he implores remains invisible, inaccessible, cold, unknown and absent. His sonnets are so many chill appeals to her pity and might well leave her unmoved. But Daniel has merits as a writer. The language of his sonnets is usually pure and their versification correct in spite of some hard elisions and forced epithets in the manner of du Bartas ("Muse-foe-Mars"). If they incline too much to rhetoric they are clear and have unity; sometimes a pale ray of imagination is shed on them; and here and there a line or two have a true beauty which revives the reader ("O clear-eyed Rector of the holy hill").

Barnabe Barnes is the antithesis of Daniel. He is a frenzied poet, or at least it pleases him to assume airs of dementia, and he escapes servility by extravagance. There is a curious mixture of factitious delirium, obscure indecency and true verbal vigour in his collection *Parthenophil and Parthenophe*. We cannot tell whether this be a very young poet who dreams unchastely and is intoxicated by rhyme, or a man of vulgar mind who swaggers of set purpose. The content of his collection is curious to consider. Comparisons, epithets, mythology, obscenities, puns, parentheses, questions and, above all, apostrophes are heaped one upon the other. We understand where we can, and probably there is not always any sense to be understood. The best lines occur in the madrigals which follow the sonnets and are of more worth than they.

On the whole, after the great sonneteers Sidney, Spenser and Shakespeare, it is Michael Drayton who bears reading best. His collection *Idea*, augmented in every new edition which appeared from 1594 to 1619, is a sort of encyclopædia in which all the familiar themes recur with others added to them. We do not know if his Idea represent one woman or several or none, if during the twenty-five years covered by the series the poet flitted from love to love or from fancy to fancy. While he hardly gives the impression of a true passion, shows little delicacy and is often vulgar, he yet is versatile and animated and more than once ingenious to the point of the fantastic. The taste for geography manifest in his long poem is betrayed in several of his best sonnets, for instance in the first, in which he represents himself as an adventurous seafarer who has sailed the perilous seas of love, and in the thirty-second and fifty-third, where all the rivers of England are humbled before that sweet stream Ankor on whose banks Idea dwells.

Another frequent characteristic of Drayton is his dramatic sense. His sonnets enclose on occasion small scenes, for instance the second, in which an inquiry into the murder of his heart is instituted, or the fifty-ninth, in which he and Love quote proverbs against each other. In this genre Drayton produced the most dramatic of sonnets, his sixty-first, in which he bids his mistress a bitter farewell, promising to forget her for ever, and then suddenly, while he grasps her hand to take leave of her, addresses to her the words by which they will doubtless be reconciled.

On the whole, *Idea* is an easily, carelessly constructed work, lacking unity but in no way inert, and with a dash and a rude bravery of style which give it value.

The loss of all the collections we have just mentioned, and also of Fletcher's *Lycia*, Thomas Watson's *Teares of Fancy*, the unsigned *Zepheria*, Percy's *Cœlia*, Willoughby's *Avisa*, the *Alcilia* of J. C., Griffin's *Fidessa*, Lynch's *Diella* and Smith's *Chloris* would hardly impoverish poetry. They may be summed up as imitations, if not mere translations, or else they are experiments in style and in conceits. But three works, signed by great names, are more beautiful than any of the others and bear many marks of sincerity, that is of a direct relation to life and their authors. They have suffered from mediocre neighbours, and their few inevitable, superficial resemblances to these have caused some recent critics to condemn them as tainted by the same unreality and produced by the same rhetoric. They are Sidney's *Astrophel and Stella*, Spenser's *Amoretti* and Shakespeare's *Sonnets*. That lofty and deep natures should have been superior to others even in sonnets is not surprising. It would seem that these true poets, with all the gamut of poetic forms at their disposal, had recourse to the sonnet when they wished to express their intimate feelings, and thus used it in conformity with its origin and for its proper purpose, not to make play with a fiction unconnected with their real life. The impression of sincerity is most simply explained by supposing that the writers were sincere, and it happens also that the few facts revealed by their sonnets are in strict agreement with the little known about their lives.

Is this to say that these sonneteers have no common ground with their forerunners? Far from it. They are like them by their exaltation, by the fact that for thousands of years lovers have repeated the same words and gestures and have sometimes been deceived into believing that they used them first. Moreover, all poets from the time of Petrarch shared an idealism which was their philosophy. Platonic thought, especially as it helped them to deify their mistress's beauty, make a virtue of their desire and assure eternal life at once to their verses and to the lady of their choice, made its way into all their minds. This is not to say that they were, properly speaking, imitators, but that they lived in a common atmosphere.

Moreover, their wish to offer worthy jewels to the object of their love led all the sonneteers to refine alike, and sometimes, when the greatest of them dived for pearls, they brought up the gems they had admired in others. Yet not only in their imagination, but also in their passion, there is a vivifying and renewing force. Even their repetitions are spoken in a new voice which is their own. Neither Petrarch, nor Ronsard, nor the most famous of the Italian and French sonneteers, could take the place of these English sonneteers, Sidney, Spenser and Shakespeare. The individuality of a great sonneteer is as distinct as that of any other great writer. In him the part of convention is slight and transparent and his true figure shines through it.

We have already spoken of the sonnets of Sidney and Spenser which are at the very heart of their poetic work. Shakespeare's sonnets are in different case, for they were written in moments snatched from work for the theatre.[1] His unequal collection, spoilt in more than one place by excessive subtlety, stained by shadows which the most attentive searchlight has not entirely dissipated, is yet the casket which encloses the most precious pearls of Elizabethan lyricism, some of them unsurpassed by any lyricism. The formidable efforts to deduce the exact history of the poet's heart from his sonnets and the publisher's mysterious dedication, and the conflict of the theories resultant on this investigation, must not be allowed to conceal either the absolute beauty of the verses or the clear lines of the drama of feeling they trace. Shakespeare tells of his fervent love for a young man of high birth whose beauty and nobility he celebrates. He devotes himself to him whole-heartedly, finds in him his joy and his consolation for all the misery of life. He also expresses the agony of his love for a capricious and fickle married woman who deceives him with his friend. To that friend he is indulgent to the point of forgive-ness, but for the woman he feels anger gradually increasing to hate.

The finest, most poignant and most passionate sonnets are those in which he gives himself, with all his love and his genius, to the young man who dazzles him even after he has been betrayed by him. The profound pathos is thrown into relief by the rare beauty of the images and the style, and by the perfection of the versification, which has a subtle melody never to be surpassed. Music is not inherent in the pattern of the sonnet, or rather in the fourteen-lined poem, three quatrains with distinct rhymes followed by a distich, a form which is less expert than the Petrarchian. But its looseness is redeemed by the infinite care with which the poet caresses words and sounds. Only the best sonnets of Milton attain to the supreme beauty of the best written by Shakespeare, and their themes and effects are entirely other.

(e) Erotic Italianism. The Licentious Poets.—Feared and denounced though it was by Puritans like Ascham, Italian voluptuousness was still seductive to poets. Its traces are everywhere, in the ardour of many sonnets and songs, in the warm colouring of more than one such historical picture as Drayton's *Barons' War*, and even in poems like Spenser's which have a very evident moral tendency. The most beautiful passages of the *Faerie Queene* are impregnated with it. Yet Spenser was tenaciously fighting the licentiousness of the Italian muse, and his work is justly renowned for its purity and lofty tone as compared with that of more than one of his great contemporaries who were still less impervious than he to the charms of the Mediterranean Circe. Marlowe and Shakespeare were among these. Under the influence of the verses and *novelle* of Italy, a sensual, lascivious poetry flourished in England, and was apt to provide libertine fine gentlemen and courtesans with their daily reading. These writings match the daring mythological paintings which the sixteenth-century artists alternated with religious pictures. The moralists had good cause to be scandalised when they listened to such stories as Marlowe's *Hero and Leander* or Shakespeare's *Venus and Adonis*, not to mention John Marston's *Pigmalion* and other analogous productions of the time.

(1) *Marlowe's "Hero and Leander."*—Marlowe's *Hero and Leander* [2] deserves careful study, not only for its real merit, but also for its great success in its author's generation and the praise, sometimes extravagant, given to it in our day.

The English Renascence is here seen at work on a legend of antiquity and trans-forming it. The original poem was written by a fifth-century grammarian, Musæus, an Alexandrian satiated with complicated dishes who fell in love with simplicity and took to a milk diet. In spite of some inevitable mannerisms, Musæus wrote an

---

[1] Doubtless between 1594 and 1602. Published 1609.
[2] Written before 1593, when Marlowe died; not completed. Published in 1598 with Chapman's continuation, another edition in that year with a sequel by Petowe. See Chabalier, *Héro et Léandre* (Paris, 1911).

exquisite poem, simple in outline, short and yet complete and harmonious, very pure although it celebrates ardent youthful love. In it Hero is the virgin suddenly awakened to love, Leander the adolescent overcome by his first passion. The idea of the final catastrophe broods over the whole work, imparting melancholy even to the description of the lover's bliss. Marot followed the Greek poet exactly when he wished to relate the beautiful story to the French, adding only that seeming artlessness which his style communicates to all his subjects. There is in fact no better method.

But Marlowe did not wish to translate. His intention was to charge his plot with all the wealth of his imagination and to give rein also to satire and irony. The tragic end of the lovers did not keep him from making merry on his way to it; he respected neither the purity of the legend nor the character of the young lovers, ennobled by courage, trial and death. In Musæus the consummation of the love of Hero and Leander is simple and natural. Although there is no nuptial rite, there is no sin. But in Marlowe, the atheist and libertine, the idea of sin does not spring from piety, but is present because he uses his poem to run counter to the beliefs of his time and because it amuses him to defy the moral sense of those about him. The provocation has a racy turn and sometimes changes the pure story into a *fabliau*. Marlowe likes to unmask the unconscious hypocrisies of his hero, even more of his heroine, and there is a hint of satire against woman in his poem. It is in the spirit of the Middle Ages rather than of paganism. But paganism of the most scandalous kind, which he did not find in Musæus, is there also, an enthusiasm for manly beauty and the gratuitous introduction of forbidden practices into the tragic idyll. We are shown Neptune in love with handsome Leander and pursuing him beneath the waters. All this medley makes *Hero and Leander* a composite and barbarous work, and it is impossible to understand Swinburne's praise of it. "That poem stands out alone amid all the wide and wild poetic wealth of its teeming and turbulent age, as might a small shrine of Parian sculpture amid the rank splendour of a tropic jungle."

Fundamentally nothing could be less Greek. Rather we have here an extravagant Ovid, a demoralised Spenser. Yet how restrained and classical the portrait of the Spenserian Belphœbe seems beside Marlowe's heroine, dressed by his unbridled fancy as a young priestess of Venus! The strangeness of her clothing is extraordinary—her lawn mantle, "the lining purple silk, with gilt stars drawn," her wide green sleeves, her blood-stained blue kirtle, her myrtle wreath whence falls a veil of artificial flowers and leaves, her pebble necklace,

> Buskins of shells, all silver'd, usèd she,
> And branch'd with blushing coral to the knee;
> Where sparrows perch'd, of hollow pearl and gold,
> Such as the world would wonder to behold,
> Those with sweet water oft her handmaid fills,
> Which as she went, would cherup through their bills.

Besides all this prettiness there are conceits: the artificial flowers of the veil are so well imitated as to deceive, and men "praise the sweet smell as she past," and they feel the exhalations of her breath; bees also are taken in, seek honey in the veil, "and, beat from thence, have lighted there again." Even worse than all this are the red spots on Hero's skirt, "made with the blood of wretched lovers slain," doubtless for the sake of the amiable girl!

In manner Marlowe comes very near the prettiness and curiosities of *Arcadia*. Elsewhere, by the way he makes his hero and heroine think, act and speak, he recalls one of Chaucer's sprightly tales or he anticipates Swift's cynicism. But always there is an underlying sensuality derived from Ariosto or even from Aretino. It is painful to see this graceful and pure theme turned into a half-satirical, half-aphrodisiac tale. Marlowe's poem is astounding by the heavy and extravagant richness of its frame as by the highly flavoured coarseness of its details.

And yet it has merits which partly explain the dithyrambic praise accorded to it. It is the work of a true poet who overloads a story without stifling it, and brings into his narrative a beguiling vigour, a great writer of verse whose touch is sure and clear although he does not always keep free of the preciosity of his time, who handles words and images with surprising decision and energy in a language which has withstood time better than that of any other man of his century. Moreover, Marlowe's irreverence is not uninterrupted; here and there he is unreservedly on the side of the lovers; he is capable of sincere passion as well as of cynicism. It was in one of his happy moments that he wrote his famous lines on love at first sight, "It lies not in our power to love or hate." The reader of *Hero and Leander* protests, but is vanquished all the same, and he ends lamenting that this poet was stopped in mid-career.

His talent shines luminously when his verses are compared with those of the poets who succeeded him, and not only those of the mediocre rhymester called Petowe, who seems to have been entirely ignorant of the Greek legend and who transformed *Hero and Leander* into a chivalrous romance. Petowe's Hero is loved by the king of her country, rejects him and is cast into prison, to stay there until a knight shall defend her honour victoriously in the lists. Leander, nameless and disguised, appears as her champion, triumphs and claims her, but she is faithful and refuses him until she sees his face, whereupon the two live happy ever after. There is here no plunge into the waters, no Hellespont, no tragedy.

But Marlowe's superiority is hardly less apparent when the sequel to his poem is read which was written by the over-learned George Chapman, afterwards famous for his translation of Homer. Chapman knew Greek and the original poem, but he is as far removed from Marlowe as Marlowe is from Musæus. He is the most unintelligible, the gloomiest and the foggiest of the Elizabethans, and thereto as much a moralist as Marlowe is a cynic. He makes the death of the lovers the punishment of their illicit love, and invents the heaviest machinery for the purpose, introducing endless new episodes into the restrained story. He fashions for Hero a new dress which makes Marlowe's seem simple. The scarf he gives her takes as long to describe as the shield of Achilles and bears stranger symbols. He cannot refrain from introducing a moral reflection into the smallest descriptive detail. If the waves buffet the swimmer's body, he says:

> And toss'd distress'd Leander, being in hell,
> As high as heaven: bliss not in height doth dwell.

In many places he touches the lowest depth of absurdity to which the astonishingly unequal poetry of the Elizabethans could fall, one beneath any watery abyss into which poor Leander sank.

(2) *Shakespeare's "Venus and Adonis"* (1593) *and the "Rape of Lucrece"* (1594).—Shakespeare's *Venus and Adonis*, which he calls "the first heir of my invention," was written at the same time as *Hero and Leander*. It was lovingly chiselled and was dedicated by the poet to the Earl of Southampton, his young and noble patron. Here again inspiration comes from a classical legend. Shakespeare has recourse to Ovid as Marlowe to Musæus; he too ministers to the taste for licentious pictures and enfranchises himself from the exigencies of drama in order to follow his fancy.

The story is well known. Venus falls in love with the young Adonis, who cares only for hunting and rejects her. In spite of her he goes back to his sport, is killed by the wild boar which is his quarry and is metamorphosed into an anemone.

Shakespeare eliminates nearly all the mythology. A powerful instinct impels him towards reality. His goddess is a woman skilled at lovemaking and ravaged by passion, and in Adonis we already have the young sport-loving Englishman, annoyed and fretted by the pursuit of a beautiful amorous courtesan whose sensuality is unbounded and who retains no prestige of divinity.

These realistic passions are framed by equally realistic pictures and episodes. The arguments of Venus are supported by the appearance of "a breeding jennet" rushing out of a neighbouring copse and at once joined by Adonis's steed, who breaks his rein in order to go to her. The horse is painted with dry precision, as by an expert. Further, the goddess vividly describes boar-hunting and hare-hunting to the youth, the one an over-dangerous sport whence she would dissuade him, the other a safe amusement which she recommends. These two specialised pictures are plainly drawn at first-hand and from observation, and the most touching lines of the poem tell of the agony of the "timorous flying hare."

It is, however, impossible not to recognise that the dominant note is struck by the voluptuous painting of the goddess's lascivious gestures and the complacent retailing of her glowing words. Thus regarded, the poem is, from the merely artistic point of view, a complete success. Shakespeare gives evidence in its stanzas of astonishing linguistic wealth and skill. He too is over-prone to conceits, but on the whole the critic has only to admire his masterliness.

Because he writes in stanzas, not, like Marlowe, in rhyming couplets, his poem has less the turn of a narrative than *Hero and Leander*. It is pre-eminently a series of pictures. If the licentiousness of the two poems is about equal, that of Shakespeare has the advantage of dealing with a mythological legend and staging a heroine neither of which could be much profaned. On the other hand, his eroticism is more elaborate and has less dash and spontaneity than that of his rival.

It seems to have been for an artistic purpose that Shakespeare in the following year chose the rape of Lucretia as the subject of a poem which forms at once a pendant and a contrast to the preceding one. Having painted the attempt of an amorous woman to seduce a youth, he proceeded to represent the rape of a chaste wife by a wretched debauchee.

The later work shows increased power and breadth, but the old defects in strengthened form. The speeches are longer than ever and less appropriate— Lucrece's supplications to Tarquin before his crime, the endless plaints which intervene between the assault and the suicide of the outraged wife. The minute descriptions, with their prettiness and conceits, are especially irritating, veiling and enervating, as they do, the tragedy of the theme. In the portrait of Lucrece, asleep upon her bed as Tarquin draws her curtains, poetry and bad taste are inextricably mingled.

From end to end of the poem the reader is exasperated by the poet's very talent, his fancy and eloquence, and is brought to regret both Ovid's quieter picture and Chaucer's artless rendering thereof. He tells himself that the limits of the sonnet and restrictions of the theatre had the happy effect of setting bounds to the poet's exuberance. An aspect of Shakespeare is revealed which could not appear so clearly in his other works, but it is on the whole the less pure side of his genius, both morally and poetically.

The judgment of his contemporaries was other, and a large part of their eulogies of Shakespeare, as of Marlowe, refers to their voluptuous poems. These provoked such imitations as Marston's *Pigmalion*, written in the same spirit, and Francis Beaumont's *Salmacis and Hermaphroditus*, and they remained the most popular specimens of the poetry of questionable character which the Puritans were wont, not without the support of forcible arguments, to rebuke.

(f) PIOUS AND REFLECTIVE POETS. (1) *Southwell, Sylvester.*—Together with licentious poems, Italy supplied pious effusions which were equally mannered and were marked by the same cult of conceits. It is very remarkable that the Catholic poet Robert Southwell (1561–95)[1] sought in Italy an antidote to the heady stanzas of *Venus and Adonis*. This ardent Jesuit, who lived in the hope of martyrdom and was indeed executed, after cruel tortures, at Tyburn in 1595, left behind him verses which are the most religious of his generation, marred though they are by the preciosity of the day. It was in prison that he conceived the idea of writing poems in which passion should become the servant of faith. In *St. Peter's Complaint* he repeats the stanza of *Venus and Adonis*. The poem abounds with forced similes, paradoxes and antitheses. Southwell, exactly like the French Malherbe who was sowing his wild oats at this moment, reproduces the mannerisms of the Italian Tansillo.

His lyric ardour is purer in the short pieces which follow his *Complaint* and form the collection called *Mæoniæ*. The most famous of them is that strange and ardent vision the *Burning Babe*, which shows the Christ-child on fire with suffering and love, and was admired by Ben Jonson. To this should be added his fourfold meditations on the Four Last Things, an ecstatic contemplation of celestial joys which is like a foretaste of Crashaw.

Southwell's Catholicism isolated him among the Englishmen of his generation. The chief part of Elizabethan poetry consisted of translations from the Huguenot poet du Bartas,[2] whose *Semaine* (1578), followed by his *Seconde Semaine* (1584), acquired extraordinary celebrity in Protestant countries. James VI. of Scotland, Thomas Hudson and Philip Sidney himself immediately translated extracts, but the special interpreter was Joshua Sylvester,[3] who from 1590 to 1599 published copious renderings of the verses of the French poet, and in 1605–6, under James I., a complete translation of his works. Both du Bartas and his translator won immediate recognition; no work of this time received more enthusiastic praise. The grandeur of the subject, which was the creation of the world, made the productions of any less ambitious muse seem petty. The grandiloquence of du Bartas was taken for pure sublimity, and, far from shocking English taste, his constant lapses from the noble to the trivial, his eccentricities, his unsmiling puerility and his enormous long-winded bombast fell in with natural tendencies and satisfied them. The composite epithets, which soon made du Bartas ridiculous in France and strikingly proved him to be out of tune with the spirit of the French language, were fitted to English and easily acclimatised in England. Even in Elizabeth's reign the glory of du Bartas was known to everyone; it was acknowledged by Spenser as by Sidney, by Drayton as by Daniel. Not, indeed, until the reign of James I. did it reach its full height, and du Bartas won yet more tardily the most honourable of all his claims to fame, that of leading Milton to choose the sacred story of the fall of the angels and of the first man for his theme. But in the great void which stood for religious poetry at the end of the sixteenth century, the appearance of the English version of *La Semaine* was an even more impressive event. Protestantism, hitherto divorced from the Muses, conceived for the first time the idea of a high epic poetry based on the Bible. Religious men who had the taste for poetry, but were scandalised by the paganism of their contemporaries, found "verses which a girl could read without blushing."

Des vers que sans rougir la vierge puisse lire.

La Semaine, I. ii. line 30.

Even of Spenser, proselytise though he did on behalf of Protestantism and

---

[1] Edited by Grosart (1872).   [2] H. Ashton, *Du Bartas en Angleterre* (1908).
[3] Edited by Grosart, 2 vols. (1876).

morality, this could not always be said. Du Bartas did not think it necessary to transpose the Bible into mythological pictures, but went straight to the Scriptures. He showed that a great and truly Christian poetry was possible, and the revelation constituted his glory, which was as brilliant as it was ephemeral.

(2) *Sir John Davies and Davies of Hereford.*—Southwell in his ardent piety stands almost alone. Only a generation after him did the example of du Bartas give rise to a truly Christian poetry. But under Elizabeth some poets who had already come under his influence followed tendencies which, amid the prevalence of the fantastic, were markedly severe, even didactic. It is true that Spenser had built up his sensual visions behind a noble moral façade, and that Daniel's reflective muse was prone to a grave thoughtfulness, yet two men who in some sort specialised in philosophical poetry may be detached from their fellows.

Sir John Davies (1569–1626), a lawyer who became a statesman, began by giving free rein to his capricious imagination in his *Orchestra, or a Poeme on Dancing* (1596), one of the most curious examples of the strange Elizabethan inventiveness. He represents Penelope as refusing to dance with the suitor Antinous, who thereupon proves to her that the exercise is both ancient and universal, since the elements and the heavenly bodies, involved in rhythmic movement, are so many dancers. On this curious theme the poet has many animated stanzas of which some attain to true poetry. Three years later, he produced a series of twenty-six hymns in acrostics to Astræa, or Elizabeth, which are full of go, and also a more serious poem on the immortality of the soul, *Nosce Teipsum* (1599), which very happily, in eloquent quatrains, reconciles imagination and logic. This poem was at the time the supreme attempt to reason in verse, for all that it did not quite escape infection from the reigning fantastic tendency. In this age of madrigals and pastorals it constitutes an anomaly.

Much more profusely, but with much less poetic swing, the Welsh poet and writing-master John Davies of Hereford (1565?–1618?),[1] almost the namesake of him whom we have just considered, wrote many poems on theological and philosophical subjects, the best known of them *Mirum in Modum* (1602), a dissertation on the glory of God and the form of the soul, and *Microcosmos* (1603), a description of the small world of man with instructions on the art of governing it. This is a vague metrical treatise on physiology and psychology. The writer continued to make verses until his death, sacred verses especially, but satires and epigrams intermingled with them. He had little poetry, but an unfailing and unmistakable edifying tendency.

(g) SATIRE.—In 1597 a young man who had just left the university wrote at the beginning of a collection of satires:

> I first adventure, with fool-hardy might,
> To tread the steps of perilous despight:
> I first adventure, follow me who list,
> And be the second English satirist.

This was Joseph Hall,[2] and his arrogant announcement was a sign of presumption rather than knowledge. No one is ever the first. Without going back to *Piers Plowman*, we find that satire had flourished in various forms since the Renascence, in Skelton and Wyatt and more recently in George Gascoigne, the author of the *Steel Glass*. It had made use of doggerel, rhymed heroic verse and blank verse, in turn. Spenser had found ample space for it in more than one of his works, and had produced one very harsh satire, his *Mother Hubberd's Tale*, which is, on the whole, the most successful of this century. Thomas Lodge, a year before Hall, published

---

[1] Edited by Grosart, 2 vols. (1873).
[2] Complete poetical works edited by Grosart (1879).

A Fig for Momus. Since Hall was certainly not unaware of all these productions, he doubtless deemed that the name of satire should be reserved for imitations of the ancients, Horace, Persius or Juvenal, whom he himself followed closely. But while he is inspired by their form, the task he sets himself is fortunately that of chastising the society of his own time, and his *Virgidemiarum*, in six books, of which three were published in 1597 and three in 1598, contains a fair number of sketches of abiding interest because their subject is contemporary manners. The twenty-three-year-old poet naturally displays in his invectives against his times a supreme self-confidence. He boldly solves every moral problem, and speaks out loudly, comparing the ways of a past he does not know to those of the present. But not only has he a certain writing talent, comparative lucidity, skill in combining words, and the ability to express himself in a lively, striking way: he is also less inclined to vague declamation than his youth might warrant. He is concrete and picturesque. He attacks the extravagance of dress, describes the costume of a dandy, makes fun of a courtier whose wig has been blown away, and, like Portia in the *Merchant of Venice*, at much this time, paints the Englishman's jumbled costume to which every country had contributed. Similarly he criticises the language of his day—

> Bibinus self can have ten tongues in one,
> Tho' in all ten not one good tongue alone—

and mocks the conceits of the sonneteers. Except for Spenser, to whom he finely renders homage, he sees in literature only the blameworthy, and like Spenser he actually, in this year of 1597, perceives only decline and barbarism in the drama. Yet there is both justice and point in his attack. He is especially indignant at the grandiloquence which Marlowe, author of *Tamburlaine*, had brought into the fashion:

> Then weeneth he his base drink-drowned spright
> Rapt in the threefold loft of Heaven's hight:
> When he conceives upon his faigned stage
> The stalking steps of his great personage
> Graced with huff-cap termes, and thundering threats,
> That his poor hearers hair quite upright sets.

As much of a classicist as Sidney, Hall protests against the buffoonery of the clowns introduced into tragedies and the consequent "goodlie hotch-potch."

Hall did not confine his strictures to literature. He draws a vigorous little picture of the hardships suffered by a tutor in a squire's household, inventing an advertisement in which all the services and compliances the squire expects of the poor man are enumerated.

> All these observ'd, he could contented be
> To give five markes, and winter liverie,

it concludes.

The Church soon robbed letters of this young and most promising satirist. Hall became a bishop, and it is remarkable that the other satirists of the period also ended as clergy, just as in France Régnier became canon of Chartres.

Such was the fate of John Marston (1575–1634),[1] the most cynical of the Elizabethan authors, whose first efforts were the licentious poem the *Metamorphosis of Pigmalions Image* and *Certaine Satyres*, most of them collected in the *Scourge of Villanie* (1598). Marston was attacked for the immorality of his *Pigmalion*, and defended himself by stating that he wrote it to ridicule the fashionable licentious paintings. The sincerity of the defence is doubtful and the same doubt attaches to all this poet's satires. Under the pretence of teaching morals, Marston allows himself to go to the extreme of coarseness both in subject and in language. He is

[1] Complete edition by Bullen, 3 vols. (1885).

certainly more virulent than Hall, but he is also more declamatory and much less accurate. In his writing there is hardly anything representative of the period. His pedantry is as excessive as his cynicism. On the whole, he is most remarkable for his gift of words. His lungs are strong and insults spring plentifully to his lips, as he ploughs up

> The hidden entrailes of ranke villanie,
> Tearing the vaile from damn'd impietie.
> Quake guzzell dogs, that live on putrid slime,
> Skud from the lashes of my yerking rime.

Here and there, amid this emphatic flow of words, something or someone is more exactly delineated, for instance the amateur of the theatre whose criticism, like the speech of Shakespeare's Pistol, is all in the verbiage of tragedies. It is also permissible to believe that under the Latin names of his characters Marston is aiming at contemporaries, that Tubrio stands for Marlowe. But generalities prevail and identifications are difficult.

At the same time as Hall and Marston, if not a little before them, John Donne (1513–1631)[1] as early as 1593 composed his first satires. The later dean of St. Paul's was then writing satiric and erotic poetry in turns. But his early verses did not appear until 1633, after his death. By reason of his extreme youth he could not be a very profound moralist, and his satires were mainly literary exercises in which, however, his originality and his fantastic bent were already apparent. Yet more impregnated than Hall with literary reminiscences, he desired to restore to the satire the rude versification used by the Romans. A precocious taste for the obscure led him to prefer Persius, who is his favourite model.

Never has English metre, the heroic metre, suffered as at his hands. He wrote so-called couplets, but allowed himself to drag the sense from one line to the next in the most violent way and to make the most singular divisions of his line. More than this, he violates the iambic rhythm over and over again and many of his lines cannot be scanned.

> If all things be in all,
> As I think, since all which were, are and shall
> Be, be made of the same elements,
> Each thing each thing implies or represents.

When he rhymes unaccented syllables—officèrs, suitòrs—the fact may be ascribed to archaism, but with little probability, since he aimed at modernism and a reproduction of the inflections of everyday speech. It is rather that he despised the laws of versification.

As for his subjects, they are traditional but reanimated by observation and by something pointed and unexpected in the way they are handled. He resumes Horace's theme of the importunate bore and that of the snob who disturbs the poet at his books and drags him out into the street where repeatedly he leaves him in order to greet some important personage.

The poet's subtle and metaphysical imagination was already finding vent, as in the satire which exposes the wretchedness of courtiers and litigators. Magistrates are the sea in which all streams lose themselves, litigators these streams which feed this sea. The queen can do nothing in the matter: she is like the calm source of the Thames, ignorant who owns the meadows flooded by its branches or the cornfields its waters inundate.

> O age of rusty iron! Some better wit
> Call it some worse name, if ought equal it,
> Th' iron age was, when justice was sold; now
> Injustice is sold dearer far.

[1] Complete edition of Donne's poems by H. J. C. Grierson, 2 vols. (1912).

With Marston and Hall, Donne represents classical Elizabethan satire. This was, however, only a small part of the satirical poetry of the period. The spirit of satire was more abundantly manifest outside the regular forms. The prose of such as Nashe, the "English Juvenal," is nothing but long, droll, Rabelaisian satire. It was, however, especially under James I. that satire ceased to be merely literary, and became the sincere and vehement expression of a pessimism which was often painful. Pure satire became frequent on the stage, not only in Ben Jonson's plays, but also in those of most of his contemporaries, not excepting Shakespeare, whose *Hamlet, King Lear, Troilus and Cressida* and *Timon of Athens* have many touches and even whole passages in the tone of bitter invective. All the dramatists mockingly or indignantly denounce vice, at least intermittently. Sometimes they inveigh against the society of their day, sometimes against mankind itself.

2. **Poetry under James I. (1603-25).**—There is something arbitrary in a separation of the poetry of Elizabeth and of James I. The division must be understood to be convenient rather than anything else, a device to assist the chronology of literary history. The poets who wrote as much in one reign as the other are numerous—Shakespeare, Daniel, Drayton, Chapman and others, and to attribute much importance to the change of sovereign would be puerile. Yet the division has the advantage that it marks an evolution which, in spite of many exceptions, caused the two first decades of the seventeenth to differ from the two last of the sixteenth century.

Elizabeth's reign has the glory of youth and growth, of national expansion and patriotic faith. The whole of literature is lit up by the victory over the Armada. Even the liveliest satires and the gloomiest pages written have a spontaneity and dash which are near to joy. We feel the intense enjoyment of the poet who is adventuring into new paths, his delight with his own creations. He derives from life, from the things he sees and from the current ideas, a pleasure perpetually renewed. He is intoxicated with the novelty of his metres and the freshness of his vocabulary. If he be Spenser he writes *Hymnes in honour of Love and Beautie*; if Marlowe, *Tamburlaine the Great*; if Shakespeare, *Love's Labour's Lost* or *Midsummer Night's Dream*. He has neither morals nor religion, except such a façade as Spenser affixed to the *Faerie Queene*. Pessimism exists for him only superficially or momentarily, a cloudy sky through which the sun is about to break.

Was it the effect of the vain attempt of Essex at a revolution which would have overthrown the old queen's unpopular counsellors? Was it the disillusionment of the dull reign of James I., when England withdrew into herself and the great hopes of expansion were frustrated? Or was it merely the weariness which followed on the long previous lyrical exaltation? Whatever were the causes, life came to seem sad, human nature perverse, society vitiated. Shakespeare wrote violent, poignant tragedies and comedies hardly less bitter. A harsh or cynical realism succeeded to the transports of former days, to the flights into ideal spheres.

Poetry had grown self-conscious; the earlier ardours and easy enjoyment of colours and words now were on the wane. Poets readily became more moral or religious, sometimes more didactic. A general more sombre or more melancholy hue was diffused over letters. While literature acquired more substance it became less capable of facile, light-hearted joy. Poetry was already a little under the shadow of the approaching great civil conflict, of the strengthened and menacing Puritanism. If it were permissible to assign an age to two succeeding generations, we would say that the second was nearer middle life than the first. Even such of its poets as reverted to the Elizabethan manner had lost the first freshness of invention; they were merely in the sequence.

(a) GEORGE WITHER.[1]—At the very end of Elizabeth's reign and under James I. several poets flourished who are variously interesting, some who had received an impulse from their predecessors and others who adventured in new paths.

George Wither, William Browne, the two brothers Giles and Phineas Fletcher and Drummond of Hawthornden may be cited as in the succession of Spenser. The spirit of the pastoral or the allegory or the refinement of the sonneteers dominates their work.

George Wither (1588–1667), the Puritan satirist, a voluminous writer, lived to see the Restoration, but all of his verses which deserve to survive were published before 1622. The son of a Hampshire country gentleman, he was educated by the rector of the parish, and his early home gave him a strong taste for the country and a love of solitary independence. His poems, which are often autobiographical, describe his rustic, unsophisticated youth. When he reached the court of James I., at the age of eighteen, he was scandalised by the lying and the licence he found there, and he satirised the court in his *Abuses stript and whipt* which appeared in 1613. The satire is general, without personal attacks, but it caused such displeasure that Wither was imprisoned in the Marshalsea. He was there for several months, and there wrote one of his most charming poems, the *Shepherd's Hunting*, published in 1615. It is a sort of pastoral in the form of a dialogue between Willy, who represents the poet William Browne, and Philarete, the friend of virtue, otherwise Wither himself. In the most famous passage the prisoner Philarete encourages Willy to resume his interrupted pastoral songs, describing to him how he beguiles his own captivity with the help of his Muse, who shows him how to enjoy in memory the natural beauty from which he is debarred. It is here that an outburst of gratitude to Nature occurs which at this date is surprising, one which contains all Wordsworth in germ:

> In my former dayes of blisse,
> His divine skill taught me this,
> That from every thing I saw,
> I could some invention draw:
> And raise pleasure to her height
> Through the meanest objects sight;
> By the murmure of a spring,
> Or the least boughs rusteling,
> By a dazie whose leaves spred,
> Shut when Tytan goes to bed,
> Or a shady bush or tree,
> She could more infuse in mee,
> Then all natures beauties can,
> In some other wiser man.

The other poems of Wither's youth are inspired by the same spirit, for instance his *Fidelia*, an elegy of love, which was followed by love songs. The satirist, who was soon to be a determined Puritan, appears in one song as a boon companion who refuses to waste himself in despair for a woman who scorns him. In *Faire-Virtue, the Mistress of Phil'Arete*, which he wrote in 1622, Wither perhaps reached his highest accomplishment, but unfortunately his prolixity and the common and heavy character of his moralising had increased, and the collection is only intermittently of value. The song of the *Constant Shepherd* is a farewell to the sirens whom the poet rejects for virtue. Yet he is still capable of enjoying the pleasures of an honest life. In a Christmas song his unconquerable love for the traditions of jollity breaks out, and he writes one of the lustiest of the poems inspired by the roast-turkey season, one full of homely merriment. With its refrain, "And let us be merry," it exhales the mirth of pagan rather than Christian festivities and heralds, two centuries in advance, the Dickens Christmas. It has Dickens's sentimental joviality,

---

[1] His poems have been edited by H. Morley (1891).

I—P

for Wither too remembers the unfortunate who receive a generous pittance on this day of feasting.

It is disconcerting to discover this mood in a Puritan, simultaneously author of *Wither's Motto* (1621), which earned him not only renewed imprisonment in the Marshalsea, but also punishment from Ben Jonson, who in *Chronomastix* defended his times against this reviler. Henceforward Wither, once a writer of gentle pastorals, gave himself up to the composition of satires in which elements of exaltation and mysticism are mingled. He became one of the prophets of the Revolution, the typical Puritan scribbler, and thus exposed himself to the ridicule of Cleveland and Butler, producing such rubbish that Pope calls him "wretched Wither " and instances him as the type of a bad poet.

Wither's merits were not only distinct from his Puritanism, but in direct conflict with it. Only his youthful verses, of which some are charming, count at all. But even in them he is unequal; his best passages occur among platitudes. He is too apt to improvise, to abuse the dangerous easiness of the line of four accents. His is work which cries out for the selector.

(*b*) WILLIAM BROWNE.[1]—William Browne (1591-1643), the friend of Wither's youth, confined himself strictly to the pastoral. His *Britannia's Pastorals* has, by reason of its extent and patriotic title, made him something like the classical representative of pastoral poetry in his country.

He was inspired by Spenser's *Calendar*, especially for his *Shepheard's Pipe* (1614), which is a series of eclogues, serious or homely by turns. In *Britannia's Pastorals*, of which the first book appeared in 1613, the second in 1616, while the third remained in manuscript until 1852, he was undoubtedly under Spenser's influence, but Sidney's *Arcadia* was his chief model. Unfortunately he imitated too closely the confusion of plots in the great romance, and the entangled adventures which form the web of his poem cannot be resumed. The principal thread is supplied by the story of the love of Celandine and Marina. Celandine becomes indifferent to Marina, who has given him her heart too quickly. She wishes to drown herself, but is saved by the river-god, who carries her off to Mona, where she is imprisoned in a cave by the monster Limos, or Hunger. From the time he loses her Celandine again loves her, searches Fairyland for her, and there finds Spenser asleep. The poem stops before Celandine's adventures are concluded.

Many other stories, nearly as long, fill the poem, which is half allegory and half mythology. Its subject is, however, of secondary importance. Its charm is constituted by a wandering fancy. It must be read, like the *Faerie Queene*, in a leisurely way, and also with indulgence for the young poet's numerous faults, his inequalities as he constantly lapses from poetry to flatness, his too heavy decoration as he strings pompous similes together and thus interrupts his narrative, his conceits, his facetiousness which does not stop short of punning, and his composite epithets after the manner of du Bartas.

Yet Browne has interesting characteristics, distinct from those of his models. His poem is written in couplets which often have a distinctly classical air, the lines marching two by two, and having an epigrammatic or proverbial turn. And the couplets are not seldom interrupted to make way for graceful songs and touching elegies.

One of the attractions of the poem is its evidence of Browne's love for his own county of Devon, his pride in its glory as the nursery of seafaring adventurers and his intimate knowledge of its natural features and local customs. Although he was beguiled into factitious and romantic pastoral poetry, Browne was capable

---

[1] Complete edition by W. C. Hazlitt (1868). Poems ed. by G. Goodwin (The Muses' Library, 2 vols., 1894). See F. W. Moorman, *William Browne: his Britannia's Pastorals*; E. Gosse, *The Jacobean Poets* (1899).

of seeing Nature as she is, and sometimes he painted her successfully. He could make English birds sing in concert, and he could bring a hunt to life or depict an effect of the dawn in a village.

Always he is cheerful. He enjoyed writing verses. He had youth and he wrote from the heart.

His *Pastorals* are certainly no masterpiece. He is a richer and less correct Racan who occupies an honourable place below the great.

(c) PHINEAS FLETCHER.—The influence of Spenser on Phineas Fletcher (1582–1650),[1] the incumbent of a small Norfolk parish, was yet more marked. Although his poems did not appear until 1631 and 1633, they were written much earlier, for he calls them "these rawe Essayes of my very unripe yeares, and almost childehood." They probably date from his undergraduate days at Cambridge.

His *Piscatorie Eclogs* are original only in substituting fishermen for shepherds. He changes only the accessories of the *Shepheard's Calendar*, and, like the Spenserian shepherds, his fishermen alternately converse of love and of religion. His reputation rests on the *Purple Island, or the Isle of Man,* a long allegory of which the elements are derived both from Spenser and from du Bartas. The Huguenot poet whom William Browne had already celebrated had no greater admirer than Phineas Fletcher, who acknowledged him as his master:

> And that French Muse's eagle eye and wing
> Hath soar'd to heav'n, and there hath learn'd the art
> To frame Angelick strains, and canzons sing
> Too high and deep for every shallow heart.

This unfortunate love for a pseudo-great poet led Phineas Fletcher into many extravagances. The presentment of his allegory is clumsy to the point of being ridiculous. The allegory itself, in which the island, with its hills, rivers and woods, represents the human body, is like a disguised lesson in physiology. The author attempts to be at once technical and poetic, and finds himself obliged to explain his verses by numerous long footnotes. He is fairly well informed on anatomy, but is unaware of Harvey's discoveries about the circulation of the blood, and considers flesh to be blood badly dried. His mistakes are, however, less regrettable than his method. In his exposition of the structure of the body he repeats Drayton's unhappy attempt to versify geography. The feat is something like that of the descriptive writers of the eighteenth century—Pope analysing a game of ombre or Delille a game of chess. Each organ is personified: Hepar is the liver, Koilia the stomach, Splenion the spleen, Visus the eye, Gustus the taste, whose wife is the garrulous Lingua, and so forth. These faculties are served by grooms corresponding to the secondary organs, the muscles or nerves. They live in the valleys, on the hills or in the towns.

All this part of the poem is a paraphrase of the description of the Castle of Alma in Book II. (Cantos 9–11) of the *Faerie Queene,* with the difference that Fletcher, in his desire to be scientific and technical, obscures the Spenserian symbolism. Spenser's stanzas xxi. to xxxiv. are interminably dragged out in Fletcher's five first cantos. From a hundred lines he draws fifteen hundred. Nothing shows better than a comparison between the two works Spenser's real genius, very great even in the passages of his poem which are least calculated to please to-day. His long-windedness appears as brevity, his strangeness as good taste and classical judgment.

In the moral part of his allegory, in which he is more at his ease, Fletcher is still the disciple of Spenser who showed the Castle of Alma or the Soul attacked by the vices and sins. Similarly Fletcher paints battles between the vices and the virtues,

[1] Giles and Phineas Fletcher, *Poetical Works,* ed. Boas, 2 vols. (1908–9).

the latter led by Eclecta, or the Church. He relates them in chivalrous language as knightly conflicts. Eclecta is a more visibly Christian Belphebe or Britomart. The historical allusions and the flattery also recall the *Faerie Queene*: the angel who comes from heaven to save Eclecta is King James I.

Yet Spenser's pupil is distinguished from his master by his greater religious fervour and by his literary form—the lighter stanza, the quickened movement, the more modern style, the total absence of archaism.

In spite of all his strange inventions and scientific velleities, this is a true poet. His images drawn from nature have no great rarity, but their grace and liveliness are their own. There is a ring in the stanzas which describe the joys of the Church reunited to good, to Christ and to God, and in the dialogue between husband and wife and the picture of their paradisial joys.

Fletcher is in some sort the connecting-link between the poet of the *Faerie Queene* and Bunyan, who described Mansoul.

(*d*) GILES FLETCHER.[1]—The poetry of Giles Fletcher (1588?–1623), also a country clergyman, was, even more than his brother's, marked by religious fervour, and bore witness to the renewal of faith and mysticism which was soon to affect many of the Anglican clergy, so aptly reprehended by Spenser for inertia and indifference. Giles Fletcher's chief poem, and almost his only one, is *Christs Victorie and Triumph* which was published in 1610. It is a young man's work and shows signs of immaturity, but exuberance and a wealth and freshness of imagination more than redeem its faults. It forms a link between Spenser and Milton, between the two first books of the *Faerie Queene* and *Paradise Regained*. Its subject is that of Milton's poem and is treated in the Spenserian manner: Christ's life on earth, His mission of mercy, His struggle against Satan who tempts Him, His final victory and the vision of the heavenly Jerusalem. Like his brother Phineas, Giles acknowledges Spenser and du Bartas as his masters, calling the latter "Bartas, my sacred Sovereign," and numbering him among "the miracles of our latter age." He is haunted by the *Semaine*, which had lately been translated by Sylvester (1605–6). As du Bartas inspires his subject, so he takes his style and his versification from Spenser. His stanza is Spenser's shorn of one line, and in his style there is Spenser's harmony and redundancy, together with an overweight of flowers and epithets, and also an inclination to antithesis unknown to his master.

There is greatness in the opening stanzas, the debate between Justice and Mercy, who in turn plead before God. The Creator is finally moved by Mercy, and the triumph of Christ in heaven is thus signified.

His triumph upon earth ensues. In the desert He resists all the temptations of the Evil One—despair, presumption, vainglory, voluptuousness, pride and covetousness. He passes through the same trials as Spenser's Sir Guyon.

There follows Christ's triumph over death in a picture of the Passion, and His triumph after death portrayed in a fervent hymn, an ecstatic description of earthly joys and regenerate man after the resurrection of the Saviour, and a final picture of the felicity of the blessed written in a spirit of exaltation. Except some of Shelley's visions, there is perhaps, in English, no other such rapturous description of Paradise. Milton is too restrained, too severe and too classical for such effects. Bunyan's heavenly Jerusalem repeats the Apocalypse too literally. Moreover, the faith of these great Puritans was too exclusive and individual. More than they, Giles Fletcher aspired to the felicity of all good Christians; he has more unction; the spirit of the Gospels is his supreme guide, and he seems to be unaware of the rigours and the terrors of the Old Testament. For all his striking youthful defects,

---

[1] Edited by Grosart for the Fuller Worthies Library in 1868 and for the Early English Poets Series in 1876. See also last note.

he has an honourable place among the religious poets of England. Religion was to him the source not of wearing scruples or of fears, but of beatific visions.

(e) DRUMMOND OF HAWTHORNDEN.[1]—William Drummond of Hawthornden (1585–1649) has a place among Spenser's successors for different reasons than Phineas Fletcher.

This Scot, who wrote the purest English, was a great man of letters, knowing the literature and the languages of the moderns as of the ancients. He was especially susceptible to the Italian influence. While his poetry is full of reminiscences, it is marked by a suave, slightly melancholy tone which makes it personal. It consists mainly of the book of poems published in 1616, a long panegyric on James VI. on the occasion of his visit to his native country, entitled the *River of Forth Feasting* (1617), and a collection published in 1623 and called *Flowers of Sion*. The poet's talent is best revealed in his sonnets, which are Italian in form, save that they end with an epigrammatic couplet. His sincere love for Nature is apparent through his sonneteer's conventions and his reminiscences. Living far from the centre of English literature, he pursued the sonnet when in England its popularity was on the wane and it was no longer methodically used by poets.

(f) BEN JONSON.[2]—In contrast to the poets just reviewed, who followed beaten tracks, we have two who were pioneers, Ben Jonson and John Donne. It was they whose influence was felt by the greatest number of their countrymen down to the Restoration.

Although Ben Jonson was first of all a dramatist, his poetic work, other than dramatic, is of fairly considerable extent. It consists of short pieces, written throughout his life, which appeared in three collections, *Epigrammes* and the *Forrest*, published together in the folio of 1616, and *Under-Woods*, published in the folio of 1641, after his death. No weight should be attached to the difference of titles, which implies no real difference of subject. All the collections are of detached poems. Complimentary verses as well as satirical quatrains are included with the *Epigrammes*, and *Under-Woods* contains poems longer than the *Forrest*, a word which merely translates the Latin form *silvæ*. These two or three hundred little sets of verses may well be considered in accordance with their character, irrespectively of the collection in which each occurs.

As is to be expected, the spirit of satire looms large in them. Side by side with the true epigrams, two or four lines long, sensible rather than biting and somewhat lacking in pointedness, Jonson presents us with a fair number of little sarcastic portraits in ten or twenty lines, not unlike the "humorous" characters so plentiful in his comedies. Some types are skilfully pilloried: the reformed gamester taught wisdom by a beating; Shift, the retired lieutenant, cadging on the citizens and answering every inquiry with "God payes"; Don Surly, who gives himself importance by an affectation of haughtiness, a pretence of disdain, a display of sarcasm and an abundance of oaths; and

> Poor Poet-ape, that would be thought our chiefe,

who "takes up all, makes each man's wit his owne," and in whom some have believed they saw an offensive picture of Shakespeare.

Ben Jonson also wrote moral satires which were on a larger scale and were nobler in tone and more sincere in expression than those of Hall and Marston. His epistle to Sir Edward Sackville inveighs successfully against patrons who grant

[1] Ed. Ward, for the Muses' Library, 2 vols. (1894), and Fréchette (1912).
[2] Ed. by Gifford (1816), and revised by Cunningham, 3 vols. (1871), 9 vols. (1875) (the poetry is in vol. iii. of the 1875 edition). For studies on Ben Jonson's poetry see E. Gosse, *The Jacobean Poets* (1889); Swinburne, *A Study of Ben Jonson* (1889); and M. Castelain, *Ben Jonson, l'Homme et l'Œuvre* (1907).

their favours arrogantly, generally to the undeserving, and who are well paid out when they reap ingratitude.

Yet more lively is his epistle to a friend, Master Colby, to persuade him to go to the wars. He advises him to flee a town where men, in the leisure of peace, lead a shameful life, and to seek the camp. It is in such poems that Jonson's personality best appears, his blunt frankness which expressed itself in harsh versification, strong rather than harmonious.

But there is more than satire in the collections. They include many complimentary lines to the contemporary writers who were the poet's friends, if not his rivals—Bacon, Camden, Drayton, Chapman, Donne, William Browne, Sylvester, Francis Beaumont, John Fletcher, Shakespeare. The verses in honour of Shakespeare, inserted at the beginning of the works of this rival, are very beautiful. While Shakespeare lived Ben Jonson's relations with him seem to have been cordial and hostile by turns, but after his death any jealousy or animosity he may have felt for him was effaced, and there remained an enthusiastic, moving admiration which produced the first unreserved and worthy celebration of his greatness.

Ben Jonson's praise was not always either as just or as fitly bestowed. Yet, when the hyperbolical flattery usual in his day is remembered, it is rather the manliness of his address to his patrons which is striking. His verses to the Sidney family and to the poet's sister, the Countess of Pembroke, are no mere sycophantic eulogy. He has fine verses on Penshurst, Sir Philip Sidney's birthplace where he had himself received hospitality, on its amenities and charms and especially on the rustic simplicity and patriarchal virtue it sheltered. This poem is far superior to his long, elaborately staged compositions, whether odes or epithalamiums, which must be regarded mainly as literary exercises in the manner of the ancients. He was the first Englishman to write Pindaric odes, with strophe, antistrophe and epode, and the experiment cannot be called a happy one. Its artifice is too apparent and the author has not the qualities which make great lyricism.

Like the poets of the French Pleiad, Jonson was more successful in his imitations of the Greek Anthology, writing beautiful elegies and, in particular, touching and noble epitaphs. In this genre he was surpassed only by Herrick, his disciple.

Love figures in his collections, but merely, it would seem, as a literary theme. The *Celebration of Charis*, which he says he wrote at fifty years of age, is very fanciful and lively, and, of the ten poems which compose it, the fourth is in stanzas of a rare and truly lyrical pattern. In general, however, his love pieces reproduce poems of antiquity. The learned Ben Jonson translated more than he invented.

His work, taken together, offers some general characteristics. He was the most learned and the most convinced of the humanists of his generation. Until Milton, he was, with his unmatched knowledge of Greek and even greater knowledge of Latin, first among them. He was little influenced by French or Italian literature, being ill acquainted with these languages, and he had not Spenser's sympathy with the Middle Ages. His culture was fundamentally Latin. The Latin muse appealed to his robust genius, with its desire for energy and tendency to moralise. It certainly was not through him alone, but it was principally through his means, that Neo-classsicism was introduced into English poetry in the seventeenth century. He makes us feel that we are on the road to Dryden.

It is, however, his second characteristic that his personality is not stifled by his Latin livery. On the contrary, it shows itself very openly. Ben Jonson was a glorious egoist, very strongly individualised, with fixed ideas which he asserted arrogantly. His pride, his contempt for ignorance and hypocrisy, his love of frankness and loyalty, his straightness, the manly affection of which he was capable: all these are manifest in his verses.

He was without certain gifts—spontaneity and fancy. His style inclines to the abstract and lacks imagery. His metres are varied, but his rhythm is not pliable. There are many hard constructions in his verses, and Dryden called his translations "jaw-breaking." But he contributed to the poetry of his country some qualities in which it was then defective: he aimed at putting much meaning into the metrical line and his composition tended to be consecutive and regular. He subordinated fire and dash to logic. He taught soundness, reflection, self-control.

This was why in the latter part of his life, and especially after 1620, many admirers and disciples were grouped about him. He spoke as a master who knew the law, and many listened. He was the central poet, king of the taverns frequented by poets. Beaumont and Herrick have sung "those lyric feasts" where "rare Ben Jonson" was king. He had his "sons," and to be of "the tribe of Ben" was glorious. Following his example, poets cultivated the epigram, rifled the Greek Anthology and impregnated themselves with classicism. His influence lasted throughout the century, but was crossed and opposed by that of his friend John Donne.

(g) JOHN DONNE.[1]—John Donne (1573–1631), who, after a secular youth, took orders at the age of forty-three, in 1615, and ended as dean of St. Paul's, is perhaps the most singular of English poets. His verses offer examples of everything castigated by classical writers as bad taste and eccentricity, all pushed to such an extreme that the critic's head swims as he condemns.

Donne was a precocious poet who began to make rhymes about 1593 and had written many of his best poems before he was twenty-five. He would therefore be, in the strict sense, an Elizabethan, were it not that his poems, with a few exceptions, were not published until after his death in 1633. They were read in literary circles before they were printed, but they exercised their large and curious influence after their appearance in book form.

At the outset of Donne's career Spenser had already won his glory, and the Petrarchian sonneteers were producing collection upon collection. The independent young poet reacted against these schools. He found pastoral poetry, mythology, the allegory, Platonism, the taste for platitudes and for copious and facile description in the fashion. He despised convention and the morals of chivalry, as he despised highly regular metres and monotonous and harmonious cadences. His violation of rhythm in his *Satires* has already been mentioned. It was hardly less in his *Songs and Sonnets* and his *Elegies*. His friend and admirer Ben Jonson said of him that he esteemed him "the first poet in the world for some things," but also that "Donne, for not keeping of accent, deserved hanging." Closely examined, this crime, for such it is, derives from his subordination of melody to meaning, his refusal to submit to the reigning hierarchy of words, sometimes from his lapses to the expressive spoken tongue, in defiance of the convention of poetic rhythm. He introduces into rhymed verse such bold innovations as were customary in the blank verse of the dramatists:

> When thou knewst *what* I dreamt, when thou knewst *when*.

To smoothly flowing lines he often prefers those, freely divided, in which the accents have an effect of shock, pull the reader up and awaken his attention.

His style is analogous. He will have nothing to do with the easy and familiar, the mythological imagery; he turns out the company of the gods and goddesses and rejects the spoils of Greek and Latin poetry. His horror for the commonplace amounts to a cult of the eccentric. At the risk of being enigmatic, he takes pleasure

---

[1] Complete edition of his poems by Grierson, 2 vols. (1912). Edited by Bullen for the Museum Library (1901). *Life and Letters*, ed. by Edmund Gosse, 2 vols. (1909). Life in *I. Walton's Lives*, ed. Morley (1888). See also M. P. Ramsay, *Les doctrines médiévales chez Donne* (Oxford, 1916).

only in the subtle. His sonnets, often such not in structure but merely in name, are akin by their subtlety to the most subtle of those which Shakespeare was writing at this time, but go far beyond them in this quality. Passion, feeling, sensuousness: all are subjected to wit. This play of wit sometimes results in astounding hyperbole: Donne excuses himself for mistaking his mistress for an angel on the ground that to imagine her other than she is would be profane. Or he incongruously brings together ideas as remote from each other as the antipodes, mingling the lofty and the mean, the sublime and the trivial. He deduces every kind of consequence from the fact that a flea hops from biting him to suck his mistress's blood. He will not let her kill this creature in which their blood has mingled, and which is therefore their bridal bed, the temple of their wedding.

In such passages Donne lapses to the ridiculous, or rather he is saved the fall by his consciousness that he is playing with his theme and his amusement at his own extravagance. More often the fantastic is combined in him with passion, a strange compound, and he writes short, disconcerting, unique poems, some with a dramatic turn, which presage Browning two centuries in advance. He suggests scenes: bit by bit, by means of scattered indications of surroundings, movements and gestures, a scene is half-discerned. The *Dream* is such a poem.

He has sudden impulses of thought which react strangely, sometimes advantageously, from the restricted modulations of the madrigal makers, for instance the opening lines of his *Good Morrow*:

> I wonder, by my troth, what thou and I
> Did, till we lov'd?

At the beginning of *Canonisation* this abruptness is mingled with a piquant discourtesy:

> For God's sake hold your tongue, and let me love.

The inverse of the Petrarchians, Donne generally rejects the lofty cult of woman, towards whom he is highly ironical. His *Elegies* realistically relate more than one nocturnal adventure, akin, but for their tone, to the *fabliaux* (the *Perfume* and others). The women to whom he writes his first verses are without virtue or faith.

When a woman seems worthy to inspire a passion, Donne holds platonic love to be a lure, or seeks, with subtle sophistry, to change it to its contrary. With what insidious arguments would he persuade his love to give herself to him entirely! His most beautiful poem is perhaps his *Ecstasy*, in which, when he has long adored his beloved, dumb and motionless, their hands and eyes meeting, he begs that their passion may have its fleshly consummation. Their two hearts are melted into one. They feel that they have become pure spirits. From this height at which they plane how little does the body matter! Poor body, which yet deserves its reward for having brought them together! To remember it is only just,

> But, O, alas! so long, so far
> Our bodies why do we forbear?
> They are ours, though not we . . .

Although Donne's love is always profoundly sensuous, it is sometimes expressed with singular force and grandeur. The thought of death ennobles him. In the *Anniversary* he sees himself persisting even in the grave. In the *Relique* he imagines himself dead and beneath the soil. His grave is opened to admit the body of another, his mistress, and on his wrist the gravedigger finds

> A bracelet of bright hair about the bone.

Henceforth both of them, because of their great love, will be honoured like saints:

> All women shall adore us, and some men.

Thus everything in Donne's early poems is in revolt against the poetic canons of the age. Their wit is indeed by itself no novelty. Wit—and conceits—abound in Sidney and in Shakespeare. But in them it is an ornament, an occasional grace. In Donne it is everywhere. It is his very genius, and fashions his feeling and his thought. He is overweighted with allusions to philosophical doctrines, even scholastic philosophy in which he was expert, and to contemporary science, even of the most abstruse description. His Muse loves those sudden flights from the material to the spiritual sphere for which Dryden gave him, and Samuel Johnson confirmed to him, the title of "the Metaphysical." He deserves it also for his obscurity, which is sometimes terrible. He is again like Browning because the very difficulty in reading him has counted for something in his success, because it became a point of vanity to be subtle enough to apprehend his subtlety, to have enough mental agility to follow his somersaults.

We have spoken hitherto only of the secular poems of his youth. They are the best. Moreover, his religious poems differ from them only in theme; their spirit is the same. He is at his best in short pieces. In his longer, more ambitious poems, like the *Anatomy of the World*, and *Of the Progress of the Soul*, also called the *First Anniversary* and the *Second Anniversary*, he is nothing short of unbearable, for all that these verses are illumined by stray lightning flashes. He was made for surprises and rapid flights, and had neither the constructive nor the staying power which could keep him long on the wing. Moreover, his quintessence of the fantastic is intolerable except in small doses, as was proved by his many imitators, the Metaphysicals of the seventeenth century. The long poems of that age are few and, except for those of Milton, negligible. But the poets produced copiously little sets of verses which are found in anthologies and are sometimes exquisite.

Like his contemporaries, Gongora in Spain and Marini in Italy, Donne carried a characteristic of the Renascence to the extreme. His poetry, otherwise very distinct from theirs, has in common with it an exaggerated subtlety, but while their refinement was especially one of style and manner, he refined thought.

CHAPTER IV

1. The Novelists and Writers of Short Stories : Greene, Lodge, Nashe, Deloney, Dekker.[1]—Poetry dominates the whole of the Renascence to such a point that it often invades the sphere of prose. True prose, simple, restrained and clear, fit not to impassion but to instruct, not to flatter the imagination but to satisfy the reason, is exceptional in this age. Many of the prose works of the Elizabethan period derive from the models provided by Lyly's euphuism and Sidney's arcadianism, which is to say that they are marked by the characteristics of poetic prose. This is particularly evident in the work of the novelists.

(a) ROBERT GREENE.—It is most noticeable in the romantic part of the works of Robert Greene (1560–92), Lyly's disciple and successor. He is of those who imitated the prettinesses and artifices of euphuism. Anthony Munday, Barnabe Rich, Melbancke and Warner are with him, but he is both a more prolific and a more pleasing writer than they. A Cambridge man who drifted into Bohemia, he wandered about Italy and Spain, where he "saw and practised such villainy as is abominable to declare," then settled in London as the hack of booksellers and companies of actors, among whom his work was much in request. At one time almost rich, at another in indigence, he led a life of debauchery among women of the street and in taverns, deserting his wife and child. Yet at heart he was an idyllist, and his euphuistic romances are on as high a moral plane as Lyly's. *Mamilia*, published in 1583, was intended to warn young men against the seemingly pure love which might seduce them to lust. He also wrote *Arbasto, Perimedes* which was imitated from Boccacio, *Pandosto*, and *Menaphon* published in 1589.

If his style and his moral tone are adopted from *Euphues*, his themes are as romantic as those of the author of *Arcadia*. *Arbasto*, for instance, is a love story as complicated as it is tragic. Arbasto, king of Denmark, placed between the two daughters of the king of France, loves one of them unrequitedly, is loved by the other to whom he is indifferent, and finally is the cause of both their deaths. The romantic character of *Pandosto* can be conceived from the *Winter's Tale*, for which it supplied the plot. *Menaphon* is an agreeable arcadian pastoral, full of very poetic passages and of graceful songs which excuse its extravagance. It proves the serenity and purity of this Bohemian's imagination. The conventional opening is really touching, the scene of the shipwreck in which a woman and her infant son are cast upon the shore, and she hushes him with that lovely cradle-song:

> Weep not my wanton, smile upon my knee.

There is an element of true feeling at the heart of these fantastic stories.

---

[1] Texts: R. Greene in *Life and Works of Greene*, ed. Grosart, 15 vols. (1881–6); Nashe, ed. Grosart, 6 vols. (1883–5); ed. McKerrow, 4 vols. (1904); Deloney, ed. Mann (1912); Dekker, *Non-Dramatic Works*, ed. Grosart (1881). The following romances separately: Greene, *Menaphon*, ed. Arber (1880); *Groat's Worth of Wit*, ed. Harrison (1923); Lodge, *Rosalinde* (Cassell's National Library); Nashe, *The Unfortunate Traveller or the Life of Jacke Wilton*, ed. Gosse (1892), and Brett Smith (1920); Deloney, *The Gentle Craft* in *Palæstre*, xviii. (1903); Dekker, *The Gull's Horne Book*, ed. Saintsbury (1902), *The Seven Deadly Sins of London* (The Percy Reprints, 1922).
  See W. L. Crosse, *Development of English Novel* (1905); W. Raleigh, *The English Novel* (1904); Jusserand, *The English Novel in the Time of Shakespeare*, 4th ed. (1902); Jordan, *Robert Greene* (Columbia University Publications, 1915).

But Greene did not always write romance. He had also a more popular and realistic vein illustrated in the series of short stories called the *Conny-catching Tracts* (1591–2), in which he turns to profit his acquaintance with every kind of ruffian, thief, loose woman and rascal in order to paint the underworld of London and initiate the reader to the whole bag of sharpers' tricks for decoying the unwary. Whether his first object be indeed, as he professes, to put the innocent on their guard against the rogues, whether his tales be not calculated to awaken an unhealthy interest in this cockney hell rather than to enforce a lesson in prudence, is uncertain. He undoubtedly enjoys retailing all the swindling, and sometimes, when he forgets himself, he is unquestionably on the side of the swindlers. His journalist's business—he is complacently recounting the happenings of disreputable streets—leads him to abandon euphuism for a simpler manner, and he thus enters on the road which led to Defoe.

The question of his sincerity arises especially in connection with his *Confessions*, the last in date of his prose works. Worn out by debauchery and poverty he brought out, one after the other, several pamphlets filled from end to end with sorrowful self-accusation. In these he avers his own conversion and deplores his errors, but this intemperate conversion involves the accusation of the companions of his debauchery, George Peele, Nashe and Marlowe, whom, without any scruple for implicating them, he apostrophises. Repentance for their atheism, lusts and blasphemies mingles with his remorse for his own backslidings, and he adjures them to be converted too. He must have been a drunkard to the end, for vinous tears have certainly watered the ink with which he pens these pages. The most famous passage is that in which this popular theatre hack denounces a new playwright who once dressed himself out in borrowed plumes taken from Greene and his friends, but now can do without them. Here we have the first evidence of the success of Shakespeare, the actor-author. At the thought of his rivalry, Greene's complaints are turned to fury, and he forgets that he is speaking of the very vanities which elsewhere he declares himself to have outlived and exhorts his former boon-companions to abandon.

(*b*) THOMAS LODGE.—Thomas Lodge (1558–1625), wiser than Greene, ended his life, after a short and fairly brilliant career, in the sober middle-class as a well-known doctor, and left behind him one euphuistic romance which is the most attractive of them all, *Rosalinde*, written in 1590 and the source of *As You Like It*. Undoubtedly Shakespeare read it with delight, and he was much in the author's debt, not only for his plot, but also for the character of his heroine. The romance is a medley, frequently charming, of monologues and witty sentimental dialogues, after the manner of Lyly, and of songs which are among the most delicately refined of the period.

(*c*) THOMAS NASHE.—Thomas Nashe (1567–1601) was, however, the real successor of Greene, the realist and satirist. Known at the age of twenty-five as the young Juvenal, he did not indeed wait for Greene's example before he gave rein to his liveliness. He was the pre-eminently picaresque author of the period and also the best equipped of the pamphleteers. Having acquired learning at Cambridge, he came to London, became Greene's friend, and flung himself desperately into every current dispute, particularly the Martin Mar-Prelate Controversy, then raging between Episcopalians and Puritans. Before he wrote about Puritans at all, Nashe dipped his pen in gall, but he distinguished and isolated one among his adversaries, Spenser's faithful friend, Gabriel Harvey, who had had the bad taste to vituperate Greene after that writer's death. Nashe mishandled Harvey for several years, and mocked his heavy pedantry so vigorously that he kept the laugh on his own side.

In prose, or at least in English prose, Nashe was the creator of a new genre. He was, from the very outset of his career, the initiator of the grotesque satirical style which is compounded of the grotesque and the lyrical. As early as 1589 he was using it against Greene's first dramatic rivals, probably Kyd and Marlowe, In his preface to Greene's *Menaphon*, addressed to the members of Oxford and Cambridge universities, he poses as defender of the classical tradition against the rodomontade and bombast of the recent authors of popular tragedies. It is difficult to make out whether he have in truth any object but to deal blows right and left, but he mocks with an astonishing vocabulary the tragedians "who contend not so seriously to excell in action, as to embowell the clowdes in a speach of comparison; thinking themselves more than initiated in poets immortalitie, if they but once get Boreas by the beard, and the heavenlie bull by the deaw-lap." He hits off the extravagance of the blank verse of *Tamburlaine* admirably when he speaks of "the spacious volubilitie of a drumming decasyllabon." But his pose as champion of a simple moderate style is no more than a pose. All his life he revelled in the frantic, and he ended by frankly avowing this taste and the models he preferred in the preface to his last book, the burlesque *Lenten Stuffe*, in which with Rabelaisian vigour he glorifies the herring, the source of the wealth of Yarmouth, "Mounsieur herring," "Solyman Herring," "Pater patriae."

Know it is my true vaine to be *tragicus Orator*, and of all stiles I most affect and strive to imitate *Aretines*, not caring for this demure, soft *mediocre gonus*, that is like water and wine mixt togither; but give me pure wine of it self, and that begets good bloud, and heates the brain thorowly: I had as lieve have no sunne, as have it shine faintly, no fire as a smothering fire of small coales, no cloathes, rather then weare linsey woolsey.

This pupil of Aretino, who also owes much to Rabelais, reviewed the manners, the absurdities and the superstitions of his day in the *Anatomie of Absurditie* (1589), *Pierce Penilesse, his Supplication to the Divill* (1592), *Christ's Teares over Jerusalem* (1593), and the *Terrors of the Night* (1594). Once he tried his hand at a romance, and being incapable of submitting to the starched style of euphuism or assuming the namby-pamby innocence of the pastoral, he resorted to the picaresque, and produced the *Unfortunate Traveller, or the Life of Jacke Wilton*. The story purports to be historical: to relate the life of Jack Wilton, a page in the reign of Henry VIII. who becomes an unscrupulous adventurer, and with whom we wander through Flanders, Germany and Italy, meeting many celebrities and witnessing some famous scenes. Wilton is present at the Battle of Marignan, at the Fall of Münster and at the massacre of the Anabaptists; he becomes the friend of Surrey during that nobleman's courtship of Geraldine; he watches Erasmus writing his *Praise of Folly* and Thomas More meditating his *Utopia*; he hears Luther's and Carlstadt's invectives against the pope and assists at the necromantic seances of Cornelius Agrippa. All these semi-historical scenes follow each other regardless of chronology and order, and with homely episodes interspersed among them. All have the vigour and concrete life imparted by a mocking imagination. It was the second part of this novel which made the greatest impression on the author's contemporaries. Its scene is Italy, and it shows in turn the magnificent Italy of the arts and the Italy of courtesans and assassins. Nashe alternates his admiration and his execration, now lures the traveller by the marvels he displays, now vituperates, as decidedly as Roger Ascham, the English who visit this land of crime, but he certainly gives much the most space to horrors. He first laid in abundant material for the later melodramatists, Marston, Tourneur, Webster and Middleton, whose land of predilection Italy was. If Nashe begins by preserving the grotesque character of his scenes of strange debauchery and incredible tortures—the furies of the Jew Zadoch who seems to parody Marlowe's Barabas—he ends by relating the history of a vendetta, seriously, intensely and passionately. His style changes. He rids himself of his habitual eccentricities, and recounts swiftly, clearly and nakedly how Cutwolfe pursued Esdras, his brother's murderer, for twenty months, came upon him, unarmed, in his chamber, was deaf to the cowardly brigand's supplications, and with brandished dagger brought him, in the hope of a respite, to damn his soul with fearful blasphemies, before his throat was cut even as he uttered the abominations which must unfailingly send him straight to hell. No words painting a wretch's abject fear of death more strongly were ever to be uttered on the stage. "Thou canst not send me to such a hell as already there is in my heart. . . . Thy over-hanging sword hides heaven from my sight." Nor, especially, was the horrible enthusiasm of Cutwolfe, as he voices his joy in vengeance, ever equalled:

> Of hell doo I esteeme better than heaven, if it affoord me revenge. There is no heaven but revenge. I tell thee, I would not have undertooke so much toyle to gaine heaven, as I have done in pursuing thee for revenge. Divine revenge, of which (as one of the joies above) there is no fulnes or satietie.

The apostrophe continues in the same strain of puissant hatred. When it is Cutwolfe's turn to be led to his death, his exaltation is the same, and before he too dies, after the most refined tortures, he again declares the glory and the joy of revenge.

This last story is in such contrast to the rest of the romance that we are moved to ask if it be by the same author. No other from whom it might have been translated has, however, been cited.

Nashe's one novel and his numerous pamphlets won him great repute and an influence which survived him. He was imitated with an energy less tumultuous than his by Dekker, and with truculency almost equal to his own by Middleton. Even his university kept a pride in his original talent. "Let all his faults sleep with his mournful chest," exhorted the *Returne from Parnassus* in 1602,

> Yet this I say, that for a mother's wit,
> Few men have ever seen the like of it.

(*d*) THOMAS DELONEY.—Quite opposite qualities constitute the merit of Thomas Deloney (1543?–1600?), who has been recently discovered as a novelist. This weaver used to be known only as an author of popular ballads, some of them historical and patriotic, and others comic or sentimental, but all of mediocre value as poetry. In his lifetime they excited the mockery of the literate, of Nashe among others. But in his last years Deloney wrote also a series of prose works to the glory of two powerful livery companies, the Weavers and the Cordwainers. He reproduces better than anyone else the spirit, the feelings and the prejudices of the craftsman's world to which he belonged. Before there were any plays to flatter the tastes of this considerable section of the London public, Deloney wrote for them these curious books, entirely given up to stories of the crafts. His *Jacke of Newbury* relates the rise of a young weaver's apprentice who marries his master's widow and prospers marvellously. It takes us into the great weaver's shop with its two hundred looms, each worked by one man with a boy to help him, one hundred women carders and two hundred spinsters, not to speak of the hundred and fifty children who pick the wool, the fifty shearers, the eighty rovers, the twenty fullers. It is not surprising that the rich owner receives a visit from King Henry VIII. and figures as an historical personage.

The series of short stories devoted to the Cordwainers constitutes a complete, if not a truthful, history of their mystery. The *Gentle Craft* is a survey of shoemakers from legendary times and a pendant to the genealogies of nobles and kings. The trade was very much of the people, with its apprentices who sang rhymes and cracked jokes while they worked the leather, with its travelling journeymen trudging from town to town, their tools, the bones of St. Hugh, on their backs. Deloney sings their annals from the beginning, from the time of St. Hugh, their patron saint, who was martyred under Diocletian. There follows the story of Crispin and Crispian, sons of the queen of Logria, who were persecuted by the Emperor Maximian but finally triumphed, so that Crispin, the saint, married the emperor's daughter. The chronicler then jumps to the fifteenth century, and relates the rise, under Henry VI., of Simon Eyre, who became Lord Mayor, founded the leather-market in Leadenhall and acquired lasting popularity by instituting a holiday on which the Cordwainers' apprentices feasted at his cost. Afterwards, under Henry VIII., Richard Castelar, who was no less rich, bequeathed his fortune to the poor and the hospitals.

Into this frame Deloney introduces a number of homely scenes. Caring nothing for historical colour, he sketches prentices and journeymen from the life, at work in the shops, singing, arguing, making love to customers who are usually maidservants from the taverns, or involved in amorous adventures which recall the *fabliaux*. Or he shows the relations between workmen and masters, the master's hearty and generous good nature in conflict with the niggardliness of his wife, and his refusal to countenance the housekeeping economies by which she would increase profits. Or again, we see the good journeyman who cannot rest when the spring comes, who asks his master to settle his account and wanders off on the broad highway to seek another shop, humming a merry song as he goes.

Deloney has two manners for the telling of all these stories. For such as are pitched in a lofty or a sentimental key he is wont to have recourse to euphuism, for as a man of the people he is behind the times. It was some years since the fine language of euphuism had fallen from its place at court and found a home with the class of humbler citizens who were straining to be genteel. But when, as happens more frequently, Deloney paints workshop scenes, making his workmen speak, he uses the clearest and nimblest and also the gayest prose of his time. He is no poet, but he has the gift of good humour, and we owe him the brightest, the most genuinely merry pages of a period in which prose was overdriven by the taste for lyricism or for truculent buffoonery. Although these stories were forgotten for three centuries, they were much appreciated by the author's contemporaries. They were of undoubted service to Dekker, who almost immediately used the life of Simon Eyre for his excellent *Shomakers Holiday*, and Heywood was probably also indebted to them, since he too greatly desired to gratify the pride of the livery companies. It is true that Deloney's realism is under suspicion. His plans did not allow him to paint any but flattering pictures of the industries of his day. He had taken an engagement to honour them. But he knew them through and through. We feel that his books bring us near to them. He gives us access to this society of citizens and craftsmen, as yet untouched by Puritanism, which from this time was one of the great forces of England and one of her storehouses of merriment and vitality.

(e) THOMAS DEKKER.—It was Dekker who in the reign of James I. succeeded Greene and Nashe as a prose-writer, although his best comedy was inspired by Deloney. He wrote not novels, but social studies and pictures of London life. He began with occasional tracts, like his *Wonderfull Yeare*, which had for subject the year 1603, in which Elizabeth died, James I. succeeded her, and one of the great plagues of London occurred. Dekker commemorates these events in a style of which the imagery and truculency recall Nashe and which often is near parody. It might almost be a poem in mock-heroic prose and the author's seriousness is always in doubt. It is true that he paints the plague in an allegory which does not lack grandeur: death is shown encamped with his army of scourges in the sin-stained outskirts of the city. His troops attack, seize the town, massacre men, women and children, loot and waste. Dekker, who aims at producing a strong effect, is prodigal of macabre description, apostrophes of the plague and hyperbole, not omitting pedantic reminiscences; and his very excess of rhetoric weakens the impression, so that we long for those simple, poignant pages in which Defoe was to tell the story of the Great Plague of 1665. The anecdotes with which Dekker relieves the gloom of his picture, and which, for the refreshment of the reader, he chooses for their amusing quality, have more merit, but they throw yet further doubt on the sincerity of the author's emotion. We have, for instance, the story of the cobbler's wife who believes herself at the point of death, and confesses to her husband and neighbours all the infidelities with the husbands of other women of which she has been guilty. Groaning, "All are sinners," her husband forgives her. But she recovers, and the wronged wives are getting ready to tear out her eyes when, happily, everyone adjourns to the tavern and anger is quenched in Bordeaux wine. The scene ends with a general reconciliation.

The story of the adventure of the wandering tinker who, in a panic-stricken country town, dares, for a crown, to carry to his grave a rich London citizen who has died suddenly at the inn, is also most entertainingly told. The tinker finds seven pounds in the dead man's pocket, and comes back to the village crying, "Have ye any more Londoners to bury, hey downe a downe dery, have ye any more Londoners to bury," but the villagers scatter before him in fright.

Dekker is more successful in comedy than in tragedy, as he proves in the *Batchelars Banquet*, that light-hearted version of the *Quinze joies du mariage* and *Cent Nouvelles Nouvelles*. It is a series of pictures of the miseries of conjugal life, that is of the unhappiness of husbands, invariably represented as good fellows, invariably deceived and invariably unfortunate. Dekker tells his story vivaciously, retailing conversations between husband and wife, throwing the part of the mother-in-law into relief, and bringing gossips and gay dogs back to life. The realism is often very lively, and would be more so were not the author too faithful to the spirit of the *fabliau*, did he not too persistently take sides against the *Legende of Goode Women*. His women are all wittingly bad. He does not allow one of them to worry her husband with good intention, to torment him by excessive affection or even by jealousy.

Greene's tracts on the rogues of London are recalled by Dekker's *Belman of London* (1608), and Nashe's *Pierce Penilesse* by his *Seaven Deadly Sinnes of London* (1606), and even more by his *Newes from Hell brought by the Divells Carrier* (1606). But Dekker had found himself when, in 1609, he wrote the *Guls Horn-Booke*, an ironic guide for a man of fashion who is duper and duped by turns. The Gull is a snob of olden times, an apprentice to the art of profligacy, and he ruffles it for his hour, plucked, the while, by tavernkeepers, swindlers and women of the street.

He reaches town from the country very ignorant, unable even to read or write but determined to live in great style. Dekker undertakes his education. He advises him on the means to his end without ever departing from that ironic style which has been called grobianism, after *Grobianus*, a work of the German Dedekind (1549), itself much in debt for its manner to Erasmus's *Praise of Folly*. To grobianise is to supply advice or praise which conceals ridicule and shows up the absurdity of its object. Ben Jonson had resort to this device in his comedy *Cynthia's Revels*, and Swift was to make admirable use of it, particularly in his *Directions to Servants in general*.

Dekker's book ranks high in this series. At first he translates *Grobianus*, but he soon emancipates himself sufficiently from its influence to be both local and original. He gives one of the richest of all the pictures of the life of pleasure in Jacobean London, following his Gull from the time he gets up until he goes to bed. He takes him to St. Paul's, then the meeting-place of idlers, adventurers and debtors pursued by their creditors. These poor wretches, empty of pocket and stomach, "dine with the good Duke Humphrey," which is to say that they fast near the monument identified with Humphrey of Gloucester, the son of Henry IV. "There you may spend your legs in winter a whole after-noone: converse, plot, laugh and talke any thing, jest at your Creditor, even to his face, and in the evening, even by lamp-light, steale out, and so cozen a whole covy of abhominable catch-pols."

Thence the Gull passes to an ordinary, where his campaigning stories dazzle his fellow-diners, or, if he pique himself on a poetic gift, he recites his own or his purloined verses. It is, however, especially at the playhouse that Dekker, himself a playwright, advises his Gull to let himself be seen. There, as might one of Molière's little marquises, he must display his person and shout his remarks, seated well to the front of the stage at the risk of getting into the way of the actors. He must defy the audience as they yell abuse at him, yawn at the most pathetic moments in the play, and noisily leave in the very middle, "with a screwd and discontented face." Thereafter the Gull goes to the tavern, where he spends much money, and is careful to call the drawers by their Christian names and to appear intimate with the host and hostess. At night he returns home, attended by a boy bearing a lanthorn, and assuming airs of grandeur in order to deceive passers-by and intimidate the watch.

Dekker's sketches confirm and complete the pictures of London life in the comedies of the time, particularly those of Jonson and Middleton. His prose has lost its heaviness and is excellent. His irony hardly ever flags, is always good-humoured, and is relieved by numerous details of fact of which the presentment is lively and accurate and original by force of its very accuracy. There is nothing left of Nashe's deforming truculency which produced not pictures but caricatures. Dekker is in direct contact with reality, preserves actual proportions and respects line and colour. He is on the road which leads to the humorists of Anne's reign. From afar he heralds Swift, and chiefly Steele and Addison, for he is a less bitter writer than Swift. Not for a whole century did another author thus combine realism and humour.

2. **The Authors of Characters : Overbury, Stephens, Earle.**—Dekker is less a novelist than a collector, an amateur of manners. Side by side with him certain writers may be placed who drew so-called "characters," imitating Theophrastus as La Bruyère did after them. They were closely connected with the satirists in verse, of whom Joseph Hall produced one of the earliest of the imitations of Theophrastus in his *Characters of Vices and Vertues* (1608). It was, however, Sir Thomas Overbury [1] who gave this genre a really literary character by the twenty-one prose portraits which he added to his poem *A Wife* (1614). There is wit and point in these drawings of types, of which he praises some while he reveals the vices of others. They are a rapid review of society by a lettered courtier attached to the feudal order and hostile to Puritans.

In 1615 John Stephens, a young lawyer, followed in the steps of Overbury with his *Satirical Essays, Characters and Others*, as did John Earle (1601?—1665) [2] with *Microcosmographie*, which was published in 1628 after it had circulated for some years in manuscript. This inquiry into society was taken up by author after author, and the resultant picture became more and more complete. In every instance it

---

[1] Complete edition by F. Rimbault (1856; reprinted 1890).
[2] Ed. A. S. West (1897).

is noticeable that the search for pointed phraseology and curious turns of speech and the wish to condense led to the advancement of prose. The art of portraiture in words was thus developed in England at the same time as in France, although in a different way. The English did not pursue it in drawing-rooms, but made their sketches in solitude. Their style had consequently a quaintness unknown to the French and often lacked good taste, but in compensation they allowed themselves considerable play of fancy, often with a happy effect.

3. **Dramatic Prose.**—Greene, Nashe and Dekker were dramatic authors, and the qualities of their prose betray their habit of appealing to a mixed public who demanded nimble speech, either clear or arresting. Other dramatists also produced prose works: Jonson's *Discoveries* is in this medium, as are Thomas Heywood's *Apology for Actors* and *England's Elizabeth*, and Middleton's *Black Book* and *Father Hubburd's Tales*. It is not, however, necessary to go outside the theatre in order to find dramatists' prose, for most of them gave it a considerable, if not the first, place in their plays, and its progress cannot be well understood without an examination of the characteristics of the numerous prose scenes scattered among the dramas of the Renascence.

Gascoigne, no later than 1566, in his comedy *Supposes*, translated from Ariosto's *Gli Suppositi*, was the first to forsake verse. Yet for many years afterwards no author resolutely made prose his only medium. John Lyly, who wrote all but one of his plays in prose, is an exception. There is no need to repeat what has been said of the characteristics of his euphuistic style which he transferred from romance to drama with little modification of its eccentric features, except such as was occasionally necessary to rapid and witty dialogue. But Lyly in this genre stands alone. In general, the playwrights of the Renascence varied their medium to suit characters and mood. Most of them alternated verse and prose, and they almost all made it a rule to use, in one play, verse for tragic and lofty passages and prose for homely and comic scenes. Marlowe did this in his *Jew of Malta* and his *Doctor Faustus*, Greene in his *Friar Bacon and Friar Bungay*, and Shakespeare in almost all his plays observed their precedent.

Shakespeare rarely keeps the two forms separate, and the plays which he wrote entirely in verse are few. They are *Richard II.* and *King John*, together with *Richard III.* which has fragments of prose. He wrote no play all in prose, not even the *Merry Wives of Windsor*, that burgher comedy in which prose dominates. His custom was to mingle the two forms. Often the principle of distribution is easy and clear: the tragic is reserved for verse and the comic expressed in prose. Clowns, and the definitely humorous characters allied to clowns, abstain from verse. This is exemplified in *Romeo and Juliet*, where the gossiping nurse is almost alone in her use of prose, and in *Henry IV.*, where all the great historical scenes are in verse and all those which centre about Falstaff in prose.

Sometimes, however, the alternation of prose and verse is much more difficult to explain. In certain passages it is hard to account for it except by a need of variety, but only rarely can no other and more subtle artistic reason be discovered to justify it. In *Much Ado About Nothing*, for instance, there are two parallel scenes, both mainly comic. In one, Benedick's friends, speaking in his hearing when he believes himself hidden, contrive that he shall think that Beatrice is in love with him. This is in prose. In the other, Beatrice's cousin and her gentlewoman similarly convince her that Benedick loves her madly, and this is in verse.

These two successive scenes are entirely different in tone, as a consequence of their difference of form, and reflection shows their diversity to be just and appropriate. Each of them gives birth to love in the heart of one of the young people. For Benedick, whose vanity is flattered, this is mainly a laughing matter,

I—Q

but it is touching and almost tragic for the shy and maidenly girl who cannot admit the feeling without pain and disturbance.

Prose is also the normal medium of certain even of the poetic characters of Shakespeare, for instance of Rosalind in *As You Like It*. That this charming heroine of a most fanciful play speaks in prose almost exclusively is at first surprising. But only prose is sudden and swift enough to render her astonishing flow of imagination and words, her marvellous nimbleness of tongue. Rosalind is the most exquisite of chatterboxes. To make her speech rhythmic would be to make it slower, to rob it of a little of its spontaneity. The voice would no longer be able to produce the desired effect of words gushing out unquenchably.

These facts are simple beside others which can be deduced from the great dramas. It is not at first apparent why one of the most outstanding passages in *Hamlet* is in prose, that where the prince, anticipating Pascal, paints the contrast which is in man, half-god and half-beast. Hamlet is on the stage with his false friends whom he suspects to be spies. How is it that the scene, at first familiar in tone and naturally in prose, does not, like so many others in Shakespeare's plays, rise into verse at the great speech, and how is it that even in this highly lyrical effusion we feel prose to be in perfect harmony with the mood? The reason is that Hamlet's words would not have had the air of confidence and carelessness which he was feigning if he had interposed verse between himself and those he addressed. Even while he expresses his pessimism, he remains on his guard against emphasis.

But the most surprising use of prose of all is Othello's, who passes from verse to prose at the most tragic moments, for instance in the first scene of Act IV. It is that in a paroxysm of jealousy, maddened by Iago's lies, he has what is almost an epileptic seizure and his speech, in its incoherence, breaks free of all rhythm. He utters cries rather than words. For an analogous reason prose is introduced into what is perhaps the most pathetic scene in the play, that between Othello and Iago in which the murder of Desdemona is determined, and Othello is constantly torn by the thought of all the beauty, grace and love about to perish. "Nay, that's certain—but yet the pity of it, Iago—O Iago! the pity of it, Iago." Here again the poet abstains from rhythm in order the better to mark the disarray of this soul, to show this nature which had been master of itself thrown off its balance and staggering in bewilderment. The terrible struggle within Othello is indicated by such abandonment of the stately measure of blank verse which up to this point had seemed the natural rhythm of his voice.

Similarly Lear in the height of his madness rejects verse, which is necessarily ruled and reasoned, or adopts it only in brief snatches, in such fragments as he utters when he wanders foolishly in the fields near Dover.

It is nearly always possible to detect in this way the poet's subtle intention when he changes from one form to the other, and to perceive that it is not haste of composition which causes him to forgo verse. Manifestly he is conscious of the value proper to prose, and does not make the mistake of turning it into poetry mechanically, universally or in defiance of sense.

In confining his clowns to prose, he is giving to special actors the mode of expression proper to their parts, one which has its ritual and traditional rhythm, although not that of verse, indeed a rhythm unworthy to be versified.

In serious passages of his plays he uses prose to produce an eloquence distinct from that in verse, partaking less of imagery and more of ratiocination. Thus Henry V., on the eve of Agincourt, proves to the soldiers that the king is not guilty of their damnation if they die in a state of sin. He speaks like a lawyer, and nothing but prose could have shown his need to exonerate himself, to argue and to prove. Similarly Brutus, rashly appealing to the reason of the Roman people, harangues them in prose, while Mark Antony, when he wishes to rouse them, inflames their passions with admirable verse.

Shakespeare was able to use prose so largely and artistically only because he had cultivated the qualities inherent in it. The extraordinarily nimble speech of Henry V., as he pleads his cause, is surprising beside the rest of sixteenth-century prose and difficult to equal in this generation. In such passages Shakespeare's prose has a ready, certain flow which was never surpassed. It is, moreover, true and not poetic prose.

Shakespeare must none the less be classified as a poet who gave some space to prose. His prose is subordinate and the essence of his work and his genius is poetic. It was other playwrights who made prose reign on the stage, especially Ben Jonson, who was a prose-writer first of all, although he often obliged himself to translate his thought into verse and did it vigorously, sometimes, in his songs, even gracefully. Prose was, however, better suited to his robust and realistic temperament, and like a good humanist he formed his prose style carefully, making close translations of Latin passages which struck him during his reading, then altering them slightly, on occasion, to adapt them to existing circumstances. We can watch the process in the curious notebook which he published under the title of *Discoveries*.[1] Nor was this all. He also meditated on the laws of language and wrote the first English grammar; and although the complete version of this work was destroyed in 1623, when his library was burnt, and only his notes for it now remain, they are enough to indicate the analytical bent which made him a contrast to his contemporaries, with their carelessness of rules and their dependence on current uses and inspiration.

A large part of Ben Jonson's plays is in prose. Not only does he nearly always use it abundantly, interspersed with verse, but it is also the sole medium of two of his comedies, *Epicœne, or the Silent Women*, and *Bartholomew Fayre*. Many will consider that prose suited his talent better than verse, for while his versification is strong, it is harsh and has no flexibility or swing. It lacks light-heartedness and sonority. His prose, on the other hand, is natural, comparatively terse and rich in concrete details. Wit and humour are not frequent in it, but it is solidly significant, accurate and often eloquent.

Prose was not spoken on the stage only in Shakespeare's and Jonson's plays, and a complete review of the subject would cover the work of almost all the playwrights of the day. But the others were ranged under these two leaders and contributed no new qualities of their own. Enough has been said to show the part of the theatre in the development of prose. It brought it near to everyday speech at a time when it tended either to formlessness or to excessive mannerism, was either unduly learned and pedantic and Latin in construction, or so overcharged with parentheses as to be obscure. Beneath the Latinised prose of the theologians, philosophers, moralists and controversialists of the Renascence, there existed this other prose of the dramatists, which was formed on the spoken language and was idiomatic and clear. It was this prose which reappeared half a century later and became general, penetrating to the genres to which it did not at first have access.

4. Literary Criticism.[2]—Criticism of literature figured considerably in the prose of the English Renascence in point of the number of the works produced, but was of mediocre value and importance. It was very little original, almost wholly inspired by theories put forth on the continent which themselves closely followed antiquity. Only rarely did critics adapt themselves to the special circumstances of the country and write with a direct bearing on the great English works

---

[1] Ed. by M. Castelain, Paris (1906).
[2] *Elizabethan Critical Essays*, ed. Gregory Smith, 2 vols. (1904). See Saintsbury, *History of Criticism*, vol. ii., book iv. (1902), and Spingarn, *A History of Literary Criticism in the Renaissance*, part iii. (1899).

which multiplied without attracting their notice. So completely did they ignore what was immediately presented to them that they are little more than abstract writers. In this as in all other fields Italy was well in advance of the rest of Europe. When the foundations of doctrine and of the social hierarchy were shaken, it was in Italy that men of letters first sought to justify their existence and win honour. Criticism had a double aim: it wished both to glorify literature and to proclaim its laws. When the Italians undertook this task, they chose the ancients for their guides. They turned to Aristotle's *Poetics* or Horace's *Ars Poetica*, where they found established the principle of the imitation of nature and the consequent doctrine of reason, objectivity and classical wisdom. Or they went to Plato, who spoke to them of an ideal of poetic beauty emanating from the individual poet, which led to an imaginative and subjective literature with the characteristics subsequently called romantic. Scaliger, with his *Poetice* of 1561, represents Aristotelian criticism, as Minturno, with his *Ars Poetica* of 1564, stands for Platonic criticism. These two writers did in some sort carry criticism to philosophic heights, but elsewhere in Europe it was humbler, more utilitarian or more matter-of-fact. In the countries not yet sure of themselves the problem was how to establish the literary claims of the national language so as to awaken ambition. Such was the object of du Bellay in his *Défense et Illustration de la langue française*. In England the moral issue was dominant, the first to be considered and the stimulus to discussion. It had, as early as 1568, the place of honour in Ascham's *Schoolmaster*, where it was the motive for opposition to Italianism, which was condemned in the name not of beauty, but of virtue.

But Ascham wrought no change. The corruption of which he denounced the inroads had, ten years later, established itself on English soil, to the scandal of serious and upright men who tended consequently to regard poetry as synonymous with depravity.

Hence the attack of a man of letters converted to Puritanism, Stephen Gosson, whose *School of Abuse* (1579) is directed against all secular literature, making no distinction between "Poets, Pipers, Plaiers, Jesters, and such like Caterpillars of a Commonwelth." His principal animus is against the theatre, but, like the Christian preachers, he extends his condemnation to cover much else. Poets he calls "the fathers of lyes," and therefore he considers poetry bad in essence. Anticipating Rousseau, he adds that it is destructive of energy and enervates and effeminates a nation.

This invective has survived because of the retort it provoked. Gosson dedicated it to Sidney, who was known for his nobility and purity of soul, and reputed the champion of the Protestant cause. While Thomas Lodge, the playwright, immediately answered it with a wholly pedantic *Defence of Poetry*, laden with classical quotations and no longer of interest. Sidney replied at leisure, apparently for his own satisfaction, since his *Defence of Poesie* was published only in 1595, long after his death. His plea for poetry constitutes one of the most eloquent and most pleasing prose works of the period.

On the whole, Sidney agrees with Gosson in holding existing English literature cheap, especially English drama, but he condemns it not for reasons of morals, but because the works he considers seem to him weak, mediocre, ridiculous, bereft of art. Of poetry in itself he has the most exalted conception. The poet is for him the first lawgiver of a society, the *vates*, superior both to the historian, who is chained to reality, and to the philosopher, who is obliged to be constantly severe and abstract. The poet paints the ideal with beguiling charm. Far from softening men, poetry has been a chief awakener of the warlike spirit and the virtues of chivalry. Even a popular, ill-rhymed ballad like *Chevy Chase*, "sung but by some blind crowder with no rougher voice than rude stile," even the Arthurian romances with all their absurdities, are a call to man's courage and his desire for glory. In conclusion, Sidney declares that, although English literature is still poor, it seems to him capable of high destinies.

The style of the *Defence of Poesie* is eloquent, frequently poetic but much less decorated, both franker and more virile, than *Arcadia*. Sidney makes fun in it of euphuism, proposes Demosthenes and Cicero as models, and protests against the abusive use of literary ornaments. "For now they cast sugar and spice upon every dish that is served at the table: like those Indians, not content to wear ear-rings at the fit and natural place of the ears, but they will thrust jewels through their nose and lips, because they will be sure to be fine."

In fact, no other critical English work as broad and as much alive was written in this period. All the important questions are stated and treated in it, whereas elsewhere there are only technical treatises and discussions on points of detail. What strikes us especially, when we seek to estimate Sidney's book as a whole, is that from beginning to end he respects the precepts of the ancients and unreservedly condemns the literary methods, his own and those of others, which were practised in his time. His *Arcadia* is in conflict with his theory. As much is true of all his contemporary authors. No sooner does one of them turn critic, than he adheres to the school of antiquity, careless whether or not his own work obey the laws he accepts and recommends.

This applies even to Ben Jonson, the playwright who discussed his art most. He poses arrogantly and defiantly as the disciple of the ancients. But while his criticism is after Horace, in practice he treats the theory he professes almost as cavalierly as his rivals, and not only disregards the unities in the strict sense of the word, but mingles the tragic and the comic. Like the others, he presents a series of historical scenes in his *Sejanus* and his *Catiline*, yet seems to imagine that he is writing tragedies in accordance with the rule.

The playwrights who had not, like Jonson, definitely ranged themselves with the humanists, never define their art. But if, exceptionally, they approximate to a theory, they show themselves inclined to echo classical judgments with which their practice is in extreme conflict. Thus Shakespeare mocks merrily at the mingling of the comic and the tragic, making fun of the plays which, like the *Pyramus and Thisbe* of Bottom and his fellows, were full of "very tragical mirth," those "lamentable comedies." He alludes to the heteroclite taste of his time, jestingly giving the list of the "historico-pastoral, tragical-historical, tragical-comical-historical-pastoral," and the others which were in favour, and he laughs at the artless, rude staging of *Pyramus* which parodied his own theatre with its childish expedients. Hamlet, unquestionably his mouthpiece, recommends to the players, on wholly classical principles, the fitting, the moderate and the probable, and is an essentially Aristotelian critic who tolerates clowns with impatience, and since he cannot suppress their part would confine it within strict limits. The play which Hamlet admires and desires to have performed is an oratorical tragedy in the manner of Seneca.

Shakespeare himself doubtless went beyond Hamlet's limitations. Out of his own ideas he chose such of them as he deemed appropriate to the young prince. Yet while he does not make him voice all his experience as an author, he lends him the more refined of his own opinions, those in agreement with the classical writers. Nowhere does he give utterance to an apology for the so modern and so broad form of drama which he himself followed. He merely, with a smile, admits to his public in the prologue to *Henry V*. that he perceives all the improbabilities of his drama, but counts on their "imaginary forces" and their goodwill to "piece out our imperfections with their thoughts."

In addition to their controversy on the morality of poetry and their consideration of dramatic art, the men of the English Renascence gave a fair share of attention to a discussion on the comparative merits of measured or reformed, and rhymed verse. The dispute arose in Italy and France, but it was the occasion in England of a long series of attacks and counter-attacks which prove it to have been waged in this country with more heat than elsewhere. It is remarkable that the first antagonists of rhyme were so carried away by their cult of antiquity that they disregarded the existence of blank verse, which seemed to them a bastard and inadequate compromise. They wished, at the same time, to abolish rhyme, which they held to be gothic and barbarous, and they claimed to make English syllables quantitative, long or short as in Latin. Some of them, like Sir John Cheke and Ascham, vaunted the iambic line, and Gabriel Harvey even championed the hexameter. It can serve no purpose to speak of the unreadable poems which Harvey, Stanyhurst, Abraham Fraunce, Campion and others—even, passingly, Sidney and Spenser—produced in accordance with these rules. The metricians of the day were exercised by the question. William Webbe, in *A Discourse of English Poetrie* (1586), shows himself the determined partisan of measured verse. George Puttenham, in the *Arte of English Poesie*, the most voluminous of the technical treatises of the period, is less willing to commit himself and holds the balance between the contesting parties. The poet Thomas Campion, author of so many charming rhymed songs, was in the enemy camp in 1602. In his *Observations on the Art of English Poesie* he condemns rhyme as improper to poetry. The only good effect of his attack was that it induced the poet Samuel Daniel to write his *Defence of Ryme* (1603), which closed this controversy of more than thirty years' standing and was the first example in England of sane æsthetic criticism applied to a special subject. Hitherto all the blows had been aimed wide. On either side there had been pedantry, abuse of authorities, ignorance of essential facts, disregard of blank verse, even confusion between the meanings of the words rhythm and rhyme. Daniel evinced a reasonableness, exactness and perspicacity unknown to the others. Even to-day it is worth while to meditate on his words. He bases himself on uses. While he denies that the admission of rhyme, which exists and pleases many nations, is a matter for discussion, he does not shirk the task of founding rhyme on reason. He does not bow down before the ancients. That rhyme makes rhythm of a kind unknown to them is, he says, their loss, who knew not this "Echo of a delightful report." Nor does rhyme preclude from measure English verse which is based on tonic accent. To complain of the shackles of rhyme is to ignore the nature of the pleasure of poetry and of its creation. The poet finds that "Ryme is no impediment to his conceit, but rather gives him wings to mount, and carries him not out of his course, but as it were beyond his power to a far happier flight." Rhyme is a means of imparting form, outline and limits to imaginative conceptions. It organises chaos. Its terminal cadence gives "a certainty" as well as measure.

Daniel has a secret preference for the stanza over the couplet, and he would reserve feminine rhymes for songs. But these are personal tastes, as he himself knows and says, and he modestly refuses to erect them into law. It was doubtless his fondness for the stanza rather than the couplet which prevented the classical school from acknowledging him as one of the best of their forerunners.

His own moderation impels him to condemn the intransigence of those who would, at one stroke, rule out all the past. But in him this moderation is accompanied by frank independence. He throws off the yoke of antiquity:

All our understandings are not to be built by the square of Greece and Italie. We are the children of Nature as well as they, we are not so placed out of the way of judgement, but that the same Sunne of Discretion shineth upon us. . . . Wee must not looke upon the immense course of times past, as men overlooke spacious and wide countreys, from off high mountaines, and are never the neerer to judge of the true nature of the soile.

From end to end of his short treatise Daniel unfolds his argument in the same wise and reasonable spirit. His pleading, often directed against the superstition of the humanists, is finely classical in form. It is oratory, less poetic and nervous than the language of Sidney's *Defence*, at times a little redundant, but exceptional in this period by its sequence, its logic and its urbanity. More than any one of his contemporaries, Daniel possessed the qualities of the perfect writer of prose.

5. **Religious Prose. Hooker. The Preachers. The Bible.**—(a) THE CON-TROVERSY BETWEEN THE PURITANS AND THE ANGLICANS. The religious literature of the Elizabethan period, first constituted by a series of violently controversial writings, ended with Hooker's serene and majestic work. The most famous of the disputes which occupied authors was that in which the Calvinists engaged the Anglican Church, the so-called Martin Marprelate Controversy. It began in 1588 and lasted for at least five years. The Marprelates used their secret printing-presses, easily moved and impossible to seize, to bring out a multitude of anonymous pamphlets, of which the authorship is still an almost complete mystery, and in which, with insulting irony, they denounced the bishops as swine, Canterbury Beelze-bubs, antichrists, foxes, dogs. The attack had a popular turn like the contemporary great French political satire, the *Satire Menippée*. Often the pamphlets had punning titles and always the tone of lampoons. The Anglican replies struck the same note. The bishops, with temporal arms at their disposal, found other defenders among the men of letters, who instinctively execrated and feared the Martinists or Puritans as enemies of secular literature. These champions of Anglican orthodoxy had no religious convictions, but they loved a fight. They were the *condottieri* of this war. They defended episcopacy in the taverns. Thomas Nashe, the disciple of Aretino, is the best known of them. The leading Martinists were arrested in 1593 and hanged, among them the Welshman Penry, who seems to have been the soul of their revolt. Sermons were censored; the gallows and the stocks were used to enforce orthodoxy; and the press was subjected to severe regulation.

(b) RICHARD HOOKER.[1]—Anglicanism was also able to make another and less brutal retort to its detractors, to adopt a persuasive tone and give reasons for its doctrine. The glorious task fell to Richard Hooker (1554–1600). In 1593 and after-wards he published his magisterial work, the *Laws of Ecclesiastical Polity*, which is both a monument of serious controversial literature and one of the first master-pieces of English prose. Hooker was engaged on it until his death in 1600.

He was a man of humble birth whose parents at first intended to apprentice him to a trade, but he showed so much precocious knowledge at school that he was sent to Oxford, where his intelligence and piety gave equal edification. He took orders, and in 1584, when he was Master of the Temple, he was drawn into a con-troversy with the Puritan Travers. Afterwards, instead of seeking honours, Hooker begged as a favour for a country living where he might "behold God's blessings spring out of my mother earth, and eat my own bread without oppositions." The dispute he had sustained had obliged him to probe and to order his ideas. In rural quiet and retiremen the composed his great defence of the established Church of England. Izaak Walton has charmingly told the story of the life of this sage, or rather of this saint, candid, shy and kind, helpless against malice and ruled and bullied by an ill-tempered woman, reading Horace while he tended his flock. His brain was, however, no less vigorous than his temper was gentle and docile. He

---

[1] *The Laws of Ecclesiastical Polity*, ed. Church and Paget (1888); book i., ed. Church (1876). For life of Hooker see *I. Walton's Lives*, ed. Morley (1888).

boldly establishes as a principle that the compromising attitude, which has given the enemies of the Church of England matter for so much reproach, is nothing else than a mark of wisdom.

To the extremists who referred everything to the Bible, Hooker retorts that man receives God's teaching from two sources—revelation in the Bible and reason, which is the gift of God. If these two ever seem to be in conflict, it is reason which must be followed. Reason is God's first-born child, and finds everywhere in nature the law which has existed from the beginning, which God gave even to Himself and observed when He created and ordained the world. God is supreme reason. All God's law is a law of reason, and every law of reason is a law of God.

As for the Bible, it reveals the supernatural truths which man could not have discovered by reason alone. It is an additional but not the only light. Hooker deems that man should be guided by all the instruments of knowledge which he possesses, together and concurrently. Papistry appeals to the authority of the Church against reason. Puritanism is essentially an appeal to the authority of the Bible against the Church and against reason also. The Church of England effects a required reconciliation, for it admits the authority of precedents and yet recommends obedience to the Bible, but teaches that all must be controlled by reason.

Starting from these principles, which are very like those held by Pecock in the previous century, Hooker was able to defend the hierarchy and discipline of his Church against the Puritans, who attacked them as unscriptural, and he could similarly defend the ritual and uses which the Puritans considered superstitious. He holds that the Bible dictates no certain laws for the ecclesiastical and the civil polity, and that positive laws are partly susceptible of change. But since he finds reason plainly reflected in existing societies, since they evidently obey a law, he defends them against the attempts which were being made to disturb and confound them. He very clearly illustrates the conservatism of the Anglican religion.

His book is eminent not only for its ratiocination and the knowledge it shows, but also for its consistently noble and lofty tone, and the amplitude of its construction which owes much to the *Summa* of St. Thomas Aquinas Yet its atmosphere is not the special and exclusive one of theological treatises, for Hooker is at least half a philosopher, and no one has done homage to human reason more finely than he.

The book is also remarkable for its style. For the first time English and not Latin is used for high generalisation. The English is indeed modelled on the Latin for which it is a substitute, markedly Latin in point of vocabulary, and often of construction also, since it uses Ciceronian periods. None the less this prose is luminous and harmonious, and equally removed from pedantry and from vulgarity. It is strictly ruled by logic and aims at convincing the reason, yet it is not without passages which impress the imagination. It is Hooker who first brought the prose of his own language to rank with that of antiquity.

His teaching was fated to be neglected and his cause to be defeated in the seventeenth century, but, besides the success of his book in his own day, he received compensation when Anglicanism was restored. Hooker's ideas, arguments, philosophy and attitude reappeared in all the great Anglican theologians. His blend of traditionalism and rationalism remains the distinctive mark of that religion of England to which he was the first Father of the Church. And outside Anglicanism, his respect and admiration for the law regulating societies recurs, hardly modified, in the famous pages of Burke.

(c) THE PREACHERS.—The same moderate and well-balanced attitude, the same grave eloquence expressed in periods, were shown in Hooker's sermons. His diffidence may have prevented them from having all their rightful effect at the time of their delivery, but they are strong though they appeal less to reason and more to conscience and feeling than his book. The serenity he displays in them was in contrast with the invectives of his contemporaries against the new Babylon. Hooker was courageous and broadminded enough to affirm the Church of Rome to be the true and sanctified Church of Christ. Far from incriminating Catholicism, he searches it for points of agreement.

He was not, however, the most renowned preacher of his own day. Public favour was accorded first to Bishop Andrewes, and then, a little later, to John Donne, both of whom were typical preachers of the age, by their defects as by their qualities.

Bishop Lancelot Andrewes (1555–1626)[1] was a very learned theologian who knew fifteen languages, who, as a philosopher, was appreciated and consulted by Bacon, and who was as famous for his wit as for his charity. His wit was, however, modified by the fads of the century: he liked to lapse into conceits and plays on words; and he weighted his prose with pedantry, scraps of Latin and Greek. His homilies made him, for his contemporaries, the Star of Preachers and the Angel of the Pulpit, and until the advent of Jeremy Taylor and Tillotson he remained the favourite of his Church. But a change in taste has dimmed his former repute. He inveighed against rhetoric, and yet was far too ready to make sacrifices for rhetorical effect, and part of his success was undoubtedly due to the perfection of his diction.

In the early seventeenth century only John Donne[2] shared his renown. Donne carried into his sermons the strange "metaphysical" subtlety which marks his verses. He considered that the preacher should not speak with "an extemporal or irreverent or over-homely and vulgar language." Certainly he put into his sermons his fantastic rhetoric, and his erudition, his knowledge of the Fathers of the Church, particularly St. Augustine. The obscurity of the preacher is no less conspicuous than that of the poet. He is prodigal of similes and metaphors; he does not always seem clearly to know whither he is bound or where he leads his hearers; his macabre imagination is betrayed by his constant and willing returns to the themes of death and the Judgment. Some of his sentences are quoted as admirable for their rhythm and emphasis, but there is not one of his sermons which exacts admiration as a whole.

(d) THE BIBLE OF 1611.[3]—Nothing else in the religious prose of the Renascence is equal in literary beauty and importance to the 1611 Authorised Version of the Bible. From Anglo-Saxon times onwards there had been many previous translations of the Scriptures, but this one remained intact and was accepted by all Protestant sects for nearly three centuries. It was not the first time that Hebrew literature influenced English thought and imagination, but it happened that 1611 marked the beginning of the period in which the Bible really circulated among all classes of the people, became the daily reading of the whole nation. It is therefore at this point important to examine its literary influence on the minds of the English.

It is perhaps especially necessary to insist on the influence of the Old Testament, for the Gospels had always been widely known throughout Christendom, independently of the Reformation. Moreover, it was the Old Testament which chiefly placed its imprint on Puritan minds and fashioned them. The Old Testament is the history of an Oriental people, the fruit of the religious genius of the

[1] Ed. by F. E. Brightman (1903).
[2] *Donne's Sermons*, selected passages ed. L. P. Smith (1923); *Ten Sermons of Donne*, ed. G. G. Keynes (1924).
[3] Reprint of the Authorised Version by W. A. Wright (Cambridge, 5 vols., 1909). See also A. S. Cook, *The Bible and English Prose Style* (Boston, 1892); J. H. Gardiner, *The Bible as English Literature* (1905); R. G. Moulton, *The Literary Study of the Bible* (1899), etc.

Hebrew race. Like the Jews, the English were, even before the triumph of Puritanism, prone to consider themselves the chosen people. As early as 1580 Lyly had said that "the living God is only the English God." This opinion, with all the intensity, the enthusiasm, the narrowness, the exclusiveness, and, on occasion, the pitilessness it implied, became general in the seventeenth century. Psalm cxxxvi., with its exaltation of the divine *mercy* which "smote Egypt in their first-born," "overthrew Pharaoh and his host in the Red Sea," and "slew famous kings," expresses admirably the frame of mind in which Crowmell's soldiers went to battle. This unconscious and blind exclusiveness must be numbered among the foundations of the modern English mentality. The Bible strengthened the religious and moral sense of the English, but, at the same time, it drew about them moral and religious limitations almost as narrow as those which confined the Jews.

This Jewish history, on which millions of the English henceforward meditated and which they assimilated, was conveyed to them in stories, lyrical poems and prophecies. The Old Testament condenses a whole literature in one book, with such unity of passion and sequence as the literature of no other country presents. It claims to be not the work of one author or of several authors of different centuries, but the Word of God, dictated to the various elect of the chosen people in turn, continued through the ages, ever growing but always the same. Yet the style of the several books is very different: the narratives are restrained, brief, sometimes dry; the lyricism is ardent, metaphorical, redundant; the prophecies often obscure, even enigmatic.

The whole is poetic in form. If not metrical in the Western sense of the word, it is divided into verses, and these give the enjoyment proper to poetry by a parallelism which is the effect of synonyms, of complementary explanation, of antithesis or of repetition. Versification of this kind has the advantage that it can, without much loss, be translated into any language. The verse has only the simple, broad rhythm which is based on the accentuation of the principal words. There is no measure, no rhyme, no prosody. St. Jerome's admirable Vulgate had shown how happily the original might be rendered in Latin. The English Authorised Version is not less beautiful.

Mr. A. S. Cook has resumed as follows those characteristics of the Bible by which it lends itself to translation better than any other poem [1]:

(*a*) Universality of interest. There is much in it for the meanest and most illiterate, and its treasures are not to be exhausted by the wisest. . . .
(*b*) The concreteness and picturesqueness of its language, appealing alike to the child and the poet, while suggesting abundant reflections to the philosopher.
(*c*) The simplicity of its structure, which requires little more from the translator than that he shall render with fidelity one brief clause at a time, and follow it by the next.
(*d*) A rhythm largely independent of the features, prosodical or other, of any individual language.

The translator's great difficulty is to find language at once simple, homely and bold, and yet not coarse. Here the 1611 translators were helped by the earlier translations, which supplied them with a choice of renderings. They rejected the most archaic of these because they had to be intelligible, but they retained a fair number of words and a larger number of turns of phrase and grammatical uses which were still clear although they tended to be of the past. Their basic material was a real Biblical dialect which had been wrought by Wyclif, Tindale and Coverdale. It is a religious language at the heart of the English language, which proceeds from it without quite losing its special identity and is charged with all the accumulated pious emotion of successive generations. It is sufficiently recognisable and

[1] *Cambridge History of English Literature*, book iv., chap. ii.

distinct to bring a lofty tone into men's voices, to be marked as sacred among the rest of their speech.

The Authorised Version of 1611 was the work of forty-seven scholars, nominated by James I., over whom Bishop Lancelot Andrewes presided. It was declared to have been produced at the king's special command and to be appointed to be read in churches. It was also adopted by the Puritans in preference to the so-called Geneva Bible.

It frequently attains to beauty, beauty which is as absolute as that of the most beautiful verses. The fact is partly due to the wealth and freshness of the language of the day, which had not yet been dessicated and dulled, and was saved, in this instance, from its habitual faults. The shortness of the verses compelled restraint, and hemmed the language in from overflowing into unending and formless sentences. It is impossible to exaggerate the benefit wrought to literature by the reverent reading and repetition of these admirable chapters. The most literate were preserved from affectation and pedantry; the philosophers acquired an alternative to dry and disfiguring abstractness; the ignorant received an ideal which lifted their speech above the level of the rude and the vulgar. A wandering tinker like Bunyan was able, with no model but the Bible, to become a great English prose-writer.

It has, however, too often been forgotten that the benefit of the Authorised Version is not unmixed. Together with its admirable qualities, the Bible of 1611 had enormous defects which did not fail to retain a long hold on the minds and therefore on the prose of many Englishmen. Partly because of the obscurity of the original texts, and partly because of many mistranslations of sense, the Authorised Version contains numerous quite unintelligible passages, verses and expressions, not to speak of the many places in which the disjointedness of Oriental thought is disconcerting to European minds.

Since it was the accepted Word of God, readers in their thousands applied themselves to deciphering sentences which were really enigmatic and often incapable of yielding sense, and they discovered allegories in them, or saw the secret revelation of a doctrine necessary to their salvation in words which had been coupled together by faithful translators at their wits' end. Think of the numbers who, by ingenious deductions, read their own wishes or desires into a sibylline verse of the Scriptures. Or, not to leave the strict limits of literature, imagine this Book of Books, with its thousand strange and obscure expressions, accepted as the norm, developing the taste for broken, apocalyptic language.

Examples could be cited of countless passages in which piety or discretion impelled the English translators to render the Hebrew literally, without daring to introduce any meaning which they had not the wit to discover in their original. We will mention only the mysterious epithet "fearful in praises" applied to God in Exodus xv. 11, or the verse which in the Book of Job refers to the divine might, "If he cut off, and shut up, or gather together, then who can hinder him?" (Job xi. 10).

Probably assiduous reading of the Bible is largely responsible for the troubled and confused eloquence, interrupted by images violently subversive of logic, of which many English writers have been guilty. Fortunately, the dangers of following the Scriptural model were combated by that great respect for strict reason which marked the classical period, already at hand, the period of analysis and ratiocination. Its first signs were perceptible when the Authorised Version appeared, and, after the Puritan Age, the reign of the understanding was established almost without contest. Two currents of thought, one mystical and the other rationalistic, flowed through the seventeenth century, and were sometimes separate and sometimes merged in each other. By 1611 the poetic fervour of the Renascence had cooled or been transformed. Bacon's work was a counterpoise to the Bible, or rather the practical and utilitarian spirit which led to the foundation of the Royal Society for Improving Natural Knowledge was balanced by the diffusion of Biblical poetry.

The result was a literature which had a double inspiration and double aspect, the two being complementary rather than antagonistic to each other. It is due to the Bible that English was less deeply modified by analysis and by grammatical definition than French, then embarking, with Malherbe, the *Précieuses* and the grammarians, on the road to somewhat dry simplification. The Bible was the great force which perpetuated in English, even in English prose, elements of poetry and of quaintness and a certain *chiaro-oscuro*, and which also maintained in thought a mysticism and an imaginative ferment increasingly threatened by strict rationalism. When it is remembered that Great Britain is the land of the Royal Society, Hobbes, Locke, Hume and Adam Smith, the economists and the utilitarians, the country in which the sense of the practical and the positive, implanted by the Normans, has perhaps taken deepest root, the immense importance is understood of the Bible which kept poetry alive, sometimes indeed at the expense of complete intellectual clarity.

6. **Philosophical Prose : Bacon.**[1]—Side by side with the religious literature, a secular literature, distinct from although not in conflict with it, was coming into existence and was concerned with philosophy and morals. Francis Bacon (1561–1626) never speaks of religion except with respect, and seems himself to have been religious, for he wrote several very beautiful prayers for his own use and professed the Anglican faith. But his work had no connection with theology or even with Christian morality. It is the product of a free spirit, of thought which adventures in new paths discovered by itself. He is the first in date of the English philosophers and one of the most eminent and characteristic of them. Moreover, he is one of the pioneers of modern philosophy in all countries.

The contrast between his great intellect and his mediocre character is one of the commonplaces of history. This client and friend of Essex who directed the legal proceedings against him, this Lord Chancellor of James I. who was obliged to acknowledge himself guilty of corrupt and abusive exercise of his office, could be summed up by Pope as "the wisest, brightest, meanest of mankind." While it may be admitted that there were attenuating circumstances to excuse him, it is impossible to deny that he made friendship and uprightness subordinate to his career. This low ambition was, however, redeemed and ennobled by another, the desire to serve mankind by the search for truth. Very early, while still at Cambridge, Bacon realised the sterility of the scholastic studies which lead to verbal controversy but never to reality. He then conceived the idea of a mission beside which all the acts of his practical life sank almost to insignificance:

I found in my own nature a special adaptation for the contemplation of truth. For I had a mind at once versatile enough for that most important object—I mean the recognition of similitudes—and at the same time sufficiently steady and concentrated for the observation of subtle shades of difference. I possessed a passion for research, a power of suspending judgement with patience, of meditating with pleasure, of assenting with caution, of correcting false impressions with readiness, and of arranging my thoughts with scrupulous pains. I had no hankering after novelty, no blind admiration for antiquity. Imposture in every shape I utterly detested. For all these reasons I

---

[1] Complete edition by Spedding, Ellis and Heath, 14 vols. (1857–74). *Philosophical Works*, ed. Robertson, 1 vol. (1905); *The Advancement of Learning*, ed. W. A. Wright, 5th ed. (1900). The *Essays* are constantly being edited. See also Abbott, *Bacon, an Account of his Life and Work* (1885); R. W. Church, *Bacon* (1884); J. Nichol, *Bacon* (1888–9); C. de Rémusat, *Bacon, sa vie, son temps et son influence jusqu'à nos jours* (1857); Ch. Adam, *Philosophie de Bacon* (1890).

considered that my nature and disposition had, as it were, a kind of kinship and connection with truth.

His first object was to acquire the knowledge which increases man's empire over the earth. At thirty years old he wrote to Burleigh, "I have as vast contemplative ends as I have moderate civil ends; for I have taken all knowledge to be my province."

Little by little, he elaborated the doctrine which he formulated in 1620 in his *Novum Organum*. He declared science to be one, and to have a practical object.

We are concerned not with pure skill in speculation, but with real utility and the fortunes of the human race. . . . For man is no more than the servant and interpreter of Nature; what he does and what he knows is but that which he has observed of the order of Nature in act or in thought; beyond this he knows nothing and can do nothing. For the chain of causes cannot be relaxed or broken by any force, and Nature cannot be commanded except by being obeyed.

Since the obstacles to the attainment of this power, which depends on science, are ignorance and error, the causes are analysed of error or the tendencies to error existing in the human mind, and here given the Platonic name of idols of the intelligence. Bacon takes pleasure in subdividing these idols into those of the tribe, the cave, the market-place and the theatre, using a curious symbolism which bears the mark of the Elizabethan age. Then he determines the true method, establishing the importance of an objective attitude to nature, and the necessity of systematic experiment, and of caution against precipitate conclusions, "for the subtlety of nature is many times greater than the subtlety of our logic." The passage from particular facts to general laws should always be made by prudent and successive degrees.

True science is the knowledge of causes which Bacon, like Aristotle, divides into material and efficient causes in the physical, and formal and final causes in the metaphysical, sphere. The search for the final cause leads to the corruption, rather than the progress, of science. Form is the true object of search, and is found in the fixed laws which rule bodies. It is the thing itself, the object in its relation to man and to his senses and understanding, as opposed to the object considered in its relations to the universe. These forms are limited in number and are the alphabet of nature. Therefore it is possible to hope that science and philosophy will in the future be complete. The great matter is to collect instances, that is facts, after which the inductive method can be followed with security. A beginning can be made with the hypothesis which yields the first "vintage."

Although Bacon may often go astray in his scientific researches while attempting to put his own method in practice, it remains none the less certain that his glorification of facts, the search for them and their classification, had a powerful effect on English thought, not, however, immediately, but after half a century. The Royal Society for Improving Natural Knowledge emanated from Bacon and was the means for the establishment of the Baconian spirit in the heart of the nation.

In the meanwhile, this man, who opened up new horizons to the understanding of his fellow-countrymen, who broke with the Middle Ages and made so bold a step forward into modern times, was chained to the past by his language. He was convinced that "these modern languages will at one time or other play the bankrowtes with books," and he entrusted his philosophy to Latin. His capital work *Instauratio magna* (1620–3) is written in Latin, as are the numerous scientific and philosophical pamphlets appended to it. Even when he wrote in English his *Essays*, which soon became popular, it was the Latin translation of them, "being in the universal language," which might, he judged, "last as long as books last."

It is therefore only in spite of himself that Bacon ranks among English prose-writers, and only in virtue of the least of his works, his *Essays,* his *Advancement of Learning,* his *History of Henry the Seventh,* his *Apophthegms New and Old,* his unfinished novel, the *New Atlantis,* and various treatises and pamphlets. One hundred years after Thomas More, whose masterpiece also was in Latin, he continued this tradition, but his attitude had less justification, since in his time every literary genre was exemplified in the national literature. It is the more surprising because he could handle English prose so surely and vigorously that he became, in spite of himself, one of the first prose-writers of his country.

He cannot be said to owe this place to his *New Atlantis,* a painfully didactic and awkwardly written description of a new Utopia inhabited by scholars after Bacon's own heart. The most characteristic monument of the imaginary island is "Salomon's House, or the College of the Six Days' Works," which is a sort of anticipation of the Royal Society and similarly destined to "the producing of great and marvellous works for the benefit of men." In its turrets for observing depth and height, and in its dissecting and vivisecting halls, audacious researches were conducted, some of which were afterwards realised, although the fantastic nature of others has become apparent. This novel is, in fact, Bacon's philosophy of science presented in romantic form by a writer without the gift for romance of which Thomas More received so fortunate a share.

The *History of Henry the Seventh* is stylistically much more remarkable. It was written to please James I. in praise of his ancestor, the first Tudor sovereign, but it has all the gravity suited to an historical work. Bacon's sagacity often appears in it, and was to show itself yet more clearly in the portraits of Henry VIII. and Elizabeth which he left behind him. No other favourable and admiring picture of the queen is as good.

It was, however, by his *Essays* that Bacon proved himself a great writer of his own language. Their title, although not their spirit, recalls Montaigne's masterpiece. While Montaigne is copious, homely, prodigal of confidences, interested in everything, prone to philosophise on whatever relates to man, Bacon is curt, almost sibylline, entirely impersonal and averse from pure speculation. He deduces general maxims only from the observations he has himself been able to make. He writes only for courtiers and statesmen like himself. His manner is intermediate between that of Montaigne's essays and that of the maxims of de la Rochefoucauld. He supplies short dissertations wholly sententious in form, supported by quotations from the ancients but founded on direct observation. The construction is stiff and formal. Like a good lawyer, Bacon, with an air of complete impartiality, balances opposing arguments before he draws his conclusion.

The essential merit lies in the density of the thought and expression, the frequent brilliancy of the poetic images, inserted never as ornaments but always to emphasise an idea, and the impressive loftiness of the oracular tone.

The moral is that set forth in the *Novum Organum,* and the design is practical and utilitarian. There are in fact two morals rather than one. Good for Bacon has a double character, according to whether it be considered relatively to the individual or the state. He is strongly imbued with Machiavellism, and praises Machiavelli for describing not what men should do, but what they do. He is doubtless aware of the difference between virtue and interest. He declares that he is so, and that nothing is of as much worth as virtue. But it is the art of success among men which is the subject of his *Essays.* He points man to the part he should play on the stage of social life, as is indicated in the sub-title of his book: *Counsels Civil and Moral.* Baudouin, its first French translator, was right to call it *L'Artisan de la Fortune.*

Within these limits the *Essays* have singular force and weight. No one has ever produced a greater number of closely packed and striking formulas, loaded with practical wisdom. Many of them have become current as proverbs. Other maxims, either cast by Bacon directly or translated from his Latin, can be extracted from all his works and added to those in the *Essays*. The value of some depends entirely on their wisdom and its forcible expression:

> He that hath wife and children hath given hostages to fortune, for they are impediments to great enterprises, either of virtue or mischief.
> Children sweeten labours, but they make misfortunes more bitter. They increase the cares of life, but they mitigate the remembrance of death.
> Lookers-on many times see more than the gamesters.

Others are remarkable by their images, at once large and terse:

> Men fear death as children fear to go in the dark, and as that natural fear in children is increased with tales, so is the other.

To show that religion is degraded by the shedding of blood, he says:

> Surely this is to bring down the Holy Ghost, instead of the likeness of a dove, in the shape of a vulture or raven, and to set out of the barque of a Christian Church a flag of a barque of pirates and assassins.

These *Essays* are the first in date of the classics of English prose, in the proper sense of the word. They are used as class-books almost as much as Shakespeare's plays. School-children learn from them to analyse their thoughts, to investigate the etymological sense of words—Bacon's words are weighted with their Latin meaning—and to formulate condensed reflections. The *Essays* also constitute a handbook of practical wisdom, enclosing in their shortest maxims an astonishing treasure of insight. There has been no more active stimulant to wit and the understanding. As compared with Hooker's great dialectical work, with its vast, developed argument and concentration on temporary and local disputes, the *Essays* are a compendium of precepts, or rather of reflections, which are true of all men, for all time and in all places.

7. **An Eccentric : Burton.**[1]—The list of the prose-writers of this time ends with an eccentric humanist. All the pedantry of the Renascence was poured into the *Anatomy of Melancholy* (1621), but vitalised by pervading humour. The author, Robert Burton (1576–1640), was a contemporary of Ben Jonson who left Oxford to become a country clergyman. He seems to have lived entirely among books, and he made his booty of Greek and Latin and of many modern authors. He was learned, knowing mathematics, astrology and land-surveying excellently well. His weapons against his gloomy, melancholy temper were scholarly jokes and the arduous work of collecting all the allusions to his affliction which his endless reading revealed. Had he followed his own inclination he would, like Bacon, have clothed his work in Latin, rather than "prostitute my muse in English." But since the "mercenary stationers" would have none of a book in the learned language, he had to fall back on the vulgar tongue. The result of his lengthy labours was an enormous quarto volume, followed, during the seventeenth century, by seven folio editions. The title is characteristic: *The Anatomy of Melancholy : What it is. With all the Kindes, Causes, Symptomes, Prognostickes and severall Cures of it. In Three Maine Partitions with their severall Sections, Members and Subsections, Philosophically, Medicinally, Historically, opened and cut up. By Democritus Junior. With a Satyricall Preface Conducing to the following Discourse. Macrob. Omne meum, Nihil meum.*

---

[1] *The Anatomy of Melancholy*, ed. Shilleto (1893; reprinted 1904).

The book contains indeed nothing which was Burton's own, for he pillaged all known books. Yet everything in it became his because he chose it and because his temperament infused into the whole a sort of unity.

His heroine, Melancholy, was not the gentle companion beloved of the romantics, the pensive maiden, contemplating the beauties of nature in sweet sadness and petting her own feelings, who was dearer than cheerfulness. To the men of the Renascence melancholy was a sickness; it was the *black distemper*, according to the strict Greek meaning of the word, and was the doctor's affair. The distance which separated melancholy from madness was short, and while Burton sometimes distinguishes between the two, he often confuses them.

The melancholy of Shakespeare's Jaques in *As You Like It* is a compound of moroseness, misanthropy, eccentricity, irony and sarcasm. It is softened only for a moment at the sight of a deer wounded to death, and this tenderness soon turns into satire against man. A fit precursor to Burton, Jaques goes on his way culling instances and proofs of human foolishness, madness and perversity. Shakespeare disowns him, finally letting Rosalind scoff at him and turn him out. If George Sand, adapting Shakespeare's comedy, made Jaques into the wise and beneficent philosopher of the piece, it was that Rousseau had formed her mind and she could neither understand nor approve melancholy as it was conceived by a man of the Renascence.

Burton, Democritus Junior, devotes his book, which is as methodically constructed as a scholastic treatise, to an enumeration of all the forms which melancholy can assume to darken the life of man. He treats of religious melancholy, which the Puritans were beginning to exemplify, and of the melancholy of love-sickness. His *Anatomy* is in fact a vast picture of human folly. It echoes not only the attack of the ancient Democritus, but also the satires of antiquity, those, for instance, of Lucian, and also more recent invectives, Sebastian Brandt's *Ship of Fools*, Erasmus's *Praise of Folly*, and, in part, More's *Utopia*, not to mention numerous sarcasms taken from Rabelais and Montaigne. "Thou shalt soon perceive that all the world is mad, that it is melancholy, dotes," and Burton finds that its madness recurs in all ages and countries, at all times of life and in every condition. Customs, uses, occupations, tastes, actions and words prove this abundantly. The existence of war bears overwhelming witness to it, and he dwells long on the madness of war, thus following More and anticipating La Bruyère and Swift, with less passion and eloquence than theirs, but with an extraordinary array of particular examples, annotations and quotations.

His reflections on his own country are curious. He first praises its prosperity and its learned king, James I., "another Numa, a second Augustus, a true Josiah." But he then shows the other side of the picture, the state of Ireland, which he calls a "dishonour to our nation," and of England, where the land seems to him uncultivated and miserable in comparison with industrious Holland. He declares idleness to be the scourge of England. "Idleness is the *malus Genius* of our nation." The Englishman will not work. Burton escapes from his grief to a Utopia, imagining a country in which every material improvement should have been effected. Yet he is not fantastic, but keeps clear of communism, ably defending the civil and ecclesiastical hierarchy.

In such digressions he shows himself a reasonable man, but more often his good sense is cloaked by eccentricity and his wisdom disguised as humour. This frenzied compiler, this scholar quoting endlessly, this writer of prose who recoups himself for his abstention from Latin by introducing numerous Latin expressions into his sentences, does not take himself entirely seriously. On occasion he makes fun of himself and his brother pedants. He can scoff at antiquaries and philosophers as vivaciously as La Bruyère, and he can give away the tricks of his trade:

> As Apothecaries we make new mixtures every day, pour out of one vessel into another; and as those old Romans robbed all the cities of the world, to set out their bad sited Rome, we skim off the cream of other men's wits, pick the choice flowers of their tilled gardens to set out our own sterile plots.

He exactly describes his own manner of writing. "As a River runs, sometimes precipitate and swift, then dull and slow; now direct, then *per ambages*; now deep, then shallow; now muddy, then clear; now broad, then narrow; doth my style flow." It is a style recognisable to a French reader who knows it in Rabelais and Montaigne. Perhaps it is with Rabelais that Burton has the most striking analogy of form, for both writers follow the curious method of emptying on to every statement their whole store of synonyms, letting fly all their epithets, compelled thereto by no necessity of meaning, but by their rather childish pleasure in displaying wealth of vocabulary, their joy in handling and feeling the words at their command.

In subject, on the other hand, Burton is much nearer to Montaigne. Although he professes to confine himself to melancholy, he reviews all the follies of man. Sometimes, when he intervenes directly and speaks of himself, relating his life or experiences, he is very close to the author of the *Essais*. His quotations, of which he has too many, do not distinguish him from the French writer, save that they are part of the very warp and woof of his style. But the rigorous divisions of the *Anatomy*, Burton's lack of a really definite and personal philosophy, his inferior penetration and his less free spirit, his fewer profound observations and greater share of pedantry and eccentricity, place him, in spite of everything, very much below Montaigne. He is more bookish, less spontaneous and keen, lets himself go less, and has not the same grace. The Frenchman walks the great high-road of students of morals and of society. Burton lives remote from beaten paths, in a hermitage of baroque construction, to which few to-day have access.

Yet this fantastic writer had in England lasting influence of a sort. The numerous editions into which his book ran up to 1676 are proof of his success with two generations. In the eighteenth century he was forgotten and could be robbed with impunity, especially by the humorist Sterne. It was tempting to make a parade of knowledge by means of the wholesale spoliation of this great folio, neglected by everyone except Doctor Johnson, whose daily reading it was. In the nineteenth century Burton's reputation was revived by Charles Lamb, who rendered him a sort of cult, including miscellaneous extracts from his writings in *Curious Fragments*, and amusing himself by imitating his methods in his own essays.[1]

A little of Burton's eccentricity and pedantry marks nearly all the prose of these fifty years. It lacked the clear, even simplicity which to the French is the proper characteristic of true prose. It was not yet entirely distinct from poetry. But it was tending noticeably to conquer more and more ground. In spite of the resistance of Latin, it had extended its sphere to include more diverse subjects. It embraced theology; it touched on philosophy; it made definite conquest of literary criticism; and it annexed the moral essay and the "characters." It shared the elasticity of the novel, could be romantic, sentimental, realistic or comic. It had

---

[1] English literature has a partial claim to John Barclay (1582–1621), who was born at Pont-à-Mousson of a Scottish father and French mother, and wrote in Latin his picaresque romance, *Euphormionis Satyricon* (1603–7), and his more famous historical *roman à clef*, *Argenis*, (1617), dedicated to Louis XIII. The latter work is, however, mainly concerned with France and had there its chief success, which gave an impulse to the pseudo-historical romances of the middle seventeenth century. In fact, Barclay was the typical cosmopolitan writer of the time, and his use of Latin, the only cosmopolitan language, is characteristic.

I—R

already an important part in the theatre. It had learnt to relate and to discuss. It could mock and it could be serious. When the poverty and uncertainty of prose before 1578 is remembered, its rapid progress is striking, and seems almost to equal the advance made by poetry. The victory of the Puritans interrupted its use for the literature, light and frivolous in form, which ceased to be produced until the Restoration, but the generation of the middle of this century used a prose which, while less diverse, attained in the higher kinds of literature to a magnificent development of those qualities of eloquence, strength and amplitude already apparent in some of the prose-writers we have reviewed.

CHAPTER V

I. Fertility of the Drama. The Difficulty of Tracing its Evolution.—
Rich as are all the manifestations of the English literature of the Renascence, its
highest glory and the most direct and original expression of the national genius
are dramatic. Elsewhere imitation and artifice play a part; aristocratic sentiment
or an ephemeral fashion is a check on spontaneity, ruling out whatever is of the
people, or colouring style or subject to make it archaic, euphuistic, arcadian or
pastoral. On occasion, the greatest authors pride themselves on exclusiveness.
Spenser writes with his eyes on the court, especially on its lords and ladies. Shakespeare, dazzled by the friendship of the young Earl of Southampton, heads *Venus
and Adonis* with two arrogant lines from Ovid: "Let the mob admire what is vile;
to me may fair Apollo serve cups filled with water of Castalia." The influence of
antiquity and of foreign countries, especially Italy, is everywhere so noticeable,
that only rarely do we receive an immediate and broad impression of the English
genius. Everything bears a little the mark of a restricted public, a set or a coterie.
The sonneteers, the anacreontics and the various humanists do not wholly belong
to their country, but owe allegiance also to foreign writers who inspire them and
whose rivals they are.

The theatre was open to all: the whole town was attracted by it and enthusiastic
for it. It was truly national. For many it took the place of the church they neglected;
to most, in this time of no newspapers and few and little-read novels, it was the
only source of intellectual pleasure. A secular temple, it provided from time to time
a communion of patriotism instead of the old communion of faith. For while the
insatiable curiosity of the public did indeed make a constant demand for stories
of foreign countries, all they wanted of them was to be astonished, amused or
scandalised. In order to please the English, the playwright had to produce scenes
constructed for the English alone. He had to please everyone in his public, but his
public was purely English. Never has any other audience been so stimulating to
writers, who received their immediate reward in tears or laughter, noisy and
multitudinous applause. And niggardly though the payment for plays might be,
the demand for them was incessant. Whenever an author found his pocket empty,
he knew that his best chance of filling it promptly was on the stage. Therefore all
the authors wrote or tried to write for the theatre. There is hardly a poet or novelist
of this period who did not at some time turn his attention to drama, not to speak of
those who gave almost all their energies to it. Certain of them who, like Daniel
and Drayton, had little gift for dramatic composition, attempted it only passingly
and withdrew before their lack of success. But the number of those who never
tried their hand at a play is small. Even Spenser wrote nine comedies, unfortunately

[1] General works: A. W. Ward, *History of English Dramatic Literature to the Death of Queen
Anne*, 2nd ed., 3 vols. (1899); F. E. Schelling, *Elizabethan Drama*, 2 vols. (1908); F. G. Fleay,
A Biographical Chronicle of the English Drama, 2 vols. (1891); *A Chronicle History of the London
Stage* (1880). For all Shakespeare's predecessors see Mézières, *Prédécesseurs et Contemporains
de Shakespeare* (1863); E. S. Boas, *Shakespeare and his Predecessors* (1896); J. A. Symonds, *Shake-
speare's Predecessors* (1884); A. Symons, *Studies in the Elizabethan Drama* (1920).

lost; Sidney, indeed, produced no more than a court masque, but he gave such a large place in his *Defence of Poesie* to the popular drama which he despised as to prove its importance to the life of this century.

This is therefore the subject which the historian of the literature of the Renascence must study principally. It is also that most difficult to consider. The sixty-two years from 1580 to 1642 seem to present an inextricable confusion of plays, such a jungle of dramatic production as is very difficult to light up with ideas. It is a puzzle to find a principle of classification applicable to the thousand or so plays extant. To trace an unbroken evolution would be infinitely desirable, but a careful examination leaves no certainty that such exists. None but inevitable changes can be perceived. It may be that there was at the beginning greater freshness and artlessness, and that the dramatist then pulled his strings more awkwardly than when practice had taught him technical skill and given him both more ease and less conviction. But many exceptions would have to be made even to these cautious generalisations. Nothing is certain but the progress and the decline of blank verse. Stiff at first, it gradually became pliable, then as free as was compatible with its rules, and finally from liberty it passed to nothingness. But there is on the whole no such passage from youth to middle age, and thence to decadence, as can form a thread for the history of the great ages of literature. The Renascence drama did not die a natural death. It was executed when it was still very much alive, so much so that the executioner was unequal to his task, and that twenty years later the alleged corpse was resuscitated, and promptly resumed, under the Restoration, a singularly active life.

The critic is, further, without the data and dates which would enable him to follow an evolution. He has to base his arguments on the extant plays without knowing how many have been lost. Thomas Heywood alone, who claims to have written 220 plays, left only thirty-five to posterity. The chronology of numerous dramatic works is purely conjectural. The life and character of the authors are almost entirely unknown. Many of them are no more than names, and there is no psychological certainty on which to rest the study of their works. The authorship of plays is very often uncertain. The habit of repeating and rearranging earlier works, that of the collaboration of playwrights—who worked at a play simultaneously or successively, or at one time simultaneously and at another successively: these factors complicate investigation over and over again. Will it ever be possible to unravel the tangle of Fletcher's work and Massinger's, Middleton's and Rowley's, Dekker's and Webster's?

It is impossible to follow with certainty the individual history of each playwright, or each company of actors who had a repertory, or each theatre which had a public. In spite of the considerable efforts which have been made, the unknown remains vaster than the known.

It would be tempting to make the classification by genres, to divide the plays into tragedies and comedies with their subsections, pure tragedy and tragi-comedy, historical drama, romantic and realistic comedy, pastoral comedy and comedy of manners and of character. But the distribution would have little correspondence with the realities of this drama which was wont purposely to mingle genres in one play, aiming at variety rather than harmony.

We are brought back to search for a central figure, and to group about Shakespeare, incontestably the greatest of all, the constellation of his rivals—his predecessors, contemporaries and successors. While, however, there is much to be gained by subordinating everything to the master, it cannot be forgotten that several critics have claimed this central place for Ben Jonson, whose attitude to his fellow-dramatists is better known, whose theory of the drama is more clearly enunciated, and whose production was spread over a longer time, thirty-six years, from 1597 to 1633, as against the twenty-three years, from 1590 to 1613, for which Shakespeare wrote.

Whatever method be adopted, it is important to realise the swarming confusion which has to be reduced to order. On almost every day of these sixty years performances were simultaneously given in the London theatres of the most dissimilar plays belonging to the most various genres, plays already old, and plays which, more often by their subject or plot than by the really fresh mental attitude or change of method they indicated, were new. What the public desired up to the end was to feel again at each performance the emotions they knew or others like them, and if possible to have dished up for them a story which had not yet been staged.

2. **The Public Theatre. The Stage. The Actors.**[1]—It has been possible to elucidate the conditions of the tangible stage and those in which actors and playwrights lived better than the dramatic evolution. We have stated that the first public theatre was built on the confines of the city in 1576; by the end of the century there were some eight of them on the north and south side of the Thames, a surprising number for a town of hardly 200,000 inhabitants and a proof of the singular popularity of dramatic representations. These took place, for lack of means of lighting, in the afternoons, generally in buildings which externally were round or hexagonal. Within, the disposition of their space seems almost always to have been the same. A courtyard, open to the sky, was the pit; around this were two or three tiers of covered galleries; and in front of the pit a large protruding platform on trestles formed the stage. Two pillars in the middle of the platform upheld the ceiling; at the back, between two doors used by the actors for their exits and entrances, another scene was overlooked by a balcony with windows, and before this back-scene there was a movable curtain.

There were no wings and no back-scenery, and only the simplest accessories—table, chairs, bushes—to indicate or rather symbolise the place of the action. Sometimes it was merely intimated on a placard to such as could read. The front-scene served almost all purposes so long as it was not necessary to represent a special place. Many scenes in Elizabethan plays pass in a vague, indeterminate place, in a street or public square, before a house or in an unspecified room.

The back-scene was used for places which had a special and distinct character. The curtain at the back rose to discover persons in a particular attitude, for instance Ferdinand and Miranda playing chess in Prospero's cell.

The arrangement was in its outline taken from the mediæval stage, which included a vague place (*platœa*) and others which were defined (*sedes, domus, loca*). The progress of the theatre in the seventeenth century brought the back-curtain more and more forward until it finally reached the front of the stage and the undefined part of the platform disappeared. Then it became possible to supersede the slight scenery of the back-scene with scenery which was erected behind the front-curtain and became increasingly multifarious, large and complicated.

On this almost naked stage the actor's person had a double importance. His costume was as rich as the stage was poor. Attention was entirely concentrated on his tragic gestures or grimaces. His declamation, in particular, was important, emphasising the value of the numerous monologues, the multiplied pointed tirades of the plays of the period. His art was therefore carried to a high pitch. English actors had at this time a reputation which reached the continent, whither they were summoned and where some of them made long tours. There were no actresses:

---

[1] E. K. Chambers, *The Elizabethan Stage*, 4 vols. (1924); J. Q. Adams, *Shakesperean Playhouses* (1920); A. Feuillerat, *Le Bureau des Menus Plaisirs et la mise en scène à la cour d'Elizabeth* (1910).

women's parts were played by boys. All the prestige which belongs to an actress went to the actors, and more than one citizen's wife was fascinated by them. Members of the Inns of Court and great gentlemen were proud of their intercourse with the profession, and in the taverns an actor cut a fine figure. Although they were almost outcasts from society, actors not only enjoyed popularity, but were also cultivated by persons whose acquaintance was most flattering to their vanity. They had a good chance to make their fortunes if, amid the dangerous temptations of their calling, they lived an orderly life and preserved a practical point of view. If they had a share in the ownership of their theatre, they were prosperous and important men, enjoying much more consideration than the frequently starveling playwrights who tried to sell their plays to the companies.

Such an actors' company as that to which Shakespeare belonged, which was patronised in turn by Leicester, by Ferdinando, Lord Strange, who became Lord Derby in 1593, and by the Lord Chamberlain, and which became the King's Company at the accession of James I., was a veritable institution. We find it playing at the Bull's Inn, at the Theatre, the Curtain and the Rose, and at the Globe, built by this company for its own use in 1599. Under James I. it owned two playhouses, the Globe in Southwark, which was used in summer, and Blackfriars, almost within the city liberties, a covered theatre in which there were performances in the winter. This company was directed by the Burbages, father and son; by Richard Burbage, one of the most famous actors of the day, from 1597 to 1619. It had its struggles, some of them sharp, in particular with the Lord Admiral's Company and with the Children of the Chapel Royal, who captivated London for a time. But it triumphed over all rivals and retained its supremacy until the theatres were closed.

As for individual actors, the famous Edward Alleyn (1566–1626), who created the leading parts in Marlowe's plays, made his fortune so effectively as director of the Lord Admiral's Company, that he became master of the royal games and of the king's "bears, bulls and mastiff dogs," which were baited in the several rings, bought a manor from Lord Francis Calton for ten thousand pounds, very munificently founded on it Dulwich College which he endowed largely, and founded other charities also.

The passion for the theatre, which attracted money to it, gave rise to speculation. Thanks to his diary for the years from 1592 to 1603, we can follow in detail the investments of Philip Henslowe, Alleyn's father-in-law, a dealer and pawnbroker. As shrewd as he was illiterate, this capitalist bought plays from authors and sold them to actors. The price of a play varied from four to ten pounds. He advanced money to necessitous playwrights and sold stage-properties to the theatres. He built the Rose Theatre, and then the Fortune and the Hope Theatres. Under Elizabeth he directed the Admiral's and Lord Worcester's Companies, and under James I., when actors were no longer protected by noblemen and the surviving companies were under the patronage of members of the royal family, he was at the head of the Queen's and the Prince's Companies.

3. **The Plays. The Public.**[1]—In 1580 the theatres possessed a repertory of plays already studied and others like them. Because these disregarded rule, they provoked the ridicule or indignation of the literate, who compared them with the works of antiquity and blushed for the national barbarism. It was deplored as early as 1578 by George Whetstone, for all that he himself was the author of a sufficiently romantic play, *Promos and Cassandra*. Sidney repeated his strictures three or four years later in his *Defence of Poesie*, and added force and brilliancy to them. He passed sentence as a humanist on gothic and popular productions, for although at heart he was, as his *Arcadia* proves, an extreme romantic, he no sooner

---

[1] C. J. Sisson, *Le goût public et le théâtre élisabethain* (Dijon, 1922).

became a critic than he was the docile disciple of Scaliger, Minturno, Castelvetro and their like. He confronted a drama which knew nothing of decorum with the law of the unities and the law which separates the tragic and the comic, and he energetically ridiculed the absurdities entailed by changes of scene and time:

> You shall have Asia of the one side, and Affrick of the other, and so many other under kingdoms, that the player when he comes in, must ever begin with telling where he is, or else the tale will not be conceived. Now you shall have three ladies walk to gather flowers, and then we must believe the stage to be a garden. By and by we hear news of a shipwrack in the same place, then we are to blame if we accept it not for a rock. Upon the back of that, comes out a hideous monster with fire and smoke, and then the miserable beholders are bound to take it for a cave: while in the meantime two armies fly in, represented with four swords and bucklers, and then what hard heart will not receive it for a pitched field. Now of time, they are much more liberal. For ordinary it is that two young princes fall in love; after many traverses she is got with child, delivered of a fair boy: he is lost, groweth a man, falleth in love, and is ready to get another child, and all this in two hours' space.

Sidney has the penetration to perceive the law by which the English playwrights were unconsciously governed. They believed themselves to be historians, and followed events step by step, forgetting the prerogatives of art which does not obey literal truth and which has the task of rearranging, eliminating, combining, constructing.

In this Sidney goes straight to the root of the matter. Quite artlessly, like the authors of the mysteries, the popular playwrights made it their business to distribute a story in scenes and to stage it. They had no conception of the necessity of a special plot, and in a large number of plays they did without one, and were thus able to produce a truly historical drama.

Sidney's condemnation would probably have been modified had he found artistic qualities of style in the drama which existed about 1580. The plays he had in mind were often ludicrous in form; the formula to which the poets conformed, one which masterpieces were soon to justify, suffered from this awkwardness. It was at the moment when Sidney was condemning contemporary drama that works were first performed which show, in spite of their defects, the evident signs of artistic labour. The capital contribution of humanism to the drama was the generalisation of the use of blank verse, the sole great innovation which the Renascence induced a conservative public to adopt universally.

More than the conscious will of the playwrights, the nature of their public decided the dramatic system—if the word may be applied to the almost unconscious work of tradition—which prevailed in England. The audiences who crowded into the Elizabethan playhouses represented every class and every trade. The queen herself might, on occasion, be seen attending a performance at Blackfriars, where the most fashionable audiences gathered. But to all the playhouses there was an affluence of the great and the lowly, the nobles and the people, the literate and the ignorant, the exquisites and the boors. Standing in the pit, the people pressed against the stage, intervening between it and the rich citizens and lords in their seats in the galleries. Mannerless coxcombs, arrogant as a Molière marquis, sat on the rushes on the stage, chaffing the actors and getting into their way. The playwright's duty was, like that of the author of a mystery, to provide food for every palate.

Thus it was that no play was written for performance on a public stage which did not combine contraries, pass from extreme coarseness to extreme refinement. There were exquisites among the audience who piqued themselves on their poetry and distilled subtle sonnets, and there were the groundlings, mainly attracted by the clowns and pronounced by Shakespeare to be "for the most part capable of nothing but inexplicable dumb-shows and noise." The great mass of the audience was, however, made up of simple folk, desirous of amusement yet willing to be edified or instructed, endowed with a curiosity at once ingenuous and ardent, and with imagination which easily moved them to tears or shouts of laughter. Neither squeamish nor sceptical, they blindly admired flights of lyricism which went beyond their comprehension, readily submitted to illusion and did not grudge their enjoyment. Such is a mixed popular audience in every country. It is an ideal, a grateful audience, perhaps the best fitted to appreciate the essentials of drama, namely the life and the human truth of its pictures.

It was the necessity of satisfying it which determined the character of the English drama of the Renaissance. Its extreme variety gave birth to the profound difference which henceforth distinguished this drama from that of France.

Hitherto too much has been attributed to race as a factor determining this divergence. Men have liked to show English drama leading to Shakespeare as an inevitable effect of the national genius, of the need for vehemence, movement, variety, imagination and also brutality which was in the blood of the English. France is represented as having advanced in an opposite direction towards Racine, because the French race was in love with beautiful proportions, harmony, fine analysis and nobility. To this theory there is the objection that these two contrasting nations, which seem at this time to turn their backs on each other, shared throughout the Middle Ages a drama which differed for each of them only in points of detail. Both peoples were impassioned amateurs of the mysteries which in both their countries not only had the same religious subjects, but were also closely akin in form and in the spectacles they provided. Moreover, France in the Middle Ages seems to have taken the lead in this matter, and to have supplied the earliest dramatic models. How could she evolve out of herself what was less fitted to her own genius than to that of a neighbouring nation, England, which accepted and kept what she gave? How could she, analogously, build for centuries the most marvellous of all the gothic cathedrals before she recognised that her natural destiny was to repeat the peristyles and colonnades of Græco-Roman architecture?

The difference between the dramatic art of the two countries must be explained less ambitiously and more certainly. The fact is that France at the time of the Renascence had disinherited the old religious drama, the only really native and popular drama, while England still preserved almost all its elements. The difference was rather in the public of the theatre in the two countries than in the national temperaments. The English theatre was still open to all men and made for them all. But the drama of the French Renascence took form after a police regulation, intended to check disorder, had in 1548 forbidden in France any popular performances of the mysteries, and therefore it was both new and a thing apart. It was subject to no influences except those of antiquity, and its appeal was to a select public of humanists and literates, with a due admixture of pedants. Nothing was left to the people but the farces and the clowning of the fairs. What was at its origin shared indiscriminately by all the people of both countries, was in France cut for a long period in two halves, with the result that the court and the literate class, the men bred on Greek and Latin, engrossed all that was noblest, while the people had the rest. For it is improbable that there was ever a large number of workmen who understood *Cinna* and acclaimed *Mithridate*. It is no more than just to credit accident with what accident mainly accomplished.

Nor can it be doubted that in England there were velleities towards a break between the art of the aristocracy and of the people. The court was greedy of dramatic representation, and some playwrights addressed themselves to satisfying the more refined tastes of the queen and the courtiers. It was naturally at the court or before the court that truly artistic drama was first attempted. The popular theatre, left to itself, threatened to persevere in disorder and coarseness, and could still be careless of elegance and style. It is in plays written for the court that these qualities, without which drama can be intensely alive but cannot survive as literature, are first plainly discernible. Since there was at this time constant intercourse between the court and the city, actors passed from the one to the other, and the same play was often given before the queen and the people in turn, so that progress stimulated by one audience was soon afterwards enjoyed by the other also. The benefit soon became general, but the search for the beautiful manifestly originated in the more cultured of the two spheres.

4. **The Plays of John Lyly.**[1]—John Lyly's plays were the first to provide models of refinement, or at least the first of all that have come down to us. For Lyly was not the first in date of the court purveyors. It is calculated that from the time of Elizabeth's accession seven plays were, on an average, given before her every year, and that about one hundred and fifty had been thus performed before Lyly's advent. Almost all of them have been lost except *Gorboduc* (1562), *Damon and Pythias* (1564) and *Tancred and Gismunda* (1586). We know of the rest only from the records of the Office of the Revels, the Master of the Revels having the duty of providing masques, dances and plays for the queen's diversion. He had to examine plays which were to be performed in her presence, whether written on purpose for her or chosen among such as had had a success with the public. Of the subsisting titles of the lost plays, so many are classical or mythological that their habitual subjects are revealed. There are synopses of masques which must have been mythological allegories of the same kind as most of Lyly's plays.

Lyly's success as author of *Euphues* and creator of euphuism seems immediately to have made him the accredited purveyor of court plays. His first play was indeed performed at Blackfriars Theatre before it was given in the queen's presence on 31 December 1581, but it seems to have been written with a view to Elizabeth's pleasure, as were most of his later plays. Lyly writes as a wit catering for an audience which likes what is witty, a man of letters appealing to cultivated people, a courtier flattering his sovereign. He seems entirely regardless of any larger public. As a refined, even a mannered, writer, he addresses himself to fine lords and fair ladies. He gives them the treat of hearing, on the stage, the antithetic style and decorative similes of that prose which was, and which remained for some ten years, the admiration of the fashionable world. No work ever bore its author's imprint more plainly than Lyly's. Each of his plays has a harmony and atmosphere proper to himself.

The most decided improvement due to him arose from his choice of prose as a medium, and a prose which, for all its artificiality, aimed at beauty. In face of the prevailing anarchy in the matter of literary form, he chose this one of the two solutions possible to him. He wrote too well, too elaborately and by too factitious methods, but in witty dialogue he attained to true art. His drama consists, for that matter, almost entirely of dialogue, for his plots are usually insignificant. His first known play, *Campaspe* (1581), is the work of a humanist whose matter is almost wholly taken from antiquity, but who remains independent in his construction. If precedents were to be found for it, they certainly would not be the comedies of the ancients, but rather the witty dialogues of Erasmus, and Lyly's pretext for uniting dialogues is a plot intended to eulogise Queen Elizabeth.

Alexander's love for his captive, the Theban Campaspe, is in conflict with his desire for glory and his consciousness of his royal duty. His love is crossed by that

---

[1] Complete works edited by R. W. Bond, 3 vols. (1902). *Campaspe* is printed in Manly's *Specimens*, op. cit., vol. ii. For critical study see A. Feuillerat's important *John Lyly* (1910).

of Campaspe for the artist Apelles whom Alexander has commissioned to paint her portrait, and who, as he traces her features, falls in love with her. Some pretty sentimentalism, relieved by mythology, is occasioned.

Round about Alexander are argumentative soldiers and philosophers who give Lyly an opportunity for having certain historic aphorisms repeated on the stage. Alexander is confronted with Diogenes, the cynic, who rejects his advances and tells him some hard truths. Their conversations are real duels in which, amid the clash of swords, we hear almost all the famous retorts with which antiquity credits Diogenes.

These scenes are in pleasing juxtaposition to arguments between the slaves of the principal characters—Diogenes, Plato and Apelles—who meet in the market-place. The slaves' jokes are, it is true, mainly plays on words which betray the grammarian, yet they have a sufficient correspondence with the slaves' masters.

The play is witty and graceful and no more, but it is so in a high degree and consistently. Its euphuism, properly so called, is concentrated in the monologues, which are an exposition of Stoic morality, surprising in this ornate dress. Alexander, standing for Elizabeth, sacrifices his love to his duty as a sovereign and marries Campaspe to Apelles. There is little construction and no passion, only a series of fine-drawn conversations. Lyly wrote nothing wittier. In itself, as an example of an artificial genre, this play is exquisite, the only perfect thing produced before Shakespeare.

In the subsequent comedies the wit persists, but it is mingled with more fancy, and also, although the scene is again laid in antiquity, with some dreamy roman-ticism. In *Sapho and Phaon* there is again an allegory which flatters the queen, and more directly than before. Elizabeth's courtship by the Duke of Alençon is probably figured. Phaon, a poor boatman of Syracuse, is endowed, by a caprice of Venus, with unmatched beauty and rendered at the same time insensible to love. On the other hand, the goddess has pierced with an arrow the heart of the chaste Princess Sapho, of whose beauty she is jealous and whose chastity angers her. Sapho, crossing the water in the handsome ferryman's boat, falls deeply in love with him, and his heart also is touched in spite of his insensibility. He consults the Sibyl, who instructs him in the art of winning a woman's heart, and whose speech anticipates Shakespeare's Rosalind when she teaches Orlando how to court his beloved.

Sapho, languishing with love for Phaon, has him brought to her room on the pretext that he possesses a remedy which will cure her. The interview between the lovers is curious, endlessly mannered, yet charming in its concealment of a declaration beneath transparent play on words.

Yet Sapho laments. If Phaon love her, she must lower herself; if he be indifferent to her, she must die. She is saved by Venus, who too is captivated by Phaon and who deprives her of feeling. But the goddess fails to win the boatman's love. Her own child Cupid abandons her for Sapho, who inherits her power. And there is nothing left for poor Phaon to do but to leave Sicily, taking with him his cult of Sapho (Elizabeth) and his eternal love for her who is impervious to love, who has triumphed over Venus and is the mistress of Cupid.

Endymion (1586) has the merit that Lyly stages in it one of the most poetic of ancient myths which he does not rob of all its original grace. Manifestly this is another eulogy of Elizabeth, to be identified with Cynthia whom Endymion loves respectfully. The allegory is, however, more complicated than those of the earlier plays and more difficult to elucidate. It has been too much a subject of discussion to allow the several suggested interpretations to be given here. Endymion, by the enchantment of Tellus, who is jealous of Cynthia, is overpowered by sleep. One of

the most romantic scenes of Elizabethan drama is that in which his friend
Eumenides arrives in Thessaly, the land of enchantments, in search of the charm
which will awaken him. He reaches the banks of a prophetic spring of which the
bed is visible only to faithful lovers, for they alone can read on it the word which
will win them their heart's desire. Eumenides, who is the faithful and unfortunate
lover of Semele, a lady of Cynthia's court, hesitates long. Shall he ask for the love
of Semele or for the deliverance of Endymion? At last friendship and duty prevail
over love, and he learns that a kiss from Cynthia will give back life to Endymion.
Awakened after a sleep of forty years, Endymion, thanks to the kiss, recovers his
youth and the right to continue his respectful courtship.

When about 1590 Lyly wrote *Midas*, he abandoned flattery for satire. The play
is inspired by the disaster which had recently overtaken the Spanish Armada.
Midas, having obtained from Bacchus that all he touches shall turn to gold, prefers
Pan's song to Apollo's, and by Apollo is afflicted with asses' ears. It is not difficult
to read in all this a parable of Philip II., ruined by his very wealth, rashly daring
to rival Lesbos, or England, and beaten in his contest with the enemy island. The
allusions are very plain. The play is hardly suited to the stage, since it lacks a plot,
and its value depends mainly on the skilfulness of the allegory.

In *Gallathea* (1587) Lyly had emancipated himself from the necessity to be
either flattering or satirical, and merely amused himself by playing variations on
the theme of love. The play has two heroines, both disguised. Each has a father
who passes her off as a man to save her from the Minotaur to whom the fairest
maiden is offered every five years. So charming are these maidens in their pages'
guise that they are loved by all Diana's nymphs. But they love only each other,
each believing the other to be a boy. Venus unravels the tangle by changing one
of them into a man.

The play has some very pretty motifs and certain elements of poetry. The
scene in which Cupid, masquerading as a nymph, uses his disguise to awaken love
in all Diana's train, and is discovered by the angry goddess, who obliges him to
undo his mischief, is attractive. That in which each of the two fathers assures the
other that he has the more beautiful daughter is amusing, as is that in which young
Hebe, momentarily threatened by the Minotaur, is saved because her beauty is
judged inadequate, and does not know whether to rejoice at her safety or to
mourn it

But Lyly, as often happens to him, stops short in his best scenes. He goes only
half-way, makes no more than a sketch. His work lacks movement, and what
construction it has is too artificial, frozen by an excess of symmetry.

His last plays are pastorals like his *Gallathea*. *Love's Metamorphosis* shows
three nymphs of Ceres, unmoved by the love of three shepherds and metamorphosed by Cupid, the first into a stone for her cruelty, the second into a flower
for her coyness, and the third into a bird for her inconstancy. Cupid would restore
them, at the prayer of Ceres, to their proper forms, but at first they refuse this
service because they prefer ignorance of the ills of love and the unfaithfulness of
man. They yield only to the boy-god's terrible threats, and even so they warn their
lovers that the stone, the flower and the bird still live in their hearts.

In the *Woman in the Moone*, his only play in verse, Lyly reaches the point
of satirising woman unreservedly. He repeats the ancient legend in his own way,
imagining that when Pandora is created she receives from each of the seven
planets something of its own nature: melancholy from Saturn, ambition and disdain from Jupiter, a warlike temper from Mars, kindness from the Sun, an amorous
nature from Venus, falseness from Mercury, and madness from the Moon. Then
Lyly amuses himself by showing Pandora influenced by each of these planets in

succession. She ends within the sphere of the moon, where she is stationed at her own desire, all women being essentially "foolish, fickle, franticke, madde."

While Lyly usually drew on mythology and ancient history for his plays, once, in *Mother Bombie* (1587–9?), he tried his hand at a modern comedy in the Italian manner which has a much complicated plot. In spite of some pleasing passages, it is weak work, without any of the necessary swing. It is in his court dramas that Lyly's characteristics must be sought.

Nothing else as artistic had yet been produced on the English stage. Lyly's composition has defects: there are weak moments in his plays and ineffective complications, a mingling of the serious and the comic which connects him with the popular drama but proves his inability to blend these opposites in one plot. While, however, there is a general lack of force, depth and true passion in his work, his language is invariably careful; his dialogue is artificial but pointed; retorts depend mainly on play on words, but are lively and well turned and have a courtliness; there is choiceness in his tone and mannerisms, originality in his subjects, even grace and fancy in his conceptions; and his work, exactly because of its artifice and its pedantry, is precisely fitted to the fashionable society for which it was written.

Lyly is a long way behind Shakespeare, but none the less he anticipates him, the Shakespeare of *Love's Labour's Lost, Midsummer Night's Dream, Much Ado About Nothing* and especially *As You Like It*. He anticipates him yet more clearly if the charming songs of his comedies be not denied him. They appeared only in a posthumous edition of his works, and recent critics refuse to attribute them to him.

5. **George Peele.**[1]—Like Lyly, the prose-writer, George Peele, the poet (1558–98), began his career as a courtier. Like Lyly, he had a taste for ornament and cared for fine language. Although he acquired a reputation for wildness, became known for an incorrigible Bohemian, his upbringing was good. He went to Oxford and for some time he wrote for the court as a man of letters and refinement and a graceful poet.

The work which was apparently his first may be called a mythological pastoral, the *Arraignment of Paris*, which was played in 1580 before the queen, whom it greets in a concluding apotheosis. Diana revises the judgment of Paris in honour of Elizabeth, to whom she awards the apple. This pastoral has hardly any construction, but is very pleasing. Peele is a less witty and more poetic Lyly. No style was ever more bestrewed with flowers than his. In his play we see Flora causing nature to blossom on the spot where Diana is about to appear and painting with flowers the portrait of Juno in yellow, Pallas in red and Venus in blue. Peele, who had lately read Spenser's *Shepheard's Calendar*, mingles mythological personages with rude, realistic shepherds. His taste is not infallible: Helen, by whose means Venus seeks to tempt Paris, is a real farm-girl, a fact which does not keep her from singing an Italian song. But these vagaries do not much spoil this fantasy. It is fragrant, lyrical, light and melodious.

The same love of decoration appears even in those of Peele's plays which were not written directly for the court. His *David and Bethsabe* is curious in this respect. Its subject gives it a place apart from other works as a link with the old religious plays. But it is differentiated from these by the spirit which animates it. Peele ignores the marvellous, knows neither God nor devil. He stages literally a passage from the Bible—2 Samuel xi.–xx.—on the pattern of the new historical dramas, treating Scripture as Shakespeare afterwards treated the chronicles.

The construction is awkward. Two stories, that of Bethsabe and that of Absalon, are developed side by side but without connection between them. The drama moves slowly. The play is cold, but the style is very careful. Peele's imagery is

---

[1] Complete works ed. by A. H. Bullen, 2 vols. (1888). Study by P. Cheffaud (Paris, 1913).

inspired by the Psalms and the Song of Songs, but all that in the Bible is great and strange becomes, when he handles it, pretty, decorative, precious, often commonplace and often unreal. Peele's descriptions are profusely flowery. It is tempting to apply to him the pretty line in his *Arraignment of Paris*—

> Ye may ne see for peeping flowers the grass.

For the rest, he is so slavishly faithful to his source that he puts nothing into his characters which he does not find in the Old Testament. He neither explains them nor gives them life.

His authorship of the other plays which have been ascribed to him is uncertain. It is most probable that he wrote *Edward the First*, one of the plays on national history, and the *Old Wives' Tale*, a parody or satire on romantic comedies in which Milton found hints for his *Comus*. The weakness of his dramatic sense is yet more apparent in these plays. He was a poet little fitted to write anything for the stage except masques and lyrical pieces.

Neither Peele nor Lyly nor anyone else had achieved striking success on the public stage when suddenly, at some months' distance, the playhouses rang with the verses of Kyd and Marlowe. In swift succession, Kyd in 1586 produced his *Spanish Tragedie*, Marlowe in 1587 his *Tamburlaine*, an unknown author his *Arden of Feversham*, and a certain Hughes his *Misfortunes of Arthur*, the best tragedy on the classical model which had appeared since *Gorboduc*.

If then the artistic drama of the court had its beginning in 1580, it was in the years 1586 and 1587 that the drama of the public stage began its famous career, in which the most diverse genres had part. *Arden of Feversham* remained one of the best examples of the realistic and moral plays given in the city theatres. The *Spanish Tragedie* was for years the most popular of the gloomy, bloodthirsty romantic dramas of these theatres, while *Tamburlaine* was their surpassing heroic play, impressive by its sublimity and fitted to inspire admiration for the superman. If it be remembered that Lyly's *Endymion* was being performed at the same time, it must be acknowledged that English drama had shown even then not only her strength, but also her diversity.

6. "**Arden of Feversham**" (1586).[1]—At this early date it is a surprise to come upon a play which bears all the marks of dramatic maturity. The unknown author of *Arden of Feversham* was no great poet, but he had to an extraordinary extent a sense of the stage, the modern stage. He was in no degree a romantic. He dramatised a real and recent crime chronicled by Holinshed. His play is, in subject and form, a typical citizens' drama, in spite of its fitful use of fine language, its inclusion of some tirades which are characteristic of the Renascence and its use of blank verse. Its merit lies in its psychological truth and its character-drawing.

Alice, wife of the wealthy gentleman Arden of Feversham, has become the mistress of Mosbie, a countryman of low birth and coarse nature who inexplicably fascinates her. The two of them plot to murder her husband, she that she may belong only to Mosbie, he out of avarice. After several failures they contrive the murder successfully, but their crime is immediately discovered, and they and their accomplices are duly executed.

The play is fundamentally moral. It really makes adultery and murder odious, embellishing neither life nor vice. But it reaches this effect not by sermonising, but by insight into the souls of the guilty, the tortures they undergo, and their meanness.

The husband is indeed drawn with a rather hesitating hand: he vacillates between jealousy and credulity, passes from just anger at the shamelessness of the

---

[1] Printed by Tucker Brooke in *The Shakespeare Apocrypha* (1908).

lovers to a blind confidence inspired by his wife's blandishments. He seems to be aware of Mosbie's treachery and yet he takes him back into favour and declares him innocent. He speaks like an honourable man, and yet there is an episode in which, in order to round off his estate, he gets possession of a poor man's land. This indecision weakens the emotional effect in that it withdraws some sympathy from the victim, but it is also a signal proof of the realism of this playwright, who refused to create a hero, to make a crude contrast between vice and virtue.

In Mosbie's vileness there is no contradiction. He has not passion for an excuse. Throughout his lovemaking with Alice he slyly nurses a grudge against her, never loses his class-hatred, which she inflames by rash words when she is suffering twinges of remorse.

Alice is a prey to an irresistible passion which, in lucid moments, she vaguely suspects to be the effect of witchcraft. She is the soul of the play: her will leads to action, decides on the murder and plans it, because she wishes to belong unshared to Mosbie. But no sooner is the crime accomplished than the spell is broken. Alice is horrified by her own deed and dies repentant.

There are whole scenes between the two lovers which grip us by their truth and their forcible portrayal of the soul. In Act III. scene v. Mosbie is shown uneasy about the consequences of the contemplated crime. He has been drinking to dull his faculties, but his anxiety persists. He realises that he is much less happy than he used to be, yet knows that the affair is in train and he cannot draw back, and so looks to the future. He must, he tells himself, get rid of his accomplices, Alice as well as the others, since he never could trust a woman who had betrayed her husband.

At this point Alice, just recovered from an access of remorse and religious feeling, arrives on the scene, carrying a prayer-book and irritated against her lover. She recalls her love for Arden in the days of her innocence, begs Mosbie to forget her, wishes again to be a faithful wife. When he protests she overwhelms him with contempt, upbraiding him as a base artificer who has bewitched and corrupted her. He answers her insults with curses, tells her that for her sake he has lost his character, that instead of falling in love with a "wanton giglote" he might have married an honest maid "whose dowry would have weyed down all thy wealth." It is he who has been bewitched, but he has done with her. He sees her as she is, without beauty; he is maddened by the thought that he ever thought her fair. And thereupon Alice abuses herself, supplicates him, declares herself ready to burn her prayer-book, appeals to his love. Mortified and filled with mean resentment, he at first answers her ironically, thoughts of money mingling with all his thoughts of love:

> O no, I am a base artificer;
> My winges are feathred for a lowly flight.
> Mosby? fy! no, not for a thousand pound.
> Make love to you? why, 'tis unpardonable;
> We beggers must not breathe where gentiles are.

Yet he gives in because it is in his interest to do so.

Even in the painting of the secondary characters there are powerful strokes. There is for instance a scene which depicts one of the nights for which the crime is planned. Arden is in a friend's house in London, and his servant Michael is to open the door to two murderers while his master is asleep. Michael is no vulgar wretch to be bought for money, but Alice has promised him that if he kills Arden or lets him be killed he shall marry Susan whom he loves. It happens, however, that he imagines the murder: he sees the assassins entering the house, slaying Arden, then saying to each other that it would be well to get rid of the servant who might betray them, and so preparing to stab him also. Upon this Michael utters in the darkness a terrible cry; his master is awakened, comes down to see what is the matter, and shuts the door which has been left open purposely. By Michael's cry he is saved for this time.

This dramatic force and truth of characterisation have led some to attribute the play to Shakespeare, assigning it to his early period. But it has a vulgarity of sentiment and atmosphere which cannot be reconciled with Shakespeare's work. None the less, it is a remarkable production, and stands first in a line of succession which was lost for some twelve years and then reappeared in dense and copious plays. The Elizabethan drama, generally romantic, could be unromantic also. There was a section of its public whose preference was for modern and topical subjects, and there were playwrights to satisfy these tastes.

7. **Thomas Kyd.**[1]—The majority, however, expected and desired romantic melodrama, and the first writer who supplied this demand was Thomas Kyd (1558–94) with his *Spanish Tragedie*. Nothing is known of Kyd save that he was the son of a London scrivener and studied law, and that Seneca's tragedies were his habitual reading. He bled Seneca white, and he translated Garnier's *Cornélie* which was modelled on Seneca.

So much can, at least, be deduced from a diatribe of Nashe's written in 1589. Seneca's influence on Kyd cannot be questioned, yet it did not cause his masterpiece to conform to the rules, as Thomas Hughes's *Misfortunes of Arthur*, which was played at Gray's Inn at the same time, did so conform, a play tragic and grave as could be desired and full of sententious dialogue. What Kyd learnt from Seneca was how to produce terror—by the ghost of his prologue who relates past events, by atrocious circumstances and by speeches heightened with striking lyrical expressions. He makes no attempt to simplify the construction of the popular drama, and he cares nothing for the unities. He takes from the Latin poet only what he thinks an English audience will assimilate, and leaves the loose, facile construction of the national drama intact. He owes to Seneca's *Thyestes* his theme of vengeance, one capable of producing the most pathetic and most fearful effects. He learns from him to envelop his whole work with an atmosphere of gloom, and adds the use of the most powerful stage expedients known to his own experience.

Young Horatio, son of the marshal Hieronimo and valiant as the Cid, is treacherously slain by Prince Balthazar and the perfidious Lorenzo at the very moment of exchanging love-vows with Bel-Imperia, daughter of the Duke of Castile. Bel-Imperia and Hieronimo swear to discover the murderers and avenge the deed. When the old father, who feigns madness in order to reach his ends and is indeed half-mad with grief, feels certain that he knows the murderers, he conceives the idea of having a play acted at the wedding of Bel-Imperia, who is obliged to marry her lover's murderer. This tragedy becomes a real one: everyone at the wedding kills himself or is killed.

Another story of revenge is a frame for this one. Before the action of the play begins, Don Andrea, Bel-Imperia's first lover, has been treacherously slain in the war with Portugal. His ghost opens the play, calling for vengeance on Prince Balthazar, who has put him to death.

A synopsis can give, however, only a poor idea of the horrors of this melodrama and the skill which made it a triumph. The fearfulness of crime is introduced into ardent, passionate scenes, making a contrast as violent as that between light and darkness. Horatio and Bel-Imperia are suddenly struck by love as he, the young warrior, is about to tell her of the death of Don Andrea, her betrothed. At once she gives him her heart. The lovers make a nocturnal assignation in the gardens of

---

[1] *The Works of Thomas Kyd*, ed. Boas (Oxford, 1901). *The Spanish Tragedie* is printed in Manly's *Specimens*, op. cit., vol. ii.

old Hieronimo, and there is a scene passionate as that between Hernani and Doña Sol, which is interrupted by the arrival of masked assassins who stab Horatio and hang his body in an arbour.

The sequel is even more horrible. Old Hieronimo, who has been awakened by Bel-Imperia's cries, comes through the shadows clad only in his shirt. He gropes his way, stumbles upon the corpse, and at this moment is joined by his wife, old Isabella. They mingle their tears and their vows for revenge. Hieronimo's final oath is in thirteen Latin hexameters, and it must have sounded like an incantation and have been as terrifying as it was incomprehensible.

Old Hieronimo's madness, whether true or feigned, overtakes him in strange accesses. He goes to demand justice of the king, and before all the court plunges his poignard in the ground. Since he is a judge, citizens petition him for justice, among them an old man who desires that his son's murder may be avenged. The judge is thereupon beside himself, draws from his breast a napkin stained with Horatio's blood, tears the plaintiffs' petitions to pieces, and finally rushes from the room, crying "Run after, catch me, if you can." Almost at once he returns and mistakes the old father for his Horatio. Persuaded from this error, he believes the old man is a Fury exciting him to avenge, then recognises the old father's true identity and goes out arm in arm in his company. Certainly no one could be madder.

In the last scene, in which everyone is killed, Hieronimo confesses to the king what he has done. When the king threatens him with extreme torture, he bites out his tongue in order not to speak again. Then he beckons for a knife with which to mend his pen, and therewith adds to the bloodshed by stabbing the father of one of his son's murderers and killing himself. Don Andrea's ghost, which appears several times over to demand revenge, may well declare itself satisfied.

It was difficult to go much farther in melodrama. This one was so good that, in spite of all ironies and parodies, there was still a demand for it fifteen years after its first performance. Ben Jonson, the classicist, made additions to it, possibly those which have come down to us and which are certainly remarkable. They consist of new touches added to Hieronimo's madness and give the play the benefit of the improvement in dramatic psychology that had been made in the interval.

The play in its original form is emphatic, declamatory and often ridiculous, yet such as to grip a simple public. The motives for action are not made clear; the characters are alive yet hardly have character. It is the element of the pathetic which veils all defects. Of all the parts in Renascence drama, that of Hieronimo was the most grateful to actors and the most popular with the public. Moreover, the play supplies the poetry of place and scenery. It respects neither the unity of place nor that of time, yet preserves, on the whole, unity of action, and it also has unity of motive, for it all centres round revenge.

This excellent and most popular motive recurs in several of the great plays: the *Spanish Tragedie* foreshadows *Hamlet*. If the principal object of literary history were to determine starting-points, more space would be given to Kyd's play than to any of the great Shakespearian tragedies. Critics admit to-day that Kyd, whose other work is less interesting and is not certainly his, may have written an early and lost version of *Hamlet*. Such a play unquestionably existed in 1589, and it is likely that its author was the creator of old Hieronimo.

8. **Marlowe.**[1]—*Tamburlaine*, in its two parts, of which the first appeared

---

[1] His collected works have been edited by F. Cunningham, 1 vol. (Chatto and Windus); by A. H. Bullen in *The English Dramatists*, 3 vols. (1884–5); by Havelock Ellis in the Mermaid Series (1887); and by C. F. T. Brooke (Oxford, 1910).

Annotated editions: *Faust*, ed. Ward, and *Edward II.*, ed. Tancock (Clarendon Press).

Critical Studies: C. P. Baker, *Dramatic Technique in Marlowe* (1913); Danchin, "Etudes critiques sur C. Marlowe," in *Revue germanique* (Jan.–Feb. 1912, Nov.–Dec. 1913, Jan.–Feb. 1914).

in 1587 and the second in 1588, astonished the public for quite other reasons than the *Spanish Tragedie*. Its author was Christopher Marlowe (1564–93), a young man of twenty-three, who had just left Cambridge. He was entirely without experience of the stage, but he compensated for this lack by the extraordinary spirit of defiance and revolt which animated his dramatic work. Novel though *Arden of Feversham* and the *Spanish Tragedie* were, they were plays which bore the imprint of the traditional morality. From end to end they denounced and condemned crime; their murders cried out for vengeance. But the new playwright dared to claim admiration for the most bloodthirsty of men, to make of him a sort of demi-god.

Nothing is more characteristic of Marlowe than his choice of his first hero. He had read a translation of Tamerlaine's life by the Spaniard Pedro Mexia and another life of him by Perondinus of Florence. His imagination was inflamed by the story of the career of this unmatched adventurer who from a mere shepherd became the most powerful man in all the world. There was no need to invent: to follow history, or legend in the guise of authentic history, was enough. What were Alexander and Cæsar beside this fourteenth-century Tartar, the conqueror of Persia and Muscovy who laid Hindustan and Syria waste, vanquished the Ottomans, and died at last as he was flinging himself upon China at the head of two hundred thousand warriors? What cruelty did not seem mildness beside his, who strangled a hundred thousand captives before the walls of Delhi, and set up before Bagdad an obelisk built of ninety thousand severed heads? What symbol could strike more terror than the white tents and banners which stood, in sign of friendship, before a town on the first day of one of Tamerlaine's sieges, the red tents and red flags which were there on the second day, in sign of pillage, and the banners and tents, all black, which beset it on the third day, in sign of extermination?

All this was so grandiose that Marlowe was dazzled. The man capable of so prodigious a destiny, of such unbridled contempt for human life, seemed to him a superior being, a superman to whom the petty rules of morality did not apply. His Tamburlaine massacres wholesale, women and children as well as men, laughs at the blood he sheds, imprisons the vanquished Emperor Bajazet in a cage, has his chariot drawn by kings whom he insults, burns a town in honour of the funeral of his wife, Zenocrate, and all the while remains entirely admirable, outside and above human judgment. He is the despiser of men and gods. Marlowe endows him with the boundless arrogance of an emancipated virtuoso and philosopher of the Renascence. Tamburlaine is the great victor, the conqueror of the world. Therefore he is in the right.

Marlowe transfigures him, not by omitting or weakening any of his atrocities, but by exalting them. He sees in him the triumph of the will to power and thinks that nothing could be finer. To glorify his Tamburlaine he goes to the romances of chivalry in search of heroes moved by an unbridled appetite for glory, and there finds the poetry a mere exterminator would lack. Like those extravagant knights, Tamburlaine is capable of extraordinary love. He lays the earth at the feet of his Zenocrate and when death takes her from him he threatens heaven with his rage.

This play, which is simply Tamburlaine's life divided into scenes, expresses the strange ardours of a young scholar who had cut himself irrevocably adrift from all restraint. A libertine in both senses of the word, Marlowe prided himself on his paganism, his rebellion, not against the dogma of the Trinity only, but against the very spirit of Christianity. His ideal was the man freed from all morality who seeks the maximum of strength and enjoyment by way of impiety, sensuality and crime. What he could not declare to the public directly, he makes his Tamburlaine proclaim upon the stage. It was to the quest of the impossible that he himself aspired,

I—S

and Tamburlaine is vowed to it at his first meeting with Zenocrate. She has come to him, all dishevelled and disconsolate, to ask him to pardon her father, the Sultan of Egypt. At this moment the man who had, an instant before, slaughtered the suppliant virgins of Damascus and had their corpses hoisted on pikes, utters the most lyrical of appeals to absolute beauty, a cry of grief because he knows and declares that what he calls upon is beyond his reach.

The like exaltation had already been felt by Tamburlaine at the thought of being king. On the precedent of Jupiter, who ousted his father Saturn from the throne in order to reign himself, Tamburlaine regards ambition as the spontaneous act of human nature:

> Still climbing after knowledge infinite,
> And always moving as the restless spheres.

The same wild rapture is sustained through ten acts, for two dramas are consecrated to this one hero Tamburlaine, who is almost always on the stage and by himself is nearly the whole of either play. It is appalling to reflect on the task of Alleyn, the actor who created the part and had to utter all this character's declamatory violence and repeated lyrical tirades. Nothing could be less dramatic or more monotonous: the same theme and same tone of passionate emphasis recur endlessly. It is true that, to captivate the sight, there are some scenes which haunted men's memories: Bajazet dying of hunger in his cage while a banquet is served to Tamburlaine, who tenders him a mouthful or two on the point of his sword; Bajazet, at the end of his endurance, braining himself against the iron bars which imprison him; his wife, Zabina, seized by madness when she sees him dead and taking her own life; above all that famous spectacle of Tamburlaine, whip in hand, drawn by two kings harnessed to his chariot to whom he cries:

> Holla, ye pamper'd jades of Asia!
> What, can ye draw but twenty miles a day?

It was never necessary to parody *Tamburlaine*: to mention it was enough. On the whole, its spectacular extravagances are dispersed, but the declamation is continuous. That men listened to this play from end to end can be explained only by supposing that the fire in the heart of the young poet caught his audience. They too must have been in a state of half-delirious exaltation. The distraught rhetoric is sustained by verse of which the unfailing sonority was as new as the subject. Marlowe began his career with a superb contempt for the popular rhymesters. He makes blank verse, hitherto without brightness or ring, thunder and echo through his play like a drum that never ceases. Other heroes, from the Herod of the mysteries downwards, had already uttered fearful blasphemies and unending rodomontade, but they had had to express them in slight stanzas or frail couplets. The verse for which men had been waiting, completely formed verse, now sounded on the stage for the first time. It was a thing too prestigious to be withstood. The wits might mock at this "spacious volubilitie of a drumming decasyllabon," at this "bragging blank verse," but, whether they would or no, they had soon, in deference to the public, themselves to beat the drum as well as they could.

The madcap was in truth a great poet whose very extravagance was justified because it expressed his nature. He produced play after play, all continuations of his first. They were perhaps less purely the expression of his temperament, but they gained by his increasing knowledge of the stage, which did not prevent them from being still mainly lyrical and oratorical. He was, however, leading a life of intense dissipation which hardly ever left him time to produce a complete work like *Tamburlaine*. He became the improviser who flings a couple of powerful scenes into a botched play.

Such was the composition of the *Tragical History of Doctor Faustus* (1588), for which he drew on one of the most fruitful of legends, but merely built an admirable framework about scenes hardly written, and clowning which reads as though the actors had been invited to fill it in as they chose.

Once more faithful to the custom of his country's stage, Marlowe divided the German legend of Faust, as he had read it, into scenes. His forceful egoism is projected into the character of the necromancer who vows himself to the devil in return for sovereign knowledge and sovereign power, and who is thus able for twenty-four years to satisfy his appetites. They are poor and coarse enough in the legend, leading him mainly to play practical jokes on the great ones of his day, the Pope and the cardinals, and to make poor wretches the butt of his magic. Marlowe takes little interest in these distractions, which he barely outlines. But when Faustus evokes the spirits of the past and obtains a vision of the Greek Helen, the poet, imagining her supreme beauty, is rapt to incomparable lyricism.

Retribution follows: Faustus has to keep his bargain with Lucifer, and tremblingly awaits death and hell. Marlowe, the atheist, alone in a Christian world, must also, at times, have felt to the full the horror of his denials and his blasphemies. He was too near faith to be indifferent. The very vehemence of his professions of impiety was a sign that his emancipation was incomplete. He shook his fist at heaven and feared at the same moment that heaven might fall and crush him. The last scenes of *Faustus* are among the most pathetic and most grandiose in Renascence drama. They stand by themselves, distinct from all the rest of this drama. They are unsurpassable, even by Shakespeare. Marlowe, incapable of a whole masterpiece, yet had genius to reach, here and there, the sublime beauty which has no degrees. When Goethe took the same legend for the basis of one of the chief accomplishments of modern poetry, he could not eclipse the poignant greatness of his forerunner's final scenes. He, who did not know how the impious tremble, could not recapture that anguish of horror.

Marlowe never again found a plot which gave him so much scope, but even in the *Jew of Malta* (1589) he sometimes reveals his lyrical power. He was doubtless led to write this melodrama by the success of the *Spanish Tragedie* and other tragedies of atrocious vengeance. His Jew, Barabas, is unjustly deprived of his goods by Christians, and by an extraordinary series of crimes avenges himself on them, and also, becoming a monomaniac, on mankind in general. Obliged to use cunning to attain his object, he is Machiavellism incarnate. His crimes must have made the hair of audiences stand on end. They accumulate until, having first delivered Malta to the Turks and then the Turks to the Christians, he falls into a cauldron of boiling water into which he had schemed to throw his last enemies.

There is only one other character who counts in this play, and he is yet more terrible, the Moorish slave Ithamore who is Barabas's tool and an incarnation of the lust of extreme cruelty.

This melodrama opens grandly, and before the Jew becomes a criminal maniac he has, like Tamburlaine, dignity and greatness. Enormously rich, we see him first in his counting-house, with heaps of gold before him, a poet intoxicated by the immensity of his own wealth and the immense power which is its consequence. As he enumerates the countries whence his treasures come, his exaltation has a mystical greatness. Something of this remains to him when he hears the governor's order that half his estate and that of the other Jews shall be confiscated to pay the tribute to the Turks, and when only he of all his co-religionists keeps his pride, remaining indignant and inflexible. It has often been said that Shakespeare dared to defy contemporary prejudice by attracting sympathy intermittently to Shylock. Yet Shakespeare's Shylock is as avaricious as he is cruel, and ridiculous through his avarice. The only true rehabilitation of the Jew is that which Marlowe attempted in his first act, where the haughty, intrepid Barabas, facing the hypocritical governor, is really a splendid figure. That he subsequently appears as a frenzied wretch is of little consequence. For a time the poet identified himself with the Jew, who may even, by the very enormity of his later crimes, have retained the strange sympathy of his creator.

Besides an unfinished play, the *Massacre at Paris*, on the massacre of St. Bartholomew, a subject which gave Marlowe his fill of horrors and attracted him by the boundless ambition of the Duke of Guise whom he made his hero, he wrote a *Dido*, which was finished by Nashe and in which he dramatised the Fourth Book of the Æneid. This play is less sombre in colour than his earlier work, but is marred in places by the worst lapses of taste. Marlowe was also able, before he died at the age of twenty-nine, to write the best of the tragedies on national history which preceded Shakespeare's, his *Edward the Second*, first acted in 1592.

Whether because Marlowe's genius had developed, or because the exigencies of historical drama obliged him to self-effacement, this play has qualities which are properly dramatic and are found in none of its predecessors. The lyrical declamation is under a new restraint. The tirades are shorter and the dialogue is better distributed in speeches. The blank verse is less strained and more pliable, nearer to the tones of the human voice. Progress in character-study is also evinced, over a numerous and diversified cast.

The subject is the truthful history of a king who is dominated by his favourites, first Gaveston and then young Mortimer. Mortimer reaches an understanding with Queen Isabella, who becomes his mistress. The betrayed king is cast into prison and put to death by the order of the two accomplices, who are in their turn executed by their victim's son.

Edward II. stands for sentimental weakness, the royal baseness which cowardice can make bloodthirsty. In Mortimer, with his unbridled ambition, Marlowe returned to one of his favourite types, and it is Mortimer who connects this play with its predecessors.

Except the death of Faustus, nothing in Marlowe's plays is more poignantly pathetic than the scene of the murder of Edward II. in Killingworth Castle by two ruffians. The end of the bad king is so miserable that he becomes an object of pity.

Edward the Second is better constructed than Marlowe's other plays, free from his habitual extravagance, humanised and less removed from contemporary drama at its average. But it shows the author's dramatic weakness the more clearly because of its very merits. This tragedy has not the lucidity necessary to character-drawing, to the weaving of a plot and to the distribution of sympathy. It also lacks variety and dramatic progression. Of the plays devoted to national history, it was, until Shakespeare, the most artistic, but a long distance separates it from the least of Shakespeare's historical dramas. The spirit of patriotism necessary to a work of the kind does not breathe in it, possibly because Marlowe, a rebel against the religion and morality of his fellow-countrymen, did not share their political passions either. Again in this play, he shows himself in revolt against the common morality, when, with lyrical exaltation, he paints the unnatural love of Edward II. for his favourite Piers Gaveston.

Marlowe added nothing to dramatic technique saving that he determined the victory of blank verse. His merit is that in his short career he set the stage on fire with the flame of his passion. Less versatile than the other prominent playwrights of his day, less able than they to conceive of multitudinous feelings distinct from his own emotions, less quick than some to catch the scenic side of things, surpassed not only by the masters, but also by mediocre playwrights, as an architect of drama and constructor of pliable and nimble dialogue, without any sense of the comic or sense of humour or any aptitude to draw a woman, Marlowe yet possessed a supreme quality which enabled him at once to lift drama into the sphere of high literature. He was a great poet, a lyrical, personal, violently egoistical poet, who carried with him his own unique conception of man and life. In spite of his atheism, he foreshadowed Milton from afar; a little of him was in the Byron who wrote *Cain*, a little in Shelley. His exclusiveness produced intensity, and the English stage was in great need of intensity. Grace, wit and fancy had been scattered on it, mingled indeed with faults of every kind, but never hitherto had it known this dash, this vehemence animating a whole play, this rapid march, as to victory, by which drama inspires the conviction that thus to move is to be alive.

It is, after all, a mistake to suppose that every work written for the stage must have specially dramatic qualities. To give an audience an impression of greatness, to cause them to tremble with enthusiasm and feel the rush towards an end—any end: this does as well. The fact is proved by Marlowe's work as by part of Corneille's. His immediate success and his powerful influence are unquestionable. Even when his plays had come to seem extravagant they remained popular. They first made the English public feel the pride of strength, and persuaded or deluded English drama into the belief that it equalled the sublimity of the ancients. As did the *Cid*, Marlowe's plays, for all their lack of patriotism, made hearts swell with a new national pride. His characters, out of scale and unnatural as they are, can dispense with probability because they have the breath of life. Their passionate declaiming, as well as the triumph over the Armada, one year after Marlowe's first play, and the pride in distant conquests, made English hearts drunk and giddy with triumphant strength. Together with the discoveries of the great seafarers, these figures on the stage enlarged, in men's minds, the bounds of the possible. These plays were a pæan to the infinity of military power, of knowledge and of wealth. The subjects Marlowe borrowed, the heroes he moulded, were no more than his mouthpieces, voicing his exorbitant dreams. Like him they sought the infinite and like him were never sated.

9. **Robert Greene.**[1]—The success of the *Spanish Tragedie* and of *Tumburlaine* took the usual purveyors of the popular stage by surprise. Their astonishment and anger are attested by the young English Juvenal, Thomas Nashe (1567–1601), who from the age of twenty was one of the group of young writing-men from the universities who did the actors the great honour of working for them. Lyly and Peele, who looked especially to the court, were somewhat loosely attached to this group. Thomas Lodge (1558?–1625) was rather connected with the public stage, which he had undertaken to defend against Gosson. He wrote about 1589 a mediocre play on the struggle between Marius and Sulla called *The Wounds of Civil War*. As for Robert Greene (1560?–1692), he was at this time turning all his energies from the novel to drama, and with Lodge he wrote, in the old didactic manner, a sort of miracle-play called *A Looking-Glass for London and England*.

As an effect of the triumph of Marlowe and Kyd, Lodge was, before long, deflected from the stage, and bade it a disdainful farewell in 1589, resolved

> To write no more of that whence shame doth grow,
> [Nor] tie my pen to pennie-knaves delight.

But Greene persisted and was obliged to conform to the altered taste. His *Alphonsus* and his *Orlando Furioso* are extravagant and declamatory enough to recall

---

[1] *Complete Works*, ed. Grosart, 15 vols (1881–6); *Dramatic and Poetic Works of R. Greene and G. Peele*, ed. A. Dyce, 2nd ed. (1879); *Plays*, ed. Dickinson (Mermaid Series, 1909); *James IV.*, by R. Greene, printed in Manly's *Specimens*, op. cit.; T. Lodge, *Complete Works* (except translations), ed. Gosse (Glasgow, 4 vols., 1872–82); *The Wounds of Civil War*, in Hazlitt's Dodsley, op. cit., vol. vii.; Thomas Nashe, *Complete Works*, ed. Grosart, 6 vols. (1883–5); *Works*, ed. McKerrow, 4 vols. (1904–8).

Tamburlaine, but bear no marks of genius. It is possible to doubt whether *Alphonsus* be an imitation of Marlowe's famous play or a parody on it.

Greene's *Friar Bacon and Friar Bungay* is another *Faustus,* called into being by the success of that play. Greene's conformity to the changed demand is, however, only apparent. His personal vein subsists, with its charm, and forms an essential contribution to the preparation for Shakespeare's work.

This element, which is Greene's own, is manifest in two plays which, among those attributed to him, were certainly written by him and which seem to have been his last works for the stage, *Friar Bacon* and *James the Fourth.*

The title of *Friar Bacon and Friar Bungay* is misleading, for it is applicable only to the secondary part of the play, in which Greene rivals *Faustus* in exhibiting the tricks played upon each other by two magicians. But side by side with this mediocre comedy there is an idyllic play on a romantic theme which often is very graceful.

Edward, Prince of Wales—a prince unknown to history—comes upon Margaret, a keeper's daughter and the belle of Fressingfield, in her dairy, and falls in love with her as she hands him a cup of milk. He commissions Lacy, Earl of Lincoln, to act as his go-between and win him the girl's heart that he may make her his mistress. Lacy discharges his trust with so much goodwill that he himself comes to love Margaret and is loved by her. At first the prince is furious and would kill the traitor, but he ends by forgiving him and uniting the lovers. The prince thus plays a part analogous to that of Alexander in Lyly's *Campaspe.* Lacy, however, wishing to try his peasant love, pretends that the king is obliging him to marry a Spanish lady. Margaret, in despair, is about to become a nun when Lacy reappears, conquers her for the second time, and marries his Griselda.

In spite of its abundant use of mythological figures, this idyll has much grace and freshness. Country air blows through it. The most charming scene is undoubtedly that in which the Prince of Wales relates how he has lost his heart to the dairymaid. He is a very young man, enthusiastic and cultivated, to whom mythological reminiscences are a natural aid to the expression of love. The character of Margaret, really a pure girl in love, has no precedent in drama. Nashe, with his usual verbal excess, calls his friend "the Homer of Women," and certainly it was Greene who, first of playwrights and before Shakespeare, had the qualities of tenderness and grace necessary to paint a pure, loving woman.

In his pseudo-historical play, the *Scottish History of James the Fourth, slain at Flodden,* in truth a stage-version of an Italian story told in Giraldi Cinthio's *Hecatommithi* (first *novella* in the third decade), Greene has drawn two very charming portraits of women. His James IV. marries Dorothea, daughter of the king of England, but loves Ida, daughter of the Countess of Arran. Rejected by Ida, who is too virtuous to be his mistress, he tries to compass his wife's death. She is, however, not killed, only wounded, and instead of bearing malice, she intervenes in time to save her faithless husband at the moment when ruin threatens him through the war which the English king wages to avenge his daughter.

Another charming scene is that in which Ida is tempted by a certain Ateukin, the tool of James IV. He finds her sitting with her mother in the porch of their castle, both women busy with needlework. The conversation of the mother and daughter, before he arrives, is full of the honesty and simple happiness of dutiful, unambitious persons. Ida answers Ateukin's offers in words both candid and noble. Virtuous as she is, his revelation of vice astonishes her:

> O, how he talks, as if he should not die!

In Dorothea, Griselda is once more recalled, but she is also a first sketch for

Shakespeare's heroines—Julia, Viola, Imogen. When she learns that her husband has signed her death-warrant, and is urged to summon her father, the king of England, to her aid, she cries:

> As if they kill not me, who with him fight!
> As if his breast be touched, I am not wounded!
> As if he wailed, my joys were not confounded!
> We are one heart, though rent by hate in twain;
> One soul, one essence doth our weal contain:
> What, then, can conquer him, that kills not me?

This pathetic scene ends in charming fancifulness, Dorothy, disguised as a man, fleeing with her dwarf Nano, and smiling through her tears at her own strange figure. She reaches a wood when she is weary and is consoled by Nano, who is as faithful but not as sarcastic as Lear's fool. We think of Rosalind arriving with the fool Touchstone in the Forest of Arden.

Greene, by his taste for the romantic and his moments of tenderness, foreshadows Shakespeare, as does Lyly by his wit, the author of *Arden of Feversham* by his psychological sense, Kyd by his tragic atmosphere, and Marlowe by his lyrical eloquence. These various gifts had yet to be united in one man and one work. Shakespeare was to gather them together and to enhance them.

CHAPTER VI

SHAKESPEARE'S PLAYS [1] (1590–1616)

1. The Advent of Shakespeare.—The relation of Shakespeare's plays to contemporary drama is the first problem connected with them which confronts the historian of literature, and the only one he can treat with the necessary fullness. For to study each of these thirty-six plays, distinct and truly independent of each other as they are, on a scale proportionate to its value and importance would be impossible where space is necessarily restricted. We can here attempt no more than the discovery of the points at which Shakespeare connects with his rivals and those at which he dominates them.

His first appearance in literary history is curious and significant. Nashe and his friends, the company of young humanists known as the University Wits, had hardly recovered from Marlowe's sudden triumph, when they were faced with another and more dangerous rival who sprang from a different world. Marlowe, Master of Arts of Cambridge, was after all one of themselves, and when once they had exclaimed against his arrogance, it did not take them long to follow in his footsteps. He was a new and a brilliant recruit for their group. But danger now threatened them from the world of the actors, from the ignoramuses whom they were wont to regard as barely able to declaim the fine passages written for them by men of letters. A well-known actors' company, the Lord Chamberlain's, were snapping their fingers at the manuscripts of the university men, the accredited producers of fine literature. An actor was taking it upon himself to write, was reshaping, clipping, adding to his company's repertory, and fashioning it anew when he did not create whole plays. Greene, who was near his end and whose sight was

[1] Life. Halliwell-Phillipps, *Life of William Shakespeare*, 2 vols., 7th ed. (1887); W J Rolfe, *A Life of Shakespeare* (1902); C. I. Elton, *William Shakespeare, His Family and Friends* (1904); Sidney Lee, *A Life of Shakespeare*, new ed. (1922); J. Q. Adams, *Life of William Shakespeare* (1923).

Editions of the Text: Reprints and facsimiles of the 1623 folio and the quarto editions. Complete annotated edition: *Cambridge Shakespeare*, 9 vols., 2 eds. (1891–3); Furness, *New Variorum Shakespeare* (1871 et seq.) (unfinished); Furnivall, *The Leopold Shakespeare*, Delius text, 1 vol. (1877); Gollancz, *The Temple Shakespeare*, 40 vols. (1894–1900); W. J. Craig, *Arden Shakespeare* (1899 et seq.); C. H. Herford, *Eversley Shakespeare*, 10 vols., 1899; W. J. Craig, *Oxford Shakespeare* (1904), etc. Separate plays edited by Clark and Wright for the Clarendon Press and by Verity for the Cambridge University Press, etc.

Studies, General: E. Dowden, *A Shakespeare Primer* (1877); Nelson and Thorndike, *Facts about Shakespeare* (1913). Miscellaneous Studies: G. P. Baker, *The Development of Shakespeare as a Dramatist* (1907); F. S. Boas, *Shakespeare and His Predecessors* (1895); G. Brandes, *William Shakespeare* (in German, 1896; English translation, 2 vols., 1898); E. Dowden, *Shakespeare, his Mind and Art* (1874); R. G. Moulton, *Shakespeare as a Dramatic Artist* (1885); W. Raleigh, *Shakespeare* (English Men of Letters Series, 1907); W. Hazlitt, *Characters of Shakespeare's Plays* (1817); Swinburne, *A Study of Shakespeare* (1880); B. Wendell, *William Shakespeare* (1894); R. G. White, *Studies in Shakespeare*, 9th ed. (1896); Darrell Figgis, *Shakespeare, a Study* (1911); A. H. Thorndike, *The Influence of Beaumont and Fletcher on Shakespeare* (1904); Stoll's study on "Falstaff" (*Modern Phil.*, Oct. 1914), on "Othello" (*Bulletin of University of Minnesota*, March 1915), on "Hamlet" (ibid., Sept. 1919); B. Mathews, *Shakespeare as a Playwright* (1913); L. Schücking, *Die Charaktere Probleme bei Shakespeare* (1919); Stendhal, *Racine et Shakespeare* (1823); G. Guizot, *Shakespeare et son Temps* (1852); Mézières, *Shakespeare, ses œuvres et ses critiques* (1860); V. Hugo, *William Shakespeare*; Stapfer, *Shakespeare et l'Antiquité* (1879–80); J. Darmesteter, *Shakespeare* (1893); Pellissier, *Shakespeare et la superstition Shakespearienne* (1915); G. Duval, *L'Œuvre Shakespearienne et son histoire* (1911), etc.

sharpened by jealousy, discovered the enemy, and in 1592 pointed out to his fellows that "there is an upstart crowe beautified with our feathers that with his

> Tyger's heart wrapt in a player's hide

supposes he is as well able to bumbast out a blank verse as the best of you; and being an absolute *Johannes fac totum* is in his owne conceit the onelie Shake-scene in the countrie."

So great was the danger that Greene advised his colleagues, Marlowe among them, to abandon the playwrights' profession. To stay in it would be to lose their time and trouble as well as their souls.

The man who was thus denounced was William Shakespeare, born in 1564, and now twenty-eight years old. Following on a period of obscurity, he was at this time enjoying a fair reputation with the actors' company to which he belonged, and his plays were being well enough received to render the most vaunted dramatists uneasy. He had been in London for five or six years, having been driven thither from the small town of his birth, Stratford-on-Avon, as much by poverty as by a passion for adventure and for the stage. It was his intention to supply the needs of his father, whose business was not thriving, of the wife he had rashly married when he was only eighteen, and of his three children. His education had been haphazard, as much a matter of miscellaneous, ardent reading as the result of his attendance at Stratford grammar-school, and he might well seem ignorant to Masters and Bachelors of Arts of the two universities. He had nothing behind him except his natural genius and his daily experience of the stage. He had no theory of literature, only the desire to interest the public, and a talent so flexible that it immediately adapted itself to every genre and imitated every note on which a poet had ever played.

There is some doubt about his first plays, for they were anonymous and for the most part rearrangements. The young actor realised that, in these years near the Armada, patriotism was the link which most strongly united the very mixed audiences in the playhouses. He therefore turned to the chronicles, and produced the scenes from national history which then were so popular. He retouched scenes from the reign of Henry VI. which showed, in turn, the exploits of Talbot, the astonishing career of Joan of Arc, the "witch," and the English disasters caused by the civil war. Nothing hitherto performed had had so much movement or diversity or shown so much understanding of the stage as this dense trilogy of plays, entirely archaic in structure and attractive mainly because of the multiplicity of its incidents.

The triumph of Kyd and Marlowe had, however, shown the playwright that the applause of audiences could be won in other ways. The innovations attracted him by their success and by the conspicuous merits which veiled their conspicuous defects. He wrote, or more probably retouched, *Titus Andronicus*, a tragedy of atrocious vengeance which reveals an imagination even more fertile of horrors than those which conceived the *Spanish Tragedie* and the *Jew of Malta*. But he knew himself able to evoke laughter as well as tears and shudders. This young man had a very keen sense of the comic and an inexhaustible, almost excessive, flow of words. He was ambitious not only of a popular success, but also of the approval of the wits, even the court wits. Lyly's witty dialogue inspired him, and with vigour unknown to Lyly he wrote *Love's Labour's Lost*, a fantasy of which the subject and the style appealed to the most cultured section of the public. At much the same time, he supplied less fastidious appetites with a farce which was a free adaptation of the *Menæchmi* of Plautus, and, that laughter might be the louder, he added to its plot, inventing two servants exactly like each other to balance the close resemblance between their masters. In this play he indulges in Rabelaisian mock-lyricism, the like of which had hardly yet been heard on the English stage.

Such are, approximately and probably, the plays which he produced before he provoked Greene's invective, those which made him so formidable a rival, in every branch of their profession he had been able to reach, to the playwrights then enjoying popular favour. His first romantic play, the *Two Gentlemen of Verona*, which definitely trespassed on Greene's own sphere, may also have been acted by this time, a fact which would explain the chagrin of that painter of the gentle love of women, to whom it must have been bitter to witness the advent of Silvia and Julia.

The playwright who had been neither to Oxford nor to Cambridge undoubtedly did these things as well as the most scholarly, even better than they. The impartial observer had to acknowledge that his lack of the regulation culture did not seem to impede him in any way. He did indeed use comparatively few mythological images, a fact which only pedants could regret, but his skill in composition was, when he chose, equal to that of any of the university dramatists, his style was as brilliant as theirs, and his blank verse no less sonorous, for all that this metre was of learned origin and the humanists had hoped to keep it to themselves.

Nothing is in fact falser than the idea that, because Shakespeare was an actor, he was disqualified as a playwright. It is none the less an idea to which mistaken critics cling, and even to-day there are those who would deny him the authorship of the plays recognised as his.[1] Mingled with Greene's invective, there is the starveling author's jealousy of the prosperous actor. We have said that, in spite of Puritan disapproval, actors in this period enjoyed much prestige with the most various classes of society and had access to every world, from the lowest to the highest. Rather than be surprised that Shakespeare, like Molière, was an actor and yet wrote plays, which were masterpieces, we might well ask if it would have been possible for him to write them in any other walk of life.

2. **His Career as a Dramatist from 1592 to 1601.**—One fact is certain: the Jack-of-all-trades whom Greene despised took rank, almost at once after Greene's attack, among the most brilliant and refined of poets, for he published *Venus and Adonis* and the *Rape of Lucrece* in quick succession. He was moreover honoured by the friendship of one of the greatest peers of the realm, the Earl of Southampton. Further, and most importantly of all, he was for six or seven years the undisputed, almost the only master of English drama. Chance and death and his own genius worked together to bring about this supremacy. Greene died in 1592, almost immediately after denouncing him. Marlowe, the greatest of his rivals, came to a sudden end next year. Kyd's death occurred in 1594. Lodge abandoned playwriting for medicine; Lyly withdrew from connection with the stage of the court; Peele plunged deeper and deeper into dissipation and wrote no more; Nashe had found his right means of expression in satirical pamphlets and novels. Until the end of the century, or at least until 1598, no one vied with Shakespeare except such mediocre purveyors of occasional plays as Anthony Munday. No important writer was his rival. It is impossible to cite a single play, either a tragedy or a comedy, which appeared in these years and had a real value to make it comparable to Shakespeare's.

It therefore is not surprising that the most unmodified praise accorded to

---

[1] The chief of the theories of this kind advanced are: (a) The Baconian Theory, that Bacon wrote Shakespeare's works, the oldest of these theories, for it dates back to 1856. See Delia Bacon, *The Philosophy of the Plays of Shakespeare Unfolded* (1857), and many posterior publications. (b) The Rutland Theory. See C. Demblon, *Lord Rutland est Shakespeare* (1913). (c) The Derby Theory. See Abel Lefranc, *Sous le masque du Shakespeare, William Stanley VIe comte de Derby*, 2 vols. (1919), and numerous articles, all containing much interesting information. (d) The Oxford Theory. See C. Palmer, *Shakespeare Identified as Edward de Vere, 17th Earl of Oxford* (1920).

Shakespeare in his lifetime dates from 1598, when Meres, a university man, classes him in the first rank of writers of tragedies and comedies. Meres, evidently well acquainted with his work, places him on a level with the ancients and cites such of his plays as had hitherto been produced, thus establishing which he wrote before his thirty-fifth year.

In this period and the three following years, that is up to 1601, Shakespeare wrote the rest of his historical dramas, his fairy-play, *Midsummer Night's Dream,* one tragedy, *Romeo and Juliet,* and all his romantic and light-hearted comedies. His youth lasted through these years and his skill grew. From 1593 onwards he was no longer a prentice to his craft. Marlowe's influence is still apparent in *Richard III.,* that portrait of a monster of crime which might be called Shakespeare's *Tamburlaine,* but its dimensions have been westernised, and it claims admiration rather for the hero's strange energy than for his cruelty and his crimes. The tragedy of *Richard II.,* the arbitrary, weak, imaginative king who is the victim of his own vagaries, is a pendant to Marlowe's *Edward the Second,* but also a contrast to it. Shakespeare departs from his model and follows his own genius for character-drawing. In *King John* no reminiscence of Marlowe remains save the eloquence of the tirades and the sonorous roll of the verse. In the trilogy formed by the two parts of *Henry IV.* and by *Henry V.,* Shakespeare's most powerful creation in the sphere of English history, his broad strokes of the brush—his mingling of the comic and the tragic, his association of Falstaff with the Prince of Wales who became the hero of Agincourt—show that his genius had reached complete independence. Here, he owed nothing to anyone but himself.

His originality is no less striking in the passionate tragedy of *Romeo and Juliet,* of which the splendour, the poetry and the pathos were not even faintly foreshadowed by any earlier work.

Every memory of Lyly's mythological imagination and witty dialogue and of Greene's sustained and tender grace grows dim and fades into oblivion before the exquisite fairy-piece, *Midsummer Night's Dream,* and before the marvellous series of the romantic plays, compounded of feeling and laughter, mocking and grave at once, *The Merchant of Venice, Much Ado About Nothing, As You Like It* and *Twelfth Night.* The poet's contemporaries seem to have felt that these plays were more clearly marked by his genius than his other work, for they gave rise to the epithets frequently connected with his name, "sweet," "witty," "gentle." The public might be taken in by the playwrights who emulated his tragedies, but there were enchanted regions in which he reigned alone over an unshared kingdom.

He did not, however, imprison himself in them. He remained alertly watchful, ready to accept interesting novelties. When, about 1598, realism made its appearance on the comic stage, mingled by Ben Jonson with satire, or tinged by Dekker, in the *Shomakers Holiday,* with sentiment, the success of the new genre provoked Shakespeare to emulation. This, rather than mere chance, must have been the origin of the *Merry Wives of Windsor.*

It was at about this time that the critics' discussion of dramatic laws, hitherto confined to the narrow world of theorists, began also to interest authors and the literate section of the public. After the publication of Sidney's *Defence of Poesie,* in 1595, men were concerned about the unities, dramatic decorum and probability. Ben Jonson brought the question right on to the stage, the stage of the Globe Theatre where Shakespeare acted, and Shakespeare had too open a mind not to be interested in it. In the several prologues of *Henry V.* he shows himself cognisant of it. But he dismissed it with a smile, trusting to the docility of his audiences and to the facile imaginative power which kept them from quarrelling with their enjoyment. From this time, however, he was raising up for himself an opposition from the humanists which was to injure his prestige. Critics came to divide playwrights into two classes: those who wrote free drama and the classicists, the first headed by Shakespeare and the other by Jonson. That amusing university comedy the *Returne from Parnassus*, played in 1601, marks the rise of this distinction which henceforth, in the opinion of some of Shakespeare's contemporaries, modified his glory.

3. **His Career from 1601 to 1608.** — About the year 1601 Shakespeare's dramatic career underwent a singular revolution. Hitherto there had been about his plays an air of youth and cheerfulness. Even *Romeo and Juliet* begins in a lively, even a rapturous, mood, and is rather a play which darkens to tragedy than a tragedy of unrelieved gloom. One of the most comic and one of the most fanciful of Shakespearean characters, Juliet's nurse and Mercutio, hold their own for a long time before the inroads of passion and the obsession of catastrophe. Not only, however, does 1601 mark the beginning of the series of great and cruel tragedies and no less tragic dramas of Roman history, but after this date such comedies as the poet wrote had lost all their gaiety. Characters intended to be diverting, like Parolles in *All's Well that Ends Well*, miss their effect. *Measure for Measure* hovers for three acts on the brink of tragedy, and escapes it finally only by an effort so violent as to cut one of the poet's most powerful works in two. Where, as in *Troilus and Cressida*, laughter persists, it is bitter, cynical and sarcastic, never light-hearted.

The question of the reason for the change arises. Did it lie in Shakespeare's own feelings or outside him? There is no doubt that as an actor-author he was increasingly prosperous. The passing danger of the rivalry of the boy-actors cannot thus have disturbed him, any more than certain sarcasms uttered by the humanists. He suffered, however, some personal sorrows. He lost his father in 1601. Above all, the sonnets prove that he endured a tragedy of the heart, was betrayed by a friend and a mistress and bitterly disillusioned in his friendship and his love. In all probability, he was also disgusted with public affairs. As Southampton's friend, he was connected with Essex, and very deeply felt the failure of the Essex conspiracy, the execution of the favourite and the imprisonment of his accomplice, Southampton. The choice in this very year of the subject of *Julius Cæsar*, and the glorification, at Cæsar's expense, of Brutus, the conspirator, can best be explained by political events and by the poet's increasing pessimism.

Yet since this was a playwright compelled to provide the public with the feast they craved, we may also ask to what degree he met a general demand for gloomier, more tragic plays. It is beyond question that in these years there was a revival of that taste for the violent and horrible which reigned at the outset of Shakespeare's career and which, by his more human and happier work, he had done more than anyone else to supersede. This revived taste was once more satisfied, both by Shakespeare's plays and by those of his rivals.

About 1598 Chapman wrote his first sombre tragedy, *Bussy d'Ambois*, followed, in 1604, by the *Revenge of Bussy d'Ambois*. John Marston gained distinction by his frenzied dramas, *Antonio and Mellida* about 1598 and *Antonio's Revenge* in 1600, not to speak of his no less ferocious comedy *The Malcontent* in 1601. This last play inaugurated a stage type—the victim of odious injustice who, in anger mixed with irony, rants against the vice which surrounds him and prepares retribution. In 1601 Kyd's *Spanish Tragedie* was rejuvenated, with very fine additions which enlarge upon the theme of old Hieronimo's madness and are possibly from the pen of Ben Jonson. In 1602 Henry Chettle produced the *Tragedy of Hoffman, or a Revenge for a Father*, of which the subject is again the now universally honoured one of revenge. Society, mankind and life were sarcastically or furiously, and as universally, denounced.

It was in this atmosphere that *Hamlet* (1602) appeared, and was followed by Shakespeare's great pessimistic dramas—*Othello* (1604), *Lear* (1605–6), *Macbeth* (1607) and *Timon of Athens* (1607), together with his no less bitter comedies— *Measure for Measure* (1603) and *Troilus and Cressida* (date uncertain). A like spirit breathes in the Roman tragedies, ending in 1608 with *Coriolanus*, a hero whose life is all one long tumult of fury and indignation.

4. Last Plays and Death (1608–16). — About 1608, when he was forty-four years old, Shakespeare abandoned the tradition of violence, leaving it to be continued for some years longer in the plays of Cyril Tourneur, Webster and Middleton, and reverted to that romantic mood which he once had found congenial. He still wrote of crimes and misfortunes, but his bitter invectives had given way to indulgence and serenity. He had, it is true, lost the light-hearted gaiety of his youth; where once he had laughed, he now, in his maturity, smiled pensively, not without melancholy. The very fantastic nature of his subjects betrays his desire to find in romance a consolation for history. The period is that of *Pericles* (1608?), *Cymbeline* (1610), *Winter's Tale* and *The Tempest* (1611), plays which were the supreme accomplishment of this prosperous actor. He was at this time about to retire to his native town, where he passed the last years of his life in peace, and died in 1616 at the age of fifty-two.

The question again arises of the reason for the changed atmosphere of the plays, whether it be the mere effect of years and the spiritual travail through which, after a phase of pessimism, the poet at last attained to peace, or whether it respond to the need of the public for relaxation. Audiences had indeed been sated with horrors and frenzied declamation. Had Shakespeare been apprised of this by the success of two young playwrights who had quickly reached popularity, Beaumont and Fletcher? The first result of their brilliant collaboration was *Philaster*, a play which is the quintessence of the sentimental and romantic, and which was performed at the Globe in 1608.

They were Shakespeare's disciples and he had nothing to learn from them. Yet, noticing how they succeeded, he may have realised that the time for gloomy tragedy was past.

While his mood softened, he conceded nothing to the cult of classic regularity which Sidney and Ben Jonson had in turn recommended. Never did he make as free with all the unities as in *Cymbeline*, except in *Pericles* and the *Winter's Tale*, where he traverses lands and seas and accompanies his heroines from the cradle to marriage. Yet, as though to show to the end that he took sides against no dramatic theory, *The Tempest* is the one of his plays which is most respectful of the unities in their broad sense. Its action passes in one day and in only one place, within the bounds of an island. Thus to the last Shakespeare demonstrated his only conviction: that all dramatic systems are good, but not one of them indispensable.

It has been ascertained that almost all those of his plays which are accepted as his supreme masterpieces were produced after 1601. Yet, owing to the strictures of the humanists, he seems in this second part of his career to have lost the unique position which was his at the end of the sixteenth century. In the judgment of contemporaries his glory was then not distinguishable from that of others, all in various ways remarkable, who stood beside him. Webster, although he owes him much, names him together with Dekker and Heywood, as ranking a little below Chapman and Jonson, those learned authors, and Fletcher and Beaumont, those well-born young playwrights. He places him on a level with two popular improvisers. The quality he praises in him is his "right happy and copious industry." We seem to hear the faint echo of animated, noisy arguments in the literary taverns or even on the stage, arguments which did not diminish Shakespeare's success with the public, but which modified his reputation among certain wits and pedants, those who were beginning to pose as dramatic critics.

After his retirement and death, Shakespeare still had fervent admirers among amateurs of the stage, and also among the actors who had been his comrades and who remembered, when they piously published the 1623 folios, the applause which had greeted his plays. But since there was no organised criticism, his works, whence all his successors helped themselves abundantly, were classed with those of his contemporaries, almost on an equality with them. That his incomparable superiority was realised at all appears only in some enthusiastic verses written by Ben Jonson, his rival, and the young Milton, in the cult which the poets Suckling and Davenant traditionally rendered to him, and in the love which the good Duchess of Newcastle conceived for him in her youth. Only when men could view him at a great distance, across nearly a century, did they discern his true stature.

5. **In What does Shakespeare's Superiority over his Contemporaries Consist? The Variety of his Gifts.**—Wherein does Shakespeare's superiority, universally recognised to-day, lie? To us it shines with a blinding light, yet it did not dazzle those round about him, whence it follows that in some way it was difficult to apprehend. There is indeed hardly a glory of Shakespeare's drama which might not be matched by a fragment or an aspect of some other play of the period. He did not—how could he?—surpass the pathos and poetic sublimity of the last scenes of Marlowe's *Faust*. He created no atmosphere of grief and horror more agonising than that which envelops Webster's *Duchess of Malfi*. Not one of his plays is more solidly constructed than Jonson's *Volpone, Epicœne* and *Alchemist*. None of his comedies is more skilfully staged than Beaumont and Fletcher's *Knight of the Burning Pestle*, none of his tragedies than their *Maid's Tragedy*. Fletcher's and Dekker's songs yield nothing to his in lyrical beauty. He has created no character more singularly original than Dekker's old Friscobaldo, and he never gives the illusion of reality more powerfully than Middleton and Rowley in their De Flores. The poignant humanity of Heywood in *A Woman Killed with Kindness* equals his when his painting is most moving. There is in Dekker's *Shomakers Holiday* a merry swing not bettered in Shakespeare's most exhilarating comedy. Every element in Shakespeare's drama might thus, in isolation, be matched by the best of the contemporary writers for the stage at their best. What, then, is distinctive in Shakespeare?

First, his combination of all the gifts which were scattered or isolated in the work of others, the multifariousness of his curiosity and the extreme diversity of his talents. From the very outset of his career this is apparent. He did not, like most of his fellow-dramatists, continue unswervingly in the path in which he made his first steps, acquiring, like Lyly, Kyd and Marlowe, a distinct manner which both marked and bounded his personality. His flexibility was marvellous. He adapted himself to the most diverse material, and seemed to use it all with equal ardour and joy. Besides the narrative poems like *Venus and Adonis* and the *Rape of Lucrece*, into which he poured all his love for lyrical beauty and command of rhymes, his first essays in drama are so astonishingly various that no one theory fits them and each of them ought to be studied separately. They correspond to and overflow every dramatic classification hitherto known—national history, tragedy, comedy, romantic and fairy-plays. But these categories do not suffice to show their variety. The word comedy includes works of Shakespeare's as distinct as *Love's Labour's Lost*, that fantasy made of sparkling dialogue, fireworks of word-play, and the *Comedy of Errors*, a farce with a much involved plot modelled on Plautus. No two of the dramas of English history have the same shape or a like movement. *Henry VI.*, little removed from the mysteries, is a chronological series of scenes from a very long reign, hardly connected with each other and without a central figure. *Henry IV.* and *Henry V.* also resume whole reigns, but they include very searching character-drawing and are persistently dominated by one personage. This trilogy is in fact massed very freely about the wild young heir to the crown, constantly in the company of the jovial drunkard Falstaff, and transformed into a triumphant king. The interest of *Richard III.* is concentrated in the monstrous Gloucester, who through fraud and murder hews himself a way to the throne, and continues his criminal course until death strikes him down. *King John* is less dominated by a royal figure, that of the vacillating and cowardly tyrant who is more the slave rather than the master of circumstances: its action turns rather upon a single crime, the murder of the young Arthur. As for *Richard II.*, it is essentially a tragedy, the dramatisation not of a reign but of a crisis: everything in it is reduced to a struggle between the bad, weak and capricious king, a sentimentalist and an egoist, and the politic Bolingbroke.

Shakespeare is never found twice at the same point. It is as though he had sworn in his youth to experiment in constructions of the most varied kinds and in the most highly contrasted moods. He shows equal aptitude for the tragic and the comic, the sentimental and the burlesque, lyrical fantasy and character-study, portraits of women and of men. To the end of his career these alternatives recur. In the two years, 1601 and 1602, he produced the light-hearted comedy, *Twelfth Night*, with its mingling of farce and romance, *Julius Cæsar, Hamlet* and *All's Well that Ends Well.* About 1608 came, in quick succession, *Coriolanus, Timon* and *Pericles.* His greatest triumphs could not induce him to sustain an attitude, and although a persistent pessimism consecutively inspired, from 1604 to 1606, the great sorrowful tragedies, *Othello, Lear* and *Macbeth,* these were differentiated by such astonishing variety of kind, presentment and dramatic movement, that the impossibility of finding one formula to fit them all is quickly apparent.

This diversity exists everywhere in Shakespearean drama. It is shown both in the contrast afforded by plays produced at the same time, and in that evolution which colours the whole series of the plays with the hues of the succeeding seasons —the fresh green of spring, the darkness of summer thunder-storms, and the melancholy splendour of autumn.

6. **Creative Force. His Characters.**—Besides his variety, the poet's capital gift was certainly that he could endow historical and imaginary beings with life, not intermittently and by flashes, like most of his contemporaries, but constantly, so that however they are modified during a play they do not lose their identity. This power was abnormally developed in him, but he wielded it easily, naturally, spontaneously, without ever giving an impression of effort. From the beginning there is life everywhere, but as he advanced towards maturity his characters came to be more boldly outlined and more complex. This is first manifest in Biron in *Love's Labour's Lost,* in the antithesis presented by Proteus and Valentine in the *Two Gentlemen of Verona,* and by Richard II. and Richard III. in the plays called after them, and in the contrast in *Richard II.* between the too imaginative king and the astute Bolingbroke. The first important comic figure is undoubtedly Bottom in *Midsummer Night's Dream,* but the clown Launce in *Two Gentlemen of Verona* and the Dromios in the *Comedy of Errors* had previously made good their claim to droll originality. From 1593 onwards, very few characters of any importance in any one of the plays did not receive from his creator the vital spark and the distinctive mark of his individuality; each one of them deserves to be named. They differ in their sex, age, state of life, virtues and vices, but all of them are alike in being alive. Since we cannot go through all their list, let us think only of those who in a single tragedy, *Romeo and Juliet,* receive their rich share of this vital gift: the lovers

no doubt have most of it, but it is also meted out to old Capulet, Tybalt the bully, the cynical Mercutio, the nurse and Friar Lawrence. Their parts may be short, they may have to speak only some twenty lines of verse, but these are enough to let the poet make them unforgettable. Multiply them by thirty-six, the number of his plays, and you have a throng than which none more alive ever issued from a human imagination. A whole world persuades audiences, or even mere readers, of its presence, with a force of realism to which very few of the real beings among whom playgoers spend their lives attain. It is principally in this respect that Shakespeare surpasses his rivals and is Shakespeare. All his contemporaries have written scattered scenes, as animated, as tragic, comic or poetic as his, but when the total number of the persons to whom they have ensured immortality is counted, it is questionable whether all of these, collected from all their plays, would counterbalance those in a single great Shakespearean play.

It is indeed not enough to say that Shakespeare's supreme gift to his puppets, that which places him far above his contemporaries, is life and animation. Animation at least is not lacking to the creations of the others, some of whom are prodigal of it. But only very rarely can they give the illusion that their characters are at once living and true. Not Marlowe, nor Jonson, nor Beaumont and Fletcher, to mention only the most illustrious of Shakespeare's rivals, were capable of the truthful character-drawing which could alone prolong the life of their puppets beyond the time of a performance. The characters of these other playwrights are almost always excessive, inhuman, arbitrary or theatrical; their aim is to produce surprise; in their feelings we do not recognise our own; their extravagance or their inexplicably sudden changes of front are disconcerting. Shakespeare's characters, whether good or bad, whether moving among the realities of history or the most romantic happenings, have an unfailing humanity which makes them plausible and keeps them within the orbit of our sympathy.

7. **The Epical Basis of Shakespeare's Drama.** — A profound difference between Shakespeare's work and that of his contemporaries consists in the greater truth, the more serious and substantial character, which fundamentally belongs to his plays in the mass. Their matter, and theirs alone, is epical as much as romantic. He alone gave so much space to the epical, and wrought it consciously, continuously and on a great scale. His six dramas of English history and three Roman tragedies, together with *Hamlet, Lear* and *Macbeth*—based on earlier and more or less legendary chronicles accepted as genuine history by him and his public—form such a whole as is found nowhere else and is the solid bulwark of Shakespearean drama. They prove the poet to have been long in contact with what was, or what he believed to be, the realities of the past. His effort to evoke and revive the past left him with a taste for truth apparent in his treatment of subjects which are hardly historical but are borrowed from the *novellieri*, for instance the themes of *Romeo and Juliet* and *Othello*. It would be possible to find yet other reminiscences of the epic mood which give substance to fiction even in his fantastic or fairy worlds, right in the heart of his romantic plays. Other playwrights often made history unreal, but Shakespeare could warrant the truth even of romance.

It is the plays devoted to national history which most plainly connect his work with the old religious drama, of which the original object was not mere pleasure but instruction and edification.

Nothing is more honourable to Elizabethan audiences than that they sought their amusement in the mere spectacle of great national events; nothing better attests the poet's greatness than his self-effacement in his work and his neglect of all the pettiness of the dramatic codes and the recipes for producing emotion. There is no apparent art. The simplicity and the greatness of conception found in the mysteries are repeated. As a child, Shakespeare may have seen the old sacred plays performed at Coventry. There is thus a link between this poet of the Renascence and the poets of the Middle Ages. Country instead of faith is his theme. He imparts knowledge of history as those old poets taught religion. Except for *King John*, the subject of which sets it some four hundred years apart from the others, these plays are a continuous history of England over a long period, the whole fifteenth century. From the day when Bolingbroke dethroned the weak Richard II. and founded the Lancastrian dynasty, until the Battle of Bosworth, when Henry VII. defeated the tyrant Richard III., ended the bloodthirsty Wars of the Roses and won the crown for the House of Tudor, Shakespeare brought the history of their country before the eyes of his countrymen, at a time when the Tudors were still reigning, Elizabeth wielding her glorious and undisputed sway. Foreign war with its triumphs and disasters, years of prosperity and of misery, glory and shame, princes heroic and abject: all succeed each other in the plays, painted almost impartially for a public enabled at once to marvel and to learn.

Shakespeare keeps this breadth when he leaves London for Rome and abandons Holinshed for Plutarch. Although no longer sustained by patriotism, he is upheld by the prestige which belongs to the great names of antiquity, and haloes about the heads of Coriolanus, Brutus, Julius Cæsar, Antony, Cleopatra. His first care still is to breathe new life into famous men and great events. He is less scrupulously respectful of truth than incapable of conceiving drama as made by the violation of truth. He is, however, entirely unconcerned to reproduce manners and costumes. Knowing nothing of the historical realism which goes by the name of local colour, he succeeds in representing the past with human truth so deep and life so intense that his work has become complementary to that of the scholar. The scholar may be left to note where the men of the past differed from the men of the present. Shakespeare marks the characteristics they share so vigorously that he eliminates twenty centuries. With him historical drama reaches its apotheosis in such scenes as that in which the Roman populace, after acclaiming Brutus, Cæsar's murderer, is almost immediately turned against him by the moving, insidious eloquence of Antony, so that men weep at the sight of Cæsar's body and cry out for the death of the conspirators.

Only Jonson followed Shakespeare along this path, but he, having more exact knowledge, was too much preoccupied with the painting of curious customs and with his own learned details to retain Shakespeare's broad epic manner. He was too ready to sacrifice the intuitive insight into human character and the play of human feelings to a literal reproduction of the narratives of Latin historians.

8. **Shakespeare's Art.**—The question whether Shakespeare be an artist is the one concerning him which was most discussed by his contemporaries and has most divided posterity. From the beginning, his natural genius, fancy and spontaneity have been almost universally recognised. But that firm reason, a concerted plan and an organising will directed his poetic force, this was for long not perceived and is still disputed by many. "Shakespeare wanted art," Ben Jonson says bluntly, and comments on the statement in a well-known passage. "He had an excellent phantasy, brave notions, and gentle expressions, wherein he flowed with that facility that sometimes it was necessary he should be stopped. ' Sufflaminandus erat,' [1] as Augustus said of Haterius. His wit was in his own power: would the rule of it had been so, too!"

Shakespeare is so abundant a writer, at times indeed to the point of excess, that Jonson inclined to deduce that he lacked self-control, that his genius ran away with him. His fellow-actors, publishing his manuscripts in 1623, gave credence to this

---

[1] "He had to be repressed."

I—T

opinion when, thinking to honour him, they stated that "what he thought, he uttered with that easinesse that wee have scarse received from him a blot in his papers." Milton echoed them even in his loving praise of Shakespeare, calling him " Sweetest Shakespeare, Fancy's Child," who warbled forth his " native wood-notes wild."

Literary judgments often rest on an antithesis. We can understand how in men's minds the learned and laborious Jonson soon came to be contrasted with the spontaneous Shakespeare. Art, by a confusion between learning and care for art, was conceded to the one, genius to the other. There was no protest against this view except that which, curiously, was advanced by Jonson himself, who had done so much to propagate it. He, in the fine verses which headed the 1623 folio, wrote:

> Yet must I not give Nature all: thy art,
> My gentle Shakespeare, must enjoy a part.
> For though the poet's matter nature be,
> His art doth give the fashion. And that he
> Who casts to write a living line, must sweat,
> (Such as thine are) and strike the second heat
> Upon the Muses' anvil; turn the same,
> And himself with it, that he thinks to frame;
> Or for the laurel, he may gain a scorn,
> For a good poet's made, as well as born.
> And such wert thou.

This irrefutable evidence of the great humanist who had known him personally is confirmed not only by Shakespeare's non-dramatic work, with all its marks of loving chiselling, but also by numerous signs of corrections, some of them considerable, in the several editions of the plays. The absence of erasures from the final manuscript is of comparatively little value as evidence. Moreover, while Shakespeare's work contains no dramatic theory, it very clearly indicates his opinions on the art of acting. The celebrated scene in which Hamlet criticises the actors and tries to inspire them to natural interpretation, equally removed from emphasis and flatness, says much for the control which Shakespeare would have had reason exercise over caprice and fancy. It is in this passage that an illuminating dictum occurs which hardly leaves a doubt that the poet could be completely master of himself even when borne on the wings of the most impetuous flights of his genius: "in the very torrent, tempest, and, as I may say, the whirlwind of passion, you must acquire and beget a temperance that may give it smoothness." What classical critic would not subscribe to this precept, even envy it?

To admit that Shakespeare gives this regulating power to wisdom is the best way of explaining the harmony which he has been able to bring into almost every one of his plays. Different though their elements be, each has its own atmosphere, and this could not regularly happen as the effect of a fortunate accident. The very freedom habitual to popular plays, the custom of mixing two or even three plots in one play, the alternation of the tragic and the comic, the concurrent use of rhymed and blank verse and of prose: all contributed to enhance the difficulty of fusing harmoniously pictures and scenes so disparate in their moods. The resultant success is the more meritorious because, like something done for a wager, it was all but unattainable. No one recipe was ever twice applicable, but each work demanded its special solution. A detailed study would be necessary to show the concealed and sure art which interweaves the threads of the double plot of the *Merchant of Venice*, finally confronting Shylock with Portia, or which in *Midsummer Night's Dream* brings together, from the opposite extremes of society, the grotesque craftsmen and the lords and ladies of Athens and, from their even greater remoteness, Titania, the little fairy, and Bottom, the boor, whose meeting has a symbolism essential to the play. Similarly, in *King Lear* the theme of filial ingratitude is repeated, as by an echo, when Lear's suffering recurs in Gloucester, the betrayal of Goneril and Regan in Edmund.

We might thus examine nearly all the plays, for a different method is used in each of them. Is Shakespeare's art less real because it is essentially mobile and varied? His tendency is to efface all its traces, and only patient study can reveal them in their secret, much-veiled lurking-places, hidden behind the illusion which art itself creates.

Take in *Hamlet* the fragment of a tragedy after Seneca which the prince causes the actors to declaim in his presence. The prince's pleasure in this passage and the impassioned pathos of the actor's delivery are proof that there is here no question of a mere parody. Even while, by the inappropriate praise he puts into the mouth of Polonius, Shakespeare makes fun of some archaic and forced language in the tirade, he clearly considers it to be in itself eloquent and effective. It is a fine piece of declamation. Here it is true that he is doing justice to a genre not his own, but he is also using this sample of noble and artificial tragedy to make, by force of contrast, his own play seem entirely natural. His characters speak while the others declaim. Or rather, his characters are not such, but merely men. Thus the contrast turns his own play from a stage representation into very reality.

9. **Shakespeare's Empiricism.**—The factor which has done most to mask Shakespeare's art is its consistency with cheerful or at least resigned acceptance of the conditions which the contemporary stage imposed on a dramatist, and which were a result of the demands and habits of the public, the poor staging and the methods of Shakespeare's brother actors. His art is essentially empirical: it takes realities into account and is not based on the abstract. He himself, speaking with the voice of King Henry V., reveals its principle:

> There is some soul of goodness in things evil,
> Would men observingly distil it out.

In no way blind to the faults of the stage of his day, Shakespeare was as aware as anyone else of the poverty of its scenery and the brutal taste of the "groundlings," "capable of nothing but inexplicable dumb-shows and noise"; he was annoyed by the misuse of clowns, who interrupted and held up the most pathetic scenes with ill-timed fooling; he was pained by the emphatic declamations of tragic actors whom he implores not to "saw the air too much with your hand" or "tear a passion to tatters, to very rags." Yet he did not, as a consequence, effect any riddance he forbids nothing. He attempted no such return to the noble simplicity of the theatre of antiquity as would soon have emptied the Globe playhouse, but endeavoured to do the best he could with the actual conditions he could not escape, galling though some of them were. Although he lacked scenery, he did not think it necessary that the action of his plays should pass in a neutralised scene, some abstract place. He counted on the facile imagination of his audience to conjure up what he could not reproduce, and helped them with the swift, vivid descriptions which he introduces into his verses. The scenery which the naked stage could not provide is supplied in the text of his plays. His characters and places are so closely associated that they cannot be separated. The name of Juliet at once calls up the Capulets' ball-room, or the moonlit balcony, or the tomb in which she lay before she died. The trees of the Forest of Arden droop and rustle about Rosalind. The storm blows upon the dishevelled Lear on the deserted heath. Hamlet waits feverishly for the ghost on the platform at Elsinore or cracks grim jokes in the churchyard. Nowhere is there more of the picturesque or of the poetry of nature than in these plays, performed with a few properties to symbolise rather than to indicate the places in which their action passed.

Similarly, instead of eliminating or disdainfully neglecting the clown, Shakespeare undertook his education, gave him direction and converted a necessary evil into good. Marlowe, an idealist, proclaimed his contempt for clowning and resolution to have done with it. In *Tamburlaine* he has turned the clown out, unless indeed, as may well have happened, the groundlings called him back to fool between the scenes and thus provide relaxation from the sustained sublimity of this enormous play. Marlowe would concede nothing to him. Yet when Marlowe came to write *Faustus* he had, willy-nilly, to compromise, and since he felt it beneath him carefully to write a part for the clown, he threw him, as it were, a sketch for his buffoonery and grimacing and let him fill it in for himself. The result is a play of which parts, the beginning and the end, are admirable, but which is a mere framework.

Shakespeare, complain as he may of the outrageousness of the clown, takes another course. After all, he appreciated the inherent drollery of this figure, his jokes, his special terms of speech, his quips and his play on words. He therefore adopts him, lets him into comedies and even into tragedies so long as he "speak no more than is set down" for him. He writes his part to fit his habitual speech, puns and all, but includes in it some better compounded and more pointed jokes. Shakespeare makes of the clown, whether he remains a boor or becomes a court fool or nobleman's jester, a sort of popular philosopher who is independent and sagacious beneath his apparent stupidity, and who passes through most of the plays without belonging to them.

Sometimes, however, he makes a real character of the clown, humanises him and gives him a sort of heart. He lends him affection, such as Launce feels for his mangy dog, or Touchstone for Celia, or Lear's fool for his master. Or he admits him into a craft. Bottom is a weaver and, with his self-sufficiency and artlessness, has character, shown for instance in his conviction that the amusement which his stupidity affords proceeds from his wit. Bottom has won a place in the foreground of a play, for the meaning of *Midsummer Night's Dream* depends on his meeting with Titania. Elsewhere the clown has the guise of a watchman, when he appears as Dogberry, a pompous idiot and the prototype of all the burlesque policemen of the stage. At the very end of his career Shakespeare brings the clown back to the state which was his originally before he became a professional jester. He identifies him with the country gaby whose name had clung to him, but whom he had forgotten. In *Winter's Tale* he is an old shepherd's son, a real thick-headed, ingenuous country lad. Thus the clown who had deserted the fields for the stage is brought back to the fold.

To sum up: Shakespeare's use of the clown is often so happy and unexpected that this character could hardly be spared from Shakespearean drama. If the clown were gone, something would be missing from the whole. The purity and nobility of the plays would doubtless be enhanced, but their meaning would be restricted and their philosophy would suffer. The poet did well to think, like Friar Laurence in *Romeo and Juliet*—

> For nought so vile that on the earth doth live
> But to the earth some special good doth give.

It was this tolerance, proper to him, which enabled Shakespeare to retain the clown longer than most of his rivals, and the fact is among those which make his plays seem more archaic than theirs. Jonson and Fletcher, more innovators than he, soon got rid of the vestiges of the primitive stage which clashed with their conceptions of realism and modernity. They did not perceive the "soul of goodness" which lurked in the clown who had become an anachronism.

Shakespeare's conservatism is more clearly shown in matters of greater consequence. He seems to have been one of the least inventive of his contemporary writers. He preferred subjects of which others had made trial. Very often he did no more than work upon existing plays. Some of his masterpieces had already been tried on the stage, for instance *Romeo and Juliet*, *Hamlet* and *Lear*. Not to speak of the doubtful *Henry VI.*, it is certain that there were plays prior to his on the same subjects as the *Two Gentlemen of Verona*, *Richard III.*, *King John*, the *Merchant of Venice*, the *Henry IV.* and *Henry V.* trilogy, *The Taming of the Shrew* and *Measure for Measure*. The same is probably true of the *Comedy of Errors*, *Richard II.*, *Julius Cæsar* and *Troilus and Cressida*.

When Shakespeare's subjects had not already been dramatised, he generally took them, even for his comedies and romantic plays, from a book, and reproduced them, on the whole, faithfully. He borrowed the theme of *As You Like It* from a novel by Lodge, that of *Winter's Tale* from a novel by Greene, and *All's Well that Ends Well* from one of Boccaccio's stories. *Othello* comes from a story of Cinthio, *Pericles* from old Gower's version of the Greek novel *Apollonius of Tyre*. The originals are known of the serious parts of *Much Ado About Nothing*, *Twelfth Night* and *Cymbeline*.

The plays of which he seems to have invented the subjects are very few, nor can it be absolutely asserted that their source will not one day be discovered. They are the *Merry Wives of Windsor*, save for some insignificant passages, *Love's Labour's Lost*, *Midsummer Night's Dream* and *The Tempest*, and they are just enough to show that, if he did not usually care to create his plays entirely, he could do it when he chose. It is remarkable that the three last of these plays have an exceptional character, that, having been voluntarily and arbitrarily created, they are of the nature of plays with a purpose, symbolical plays. Each of them illustrates an idea.

Some young men have sworn to devote themselves entirely to study and have forsworn love. Love comes to rouse them from their studious retreat; they find that they have taken a wrong course, that love is the supreme master of knowledge and wisdom. They repudiate their semi-monastic vows and give themselves up to the joys of love. Such is the theme of *Love's Labour's Lost* and the manifest moral of this fantastic comedy.

What laws does love obey? How is the thread which binds hearts spun and how is it sometimes broken? Who can explain sudden changes of feeling, the interplay of sympathy and antipathy? Helena loves Demetrius, and Demetrius Hermia, whose heart is all Lysander's. Suddenly Lysander as well as Demetrius gives his love to the despised Helena. Soon afterwards, happily, the hearts which had gone astray beat true again. What has occurred? The play tells that fairies with souls as light as their bodies tangle and untangle the skein of human caprice. Oberon would help the lovers to an understanding, but the elf Puck, his giddy, mischievous servant, carries out his orders wrong. The fairies themselves can be blind as men. Oberon and Titania love, quarrel, are jealous of each other, are reconciled. Because the juice of a flower is dropped on her eyes, little lovely Titania is enamoured of a bragging blockhead of an artificer who wears an ass's head, and she remains under the spell until she is released by the counter-charm. For such is the poet's answer to those who asked him the reason of the heart's vagaries. Spells are worked by mysterious beings who themselves are the sport of enchantment. He explains, then vanishes with a mischievous smile. Such is the theme of the *Midsummer Night's Dream*.

The Tempest, written at the other end of Shakespeare's career, is also full of symbolism. Prospero is a magician who by his art has subjected the man-beast personified in Caliban and the invisible elements personified in Ariel. A king whom treason has disinherited, he has resolved to bring his triumphant enemies low and deprive them of power. He draws them to his lonely island, where he has them at his mercy, but his object is to pardon them and change their hate to love, to marry his daughter Miranda to Ferdinand, the son of his enemy.

These are plays of which the conception is individual and arbitrary and proportionately significant. But among the rest of Shakespeare's drama they are exceptional, for usually he seeks not to interpret or guide life, but to present it. There is no symbolism in most of his plays except such as it may please the ingenious hearer to introduce. *Hamlet*, universally acknowledged to be the one of his tragedies most laden with thought, touches on many problems—vengeance, suicide, love—but advances a solution for none of them. The tragedy provides the spectacle of the trouble of Hamlet's soul and attempts no more.

Content, as a rule, "to hold, as 'twere, the mirror up to nature," and to show "the very age and body of the time, his form and pressure," Shakespeare gives fewer direct lessons than the dramatists who, like Ben Jonson, pose as censors of morals. Systematic thinking has marked his work less clearly than that of the revolutionary Marlowe. He has not Massinger's tendency to oratorical discussion of a thesis.

10. **Shakespeare's Philosophy.**—Much has, nevertheless, been said of Shakespeare's philosophy. So many reflections on life occur in his plays as to produce the illusion that he was endowed with superior wisdom. It is tempting to imagine that the collection of the scattered fragments of his thought would constitute a body of doctrine which would yield an answer, his answer, to the riddles of life.

In truth, no Shakespearean system exists; this philosophy vanishes if we seek to grasp it. Its numerous contradictions soon become apparent, and its incoherence, which is no less than that of reality. They escape disappointment who hold that had the poet had a message to deliver he would have placed it in his non-dramatic work, more especially his sonnets, and that he did nothing of the sort. There is nothing in Shakespeare's philosophy which is distinctive or carries conviction. The miracle is not in the abstract thought his works contain, but in that extraordinary pliability which let him put the most divergent, most striking and most ingenious arguments in the mouths of his characters in support of their passions or interests. Each of them, from the kings to the clowns, has indeed a philosophy, which he makes singularly clear. Each judges life in his own way, from his own angle, whence he may utter a remark strikingly true, and profound also, in many instances. But all this is the emanation of a vigorous dramatic genius. These scattered reflections, evoked by circumstances and deliberately self-contradictory, derive strength from their appropriateness, and are penetrating by the feeling of which they are born, as they are beautiful by the poetry of the words which clothe them. But it is vain to hope, by gathering them together, to attain to a higher wisdom which was the poet's. They are not maxims accumulating to produce a total result. Their number is commensurate only with the diversity of human judgments, and reveals only the playwright's marvellous versatility and his consciousness of the relative nature of all things. Hence philosophies constructed from the ideas scattered through the plays have been frail and mutually contradictory. Protestants, Catholics and free-thinkers have with equally plausible arguments claimed Shakespeare for their own. He enunciates principles akin to those proverbs and popular sayings, all equally striking, all true within their limits, which contradict each other; one of them can often be matched by its exact contrary—"Like father, like son"—"A père avare fils prodigue." Hamlet, discouraged by the something "rotten in the state of Denmark," has cause to hesitate, exactly as Henry V., seeing "some soul of goodness in things evil," has reasons for acting, finds that the very obstacles in his path are motives for action and hope. Each temperament and every circumstance has in the plays its appropriate philosophy. No higher doctrine embraces and resumes them all.

Nevertheless, the deduction is allowable that the playwright's thought rarely went beyond earthly life, that if he sometimes glanced further he soon brought back his gaze to this world, which seemed to him man's all. He does indeed admit with Hamlet that human reason is limited and surrounded by a great mystery:

> There are more things in heaven and earth, Horatio,
> Than are dreamt of in your philosophy.

Yet Hamlet himself says, "To die: to sleep; no more," for all that he keeps

> The dread of something after death,
> The undiscovered country from whose bourn
> No traveller returns.

Other characters in the plays make more decided denials. It may mean nothing that Macbeth, the murderer, thinks

> Life's but a walking shadow, a poor player
> That struts and frets his hour upon the stage
> And then is heard no more: it is a tale
> Told by an idiot, full of sound and fury,
> Signifying nothing.

It may mean no more that Jaques, the melancholy philosopher, believes

> All the world's a stage,
> And all the men and women merely players.

Touchstone, the fool, may be left responsible for his limited view of life:

> "It is ten o'clock:
> Thus we may see," quoth he, "how the world wags:
> 'Tis but an hour ago since it was nine,
> And after one hour more 'twill be eleven;
> And so, from hour to hour, we ripe and ripe,
> And then, from hour to hour, we rot and rot;
> And thereby hangs a tale."

It is, however, difficult to think that Prospero did not voice the poet's mature opinion when, reflectively, he averred that:

> We are such stuff
> As dreams are made on, and our little life
> Is rounded with a sleep.

This is to speak as a philosopher of antiquity rather than a Christian. Yet the saying was not such as to scandalise an audience of the Renascence or to mark Shakespeare's plays as more impious than those of his contemporaries. Marlowe had written more audacious lines. Shakespeare did no more than find rare and unforgettable forms in which to enclose the secular thinking of the men of his time.

11. Poetry of Form. Style. The Power and the Excesses of Shakespeare.— Shakespeare's personality, which he deliberately effaced behind his work and made subservient to the conditions of the stage, asserted itself irrepressibly in the form of his plays, his style and his versification. There all the wealth of his gifts found vent. Marked though the characteristics of the period be, the form of his work is unique and incomparable, impaired by faults as brilliant as the colours in a golden pheasant's tail. He was afflicted by all the diseases of style proper to his century, one after the other, as well as by its happy bravery, and he blended them in a style entirely his own, which transforms its constituent elements and harmonises disparities as numerous as though they had been assembled in each play in fulfilment of a wager.

His dramatic gift alone would have secured his immediate popularity, but would hardly have ensured his glory. The first dramatist was also the first poet of his day and one of the first of all time. The poet is not only revealed by the hundred exquisite songs with which the plays are strewn. The ardent passion for beauty which is the distinction of the sonnets, and causes the best of them to reach the high-water mark of beauty in English poetry, attains in the plays to results as fine, and there has a diversity of mood and accent impossible to the sonnets with their monotonous theme and form.

Most often the fusion of dramatic and lyric elements is perfect, absolute and beyond analysis. A whole scene is lifted to a higher mood while the proportions of its constituent elements are unmodified, and thus the pleasure of truth, which is retained, and the added pleasure of beauty are blended in strict unity.

Beauty comes of the perfection of the style and the versification, the rarity of the images and the accompanying music. No purely lyrical poetry in English weds words or metaphors more triumphantly or contains more varied, richer or more delicate sonorities than those which Shakespeare spontaneously and inexhaustibly produces in the blank verse of his plays. Yet the pleasure of an emotion properly dramatic is nearly always added to the pleasure of lyricism, which therefore is saved from the egoistical dilettantism fatal to enchantment. A special glory belongs to the poet who, without sacrifice of probability, inspires other hearts than his own with the highest lyrical emotions and causes other lips to utter them, while at the same time he follows or urges the progress of the action which decides the fate of his puppets.

In the capital scenes of the great tragedies—the duologues of Romeo and Juliet, Hamlet's soliloquies, the scene of the awakening of Othello's jealousy, of Lear's passionate railings or of Macbeth's hallucinations—this poetic prestige overlies a pathos which could exist without this splendour but is transfigured by it. All the translations have allowed this supreme enchantment to escape, and give, therefore, only an incomplete comprehension of the total effect. When Iago sees Othello, already ravaged by the jealousy he has put in him, coming towards him, and says:

> Not poppy, nor mandragora,
> Nor all the drowsy syrups of the world
> Shall ever medicine thee to that sweet sleep
> Which thou ow'dst yesterday,

something infused in the beauty of the rhythm and the syllables transforms Iago into an infernal magician. He has been a vile rascal; he becomes a demon.

The defects of this rich genius for words are almost as glaring as its qualities are dazzling. There is on every occasion such a multitudinous flow of words and images to Shakespeare's mind as nothing seems able to dam. Ben Jonson, noticing this irrepressible impetuosity, regretted that it could not be checked: "Sufflaminandus erat." Images gush forth, beautiful or strange, but without order, redundant and sometimes injurious to dramatic probability. Old John of Gaunt in agony breathes out his love for England in multiplied, piled-up similes, interrupted, resumed, inexhaustible. His tirade would weary the lungs of a young, strong man. The wounded soldier who relates to Duncan Macbeth's victory over the rebels heaps frenzied metaphors on to emphatic similes.

Even more often the poet yields to the temptation to be subtle. He plunges into subtlety confidently, sure that he can find a way out of the labyrinth. In the sonnets, when he is speaking in his own person, he uses and misuses subtlety immoderately. His narrative poems are full of it and it is the very web of the unending lamentations of Lucrece, Tarquin's victim. Almost all his characters, whether tragic or comic, show unexpectedly a taste for the like quintessence of wit, a joy in splitting the finest hairs. The young queen, wife to Richard II. (Act II. scene ii.), when she is uneasy about her husband's absence, involves herself, with a courtier who seeks to dispel her anxiety, in the maziest of arguments about her presentiment of evil. The most subtle sonneteer would find it difficult to follow the slender threads of these highly abstract analyses, in which the play of verbal antithesis is so fine-drawn that even a slow reading hardly discovers its clues. However keen our perceptions may be, we have little chance of unravelling the almost invisible threads of such a skein while we are listening to a play. Shakespeare has become a wit rather than a poet and, like a tight-rope walker, is carried away by pleasure in his own agility. Not all his experience of the theatre can defeat his joy in overcoming difficulties.

This lack of moderation is the limitation of his dramatic genius and his realism. It brings on to the stage a superfluity of lyricism both ill-timed and out of place. It endows the most divergent characters, even the dull and the foolish, with an improbable command of language and power of analysis.

In part the defect is to be ascribed to the age, but it is mainly due to Shakespeare himself. In fact, it is probably true that, except the fuliginous Chapman, lost in metaphors and drowned in subtleties, Shakespeare has a more difficult style than any other Elizabethan dramatist. Marlowe's eloquence, Jonson's vigorous realism, Dekker's easy grace, Middleton's dry precision, Fletcher's rather superficial distinction and Massinger's oratorical swing make their plays more lucid than his, leave fewer difficulties to be solved and knots to be untied. Although in many passages, and nearly always in the most beautiful, Shakespeare shows himself capable of complete clarity and frank simplicity, he yet had a personal taste for a twisted, slightly enigmatic mode of expression, for variants on the current uses of speech, and the hearer and even the reader must consequently exert ingenuity to understand him. This habit of mind, usually dropped when a play reaches its intensest moment, is especially manifest in secondary scenes in which the dramatic instinct does not restrain him. It expresses a natural tendency which needed to be contained and checked by a superior necessity of the action of the play.

12. **Shakespeare's Universality.**—We have shown, more or less clearly, the link which joins Shakespeare to his contemporaries, how he was like them and how he surpassed them. The study has been much too limited for a poet who, in Jonson's words, "was not of an age, but of all time." So astonishingly widespread is his glory, that it might also be said that "he was not of a land, but of all lands." We ought to notice certain other characteristics which distinguish him from his English rivals less than they place him in opposition to the classical drama. The most important of all is the frequent complexity of his characters, which, as a rule, are not represented only within the short span of a crisis. Shakespeare took advantage of the wide allowance of space under his dramatic system, the twenty or so scenes into which each of his plays is, on an average, divided, and showed his heroes at various moments of their lives, in changing situations and in colloquy with different persons. They are not obliged to sustain one attitude, but have time to move and alter. No simple principle accounts for them. They have life and life's indefiniteness, and therefore they are not always fully intelligible, but are mysteries. It is even possible to ask whether Shakespeare himself understood them all. Had he analytical comprehension of Hamlet? The watchmaker understands the watch he has made, but "it is a wise father who knows his own child." Thus it is that

many Shakespearean beings, whose reality cannot for an instant be questioned, do not admit of too precise investigation or are differently interpreted by different critics. But even as they evolve and their complexity increases, an art of which the secret escapes us preserves the illusion of their identity through all their changes.

Another great characteristic of Shakespeare's genius is an undefinable alertness and mobility which keep attention on the stretch. His prodigious vitality remains unimpaired after three centuries. It seems to grow every time he is read. Something of the mystery belongs to him which Enobarbus noticed in Cleopatra's charm:

> Age cannot wither her, nor custom stale
> Her infinite variety: other women cloy
> The appetite they feed: but she makes hungry
> Where most she satisfies.

No other literature, whatever its beauty, does not seem monotonous after Shakespeare. Free of every theory, accepting all of life, rejecting nothing, uniting the real and the poetic, appealing to the most various men, to a rude workman as to a wit, Shakespeare's drama is a great river of life and beauty. All who thirst for art or truth, the comic or the tender, ecstasy or satire, light or shade, can stoop to drink from its waters, and at almost every instant of their changing moods find the one drop to slake their thirst.

CHAPTER VII

1. George Chapman.[2]—Shakespeare's rivals were found, as might be expected, in the camp of the humanists. The hostility first shown to him by Greene and the University Poets was renewed by Chapman and Jonson. Not that these playwrights took from him, more than others, his foremost place in the popular favour, but they seem, from time to time, to have trumpeted more loudly than the rest their literary qualifications, the attainments which they could contrast arrogantly with Shakespeare's slight equipment of learning, his "small Latin and less Greek."

George Chapman (1559?–1634), famous for his translation of Homer, began to write plays somewhat late in life, when he was nearly forty years old. In so doing he seems less to have followed a vocation than to have been attracted by the extraordinary popularity of the theatre. Men who would in any other period have held aloof from the stage at this time wrote comedies and tragedies for the sake of applause as much as money.

Saving that he was a great reader of Greek and Latin authors, not excepting the Neo-Latinists of the Renascence, on whom he drew considerably, Chapman was all but destitute of the qualities we esteem classical. Almost more than any of his contemporaries, he lacked the faculty of composition and clarity of intelligence. He possessed, on the other hand, and to a rare degree, the romantic exaltation of the Elizabethans with its qualities and defects. He shared their flights and falls, their audacities of style, their moments of nobility and splendour, their long intervals of senselessness and obscurity. Saved from extravagance when he was kept within bounds by the author he was translating, he was apt to flounder when he adventured alone. He had not the guidance of reason or good taste or even that of mere good sense.

His magniloquence and his assured self-confidence were none the less imposing. He made others share his own belief that he was possessed of a poetic demon. It is to-day generally accepted that he is the rival poet to whom Shakespeare, in his sonnets, gives praise mixed with irony. He speaks of "the proud full sail of his great verse," and of

> his spirit, by spirits taught to write
> Above a mortal pitch.

Chapman's talent has most relation to the frenzied genius of Marlowe, whose senior he was by five years and whose impetuous eloquence he admired. He concluded Marlowe's *Hero and Leander*, revived Tamburlaine's declaiming in his tragedies, and followed the example of Marlowe's *Massacre at Paris* by seeking subjects for gloomy plays in contemporary French history.

---

[1] Mézières, *Contemporains et successeurs de Shakespeare* (1863).
[2] Ed. R. H. Shepherd, 3 vols. (1889); selected plays published in the Mermaid Series, ed. W. L. Phelps (1895); *All Fools* and *The Gentleman Usher*, ed. T. M. Parrott (Belles Lettres Series, 1907); *Bussy d'Ambois* and *The Revenge of Bussy d'Ambois*, ed. Boas (Belles Lettres Series, 1906); *Plays and Poems: the Tragedies*, ed. Parrott (1910); *Charlemagne*, ed. F. Schoell (Princeton University Press, 1920). See F. Schoell, "Une source nouvelle de Chapman," in *Revue Germanique* (July–August 1923).

His best-known tragedies are *Bussy d'Ambois*, which may have been written as early as 1598, although it was not published until 1607, the *Revenge of Bussy d'Ambois* (Ambois stands for Amboise), published in 1614, and the *Conspiracy*, followed by the *Tragedy of Charles, Duke of Biron*, both published in 1608. The subject of the two first of these plays goes back to the reign of Henry III. of France. They are concerned with Bussy, the famous bully and lover of the Countess of Montsoreau whom Dumas made so popular two hundred and fifty years later. Biron is the marshal who was the friend of Henry IV. and who betrayed his master, was pardoned, repeated his offence while he was ambassador in London, was called upon to confess what he had done, and, on his refusal, put to death in 1602. Chapman closely follows the English translation, published in 1607, of the versions of this affair by Serres and Mathieu. Since Henry IV. was still alive he could hardly have found a more recent topic. The French ambassador protested, in spite of the fine part which the king is made to play, and backed his protest by citing a prohibition to actors to bring any living Christian king on to the stage. Both the events and the characters of the play are historical. Chapman is one of the few authors of the day who attempted to represent Frenchmen without caricature. But his work is diffuse; it contains too much speechifying and too little movement. The characters are monotonous: Biron is too constantly an arrogant braggart. Yet, for all that this central figure is swollen with conceit and animated by immoderate ambition, the ten acts devoted to him are Chapman's most measured and correct contribution to tragedy.

Dramatically, however, *Bussy d'Ambois* is Chapman's most interesting work. In it this learned poet, whose head was filled with mythology, this impetuous, fuliginous lyricist, is seen at work upon a melodrama.

Following an unknown source, he shows a complete ignorance of the real France, but has no satirical intention. He mingles authentic facts with his own inventions. He transforms Bussy into a stage hero, after Marlowe, and lends him a power of wild declamation. This Bussy has placed his incredible valour at the service first of the Duke of Anjou, the king's brother, and then of the king himself, and the courtiers rage and tremble as much at his unbounded freedom of speech as at his sword-play. He avenges himself for their insults in the time of his poverty and friendlessness. He wins the favour of the Duchess of Guise in the teeth of the duke, not because he loves her but out of bravado and revenge. He claims the right himself to do justice to himself. Unfortunately he is not only the vehicle for the poet's independence, but must also bear the burden of his foggiest metaphors.

But the really original character in the play is the Countess of Montsoreau (or Montsurry, as the author calls her), to whom Chapman gives the romantic Christian name of Tamyra. This study of a devout woman, a Puritan in love, is, if not very true or coherent, both interesting and new. Situations proper to comedy are introduced in the midst of the most tragic plot. Tamyra is known at the court of Henry III. for her virtue, loves her husband and is loved by him. Her good conduct is conspicuous in the dissipated society in which she moves. When the Duke of Anjou coarsely seeks to seduce her, she answers him firmly and wittily and with proper indignation at his cynicism. When she is rallied for her faithfulness to her husband, she replies nobly and gravely, as a matron should. Yet at the very moment when she is thus finely defending herself, she has ceased to be a virtuous wife. Irresistible passion had, from her first meeting with him, swept her on towards surrender to the brilliant Bussy in all the bravery of his daring. She is dazzled so that she can hardly hide her feeling from other women. It is all she can do not to betray her jealousy of the Duchess of Guise whom she believes Bussy to love, and whose guilty passion she blames with her lips while she envies it in her heart. Love has stricken her suddenly and irresistibly; she is the victim of fatality. When she has made up her mind to sin she still preserves the appearance of virtue, not only before her husband, whom she betrays, but also before her confessor, the Friar, her tool and accomplice, and even before the very lover to whom she gives herself. This dualism, persistently continued to the end of the play, is as much in the nature of a satire on feminine hypocrisy as part of the portrait of a real woman. Bussy, when once he is Tamyra's lover, cannot refrain from mocking her Puritan scruples, whereupon she tremblingly invokes the God whose wrath she fears, but immediately afterwards, when her husband returns, makes up for her piety by a double dose of lies.

All through these scenes we feel that Chapman is on the brink of a very bold and very penetrating psychological study, but his hand is not sure enough and he deviates into the improbable. The idea of treating frailty and hypocrisy no longer, after the manner of the *fabliaux*, as comic, but as grievous and agonising, is interesting. With a little more knowledge of the heart, Chapman might here have written Shakespearean scenes. But he would first have had to render his Tamyra plausible, and this he fails to do. In the remainder of the play she endures so much torture that she becomes pathetic. Her husband, when he knows himself betrayed, compels her, stabbing her with his dagger, to write a letter which causes Bussy to fall into an ambush. The remorse she still feels wrings from her a cry which is really moving:

> Heaven, I ask thee remission of my sins,
> Not of my pains.

The story of the love of Bussy and Tamyra forms the best part of this unequal tragedy, and deserved to save it from Dryden's absolute condemnation, merited though this be by the copious declaiming of Bussy, whose life certainly gave him no right to the pose of a champion of virtue assigned to him by Chapman. Dryden had Bussy's tirades in mind when he defined this play: "a dwarfish thought, dressed up in gigantic words, repetition in abundance, looseness of expression, and gross hyperboles; the sense of one line expanded prodigiously into ten; and, to sum up all, uncorrect English, and a hideous mingle of false poetry and true nonsense."

As compared with this first play on Bussy, that which shows the hero's revenge is as much less dramatic as it is more reasonable. It is Chapman's *Hamlet*. The hero, this time, is Clermont d'Ambois(e), Bussy's brother, whom Bussy's ghost incites to vengeance, but who is too philosophical not to hold violence in horror, so that he delays long before he accomplishes his task. When he has avenged Bussy he kills himself.

It is something of a surprise to find that Chapman also attempted comedy, and not without success. His best comedies are *All Fools*, printed in 1605, and *Monsieur d'Olive* and the *Gentleman Usher*, published in 1606. Here he abandons his forced, uneasy lyricism, if not his habit of moralising. The value of the plays lies in a certain pleasant romanticism rather than in their character-drawing. *All Fools*, modelled on Terence, is a lesson to fathers: the indulgent and the severe father are painted in contrast, Chapman sympathising with the more benign of the two. *Monsieur d'Olive* is nearer being a comedy of character: it represents a gallant whose unfailing quick-wittedness and coolness are amusing, but who is dropped all too soon in favour of another plot. Chapman's best claim to merit as a writer of comedy rests on his collaboration with Ben Jonson and Marston in *Eastward Ho*, but it is nearly impossible to determine the part he had in the composition of this excellent satire on middle-class manners of which we shall have to speak later.

2. **Ben Jonson (1573?-1637).**[1]—Chapman had almost nothing of the humanist except his erudition. By temperament he was a romantic, and saving when he took a ghost from Seneca or a theme from Terence, he followed the free methods of the popular English theatre. The man who resolutely took up the position of a disciple of the ancients, and attempted, under their inspiration, to reform the English stage, was Ben Jonson. He it is who in his own time and ever afterwards provided the typical antithesis to Shakespeare. The honour is one he deserves, because his works have real value and because his attitude was conspicuous.

His lengthy career as a dramatist (1597-1633), the relatively large amount of extant information regarding his life and character, his combativeness which brought him into conflict with several of his fellow-playwrights, the numerous allusions and satirical portraits in his plays, his expositions of theory and his sarcastic references to his public, perhaps make him, rather than Shakespeare, the rightful centre for a study of Renascence drama. He belongs moreover to the generation, born some ten years after Shakespeare, which was the most prolific of variously talented writers. He was the contemporary of Dekker, Marston, Middleton, Fletcher, Tourneur, Webster and Thomas Heywood, with every one of whom he was connected: he was the friend of some and quarrelled with several others.

In one sense, if the mark of originality be resistance to the general current, he was more original than Shakespeare. Shakespeare accepts the conditions of the stage of his time, is aware of its shortcomings, but resigns himself to them with a smile. His relations with his public remain sympathetic. Jonson, however, is in angry and arrogant opposition to the Elizabethan stage, and sets up his own tastes, ideas and theories, all derived from the ancients, against the popular taste. Shakespeare follows with docility the course of the stream; Jonson flings his vast bulk against it.

A pupil, at Westminster School, of William Camden, the famous antiquary, and a graduate of Cambridge, Jonson was truly learned. Throughout his life he copied into a notebook passages which struck him during his reading of the ancients, and he repeatedly had recourse to these excerpts when he was writing, adapting them, if necessary, to the circumstances of his own time. He was acquainted not only with the great writers of antiquity but also with forgotten, mediocre authors and with the commentators and critics. He was as well read in the historians as in the poets. When he brings antiquity back to life his work is amply documented and he betrays an accurate conception of manners and customs. When he paints the society of his own day, he has made an equally careful preliminary study, notebook in hand, and has, like a modern impressionist, brought together numerous details from the life, picturesque touches, strange things he has seen and speeches —especially foolish speeches—which he has heard.

(a) HIS COMEDIES.—Temperamentally Ben Jonson was a satirist and his education made him a realist. His first play was indeed a half-romantic comedy, *The Case is Altered* (1597), an amalgam of the *Captivi* and the *Aulularia* of Plautus, but in 1598 *Every Man in His Humour*, his first celebrated and really personal work, revealed his true tendencies. Its scene was first laid in Italy, but almost at

---

[1] Ed. by Gifford in 9 vols. (1816); this edition revised by Cunningham in 9 vols. (1875), and in 3 vols. (Chatto and Windus, 1889). Ed. by C. H. Herford, in the Mermaid Series, 3 vols. (1893-4). Critical editions of many plays in Yale Studies. The *Alchemist* and *Eastward Hoe*, ed. by F. E. Schelling in Belles Lettres Series. *Every Man in His Humour*, ed. by Percy Simpson (Oxford University Press, 1919). *Catiline, His Conspiracy*, ed. L. H. Harris (1921).
Studies: M. Castelain, *Ben Jonson: l'Homme et l'Œuvre* (1907); Gregory Smith, *Ben Jonson* (English Men of Letters Series, 1919); Mézières, *Prédécesseurs et contemporains de Shakespeare* (1881); P. Reyher, *Les Masques anglais* (1909); W. Hazlitt, *The English Comic Writers* (ed. 1903); A. C. Swinburne, *A Study of Ben Jonson* (1889); J. A. Symonds, *Ben Jonson* (English Worthies, 1886).

once he changed it to London, showing clearly that the characters he has sketched are English.

We are introduced to a set of eccentrics. Each has his particular "humour," his prevailing mood or rather his oddity, mental habit, or fad. Jonson wishes to make eccentricity the capital characteristic on which all others depend, but it is individual oddities that he mainly portrays. His method is that of Dickens, whose cheerfulness he however lacks, for he is a satirist rather than an amusing writer, and painstaking rather than spontaneous. The fixed, narrow limits of his characterisation were opposed to the uses of his contemporary playwrights, who gave their characters full play, developing them spaciously and endowing them, even to excess, with complexity and the faculty of growth, so that they sometimes became incoherent. These other dramatists made stereotyped oddity the characteristic only of their secondary characters. It was only to the Pistols and the Nyms that Shakespeare gave "humours." Jonson bestows them on all his characters and especially the principals. In his play there is an old gentleman who is exaggeratedly worried because his son, a young poet, is sowing his wild oats: it is the father's "humour" thus to plague himself. There is a merchant whose "humour" it is to be a jealous husband; two young self-confident and foolish fops, the town gull and the country gull, exist but to be duped; an honest, optimistic magistrate has unshakable faith in the virtues of a cup of sack; and Bobadil, a blusterer of a new kind, takes everyone in by his decorous manners, his reticence like that of a man sure of himself, and the calm voice in which he utters his improbable boasts. Bobadil rivals Falstaff in ready lying, but remains a quite distinct and original type.

In that he excludes romanticism and is careful to sustain the comic tone of his comedy, Jonson shows himself the disciple of the ancients. There is no mingling of more sensational elements. He had the sense of the appropriate in so high a degree that in the second edition of his play he eliminated, as too warm in tone and pitched in too lofty a key, an eloquent apology for poetry which occurs in the first edition.

The structure is, however, no closer than elsewhere and no progress towards true unity is evinced. This initial work and the plays which followed it immediately are rather reviews of grotesque types than strongly constructed comedies. It is very remarkable that Jonson assimilated classical qualities only gradually, one by one, it might be said, and never displayed them all in one work. At this stage he could not yet take credit, as he does in the prologue printed in 1616, for having got rid of anything more than the gross licence and puerilities of staging which Sidney had derided.

He was, moreover, self-deceived when he thought that he had substituted real men for stage "monsters." With his inclination to notice only obvious individual peculiarities or the violent actions of exceptional persons, his almost total disregard of fundamental feelings common to mankind and his ignorance of love, Jonson never got near to nature in the classical meaning of the word. To find in his plays a character who is merely a man or a woman is almost impossible. In this, the essential respect, Jonson is far less classical than Shakespeare.

In his later comedies his satirical attitude is accentuated. In *Every Man out of His Humour* he himself is Asper, the harsh and pitiless judge of whatever is ridiculous or vicious, a cynic descended from Diogenes. Like Persius or Juvenal he cries:

> I'll strip the ragged follies of the time,
> Naked, as at their birth,

and

> with a whip of steel
> Print wounding lashes in their iron ribs.

More than one of the grotesques in his play is probably the caricature of an actual person who was recognised by a section of the public. But the portraits undoubtedly exaggerate the eccentricity and extravagance of their subjects: Deliro, the idolising husband consistently rebuffed by his wife; Puntarvolo, the mad, quixotic gentleman who lives a chivalrous romance, entering his house as though it were a strong castle, winding the horn that his door may be opened to him, making his own wife come to the threshold in response to his knight-errant's challenge; Fastidious Brisk, the courtier absorbed by his own dress and fatuous as a Molière marquis, who fights with another courtier a comic duel in which not a drop of blood is shed, but the two lacerate each other's smart clothes and ornaments; Fungoso, the law-student who imitates Fastidious Brisk and extorts money from his father to copy his clothes but can never keep up with his model, who has always adopted a new fashion just when the copy is complete; Sordido, the miserly father and assiduous peruser of almanacks, who thinks of hanging himself in order to prove the prophets wrong.

It is curious to find this extravagance within a realistic framework and introduced in the tones of realism. This play and its predecessor reproduce so much that belongs to the manners of their time, that London and London life in 1600 might be partly reconstituted with their aid. Much trouble and investigation has gone to produce the abundant details, and yet the result is ungrateful, tedious in the extreme, scrappy and seldom amusing. We are surfeited with satire and sigh in vain for a scene which would simply show humanity. The approval which Jonson constantly claims from his audience, and his ill-will to everyone and everything and faith in himself and his own superiority are moreover irritating. His preoccupation with himself is in contrast to the modesty with which Shakespeare invariably sinks his personality in his work, is never to be found or seen. Jonson deems his personal quarrels interesting enough to furnish scenes for his plays or even whole plays. He, the representative of reason, morality and knowledge, does not fear to bring his enemies upon the stage. Cynthia's Revels (1601) and, even more, The Poetaster (1602) are so many acts of homage to himself, not to mention the prologues, epilogues and inductions in which he obtrudes his personality.

In The Poetaster he is Horace, whose friend is Virgil, whose admirer is Augustus, and to whom the bad poets Crispinus (Marston) and Demetrius (Dekker) are jealous enemies. Nothing opposes him save foolishness, envy and malignity. The whole of this Roman allegory is constructed for the author's greater glory. Latin poetry is used to provide him with a sort of apotheosis. The aggressive character of his early work connects him with ancient Greek comedy, with Aristophanes and his direct and personal satires. But, unlike the Greek dramatist, Jonson is incapable of generalising his antipathies, of transforming them into broad lessons on politics and morality.

These plays do not represent the whole of Jonson's achievement. The series of his personal plays provoked retorts from Marston and Dekker and mainly gave matter for what has been called the War of the Theatres, each antagonist having his playhouse whence he let fire on the enemy. Subsequently Jonson rose to the level both of tragedy and of high comedy. The great comedies of the period of his maturity, Volpone, or the Fox (1605), Epicœne, or the Silent Woman (1609), The Alchemist (1610) and Bartholomew Fair (1614), are among the most remarkable of the dramatic works of the English Renascence.

In these he does not merely pass types of eccentricity in review. He turns his powerful intellect to the construction of his plays and endeavours to make them strong as Roman buildings. Far from drawing on the old repertory of subjects, according to Shakespeare's habit, he invents everything, his matter, plot and characters, which are in turn the creations of his logical mind and the fruits of his direct observation of eccentricities.

Of all these plays, it is *Volpone* which is the most powerful and also most in the tradition of the morality-plays. It is a violent attack, not unreminiscent of Marlowe's extravagance, on cupidity and mean avarice and Machiavellism. Since it contains hardly anything to balance its display of vices, the view it gives of human nature is cynical, analogous to that so persistently put forward by the French *théâtre rosse* of the end of last century, for which school of drama Jonson might have provided most striking models.

Volpone is a Venetian magnifico, old, rich, childless and a passionate devotee of every form of enjoyment, in particular the enjoyment of gold. Surrounded by false friends anxious to inherit from him, he gives out that he is dying, and by persuading each of them that he is the heir designate obtains magnificent presents from them all. Any one of them, out of a frenzied cupidity equal to Volpone's own, is capable of sacrificing honour, child or wife to his chance of engrossing the inheritance. Between Volpone, the Fox, and these appropriately named beasts of prey —the lawyer, Voltore or Vulture, the dying Corbaccio or Old Crow, and the Merchant, Corvino or Little Crow—the intermediary is Mosca or Fly, Volpone's parasite and a trimmer of infinite resource. There is something famished and superhuman in the passion of all these characters. Volpone's thirst for gold is as vehement, if not as poetic, as that which torments Marlowe's Jew of Malta. Yet the enormity of the fraud he has organised is an even greater joy to him than his gold. For sheer ferocity, no scene has ever surpassed that in which the aged, crippled, blear-eyed Corbaccio, with one foot in the grave, comes to sniff at the body of the man whose death he has discounted, or that other scene in which Corvino, whom a trifle has roused to vent a fit of terrible jealousy on his wife, the pure Celia, drags her, by threats and violence, to the presence of Volpone, who has made this surrender a condition of the succession to his property. In yet another and no less ferocious scene, Volpone, who has been given up to justice, is shown standing his trial. Each of his dupes comes forward to speak for him, each of them warmly eloquent, improving on the statements of the rival he uneasily watches, and inventing the most abominable lies, even against a son or a wife, to exculpate the accused man.

The playwright's vigour, his clever manipulation of the threads of his plot and the strong construction render almost credible the inhuman situation which is the subject of the play. But its success is void of the element of fun, for the atrocity of the satire excludes laughter. In *Epicœne*, however, Jonson aims at producing merriment. For once he sacrifices his moral to his design of pleasing the public. The play is intended, he says,

> . . . for ladies; some for lords, knights, 'squires;
> Some for your waiting wench, and city wives;
> Some for your men, and daughters of Whitefriars.

He has suddenly passed from one extreme to the other. His theme is no longer execrable vice, but a whim, an oddity. Fundamentally *Epicœne* is of the nature of a farce, but it is at least as robustly constructed as *Volpone*, so that Dryden regarded it as the model of a well-made comedy. The chief character is Morose, an egoistical bachelor who nowadays would be called a neurasthenic. His special "humour" is his abhorrence of noise. He lives in a blind alley, and makes war on all who cry their wares in the street, has his front-door muffled, keeps his shutters closed, and quilts his staircase. His servants have orders to answer him only by signs: his own voice is the only noise he will tolerate. Jonson took this character not from

I—U

real life, but from the pages of the Greek rhetorician Libanius, and he lodged him in London among thoroughly English eccentrics.

The subject of the comedy is Morose's marriage to a young girl reputed to be always silent. He marries her in order to disinherit his nephew to whom he has taken a dislike. But the girl has been secretly chosen for his uncle by this mischievous nephew, and she is no sooner married than she proves talkative and noisy to the last degree. The wedding is an excuse for a boisterous hubbub which maddens the old man. He wants a divorce before the day is out, and pretexts for it are vainly sought in a learnedly grotesque consultation with pretended lawyers. Finally the nephew agrees to save his uncle in return for a goodly sum of money, paid cash down, and reveals that the bride is a youth disguised for the occasion.

The situation lends itself to scenes of pure clowning: Morose is surrounded by a most heteroclite company all, naturally, as noisy as they can be—a barber, a coxcomb, an amateur of sport and a whole society of *précieuses ridicules*. Energetically, perhaps too assiduously, the play calls for laughter. Even when he is writing farce, Jonson is weighted with the spoils of his learned reading and the raw scraps of realism which he pours into his prose. The fruits of his observation mingle strangely with curiosities he has culled from the ancients. He is too little spontaneous; like Flaubert, he is too industrious and too learned to evoke light laughter.

In *The Alchemist* he returns to satirical comedy. Once more he is denouncing rogues. Face, a servant, brings a swindler named Subtle to his master's house while the latter is absent in London. Subtle poses as an alchemist, and the hope of the philosopher's stone causes men of every kind to have resort to him—a lawyer's clerk, a tobacco-merchant and a great gentleman, Sir Epicure Mammon, who is constantly preoccupied by dreams of magnificence and voluptuous desires. Among these seekers after gold are two Puritan Brethren of Amsterdam who give the playwright his first real chance to ridicule the sect hostile to the stage. In this remarkably constructed comedy, which, unlike its predecessors, has a theme of lasting interest longer-lived than alchemy—the exploitation of the foolish and the vicious by unscrupulous rogues who dazzle them with riches—prominence is chiefly given to the rhetoric of Sir Epicure, whose rodomontade recalls Marlowe, and to the intrigues of the Puritans. The whole of this nascent sect is resumed in the sinuous, politic and adroit Parson Tribulation Wholesome and in the stupid, violent, uncompromising Deacon Ananias, whom, not without difficulty, the parson forces to accept the doctrine that the end justifies the means. Ananias is horrified at the idea of having recourse to a pagan like Subtle, but Tribulation reproaches him for ill-timed zeal and pictures to him their sect enriched and made powerful by gold, no longer obliged to intrigue pettily and fish for small bequests. Finally, after prayer and fasting, the Brethren of Amsterdam decide that they will avail themselves of the alchemist's services. In the end duper and dupes are, needless to say, duly punished.

Bartholomew Fair returns, with more insistence, to the attack on Puritanism. The chief character is Rabbi Zeal-of-the-Land Busy, a man of low origin who has acquired a great renown for sanctity and who, like Molière's Tartufe in Orgon's family, has wormed himself into the confidence of the well-to-do Widow Purecraft until nothing is done in her household without his advice. Thus, when Mrs. Littlewit, the daughter of the house, is seized with a longing to eat pig from the fair, Busy's consent is first asked and is given on condition the pig "be eaten with a reformed mouth." Everyone then sets out for the fair, where Busy guzzles more than anyone else, and in his cups upsets a hawker's basket of gingerbread, which he calls a "basket of popery." He is put in the stocks, and concludes by interrupting a puppet-show which he regards as a symbol of the public stage, that abomination of abominations.

Jonson certainly wrote nothing more entertaining than this play. It would, however, have been more completely diverting had he drawn his Puritan more decidedly, had he not made him, by turns or simultaneously, an arrant hypocrite and an enthusiast as convinced as ridiculous. He should have chosen one or other of these alternatives. Similarly, his Mistress Purecraft is both a good and pious dupe and an intriguing widow to whom religion is a means to remarriage. These inconsistencies spoil the most animated and swarming, although far from the noblest, of Jonson's plays. The fair gives him an excuse for introducing a whole rabble of sharpers, vagabonds and ruffians and a whole troop of boobies, oddities and madcaps who haunt the stalls. All his comedies are rich in details taken from life and glimpses of actual manners, but no other as much so as *Bartholomew Fair,* for which he certainly made copious notes on the spot.

It was the last of his great comedies. After its appearance he ceased for nine years to work for the stage, and resumed playwriting as an older and enfeebled man of lessened powers, producing five further plays in the period cruelly called his dotage. They are the *Devil is an Asse* (1616), the *Staple of News* (1625), the *New Inn* (1629), the *Magnetic Lady* (1632) and *A Tale of a Tub* (1633). Mediocre though they be, the observation they show of manners and passing fashions makes them interesting to this day to the social historian.

(b) HIS ROMAN TRAGEDIES.—Jonson made two attempts at historical tragedy, his *Sejanus* (1603) and his *Catiline* (1611). Both, but especially the first, were inspired by the desire to emulate Shakespeare, the great success of whose *Julius Cæsar*, in 1601, had proved that the public could be interested in a subject taken from ancient history. Jonson was conscious that his knowledge of Roman history was far more exact than his rival's. He must have laughed at Shakespeare's anachronisms, if they did not scandalise him. Shakespeare's Rome was London, and he had a very scanty and inaccurate knowledge of Roman customs and manners, of all that goes to make local colour. His only guide was Plutarch, who is a psychologist and moralist first of all, who writes of a period remote from his own and who, further, is a Greek, all of which prevents him from paying attention to scenery.

Shakespeare's shortcomings were supplied by Ben Jonson, whose tragedies are completely historical, reinforced by a thousand accurate details taken from the many and various poets and historians he had read. He studs his *Sejanus* with translated quotations, small incidents and curious touches borrowed from the authors of the period: Suetonius, Juvenal, Tacitus and Seneca. When he published the play he could cite the very editions which had been his sources. But while Shakespeare chose a subject familiar to everyone who had any culture at all, one made illustrious by the names of Cæsar, Brutus, Antony and Octavius and centring round the most famous episode in Roman history, Cæsar's murder in full Senate, Ben Jonson's erudite reading and disdain of the immediately popular turned his choice to the far less known career of Sejanus, whose triumph and fall he depicts. With his dominantly satirical temperament, he was attracted to this episode of the Roman decadence which shows vice and meanness conspicuously, rather than to the grandeur of such a struggle as that between a Cæsar and a Brutus.

It is in truth especially by his learning that Ben Jonson is removed from his forerunner. It would be false to think that he attempted to bring classical unity back into historical drama. He too used the expedient of a series of great, animated pictures, and they are neither less numerous nor less various than Shakespeare's. The action of his plays is perhaps a little closer knit, but this is a difference not of kind but of degree. It might even be said that Jonson gives more space than

Shakespeare to homely scenes in the spirit of harsh, satirical comedy. No less than Shakespeare does he depart from the type of tragedy which *Gorboduc* inaugurated and Sidney recommended. His ambition to be an historian, to reproduce the manners and customs of imperial Rome faithfully, made a number of separate scenes even more necessary to him than to Shakespeare.

Sejanus is so strongly constructed, presents history so honestly, and is so full of vigorous and exact touches, that it cannot be read even to-day without respect for the author's learning and energy of mind. He reproduces forcefully the umbrageous, perfidious, cringing, sinuous Tiberius who enjoys watching popular hatred accumulate against his favourite, and delivers that unfortunate to the people as soon as he begins to fear him. Jonson supplies a moral explanation of the fall of Sejanus in his impiety—his mockery of all the deities save the goddess Fortune, to whom indeed he renders homage, but whose images he throws down when she answers his prayer unfavourably. The philosophy of Sejanus is, like that of Marlowe's sinners, Machiavellian. With special force Jonson paints imperial corruption and the plague of informers. His pictures of manners overshadow his character-drawing. Thus we have the scene in which Livia plots the murder of her husband Drusus with Sejanus and her doctor Eudemus, and discourses learnedly of make-up and rouge while she continues her toilet; the scene in which an agent of the emperor, after hiding informers behind the door, entraps the honourable Sabinus by declaiming against tyranny in his presence, until he too begins a rebellious speech, at the first word of which he is led off to the Gemoniæ; and finally the famous scene in which the tortuous letter of Tiberius is read to the senate and the anxious servility of the senators is displayed as, one after the other, they fawn on Sejanus, then shun him like the plague, and finally, with one accord, clamour for his death.

Everywhere there is strength, dignity, knowledge—indeed too much knowledge, too much erudition, too much massive, dull speechifying. The sources of true dramatic emotion are never sounded. Thus Sejanus is shown arranging with Livia the disappearance of Drusus, whom they decide to murder, but there is no scene to show Sejanus persuading Livia to this act, the scene to which a Shakespeare or a Racine would have given precedence over all others, making it the great moment of the play. The psychology of *Sejanus* is little less elementary than that of the moralities, which divided mankind into good and bad. None of the characters goes through any interior conflict. The honest senators are not tempted, the informers suffer no remorse. The characters are very close to history, too close perhaps, for they remain remote from us. They are not brought nearer by imagination and dramatic sympathy.

Jonson, on his own confession, felt some repentance for his transgression of classical laws in this play, the liberties he took with the unity of time and his failure to use choruses. He did better in *Catiline*, in which he announces his intention to be correct and draws nearer to Seneca. This tragedy opens with a speech by Sulla's shade, who appears to Catiline. Each act, except the last, ends with a chorus. The subject, confined to Catiline's conspiracy without going back to its causes, is more restricted in time. But these entirely external differences do not prevent this play from being cast in the mould traditional in England. It is divided into twenty scenes. Its action is less straightforward than that of *Sejanus*, because in the two first acts Jonson transposes history for the purposes of poetry and satire, while in the other three he follows history step by step, so literally that he reproduces Cicero's first Catilinarian oration almost in its entirety. Faithfulness in this part of the play is very like slavishness.

On the whole, *Catiline* is inferior to *Sejanus*. The characters are drawn less vigorously and clearly. It is impossible to tell whether Catiline be actuated by cupidity, anger or love for his mistress Orestilla. Does he really love Orestilla or does he make her his tool? We do not know. Cicero is as wordy and complex as history shows him. He retains all the vagueness of mere history, for Jonson does not so much interpret documents as empty their contents into his tragedy. No light supplied by the poet is shed on the actors in the drama, whose figures are clear or dim as history left them, even such confused history as that constituted by the conflicting narratives of Cicero and Sallust.

In this imperfect play there is, however, one whole act which is as much of a success as anything Ben Jonson ever wrote. It is the second act, which was invented by the playwright and illustrates the same truth as Scribe's *Verre d'eau*, namely that the greatest events of history sometimes have the most trifling causes.

How was the conspiracy discovered? To tell us this, Jonson transports us to the house of the young and beautiful courtesan Fulvia. She is jealous of Sempronia, a scholarly and lettered patrician who makes up for her faded charms by her wit and her hospitable table. Sempronia, visiting Fulvia, recommends Catiline as a candidate for the consulate, and no more is needed to secure him the courtesan's ill-will. Her lover is Curius, who happens to be among the conspirators and whom she dismisses because he is ruined. He thereupon breaks into vague threats, telling her she will wish him back, for presently he will be one of the masters of Rome. Her countenance changes; she recalls him, and with flattery and caresses extorts from him his secret, giving him her love once more on condition that he betray Catiline. Thus Cicero is warned and enabled to compass the ruin of the conspirators. These cynical scenes are in Jonson's most spirited vein, already displayed when he was writing *Volpone*. Ferocious satire is the special distinguishing mark of his talent, and recurs at the most impressive moments of his tragedies as of his comedies.

Yet there was a poet in this robust and harsh writer. The fact becomes clear as we read his fragment of a pastoral, the *Sad Shepherd, or a Tale of Robin Hood*, in which he pleasantly disposes factitious pastoral graces about the popular archer and his companions. It is made even clearer by the numerous masques which he wrote for the court of James I. No one composed a greater number of books of words for the magnificent operas which were then the supreme luxury of the king and his lords. No one turned them more cleverly, wrote them better or gave them more variety or charm. The blunt-speaking playwright whose blank verse was hard, unpliable and without ring, had an unexpected facility when he was busy over these diversions in which allegory, mythology and the fairy-tale reigned. Many songs and short lyrics can be culled from them to protest against the too narrow judgment we might be tempted to pass on his otherwise massive and prosaic spirit. Poetry must indeed have been in the air in those days. How otherwise could it have lodged, abundantly and in endearing guise, in a corner of the work of this robust craftsman whose cynical realism inclined him to prose? His nature was broader and richer than appears from his theories. He was capable of such lyrical fancy as Molière, in a more sober age, never matched.

3. **John Marston (1575?-1634).**[1]—Of the two dramatists against whom Jonson was most implacable early in the seventeenth century, Marston and Dekker, Marston engaged him most and received his hardest knocks. The conflict was between two satirical, arrogant men, of whom Marston was foul-tongued into the bargain. His first literary essay was the collection of satires or rather coarse insults called the *Scourge of Villainy* (1598), of which we have already spoken. Subsequently, for eight or nine years, he tried his fortunes in drama, and met with

---

[1] Works edited by Bullen, 3 vols. (1887).

very fair success before he abandoned writing entirely and gave himself up to a long, silent ecclesiastical career.

His dramatic production belongs to the most glorious and most intensely active period. Although an industrious student, his temperament inclined him to romantic drama. Yet shreds of the garment of Seneca clung to him, notably the ghost he took from Seneca's *Thyestes* and the conceptions of atrocious vengeance and of the horror of crime. He might, however, have found all this equally well in Kyd and Marlowe, and his first tragedies, *Antonio and Mellida* and, even more, *Antonio's Revenge*, show the influence of the *Spanish Tragedie*. Here, as in his satires, Marston seems to wish to attract attention by the most tumultuous violence, by using more furious and eccentric language and greater coarseness than any other writer. A contemporary comic author calls him "a ruffian in his style." Since elsewhere he gives unquestionable proofs of vigour of mind, it is his sincerity, rather than his talent, which is suspect. He declaims more rabidly than Marlowe, describes with metaphors almost as foggy and disjointed as Chapman's, piles up pedantic, trivial and mouthfilling words. This is the very Crispinus caricatured by Jonson in *The Poetaster*, who, after a dose, vomits up a fantastic rigmarole. Marston's description of a storm in *Antonio and Mellida* is an example of his extravagant bad taste. Yet there is something impressive in his very turgidity. The description which opens the prologue to *Antonio's Revenge* is hardly less exaggerated, but it leads up to lines so powerful that Lamb admired the whole with reason, as a fit prelude to a story which might be classed with the tales of Theban atrocity or the legend of Pelops. Marston's most detestably emphatic passages are interspersed with nervous eloquence. Similarly, his most sombre melodrama is lit up by flashes of true poetry, as in that scene of the *Revenge* (Act III.) in which, in a graveyard at midnight, Antonio strangles a little boy who is the youthful son of his father's murderer, whom he has hitherto treated as a brother and who trusts him entirely. The ghost of Antonio's father cries out for vengeance and shames him out of his pity. These romantic shudders connect Marston with Kyd and Webster.

There is also much of Shakespeare in him, or rather, since *Antonio's Revenge* is possibly prior to *Hamlet*, he has more than one point of contact with Shakespeare. This is even more apparent in his comedy, *The Malcontent* (1601?), than in his tragedies. He introduces into this play a character who ironically comments on actions and personalities, underlines whatever is ridiculous or vicious, and deals blows right and left, and who voices Marston's own pessimism and cynical view of human motives. *The Malcontent* might be called a *Hamlet* which only a happy ending saves from tragedy. In some respects it also anticipates *Measure for Measure* and even *The Tempest*.

The Malcontent is a Duke of Genoa who has, owing to his over-trusting disposition, allowed himself to be supplanted by a usurper. He returns to his duchy in the guise of a cynic, becomes the usurper's helper, reveals to him the plots hatched against him, and takes his part when he in his turn falls from power. Finally the usurper, having suffered a change of heart, cedes his place to the Malcontent, who, with contemptuous clemency which foreshadows Prospero, grants a general pardon to the guilty. The interest of this ill-constructed comedy, with its very romantic episodes, lies in the sneers and the invectives of the Malcontent. The play centres in this true satirist who inveighs against all and sundry and proffers cynical reflections. It has, moreover, here and there, striking situations of which some are new. There is a scene, recalled by Jonson in *Sejanus*, in which the courtiers crowd round the Malcontent when he is in favour, but leave him shamelessly when the duke looks coldly at him; and another in which the usurper's wife, who with her lover has plotted his death, hears at a court ball the false news that he is dead and interrupts her informer by calling for music. Ford remembered this last incident when he wrote the *Broken Heart*. Over and over again in this play there are bold and compact touches. The sarcasm which was to be Hamlet's is expressed more vulgarly and often coarsely. The Malcontent, consoling the usurper for the loss of the duchy, exhorts him as follows: "Come, be not confounded. . . . Think this: this earth is the only grave and Golgotha wherein all things that live must rot; 'tis but the draught wherein the heavenly bodies discharge their corruption; the very muck-hill on which the sublunary orbs cast their excrements."

The work is on the whole unpleasing, obscure in style and muddled in construction, but it is forceful, varied and not without interest. It proves that plays of the type of *Hamlet* were popular before the appearance of the ultimate *Hamlet* which was Shakespeare's. It seems to have been Marston who introduced the fashion of inveighing against society and life in a mood of lyrical irony. He attempts to outdo others by shouting louder than they. He often recalls or anticipates Shakespearean subjects, and for moments at a time he does not lose too much by the consequent comparison.

Marston's other comedies are less gloomy and have, as well as more cheerfulness, some flashes of tenderness. The *Dutch Courtesan* (1604) is a pendant to Dekker's *Honest Whore*, and the order in which the two plays appeared is doubtful. The heroine is no penitent Magdalen, cleansing her soul by sacrifice, but a passionate and potentially criminal woman.

Francischina, a courtesan, has for some time been loved by young Freevill, a libertine who has sown his wild oats and aspires to the hand of a pure young girl, Beatrice. He introduces the courtesan to one of his friends, an austere and morose young man named Malheureux, who falls in love with her at first sight. But she is still in love with Freevill and is furious at the thought of his approaching marriage. She wants to get him back and rejects the advances of Malheureux until, seeing that all her efforts are vain, she tries to use her suitor to compass the death of the lover she has lost. But Malheureux is no criminal: he warns Freevill, who agrees to disappear temporarily in order that his friend may announce his death to Francischina and receive her promised reward. She, however, like another Hermione, has no sooner heard that Freevill is slain than she gives way to grief and anger. She wants to have Malheureux hanged, and only Freevill's return saves him.

Meanwhile the course of Freevill's love for Beatrice has been crossed as the result of Franceschina's plotting and his own desire to put his beloved to trial. Beatrice believes that Freevill is dead and has been unfaithful. She is miserable and has thoughts of killing herself, but in the end everything turns out well.

In spite of the happy ending, there is little of comedy about the plot. Yet the play, which aims chiefly at affording amusement, never greatly disturbs equanimity and is really diverting. The principal plot is relieved by another, purely farcical, which shows a sharper's tricks, the practical jokes played by the rogue Cockledemoy on a miserly, stupid and ridiculous citizen. Miscellaneous obscenities are scattered here and there and spoken by episodic characters.

The psychology is slight and the portrait of the courtesan rudimentary, yet there is something of everything in this play, even feeling and grace. Marston professes a desire to contrast the purity of legitimate love with the base and dangerous love of courtesans. His Beatrice is not without charm and Freevill courts her with a certain warmth.

The most individualised character is, however, Crispinella, Beatrice's younger sister. This child of fifteen, small of stature, terrifyingly outspoken, an innocent girl who talks like a trooper, who calls a spade a spade and utters everything she knows or thinks, is the ancestress of all the alarmingly frank young people of Restoration comedies. Marston is, naturally, too foul-mouthed to keep her within the limits beyond which frankness of this kind is disgusting rather than amusing. But he makes it very clear that, for all her loose talk, he intends to preserve both the true virginity and the real goodness of heart of his Crispinella. Artistically, her chief defect is that she is too self-conscious, too cognisant of her implications, yet she has to her credit some spontaneous, apposite and amusing sayings.

She was certainly inspired by the witty and incisive Beatrice of *Much Ado about Nothing*, and her relations with her elder sister recall those of Beatrice with her cousin Hero. It is a great pity that this happily conceived character is often soiled by cynicism, to the detriment of the pleasure which decent people might otherwise derive from her.

The same coarseness mars the *Parasitaster or the Fawn*, of which the idea is ingenious. The Duke of Ferrara is distressed by the coldness of his son Tiberio, who will not consent to marriage even with the fair Dulcimella, daughter of Gonzago, Duke of Urbino. The duke pretends to ask her hand for himself, and sends Tiberio to Urbino as his ambassador. Meanwhile, like the Malcontent, he adopts a disguise. As the Fawn, a privileged cynic, he establishes himself in Gonzago's court both to watch over his son and to observe the manners of the courtiers. There are curious sights to be seen there, and some ugly characters—an abominably jealous husband whom his virtuous wife at last succeeds in taming, a man who brags of his love affairs in high places and has in fact lost his heart to a washerwoman, a youthful courtier who declares his passion to all the ladies indiscriminately.

Dulcimella has, however, fallen in love with Tiberio. To impart warmth to this icy suitor, she uses the same device as Molière's Agnes, making Gonzago, her foolish father, her go-between. He conveys to the young man her pretended anger at his attempts to win her, and thus instructs him in the course he should pursue. In this way she makes sure of getting him for her husband.

To sum up: this play contains a successful comic character—old Gonzago, the solemn idiot, reminiscent of Justice Shallow and Polonius, who never doubts his own sagacity even when he is being led by the nose—and some pretty love-scenes between Dulcimella and Tiberio. Dulcimella is like a coarse copy of one of Shakespeare's daring heroines. She has none of their poetry and not more than a quarter of their wit.

Marston's signature is also affixed to a powerful play, *The Insatiate Countess*, which depicts the furious love-affairs of a woman of the Messalina type and was printed in 1613. This work seems, however, to owe far less to Marston than to the actor William Barkstead who was his collaborator.

Marston is, further, one of the three signatories of *Eastward Ho* (1605), a play which is among the best of the Renascence comedies and which he wrote in collaboration with Chapman and Jonson. This work, which unites qualities evinced in none of the plays written by its authors separately, is curious. It is difficult to distinguish what each contributed to it, but certainly Chapman nowhere else shows such vigour and realism, Jonson so much light-heartedness or Marston such decency.

The very simple theme recalls the moralities. The industrious and the idle apprentice are drawn side by side, and they furnished Hogarth, when the play was revived in the eighteenth century, with the subject of one of his best-known pictures.

Touchstone, a very worthy city goldsmith, has two apprentices, the dissipated and extravagant Quicksilver who spends his leisure among gamesters and tipplers, and the orderly, respectable and virtuous Golding. Quicksilver, drunken and insolent, is suspected of theft and turned away, and he afterwards lives by his wits, is thrown into prison and is in danger of the gallows. He is, however, saved by his repentance, his piety during his imprisonment and Golding's intervention, and in the end meets no worse fate than marriage with a girl he has debauched. Golding, meanwhile, receives the hand of his master's younger daughter, becomes a deputy-alderman and judges his fellow-apprentice, saving him out of the goodness of his heart. He is a model apprentice, model son-in-law, model husband and model friend.

The two apprentices are balanced by Touchstone's two daughters, the younger well-behaved, sweet-tempered and modest; the elder, a minx, ambitious to be fashionable, who, with the connivance of her pretentious mother, marries not an honest apprentice, like her sister, but a certain Sir Petronel Flash, a regular adventurer. She flatters herself that she will ride in her coach and be mistress of a fine house. But the house is Sir Petronel's invention, and while she is journeying thither very dashingly, having first shown her contempt for her citizen family, Petronel is planning to flee to Virginia with her dowry. He is put into prison, and vanity is duly brought low, the elder sister being obliged to implore mercy from the younger and from her father, to both of whom she has been amply disdainful.

This morality-play has much animation. It affords some vivid glimpses—the apprentices living in their master's household, the interior of his shop, vainglorious Gertrude starting off in her coach, dazzling all the neighbours. The apprentice Quicksilver, an assiduous playgoer, recites lines from the *Spanish Tragedie* in his cups. In a tavern the madcaps of the town are seen all agape while Captain Seagull relates to them the marvels of Virginia, where the first settlers were soon to meet with an evil fate.

In a scene laid by the Thames, Sir Petronel and Quicksilver, the one as drunk as the other, plunge into the water during a storm in order to swim to Captain Seagull's ship, and are cast up on to the river-bank. Still fuddled, they imagine that they have landed in France.

The drawing of the characters, especially the less virtuous of them, is vigorous, Quicksilver with his scapegrace high spirits, his rascality and his conversion and the moral ballads in which he embodies his adventures for the edification of his prison-mates; Gertrude with the airs she gives herself and the romantic dreams in which she still indulges long after misfortune has overtaken her: these are memorable portraits.

There is throughout this play a lively realism which gains credence for the moral concealed beneath its varied and comic incidents. And all goes merrily forward to the end. No structural devices obtrude themselves.

Whatever part Marston may have had in the writing of this play, it does him greater credit than any which he produced by himself. Nevertheless, these last also, in spite of the extravagance of some and the crudity of all and their element of imitation, are proof that the playwright possessed an incisive, nervous and often original talent which was of service to several of his contemporaries.

4. **Thomas Dekker (1570?–1641).**[1]—Although Jonson associated Marston and Dekker in his attacks, they are no less different from each other than they are from him. Both of them did indeed write plays in which all the liberty and also all the licence of the English stage are to be found, but while Marston's habitual cynicism and pessimism connect him with Jonson, there is in Dekker's work a vein of poetry and optimism, a tenderness and charm, which the other two play-wrights lack. While Marston and Jonson are, like Chapman, manifestly under the influence of Marlowe with his passionate rhetoric and violent and excessive

[1] *The Dramatic Works of Thomas Dekker,* reprinted by Pearson, 4 vols. (1873). Selected works in the Mermaid Series, ed. Rhys (1895); *Shoemaker's Holiday,* ed. Warnke and Proescholdt (Halle, 1886); *Old Fortunatus,* ed. Smeaton in the Temple Dramatists (1906); Jonson's *Poetaster* and Dekker's *Satiromastix* in the Belles Lettres Series (1913).

characterisation, Dekker takes us back to Robert Greene, who, in spite of the air of pedantry intermittently imparted to his style by too much mythology, was the one of the earlier dramatists least disturbed by the Renascence and most independent of antiquity. Dekker is in the succession to Greene by his prose writings, which are for the most part pictures of life among the London populace, the low life of the town with its misery, vice and eccentricities. In many little street scenes this author, who had to boil his pot, has assembled the results of his own observation and of his reading of the satirists, has collected pithy sayings and good-tempered jokes. He is something of an improviser and an artist only by snatches, but he is alive and spontaneous; his pen runs easily and he is pleasing.

His plays also connect him with Greene. A composite romanticism was inherent in him: he rebelled against all law, mingled elements taken from any and every source, combined homely realism with the immoderately romantic. He recalls Greene by the freshness of some of his scenes, and by his joy in life which endured through an existence prolonged in poverty from day to day, and even through the gloom of a debtors' prison. Like Greene, he excels at creating gentle, feeling women who are devoted and tender. He had, however, an advantage over Greene in that, when he began to write plays, English drama was no longer in a rudimentary state, but was completely constituted, fully organic and experienced. Even for his most loosely written improvisation, this progress was of service to Dekker.

Nothing is known of him, but it may be suspected that he sprang from the people of London and was irregularly educated. London was often his theme and the citizens were always his public. He wrote for the stage from 1597 onwards, at first as a subordinate. He was several times in prison, once for three years, from 1613 to 1616. From 1638 all trace of him is lost.

Ben Jonson's attacks give glimpses of him. In his person Jonson regarded him as a poor devil, down at heels and out at elbows, a jaundiced vagabond, and in his author's capacity as a "play-dresser and plagiary," a complete ignoramus without Greek or Latin, fatuous and jealous into the bargain, and willing to do anything for money. His representative on Jonson's stage is hired in order to insult Horace, who is Jonson himself. His foolish inventions are said to be growing apace like ill weeds. To this Dekker retorts by an amusing picture of the arrogant Horace-Jonson sweating in travail as he produces an ode and seeks for rhymes.

This poor ignorant wretch, this patcher and piecer, has, however, certain advantages over Jonson. More than he and as much as anyone else in this period, he has the gifts of grace and freshness. No burden of reading weighs him down. No habit of analysis cumbers him, and at his best he reproduces the animation of life very directly. He dramatises persons who live and awaken sympathy. On occasion, he has the lyrical gift; from time to time he sings a song which is winged, light and exquisite. While he hardly ever makes a unified and well-constructed play, while he has little logic and coherence and no philosophy whatsoever, he yet stands in this age for the dramatic poet who is so by instinct, who is of the people and artlessly romantic.

Impecunious as he was, he was all his life obliged to collaborate with anyone and everyone, with mediocre playwrights like Chettle, Haughton and Day, with the most famous of them all—Jonson himself, Middleton, Drayton and especially Webster—and later with Rowley, Ford and Massinger. He did not often have time to work as an artist and by himself. Only some eight or nine plays written by him alone are preserved and the merit of only four of these is eminent: the *Shomakers Holiday* (1599), *Old Fortunatus* (1600) and the two parts of the *Honest Whore* (1604).

This child of London writes especially of London and for the cockney people. Others were doubtless painting very lively pictures of the city at the same time, but they worked in a satirical or derisory spirit. Jonson displays the vices and oddities of the town. Beaumont, in the *Knight of the Burning Pestle*, makes fun of the unsophisticated ignorance of the citizens and their romantic imagination. Middleton shows himself intimately acquainted with the deeds and ways of rogues and gallants. But Dekker is, with Thomas Heywood, almost alone in his sympathy for the world of the craftsmen and the ragtag and bobtail of the streets.

The constant quarrels between the companies of actors and the civic authorities must not give the impression that the mass of the citizens were hostile to the stage The contrary is true of all save the still narrow circle of the devout. The city as a whole was stage-struck, to such a point that poets, laureates and dramatists had arisen to work specially for the citizens, pamper their tastes and vanity, and hold up on the stage a flattering mirror in which they saw their own embellished reflection. Dekker was one of their authors, but he had a natural love for the task which was to others a mere source of profit.

The powerful livery companies, proud of their wealth, numbers and origin, had, exactly like the nobility, both a semi-legendary history and historians. Deloney traced the glorious annals of the Drapers and the Shoemakers, beginning with the lives of their patron saints and ending with his own time. We have seen how spiritedly he combined realistic anecdotes and ancient tradition when he told the story of Simon Eyre, the glorious shoemaker of the reign of Henry VI., who from a mere apprentice became Lord Mayor, built the leather-market in Leadenhall, and founded a holiday and banquet for the apprentices. Dekker dramatised Deloney's novel. He makes Simon Eyre his hero, takes us into his shop and introduces us to his wife and workpeople. Life in the workshop is not all a virtuous idyll, for Dame Margerie, Eyre's wife, is crabbed and vain, the workmen quarrel among themselves and even with their master, and while the foreman is steady and self-possessed, the second is a drunken wag and a mischievous scamp. But merriment and heartiness are dominant. Simon Eyre's own jovial temper makes him unique; his very insults sound cordial. His language is emphatic and nonsensical as Pistol's, for he has learnt long words in the playhouses without understanding them, and uses them constantly, perpetrating many malapropisms. Simon Eyre is always in a good temper, in magnificent health, and fond as an apprentice or a sheriff of eating and drinking. His good fortune fills him with joy, but neither bridles his tongue nor lessens his jollity. He always treats his men as brothers, drinks and jokes with them and in his own way loves them. He is the king of London apprentices, and celebrates his accession by raining cakes and ale upon them.

Only an open, slightly superficial nature could so overflow with cheerful merriment. Shakespeare was incapable of gaiety so unthinking; moral reflections, not without sadness, are cast on his Falstaff, who belongs to exactly the same year as Simon Eyre.

Dekker is always in the sun, always enjoying a trivial, easygoing cheerfulness. He does not trouble to explain Simon Eyre's rise, cares nothing for the real psychological problem. He does not drain his cup, but merely sips its froth.

He heightens the impression of facile happiness by the love-story of the principal plot. Lacy, nephew of the Earl of Lincoln, loves Rose, the Lord Mayor's daughter. Both earl and mayor oppose the match from pride of class. Lacy then deserts the regiment he commands, letting it go to fight in France without him, and disguised as a Flemish workman he works for Simon Eyre in order to be near his beloved. He ends, of course, by running away with her, and the father and uncle, after holding out for some time, are reconciled by the king.

Dekker's cheerfulness is everywhere, like an atmosphere about the play, like sunlight shed on gutter or dust-heap and making joyous reflections. Even smutty words are bright in this gay light and gather no sinister suggestiveness in the shade. All men are good at heart, prone though they be to sin. Citizen Hammon courts Jane whose husband, Ralph, a journeyman shoemaker, has been pressed for the French war. He finds her in the seamstress's shop in which she is seeking to earn a livelihood until Ralph comes back. He desires her, plans to seduce her, and desires her the more for her resistance. He then repeats to her a false report, in which he seems himself to believe, of her husband's death. In her grief, she at last yields to his importunities, and the marriage is about to be celebrated when Ralph returns, limping from a wound, and learns what has happened. With the help of his brother shoemakers he stops the bridal procession, and his young wife then flies to his arms, preferring his poverty to all Hammon's money. For a moment Hammon does not acknowledge himself beaten, but attempts to buy Jane from Ralph. But he is, at bottom, a good fellow, and when Ralph is indignant he cedes both wife and money to him. Everyone in this play has a good heart.

A charming rose-coloured vein of feeling runs through it. It is perhaps more genuinely and virtuously merry than anything else in Renascence drama. Romantic and realistic elements are nowhere else so easily and prettily blended. A realism neither hard nor cynical combines well with a romanticism which is not extravagant, exactly as Dekker's very simple blank verse is happily allied to his picturesque prose. His sympathy with his humble folk brings them near to his great ones, so that characters are better unified than in other plays; class-barriers are broken down; the king's jovial good humour makes him one with his people, and the poorest are ennobled by their delicacy of feeling.

For Dekker is a true poet. Lamb could say of him that he "had poetry enough for anything." This poetry is more evident in a strange and unequal play which has many absurdities but includes some beautiful scenes, *Old Fortunatus*.

Dekker, a popular author who had not lost contact with the spirit of the Middle Ages, wrote a true morality-play on an old German legend already staged in England. Old Fortunatus is endowed by Fortune with an inexhaustible purse, which he has chosen to receive rather than wisdom, health, beauty or long life, and the gift of his choice brings him unhappiness. It causes his death and also that of his two sons, of whom one is virtuous and the other vicious.

The son's adventures are woven of strange buffoonery. But the play opens grandly and poetically. Fortunatus, poor and old, has lost his way in a wood when the dazzling vision comes to him of Fortune with her train of crowned ragamuffins and enslaved kings, the ragamuffins singing her praises and the kings cursing her. With royal disdain Fortune replies to them, enumerating the marks of her power. Then she notices the poor old man and offers him any one of her gifts; but as she gives him the purse he craves she blames his unworthy choice, and warns him that he will "dwell with cares and quickly die." This first and completely lyrical scene, made of harmonious and clear verses, is one of the most poetic in the drama of the period.

The *Honest Whore* is Dekker's best-known work. In spite of some Elizabethan eccentricity and whimsicality, it might be called a domestic drama. The definition fits at least the principal plot, the secondary theme being a buffoonery about a patient husband, resigned as Griselda, whose improbable placidity is unmoved even by the most outrageous insults and affronts.

The adventures of Bellafront, the whore, are very different. Among the young cynics who are her habitual companions, she one day notices the young lord Hippolito, who is in great though silent grief because he believes the girl he loves to be dead. His friends have dragged him to Bellafront's house to distract his thoughts. The courtesan falls in love with this silent man, so different from the others, but he disdainfully rejects her advances, thinks that her sighs are so many baits to her traps and that her tears for her lost chastity are false. He tells her all the shamefulness of her trade. She is converted, denies herself to her lovers, endures poverty, and dismisses even Matheo, her first seducer, declaring that she can accept nothing but marriage from him. He rejects this demand with a sneer, but is finally compelled to grant it by the Duke of Milan.

The first part of the play ends with this rehabilitation of Bellafront. The second part has truth which is more poignant and of a rarer kind. Matheo, married against his will, is a debauchee and gamester who loses all the money of the household. Determined to "fly high," he has no regard for his wife, but robs her of everything, even her dress, which he sells that he may gamble. He makes her live in a hovel of which all the furniture goes to the pawnbroker, steals in order to play again, urges his wife to resume her old trade and brings her customers. She, however, is now completely virtuous; not only does she resist her husband's infamous persuasions, stripping herself, the while, of everything for his sake, but she even repels the advances of Hippolito, who converted her and whom she loved. He is now married to the beautiful girl he once, in error, had mourned, but he seeks, nevertheless, to seduce Bellafront. His gold, his presents, his eloquence and his vaunting of the splendour of courtesans are, however, all in vain: in reply she recalls to him his sinister picture of women of ill-fame.

Unknown to her, her father, Orlando Friscobaldo, the most original character in the play, is beside her to sustain her. This old gentleman of strict morals has refused to see his daughter since her fall. She has been dead to him. Learning, however, that she is married and wishes to live virtuously, he enters her house disguised as a servant. While he feigns to be hot-tempered and brutal, he watches over her like a Providence. He first gives money to her husband, and then, finding him incorrigible and cruel to her, arranges his arrest for theft and thus has him at his mercy. When he has tamed him he forgives him, and offers his house and money to him and his wife. The struggle between Friscobaldo's sense of honour and his fatherly love is painted with extreme vigour and originality. Without analysis or soliloquies, the old man's vacillations are shown, the sudden alternations of his fury and his love, his unending care for his daughter and untiring devotion to her, hidden beneath his taunts and his apparently inflexible severity. He resolves himself to test the thoroughness of her conversion, and every time her virtue is proof against a new trial he is unable to contain his joy, and more than before allows his heart to guide him.

Friscobaldo is not merely interesting in himself. He is the first of a long line of characters who are probably dear to every public, but are especially so to the English. Nowhere else is gruff benevolence as much loved, whether in novels or on the stage, as in England. The English like to think it part of their national character, in contrast to the polite manners of southern nations which hide, as they think, a lack of virtue and cordiality. A good heart and a rough exterior make their ideal.

The Bohemian Dekker had really great gifts. He could impart poetry and life. His work, badly put together, may seem formless beside Jonson's. But Jonson's plays cannot match Dekker's cheerfulness, his true feeling, or the characters at once alive and attractive whom he created more than once, and of whom at least Simon Eyre and Friscobaldo deserve to be models. They are worthy to rank with Shakespeare's people, from whom, however, they are not copied. In the plays in which Dekker collaborated his poetry and tenderness recur. His handiwork can be recognised in the most pleasing passages of the *Witch of Edmonton*; which he wrote with Ford and Rowley, and of the *Virgin Martyr* which he wrote with Massinger.

5. Thomas Heywood (1575?–1650).[1]—It is Thomas Heywood whose tenderness and pity bring him nearest to Dekker. Lamb called this pathetic author "a sort of prose Shakespeare." He was rather, perhaps, a prose Dekker, a Dekker shorn of lyricism, fancy and gaiety, able to create dramatic and moving situations rather than strongly individualised characters. Yet because he found it easier than Dekker to do without romance, he was, in some of his plays, more successful than he in realising the ideal citizen drama.

Like Dekker, Heywood is closely connected with London, and the great body of his works constantly betrays his desire to minister to the tastes and even the vanities and prejudices of the citizens and their guilds. He was well educated, a Cambridge man. His knowledge was extensive and he was a very productive writer who attempted many literary forms and the most various subjects. As early as 1596 he was a resolute devotee of the stage, and, like Shakespeare, he was both an actor and a playwright. He was the most prolific of the Elizabethans. He claims to have been the chief author of two hundred and twenty plays of which only twenty-four have reached us. Of all English dramatists, he was the one who came nearest to the fertility of the Spaniards. Quantity is often reached at the expense of quality. This copious writer is an improviser never stayed by artistic considerations. At his best, he attains to clarity and fluency, and he desires no more.

His subjects are extremely varied. He draws on English history, ready to flatter the simple and artless patriotism or the Protestantism of his public. He appeals to their sense of honour and of morality. The better to reach his ends, he usually confines himself to England, rejecting the fashion for the exotic which attracted writers to the south, and especially to Italy.

Among his plays intended to flatter the self-satisfaction of the Londoners, the most extravagant is unquestionably the *Four Prentices of London*, which was performed towards the end of the sixteenth century. More than any other play, it panders to the vanity of the citizens. Their reading of degenerate chivalrous romances so easily went to their heads, that there was hardly an apprentice among them who did not conceal a Don Quixote. Heywood represents four youths, sons of the expropriated Earl of Bulloigne (or Bouillon), who has taken refuge in London. They have been apprenticed to a mercer, a haberdasher, a goldsmith and a grocer, and do their duty well until their blood is stirred by an appeal in the streets for soldiers who will go to Jerusalem. They thereupon enrol themselves, and each of them subsequently encounters adventures extraordinary enough to dim the glory of Amadis. At last the brothers meet in Jerusalem. Each of them has won a crown, but Godfrey, out of humility, asks that his may be of thorns.

The adulation of the city is unbounded. Each exploit of any one of the apprentices is credited to his guild, which he never forgets. On his shield each bears the emblem of his trade. Heywood dedicated the printed edition of his play to "the Honest and High-Spirited Prentises," and it was his good luck that its publication coincided with the rising of the trained bands. He was not the man to make fun of the doltish, bragging London militia.

There is the same flattery in his less romantic plays, for instance in the two parts of *King Edward the Fourth* which show the siege of London and the defeat of the besiegers by the Lord Mayor and citizens. *If You Know Not Me, You Know No Body, or the Troubles of Queen Elizabeth,* celebrates the building of the Royal Exchange by Sir Thomas Gresham, and the *Faire Maid of the Exchange* gives a realistic picture of a part of the city and the shops which clustered about the

---

[1] *The Dramatic Works of Thomas Heywood,* reprint by Pearson, 6 vols. (1874); selected plays in the Mermaid Series, ed. Verity, 1 vol. (1888); *A Woman Killed with Kindness,* ed. Ward (1897); ed. Cox (1907); *The Captives,* ed. Judson (Yale University Press, 1921).

Exchange. The hero of the latter play, the lame man Cripple, who is distinguished by his sincere love and his unselfishness, is a public scribe in humble circumstances. The *Faire Maid of the West* sounds a patriotic note in a wider atmosphere. Heywood celebrates in it the adventures of seafarers, and very vigorously reproduces life in the port of Plymouth at the time of the expedition of Essex to the Azores.

Already in these plays Heywood plainly shows his preference for dramas having a moral tendency and dealing with cockney life. *Edward the Fourth* tells the story of the king's love for Jane Shore, the goldsmith's wife, how he seduced her and raised her to grandeur, and how she fell and with her unhappy husband died in misery. There is, however, another series of plays which show Heywood's powers in their pure state, hardly adulterated by romanticism or by his historical ambitions. In them he continues a line of plays which began in 1587 with *Arden of Feversham* and which can, at intervals, be traced through works lost save for their titles, and through a few still extant.

This was a series of domestic dramas. One the most striking contributions to it is the anonymous *Warning for Fair Women* which was published in 1599, and which dramatises an actual event, the murder of a London merchant, George Sanders, by his wife's lover, with her consent. It is a realistic representation of a crime of passion analogous to *Arden of Feversham*, and insists on the punishment and remorse of the guilty lovers. A dumb show precedes each act and indicates the relation of this play to the old moralities.

The *Yorkshire Tragedy*, which was published in 1608 as a work of Shakespeare's, has a more modern aspect. It is very short, and powerfully epitomises the crimes committed by a debauchee who has come home in a state of frenzy after losing all his fortune at play. He knows that his wife is ruined, that his children must be beggars, and in a fever he turns to indiscriminate slaughter. The play moves violently and furiously; the dialogue is breathless and spasmodic; the murderer is like one possessed. Beside himself with remorse for having rendered his wife destitute, he overwhelms her with ignoble insults and blames her for all their misfortunes. Yet we feel that he loves his children even as he strangles them. He is a madman impelled by a diabolic force who strikes right and left—wife, children and servants. Brought to a halt, and in the presence of the wife he has wounded, he recovers his senses. Literally, he feels that a devil has gone out of him, and liberated, exorcised and repentant, he goes out to his punishment.

These are such realistic plays as convict sinners among an audience and compel them to confession. They are the most moral and, in one sense, the most classical contribution of the Elizabethans to drama. They respect the essential unity, that of subject. They go straight to the point, rapidly and luminously. Nothing else is so unencumbered, has a gait so unaffected, reaches its conclusions so unmistakably.

Heywood's finest and most characteristic work belongs to this school of domestic drama, but in his gentler vein he avoids crime, and does not present adultery save as a tragedy which inflicts suffering and provokes remorse. He abstains from bloodshed unless a well-known theme constrains him to it, for instance that of the *Rape of Lucrece* printed in 1609. This is an unequal play which very forcefully depicts the terror in Lucretia's house after her rape.

His masterpiece is *A Woman Killed with Kindness*, performed in 1603. Nothing in Elizabethan drama is simpler, in matter and form, or more moving than this play. It has indeed two distinct and badly connected plots, but only one of them, that which names it, is important.

A happy and virtuous married couple, whose felicity communicates itself to the audience, is first presented. But their home is ruined by the generosity of the husband, Master Frankeford, who gives shelter to a poor gentleman named

Wendoll, and bestows his confidence on him. Wendoll conceives a fatal love for Frankeford's wife, and although he is aware of the vileness of his passion, he struggles against it in vain. When, during Frankeford's absence, he is left alone with his hostess, he avows his feelings, and the young woman, who is at first horrified and stupefied, is presently under the sway of this passion, able to overcome gratitude and honour. She wavers, then succumbs: it is as though she were seized by sudden giddiness and could not do otherwise than fall. A faithful servant informs the master of the house of what has happened. At first he is incredulous, tries to banish his suspicions, plays at cards with his friend and his wife. But, strive against it as he may, he finds himself twisting everything they say and reading double meanings into all their words. Feeling that he must have certainty, he alleges that he is obliged to make a journey, and starts at night, in spite of the protests of his wife, who would stop his going, and of his friend, who offers to accompany and protect him. He returns suddenly to find the guilty couple in each other's arms. Nothing is more poignant than this return:

> Astonishment
> Feare and amazement beat upon my heart,
> Even as a madman beats upon a drum,

he says, as he approaches the room where the lovers are asleep, and when he reappears, after witnessing their guilt, he is as much ravaged by emotion as Macbeth issuing from Duncan's chamber. Yet he has not killed them, for he will not send two precious souls to hell. With withering contempt he turns his false friend out of his house, and when his wife, on her knees, weeps and implores for mercy, he forces her to acknowledge the enormity of her fault and shows her their two children:

> On whose white brows thy shame is charactered.

He then pronounces her sentence. He will punish her only with kindness. She must retire, with all her possessions, leaving nothing behind her, to a manor he gives up to her. She shall have money and servants, but she must never attempt to see him or her children again nor ever write to him. She has died to him.

She goes, forgetting the lute on which she has been wont to play, accompanying her own voice in delightful songs. He sends it after her, and his messenger overtakes her on the road, plunged in grief. Wendoll, hidden there, is the unseen witness of her unhappiness for which he is responsible. She asks the messenger to tell her husband that he has found her in tears, longing for death, and that she has sworn neither to eat nor drink. The lute is, by her order, broken against the coach-wheels:

> As the last music that I e'er shall make.

When Wendoll comes out of his hiding-place to speak to her, she screams in terror. Her lover has become for her a demon from whom she flees in horror, and Wendoll feels himself a Cain, a wanderer on the face of the earth.

Mistress Frankeford is next discovered in her place of exile and resigned to death. Her sole remaining desire is to see her husband before her life ends, and he has pity on her, reaches her in her last moments, and solemnly grants her his pardon sealed by a kiss.

Moral loftiness and poignant melancholy impregnate this play. The unfaithful wife who is torn by remorse in the very act of sinning has nothing in common with Alice, the murderess of Feversham. Wendoll, save for a final, regrettable and superfluous touch, is entirely other than the vile Mosbie. If Heywood makes his heroine fall with a suddenness which is improbable, he succeeds in conveying the fearful fascination of passion. Above all, he depicts, with a humane sympathy then exceptional, the wife's remorse and the pity of the husband, whose love subsists although his moral dignity allows him no base compromise. Customs have so changed that his kindness may to-day seem like pitiless severity. But Frankeford was Othello's contemporary; the stage he walked was that on which terrible vengeances, after the Italians, were frequent. When his time and the circumstances in which he was created are taken into account, he is seen to breathe a singular gentleness which was victorious over violent and ferocious instincts.

Nearly thirty years later, Heywood returned to the theme of pity and pardon in a less celebrated and less pathetic play, but one which is perhaps more modern and which shows great delicacy of feeling, the *English Traveller*, printed in 1633. The hero, young Geraldine, is certainly among those who won for Heywood the praise that "his gentlemen are the most refined and finished of gentlemen." He is a candid youth who does not know that platonic love may be dangerous to himself and others, and who suspects no treachery in the woman he loves or in his friend. He is in love with a girl who reciprocates his feeling, but on returning from a long journey on the continent he finds her the wife of Wincott, an old gentleman. Wincott makes friends with him and encourages his visits. Geraldine and Mistress Wincott confess to each other that their love subsists, yet do not fail in their duty, but agree to unite after Wincott's death. Meanwhile, however, Geraldine introduces to the Wincotts' house his friend Dalavill, who wins Mistress Wincott's love while he pretends that he is courting her sister. He becomes her lover and together with her mocks Geraldine's coldness. When an accident reveals to Geraldine that he has been doubly betrayed, his first thought is to kill the guilty pair, but he recoils from bloodshed and will not send them to damnation. He decides on another journey, and when Mistress Wincott, out of prudence, feigns regret at his departure, and reminds him of their vows, he tells her what he knows and blasts her with his contempt. Her eyes are thus opened to the enormity of her crime. She dismisses her lover in horror and dies suddenly, leaving behind her a letter in which she acknowledges her fault and declares her admiration for the man whose moral greatness has saved her soul by causing her to feel remorse.

These plays are the most characteristic and the finest productions of a playwright whose work is rich, diversified and extremely unequal, but who has created, here and there, some strong and simple situations appealing to feelings shared by us all. Amid the violence and ferocity habitual to the stage of the time, these scenes are restful. Heywood had a sure guide in his moral sense, which was so informed by pity that it had nothing in common with the rigidity of extreme Puritanism, and which holds good for all countries and all ages.

6. Thomas Middleton (1570 ?–1627).—Thomas Middleton,[1] chronologer of the city and more than once in charge of civic masques and pageants, had as strong ties with London as Dekker and Heywood, and depicted, as they did, the life of the town. Instead, however, of flattering the citizens, he was diverted by them. It pleased him to show up their foibles and their vices. He thus connects with the Jonson who wrote *The Alchemist*, the *Silent Woman* and *Bartholomew Fair*, with the difference that he seems less anxious than Jonson to point a moral. He has a taste for cynical pictures and a natural tendency towards the most licentious implications, although as a rule he abstains from the more brutal obscenity of such as Marston.

Hardly anything is known of him save that Jonson considered him "a base fellow," whether as a man or as a writer does not appear. In 1604 he wrote some satirical tales of low life in London, after the manner of Greene and Nashe. They

---

[1] *The Works of Thomas Middleton*, ed. Bullen, 8 vols. (1885–6); selected plays, ed. by Havelock Ellis with preface by Swinburne, 2 vols. (Mermaid Series, 1890); *The Spanish Gipsy* and *All's Lost by Lust*, ed. Morris (Belles Lettres Series, 1907); *A New Wonder, a Woman Never Vexed*, Hazlitt's Dodsley, vol. xii.; *A Match at Midnight*, ibid., vol. xiii.

form a parallel to Dekker's efforts in the same direction, and are entitled the *Black Book* and *Father Hubbard's Tale*. Incisive, picturesque and moving rapidly, they show a very complete acquaintance with the disreputable society in which the scene of the author's comedies was also laid. The *Black Book* is the more cynical of the two collections, the other being more poetic, its mood softened by a pity for the weak and poor of the world which recalls Dekker.

(*a*) MIDDLETON'S COMEDIES.—Middleton tried several paths before he found his right one, attempting romantic plays like *Blurt, Master Constable*, very strongly influenced by Shakespeare, and pseudo-historical plays, for instance the *Mayor of Queenborough* which deals with the Saxon invasion. He collaborated with several authors, principally Dekker, and finally he found his vocation in light comedy. He himself alludes, in a prefatory address to the readers of the *Roaring Girle*, to a change in the public taste analogous to that which affected dress. "Now, in the time of spruceness, our plays follow the niceness of our garments." It is not certain that the general taste had changed as much as Middleton asserts, but what he says doubtless applies to the special public for which he wrote, "the termers," gay young sparks who flocked to town in the autumn. He might have been the purveyor of some London Palais Royal theatre of the reign of James I.

He produced from 1604 to 1612 a series of highly-flavoured farcical comedies, distinguished by the vivacity of their scenes, their skilful construction and the very direct acquaintance they show with the least desirable circles of London society. The best of them are *Michaelmas Term* (1604), *A Trick to Catch the Old One* (1606?) *A Mad World, My Masters* (1606), *Your Five Gallants* (1606) and *A Chaste Maid in Cheapside* (1612).

The first of these, *Michaelmas Term*, is in its own genre not far removed from a masterpiece. Its spirit is that of the *Conny-Catching Tracts*. It shows a young man from the country drawn into a life of pleasure, induced by sharpers to gamble and spend money and brought by need of cash into the clutches of a usurer who finally seizes his estate. Quomodo, the usurer, is a draper, and has two attendants who help him to ensnare Easy, the dupe. A forerunner of Harpagon, he dispenses no money, but sells his cloth to poor Easy, who cannot get rid of it except, at a third of the price he gave for it, to a purchaser who conceals Quomodo himself. Easy cannot honour the bond he has signed and has to pledge his property. This theme is treated by Middleton with all possible accuracy. Save that the scoundrels are too prone to assume disguises, nothing could be more natural than the cheating scenes. Poor Easy, who is not foolish but merely unsophisticated, meets disaster by a mathematical necessity; his ruin is inevitably deduced. Shakespeare himself was not more skilful when he showed how Iago duped Othello. In the borrowing scene, long as it is, there is not a detail which does not tell, and the basis is a very sure and very acute psychology. The genre is not elevated, but, such as it is, it reaches perfection in this play.

All Middleton's other comedies are worth analysing. They include examples of complete cynicism like *A Trick to Catch the Old One*, a merry farce in Regnard's manner, in which Middleton claims sympathy for an extravagant nephew who makes his rapacious uncle his dupe. In *A Mad World, My Masters*, a bully plays abominable tricks on his grandfather, whose heir he is, but who will give him nothing. In the end the laugh turns against the grandson, who becomes the victim of his own misdeeds. Sometimes Middleton recalls the moralities, for instance in *Your Five Gallants*, which passes swindlers and ruffians in review, finally meting out due chastisement to them. The five types represented are "the broker gallant," "the bawd gallant," "the cheating gallant," "the pocket gallant" and "the whore gallant." At other times this playwright produces a real merry, nimble farce like *A Chaste Maid in Cheapside*, which is wholly laughter-provoking and which very skilfully interweaves several plots, each one more ribald than the other. Its matter is the adventures of several households, and the action leads at a furious pace to a comic conclusion: a barren and an over-prolific couple, a triangle in which the complacent husband enjoys his ease at the expense of a dissipated spendthrift, and a pedantic simpleton of a student who ends by marrying a red-haired Welsh-woman of slight virtue. These situations lead to wildly farcical incidents, through which runs the course of the true love of yet another couple who succeed in getting married in spite of their parents. When we read this comedy we have to acknowledge that no writer of vaudeville at the present day has more skill or adroitness than Middleton, the most modern of the humorists of the Renascence.

To all his comedies, including the last, his observation of realities gives substance. He paints the manners of his time. In *A Chaste Maid* there is a scene which sketches a christening-party from the life. We meet at this junketing all the gossips of the neighbourhood, and certain Puritans who find most pious pretexts for drinking deep. One character in *A Mad World* is more than farcical, a true portrait, probably drawn from life—Sir Bounteous Progress, a grandfather and rich old knight who practises in his country house the most liberal hospitality. He has an artless respect for titles, and is never happier than when he shelters or believes he shelters a lord beneath his roof. At the same time he is cheerful and sociable, addicted to the pleasures of the table and still a follower of women. He entertains at great expense a London countesan who deceives him barefacedly. He no sooner learns that she has taken to her bed than he concludes that she is about to bear him a son, and is beside himself with pride at the vitality he still retains. This little spare old man in his long doublet is full of go and optimism. The play subjects him to trial after trial, but his good humour is never defeated. Were he not so void of sentimentality, he might be one of Dekker's characters.

Middleton, however, was not so complete a realist as to have no share of Elizabethan fancifulness. Even Quomodo, the crafty usurer of *Michaelmas Term*, has in his composition a grain of pleasant imagination, almost of poetry. He is genuinely carried away by the thought of the property out of which he cheats poor Easy. He sees himself riding thither with his wife and children, harvests his crops in imagination. For all his rapacity, he has a quite idyllic vision of felicity and a heart which melts like that of any worthy citizen and good father. It is true that when once this fancifulness is let loose it outruns all bounds. Quomodo, wishing to know how his son Sim will behave as owner of the land gained by his father's craft, and how Thomasine, his wife, will weep when he is no more, feigns to grow ill and die. He has cause to rue his device, for Thomasine's pity for her husband's poor dupe has turned to love, and she immediately marries Easy, reveals to him the treachery which has victimised him, and helps him to recover his property. Quomodo reappears to find that he has lost everything, his wife as well as his money.

The initial realism has given place to whimsicality. Thus even Middleton's realistic comedies sometimes depart momentarily from the probable, and the imaginative among his audiences are grateful for not being constantly tied to the dull earth.

(*b*) THE TRAGEDY MIDDLETON WROTE ALONE.—His comedies are only half Middleton's work. It is strange to see him turning, at the height of his success, from the kind of work which had so well repaid him and attempting tragedy. To-day opinion inclines to attribute to 1612 the only tragedy which he wrote without a collaborator: *Women Beware Women*. It dramatises the true adventures of an Italian courtesan, Bianca Cappello (1542–87), and may have been suggested by the success recently encountered by the *White Devil*, a play on the life of another

Italian courtesan, Vittoria Accorombona, written by Webster, with whom Middleton seems to have been on terms of friendship. Vice and crime are portrayed with equal horror in the two tragedies, but there is a striking contrast between the melodramatic genius of Webster and the realistic genius of Middleton, who seems instinctively to have brought his sinister subject as near everyday life as possible.

The beginning of his play is truly admirable. It is pervaded by a gentle atmosphere of honest worth and love, so that the subsequent abominations are proportionately thrown into relief. Leontio, a young factor, beings home to his poor dwelling in Florence his Venetian bride, who is both marvellously beautiful and nobly born. It has been a love-match, and Bianca accepts her humble lot cheerfully. Leontio's mother, when once she has scolded her son for having kept his marriage secret, receives his young wife affectionately. But Leontio is obliged to leave home almost immediately. He is discovered in the street hesitating between love which holds him back and duty which drives him forward. Bianca, at her window, calls him with looks and voice, but as he is about to yield to her he summons all his courage and departs with a last farewell. Bianca, on her balcony, weeps while her mother-in-law mildly reproaches her. Leontio has hardly gone when the street fills with townsfolk, apprentices and merry urchins, assembled because the duke is about to pass. It is the day on which the duke and his nobles ceremoniously visit St. Mark's. The magnificent procession passes beneath the windows of the two women.

"Did not the duke look up? Methought he saw us," says Bianca, and the scene ends on this uneasy note. First the old mother and then the young wife are afterwards ensnared by a great lady, Livia, who acts as procuress to the self-indulgent duke. A very remarkably contrived scene, which has a powerful theatrical effect, shows Livia and the old woman playing chess in the foreground, while in the background Bianca is thrown into the arms of the duke, whose promises turn her head and whose power terrifies her so that, although she protests desperately, he finally overcomes her resistance, as much by force as by persuasion. When she is seen again, after she has lost her virtue, the tumult of her soul is such that, while she withers the procuress with scorn, she declares herself ready to accept her dishonour, since she has nothing left to do but to be shameless to the end. Her decision taken, she is feverishly gay, resolved to be what guile and treason have made her.

The return of the trustful Leontio is very pathetic. He arrives joyfully, descanting like a poet on the honourable happiness which marriage has brought him. He is stupefied by the coldness and hostility with which Bianca receives him, and in despair when he understands the truth. The scene ends with a sad soliloquy which balances the opening pæan of joy and in which Leontio envies the peace of the unmarried.

The remainder of the tragedy recounts the crimes by which Bianca and the duke attain to marriage, to die soon afterwards in the moment of their triumph. Another and parallel plot is concerned with the incest of an uncle and niece, also directed by Livia, who is a corrupter of good women and responsible for the title of the play. The end, a general massacre on the occasion of a masquerade, is linked up with the inventions which figure in the *Spanish Tragedie*, and gives Middleton's tragedy a place in a known series. Its first part is, none the less, original and poignant.

(c) THE TRAGEDIES WHICH MIDDLETON WROTE WITH ROWLEY.—Middleton's other tragedies or tragi-comedies were all written in collaboration with William Rowley (1585?–1642?), his junior by about ten years. Rowley, an author-actor like Shakespeare, wrote almost always in collaboration, so that his own talent is difficult to distinguish. He left, however, of his unaided work, one tragedy, *All's*

Lost by Lust (1619), and two comedies, *A Match at Midnight* (1623) and *A New Wonder, a Woman Never Vexed* (1631), whence it may be concluded that his literary culture was mediocre and his versification irregular and rhythmically defective, but that he had experience of the theatre and a sense of tragic and comic stage-effects which made a wide appeal. Middleton, an expert in comic dialogue, gives in his one tragedy too much space to lyrical soliloquies and tirades. Rowley's influence is presumably accountable for the more lively dialogue of the later plays and also, doubtless, for the unfortunately numerous farcical effects in such parts of them as are comedy. But it is impossible to do more than conjecture the contribution of either playwright to these undivided plays which they both signed—Middleton's name always preceding Rowley's. The chief of their joint productions are *A Fair Quarrel* (1616), *The Changeling* (1621), and the *Spanish Gipsy* (1623). All three are, for different reasons, among the most interesting of the dramatic works of the Jacobean period.

A Fair Quarrel has two plots, but the principal one, which names it, is reminis-cent of *Hamlet*; it is a *Hamlet* transposed to a lower rank of society. Young Captain Ager is, in the course of a quarrel, called the son of a whore by his colonel, a brave but violent-tempered man whom he has greatly admired. He is angry on behalf of his mother and a duel seems inevitable, but Ager cannot fight save in a just cause. Cautiously and in fear and trembling, he sounds his mother, who is indignant that her son should doubt her and strikes him. Exulting in her anger, he then tells her that she has filled him with joy and that he will now fight the man who has insulted her. She, horrified and imagining him dead already, thereupon retracts and declares herself guilty. With death in his heart Ager then declines the duel, and apologises to his adversary, who calls him a coward. The new and undeserved insult restores his spirit and gives him the right to fight. He wounds his colonel, who, believing himself at the point of death, acknowledges that he has been in the wrong and withdraws the insult to the young man's mother, confessing that he uttered it in a moment of temper.

Although Lady Ager's change of attitude is very sudden, the scene between her and her son is really dramatic, its course guided by a very sure hand.

The plot of the *Spanish Gipsy*, a more fantastic and less serious tragi-comedy, is much more complicated. The self-styled gipsy is a great Spanish nobleman who is obliged, after killing another nobleman in a duel, to flee his country. He returns thither with his wife, children and some followers, all disguised as gipsies, idyllic gipsies who constitute a free society, having its own laws and customs. From this utopian gipsy state all vice is banished: no man cheats or steals or is dissipated. Otherwise these are like true gipsies, who tell fortunes, sing, even act plays. Many suitors are attracted by the beauty of the chief's daughter, Pretiosa. The spirit of the pastoral reigns in this part of the play.

The tragedy is contained by another plot which has some really moving scenes. Young Roderigo, son of the corregidor of Madrid, abducts a pretty girl, with the help of his friends, one night when he is heated with wine, takes her to his room and violates her. At dawn on the morrow, the victim—Clara, daughter of Don Pedro—is horrified when she awakes in the place of the crime, in unknown sur-roundings. She perceives through the window a large garden with an alabaster fountain in its centre. She returns home, determined to discover her seducer, and refuses to marry a young man she loves because she can contemplate no reparation except marriage with her ravisher. Long afterwards she is hurt in a street accident and carried to a neighbouring house. When she recovers consciousness, she finds herself again in the scene of the crime. Her father, who is tending her, looks through the window, at her request, and describes to her the beautiful garden she has seen already with its alabaster fountain. Thus recognition is accomplished, and the heroine finally marries her ravisher, who ever since the fatal night has been consumed by remorse and has wished to repair his wrong to her. These incidents might be melodramatic, but Middleton's habitual realism gives them a striking air of truth.

Incontestably, however, the masterpiece of the collaboration of Middleton and Rowley is *The Changeling*, which would rank with the Shakespearean tragedies were it not disfigured by a coarse and worthless secondary plot, without connection with the principal story.

The hand of the youthful Beatrice, daughter to the governor of the castle of Alicante, is officially granted to the Lord Alonso. But the Lord Alsemero supervenes and falls in love with Beatrice, believing her free. She returns his love and they exchange vows. This opening of the play moves swiftly and is charming. Beatrice vainly implores for a postponement of the marriage her father has arranged for her. He attributes her averseness to childishness, maidenly shrinking, and it seems inevitable. In the governor's suite there is, however, a poor gentleman named De Flores, an adventurer whose dark, pustulous and terrifying countenance bespeaks his vice. He has long hovered persistently and obsequiously about Beatrice, impelled by a love at once servile and audacious, mean and forceful. She has repelled him with sarcasm and insults. She feels for him invincible loathing, as for a reptile, combined with secret horror, but he refuses to be discouraged and is ready to do anything to win a smile from her.

Since no coldness from Beatrice discourages Alonso, Alsemero conceives the idea of preventing his marriage with Beatrice by provoking him to a duel. But Beatrice, trembling for the life of the man she loves, determines that De Flores, who will do her bidding at a word, shall save her. She therefore flatters him and gives him to understand that she wishes Alonso to disappear. She plans to pay her tool with much gold which will enable him to escape after the murder, but he, the while, has no prize in view save herself.

The crime is accomplished, and De Flores returns to Beatrice to claim not the reward she intends, but that which he desires. He rejects her proffered gold although she doubles and trebles its sum. Their shared crime puts her in his power, and finally, like a hawk with its prey, he carries her off with him:

> 'Las ! how the turtle pants!

These incomparable scenes are followed by others which are unfortunately inferior, some of them extremely licentious. They show that De Flores remains true to himself. Beatrice does indeed marry Alsemero, for whose sake she has become a murderess and as a consequence has lost her purity. But the mark of De Flores is upon her. His intrepidity inspires her with unwilling admiration. Alsemero, when he comes to know of the murder, repudiates his young wife in horror, showing how different is his love from that of De Flores, which no scruple can shake. The two accomplices are arrested, but, rather than fall into the hands of Justice alive, De Flores stabs first Beatrice and then himself:

> Yes, and her honour's prize
> Was my reward; I thank life for nothing
> But that pleasure; it was so sweet to me,
> That I have drunk up all, left none behind
> For any man to pledge me.

These terrible adventures are recounted and these criminal passions and horrifying characters are drawn restrainedly, briefly, rapidly and dramatically, but not oratorically. There is no regularity in the breathless, disjointed verse, but it is nervous and full of movement.

(d) MIDDLETON'S LAST PLAYS.—Yet other plays, famous for different reasons, were written by Middleton by himself: *The Witch* (before 1622) and *A Game at Chess* (1624).

The Witch owes its renown less to its own merit than to its resemblance to *Macbeth*. When, in 1623, *Macbeth* was first published, it seems to have included several passages borrowed from *The Witch* by actors desirous of rejuvenating a play then already old. But Middleton had taken much more from Shakespeare than he gave to him. His witches descend from Macbeth's weird sisters, although they are almost comically realistic. They belong to a play founded on a legend of Alboin, king of the Lombards, properly a story of atrocities, but one which is not here treated seriously.

A Game at Chess is a curious political allegory directed against Spain. Because of its allusions it was astonishingly successful. No other play in Renascence drama was as profitable. The subject is the attempt of Spain, ultimately directed by Ignatius Loyola, to lay hands on England. Played immediately after the rupture of the negotiations for the Spanish match, the projected marriage between Prince Charles and an Infanta of Spain, it assigns a shady part to the Spanish ambassador, and the playwright was obliged to go into hiding in order to escape the consequences of his daring. The value of the play is mainly topical, but it is also no less ingenious than audacious. The characters are the chessmen, the white pieces being the English and the black the Spaniards. Middleton's skill, already frequently demonstrated on the stage, is again made manifest.

It is only because he had no high ambition that he is not in the first rank of writers. Although not without literary conscience, he had neither Fletcher's poetry nor the artistic scrupulosity of Webster. Nor had he the humanity of Heywood and Dekker. The tone of his tragedies, as of his comedies, is generally hard and dry. But in his power to convey the impression of reality he surpasses them all. While he is far from excluding the romantic from his work, his distinction is that he can make the strangest incidents familiar. The moral intention of his plays, especially of his comedies, often suffers by unclean double meanings and implications. Yet it exists: he is indubitably a satirist and to flatter vice is not his habit. His villains are usually punished as they deserve, and as a rule he neither disturbs nor goes counter to the conception of justice. However much it may be necessary to qualify praise of Middleton's considerable body of work, he remains a definitely original member of the great company of the dramatists of his time, whether we consider his comedies, in which he excels by his amused observation of contemporary rascality, or his tragedies, in which even improbable situations are convincing because he could impart an appearance of truth. Middleton neither gave sympathy freely nor could attract it in any great degree. But his work is nervous and dexterous and moves swiftly.

7. **Cyril Tourneur (1575 ?-1626).**[1]—Two men of whom we know nothing, Tourneur and Webster, put new life into melodrama at a time when, towards the end of his career, Shakespeare was abandoning tragic for romantic plays.

Cyril Tourneur, who published some mediocre poems, left behind him two sombre tragedies, the *Revenger's Tragedy*, printed in 1607, and the *Atheist's Tragedy*, in 1611.

The first and by far the most powerful of these is like a gloomy morality-play in an Italian dress. In an unspecified town in Italy, having a court at which debauchery and cruelty reign, there are an infamous duke and duchess and their appropriately named offspring—Lussurioso, their son, Spurio, the duke's bastard, and Ambitiosio and Supervacuo, the duchess's sons by a former marriage.

---

[1] Plays and poems ed. Churton Collins, 2 vols. (1873); plays of Webster and Tourneur ed. Symonds in the Mermaid Series, 1 vol. (1888).

Vindice, or the Avenger, whose betrothed the duke has first tried vainly to seduce and then poisoned, takes it upon him to punish this monstrous family. Punishment is his function, as it was that of the young Hamlet, to whom he owes more than one characteristic. He enters the service of Lussurioso, of course in disguise, and is commissioned by him to corrupt his own sister, Castiza. Desiring to test her, he fulfils his charge. Castiza resists, but her mother proves corruptible and attempts to bend her will in a really tragic scene in which the girl's horror is painted with singular force. She cannot believe that it is her mother who would persuade her to sin:

> Mother, come from that poisonous woman there.

No less impressive is the scene in which Vindice and his brother Hippolito, dagger in hand, drag their mother along by the shoulders and, under threat of death, force her to retract, show her the ignominy of her own conduct, and oblige her to reconsider and reform. Castiza enters at this moment and pretends that her mother's arguments have convinced her so that she is ready to yield to the duke's son, and the mother, in her better mind, is horrified to contemplate what she has done.

Here Tourneur, showing a son who by violence obliges his mother to recognise her fault, is manifestly in debt to *Hamlet*. Yet while he imitates he retains his independence. In his play the situation is blindingly clear; Vindice never doubts his task. As in a morality-play, there are only two colours—black and white. The effect on the spectator is immediate and irresistible. Nothing here is "sicklied over with the pale cast of thought." No play of the period reaches greater dramatic intensity more clearly and swiftly.

In his *Atheist's Tragedy* Tourneur attempts to draw a character, but lacks the necessary originality. D'Amville, his atheist, is too reminiscent of Marlowe's Machiavellian monsters, and the play is very inferior to its predecessor. Yet both are set in an atmosphere of crime and vice which certainly influenced the more poetic plays of Webster.

8. John Webster (1575 ?–1624 ?).[1]—Of all the Elizabethans, it is John Webster who, after long oblivion, was most belauded by the Romantics. About the man it has been possible to discover hardly anything. He was born between 1570 and 1580 and he disappeared in 1624. He wrote for the stage from 1602 onwards, serving for five years a sort of apprenticeship as collaborator with Heywood, Middleton, Marston and, especially, Dekker, but his part, doubtless a subordinate one, in the works to which he contributed cannot be distinguished. His two masterpieces were produced between 1611 and 1614. He relapsed after them to mediocrity, and of his later work only his Roman play, *Appius and Virginia*, which dates from about 1620, has some merit. His authorship of it is to-day disputed, certain critics assigning it to Heywood.

He survives as the author of the *White Devil, or Vittoria Corombona*, played about 1611, and the *Duchess of Malfi*, about 1614. These tragedies are enough to prove his talent.

The first is one of a series of studies of courtesans which appeared one after the other within a few years. It seems to have been Marston who broke the ice with his *Dutch Courtesan*, which the feeling Dekker answered by appealing for pity for his Bellafront. Shakespeare's Cleopatra was an entirely original variation on the same theme. But Evadne, in the *Maid's Tragedy* by Beaumont and Fletcher,

---

[1] Dramatic works ed. Dyce, 4 vols. (1830); ed. W. Hazlitt, 4 vols. (1857); plays of Webster and Tourneur ed. Symonds in the Mermaid Series, 1 vol. (1888).

For studies of Webster see E. Gosse, *Seventeenth Century Studies* (1883); E. Stoll, *John Webster, the Periods of his Work* (1905).

Bianca, in Middleton's *Women Beware Women*, and Webster's Vittoria are closely analogous and all appeared round about 1611. Webster's and Middleton's plays are pendants to each other with their atrocities, their Italian atmosphere, and the equally brilliant and criminal careers of the historic courtesans they portray, Bianca Cappello and Vittoria Accorombona.

From the beginning, the English dramatic Muse was apt to sojourn in Italy. Shakespeare early transferred himself thither in imagination, in *Two Gentlemen of Verona, Merchant of Venice* and *Romeo and Juliet*. But not until the seventeenth century did Italy become the conventional site of stage-representations of unbridled passion and gloomy atrocity. The novel, led by Nashe, was in this ahead of the stage. Marston with *Antonio and Mellida*, *The Malcontent* and *The Fawn*, Shakespeare with *Othello*, Jonson with *Volpone*, and Tourneur with the *Revenger's Tragedy*, accustomed their public to see Italy as the natural home of voluptuous pleasure, bloodshed and death. None, however, Italianised their scenes more exclusively and intensively than Webster. He specialised in Italy at a time when Fletcher and his collaborators were beginning to turn their attention to Spanish heroism.

Webster's genius is seen in the *White Devil*, especially in his portrait of Vittoria, the courtesan, whose licence scandalised Rome at the end of the sixteenth century. It is she who is the white devil. He makes her guilt clear, but at the same time conveys an impression of her fascination which he seems himself to feel. He is all admiration for this woman's beauty, the energy of her ambition and the presence of mind with which she faces desperate situations. As the wife of a poor gentleman, she is courted by Brachiano, Duke of Padua, and she convinces him that he must marry her, first ridding her of her husband and himself of his virtuous wife. The double murder is accomplished, but suspicion rests on those who profit by it. Vittoria is summoned before an imposing court, over which the Duke of Florence and his brother, Cardinal Monticelso, afterwards Sixtus V., preside. Accusations, both accurate and damning, are heaped upon her, but she meets her judges superbly, and with head held high turns their attack against them, reducing their proofs to nothingness and causing more than one of those present to waver. This scene on a large scale is admirable. Vittoria is none the less condemned to seclusion in a house of convertites, but escapes from it with her lover's help. They are pursued by the vengeance of the Duke of Florence and killed one after the other, Vittoria holding out until she has exhausted every resource of invention, cunning and courage. Even in her last hour she defends herself haughtily and, counting on the effect of her beauty, bares her bosom and walks to meet her assassins. She dies at last, confronting Fate with her last words:

> My soul, like to a ship in a black storm,
> Is driven, I know not whither.

Beside her is her brother Flamineo, her tool who has debauched her to advance his fortunes and whom she uses for her love-affairs. It is he who causes her unwanted husband to disappear. He is vice incarnate, but his intrepidity in ill-doing, his lucid intelligence and his moments of real valour make him, abject as he is, not altogether mean.

These characters are placed among many others and meet with singularly atrocious adventures. The melodramatic expedients, increasingly employed in every succeeding scene, are endless: Brachiano's wife dies because her husband's portrait, which she has the habit of kissing every evening, is poisoned; a magician causes Brachiano to witness the execution of the double crime he has ordered; the sister who has been slain appears unmistakably to the brother who mourns

her and will avenge her; Brachiano's murder is accomplished by pouring poison
into a helmet afterwards riveted on to his head by an armourer, and he dies in
atrocious pain while his enemies, disguised as Capuchins, reveal themselves to him
in his last moments, telling the tale of his crimes and promising him damnation.
The play is, moreover, spectacularly gorgeous: while the Conclave is in session,
servants are shown passing backwards and forwards, carrying dishes for the imprisoned cardinals; afterwards the election takes place, and the new pope appears
in great ceremony, uttering Latin formulas. Never has there been a more perfect
fusion of pure drama, which is an effect of representing character and passions,
and melodrama, which is based on the horror of physical impressions and on
spectacular strangeness.

The *Duchess of Malfi*, a more closely knit play, makes the same appeal. The
theme is persecuted virtue, a variant on the so popular one of revenge. There is
again a question of vengeance, accomplished, as in the *Spanish Tragedie*, by strange
means. The avengers are, however, moved by considerations due to their shortness
of vision, as, for instance, fury at a misalliance, or they have low motives, like the
desire to get possession of their victim's fortune. The victim, the Duchess of Malfi
(or Amalfi), is all goodness and innocence, and is driven to madness and death
by her brothers because she has secretly married her steward, the virtuous Antonio.

The tragedy is full of Shakespearean reminiscences: the duchess recalls Desdemona, and Cariola, her woman, Emilia in *Othello*. Bosola, the monster, the tool of
the two brothers, is modelled on Iago. The anger of Ferdinand, the criminal brother,
against Bosola, after the murder he himself has ordered, is like that of King John
against Hubert when he believes him to have put Arthur to death. The remorse
of the other brother, the cardinal who can no longer pray, is a parallel to that of
Claudius in *Hamlet*. Every such comparison would merely show up Webster's
extreme inferiority, were it not that he substitutes for the psychology, at which
Shakespeare principally aims, a search for the pathos inherent in situations and
even in material effects. It is this search which is proper to melodrama. Webster
has a strange power of evoking shudders. His means are sometimes the more
effective for their simplicity. The duchess, compelled by fear of her brothers to
keep her marriage secret, is discovered in her chamber conversing with her husband,
Antonio, her heart filled with joy and love. Antonio leaves her without her knowledge; she continues to speak, thinking he hears her, but her listener is now one of
the brothers she fears, to whom she thus betrays herself. Whoever watches the play
feels a catch at his heart, as he perceives her error while she is still unaware of it.
The impulse is to cry out to her to beware. Some of Webster's devices are, however,
much less innocent than this one. The avenging brothers revel in macabre inventions to torture their poor victim: one of them, feigning to give her his hand, leaves
a severed hand in her grasp; she is shown wax figures which represent the murder
of her husband and children; the inmates of a madhouse are let loose in her palace.

These inferior artistic expedients are, however, relieved by the poetry of melancholy and death which dominates the whole tragedy. Webster is a true poet, the
author of some of the most beautiful songs of the Renascence, and throughout,
in the very web of his style, are images, funereal in mood, which have the breath of
graveyards upon them, yet strike and stir the heart. More than this, the play
contains the character of the duchess. At first, although her love endears her, she
is not original, but she is transfigured by persecution and becomes in her despair a
lofty and solemn figure. Throughout her cruel trials she never fails to ennoble
the tragedy by the sombre poetry of her speech. Her reason is proof against all
the assaults upon her. Cariola, her woman, struggles and cries out when she is
faced with death, but death cannot make the duchess tremble. So beautiful and

so noble does she remain in death that her brother, who has ordered her death, cannot bear to see her face:

> Cover her face; mine eyes dazzle; she died young.

Not until Edgar Poe was there another genius as completely morbid as Webster. His highly special and restricted talent was active only in one genre and accomplished only two memorable plays. He was an artist, but a painful and laborious one. The effort to which production compelled him recalls Ben Jonson. His preface to the *White Devil* shows that, like Jonson, he knew the *limæ labor et mora*, that, like him, he despised popular improvisations and the judgments of the public. A contemporary satirist made fun of the trouble writing was to him:

> How he scrubs: wrings his wrists: scratches his pate!

But Webster gloried in his own painstaking. He would have attempted the most difficult form of art, for it was his desire to compose, in despite of the prevailing taste, a regular sententious tragedy, respectful of the unities, lofty in style, having its chorus and messenger. The aspiration was curious in one who stands for the triumph of melodrama raised to the level of true poetry.

9. **John Fletcher (1579–1625)** [1] **and his Collaborators.**—The production of the considerable body of work very inexactly specified, in the 1647 folio, as by Beaumont and Fletcher, began about 1607. In fact, it included, besides some plays written by the two friends together or separately, many others written by Fletcher with various collaborators and produced during the ten years after Beaumont's death. In the 1679 folio, which is complementary to that of 1647, there are as many as fifty-seven plays. This is the most considerable of the dramatic collections of the time which have been preserved. Its only unity is supplied by the personality of Fletcher, which holds together the parts of this vast whole.

John Fletcher, born in 1579, was the younger son of a clergyman who became bishop of London and member of a family of birth and culture in which literary talent was frequent. He went to Cambridge and moved in the best society, but his father died when he was only seventeen and left his family poorly provided. Need as much as taste seems to have urged him to write for the stage. He had natural gifts, such as must have ensured his success, and he was very clever at making the most of his reputation as soon as he had won it. He did not write only for his own satisfaction. He organised what may be called a play-factory of a superior kind, and throughout his life he resorted to collaboration in order the more rapidly to meet the demands of the actors and the expectation of the public.

He cannot indeed be said to have inaugurated collaboration. The practice was current before him, yet among renowned playwrights it was exceptional. Shakespeare hardly ever had recourse to it, and Jonson seldom. The best of the works of Marston, Dekker, Chapman and Webster are signed by one name, save only *Eastward Ho*. It was the almost simultaneous association of Middleton and Rowley and of Fletcher and Beaumont which made something like a regular institution of collaboration. No one, however, not Middleton himself, collaborated as constantly as Fletcher.

(*a*) FLETCHER'S COLLABORATION WITH BEAUMONT.—About 1607, when he was twenty-eight years old, Fletcher associated himself with Francis Beaumont (1584–1616), then twenty-three years old. Like himself, a man of good family,

---

[1] *The Works of Beaumont and Fletcher*, ed. Dyce, 11 vols. (1843–6); Variorum edition, 12 vols. (1904 et seq.); ed. Glover and Waller (Cambridge English Classics, 10 vols., 1905–13); *The Best Plays of Beaumont and Fletcher*, ed. Strachey, 2 vols. (1887); *The Faithful Shepherdess* (Temple Dramatists, 1887); *The Knight of the Burning Pestle* (ibid., 1898); ed. Murch (Yale Studies in English, 1908); *The Maid's Tragedy*, ed. Thorndike (Belles Lettres Series, 1906); *Philaster* (ibid., 1906); *Henry VIII*. and *Two Noble Kinsmen* are included in many editions of Shakespeare.

Beaumont was the son of a judge and the younger brother of Sir George Beaumont, a distinguished religious poet of the Puritan party. Francis went to Oxford and subsequently read law in London. He was the friend of Drayton and Jonson and a frequenter of the Mermaid, the famous literary tavern. He and Fletcher lived together near the Globe Playhouse, sharing everything, until Beaumont married in 1613. He died soon afterwards, in 1616.

The two friends worked side by side, yet sometimes wrote separate plays: thus Beaumont in 1607 produced, by himself, his mock-heroic comedy the *Woman-Hater*, and Fletcher, in 1610, his *Faithful Shepherdess*, a pastoral which is imitated from Guarini's *Pastor Fido* and contains charming fluent and harmonious passages in which the poet gives scope to his lyrical talent.

Mainly, however, they collaborated, producing together the excellent domestic comedy *Scornful Lady* (1610), the *Knight of the Burning Pestle*, most nimble and amusing of parodies, the tragi-comedy *Philaster* (1609), and two pure tragedies, the *Maid's Tragedy* and *A King and No King* (1611).

All these plays show a surprising knowledge of the stage. Reasons of style and versification have led recent critics to attribute their best parts to Beaumont, a conclusion supported by Fletcher's failure to produce anything as remarkable in later years. However this may be, several of these works must be studied at some length, for they mark both the apotheosis of dramatic skill and the beginning of the decline.

The flexibility and what may be called the modernism of the drama of the period cannot be thoroughly understood without knowledge of the *Knight of the Burning Pestle*. Partly a burlesque or parody, this is a play hard to define, to which many diverse elements have contributed, all blended so as to prove the dexterity of the authors and produce a very curious and very merry comedy, alive although it lacks depth, which might, in many respects, have been written yesterday. It has analogies with the "revues" which make fun of current fashions and events. Almost alone of its kind during the English Renascence, it emphasises the astonishing variety of the drama of the period.

The play has a twofold object. First, it mocks the craze of the citizens for romantic literature, for the adventures of knights-errant, the tales of Amadis of Gaul and Mirrors of Chivalry. Such reading turned their heads, like Don Quixote's, made them dream that they were the heroes of marvellous adventures. If Heywood's *Four Prentices of London* be recalled, it will be seen that Beaumont and Fletcher did not gratuitously invent this taste, that they had their reasons for endowing the citizens with some of the extravagance of Don Quixote, whose history was published in 1605 and very probably known to them, although it had not yet been translated. Secondly, the play makes fun of the vanity of the city, the desire to be glorified on the stage which such as Munday, Chettle, Dekker and Heywood were wont to gratify. Sarcasm, invariably merry, is aimed at the plays which crowned the citizens with an aureole, flattered the martial vanity of the apprentices, their pride in the trained bands.

The mockery is extraordinarily dexterous. The scene is laid as much in the front of the house as on the stage. A worthy grocer and his wife, seated in a playhouse, are uneasy because the prologue announces a play called "The London Merchant." They are afraid of "girds at the citizens," of which they have already had more than their fill; they call for something else, and insist that Ralph, the goodman's apprentice, shall play a part which shall be all to the glory of the Grocers' Company: he shall be the Knight of the Burning Pestle. Nor does this end the part of the grocer and his wife: their remarks, indignant and enthusiastic by turns, and always artless, are a commentary on the parody they see performed and accept in all seriousness. It is astonishing that the double parody, the exploits of the Knight, Ralph, being superimposed, as by an afterthought, on the original material, pursues its course from end to end without confusion or impediment. Every mood is deliberately introduced: burlesque rhymed verse, light songs, eloquent blank verse and the realistic, racy prose of the citizen and his wife succeed each other. Drama has never been more adroit; it had, in this respect, nothing more to learn. The skill is prestigious and the interest never flags. Yet all the while we feel that qualities of this order are supplanting others, that the aim is amusement rather than the study of character. The inevitable comparison with Don Quixote shows up all the superficiality of this comedy, its accidental and ephemeral nature. It mocks a mere fashion which never went below the surface. The quixotry of the city of London was never more than skin-deep. Practical England, already democratic enough to suffer the easy manners of the grocer and his wife, was never Spain. The play is made to afford an hour's amusement; it is a side-splitting exhibition of sleight-of-hand.

The serious plays have the same qualities and same defects. The very celebrated *Philaster* is a tragi-comedy highly reminiscent of Shakespeare. Its hero, Philaster, recalls sometimes Hamlet and sometimes Othello; the youthful Euphrasia, who disguises herself as a page named Bellario, in order to have access to Philaster, is Viola in *Twelfth Night* softened and sentimentalised, deprived of aim, wit and hope, so selfless in her love and idealised that she all but vanishes into thin air. This play, when carefully examined, reveals the method of its authors: they form a new whole by fusing various Shakespearean scenes and characters, taken here, there and everywhere. They skim Shakespearean drama, in the hope that by collecting abbreviated versions of his most striking passages they will attain to superior beauty, supreme refinement. In fact, when they transplant their flowers, they cut them off from the earth which nourishes them. They make the real unreal, yet do it with undeniable skill. The play is full of melodious tirades, graceful similes and images; the flowery, pleasant style is far less difficult than Shakespeare's. These playwrights charm more quickly than he, if for a shorter time.

The *Maid's Tragedy*, their masterpiece, has, together with similar characteristics, more substance. It is a tragedy of unknown source, its subject apparently the invention of the authors. It departs from the epic manner and tends to be romantic. The factitious and forced sentiments of the characters reflect, however, with fair accuracy, manners which were new in the Stewart period. The situation on which the play is based is that an absolute king, reigning by divine right, is reputed unassailable whatever be his acts; his courtiers regard loyalty as their first duty; and society is dominated by the cult of honour in the Spanish sense of the word, with the element of singularity and spuriousness which must necessarily accompany it. The English court under James I. and Charles I. and after the Restoration had more than one analogy with the theme of this tragedy. The spirit of the Cavaliers already prevails in it.

The king has made Evadne his mistress, and to cloak his relations with her marries her with all solemnity to the honourable but weak Amintor, who knows nothing of the royal amours and who repudiates Aspasia, his betrothed, for the sake of this marriage. On the night of the wedding, Evadne informs Amintor that he will be her husband only in name and that the king is her lover. Evadne's brother, the general Melantius, returns from the wars and perceives the melancholy which Amintor, his intimate friend, fails to conceal beneath an appearance of cheerfulness. He persuades him to confidence, and although he finds him loyally resigned to his misfortune, yet resolves to punish the king. His sister Evadne shall kill him. In a violent scene, Melantius tames this proud woman, even threatening her with his dagger, makes her see the enormity of her fault and inspires her with the determination to slay her lover. She fulfils her promise, binds the king while he lies asleep in bed, then awakens him, gives vent in speech to ferocious hatred and, stabs him. When, blood-stained knife in hand, she appears before Amintor, thinking she has won back his love, all she obtains from him is a cry of horror, and in the hope of a word of pardon she turns her knife against herself and falls dead at his feet.

Aspasia, whose unhappy lot names the play, is a colourless character. From the moment of her desertion she does no more than seek death, and she finally succeeds, when she is disguised as a man, in getting herself killed by Amintor's sword. But except for her this tragedy presents a rapid and powerful sequence of the most effective scenes, so well contrived, so eloquent and so intense that the improbability of the characters is unnoticed. A penetrating study is necessary to discover the truth hidden beneath an admirable exterior, the fact, namely, that this tragedy is striking rather than true or profound.

Except for Melantius, who is drawn strongly and sustainedly, the characters present many difficulties and inconsequences which resist analysis. Amintor is not only exasperating but also incomprehensible. His loyalty may indeed prevent him from striking at the king who has unworthily deceived him, but what is there to keep him from killing Evadne when she declares her shame and defies him? Why does he consent to cloak her infamy by assuming cheerfulness?

Even Evadne, haughty, brave, shameless, fierce and superb, is rather an admirable acting part than a consistent character. If she be not amorous but ambitious, why does she agree with the king on the concealment which robs her of the prestige and power of an avowed royal mistress? If she be merely ambitious, why is her conversion so sudden and complete? That she should yield to her brother's virile strength is comprehensible, but not that she should turn lovingly to the vacillating Amintor. What we know of her prepares us ill for her ferocity in the scene in which she kills the king: we are too ignorant of the details of her fall to be convinced by her explosion of hatred. Was it that she cherished in her heart feelings deeper than the ambition which alone urged her to her first fault?

These defects are, however, apparent only on reflection. The scenic and dramatic qualities of the work are surprising. The concentration is equal to that in the French tragedies. There is no secondary plot, for Aspasia's fate is linked up with that of Evadne. The unity of place is, in its broad sense, preserved, and the unity of time is respected: the whole of the action takes place in the town of Rhodes on the eve and morrow of Evadne's wedding-day. Throughout, the play is rendered easy by its harmonious verse and its graceful language which even to-day is not out of date.

(b) FLETCHER'S COLLABORATION WITH SHAKESPEARE.—It seems to have been after Beaumont's marriage, in 1613, that the two friends separated and that Fletcher for a time collaborated with Shakespeare. At least, it is admitted that *Henry VIII.* and the *Two Noble Kinsmen* are plays by Fletcher or, according to the most recent criticism, by Fletcher and Massinger, which include certain passages by Shakespeare.

Shakespeare's custom was not to work with a colleague, but to recast the plays in his company's repertory which had come to seem old, putting new life into them. In his last years, however, when he had already severed his connection with the stage and left London for Stratford-on-Avon, some of his sketches for plays may have remained unfinished, and he may have entrusted their completion to the most brilliant of the younger dramatists. The study of the two plays in question is interesting in itself. One of the noblest women's characters, Catherine of Aragon, whom Henry VIII. repudiates, is apparently drawn by Shakespeare. The collaboration of the poets is also interesting: Fletcher's habitual adroitness and rather too facile graces of style can be distinguished side by side with the more robust and truer touches of Shakespeare's genius.

(c) FLETCHER'S UNAIDED WORK.—Fletcher by himself wrote, or signed alone, a certain number of plays, some tragedies and tragi-comedies and, more especially, some comedies. They are all abundantly romantic. The best of the tragedies are *Valentinian* (1614) and *Bonduca* (1614), of the tragi-comedies, the *Humorous Lieutenant* (1619) and the *Loyal Subject* (1618), and the best known of the comedies are *Monsieur Thomas* and *The Pilgrim* (1621). Everywhere Fletcher shows his inherent understanding of the stage, lively ease in dialogue and elegance of style. But when he is thus uncontrolled by a collaborator, his lack of regular constructive power is apparent: in the tragedies, characters as well as situations are romantic and sentimentality is substituted for passion; in the comedies, the search for curious incidents has precedence over character-study, and indecency, instead of coarseness, appeals for laughter. The favourite man's character is a witty profligate like Mirabel in the *Wild Goose Chase*, who affects an unbridled corruption far beyond reality and makes cynical love to all women, one who is capable of true love, but bound by his own declarations to flee marriage. The heroines by their extraordinary freedom of speech travesty the mischievous audacity of Shakespeare's Beatrice and Rosalind; they listen to men uttering words with the most indelicate implications and reply almost in the same language.

Fletcher a little compensates for these blemishes by a poetry which never leaves him: at its lowest it consists in elegance and distinction of language; when it gives itself free rein it produces the numerous exquisite songs scattered through his plays of which the glory is such that they are worthy to be compared even with Shakespeare's.

He is also particularised by his special versification, distinct not only from Shakespeare's, but also from that of Beaumont and all his other contemporaries. It is by this that it has been possible to determine his part in the large collection of plays attributed to him and his principal associate. Shakespeare progressed throughout his career towards greater prosodical freedom, an increased flexibility which would allow him to adapt his blank verse to every kind of mood. Hence his varied divisions of the line, his light or weak endings and the practice which grew upon him of continuing a phrase from one line to another. Fletcher chose a line which in two out of three cases ends in one and sometimes in several hypermetric syllables. This soft but effeminate prolongation of sound hardly allows the voice to rise; it is like an oversoft cushion into which the foot sinks. It makes it impossible for the sense to be continued from one line to the next. This practice of Fletcher's is carried to the point at which it becomes a mannerism. It has the effect of shortening his sentences so that they are apt to be restricted to the line. Rhetorical effects are obviated, but there is, at the same time, a loss of scale. His style belongs to the future rather than the past, and was much in favour in the Restoration period, when Shakespeare was considered to make too difficult an appeal to the mind and to be archaic.

(d) FLETCHER'S COLLABORATION WITH MASSINGER.—After Beaumont's death Fletcher, who had the habit of collaboration, found other partners, and there is hardly a contemporary playwright who did not work with him. The names of Jonson, Field, Tourneur and Rowley are associated with his. The chief of his coadjutors was, however, Philip Massinger, who, before he ventured alone, produced ten plays with Fletcher in the four years from 1619 to 1622. Fletcher's junior by four years, he was in some sort his assistant and pupil. Fletcher, master of the play-factory, seems to have paid him for his work and taken sole credit for the plays they produced together, Massinger uttering no protest. The protest was, however, voiced, even immediately, by others, and recent criticism has established that Massinger took a considerable part in the composition of some of the most popular plays attributed to Fletcher only. Among these are the historical tragedies *Thierry and Theodoret* and the *False One* (1620), the comedies *Little French Lawyer* (1619), the *Spanish Curate* and the *Beggar's Bush*.

It seems to have been Massinger's subordinate task to write preliminary and concluding scenes, while Fletcher kept the critical scenes to himself. But the laborious junior often exceeded these narrow and ungrateful limits. More than Fletcher, he felt the need for regular composition; he had a taste for moral problems and a real genius for dialectical scenes and for legal discussions. The collaboration produced plays of rather mixed and unequal character, although Fletcher's facile verve and Massinger's intellectualism are sometimes happily complementary to each other. We shall presently deal with Massinger's independent work, but it is impossible to consider this collaboration without noticing the extreme merit of the tragedies of *Thierry and Theodoret* and the *False One*. In the former the self-denial of the pure Ordella is contrasted with the cruelty of the lascivious Brunehaut. The *False One* has the same theme as Corneille's *Mort de Pompée* and its brilliant eloquence was not surpassed, if indeed it was equalled, by the French poet.

Before leaving Fletcher's work and particularly its most famous part, that written in collaboration with Beaumont, we would wish to establish what were its distinguishing marks, wherein lay his charm and his weakness. The floating islets of this poetry are pleasant to see and give an illusory impression of stability, but soon they are revealed as unattached and unsolid, unbound to the deep earth, so many agglomerations of waste matter to which deposits from every quarter have blown or drifted forming a thin layer of vegetable soil. Thus does the poetic work of Beaumont and Fletcher float on the surface of Renascence literature. Hardly a single tie connects it with deep and true feeling, but at first sight its charm is ravishing. Hazlitt has justly compared the plays of these poets to beautiful trees which are crowned with blossom but cannot bear fruit.

CHAPTER VIII

SHAKESPEARE'S SUCCESSORS. DRAMA UNDER CHARLES I—(1625-42)

1. **Philip Massinger (1584-1639).**[1]—The playwrights of whom we still have to speak belong to the reign of Charles I. and should therefore have place in the next book of this history. But they are, in the early part of their career, so entangled with their predecessors that they cannot easily be separated from them. To study them is to continue the earlier subject. It therefore seems best to pursue the study of the drama uninterruptedly until, at a fast approaching date, the theatres were closed. When Charles I. succeeded in 1625 only seventeen years of life were left to them.

The playwright who, after Fletcher, dominated the stage by the number and quality of his plays, had long worked with him as a subordinate. To Philip Massinger thirty-seven plays are attributed of which only eighteen are extant. The remnant suffices to outline a figure in literature which was both distinct and distinguished, although not entirely original. In his outstanding qualities, Massinger was a composite of Fletcher and Jonson. The incidents and characters of his tragedies are romantic as Fletcher's, and he reproduces vices and whims as far removed from the ordinary as those drawn in *Volpone*. Yet something in his plays is proper to himself, for he cast in the readymade moulds more doctrine and the product of greater reflective powers than his precursors. His drama is the drama of ideas. He seems to have been impatient of the restrictions of the stage and the necessity of making sacrifices to the lower elements in the public taste. Yet, because he wished to succeed, he submitted, and there is as much use of material expedients in his plays and as much indecency in his comic dialogue as in the work of any other playwright. When once, however, he had made these concessions, he allowed himself to exalt nobility of sentiment and eloquently to descant on the ideas which we feel that he held dear.

He began late. He was more than thirty years old when he is first discovered obscurely working for the theatre, more than forty when he produced the first works signed by his name alone. The son of a servant of the Pembroke family, he was sent to Oxford. After seven years of silence he is found at work and in Henslowe's pay, so poor that he had served one term in a debtor's prison. Although he was associated with Fletcher, who may be called the Cavalier poet, he did not share his mental attitude. He had no weakness for the court or the courtiers, and he could not, in spite of the risk of incurring censure, keep off the subjects of politics and religion. The ideas he expresses were opposed to those of the playgoing public. He did not flatter the patriotism of audiences and he had no respect for the divine right of kings. In *The Bondman*, he gives a sympathetic representation of a revolt of slaves against their masters, showing himself a kind of socialist. He

---

[1] Dramatic works, ed. Gifford, 4 vols. (1805, reprinted 1850); same text ed. Cunningham (1870); selected plays ed. Symons (Mermaid Series, 2 vols., 1904). Studies: Cruickshank, *Philip Massinger* (Oxford), 1920; M. Chelli, *Le drame de Massinger* (capital work) (1924); appreciation by M. de Tréveret in *Revue de l'Enseignement des Langues vivantes* (1886-7).

had the audacity to present to a public fed on declamations against popery the figure of an admirable Catholic priest, actually a Jesuit and yet endowed with all the virtues. In view of the danger to which he exposed his plays when he thus went counter to popular prejudice, we can hardly doubt that in such instances he was expressing cherished personal opinions.

We have already noticed the considerable mass of work which he accomplished together with Fletcher and his talent for manipulating ideas which this collaboration revealed. He is responsible for the very fine scene in the *False One* in which the counsellors of the king of Egypt discuss the advisability of murdering the fugitive Pompey. Here already his didactic genius has scope: he substitutes eloquence, even rhetoric, for the style which is properly dramatic. In his very interesting *Virgin Martyr* (1620), which he wrote with Dekker, he found an opportunity for self-revelation: he enjoys himself as he opposes the arguments of the Christians to those of the pagans.

A comparative study of this play and *Polyeucte* would bring into relief, in a most interesting way, the state to which the English stage had evolved at this moment. The spirit of the miracle-plays was still dominant. The playgoing public was still unsophisticated, still made its old demand for lively and curious shows. Literally, playgoers had to be confronted with whatever was presented to their minds. Everything still took material form for them. Thus the persecuting fury of the pagan Theophilus is personified in the demon Harfax, his servant, and the Christian enthusiasm of Dorothea, the virgin martyr, in the young page Angelo, who is in truth her guardian-angel and whom Dekker—his hand is felt here—has adorned with his most melodious poetry. The sufferings of the virgin and of the other Christians are detailed in all their variety of horror. The grace by which Theophilus is finally converted is symbolised by a basket of flowers and fruit brought to him to the sound of celestial music. His very remorse assumes a material form: he sees the ground beneath his feet paved with the eyes of the thousands of Christians he has martyred. Thus Massinger preserves all the powerful and popular allurements of the public stage while he devotes his better abilities to the discussion of ideas. He could not have won acceptance for his ideas unless he had abundantly satisfied that appetite for the concrete which long habit had bred in his audiences.

Presently we find him working alone, unhelped and unhindered. He wrote several comedies: *The City Madam* (1619), *A New Way to Pay Old Debts* (1625), *The Guardian* (1633)—and many more tragedies and romantic plays: *The Fatal Dowry* (1619), *The Duke of Milan* (1620), *The Unnatural Combat* (1621), *The Maid of Honour* (1622), *The Bondman* (1623), *The Renegado* (1624), *The Roman Actor* (1626), *The Picture* (1629), *The Emperor of the East* (1631).

The one of all these plays which had the most lasting success was a comedy: *A New Way to Pay Old Debts*. Revived in the eighteenth century, it has kept a place in theatrical repertories. It is vigorously constructed, in Jonson's manner, but even more than Jonson's plays it lacks the true *vis comica*. The leading rôle, that of the usurer Sir Giles Overreach, extravagant as Marlowe's Barabas or Jonson's Sir Epicure Mammon, is in no way amusing. Sir Giles is a monster of cupidity to whom gold is a means to power and power a means of expressing cynical inhumanity. He is also an atheist, stayed in his course by nothing in heaven or on earth. He enjoys the misfortunes of a nephew whom he has expropriated, and whom he ignominiously turns out of his house. His aim is to marry his daughter to a peer, not because he loves her, but in order that from the position this connection will give him he may insult all the gentlemen he has plundered. He enlarges on his opinions and feelings with an improbable frankness, as when he declares that nothing affords him greater pleasure than the fears of the women and children his machinations have rendered destitute. Although his scheming is finally defeated and he made a laughing-stock, and although he lives within a skilful plot sustained through scenes which are serious and comic by turns, he belongs not to comedy but to satire, and cannot provoke laughter. The same is true of Luke in the *City Madam*, a very demon of ingratitude, hypocrisy and malice whose turpitude would be excessive in a melodrama, and who as the central figure of a comedy is doubly repulsive, by his unequalled moral perversity and by his improbability.

It is in serious drama that Massinger really shows his powers. In all the plays we have noticed there are at least fine and eloquent passages and striking scenes. Two among them may be taken as affording the best illustration of the playwright's special talent.

Of the *Roman Actor*, Massinger himself states, "I ever held it the most perfect birth of my Minerva." There is undoubtedly a reminiscence of Jonson's *Sejanus* in this picture of the debauchery and cruelty of imperial Rome, but the play is none the less original. The subject is the love of Domitian and the imperious and sensual Domitia, the wife of a senator. Taking advantage of the emperor's blind passion, she gives the rein to all her caprices, even to desiring the indulgence of the frenzied passion she has conceived for the actor Paris while she has watched his performance. Domitian, when he is informed of this affair, kills Paris, but hesitates to order the immediate execution of his mistress. His vacillation costs him dear, for Domitia, infuriated by the death of Paris and knowing her own life in danger, takes the initiative. She conspires with all the victims of the emperor's lust and tyranny and, although he is warned by a soothsayer and takes many precautions, he is stabbed by the ladies of the palace with Domitia at their head. She pays the death-penalty, but the tyrant has fallen.

These vigorous and skilful scenes are very effective. Yet they are no more than a framework for the more original scenes in which Paris figures, now discussing with his brother-actors his profession in which he believes and which he follows enthusiastically, now pleading before the Senate when he is accused of allowing on the stage allusions offensive to the state. This last scene gives him the opportunity to utter, in a lofty speech, the best of that judicial eloquence which is a distinction of Massinger's dramatic work. Paris, however, does more than plead. Within this play he successively acts in three plays or fragments, taking the parts of a doctor who cures a miser of his avarice, a lover who implores his unfeeling mistress, and a servant who, in his master's absence, suffers the solicitations of that master's wife and yields to her for fear of her revenge. The part of Paris gives scope for the display of such a variety of talents that, from an actor's point of view, few are richer or more tempting. The character is, moreover, traced skilfully and with a sure hand. Paris's sincere faith in the moral influence of his art attracts sympathy, and his plight, when very respectfully he refuses Domitia's advances, is touching. He does not love her, but he knows that if he repel her she will cause his death. His first thought is, very naturally, for his own safety, but his imagination is presently caught by the idea of a glorious, a theatrical death. What more magnificent situation could there be than that of an actor refusing an empress? He thus goes to his death as a believer goes to martyrdom.

This play, all violence, tumult and crime, should be contrasted with another, the *Maid of Honour*, the most classical Massinger ever wrote, one in which a simple plot is smoothly unfolded and which has unity of action and a regular construction. The central figure is, moreover, a true heroine who incarnates virtue, love and honour. Camiola, the maid of honour, might be one of Corneille's heroines, and like them she has been subject to Spanish influence. She seeks glory in virtue, and is mistress of her heart, for all that it beats passionately. Chimène and Pauline have in her an elder sister whom they never knew.

Camiola, who is rich, is courted at one and the same time by an opulent and highborn coxcomb—a grotesque who never makes us smile and is the sole blemish of this fine play—by an abject court favourite, by a young page ready to make any sacrifice for her, and by the king's natural brother, the handsome, brave and seductive Bartoldo. She loves Bartoldo, but refuses him because he is a Knight of Malta and would break his vow of celibacy if he married her. He would fall short of the ideal, and she would have his glory all intact. Thus virtue forbids her to follow her heart, and the discouraged Bartoldo sets out as a volunteer for a distant war, where he shows prodigious valour, but is made prisoner. His ransom is fixed at an enormous sum, and his brother, the king, who hates and fears him, is glad to be rid of him and does not pay it. But Camiola, in a transport of love and pity, goes back upon her word; she sends the prisoner both the required sum of money and the promise to marry him which will lead him to accept her gift. Bartoldo, after giving vent to his boundless joy and gratitude, leaves his prison. The very princess against whom he has fought is, however, smitten with sudden and irresistible love at the sight of his martial beauty. She takes the initiative, declares her passion and offers him her hand. Dazzled by such unheard-of good fortune, he forgets Camiola, his vows and his debt. When the marriage is about to be celebrated, Camiola protests, shows the king the signed contract between her and Bartoldo and recalls all she has done. The princess indignantly repudiates her betrothed who is seized by remorse and begs for pardon. Camiola thereupon declares that all shall know the marriage on which she has decided, and while her lovers tremble in hope and suspense she advances towards a reverend Father who, at her request, receives her to give her to the Church, for she has determined to take the veil. But first she shows Bartoldo how to recover his honour: he must resume the cross of Malta and fight the enemies of the Faith.

Never had a worthier or nobler play, or one more discreet in its use of the means to produce great effects, been seen on the English stage. Camiola steps nobly and bears herself greatly. The virtue she personifies is indeed too complacently eloquent and at times theatrical. Yet she is not all pomp and speechifying. She loves and suffers; she really has a heart.

Elsewhere Massinger has used and also misused sensational stage expedients, but here he has shown the natural tendency of his pure and grave talent. It is in this play that his aspirations are best realised. Throughout his work, however, we are conscious of his probity as a writer. His hand is very sure and his verse remains rhythmic and harmonious in a period in which the versification of most authors is dislocated, and blank verse, by the accumulated effect of repeated licence, has lost its cadence and all but ceased to exist. It is true that all Massinger's modifications are not improvements. He is carried away by a talent for oratory, so that he is often strained and monotonous. His imagination lacks spontaneity. He has a certain number of rare but unvarying images which he repeats from play to play, sometimes clothing them in identical words. It has even been possible to make a list of these. Massinger is rather an industrious than an inspired poet, and his plays do not, like those of some of his less correct rivals, give either the surprise or the enjoyment of lyricism. Taken altogether, however, his massive and often noble work is such that it redeems his age from the charge of decadence.

2. John Ford (1586-1639 ?).[1]—John Ford, who was the same age as Massinger, produced, at the same time as he, work which was narrower than his but

---

[1] Works ed. Gifford and revised Dyce, 3 vols. (1869 and 1895); selected plays ed. by Havelock Ellis in the Mermaid Series (1888); 'Tis Pity She's a Whore in the Belles Lettres Series.

bore more clearly the impress of its author's personality. He belonged to a good Devonshire family and was in 1602 admitted to the Middle Temple. This is as much as is known of his life. To imagine his person we are helped only by two lines which show a pensive and solitary figure:

> Deep in a dump John Forde was alone got,
> With folded arms and melancholy hat.

His drama is influenced by Burton's famous *Anatomy of Melancholy* which appeared at the same time as his first plays. Some youthful verse and prose, still extant, reveal him as an amoral pagan, convinced of the fatality of passion and the power of love to justify itself. His work betrays a morbid temperament, curious of the strange and attracted by the perverse, yet a true poet who wrote carefully, harmoniously and restrainedly, and whose nature inclined him to a dramatic form more classical than that affected by his predecessors.

He collaborated with Webster, Rowley and Dekker, but was less prodigal of his co-operation than his contemporaries. The best known of the plays he thus produced is the *Witch of Edmonton*, of which Dekker seems to have been the principal author. The essential part of as much of Ford's own work as has been preserved consists of five plays, the *Lover's Melancholy,* '*Tis Pity She's a Whore*, *The Broken Heart*, *Love's Sacrifice* and *Perkin Warbeck*, all written between 1627 and 1633.

The last-named is a drama of English history, the final example of a genre, once popular, which was neglected after the end of the sixteenth century. *Perkin Warbeck* is a well-contrived and fairly interesting but rather flat play. Nothing in it is either new or original.

In this it is unlike Ford's other plays. Even the weakest of them, the *Lover's Melancholy,* is attractive because of its delicate handling of emotions and the graces of its style. *Love's Sacrifice*, in spite of reminiscences of *Othello*, is often new and striking. Bianca has no precedent. She is a young and beautiful girl, humbly born, who becomes the wife of the Duke of Pavia. When Fernando, a fine gentleman and the duke's favourite, pays court to her, she rejects his advances indignantly, yet she loves him and soon after, by a sudden change of attitude, offers herself to him, declaring she will kill herself on the morrow. Her heroic passion imparts greatness to Fernando, who refrains from desecrating her purity and sends her away. Yet they meet again, and they are about to yield to their passion when the duke, who is warned, surprises them together and stabs Bianca.

The irresistible force of love is more clearly illustrated in '*Tis Pity She's a Whore*, which has incest for its theme. This crime was not now staged for the first time, for it figures importantly in *A King and No King*, where Beaumont and Fletcher complacently describe the passion of King Arbaces for his reputed sister. Here, however, the discovery, at the end of the play, of the true origin of Arbaces changes incest into legitimate love. Ford's play contains no such palliative. It is, without question, his sister Annabella whom Giovanni loves passionately, and the savour of the incest is one of the components of the exaltation of their feelings for each other. The passionate ardours of Romeo and Juliet are repeated after the lapse of a generation and are seasoned with vice and guilt. Nothing better shows the development and the decline of the drama: no longer content with normal passions, it was seeking satisfaction in perverted pleasure. Giovanni is not only in love; he is also a theorist who apologises for his crime. The scenes between the guilty pair have a warmth which proves that Ford sympathised with them in the intoxication of their passion and in their sin. The play does indeed conclude on the note of horror, bloodshed mingling with voluptuousness. When Annabella, now another man's wife, is seized with remorse and refuses herself to her brother, he kills her and reappears with her heart on the point of his dagger, so that the morbid and the melodramatic are combined. This story of incestuous love occurs in a play which has several other plots, all of them detestable and none more so than that in which Ford tries his hand at clowning. But the poetry of fatality which pervades the principal episode is undeniable.

The *Broken Heart*, a tragedy which is full of the melancholy of unhappy love and suffering virtue, is much more harmonious and has a moral much less suspect. The scene of the action is laid in Sparta, doubtless in sign of the heroism of tortured hearts. Penthea, who loved Orgilus, has been forced by the tyranny of her brother Ithocles to marry the rich and jealous Bassanes. Her heart is still faithful to Orgilus, but while she makes him a declaration of undying love, she tells him that she is resolved never to fail in her wifely duty. The struggle within her breast is, however, such that she gives way to madness and is heard to utter sad and strange words. She swears never to eat again in order that her rebellious blood, which impels her to adultery, may cease to flow. She then dies.

But her brother Ithocles, who has been so hard to her, himself learns the power of love. He loses his heart utterly to fair Calantha, the king's daughter, and his passion enlightens him on his cruelty in parting Penthea and Orgilus. In a scene between him and Penthea, he begs her pardon for his past conduct. He listens to her vehement reproaches in silence, and finally touches her so that she consents to help him with Calantha. Calantha is quite ready to love the young hero, and their marriage has been determined when Orgilus, who has sworn vengeance, stabs Ithocles.

There is here a scene of which the *bravura* is imitated from Marston's *Malcontent*. While Calantha is dancing at a court ball, all joy at the thought of her approaching marriage, she hears first that the king, her father, has just died, then that Penthea has that moment breathed her last, and finally that Ithocles has been stabbed. The Spartan princess responds only by asking the musicians to play a livelier air. When the dance has ended, she repeats the news she has just received to the court. She has become queen and it is as a queen that she speaks. She fulfils her first duty by ordering the murderer of Ithocles to be executed; then, in the temple in which the coronation ceremony is to be performed, she informs all present that, while they thought she was dancing unfeelingly, she received a mortal wound. And when she has kissed the dead lips of Ithocles and placed a ring on his finger, she dies of a broken heart to the sound of a dirge which she herself has "fitted" for her end.

On analysis, the scenes of this play are seen to be unreal and its situations romantic, but its atmosphere of subtle and poignant pity and its harmony remain. Its value is in its poetry, in the impression it constantly gives of suffering virtue and implacable passion. Ford, by the belief in fatality which dominates his work, joins hands with the Greeks, not by an effect of mere artistry but in virtue of a special temperament. The impression he makes is as deep as it is painful. His plays move in a heavy, still and thundery atmosphere. Their lack of even the lightest breath of lively and wholesome air is disquieting. Ford's persistence in painting exquisite suffering and the refinements of perversity is a manifest sign of decadence, yet it constitutes his originality which outweighs his reminiscences and his borrowing.

3. **James Shirley (1596–1666).**[1]—James Shirley, whom Lamb calls "the last of a great race," was a more prolific and a more adaptable writer than Ford. His plays are among the most correct and the most outstanding of those which

[1] *Dramatic Works and Poems*, ed. Gifford and Dyce, 6 vols. (1833); selected plays ed. Gosse in the Mermaid Series, 1 vol. (1888).

appeared in the reign of Charles I., that is from 1625 until the theatres were closed in 1642. But while Ford's work struck, with all its faults, a note which was new and sometimes very penetrating, Shirley at his best did no more than continue cleverly what Jonson, Fletcher and Massinger had begun, imparting nothing peculiarly his own.

Shirley was an educated man who had been through both universities, and a fair poet who wrote a *Narcissus* inspired by Shakespeare's *Venus and Adonis*. He was first a schoolmaster and then a Protestant clergyman, but gave up his living when he was converted to Catholicism. He began to write for the stage when he was about thirty years old, won favour at court and was commissioned to compose masques which enjoyed a very high repute. He had the lyric gift of his predecessors and the song, "The glories of our blood and state," which occurs in one of his plays, is in every anthology. His production was checked by the Revolution. He was of the king's party and went into exile in France after the failure of the Royalist cause, afterwards returning to England and to his schoolmaster's calling. He had the satisfaction of witnessing the Restoration and the revival of his plays, but he died in the Fire of London in 1666. He is thus a link between two periods of dramatic history.

He gained distinction in tragedy and in comedy. More than Massinger, and especially more than Ford, he had the adaptability necessary to success in these opposite fields.

His two best tragedies are *The Traitor* (1631) and *The Cardinal* (1641). *The Traitor* is based on the famous story of Lorenzo de Medici to which Musset returned in *Lorenzaccio*. The psychological interest of Musset's play, the portrayal of a man of noble character, ruled by republican opinions, who becomes vicious while he seeks to corrupt the Duke of Florence in order to ruin him, is wanting in Shirley's tragedy. Shirley's Lorenzo is impelled to betray the duke by the mere ambition to usurp his throne. He is throughout an underhand and hypocritical scoundrel. The interest of the play lies in his intrigues and in the skill with which he lays his plots and diverts suspicion from himself. On occasion he simulates republican sentiment, but only in order the better to ensnare his dupes. The play undoubtedly includes effective scenes, but the most striking of them are too closely imitated from Cyril Tourneur's *Revenger's Tragedy*. The tragedy is, however, well constructed and carefully written.

The Cardinal, which Shirley himself esteemed his masterpiece, is in the class of tragedies of bloodshed and horror and connected with Webster's *Duchess of Malfi*. It has enough of the tragic force of this model to show that great sombre subjects persisted to the end in the drama of the Renascence. Structurally it is weaker than *The Traitor*.

Because Shirley's comedies are partly realistic, because they paint manners and fashions and literary crazes which changed with years, they are newer than his tragedies. While he cannot create really original characters, he adroitly sketches scenes from the life of the well-to-do classes of his day. This understanding of contemporary society keeps alive *The Wedding* (1626), *The Changes* (1632), *Hyde Park* (1632), *The Gamester* (1633) and especially the *Lady of Pleasure* (1635). This last play, which is full of arguments between a husband and his wife, she desiring always to be in the mode and he fearing that she will ruin him, is the prototype of more than one comedy of the succeeding age. In spite of its inferior vigour and wit, it foreshadows Vanbrugh's *Provoked Husband*, and even, one hundred and fifty years in advance, Sheridan's *School for Scandal* and the differences of Sir Peter with Lady Teazle.

Besides these comedies of manners, Shirley wrote others which are romantic and might equally well be called tragi-comedies. In these he shows himself the faithful disciple of Fletcher, like whom he is sometimes influenced by Spain. Spanish drama was beginning to be known and it was not therefore to Spanish stories that Shirley had recourse. For the *Young Admiral* he went straight to Lope de Vega and for *The Opportunity* (1634) to Tirso de Molina. The one of his romantic comedies which he himself esteemed the best is *The Imposture*. In this an ambitious aspirant to the hand of the daughter of the Duke of Mantua seeks to get rid of a formidable rival, the son of the Duke of Ferrara, by causing a meeting between him and a mistress of his own whom he has substituted for the high-born maiden.

To sum up: Shirley's comedies can be read with a calm pleasure, for his ingenuity is sometimes satisfying, his pictures of contemporary life are sometimes interesting and his elegant style is generally meritorious, but he never affords the lively enjoyment which his predecessors supplied, at least intermittently. He continued a tradition to which he gave no freshness and contributed nothing very new.

4. **Glapthorne and Brome.**—It was especially by his merits as a writer that Shirley surpassed all the later playwrights [1] except Ford. There was, for instance, Henry Glapthorne, who between 1635 and 1642 wrote several plays of which the best, *Argalus and Parthenia*, is borrowed from the *Arcadia*. He does not lack a certain grace, but his debased blank verse is like halting prose and awakens a longing for prose. Richard Brome's verse is more regular and his plays have more savour. He was first the servant and then the friend of Ben Jonson, who affectionately calls him his son. Brome has his master's realism and gives numerous sketches of London life. He is also the disciple of Dekker, who likewise calls him son, and he alternates romantic comedy with comedy of manners. The most interesting of his fifteen plays are the *City Wit, or the Woman wears the Breeches*, and *A Jovial Crew, or the Merry Beggars*. The first of these is a light-hearted satire on the pretensions of rank and wealth, and deals shrewd blows at the citizens whose care for profit made them careless of honour. *A Jovial Crew, or the Merry Beggars* echoes Dekker's sympathy for the unfortunate, and includes the character of a certain Springlove, happy when he is in the open air, tramping the fields and the lanes, who recalls Autolycus in the *Winter's Tale*, but is an honester man than he.

Brome should have been more ambitious and less humble. He introduces himself modestly as a man of no account, calls himself not a poet but a playmaker. Yet he seems to have taken conscientious pains with his work. While his is a prosaic spirit, while he is usually attracted by realities of no elevated order, he is, none the less, both observant and vigorous.

5. **Other Playwrights of the Second Rank.**—This review of the dramatic writers of the Renascence has hitherto included only the principal names. To be complete it should also deal with a fair number of authors of the second rank, of whom some have merit, and with several anonymous plays of which certain are highly interesting.

Some of these plays were ascribed to Shakespeare by contemporary publishers

[1] Of the playwrights of the second rank noticed hereafter only a few have been the subject of special modern publications, namely:

Richard Brome, *Dramatic Works*, in 3 vols. (1873), and H. Glapthorne, *Plays and Poems*, in 2 vols. (1874), both reprinted by Pearson.

Davenant, *Dramatic Works*, 5 vols. (1872–4), and Shakerley Marmion, *Dramatic Works* (1875), both ed. by Maidment and Logan.

The works of Thomas Nabbes are included in vols. i. and ii. and the works of Robert Davenport in vol. iii. of *Old English Plays*, new series, ed. Bullen, 3 vols. (1887–90).

Sir John Suckling, *Poems and Plays*, ed. Hazlitt, 2 vols. (1892).

Two comedies by John Day are included in *Nero and Other Plays* (Mermaid Series, 1888).

Such of the works of the other playwrights as have been reprinted are included in *Dodsley's Old English Plays* (1st ed., 1744, re-ed. by Hazlitt, 15 vols., 1874–5).

or have been attributed to him subsequently.[1] Among them are two on the national history which are very remarkable, *Edward the Third* and *Sir Thomas More*, and also an excellent comedy, the *Merry Devil of Edmonton*, and a romantic play, the *Two Noble Kinsmen*, of which Fletcher was the principal author, although most critics admit that Shakespeare had a hand in it. These plays from the Shakespeare apocrypha must be added to those already studied, *Arden of Feversham* and *A Yorkshire Tragedy*. They are the most noteworthy of a considerable group of which the authorship is conjectural. Another anonymous play written with much talent is *Nero*,[2] printed in 1633. It is the work of a mediocre playwright who was both a scholar and a true poet.

To the authors already cited, certain others who wrote in the last years of Elizabeth should be added: William Haughton, the prolific Henry Chettle who collaborated with several of the famous playwrights, and Henry Porter, author of a rather broad but strong farce, *Two Angry Women of Abingdon*.

Under James I. there flourished Robert Armin. Barnabe Barnes, Gervase Markham and, especially, John Day. The last named wrote amusing comedies, the *Isle of Gulls* (1606), *Law Tricks* and *Humour out of Breath* (1608), which are inspired by Shakespeare, but which, since they lack sparkle and dash and betray a search for symmetry and for epigrams, rather recall Lyly. Day's most original work is the *Parliament of Bees*, a fantastic production which is in the nature of a masque, or rather like a series of eclogues. The actor Nathaniel Field (1587–1633), who was educated on Jonson and Chapman and collaborated with Fletcher and Massinger, wrote good-humoured antithetic comedies, *A Woman is a Weathercock* (1610) and *Amends for Ladies*.

Under Charles I., Thomas Randolph (1605–35), a young Cambridge man, gave promise of a brilliant career. His comedy, the *Muses' Looking-Glass*, is a satirical review of vice, with a realistic framework hardly less amusing than that provided for the *Knight of the Burning Pestle*; and his pastoral, *Amyntas, or the Fatal Dowry*, inspired by Tasso and Guarini and written with careful art, is one of the best examples of this artificial genre. Randolph died, however, at the age of thirty. Sir John Suckling (1609–42), a great admirer of Shakespeare who is better known as a lyrical poet, had dramatic proclivities, and both his tragedy *Aglaura* (1639), and his amusing comedy, *The Goblins*, won him applause. Literary history is, however, especially interested in the playwrights who were links between the stage of the Renascence and of the Restoration. Lodowick Carlell, who produced the *Deserving Favourite* in 1629 and *Arviragus and Philicia* in 1639, accomplished, in 1664, an adaptation of Corneille's *Heraclius*. Robert Davenport, author of *A New Trick to Cheat the Devil* in 1639, wrote, in 1661, the *City Night-Cap*. Thomas Killigrew was author of *The Prisoners* in 1641, and of tragic and comic plays under Charles II. Sir William Davenant (1606–68) produced five plays under Charles I., of which the most interesting, the *Platonic Lovers* (1636), was acted in the last years of the Commonwealth, and he also inaugurated Restoration drama with his *Siege of Rhodes*.

These dramatists betray the influence of the new age by their imitation of Spanish and French writers of romance. Carlell's plays are based on d'Urfé and Mademoiselle de Scudéry, as are those of Davenant, whose taste for sentimental heroics and the casuistry of love blazed the track for the heroic plays of the reign of Charles II.

6. **The Closing of the Theatres. Conclusion.**—Dramatic production, abundant

---

[1] *The Shakespeare Apocrypha*, ed. Tucker Brooke (1908); A. W. Pollard, *Shakespeare's Fight with the Pirates* (1920).
[2] *Nero and Other Plays* (Mermaid Series, 1888).

to the last, was suddenly checked in 1642, when the theatres were closed by Parliament. After the playhouses had struggled for existence against the Puritans for three-quarters of a century, and made them their laughing-stock, it was to the Puritans that victory finally fell. The stage had no sooner become popular than the war had been declared. Gosson was writing his *School of Abuse* in 1579; in 1583 the Puritan Philip Stubbs renewed the attack much more vigorously with his *Anatomy of Abuses*, in which he claims Biblical support for his condemnation of the drama. His book provoked many replies—from Lodge, Nashe, Field, Gager, Heywood and others. Fifty years later a pendant to it was supplied by the famous *Histriomastix* of William Prynne (1632). This fierce denunciation from the pen of a fanatic was the result of seven years of work and reached enormous dimensions. It is a depository of all the accumulated diatribes of the Fathers of the Church and the moralists against plays and actors; and it was also a direct attack on the court, where at this time dramatic art found its sole support. The companies of actors had been protected by various noblemen under Elizabeth, but from the time of the accession of James I. they all depended on the king or the queen, and such concentration was accentuated under Charles I. Prynne stigmatised as "notorious whores" the leading actresses, whom Queen Henrietta had brought over from France, and he paid for his insults when he was sentenced to lose his ears in the pillory, to pay a heavy fine and to be imprisoned at the king's pleasure. Nine years after the appearance of his book, Parliament, having barely secured its triumph over the king, ordered the closing of the theatres. Their association with royalty proved unfortunate for them. The demolition of all the playhouses was decreed; all actors seized were ordered to be whipped; and everyone who attended a dramatic performance was made liable to a fine of five shillings. For eighteen years the theatres, which had been places of intense, noisy life, were silent. When they were once more thrown open, their repertory was largely new and their audiences were largely different.

It behoves us, before we conclude, to take a general view of the drama, the great home of the literary activity of the English Renascence. When extant plays and plays which survive only in their titles are added together, their total number comes near a thousand, and this luxuriant prolificity was concentrated within narrow limits of time. Only sixty-three years separate the date on which the first public theatre was opened from that on which all the playhouses were closed. It is easy to conceive of a man who in the course of his life was present at the first performances of all the works which made the English stage illustrious. Born in 1567, he might have seen Lyly's *Endymion*, Marlowe's *Tamburlaine* and Kyd's *Spanish Tragedie* when he was about twenty; Shakespeare's *Romeo and Juliet* and *Henry IV.*, Ben Jonson's *Every Man in His Humour* and Dekker's *Shomakers Holiday* when he was about thirty; *King Lear* and *Macbeth*, Jonson's *Volpone*, Cyril Tourneur's *Revenger's Tragedy* and Fletcher's *Faithful Shepherdess* at about forty; Beaumont and Fletcher's *Maid's Tragedy*, Webster's *White Devil* and Middleton's *A Chaste Maid in Cheapside* at about forty-five; the first plays in which Beaumont and Fletcher and Middleton and Rowley collaborated at about fifty; Massinger's *Roman Actor*, Ford's *'Tis Pity She's a Whore* and Heywood's *English Traveller* at about sixty; Shirley's *Traitor* and *Gamester* and Davenant's *Platonic Lovers* in his later sixties.

Would he, witnessing this sequence of playwrights and plays, have perceived an evolution? The family likeness between most of these works, all composed on the same principle, might have hidden it from him. Nearly all of them divide a whole story, seldom invented by the author but rather taken from books, into scenes. They thus share their descent from the mystery-plays of the Middle Ages, and like them appeal, in their scenes, by turns to the imagination, the understand-ing, the feelings and the senses. Like them, they endeavour to interest the whole of man and of mankind and not merely learned and fastidious persons. Like them, they almost invariably mingle comedy and tragedy.

Their likeness to each other is the result of this conception of drama which they have in common, and the breadth of the principle on which they depend produces, at the same time, their diversity. There was no importation from antiquity of regularity of structure, and therefore no predominance of classical principles of construction which, since a playwright merely accepts them, are necessarily impersonal and have a clearly eliminating effect. There is nothing academic about these plays, not even about those of the classicist Jonson. A lively air blows through them all. The place given, even in tragedy, to a homely comic element is a correc-tive of romanticism and imparts realism everywhere. The poetry diffused over all and the habitual lyricism are controlled, tempered and vivified by this realism. Nothing is quite cut off from the earth, entirely in the clouds, in a world of abstraction. The element of direct observation, the reflections of real life which occur in some scene of every play, give abiding interest to parts of even the most mediocre and factitious production.

The very free field given to the dramatists also enabled them to let their per-sonality have play. Each of them could, according to his temperament and powers and his opportunities of observation, imprint his own mark on his work. Ignorant though we are of the limits of the individual accomplishment of playwrights, and in spite of the difficulties due to the custom of collaboration, we easily distinguish certain very distinct figures. Nothing is less liable to be confused than Lyly's courtly wit, Marlowe's rabid ardour, Dekker's tender, sentimental realism, Marston's cynical harshness, the robustness of Jonson's thought and style, the sombre, melodramatic poetry of Webster, Heywood's simple pathos, Middleton's dry, cutting manner, the skilful and elegant romanticism of Beaumont and Fletcher, the rhetorical vein of Massinger and Ford's disquieting subtlety, not to mention the superior genius at the centre of this constellation, "myriad-minded Shake-speare," who is not to be contained by a couple of epithets.

The gifts of life, variety, poetry and realism lead us to overlook defects which are numerous and sometimes enormous—loose, disjointed, clumsy or overweighted composition, the assignment of overmuch space to broad, low buffoonery, the cult of melodramatic effects, the lavish introduction of physical horrors and macabre subjects, the frequent lack of execution and of loftiness of aim, consequent on the desire for immediate success.

In what is the evolution of this drama perceptible? Is it to be found elsewhere than in the differences between authors? Does it consist in a rise which culminates in Shakespeare's masterpieces and a subsequent decline? Even if, with infinite difficulty, Shakespeare be abstracted from the field of consideration, we perceive, as is natural, that the qualities properly of the stage were almost constantly acquiring that additional skill which only experience can confer. There is something archaic about the first plays even of the great period, about the too plainly deliber-ate clash of wits in Lyly, and about Marlowe's vast declamations. Dramatic style is gradually fashioned and made flexible; the metrical line, at first too rigid, relaxes and loses its monotony; prose is more frequently used and grows nimbler; tone approximates increasingly to the natural, normal voice. Conventional characters bequeathed by the miracle-plays, personified vice and the clown, give place more and more to real beings or those who aspire to be such. The clown has neither place nor date; he is a comic actor rather than a character. He does not long survive Shakespeare, who uses him with extreme skill yet never quite cleanses him of his original taint of unreality. His disappearance marks the advance of drama, not indeed towards more truth, but towards more realism. In the work of Jonson, Middleton, Fletcher and Ford, hardly any subsists in the externals and the equipment of plays which is not modern. Their plays are, therefore, sometimes astonishingly near to ourselves although very little separates them from their predecessors. The same force of realism sweeps away, little by little, the fantastic and fairy elements which become less popular. The appeal to imagination loses strength and daring. If characters and situations tend to be less true to nature, it is not that the poets give more space to dreams, but that, as their knowledge of feeling grows less sure, they show an increased inclination for sensation.

They draw nearer to reality in externals while in essentials they become more remote from it: comedy shows a preference for eccentricity and anomalies, and tragedy passes from the epic to the romantic.

It cannot be denied that the romantic was there from the beginning, but from decade to decade it developed and little by little superseded the historical character which at first belonged to many plays. Dramas of national history ceased, with hardly any exceptions, to be written after the sixteenth century. Except for a few excursions into Roman or foreign history, subjects came to be supplied by romances, whether Italian, Spanish or French. More and more, the portrayal of normal thought and feeling made room for that of the extraordinary and complicated, whether superhuman or morbid. In order to hold the attention of audiences much used to plays, dramatists sought to astonish them, or supplied them with the most highly flavoured dishes. From the love of Romeo and Juliet, drama proceeded to the incestuous passion of Giovanni and Isabella. From portraits of English kings and lords not unfaithful to history, whence the playwrights took them, it passed to monarchs increasingly exotic and imaginary. Comic characters drawn mainly from life—Juliet's nurse, Falstaff, Justice Shallow—evolved to the excesses of Volpone or Overdone.

Avoid him as we may, we return inevitably to Shakespeare. It was he who humanised the initial violence of this drama, and at his death it tended once more to become remote from the central truth—that of character and feeling.

BOOK V

THE END OF THE RENASCENCE (1625–60)

CHAPTER I

PROSE FROM 1625 TO 1660

1. **Literature under Charles I. and the Commonwealth.**[1]—The period which extends from 1625 to 1660 is filled with the political and religious strife of the reign of Charles I. and the triumph of Puritanism. It is usual to consider this time as one in which the previously expansive development of literature was restricted and thought was concentrated on a single book—the Bible. The fact that the dominant figure is that of the great Puritan poet Milton favours this view. The Puritanism which closed the theatres did indeed give a character of strictness to the new age and bring it into contrast with the profane and licentious Renascence. Not only, however, did humanism persist as a force and affect no writer more powerfully than Milton himself, and not only are freethinking and freedom of manners still apparent in the poetry of the Cavaliers, but beyond this the religious movement of the age was not exclusively due to the zealous Calvinists who were able for a time to establish Presbyterian discipline in the country, or to the Independents who rebelled against this discipline and claimed that the individual had a right to interpret the Bible according to the light that was in him. Anglicanism, lukewarm and indolent under Elizabeth, acquired new life from the struggle. The pious fervour of the middle years of the seventeenth century was wrought at least as much by the zeal of Episcopalians, not excepting those of them who reverted to Roman Catholicism, as by the subversive passion and sombre religion of their adversaries. In no other period of their history did the Anglicans produce works, both in verse and prose, which were as noble and had as much unction. Literary production was at this time much more various than it at first seems to be. Yet it is undeniable that the religious revival gave this generation its general character and distinguished it from the preceding one. In exchange for the liberty it partly lost, it acquired seriousness, a severe dignity. Rich humanity, unlimited curiosity, the sense of the comic mingling with the sense of the tragic in the portrayal of life: all gave place to a passionate controversy on the forms of the Christian religion and a search, so constant that it was an obsession, for the way of salvation.

2. **Sir Thomas Browne** (1605–82).[2]—The contrast is perhaps most apparent in prose. There were no more novels, no more diverting pictures of

---

[1] See E. Dowden, *Anglican and Puritan* (1901); Ackland, *Little Gidding and its Inmates* (1903); and Shorthouse's historical novel, *John Inglesant* (1881).
[2] His works were edited in 4 vols. by Wilkin (1835–6); in 3 vols. by Sayle (1904); in 3 vols. by Morison (Pitt Press Series, 1922); in 3 vols. (Golden Cockerell Press, 1923). Principal works in 1 vol. in the Camelot Series (1886).
See also Leslie Stephen, *Hours in a Library*, 2nd series (1876); E. Gosse, *Sir Thomas Browne* (English Men of Letters Series, 1905); and study in French by J. Milsand in *Revue des Deux Mondes* (1858).

manners, no entertaining fruits of invention; there were not even the disinterested lucubrations of humanists whose reading amused them. The passage from Robert Burton to Sir Thomas Browne is in this respect very characteristic. The contrast between them is shown up by the very resemblances which make it possible to compare them. Like Burton, Browne was a very learned man, a humanist astonishingly widely and variously read. He was familiar with secular and sacred authors; he lived in studious retirement, complacently following the thread of his thought. He too was an eccentric, and his posthumous vicissitudes were like those of Burton, for he was all but forgotten in the eighteenth century and was restored to honour by Lamb and the romantics.

But they differed even more than they resembled each other. Burton was a clergyman, hauntingly preoccupied with medicine. He himself states that he was "by his profession a divine and by his inclination a physician." His whole book shows his taste for observing facts and details, rather than a desire to inquire into the origin and end of man.

Browne, on the other hand, was a physician by profession and a divine or preacher by inclination. He was a mystic. Outwardly, his life passed happily and calmly, reflecting in no way the troubles of the civil war. He was a Royalist and an Anglican, but he did not compromise himself and his peace was not disturbed. The exercise of his art won him much renown. He devoted his leisure to studying the antiquities of Norwich, where he lived. He applied Bacon's method to the examination of the fauna of the district and natural phenomena. His science is, like Bacon's, oddly mixed with prejudice, ignorance and ingenuousness, as appears in the most extensive of his works, *Pseudodoxia Epidemica, or Enquiries into very many received tenets and commonly presumed truths* (1647), the very book in which he proposes to criticise and rectify current errors. Nothing gives a better idea of the state of popular science than to note some of the errors he combats: "that Crystal is nothing else but Ice strongly congealed"; "that a diamond is softened or broken by the blood of a goat"; "that an Elephant hath no joints"; "that a Wolf, first seeing a man, begets a dumbness in him"; "that the flesh of Peacocks corrupteth not."

Browne himself, partly owing to his respect for the Bible, retains some errors of this kind. He refuses to accept the system of Copernicus and maintains that the earth is the centre of the universe. He believes in astrology, alchemy, witchcraft and magic. His evidence as a doctor caused two poor women to be put to death as witches.

His mind held a curious medley. In spite of his real and often deep knowledge of natural science, he kept a taste for miracles. This learned man is especially impressed by the narrow limits of science. He reveals his complex soul in the most celebrated and most curious of his books, *Religio Medici*, which he wrote before he was thirty, that is before 1635, and which was published in 1642 and translated into Latin, Dutch, French and German. Guy Patin, who knew it in Latin, says that it was much esteemed in Paris and considers that it proves the author's wit— "Il y a de gentilles choses dans ce livre."

Neither prettiness nor wit is the dominant quality of this work in which the author defines his religion. "I am, I confess," he informs us, "naturally inclined to that which misguided zeal terms superstition." Anglican though he was, he deals so gently with Catholicism that he has been suspected of being a Catholic. He tells us that he "could never hear the Ave-Mary bell without an elevation." He is full of sympathy for all Christian sects and even of pity for infidels. He prides himself on being a cosmopolitan without national prejudice. At times he might be mistaken for a scholar or deist of the eighteenth century. But this is a superficial resemblance, for he ignores the cult of reason, mental travail invariably leading him to contempt of knowledge. "It is better to sit down in a modest ignorance and rest content with the natural blessing of our own reasons, than buy the uncertain knowledge of this life with sweat and vexation, which death gives every fool gratis." Thus, while he constantly uses his reason, he has no hope of learning by it the things of greatest moment to him. His appetite for faith is great. Far from rejecting religion because it demands concessions from reason, he would have it yet more exacting:

> As for those wingy mysteries in divinity and airy subtleties in religion which have unhinged the brains of better heads, they never stretched the *pia mater* of mine. Methinks there be not impossibilities enough in religion for an active faith. . . . I love to lose myself in a mystery, to pursue my reason to an *O altitudo !*

Far from envying the early Christians the miracles which they witnessed and which compelled them to believe, he considers that their experience would make his faith too little meritorious. Moreover, he sees miracles everywhere, even in existence at its simplest. "Now for my life, it is a miracle of thirty years, which to relate were not a history but a piece of poetry, and would sound to common ears like a fable."

His habitual themes are those of the preacher—the vanity of glory, the nearness of death. He renews them with singularly erudite reminiscences which rekindle the ashes of the most remote historical past, and with constant references to the universe and to cosmographical facts. Hence there is frequently a strangeness and also a loftiness in his writings: thoughts and images are magnified; he imparts a great scale which is natural to him.

The fantastic character of the period is revealed. Browne has affinities with Donne and the "metaphysical" poets. When he wishes to mock man's vain efforts to perpetuate after death a body vowed to destruction, he speaks of:

> Egyptian ingenuity . . . contriving their bodies in sweet consistencies to attend the return of their souls. But all was vanity, feeding the wind and folly. The Egyptian mummies, which Cambyses or time hath spared, avarice now consumeth. Mummy is become merchandise, Mizraim cures wounds, and Pharaoh is sold for balsams.

He gives rein to his fancy in the *Garden of Cyrus*, which is a dissertation on quincunxes. Disposition in quincunxes and the number five gradually take on for him a mystic value. He finds quincunxes everywhere—in the sky, on the earth, in the mind of man, in the notes of music, in the optic nerve, in the roots of trees, in leaves. His strangeness of thought is indeed excused by a vein of humour: his capricious leavetaking of his subject is famous. He has worked late into the night; the stars are waning and urge him to rest. "But the quincunx of heaven (the Hyades) runs low and it is time to close the five ports of knowledge. . . . To keep our eyes open longer were but to act our Antipodes. The huntsmen are up in America and they are already past their first sleep in Persia."

Even when Browne deals with the subject he has most at heart—oblivion—he gives free play to his dilettante imagination. His *Hydriotaphia, or Urn Burial* (1658), was inspired by the discovery in a field of some fifty urns containing the remains of human bones. This induced him to meditate on death and on oblivion which soon covers up man's traces, and he was able to air his vast erudition regarding the various ancient modes of burial. He considers that the hope of a survival in memory, which, even in primitive man, was a mad hope, becomes such in a much greater degree as the world grows old and nears its end:

> Twenty-seven names make up the first story before the flood, and the recorded names ever since contain not one living century. The numbers of the dead long exceedeth all that sh all live. The night of time far surpasseth the day, and who knows

when it was the equinox? Every hour adds unto that current arithmetick, which scarce standeth one moment. And since death must be the *Lucina* of life, and even Pagans could doubt whether thus to live were to die; since our longest sun sets at right descensions, and makes but winter arches, and therefore it cannot be long before we lie down in darkness, and have our light in ashes; since the brother of death daily haunts us with dying mementos, and time that grows old in itself bids us hope no long duration —diuturnity is a dream and folly of expectation.

Thus Browne, as he writes, sometimes recalls Montaigne by his confessions, sometimes foreshadows Pascal by the greatness of his cosmic visions. But the insistence with which he places himself in a favourable light, his care to establish himself on a pedestal, awaken a regret for Montaigne's greater spontaneity and less discreet confidences. Browne remarks on his own courage, charity and pity for another's ills, and congratulates himself on his freedom from pride, although, while he lacks the scientist's pride in reason, he possesses the pride of the mystic who believes that his nature is exceptional and that he is privileged to meditate as men rarely do and to receive direct revelations. At the same time, Browne is differentiated from Pascal by what may be called his complacent redundancy. In this there is something of literary artifice, a too apparent rhetoric, and there is also a taste for the eccentric which is evidence of less intense and less inexorable seriousness than belonged to Pascal.

He is, in fact, an artist rather than a thinker, and more interesting as a writer than as a man. His prose is admirable. His style is very distinct from Burton's. His sentences are short, clearly outlined, and modern and restrained in construction. He dates by his vocabulary, for he is a great latiniser. Words which Burton leaves in Latin, in the middle of a sentence, are retained but anglicised by Browne. His love of the noble shows itself in his preference for long, learned terms. But his search for latinised words is also inspired by his love of cadences. He believes in the music of periods as the poet does in that of verse. He had a passion for harmony, loved it in the sound of organs, even found food for it in the music he heard in taverns. "There is something in it of divinity more than the ear discovers: it is an hieroglyphical and shadowed lesson of the whole world and creatures of God— such a melody to the ear as the whole world, well understood, would afford the understanding." This passion led Browne instinctively to choose the most melodious words, those which make his sentences musical. So subtle is his use of sonorities, that few poets afford in their verses a better feast to the ear than does this mystical doctor in his prose.

3. **The Anglican Clergy. Jeremy Taylor.**[1]—Sir Thomas Browne, religious though he was, was in a sense independent and a follower of his own fancy. But the renewal of piety in the very heart of Anglicanism caused some memorable pages of English prose to be written. Under Charles I. and the Commonwealth, Richard Hooker and John Donne found worthy successors. Archbishop Laud (1575–1645) was the head of the Church established under Charles I. and also, since he attempted to impose the Anglican liturgy on England and on the Presbyterians of Scotland, an architect of the civil war as he was one of its first victims. He was much hated, and although he opposed Rome he received the supreme insult of an accusation of popery. He was not brought back to Catholicism, but the circumstance that his chief adversaries were the Puritans and the Presbyterians led him to revive everything in Anglicanism which could strengthen the hierarchy, discipline and

---

[1] Complete works, ed. R. Heber, 15 vols. (1822); ed. C. P. Eden, 10 vols. (1847–52); *Holy Living and Dying*, in Bohn's Library; *The Rule and Exercises of Holy Living*, ed. Waller, 2 vols. (1900).
See E. Gosse, *Jeremy Taylor* (1904); G. Worley, *Jeremy Taylor, a Sketch of his Life and Times* (1904).

ceremonial. He desired to give the Anglican form of worship the pomp which distinguishes it from Calvinism and is the mark of the High Church.

This Anglicanism in love with tradition and solemn ritual, respectful of the hierarchy and of fine discipline, gained at this time the adherence of the leading members of the Church of England, except such of them as crossed the barrier and definitely became Roman Catholics, like the Benedictine historian Augustine Baker and Crashaw the poet.

George Herbert (1593-1633),[1] known especially for his poem *The Temple*, left behind him only the few pages of prose which are his picture of a country clergyman, the *Country Parson*. This is among the most characteristic of the prose writings of the time. From a wit and man of fashion, Herbert, towards the end of his short life, became rector of Bemerton, where he was distinguished for his fervent and fastidious piety. His experience was his guide when he drew his ideal portrait of a good parson, in simple, smooth prose which is in contrast to his subtle and often enigmatic poetry. He tells what should be the life, the character and education of a country clergyman, how he should pray, preach and behave on Sundays, how he should keep his church and what rule he should follow, and cause to be followed, in his house, what he should do and say during his pastoral visits. He allows him a time for recreation, in contrast to the morose Puritans. Nothing is more pleasing than his neat, smiling, comfortable church, of a type reproduced in England by the hundred until it became the regulation model. Everything in it signifies the mean between two extremes, between superstition and carelessness, between the gilded luxury of a Catholic cathedral and the depressing nakedness of a dissenters' chapel. Hooker's just mean is realised in the decoration of the church.

George Herbert was one of the intimate friends of Nicholas Ferrar, who founded at about this time the curious community of Little Gidding, a very characteristic expression of the Catholic aspirations of the High Church party. Ferrar, a man of business, who was highly educated, had been in Parliament and had travelled much, refused to respond to the appeal of Rome because he was scandalised by Italian morals, but desired to transport to England certain practices of Roman discipline which he admired. He retired in 1625 to the village of Little Gidding, and there founded a sort of Protestant monastery in which he lived with his family, as in a devout retreat, apportioning certain hours to prayer, reading and work. He was approved by Laud, who ordained him deacon, and visited and praised by Charles I. There is a recent and attractive description of this community, living piously and practising the highest principles, in J. H. Shorthouse's mystical novel, *John Inglesant*. It had something in common with the French Port-Royal, but while Port-Royal was Catholic in an austere spirit akin to Calvinism, Little Gidding, in a Protestant country, almost yearned for the Roman tradition which it attempted, a little romantically, to revive. The community was abolished by Parliament in 1646. Ferrar's books—he died in 1637—were destroyed and his house and church pillaged.

The spirit of gentleness and poetry by which such as Herbert and Ferrar were animated recurs in the work of the great Anglican preacher of the middle of this century, Jeremy Taylor (1613-67), who has been called the Shakespeare and the Spenser of the pulpit, the English Chrysostom and the most eloquent of theologians. He distinguished himself as a preacher as early as 1634, when he left Cambridge, was patronised by Laud and became chaplain-in-ordinary to Charles I. As chaplain of the royal army during the civil war he was made prisoner and deprived of his benefices. He retired to Wales, where, to secure a livelihood, he founded a school.

---

[1] *A Priest to the Temple*, ed. Waller (1901).

I—Z

The Restoration brought him the Irish bishopric of Dromore, and so many cares and controversies as accompaniments to the episcopal dignity that he sighed for a country living. He was obliged to expel thirty-one clergymen who were refractory to the Episcopalian order, and his liberality and kindliness made the necessity for persecution really painful to him.

The misfortunes of their Church had indeed turned the Anglicans into champions of religious liberty. After hunting down Catholics and Puritans for fifty years, and severely prohibiting Puritans from preaching, they were now demanding toleration. Taylor became their mouthpiece, without recantation, for he was tolerant by nature. This characteristic gives its high value to his great treatise *A Discourse of the Liberty of Prophesying with its just limits and temper, showing the unreasonableness of prescribing to other men's faith and the iniquity of persecuting differing opinions* (1646). He founds his argument on the difficulty of interpreting Scripture and on the fallibility of councils and theologians. Save that he insists that the Creed must be upheld, he is tolerant to a degree which in this age might well seem absolute. His other great work is *Holy Living and Dying* (1650). But his numerous sermons rank above his books.

They are distinguished less by logic than by imagination—an imagination fed by copious reading and by an extensive classical culture on which he constantly drew, and animated by his charmed contemplation of nature. Taylor is a prose poet, and as a poet is closely akin to the great Elizabethans. He conceives an imaginative interest in the objects he describes, although he is first directed to them only by the desire to render his thought clear and concrete. As he follows up his similes and develops them, he sometimes recalls the fancy or even the slightly mannered ingenuity of the poets of the Renaissance. The idea of a rose induces him to paint it in detail, that of the sunrise to describe its successive phases. It happens to him to say that prayer rises like a lark, and thereupon he gives himself free rein:

> For so have I seen a lark rising from his bed of grass, and soaring upwards, singing as he rises, and hopes to get to heaven and climb above the clouds; but the poor bird was beaten back with the loud sighings of an eastern wind, and his motions made irregular and inconstant, descending more at every breath of the tempest than it could recover by the libration and frequent weighing of his wings, till the little creature was forced to sit down and pant and stay till the storm was over; and then it made a prosperous flight, and did rise and sing as if it had learned music and motion from an angel, as he passed sometimes through the air, about his ministries here below: so is the prayer of a good man.

No poet could have better observed the bird soaring heavenward or described it with more sympathetic emotion. Such *bravura* passages could be extracted from many of Taylor's pages. They impart a charming grace and freshness, but the preacher who voices them may be accused of lingering on the path of duty to play and cull flowers. They rob his eloquence of some force of urgency. The logician is obscured by the artist.

Yet at times Taylor is forceful and great, as in the magnificent passage in which he shows death to be easy and simple, if but it be shorn of its pomp and "solemn bugbears."

> It is the same harmless thing that a poor shepherd suffered yesterday, or a maid-servant to-day; and at the same time in which you die, in that very night a thousand creatures die with you, some wise men, and many fools; and the wisdom of the first will not quit him, and the folly of the last does not make him unable to die.

Taylor was, moreover, not only an observer of inanimate nature, but also a psychologist of great delicacy who knew the heart of man. No one else has spoken

of the love between husband and wife, its frailty soon after marriage and the
strength it acquires by mutual trials, with as much insight and poetry as this
clergyman in his sermon on the marriage-ring.

A delightful anthology can be compiled from his work. His prose is the most
varied in tone and the most modern of his time. He had his share of the seductive
gift. He had a broad sympathy for nature, human and other, and to this he added
a taste for reading the profane authors of antiquity. He quotes Petronius and the
Anthology neither pedantically nor apologetically but spontaneously, because
some anecdote or line of poetry has enriched his memory. He is a proof that the
best of the clergy had absorbed the culture of the Renascence and become the
depositories of literary and poetic sensibility. Henceforward it is possible to regard
their rôle as enlightened purveyors of civilisation confidently and hopefully,
whether they occupy an episcopal see or their lot be cast in a humble parish.

Many other names [1] would have to be added to those already cited in order to
give a just idea of Anglican activity in these years. Religious prose was enriched
by the sermons of Robert Sanderson; by the penetrating mysticism of Thomas
Traherne's *Centuries of Meditations*, available only in manuscript form until they
were recently published together with his remarkable verses; by the Biblical
criticism and pure and simple sermons of Henry Hammond; by John Hales's
Golden Remains; and by a *History of the Reformation* (1661) by Peter Heylin, an
aggressive and acrimonious controversialist who also wrote a history (published
in 1656) of his travels in 1625 in France, a work without sympathy for the people
described, but pungent and picturesque. William Chillingworth's *Religion of
Protestants* (1638) made more noise, as did, in 1649, the famous *Eikon Basilike, the
Portraiture of Sacred Majesty in his solitude and sufferings*. This last book, probably
the work of John Gauden, purports to be written by Charles I. himself. It made a
martyr of this king and crowned the house of Stewart with an aureole. It is famous
both on its merits and on account of the answers it provoked.

4. **The Puritans. Baxter and Milton.**—The Puritans were no less active
than the Anglicans. On the whole, it was they who from the beginning took the
offensive. Violence and even trivial coarseness marked their pamphlets in the reign
of Elizabeth and figured also in Prynne's exposition of the case against the theatres,
his *Histriomastix* of 1632, in many attacks on episcopacy and, above all, in several
of Milton's treatises. While Anglican prose was generally characterised by suavity
and unction, Puritan prose was predominantly harsh. Jeremy Taylor and Milton
present, in this respect, a typical antithesis. But an exception must be made in
favour of moderate Presbyterians, like the five writers who signed their anti-
Episcopalian treatise by the name Smectymnus, made up of their combined
initials. Their group was headed by Stephen Marshall (1594–1655) and Edmund
Calamy (1600–66), who were dignified in controversy. The same moderation distinguishes the considerable works of Richard Baxter (1615–91),[2] the most prolific
of the prose-writers, whose *Saints' Rest* (1650) is a classic of religious literature, and
whose *Reliquiæ* is an inexhaustible mine of information on the ecclesiastical history
of the period. His simple style is neither brilliant nor nervous, yet much superior
to that of his contemporary, John Owen (1616–83), who has been called the
greatest of the Puritan theologians, but is in truth a writer of diffuse and
unattractive prose.

The controversy gives the impression that the Puritans conducted it with

---

[1] Thomas Traherne, *Centuries of Meditations*, ed. Dobell (1908); John Hales, *Works*, ed.
Dalrymple, 3 vols. (1765); W. Chillingworth, *Works*, Oxford (1838); *Eikon Basilike*, ed. Phillimore
(1879; reprint by E. Scott, 1880); P. Heylin, *Ecclesia Restaurata*, ed. J. C. Robertson (1849).
[2] R. Baxter's *Works*, ed. by Rogers, 4 vols. (1868).

violence and fierceness because of the extent to which it is dominated by Milton's [1] genius. The numerous pamphlets in English which the great poet composed in his middle age, from 1641 to 1660, form the most extraordinary monument of the prose of the middle seventeenth century. A study of his contemporaries proves these treatises to be characteristic rather of the man than of his time, but very great writers are privileged to set their mark on their age, and to think of Puritan literature is at once to remember the name and work of Milton.

His case is peculiar. He was a poet, believing profoundly in his destiny as a poet and despising prose, when he deemed it his duty to leave the studies properly his on one side and to plunge into the thick of the fight, where he remained until its conclusion. Before this episode he rhymed *L'Allegro*, after it he sang *Paradise Lost*. But between the ages of thirty and fifty he gave up verse almost entirely, which meant to him that he renounced his glory. His descent into "the cool element of prose" was the greatest sacrifice he could make to his cause. "I should not," he says, "choose this manner of writing, wherein, knowing myself inferior to myself, led by the genial power of nature to another task, I have the use, as I may account, but of my left hand."

The change was painful as a mutilation to this incomparable artist in verse. The strong force of lyricism which was in him troubled the style of his pamphlets, when it was no longer contained by art, and made his prose unique and very curious, its faults as excessive as its beauties.

The pamphlets, each consequent on an incident of the political and religious struggle, have a narrow and special character. Their subjects are often out of date, so little interesting to the modern reader that they would be neglected were it not that they contain Milton's numerous self-revelations, scraps of information about his life and ideas, and also some magnificently eloquent passages.

He first fought in the ranks of the Presbyterians and against the prelacy in pages in which the coarsest sarcasms about his adversaries alternate with the superb flights to which he is impelled when he speaks of his poetic mission.

After his wife had left him, his puissant egoism caused him to write four successive treatises in favour of divorce. In these he scornfully upbraids custom to which most men are slaves, and from his own unfortunate experience he deduces immediately the necessity of abolishing the marriage law. His marriage has been a failure: hence the institution of matrimony is, in its existing state, evil. There is no true marriage save the union of souls. Milton describes the despair of persons unhappily married. He has recourse to the ancient parable of Eros and Anteros, love and its contrary which falsely resembles it, to show that even virtuous men may be deceived by appearances. A loveless marriage is "nothing but the empty husk of an outside matrimony, as undelightful and unpleasing to God as any other kind of hypocrisy." The Bible admits and counsels divorce, and man's law is therefore impious when it forbids it, and so condemns Christians "to grind in the mill of an undelighted and servile copulation . . . oft-times with such a yoke-fellow, from whom both love and peace, both nature and religion mourns to be separated."

Milton does not desire the intervention of the law, but considers that it falls to the head of a family to decree a divorce, for which action he requires no more than the consent of the persons concerned or, failing the wife, of the husband only. Here Milton is giving vent to his contempt for women, who to him are always Eve or Delilah. His genius is at once Biblical and Roman, and he supports his thesis with

---

[1] Complete works of J. Milton, ed. Mitford, 8 vols. (1851); prose works, ed. Symmons (1806); ed. Griswold, 2 vols. (1847); selected prose, ed. Garnett (1893).
   See D. Masson, *Life of John Milton*, 6 vols. (1859–80); and in French, A. Geffroy, *Étude sur les pamphlets politiques et religieux de Milton* (1848); P. Chauvet, *La Religion de Milton* (1909); D. Saurat, *La Pensée de Milton* (1921).

arguments taken from the pagans as well as from the Jews. He quotes a saying of Paulus Æmilius. He considers only men's interest, and in certain passages of these treatises comes very near the doctrine of free love, so that he makes us think of the Shelley of *Epipsychidion*. His individualism is carried to such lengths that it becomes anarchy. The memory of his suffering influences him, the idea of freeing himself, his happiness, his work and his genius from the bonds into which he had imprudently entered. There are moving and penetrating passages in which he recounts the dangers of an unhappy marriage, greater for the young and very pure man, quite ignorant of women, than for the rake who is more informed and better armed for his own defence.

In these treatises, which assume the form of a proposal for a law, the cry of a disappointed and angry man is distinctly heard. Nothing Milton wrote is more characteristic of his haughty and absolute pride.

This campaign had, however, the effect of rendering him suspect to the Presbyterians, his recent allies, who now had the upper hand in Parliament and were imposing their ecclesiastical discipline on the whole country. His treatises on divorce had to be secretly printed, and the new yoke irked him. He resumed against the Presbyterians the struggle for freedom which he had begun with them and against the Episcopalians. His aversion from any censure of the press caused him to publish the most eloquent of his prose works, *Areopagitica, a Speech for the Liberty of Unlicensed Printing* (1644).

Here he appeals both to patriotic pride and to the passion for liberty. He desires that England shall champion the noble cause he advocates, and he has a vision of his country regenerate by the abolition of intellectual tyranny:

> Methinks I see in my mind a noble and puissant nation rousing herself like a strong man after sleep, and shaking her invincible locks: methinks I see her as an eagle muing her mighty youth, and kindling her undazzled eyes at the full midday beam; purging and unscaling her long abused sight at the fountain itself of heavenly radiance; while the whole noise of timorous and flocking birds, with those also that love the twilight, flutter about, amazed at what she means.

He admits that books acknowledged to be maleficent should be proscribed, but is opposed to censure as a preventive measure, giving his reasons in a passage as lofty and beautiful as his most famous verses and as lastingly young.

His temperament carried him to extremes, and he next placed his impetuous rhetoric at the service of the Independents. He wrote in justification of the execution of Charles I. and replied in *Eikonoklastes* (October 1649) to the *Eikon Basilike* which Charles I. was supposed to have written in prison. Then, since the insular quarrel had become European and to be read on the continent was important, he replied to the learned Saumaise's *Defensio regii* by his Latin *Defensio pro populo Anglicano*, and to Peter du Moulin's attack, *Regii Sanguinis clamor ad cœlum adversus Parricidas anglicanos*, by his *Defensio secunda*, which was followed by other pamphlets.

At the end of the Commonwealth period he returned to English in order once more to claim liberty of conscience, to demand the suppression of an established and endowed Church and to protest against the reinstatement of the monarchy. The Restoration put a stop to his polemical career. But he accomplished other prose work during his life, wrote a *Treatise on Education* in 1644 and published a *History of England* in 1670 and a *Brief History of Moscovia*. He also left among his papers a curious Latin manuscript, *De Doctrina Christiana*, in which his own bold and heterodox ideas on Christianity and morality are exposed. He reveals himself an Arian, hostile to the doctrine of the divinity of Christ, and recommends polygamy.

Large as is the part of prose in his literary productions, he regarded it always as an inferior instrument, useful for practical ends and in controversy. His prose is the improvisation of a humanist, who reserves his art for his verse and is therefore careless of the shape and limits of his sentences. It makes formidable reading. It is best understood when it is read aloud, so that the inflections of spoken words can be followed, as though they had not been confided to print. Yet the troubled vehemence leaves room, here and there, for admirable images and for powerful sarcasm, provoked by enthusiasm or anger. Moreover, Milton constantly reveals himself in his prose. We see the impetuous idealist, scorning the immediate and the real, building up a religion and a republic which might have existed only if all men had been like himself, cut to his measure. He was unquestionably a Puritan, but his outlook is so personal that he often expresses the opinions of no group and is representative only of himself.

5. **The Eccentrics. Urquhart, Fuller, Walton.**—A certain number of the prose-writers of the middle seventeenth century are difficult to class, because of their subjects and of something individual or even eccentric in their manner. There was as yet no literary norm and fancy still had free play.

The most singular of them is certainly the Scot, Sir Thomas Urquhart of Cromarty (1611–60),[1] whose original writings are examples of pedantry, wordiness and grandiloquence, and also of such vanity and vaingloriousness as cannot easily be matched. Their mere titles are stupefying—*The Trissotetras, Pantochronocanon, Ekskubalauron, Logopandecteision*—and words no less formidable swarm in their text. Urquhart had, however, the happy idea of employing his verbal vigour on the translation of Rabelais (1653), and the result was something like a masterpiece—not an exact rendering, but an adaptation which keeps the spirit of the original while the author improves on his model and gaily multiplies the synonyms and epithets of which Rabelais had already been prodigal. Like Rabelais, he makes use of every form of speech—archaisms and neologisms, jargon and slang.

Thomas Fuller (1608–61) [2] is predominantly witty and pointed. This Anglican clergyman, who served the Royalist cause and wrote the *Church History of Britain* (1655), must yet be placed rather among the antiquaries or the moralists than among the ecclesiastical writers. Of his books, his *Holy and Profane State* (1642) and his *Worthies* (1661) are most read. The former presents a series of model types in various social positions—a good father, a good soldier, a good schoolmaster, a good yeoman and others—with many historical examples. The *Worthies* gives, in the author's fantastic manner, much precious information about distinguished Englishmen and their birthplaces. It is thanks to Fuller that many significant anecdotes have been preserved, and, although he has collected much gossip, he also shows, in his more specially historical works, a critical understanding of documents which inspires confidence.

An amiable optimism illumines his style, and his love of conceits gives it relief and connects him with the so-called "metaphysical" poets of his generation. Many of his definitions are still celebrated, for instance that of the good yeoman, who "is a gentleman in ore, whom the next age may see refined; and is the wax capable of a gentle impression, when the prince shall stamp it"; and that of a negro, the image of God "cut in ebony," and also his saying that "the soldier at the same time shoots out his prayer to God and his pistol at his enemy." Fuller often sacrifices complete accuracy to pointedness, but in this he has, after all, no

---

[1] Works edited for the Maitland Club (1834).
[2] T. Fuller, *The Church History of Britain*, ed. Brewer, 6 vols. (1845–8); *The History of the Worthies of England* (reprinted 1840); *Collected Sermons*, ed. Bailey and Axon, 2 vols. (1891); *Good Thoughts in Bad Times*, etc., ed. Waller (1902). See also M. Fuller, *Life, Times and Writings of T. Fuller*, 2 vols. (1884); C. Lamb, *Specimens from the Writings of T. Fuller*, in L. Hutchinson's ed. of Lamb, vol. i. pp. 142–50.

other object than to keep the reader alertly attentive to his wise and humane counsels on morality.

No figure in the literature of the period is, however, more endearing than the one still the most popular, Izaak Walton (1593–1683),[1] who is outside all the catagories. His long life prolonged the Elizabethan age to the Restoration. He is a link between Marlowe and Dryden. Almost without literary education and never intended for a writer, he long kept an ironmonger's shop in Fleet Street. But even so he was attracted by the intellectuals. He was the parishioner and humble friend of John Donne, knew Drayton and Ben Jonson, often went fishing with the scholarly ambassador Wotton, and was frequently in the society of the wits and also, since he was a good Anglican, of the divines. All his life he kept a love for poetry such as he knew it in his youth, for its mingled grace, strangeness and artifice, and more than once he inserts verse in his simple and homely prose. In 1640 he had written his life of Donne, but it was mainly during the leisure he enjoyed after he retired from trade in 1643 that he developed a taste for relating his impressions and memories.

He is a delightful biographer. To his life of Donne he added those of Sir Henry Wotton, Richard Hooker and George Herbert, all of which were collected in one volume in 1670. Their charm is partly due to the fact that Walton only wrote lives of men for whom he had a liking and with whom he was to some extent familiar. He was, indeed, a mere child when Hooker died, but he had ties with those who knew the great divine well. Nor had he ever more than a glimpse of Herbert, but the two had friends in common. Thus it is that all Walton's biographies have a charm of intimacy. He had, moreover, heartiness and simplicity of soul; he was cheerful, good-natured and shrewd; and his books derive from his personality an exquisite fragrance. His writing is fitted to give the highest pleasure. The question has been raised whether his style be merely his natural form of expression or whether a concealed art, a hidden laboriousness, should be discerned in it. He had had no regular education, but he had trained himself by reading and by conversation with men of letters, even refined men of letters, whom he had known in his youth. It was his singular good fortune to love their mannerism and not to be infected by it. A very lively inclination took him to the poets and he was, in his hour, a poet himself. In the *Compleat Angler* we see him trying to recall songs which once had pleased him. When memory fails, when a verse escapes him, he puts down his rod and, reclining on the grass, spends an hour on remaking the forgotten lines. His invention and his memory collaborate.

It is for reasons of this kind that the style and the narratives of his Lives are so attractive. Quietly, a little slowly, always clearly although not in accordance with any strict order, he relates facts which he has conscientiously verified and impressive particulars which without him would never have reached us. Without him, we would hardly know the character of the eminent men of whom he speaks, and the loss to us would be great. It is, however, he himself, with his gentle religion and serene philosophy, who even here interests us most.

His optimism is even more apparent in his *Compleat Angler*, which has become a classic. Few books of this time have gone through as many editions and are more read and as much loved to-day. Walton put into it not only his large experience of fishing, but also the reflection of his nature and the secret of his happiness. It is perhaps the only handbook of an art or craft which ranks as literature, and it seems to have won its place without seeking it.

---

[1] *The Compleat Angler*, ed. A. Lang (1896); Le Gallienne (1897); Buchan (1901), etc.; *The Lives of Donne, Wotton, Hooker, George Herbert*, ed. Bullen (1884); A. Dobson, in 2 vols. (1898). See also S. Martin, *Izaak Walton and his Friends* (1904).

The respectable pleasure which Walton takes in fishing turns into universal optimism and thanksgiving to God for the benefits lavished on the earth. How easily a wholesome and delightful life can be led on the banks of a cool "gliding stream" on fine summer days! What madness to join in the rush for money or pleasure! How perfect life would be if all men were anglers and had anglers' souls! Everyone else seems to be obstinately shunning the only true joys to be had here below.

It should be noted that this book appeared in 1653, on the morrow of the civil war, when the country laboured under Cromwell's yoke and all Walton's friends were in the camp of the vanquished. He was sixty years old; he had lost his first wife and the seven children she had borne him. But public and private ills left no trace on the angler's smiling spirit, any more than the tortures he inflicted on the poor frogs he used as bait altered his benign countenance or modified the unction of his advice to his pupil. His joy in life was even distilled into kind words concerning those small victimised reptiles.

Walton was, but for this, the best fellow in the world. His joy was always inspired by love for the fields and the streams or by the rhymes which sang in his memory, and it was accompanied by a strong preference for decency in which there was no taint of sullen prudery. We can understand his attraction for the huntsman whom he met accidentally and converted to his ruling passion, winning him from the more brutal joys of his own form of sport, and to whom he passed on his morality, that of a man as averse from austerity as from gross self-indulgence.

This book, which has the form of a dialogue between the angler and his pupil, is a transformed pastoral. Here and there the factitious element in the older pastorals subsists, and can be recognised in some entirely poetic locutions, but these are excusable on the lips of an old man mindful of the ornate expressions which charmed his adolescence. Elsewhere all is agreeable realism, the simple painting of an English countryside, its meadows and streams, its clean inns where the fare is excellent and the sheets smell of lavender. The book is good-humoured as a holiday in the open air.

The excellent Walton, sincerely pious and moral, makes it his duty to savour the good things of this world in order to do homage for them to the Creator. His sensuousness is unctuous and purified. He enjoys the air, the aspects of the sky and the land, the sunlight and the warm summer showers. His greed is well-behaved and moderate, but its very moderation is like supreme epicureanism. He loves verses and songs and likes them to be fanciful. By his origins he belongs to Merry England, and he made its spirit survive into the gloomiest and most morose period of English history. He kept for himself a fresh and sweet retreat from the political storms. He was no hero, but a sage endowed by Fate with a lively taste for nature, a grateful soul and an excellent stomach.

6. **Other Writers of Prose.**—The middle seventeenth century can claim other prose works in several genres. England, later than France, produced memoirs: the *Autobiography* of Lord Herbert of Cherbury (1588–1648), who also wrote a history of Henry VIII.; and the *Memoirs* of Sir Kenelm Digby (1603–65), which were in manuscript form until 1827, and in which real adventures are curiously disguised by fictitious names, so that they have a resemblance to a Scudéry novel. The period with which they deal, if not the date at which they were compiled, would cause the addition to this list of the Puritan *Life of Colonel Hutchinson*, by his wife, and the Royalist *Life of the Duke of Newcastle*, by his second wife. Both these works are studied in the next volume of this history, as is Clarendon's *History of the Rebellion*, which is famous for its portraits. Two considerable men are also assigned to our next volume—Hobbes, the philosopher, and Bunyan, the Puritan

allegorist. Here we have only to mark the wealth of the period which is our subject by naming the writers who belong to the two periods. It should, however, be stated that one of the strongest replies to Hobbes's *Leviathan* was from the pen of the Puritan James Harrington (1611–77), who in his *Oceana*, published in 1656, ·proposes a republican Utopia in opposition to the absolute monarchy advocated by Hobbes. But Harrington's political romance lacks the imaginative qualities proper to its genre, those which Thomas More could so brilliantly impart. Moreover, although it is full of the reflections of an experienced and sagacious man, its style is dull, and it has not the astonishing structural force and verbal exactness which made Hobbes a precursor and a pioneer of modern prose.

This period could also lay claim to the learned John Selden (1584–1654), whose legal treatises are almost all in Latin, but whose table-talk, collected and published by his secretary in 1689, long after his death, delighted the classical age with its abundant good sense and occasional discreet irony. The civil war also synchronised with the beginning of the career of Henry More (1614–87), the most celebrated of the Cambridge Platonists. He wrote, first in verse and then in prose and both in English and in Latin, a series of works which bear the imprint of a dreamy mysticism not far removed from occultism, and are accessible only to the few initiate, so that they are in contrast to the practical and earthbound literature of the age in which the author ended his life.

CHAPTER II

POETRY FROM 1625 TO 1660

1. **Long Poems which were Failures.**—At the death of James I., in 1625, Spenser's influence was almost exhausted, surviving only in Milton. It was Ben Jonson and especially John Donne who now had disciples and imitators. Poets were numerous down to the Restoration, but, except for Milton, they were the poets of the anthologies whose memory lives only in slight lyrics or collections of small poems.[1] The ambition to write works on a vast scale had not died out, but the efforts to realise it were failures. The epical ambition which was then common to Europe, and which produced more than one pitifully abortive poem in France, was no more successful in England. Long romances in verse and attempts at classical epics constitute what is dead in the literature of the time: their titles and the names of almost all their authors are forgotten. They have been collected only by the historical zeal of the present day,[2] and to name them will sufficiently show how abundant was the unfortunate production in this genre.

They consist of metrical romances, like Patrick Hannay's *Sheratine and Marina* (1622), the *Leoline and Sydanis* (1642) of Sir Francis Kynaston, who had previously modernised Chaucer's *Troylus and Criseyde*, and W. Chamberlayne's *Pharonnida*, in six books (1659). There are also mythological narratives: Shackerley Marmion's *Cupid and Psyche* (1637) and William Bosworth's *Arcadius and Septa* (1651); long religious narratives like Edward Benlowes's *Theophila*, in nine cantos (1652), and epics like Davenant's *Gondibert* (1650), which is in quatrains, and Cowley's *Davideis* (1656), which is classical in manner and has a Hebrew theme.

Inevitably poetic qualities and readable passages are scattered here and there in these ambitious works, but on the whole they were stillborn, and have no importance in literary history save that a path leads over their graves to Milton's *Paradise Lost*.

If dead poetry be left on one side, and the attempt be then made to classify the poets of the middle seventeenth century, they are seen to fall into two main groups, separated by the differences which make the history of this troubled period. There are first the secular poets, all in the Royalist ranks and therefore known as Cavaliers, and secondly there are religious poets, subdivided into the Anglicans and the Puritans. The division is social rather than literary, but it is simple and convenient, and corresponds sufficiently to the diversity of inspiration.

2. **Thomas Carew (1598?-1639).**[3]—The poet who first, before the civil war, showed what the spirit of the Cavaliers was to be, and first was affected by the combined influence of Jonson and Donne, was Thomas Carew, a gentleman of the

---

[1] E. Gosse, *Seventeenth Century Studies* (1883); B. Wendell, *The Seventeenth Century in English Literature* (1904).

Collections of verse: *Cavalier and Courtier Lyrists* (Canterbury Poets, 1891); G. Saintsbury, *Seventeenth Century Lyrists* (undated); H. J. Massingham, *A Treasury of Seventeenth Century English Verse* (1919); H. J. C. Grierson, *Metaphysical Lyrics and Poems of the Seventeenth Century* (1921).

[2] *Caroline Poets*, ed. Saintsbury, 3 vols. (Clarendon Press, 1906-21).

[3] *Poems of T. Carew*, ed. Ebsworth (1893); ed. Vincent (1899); also in The Muses' Library.

court of Charles I. who was a reputed wit. He was a courtly and polished love-poet whom his rivals suspected of working long at his elegant verses. The logical good order of the classicists rules his mind even when, in his poems to Celia, he returns to a theme of the Petrarchists. He can isolate a thought, follow it up faithfully and balance its several parts, and many of his light sets of verses have won, in consequence, a place in anthologies. He has little sensibility—he had indeed a reputation for dryness—but his sensuous ardour enables him to avoid the coldness of gallantry. Such, in any case, is the character betrayed by his longest poem and his masterpiece, *The Rapture,* unfortunately no less indecent than the verses of Aretino. It is an invitation to Celia to flout "the Giant Honour" and enjoy forbidden pleasures without scruple. The Paradise he paints to her is one of the most licentious even of those inspired by the Italian Renascence. His attack on honour recalls Sidney's *Astrophel* and especially Donne's *Elegies.* He is also inspired by the speeches of Petronius in the anonymous tragedy *Nero* (Act IV. scene vii.), but in libertine audacity he outdoes his models.

Carew is connected with Donne by the fine elegy with which he honoured his memory. The poem has more feeling than is customary with Carew and is, moreover, one of the best pieces of criticism written in this period. No one has pointed out more accurately than Carew what was new in Donne, his contempt for outworn ornament and his need of personal and virile expression. Yet Donne left few traces upon his style. If Carew has none of the master's flashes of genius, he escapes the worst faults of his style. In his commendatory verses he shows that his thought was vigorous and direct, especially in those to George Sandys, who, after translating Ovid, gave up secular poetry and translated the Psalms. Carew confesses that he dare not greet "the holy place with his unhallowed feet," but that his Muse, like "devout penitents of old," stays "humbly waiting at the porch," listening to the sacred strains. Yet he thinks that one day his eyes,

> Now hunting glow-worms, may adore the sun,

and that:

> My eyes in penitential dew may steep
> That brine which they for sensual love did weep.

The poem is beautiful, and so restrained that it seems sincere. It is consistent with Clarendon's account of the poet's edifying death.

His was, however, a death-bed conversion. All his poetry is the work of an amorist, such as Milton despised. He writes "persuasions" to love, madrigals, complaints and reproaches, addressed to a mistress, lines to his "inconstant mistress," who shall be "damned for her false apostasy," to Celia singing, to Celia when he sends her red and white roses:

> In the white you may discover
> The paleness of a fainting lover,
> In the red, the flames still feeding
> On my heart with fresh wounds bleeding.

In the famous song, "Ask me no more," he finds all the beauties of nature united in his mistress—the rose of June:

> For in your beauties, orient deep,
> These flowers, as in their causes, sleep;

the "golden atoms of the day" which "enrich her hair," the nightingale's song:

> For in your warm, dividing throat,
> She winters, and keeps warm her note.

The theme is commonplace, but in the harmonious quatrains of this song it is turned with perfect elegance.

Carew's work is slight, much distilled, but some warmth of imagination and a certain fancy temper its coldness. The style and the versification are so polished that Waller and Denham, the acknowledged pioneers of the classical school, could hardly improve on them.

3. **The Cavalier Poets.**—Carew is the typical court poet. Sir John Suckling (1609–42)[1] typifies the Cavaliers, their loyalty, dash, petulancy, frivolity, easy morals and wit. Rich, spendthrift, valiant, a gamester and a gallant, an amateur of the drama who wrote four not unsuccessful plays and a faithful admirer of Shakespeare, Suckling mocked at the pains which Carew took to polish his verses. He was himself an improviser, one whose work is very unequal but who writes with irresistible swing. It is his light, impertinent tone which characterises him. He recalls Donne when he rallies woman on her capriciousness or himself on his inconstancy; but while he has the master's hyperbole he leaves his metaphysics alone. He discharges his mockery in the form of little, swiftly moving, neatly turned songs, irony sometimes hiding the madrigal, as in "Out upon it." His ease and flippancy are French rather than English, and it has been thought that a sojourn which he made in France before he was twenty influenced his Muse. Less slight than the rest of his work is the *Ballad upon a Wedding* in which a farmer describes, in picturesque language, a wedding at which he has been present. Here there are many lively and homely descriptive touches, as well as wit and spirit. Suckling puts new life and freshness into the conventional epithalamium. Not until Thomas Moore did anyone else show such skill at writing charming verses about nothing. "Natural, easy Suckling," as Congreve's Millamant calls him, whose life was short and who versified only as a pastime, had a considerable production. Beneath his apparent frivolity there was, as his poems prove, romantic generosity, and even, as his letter to Henry Jermyn shows, a power of reflecting on politics. His treatise *An Account of Religion by Reason*, in which he combats the Socinian heresies, is proof that he also cared for religion. The contrasts in him are characteristic of a time in which libertinage often rubbed shoulders with piety.

Richard Lovelace (1618–58)[2] was neither as correct as Carew nor as natural as Suckling. This most handsome Cavalier whose fine figure fascinated the ladies, this faithful follower of the king who was twice imprisoned and finally ruined for the cause, so that he ended his short life in the most abject poverty, was a very unequal poet. In his *Lucasta* (1649) the cold, hyperbolical compliments of the degenerate sonneteers occur side by side with Donne's obscure extravagance. The lack of art in his work is as apparent as its mannerism, and almost all of it has been forgotten. But it was his fortune to make two or three songs in which his sense of honour is in manly alliance with his love. It was he who wrote to Althea from prison:

> Stone walls do not a prison make
> Nor iron bars a cage;
> Minds innocent and quiet take
> That for an hermitage.
> If I have freedom in my love,
> And in my soul am free,
> Angels alone that soar above
> Enjoy such liberty.

It was he who wrote "to Lucasta on going to the wars,"

> I could not love thee, dear, so much,
> Loved I not honour more.

Because of these few short poems, Lovelace has the glory of having expressed the ideal of the Cavalier.

---

[1] *Poems, Plays and Other Remains of Sir John Suckling*, ed. Hazlitt, 2 vols. (1892); *The Works of Sir John Suckling*, ed. Thompson (1910).
[2] *Lucasta*, ed. Hazlitt (2nd ed., 1897).

He shares it with Montrose (1612–50), the noble Scottish champion of Charles I., whose brilliant victories were followed by disaster, death and quartering, if the Royalist hero of Scotland really wrote the fine loyalist verses attributed to him.

John Cleveland (1613–58),[1] a Royalist like these other poets, who, unlike them, was of humble origin, was very different from them. He was, above all, a satirist, and he enjoyed in his own century a popularity which his vigour and his wit deserved. But his countless slight topical allusions make him difficult to read to-day. He was, moreover, one of Donne's most determined imitators, and conceits abound in his poems. The best known of them is the *Rebel Scot*, a fiery attack on the nation which had just delivered Charles I. to the Parliament. This satirist, with his rude style, often, while turning an epigram, wrote such isolated couplets as Dryden affected, and in spite of his metaphysical strangeness he blazed the track of political satire for that poet. He did not, however, write only satires. He composed love-poetry in which a touch of real nature varies, from time to time, the extravagant gallantry, and he made some curious lyrical essays in which he was one of the first of poets to realise the value of the anapæst.

It is tempting to connect Lord Herbert of Cherbury (1583–1648),[2] George Herbert's elder brother, with these Royalist poets. He is, because of his curious *Autobiography*, better known for his prose than for his verses, which contain a subtle quintessence of poetry. His handsome person, his extravagant valour, his passion for duelling and his refined gallantry, made him a representative Cavalier, and his *Ode upon a Question moved, whether Love should continue for ever*, gives him a high place among the Petrarchists and the disciples of Sir Philip Sidney.

4. Robert Herrick.—Midway between the Cavaliers and the Anglicans, Robert Herrick (1591–1674),[3] the most gifted and the most exquisite of all these poets, has place. The anacreonticism of the poetry of his youth makes him one of the Cavaliers, and since, at the age of thirty-eight, he accepted a Devonshire living and did his best to convert his Muse, he is also to be numbered among the Anglicans. His only collection of poems, the *Hesperides*, published in 1648, contains his "works both human and divine." The former consist of 1,129 short sets of verses, the latter of only 271, and the proportion may be taken to be that in which his inspiration was secular and sacred.

This son of a London goldsmith, who from Cambridge returned to London and a life of dissipation, who in the reign of James I., while his youth lasted, was a frequenter of the literary taverns, this lover of wine, women and song, and "son" of Ben Jonson, was induced to take orders only for the sake of a livelihood. When he bade a sad farewell to London and his Muse and departed to his living of Dean Prior, in Devonshire, he resolved, like a man of honour, to be a good parson. But he had no enthusiasm for his new duties. The change was too great for this charming rhymester cast up among the savages. He petted both his Muse and a few of his female parishioners. Then, little by little, helped by his recollections of pastorals, he acquired a taste for the rich countryside in which he found himself and for the uses of rustic life. He became attached also to his church and his little vicarage; he trusted in the good people's God, to whose infinite indulgence he could leave the

---

[1] Edited by Saintsbury in *Caroline Poets*, op. cit.; *The Poems of John Cleveland*, ed. Berdan (1911).

[2] His poems were published by Collins in 1881, and were edited by Moore Smith for the Clarendon Press (*Poems English and Latin*) in 1923.
See Rémusat, *Herbert de Cherbury* (Paris, 1874).

[3] *Hesperides*, ed. by Pollard, with introduction by Swinburne, in the Muses' Library, 2 vols. (1891); by Saintsbury in the Aldine Poets Series, 2 vols. (1893); by Rhys in the Everyman's Library, (1908); by F. W. Moorman (1921).
See F. W. Moorman, *Robert Herrick, a Biographical and Critical Study* (1910); F. Delattre, *Contribution à l'étude de la poésie anglaise au XVIIe siècle* (1910; the capital work on Herrick).

frolics of his youth and certain lapses of his maturity, whose anger would not be roused because the very secular *Hesperides* were printed side by side with the *Holy Numbers.* "Jocund his Muse was, but his life was chaste," he said of himself. It was self-flattery. His portrait at the beginning of the *Hesperides* shows a torso like that of a merry Priapus, a sensuous, mocking mouth beneath an aquiline nose, a head bristling with crisp, luxuriant hair, a chest left bare. This is a real pagan from a garden where Cupids dance in a ring, while Pegasus, standing on a hillock, is poised for flight.

Herrick's works are by themselves an anthology, a collection of short poems brought together on no principle and without any order. He adopts "sweet disorder" as an æsthetic principle, loves it in poetry as much as in women's dress. He goes farther and mingles the coarsest epigrams with poetry that is winged and delicate. Every contradiction of his mobile spirit, all his fleeting feelings and thoughts, are grouped haphazard. Even his "many dainty mistresses" sometimes clash, and we can only hope that, if they were real, they were successive. He hates monotony, sharing the national craving for variety so conspicuous in the drama. He alternates the pretty with the ugly, the fragrant with the evil-smelling. But nothing really counts in his work except its exquisite qualities, which exist in profusion.

On occasion, Herrick was capable of sustained effort. He has some epithalamiums and some rustic pieces, like the *Hock Cart, or Harvest Home,* which have spirit and savour. One of the most famous of his poems is *Corinna's Going A-Maying,* which contains five fourteen-lined stanzas. It is among the most charming of songs of the dawn, fragrant with flowers, rich as a poem by Spenser, and it has the merest hint of the ingenious fancy of the metaphysical poets:

> Rise, and *put on your foliage,* and be seen
> To come forth, like the Spring-time, fresh and green
> And sweet as Flora.

This poem has become the classic of all the English songs on May.

But Herrick's truest imprint is on the multitude of his tiny poems which seem to be made of a breath of air—charming madrigals, love-fancies, addresses to flowers, brief epitaphs. The light joy of a frivolous heart, a fancy pleased by whatever has grace or beauty; the slender melancholy of a reveller who remembers how ephemeral is that which charms him: such are his moods, and to the latter of them he returns again and again as he watches the flowers in his garden—the roses, the daffodils, the blossoms of the fruit-trees, the meadows which "have been fresh and green" and are left "to lament." The essence of this mood is in a trifle about cherry-blossom:

> Ye may simper, blush and smile,
> And perfume the air awhile;
> But, sweet things, ye must be gone,
> Fruit, ye know, is coming on;
> Then, ah! then, where is your grace,
> When as cherries come in place?

Never again did a poet of the west have so light a touch. The secret seems to be kept by Japan or China.

His epitaphs are endlessly graceful. They do not weigh down the graves on which they are but poised with the delicate grace of flowers, for instance that upon a child:

> Virgins promised when I died
> That they would each primrose-tide
> Duly, morn and evening, come,
> And with flowers dress my tomb.
> Having promised, pay your debts,
> Maids, and here strew violets.

When this voluptuary was in bed with fever he called on music to dispel his pain:

> Then make me weep
> My pains asleep;
> And give me such reposes
> That I, poor I,
> May think thereby
> I live and die
>   'Mongst roses.

Everywhere his simplicity is seasoned with a strangeness—*Mad Maid's Song, Grace for a Child, A Night Piece for Julia*. He is inspired by the Anthology and by Jonson, who had made fine translations from it; but while Jonson took extreme pains, Herrick seems to sing spontaneously. He can be reminiscent, recalling Marlowe's pastoral or Shakespeare's fairies or Herbert's pious verses, but whatever he takes is transposed and lightened. He reverses La Fontaine's otherwise just verdict on the English, that they "think profoundly." Herrick thinks, feels and writes lightly. He touches nothing; he barely skims its surface. For he was without moral sense. He knew only delicate enjoyment, neither satiety, passion nor remorse. He is the most epicurean of the moderns. His life, in the time of the civil war and so near to Milton, seems a defiance, and his metres, fluid as water, and his delicately varied stanzas, are surprising in their proximity to regularised verse, to the couplet which Waller and Denham fixed and stabilised and which increasingly became the vehicle of didacticism. Herrick, born in the Elizabethan age, was in the succeeding period the perfect artist in slight verse, while Milton, with his sovereign art, reigned over grander poetry.

5. **The Anglican and Catholic Poets.**—Herrick, a pagan clergyman, represents no more than the lax Anglicanism of his time. The renewal of faith within the Catholic Church, provoked by the Protestant attacks, had its counterpart in England in the revived fervour of the Anglican clergy whom the Presbyterians attacked. We have seen the effects of their stimulated zeal on the prose of preachers and controversialists, and it also left its mark on poetry. Hooker had exemplified Anglican weightiness and the Anglican grasp of political principles. In the seventeenth century the ardour of many Anglicans reached even to mysticism. The pious fervour shown under James I. by the brothers Phineas and Giles Fletcher became widespread under Charles I. and during the persecutions of the Commonwealth. Reason became the ally, sometimes the subordinate, of imagination and sentiment. Fancy and a certain singularity were added to them, partly in consequence of the changed literary models. Poets were inspired no longer by Spenser but by Donne, whose influence was even more marked on the pious poets than on the Cavaliers.

The double tendency perceptible under Charles I. and during Laud's tenure of power, on the one hand towards the restoration of the religious practices, the material accompaniments and the very millinery of Catholic ritual, and on the other towards a renewal of monastic asceticism, was combined with a taste for the metaphysical element in the sometimes truly beautiful and always curious writings of such as Herbert, Crashaw, Vaughan and Traherne.

(*a*) GEORGE HERBERT (1593–1633).[1]—The most popular of Anglican poems is George Herbert's *The Temple* which appeared in the year after the author's death. The son of an admirable mother, whose "autumnal beauty" Donne celebrated, Herbert was the younger brother of the Lord Herbert of Cherbury who was a soldier, statesman, poet and deist philosopher. He had a brilliant career at Cambridge,

---

[1] *The Complete Works of George Herbert*, ed. Grosart, 3 vols. (1874); *The English Works of George Herbert*, ed. G. H. Palmer, 3 vols. (1895) (the best critical edition, new ed., 1920); Walton, *Life of George Herbert* (often reprinted); J. J. Daniel, *Life of George Herbert* (1893).

won the affection of James I., and had already embarked on the life of a courtier and politician, when, at the age of thirty-seven, he took orders and became rector of Bemerton, in Wiltshire, where he died three years later. All his verses are the expression of his piety as a man and as a priest. *The Temple* is a singular work, full of faith and fervour and also of subtlety, ornament and point.

Herbert's theory is that a man should dedicate all his gifts to God's service, that a poet should make the altar blossom with his poetry. He was no Puritan, but valued the beauty and neatness of the church in which he officiated, and loved cheerfulness and the mirth which avoids coarseness:

> All things are big with jest; nothing that's plain
> But may be witty, if thou hast the vein.

He offered up to God all that was graceful and ingenious in his mind. A most intelligent, sagacious and penetrating observer of himself and others, and a man of wit, learning and cultivation, he spared no means to inculcate his faith. His profound sincerity led him to detest sermons made up of solemnity and grandiloquence. He liked simple, homely, even trivial language. The subtlety of which he made too much use was natural to him, part of his very mind and the outcome of the unusual association of his ideas and sequence of his images. He is of all Donne's disciples the one most like him. He is the saint of the metaphysical school. His poetry constantly offends taste, but often gives the impression of a sort of sublimity.

Although he was passionately fond of music, and was wont to accompany himself on the lute or viol while he sang his own hymns, and although his metres are marvellously expert and varied—in almost every one of his poems there is a special combination of lines and rhymes, and to seek to make a list of his different stanzas is hopeless—the melody of his verses is not facile. Sometimes so closely packed as to be hard, they are usually nervous and original, the latter even to the point of the fantastic, and they are sharpened with humour, racy of the people and often aphoristic or proverbial in form.

Herbert's characteristic is that he expresses everything by imagery, endeavours above all else to be concrete. This constitutes his merit and also, because it sometimes leads him to dwarf an idea, a defect. Another of his defects is that he is subtle to the point of obscurity, strange to the point of the enigmatic.

The short and frequently quoted poem *Virtue* exemplifies both what is excellent and what is dubious in Herbert's accomplishment. The idea is that all fair things of the earth, the day, the rose's hue, the charm and music of the spring, must die, but that virtue lives though the whole world burn. While the cadence of the quatrains is perfect, certain of the images are surprising and disquieting. The "angry and brave" colour of the rose "bids the rash gazer wipe his eye"; spring is "a box where sweets compacted lie," and the virtuous soul "like seasoned timber never gives."

But Herbert could do better than this. The lines of his *Elixir* are deservedly included among current quotations. For Herbert the true elixir, the stone "that turneth all to gold," is:

> In all things Thee to see,
> And what I do in any thing
> To do it as for Thee.

The second verse runs:

> A man that looks on glass
> On it may stay his eye;
> Or if he pleaseth through it pass,
> And then the heaven espy;

And the fifth:

> A servant with this clause
> Makes drudgery divine;
> Who sweeps a room as for Thy laws
> Makes that and th' action fine.

The poem called *The Quip* is all life, significance and surprises. Its twenty-four lines resume all Herbert's life, his resistance to the ironical appeals of the World, Beauty, Money, Glory and Wit, who in turn ask him why he shuns them. His only reply is:

> But thou shalt answer, Lord, for me.

Such short poems as *The Pulley* and *The Collar* are moving in their strangeness. In the latter the poet cries out at the restraints his piety imposes on him:

> Sure there was wine
> Before my sighs did dry it; there was corn
> Before my tears did drown it.

He determines that he will "suit and serve his need":

> But as I raved and grew more fierce and wild
> At every word,
> Methought I heard one calling, "Child";
> And I replied, "My Lord."

There is great power in the poem in which he apostrophises Death:

> Death, thou wast once an uncouth hideous thing,
> Nothing but bones.

Now Death has lost its sting:

> But since our Saviour's face did put some blood
> Into thy face,
> Thou art grown fair and full of grace,
> Much in request, much sought for, as a good.

Nothing is more stimulating than to read these short poems, which are so much alive, so strange and so weighted with meaning, their faults of taste redeemed by their flashes of poetry.

(*b*) CRASHAW.—Richard Crashaw (1612–49),[1] who was more than twenty years younger than Herbert and a great admirer of *The Temple*, did not remain within the Anglican fold. When he was about thirty-three he became a Catholic, and he ended his life in Rome as secretary to Cardinal Palotta. He began by writing the verses of an amorist and humanist. While still at the university, he was an expert Latin poet. To the models of antiquity he added models taken from Spain and Italy, for he fell under the spell of the colour, the exaltation and the melody of the poetry of these southern countries. He was attracted not only by these glowing qualities, but also by the extravagant preciosity of such as Marini and the ardours of the Spanish mystics. It is after their fashion rather than Donne's that he is metaphysical.

The first collection of his poems to be published after his death was called the *Delights of the Muses*, and includes a celebrated translation or rather paraphrase of a poem by a Jesuit on the nightingale's song, *Music's Duel*. Never did English show more virtuosity than when Crashaw analysed the bird's trills. The extraordinary wealth of his vocabulary is as astonishing as his infinitely subtle observation of every change in the bird's "quick volumes of wild notes."

His earliest poem, *Wishes for the Supposed Mistress*, is rhythmically unique,

---

[1] *Complete Works of Crashaw*, ed. Grosart, 2 vols. (1887–8); *Poems*, ed. Waller, Cambridge English Classics (1904); ed. Tutin (1904). See E. Gosse, *Seventeenth Century Studies* (1897).

and has a verbal vigour which is prestigious. In it he enumerates the gifts which he would wish his beloved to possess, gifts amounting to impossible perfection, since they include every beauty of face, mind and heart.

It is, however, his sacred poems which contain the chief share of Crashaw's enthusiasm and what may be called his voluptuous exaltation. He published in 1646 a collection of poems written before his conversion and called *Steps to the Temple*. In this he translates, under the title *Sospetto d'Herode*, the first canto of Marini's poem on the Massacre of the Innocents, and overweights it with ornament. Even more characteristic is *The Weeper*, a litany in praise of the Magdalen's tears which includes every conceit ever inspired by a weeping mistress, together with many others invented by the poet, all transposed into a religious key. Cruel outrages on taste alternate with admirable poetic visions. Of Magdalen, he says, "upwards thou dost weep," because her tears go to heaven:

> Every morning from hence
> A brisk cherub something sips,
> Whose soft influence
> Adds sweetness to his sweetest lips.
> Then to his music, and his song
> Tastes of this breakfast all day long.

> When some new bright guest
> Takes up among the stars a room,
> And Heaven will make a feast,
> Angels with their bottles come;
> And draw from these full eyes of Thine,
> Their master's water, their own wine.

But how he compensates by his vision of the saint's grieving countenance:

> Not in the evening's eyes,
> When they red with weeping are,
> For the Sun that dies,
> Sits sorrow with a face so fair,
> No where but here did ever meet
> Sweetness so sad, sadness so sweet.

> Sadness, all the while
> She sits in such a throne as this,
> Can do nought but smile,
> Nor believe she sadness is;
> Gladness itself would be more glad
> To be made so sweetly sad.

While yet an Anglican, Crashaw conceived ardent veneration for Saint Teresa, and he returned to her as a Catholic in order to write his most magnificent hymn, the *Flaming Heart, upon the Book and Picture of the Seraphical Saint Teresa*. The flight of holy love which ends this poem is perhaps the most ardent product of English religious poetry.

Crashaw's faults are conspicuous and not one of his poems is exempt from them. There is not one which can be quoted from end to end without offending taste by some absurdity. Although Herbert abounded in conceits, several of his numerous poems are free from them. But Crashaw scattered them everywhere. Yet he possessed certain properly poetic qualities in higher degree than Herbert. While he was less intellectual than the older man, and while his language was less simple and precise, he had more warmth, colour and harmony. His lyric flights have been equalled only by Shelley. By the strangeness and obscurity of his poetry and the flashes which light it up, and by the frequently charming and invariably melodious lack of precision in his style, he has curious analogies with the best of the recent symbolists. His poems are approximations to thought, full of music and imagery.

(c) VAUGHAN.—Unequality is also a characteristic of the verses of Henry Vaughan (1622–95) [1] the mystical Welsh doctor who was born in the land of the ancient Silurians and liked to call himself a Silurist. He began by writing secular poetry which betrays Ben Jonson's influence—*Olor Iscanus,* finished in 1647; but an illness detached him from the world and turned his thoughts to spiritual things. He became impregnated with the poetry of George Herbert and imitated him, writing *Silex Scintillans,* which appeared in two parts in 1650 and 1655. He is perhaps the seventeenth-century poet who has been most scorned and who most surprisingly recovered his place in the public estimation. His verses were long taken to typify the obscure, the platitudinous and the inharmoniously rude.

As we pass from one to another of his poems, we also change from absolute blame to supreme praise. Only a few have indubitable value, but these are pure gold. In them Vaughan is more melodious than Herbert; his mysticism is more fluid and less argumentative and his imagination is mellower. He prays not in a church like Herbert, but in the open air. His own picturesque country has inspired him with love for nature, and this feeling mingles with his Christian meditations and imparts to the best of his work something which is romantic and modern. Vaughan has a hermit's soul. The large number of his poems which are too directly inspired by Herbert are usually inferior to their model. He lacks the art to construct even a few stanzas, nor can he conclude a poem. His versification is far less skilful and varied than Herbert's, and almost always his verses read like an improvisation, often an awkward one. But his meditations on life and death, in the face of changing nature, are graced by new images. There is, for instance, a poem in which he tells that he has lost one dear to him and his heart is heavy. He walks in a field

> Where sometimes had seen the soil to yield
> A gallant flower,
> But winter now had ruffled all the bower.

Then he digs in the soil:

> And by and by
> I saw the warm recluse alone to lie,
> Where fresh and green
> He lived of us unseen.

The poet weeps upon the earthy bed:

> Then sighing whispered, "Happy are the dead!
> What peace doth now
> Rock him asleep below!"

He then prays that he may again see him whom he mourns.

On another day he meditates before a waterfall, of which the "transparent, cool and watery wealth" falls,

> As if his loose, liquid retinue stayed
> Lingering, and were of this steep place afraid,
> The common pass
> Where clear as glass,
> All must descend
> Not to an end,
> But quickened by this deep and rocky grave,
> Rise to a longer course more bright and brave.

The waterfall is to him a symbol of life and death.

It is part of his originality that he felt the poetry of childhood. His *Retreat* anticipates Wordsworth's famous *Ode on Intimations of Immortality.* It is with

---

[1] *Poems,* ed. Chambers, 2 vols. (1896, reprinted 1905); ed. L. C. Martin, 2 vols. (Oxford, 1915.)

the same regret for vanished glory and purity that Vaughan reverts to his childhood:

> Happy those early days when I
> Shined in my angel infancy!
> Before I understood this place
> Appointed for my second race,
> Or taught my soul to fancy ought
> But a white, celestial thought;
> When yet I had not walked above
> A mile or two from my first love,
> And looking back, at that short space,
> Could see a glimpse of his bright face.

The whole poem is exquisite; it has not a discord. Yet it is perhaps not here, but in the poem which begins, "They are all gone into the world of light," that Vaughan reaches artistic perfection, is happiest in his choice of rhythms and images:

> I see them walking in an air of glory,
> Whose light doth trample on my days:
> My days which are at best but dull and hoary,
> Mere glimmering and decays.

Despised though Vaughan was by his contemporaries, at least his glorification of childhood was emulated by Thomas Traherne, who was born about 1634 and whose poetry and prose, up to a few years ago (1903), existed only in manuscript. Traherne's poems are, for the most part, inartistic, yet include some admirable achievements, like *The Wonder*, which expresses a child's wonder at the body in which his soul is lodged and the world into which he is transported. Traherne continues Anglican mystical poetry down to the Restoration.

(*d*) OTHER RELIGIOUS POETS.—We have to go back a little in order to make room for the Catholic poet William Habington (1605–54), a pupil of the Jesuits of Saint Omer who wrote verses of pure love to Castara, telling like beads his metaphysical fancies, which would be more excusable in a more imaginative and passionate poet.

There is more to interest in Francis Quarles (1592–1644), an Anglican with Puritan tendencies and a man of the world converted to piety, who published, as well as other work, his very popular *Emblemes* in 1635. He was an improviser, almost a journalist in verse. The *Emblemes* are a series of rhymed meditations commenting on verses of the Bible and corresponding to the illustrations which Herman Hugo, a Jesuit of Brussels, inserted in his book *Pia Desideria*.

With untiring energy, Quarles adds meditation to meditation, and his metrical commentary is very often commonplace. His language is frank and while not less extravagant is less obscure than that of his contemporary poets. Since he appeals to the great mass of readers, he banishes very rare words from his vocabulary and over-refinement from his style. Even his bad taste is within everybody's reach. He is a metaphysical poet for the many.

6. **Puritan Poetry. Marvell.**—The Puritans also had their songsters, who, while they were less numerous than those of the other party, included one of the most endearing and another, much the greatest of the poets of the century—Marvell and Milton.

It is impossible not to place among the Puritans Andrew Marvell (1621–78),[1] who under the Commonwealth was tutor to the daughter of Lord Fairfax, the great Parliamentary general, and who subsequently was Milton's friend and with him secretary to the Privy Council. He was the most inspired and affectionate of Cromwell's panegyrists, and after the Restoration he carried on in verse and prose the

---

[1] *Complete Works in Prose and Verse*, ed. Grosart, 4 vols. (1872–5); *Poems and Satires*, ed. Aitken in 2 vols. (1892), and in 1 vol. for the Muses' Library (1898). See A. Birrell, *Andrew Marvell*, English Men of Letters Series (1905).

struggle for religious and political liberty. Yet it must be recognised that no one could be less like than Marvell to the conventional harsh and gloomy Puritan, the enemy of all worldly and artistic amusement, for ever mouthing verses of the Old Testament in order to denounce the sins of the world.

This figure is dispelled as we look at Hanneman's portrait of Marvell, a man thirty-seven years old, with brilliant, living eyes, a laughing, mocking mouth and a calm brow, or as we read the verses which the poet wrote in his thirtieth year, alight, as they are, with human love and feeling for nature. Even in the poems of his maturity and in his pamphleteer's prose the gaiety is apparent of a jovial and mirth-loving spirit. On the whole, religion has far less place in Marvell's verses than in those of the Anglicans we have just considered. While he wrote many verses which witness to the sincerity of his faith, he made both more numerous and finer poems filled with the joyous humanism and the cordial, vital quality which prove him a son of the Renascence. Undoubtedly he revered the Bible, but he also loved wine, women and song.

He wrote his essentially poetic works at Nunappleton, Lord Fairfax's country-seat, where he lived from 1650 to 1652. He is inspired by the country, but not, like earlier poets, by the country seen in accordance with the pastoral convention. The desire for a more precise, for a local poetry, was already making itself felt, and one of the first poems which fulfilled it was John Denham's *Cooper's Hill*. But while a landscape was to Denham no more than the starting-point for historical and moral reflections, Marvell indulged far more fully in the happy contemplation of natural scenery. Before him only Wither had expressed, amid much rubbish, the intimate enjoyment he drew from fields and woods. Marvell spontaneously returned to this theme which was to be so dear to the Lake Poets. He is very Wordsworthian in *Upon the Hill and Grove at Billborough*, in which he describes a sort of natural terrace whither Fairfax, after his retirement, was wont to resort in search of quiet and of a meditative mood.

Marvell relates his own feelings in the longest of his poems, *Upon Appleton House*, in which he shows that he is familiar with the aspects of the country and its trees and birds, and that he has studied and compared the songs of birds. He anticipates Wordsworth in preferring the song of the dove to that of the nightingale. As he walks, he can

> . . . through the hazels thick espy
> The hatching throstle's shining eye,

and watch the woodpecker at work. He almost identifies himself with the birds and growing things:

> Thus I, easy philosopher,
> Among the birds and trees confer;
> And little now to make me wants
> Or of the fowls, or of the plants.

He calls to the birds in their own songs, "their most learned original." The leaves trembling in the wind are to him Sibyls' leaves:

> What Rome, Greece, Palestine, ere said,
> I in this light Mosaic read.
> Thrice happy he who, not mistook,
> Hath read in Nature's mystic book.

To be covered with leaves is a delight to him:

> Under this antic cope I move,
> Like some great prelate of the grove.

He calls upon the leafy shoots to cling to him:

> Bind me, ye woodbines, in your twines,
> Curl me about, ye gadding vines.

This is the exalted love for nature of a romantic, but a hint of strangeness and of Elizabethan pedantry are mingled with it.

Marvell's feeling for animals, his suffering when they suffer, is voiced with infinite gracefulness in his semi-mythological poem the *Nymph Complaining of the Death of her Fawn*.

He was the first to sing the beauty and glory of gardens and orchards. In them he tastes his dearest delights: it seems to him that all creation is

> Annihilating all that's made
> To a green thought in a green shade.

Marvell's *Garden* foreshadows Keats by its sensuousness, and Wordsworth by its optimistic and serene meditative mood.

Yet he preferred wild to cultivated nature. It is in the spirit of charming Perdita in *Winter's Tale* that, in the *Mower against Gardens*, he protests against artificial gardening processes—grafting, budding and selection.

The feeling for nature which, in the poems we have mentioned, is expressed in its pure state, is readily introduced into poems which are otherwise inspired, by Christianity or by love, nowhere better than in the famous *Song of the Emigrants in Bermuda*. Here Marvell imagines that he hears a Puritan refugee from the Stewart tyranny singing praises to God as he rows along the coast of an island in the Bermudas, "safe from the storm's and prelate's rage":

> He hangs in shade the orange bright
> Like golden lamps in a green night,
> And does in the pomegranates close
> Jewels more rich than Ormus shows.

Sometimes Marvell returns to the pastoral, but he gives it a new emphasis of truth, even of realism. The short idyll *Ametas and Thestylis making Hay-Ropes* is very original and graceful, and there is also the touching complaint of *Damon the Mower*, who, working beneath a burning sun, laments his Juliana's hardness of heart.

Love poems are not numerous in Marvell's work, but among several which are graceful (*The Gallery*) or slightly ironical—denouncing woman's tricks, artifices and coquetry (*Mourning, Daphnis and Chloe*), a few hold us by their passion. His lines *To his Coy Mistress* have Donne's strength and passion without his obscurity or bad taste, and run easily and harmoniously. They are the masterpiece of metaphysical poetry in this genre, and they also show a return to the anacreontic theme, "Gather ye rosebuds while ye may." But it is repeated with a new intensity. It issues from a heart truly deep and passionate, and the love which is demanded is violent and forceful:

> Now let us sport us while we may,
> And now, like am'rous birds of prey,
> Rather at once our time devour,
> Than languish in his slow-chapt pow'r.
> Let us roll all our strength and all
> Our sweetness up into one ball,
> And tear our pleasures with rough strife
> Thorough the iron gates of life.
> Thus, though we cannot make our sun
> Stand still, yet we will make him run.

These lines are the very essence of the poetry of Marvell, that strange, sensuous, passionate Puritan. He had, however, another vein. He was an ardent patriot, and patriotism rather than piety may be said to have dictated his verses on Cromwell's protectorate and death. It is the dominant note of his *Horatian Ode upon Cromwell's Return from Ireland* (1650), *First Anniversary of the Government under*

His Highness the Lord Protector (1655), and *Poem upon the Death of His late Highness the Lord Protector*. A sort of competition of poets, in which such as Waller and Dryden took part, was provoked by the great man's death, and Marvell carried off its prize because in his verses the man speaks through the poet. They are penetrated with emotion. Better than the others, Marvell gives the impression of the greatness of him he sang and the immensity of the loss his death occasioned.

After the Restoration Marvell pursued only the art of satire, in prose and verse, and this phase of his accomplishment is better studied elsewhere. We have said enough to show in how far he was original as a pure poet. Nature endowed him richly: his sincerity and straightness of vision sufficed to raise the metaphysical school, to which he belonged, from its state of decline, and to bring it back from extravagance to reason without alienating fancy. In the history of the feeling for nature his place is considerable. He expressed himself with liveliness and happy audacity. But he paid too little regard to versification. His lyrical work is written almost entirely in rhymed eight-syllabled couplets, a pleasant metre, but one so easy that it tempts to carelessness. In the formation of his stanzas, Marvell shows himself one of the least varied and inventive poets of his time. To rank among the greatest, he should have had a more exacting standard of art, and perhaps a more wholehearted devotion to poetry, as well as those supreme qualities of mastery of the word and the line which are the glory of the other Puritan poet, John Milton.

7. **The Precursors of the Classicists.**—(*a*) ABRAHAM COWLEY. Of the poets of the middle seventeenth century, a few are a link between the past and the present, between the Renascence and modern times. Their merits should be considered relatively rather than absolutely. Their interest has come to be mainly historical, to lie in the evidence they afford regarding new intellectual and literary tendencies, especially such of these as affect literary form.

In their first rank is Abraham Cowley (1618–67),[1] who was the most famous of them in his lifetime, enjoying a greater reputation not only than Herrick, who was almost unknown, but even than Milton. Milton himself considered that Cowley was one of the three great English poets, the other two being Shakespeare and Spenser. His renown long outlived him, yet lessened with the passage of years. Dryden said of him that, "though he must always be thought a great poet, he is no longer esteemed a good writer," and Pope, who owed him much, almost pronounced his condemnation a generation later:

> Who now reads Cowley? If he pleases yet,
> His moral pleases, not his pointed wit;
> Forgot his epic, nay Pindaric art,
> But still I love the language of his heart.

Yet, when Doctor Johnson wrote his *Lives of the English Poets* in 1778, he began with Cowley. Cowley existed for him, for all that he complacently gives the list of his faults. Cowley headed the moderns; his predecessors were out of date. Everything about Cowley assigns him to a transitional position: he was the last of the metaphysical poets and in many respects he foreshadowed the English classicists.

He was marvellously precocious. Several, and not the least distinguished, of his poems date from his adolescence. As a good Anglican and a faithful Royalist, he might be reviewed among the Cavalier or the religious poets of the middle of this century. Equally, he deserves to be numbered among the disciples of Donne. His knowledge of the ancients, whom he imitates, entitles him to be considered a humanist. But with these characteristics certain others are mingled which are new

---

[1] *Complete Works*, ed. Grosart (1881); *Poems*, ed. Waller (Cambridge, 1905); *Essays, Plays and Sundry Verses*, ed. Waller (Cambridge, 1906). See S. Johnson, *Lives of the English Poets* for Life of Cowley; E. Gosse, *From Shakespeare to Pope* (1885); *Seventeenth Century Studies* (1897).

and which modify them. With all his piety, his fantasy, his pointedness and his Pindarism, Cowley is, first of all, an intellectual. He was the friend of Hobbes and admirer of Bacon, a founder of the Royal Society and a devotee of science who was made an M.D. of Oxford and was a student of botany.

Entirely without mysticism, capable of affection but not of passion, a sincere friend and a tepid lover, his mind dominated his heart and imagination. It was less pure reason which ruled his faculties than wit, the active and voluntary play of his combined intellect and fancy. His poetry, which never glows and is often imitative and cold, is full of learned reminiscences and scintillates with witticisms.

His love verses in the fashion of the day, published in 1647 in the collection called *The Mistress*, are new versions, by a practised but untemperamental versifier, of the current themes of amorists. He succeeds only when he is amusing himself without any attempt to show feeling, as in the ballad called *The Chronicle*, in which he jestingly enumerates the mistresses who have reigned over his heart in succession. These are charmingly dexterous verses which we are not asked to take seriously. Herrick also gives the list of his mistresses, but with a tinge of melancholy which gains credence for himself and indulgence for his fickleness. Cowley's poem is no more than a set of pretty *vers de société*.

Cowley's great poetic ambitions have survived only as witnesses to his humanist's zeal. He conceived the idea of writing verses after Pindar. Ben Jonson had made a passing essay in this direction, but Cowley applied himself diligently to the task. He thought, as he relates in his copious commentary, to reproduce Pindar's enthusiasm, the boldness of his images and the freedom of his strophes. In truth, conceits, hyperboles and antitheses, copied from Donne, fill his long, irregular stanzas, in which homely, even indecorous, imagery alternates with grandiloquence. The result would be unreadable were it not lightened by flashes of wit. Here Cowley inaugurates a fashion, that of the irregular, debased Pindaric ode.

He dreamt of emulating the epics of antiquity, a dream notoriously common to all European countries during this century. It is accountable for Cowley's *Davideis*, which was intended to have twelve cantos but ends with the fourth. This poem is in the succession of Saint-Amand's *Moïse Sauvé* (1653) and of Chapelain's *Pucelle*, which also appeared in 1656, of poems, that is, which apply a form derived from antiquity to a Christian subject. Cowley anticipated Milton in going to Homer, and even more to Virgil, for a mould in which to cast his Biblical matter. Unlike Boileau, he believed that a poet who was born a Christian ought to use the themes provided by Christianity.

Davideis begins with a vision of Hell, where there is uneasiness because of the progress of David, which Lucifer proposes to stem. With the help of Envy, the Prince of Darkness breathes jealousy into the heart of Saul. A second scene shows Heaven watching over David. Structurally all this opening is strikingly analogous to *Paradise Lost*. Structurally only, for Cowley's Lucifer is still a mediæval monster, howling and brandishing his tail. And in the sequel the two poems follow opposite courses. Instead of reproducing the first of dramas, which decided the fate of mankind, Cowley stages a minutely detailed story following the Biblical narrative, but attempting to animate it by realism and to give it relief by pastoral touches. A very insipid conventional pastoral relates the love of David and Michal. The realism destitute of any local colour is obtained by modernising and vulgarising Scriptural indications. The College of the Prophets in which David takes refuge is, on Cowley's own showing, modelled on an English university—it is supplied with an excellent library.

Cowley yields to the temptation to antitheses and epigrams afforded by his rhymed lines, disposed in couplets, and his sacred poem resembles the

Bible less than it heralds the *Rape of the Lock*. His temperament was no more epical than it was Pindaric. He lacked grandeur of imagination, but not ingenuity. His best work is contained in his *Miscellanies*, on which he himself set little store, and which he filled with occasional verse. Here we find the poems which show him at his best as a man, that *On the Death of Mr. William Hervey*, a Cambridge friend, and that *On the Death of Mr. Crashaw*. Cowley, an Anglican and man of the world, pays warm tribute to the Catholic and religious poet, and the generosity of his feelings is equalled by the justice of his judgment on the verses of the "Poet and Saint."

But wit is, more than aught else, the mark of Cowley. It is not surprising that one of his small masterpieces is the ode *Of Wit*. He defines wit in the classical manner, and, prodigal as he is of it himself, he would have it used moderately. He condemns wit which is not controlled by reason or which is displayed too lavishly—and adds:

> Rather than all things Wit, let none appear;

he will have neither puns nor forced similes nor bombast. True wit is harmonious.

This very witty disquisition against wit, with its abundant imagery, ingenious to the point of subtlety, is curious.

Cowley's very remarkable poem *Against Hope* has the same character. It consists, from one end to the other, of subtle definitions of hope, so witty and so just in their strangeness that it is impossible not to admire the poet's virtuosity. He is on the tight-rope and we expect, at every moment, to see him lapse into bad taste. But, more sure-footed than Donne, he keeps his balance. Crashaw answered this attack on hope by a defence. The retort is very beautiful and more poetic than the condemnation: the comparison of the two poems shows that Cowley lacked the qualities which are properly lyrical, but his brilliant ingenuity remains dazzling.

With years, Cowley's intellectualism was accentuated. He was on the way to "the age of understanding." He wrote verses on *Reason* in which he defines his piety and in which, like a good disciple of Hooker, he takes up the contrary position to the illuminates and the mystics. After the Restoration he addressed an ode *To the Royal Society* which is an eloquent tribute to Bacon. He was of those who thought that God reveals Himself in experimental philosophy, and he celebrates the great philosopher who, as Moses brought the Children of Israel to the Promised Land, led the minds of men from bondage to the schoolmen into the freedom of experimental science:

> From words, which are but pictures of the thought,
> 　(Though we our thoughts from them perversely drew)
> To things, the mind's right object, he it brought:
> 　Like foolish birds, to painted grapes we flew;
> 　He sought and gathered for our use the true.

This significant poem concluded Cowley's unequal work. Without his defects as a writer and a versifier, he would have commanded more respect from succeeding generations. He had, however, no ear for sweet sounds. His best verses have a dry precision and are lacking in melody. He is too much given to expletives, and his rhymes are poor, often falling on weak words. He made some unhappy attempts at imitative harmony, to which he thought to attain by a singular violence—contractions and elisions which shock the ear. The classicists who followed him were affiliated to him intellectually, but did not acknowledge him as their true forerunner. It was Waller and Denham whom they honoured as the pioneers of the road they trod. To-day the pleasant prose of Cowley's *Essays* is more read than his verses.

(b) EDMUND WALLER.—Edmund Waller (1606-87) [1] was born in the year in which *King Lear* was played and died in the year in which Dryden published the *Hind and the Panther*. His long life links up two periods separated by a political convulsion and a literary revolution. During the time of civil disturbance he played a more important part than his fellow-poets. A very rich man, and a member of Parliament whose eloquence gave him influence, equally removed by his moderation from the uncompromising Royalists and from the king's enemies, he attempted to pursue a conciliatory policy which was doomed to fail. That he was no hero became clear when the plot which bears his name was discovered in 1643, and he saved his life by turning informer. He was condemned to pay a considerable fine and exiled from England, and he crossed to France, where he lived for eight years, becoming acquainted with French writers. He returned to his country in 1651 upon receiving a pardon from Cromwell, on whom he wrote a panegyric and whom he celebrated after his death; yet when the Restoration supervened he welcomed Charles II. in verse. He returned to Parliament, where his speeches were wont to be well received by a full house. He resumed his campaign in favour of liberal principles, was an advocate of pardon and toleration, and died on the eve of the Revolution. He left behind him a reputation for wit and his retorts are famous.

Throughout his life he wrote verse, but only occasional verse. He did not pride himself upon inventiveness. The aim which he set before himself in his youth was like that which the young Pope proposed to follow. "Methought," he is reported to have said, "I never saw a good copy of English verses; they want smoothness; then I began to essay." Smoothness does indeed distinguish all the short poems he left to posterity—panegyrics, eulogies of the king and queen and Cromwell, patriotic poems, love poems, literary eulogies of Ben Jonson, of John Fletcher and, under the Commonwealth, of Roscommon, jesting verses like the *Battle of the Summer Islands* and, finally, pious verses. Their date matters little. Elegance, correctness, a certain studied grace, something cold and stilted, belong to them all. The wit of the metaphysical poets recurs in Waller, but is attenuated, diluted and purified. He is much less ingenious than Cowley, but also less apt to horrify taste. It is Thomas Carew whom he most resembles. The madrigals he sings to Sacharissa recall Carew's more decent verses by their distinction within a narrow compass, their regularity of structure and their adroitness. His well-known poems—*The Bud, Go, lovely Rose* and *On a Girdle*—are models in this genre.

His imagery is clear and well sustained. He does not always avoid the pedantry of the Renascence and he sometimes uses ornamental mythology unjustifiably, but in these respects he is more discreet than many of his contemporaries. In his political and patriotic poems, in rhymed couplets of ten syllables, he is dignified and lofty. The fine verses he wrote towards the end of his life to express the serenity which accompanies old age might serve as text for an examination into the birth of classical qualities in literature. Here imagery is not strange or precious, but noble and strictly governed by the idea behind it. The lines are disposed in couplets each containing a full sentence. It is especially by the qualities which he displayed in this poem that Waller had an influence on literature. Dryden says that "the excellence and dignity of it [rhyme] were never fully known till Mr. Waller taught it: he first made writing easily an art; first showed us to conclude the sense, most commonly in a distitch." Others, including Sandys, the translator of Ovid, did this before him, but it was Waller whom the classicists delighted to honour. His celebrity as a man doubtless contributed to the fortunes of his poetry. He was known to the French at a time when it was France who could place the hall-mark

[1] *The Poems of Edmund Waller*, ed. G. Thorn-Drury (The Muses' Library, 1893). See E. Gosse, *Seventeenth Century Studies* and *From Shakespeare to Pope*, op. cit.

on literature. He earned the friendship of Saint-Evremond and the admiration of
La Fontaine, and Corneille was flattered to learn that he had the habit of translating a passage from his tragedies as each one appeared. Waller had the qualities,
or rather the lack of defects, to meet the tastes and needs of a new age which cared
less that an achievement should be original than that it should be correct and polite.

(c) JOHN DENHAM.—The other pioneer of classicism was John Denham (1615–
69),[1] whose strength is praised by Pope in the same line as Waller's sweetness.
The renown to which Denham attained by a small literary production is proof of
the appetite of the age for regulated poetry. An official, a good Royalist and the
son of a magistrate, he owed his fame, save for a few occasional poems, to his half-
descriptive, half-didactic *Cooper's Hill* which appeared in 1642. It has been called
the first example of local description, but in the main it is a meditation inspired by
a place of many historical memories, near the Thames, Windsor Forest, the ruins
of an abbey which recall the destruction of the monasteries, and Runnymede Field,
where Magna Carta was signed. What description there is has a moralising turn.
The Thames serves as a term of comparison for moral and even literary qualities,
for instance in the four famous lines which the author added to the 1653 edition,
and which became for the classicists a slogan, the æsthetic motto inscribed upon
their banner:

> O could I flow like thee, and make thy stream
> My great example, as it is my theme!
> Though deep, yet clear; though gentle, yet not dull;
> Strong without rage; without o'erflowing full.

To-day it is difficult to understand the brilliant success and long renown of
this poem. More than half a century later Pope was inspired by it to write his
Windsor Forest.

Among his miscellaneous verse, two poems are witness to Denham's taste for
metrical literary criticism. In his epistle *To Sir Richard Fanshawe upon his Translation of Pastor Fido*, he outlines, in some sort, a translators' art of poetry. He wishes
them to be not slavish, but free and animated. His advice is expressed in well-
turned couplets which Pope might have included in his work without alteration.
His antithetical style throws his ideas into relief, and he uses the decasyllabic
couplet to mark his meaning by the balance between the parts of a line.

The octosyllabic couplets of his elegy on Cowley are also thus used. This poem
passes English poetry in review and places Cowley at its summit of accomplishment, Cowley who added the natural wit of Shakespeare and Fletcher to the art
of Spenser and Jonson, and whose fancy was always governed by his judgment:

> His severe judgement (giving law)
> His modest fancy kept in awe.

He did not, like Jonson, "plunder all the Roman stores":

> Horace's wit and Virgil's state,
> He did not steal, but emulate!
> And when he would like them appear,
> Their garb, but not their clothes, did wear.

Denham may assign too high a place to Cowley, but as he praises his friend he
defines his own taste.

Slight though the figures of these two poets may seem, as also that of Davenant
(1606–68),[2] author of the epical romance *Gondibert*, who is often associated with
them, their adoption as models by the Restoration writers is proof of a changed

---

[1] *Poetical Works of John Denham*, in Chalmers's *English Poets*, vol. vii.
[2] *The Works of Sir William Davenant*, 5 vols. (Edinburgh, 1882–4).

literary ideal. The age of the understanding, unable to take pleasure in the exuberant fancy of such as Spenser and shocked by the sleight of hand of the metaphysical poets, was at hand. The new literature was called classical, but the word signified that it sought restraint rather than inspiration from the ancients. Were the title conferred by study of the great art of antiquity, he who would deserve it above all others would be the Englishman who wrote *Paradise Lost* and *Samson Agonistes*. Nothing produced in the next century was as deeply marked by Græco-Roman influence on poetic form or showed as broad and as accurate an understanding of the beauty of ancient art.

CHAPTER III

MILTON

1. **John Milton (1608–74).**[1] **His Early Poems.**—Wither ceased to be a poet before he became a Puritan; Marvell was numbered among the Puritans more by force of circumstances than as the result of his temperament. Milton, the only poet who identified himself with Puritanism, had so strong a personality that he cannot be taken to represent anyone except himself. Wordsworth spoke truth in his famous line:

> Thy soul was like a Star, and dwelt apart.

As a poet, he dominates his century from so great an altitude that he cannot be merged in it. He did indeed sing the praises of certain of his predecessors, declare that Spenser was his master, praise " Jonson's learned sock," and render homage to Shakespeare in feeling lines. But the ties which connect him with them are weak. His firm mind was proof against Spenserian exuberance; his ear was too delicate for Jonson's harsh, prosaic verse; his superb egoism substituted a single theme, the problem of morality as he himself saw it, for the innumerable aspects of Shakespeare's work, the interest which he extended to every one of life's manifestations. He speaks only for one soul, his own, which was indeed strong and lofty. Alone among poets he endeavoured to blend the spirit of the Renascence and of the Reformation. Spenser had attempted this superficially, writing moral and religious legends beneath the pictures which he painted like a great sensuous artist, but his juxtaposition of the two elements did but make their incompatibility more glaring. Milton was the first to conceive, from the outset of his career, a work which combined the perfection of ancient art and the intimate moral ardour of the Bible. He had experienced within his own heart the conflict of the opposing forces—paganism and Christianity, nature and religion—and he composed their differences in his own way. The proportion in which the two elements are present in his work varies with his years, but from the beginning his powerful will mingles with them harmoniously. No other English poet was at once so profoundly religious and so much an artist.

Milton was born in a London family in easy circumstances, Christians who were not exaggeratedly strict, but succeeded in pursuing art as well as morals. His father was both pious and passionately devoted to music, and the young Milton's natural

---

[1] *Works* in verse and prose, ed. Milford, 8 vols. (1851); *Poetical Works*, ed. Browne (Oxford, 2 vols., 1866); ed. Masson, 3 vols. (1874), in the Golden Treasury Series, 2 vols. (1875) and in Globe edition, 1 vol. (1877); ed. W. A. Wright (Cambridge, 1903); W. Raleigh (1905), etc. Numerous annotated editions of the separate poems.
Biographies: Samuel Johnson, *Lives of the Poets*; D. Masson, *Life of John Milton*, 6 vols. (1859–80); Mark Pattison in English Men of Letters Series (1879); R. Garnett (1890).
Studies: Stopford Brooke, *Milton* (1879); Sir W. Raleigh (1900); W. P. Trent (1899); Williamson (1905); S. B. Liljegren, *Studies in Milton* (1919); Voltaire, *Essai sur la poésie épique* (1726–9); article in the *Encyclopédie* (1771); Villemain, *Notice sur Milton*; R. de Véricourt, *Milton et la Poésie épique* (1838); Taine, *Littérature anglaise*, vol. ii. (1863–4); de Guerle, *Milton, sa vie et ses œuvres* (1868); Schérer, *Études critiques de littérature contemporaine* (1863–95); J. Telleen, *Milton dans la Littérature française* (1904); D. Saurat, *La Pensée de Milton* (1920); J. Douady, *La Création et le Fruit défendu selon Milton* (1923).

gifts, together with his success at school and the merits of his first verses, caused him to be consecrated to poetry and glory from an early age. Father and son seem to have shared the faith that such was his destiny. They had no thought of worldly renown, but believed in an indeterminate yet sublime vocation. The boy's preparation was intensely laborious: from the age of twelve it was his habit to work until midnight. He became a remarkable humanist, rivalling Buchanan as a Latin poet, and he also wrote verses in English, although his exacting standard, which left him long dissatisfied with his own art, led him to delay beginning his great works in the mother tongue.

It was at first intended that he should take orders, but he abandoned this plan when Laud was tyrannising over the Church of England and exciting Puritan indignation by Romanising Anglican ritual. Thereupon he devoted himself entirely to preparation for his poetic mission.

Meanwhile the youth, handsome and pure, knew the temptations of love and confided the first stirrings of his heart and senses to Latin verses: the charm of the fair young girls he saw in London parks, the disquieting voluptuousness of spring, the loves of the earth and the sun bearing fruit at the year's renewal. He could readily have yielded to the pleasures of love and to the joys of wine also, for he knew that it was Bacchus and Venus who had always inspired the Muses. But he also knew them fitted to inspire only workaday poets. He who aspired to the highest poetry, whose ambition it was to be an epic poet, must drink only pure water and have a youth chaste as that of a priest. Such, he resolved, his own youth must be.

(a) ODE "ON THE MORNING OF CHRIST'S NATIVITY."—He was at this time twenty years old. After some interesting essays, some fine verses to Shakespeare and the superb *At a Solemn Music*, which weds Voice and Verse, he wrote, in 1629, his first masterpiece, the ode *On the Morning of Christ's Nativity*. It contains hardly a trace of the "metaphysical" strangeness then so popular, and so seductive to a young mind. In the opening verses of the hymn there is indeed some mannerism. The earth is said to veil herself with snow rather than that her Maker should see "her foul deformities":

> Only with speeches fair
> She woo's the gentle air
> To hide her guilty front with innocent snow.

But this is all. As the poem continues it grows greater and purer. It is admirable when it depicts the straitening of Satan's kingdom at the Nativity, and an incomparable series of stanzas celebrates the end of paganism. "The oracles are dumb"; "the Lares and Lemures moan with midnight pain"; the gods of Phœnicia and "the brutish gods of Nile" take flight. The day has dawned before which all the powers of darkness are dissipated.

Nothing as marvellous had been written in the mood of this ode. The stanza of eight lines of different measure, closed by an alexandrine, has both swing and majesty. The poem has, above all, that which no one else has possessed in the same degree as Milton—absolute perfection in the choice of words and sonorities. From the line "The oracles are dumb" onwards there is that intimate blending of sound and sense which makes Milton the most untranslatable of English poets. There is no apparent effort after imitative harmony. The interpenetration of sound and meaning is undefinable and mysterious. Proper names, the names of gods and goddesses, are marvellous in themselves because of the place given them. The imagery is restrained and has an unequalled power of suggestion. Milton was well versed in all these pagan religions which he condemns, and was charmed by the strange forms they sheltered: "the pale-eyed priest from the prophetic cell" inspired by the oracles of Apollo, "the Flamens at their service quaint," "mooned

Ashtaroth," "the Tyrian maids" who "their wounded Thammuz (Adonis) mourn,"
the worshippers of Moloch:

> In vain with cymbals' ring,
> They call the grisly king,
> In dismal dance about the furnace blue—

and the sorcerers of Osiris:

> In vain with timbrel'd anthems dark
> The sable-stolèd sorcerers bear his worshipt ark.

To evoke these visions, the young poet uses all the resources of a language
enriched by the Elizabethan treasure. He employs energetic abbreviations and
composite epithets imported by the translator of Du Bartas, but among the riches
at his disposal he makes a severe choice. He keeps only the exquisite, reaches the
limits of stylistic effect, but never lapses to obscurity or bad taste. To-day it seems
incredible that the surprising beauty of this ode, at once so imaginative and so
classical, did not impress the poet's contemporaries with its sublime perfection.

Thus Milton was already dedicating his highest art to the service of his religion.
He did other work which was on a larger scale, but he never surpassed this ode.

(b) "L'ALLEGRO" AND "IL PENSEROSO."—Milton was still at Cambridge when
he wrote the ode On the Nativity. He went thence to his father's house at Horton,
in Buckinghamshire, having abandoned all thoughts of a practical career and
resolved to devote himself entirely to study and poetry. From 1632 to 1638, when
only rural leisure interrupted his solitary labours, he produced, one after the other,
the rest of his entrancing early poems.

We have noticed the lively taste for the country which distinguished Wither
and Marvell. That poets who inclined to Puritanism and were genuinely repelled
by the vices of the court and the town should seek "unreprovèd pleasures free"
in the country was natural. Milton's work in the years which he spent in Horton,
not far from Windsor, in a fine wooded country, well watered, rich and green,
shows deep feeling for Nature.

This is nowhere clearer than in the first poetry he wrote there: L'Allegro and
Il Penseroso. These short pieces are partly descriptive and partly poems of feeling;
they reveal a landscape less than the poet's state of mind. Milton is discovered in
search of the greatest of pure pleasures, or rather making a diptych to represent
the two aspects in which pleasure appears to him at different times, the alternation
of his mirth and gravity. There is not, as in Hercules' choice in the fable of Prodicus,
conflict between duty and desire. There is no element of the tragic: nowhere else
indeed does this pure poet show himself so sportive. He recurs to the theme of the
little poem at the beginning of the Anatomy of Melancholy in which Burton, in
alternating and antithetic stanzas, relates the charms and curses of melancholy.
He is also inspired by the delightful song in John Fletcher's Nice Valour—"Hence,
all you vain delights!" Like Fletcher and unlike Burton, Milton finally gives his
preference to melancholy, but he first recounts all the benefits of mirth. His novelty
consists in his careful observation, at first hand, of the country. The aptness of the
word "twisted" to describe the eglantine may be disputed, but elsewhere there is
only truth and pure poetry. He paints, on the one hand, all the joys which life and
Nature, in their laughing guise, can bring a man—the spring, the morning, the
lark's song, the sunrise, the men and women at work on the land, their rustic
meals, the harvest, the stories told at night by the chimneyside, and in "towered
cities," "the busy hum of men,"

> And Pomp and Feast and Revelry
> With Mask and antique Pageantry;

as well as the plays acted on "the well-trod stage," and the pleasures of "soft Lydian airs."

On the other hand, he describes the yet more penetrating pleasures of solitary meditation, sunset, the nightingale's song—moonlight, on the dry " smooth-shaven green," and to hear

> the far-off curfew sound
> Over some wide watered shore.

Or else the Penseroso, among his books in "some high lonely tower," reads philosophy or science, or he will

> Sometime let gorgeous Tragedy
> In scepter'd pall come sweeping by,

until the morning appear, not in pomp but " civil-suited." His walks are among the " archèd walks of twilight groves," or " the studious cloisters"; he no longer haunts the playhouses but, instead, the gothic cathedral, where he hears "the pealing organ blow."

The subsequent over-indulgence in description may make the lines of this double picture seem too facile and summary. Yet no later work was able to obscure the charm of these two poems or to equal their graceful restraint. Each seems to be no more than a collection of observations, yet each has, in the feeling which dominates it, unity. Each calls into being its own spirit, the rosy nymph of Mirth:

> So buxom, blithe and debonair,

with her "wreathèd smiles," which "love to live in dimple sleek," tripping " on the light fantastic toe" and leading in her right hand "the mountain nymph, sweet Liberty," and "divinest Melancholy," "whose saintly visage is too bright," and is therefore "o'erlaid with black, staid Wisdom's hue," the "pensive Nun, devout and pure,"

> With even step and musing gait,
> And looks commercing with the skies,
> Thy rapt soul sitting in thine eyes.

Nothing could be simpler than the form of this diptych: it is in rhyming couplets, each line having four accents, the very metre of which the facility led other poets to be diffuse and garrulous. But here it is held in check by an artist who rejects all but the exquisite. Milton uses learnedly what is licence in many other versifiers. He varies, at will, the calmer iambic and the abrupter and lighter trochaic measure. These two poems, which contain altogether 328 short lines, are filled to overflowing with the results of accurate observation and are an inexhaustible lesson in art. At the same time they display the whole of Milton's register, the extreme notes of the gamut of his feelings at this time. The register is short: it excludes sin, evil and pain, hardly includes mankind except as a passing spectacle, and has no place for any feeling which is not both very pure and very egoistical—the intimate pleasures of contemplation and study. Milton's soul held, as shall be seen, what was greater and better than this: he was capable of sublimity, devotion to a cause, and submission to great sacrifice. The theme of *L'Allegro* and *Il Penseroso* merely is, in the last analysis, the search for the pleasures to which he was most susceptible, and his final preference is for the most solitary and unsociable of them, for melancholy.

Curiously he excludes love from his sources of felicity. This young man of twenty-five had turned his gaze heavenward and almost dreamt of a hermit's cell. Even in *L'Allegro* there is only one, and the vaguest, allusion to a fair lady living in a neighbouring castle " bosomed high in tufted trees."

Perhaps Horton had quenched the ardours which London once had kindled, or perhaps the poet deliberately confined himself to rustic themes in these poems. The conclusion is that he did not yet give himself free scope in English verse.

(*c*) HIS MASQUES. "ARCADES." "COMUS."—The moral problem is posed in the subsequent poems, which express, in allegorical or veiled form, the conflict in the poet's heart. Externally Milton observed the fashions of the Renascence. He wrote masques, those sumptuous operas which were the dazzling fringe of the dramatic art reproved by the Puritans, or he had recourse to the pastoral fiction. But this is true only of the outer form of his poems, which alone conformed to the spirit of the age. Every emanation of Milton's thought was inwardly austere and grave.

Arcades, the fragment of a masque, is a fine compliment in verse to the Dowager Countess of Derby, whose praises Spenser had sung when she was the wife of Lord Strange. It shows the genius of the woods at his work of protecting the trees and plants, or listening, at night, to the music of the spheres. Soon afterwards, Milton wrote for the same family the words of a complete masque, *Comus*, for which Henry Lawes supplied the music.

The occasion was the appointment, in 1634, of the Earl of Bridgewater as Lord President of Wales and his choice of Ludlow as a residence. His daughter Alice, who was barely fifteen, and his two sons, who were younger still, were the principal actors in the masque. Alice is represented to have lost herself in the wood on her way to the castle, to have become separated from her two brothers and to be misled by Comus, the lustful magician, who makes a vain attempt on her virtue. She is saved once by her brothers, who put Comus and his crew to rout. But enchantment has deprived her of the power of movement and she is set free only by the intervention of the nymph Sabrina, who personifies the Severn. The sister and brothers afterwards return to the castle. Throughout the maiden is protected by a tutelary genius, "the Attendant Spirit," disguised as the shepherd Thyrsis, and it is with the help of his counsels that Comus is vanquished. When once she is saved, the Attendant Spirit, after finally exhorting mankind to virtue, departs to his celestial abode.

The plot is seen to be very slight. Milton goes back, beyond Renascence drama, to the simplicity of the early morality. He is without dramatic sense or the sense of the stage, and the masque is full of monologues and lengthy tirades. When the brothers have lost their sister, they discuss, in 160 lines, whether her virtue be in danger or whether she have in herself her means of defence. The Attendant Spirit then supervenes and continues the discussion for other 170 lines before any step is taken to save the maiden.

There are many charming, delicate descriptions in the masque, too subtle to be appreciated or even, perhaps, immediately understood, as they are heard on the stage.

The didactic intention is so apparent that it deadens the required emotion and prevents anxiety. Such confidence is felt in the strength of virtue that there can be no doubt of the event. The girl herself feels fear as little as temptation. Comus, god of drunkenness and lust, has nothing of the true voluptuary. He shows the bones of anacreonticism too nakedly. His banqueting and drinking could never have troubled the maiden's senses; his schoolman's arguments are too cold to shake her. We could understand Spenser's Sir Guyon succumbing to the treacherous lures of Acrasia's bower, but Milton's heroine never has the possibility of falling. She is able to understand only the outer meaning of the words by which Comus seeks to induce her to sin.

Everything which might be dramatic is frozen or suppressed. The characters remain abstract as virtues or vices. The only happy stage effect is that produced when the girl enters the wood which Comus haunts and calls her brothers by her song to "sweet Echo." All the rest is poetry addressed to the ear or the mind. The pleasure of a spectacle is not provided any more than dramatic emotion.

These are grave omissions. In its old age the Renascence was letting go of part of its treasure. But in this masque there are compensating novelties which are admirable. The exclusive, absolute purity may not be very dramatic, but it keeps to the heights of lyricism. This is a white, immaculate hymn to virtue. The very passages which offend the dramatic sense are beautiful in themselves, for instance the elder brother's speech or that in which the girl repels Comus. The descriptions made with so much art are little fitted to be heard on the stage, but they charm when they are read, mingling, as they do, realistic touches and subtle classical reminiscences. Above all, the style is pure as the moral. It is a new style, but one enriched by its Elizabethan past and by the quintessence of antiquity: everything has been sifted until only the perfect remains. There is less movement than with the Elizabethans; the pace seems to have slackened since Shakespeare and Fletcher; but this style, long cherished and learnedly chastened, has reached the highest degree of perfection, is pithy and mature in the extreme. In the blank verse and even more in the rhymed passages of *Comus*, especially in the admirable songs, this is apparent. Less spontaneous than "the native wood-notes wild" of the Elizabethan stage, Milton's songs are exquisite garden-flowers. The complete purity of versification and crystalline music of syllables in the song to Echo, the appeal to the nymph Sabrina, and the invocation "By the rushy-fringèd bank" are unequalled.

Hardly more than twenty years separate *Comus* from *The Tempest*, but the change wrought in this short time is understood when Shakespeare's Ariel is compared to Milton's Attendant Spirit. The winged spright, trembling with eagerness to serve man, has given place to the angel with a moral mission who is clear about what he has to do and is not to be turned from his path. Both spirits leave the earth when their task is done, but while the Miltonian angel ascends to heaven amid moralising, mythological visions, his last words a plea for chastity, Ariel takes flight like a butterfly.

While Shakespeare is lost among his creations, Milton is in truth the only living being who exists in his own work. His heroine is himself; Comus tempts as he has been tempted; she resists as he did; he speaks every word in the poem; Comus merely expresses the appeal to the senses which young Milton felt. The moral of the masque is Milton's moral—high, disdainful and solitary. The final impression is one of virtue remote from mankind and above it, sure and haughty virtue, ignoring the multitude. For the Milton of *Comus*, as for the Calvinists, the number of the elect is few. The Attendant Spirit guards, on his own showing, not the wicked or the half-good, but only the pure. These are chilly altitudes. How many who saw the masque played must have felt that they were excluded from the small band of the elect!

(*d*) "Lycidas."—Less indirectly, Milton related the conflict in his own heart in the elegy called *Lycidas* (1637), which was the last of his early poems in English. It is occasional verse in the conventional pastoral form, and was one of some twenty laments written by young Cambridge men on the death of Edward King, who had been much loved at the University, and who seemed assured of a brilliant future when he was drowned in a shipwreck near Anglesea. Milton and King were probably not very intimate. The grief of a bereaved friend is less apparent in this poem than in the Latin elegy *Epitaphium Damonis*, in which a year later Milton mourned the loss of his beloved Deodati. Emotions are, however, of several kinds. That in *Lycidas* is born of the fact that Milton, thinking of King's fate, is brought back to himself, and it springs also from the highest and rarest of all sources of feeling—the beauty of verse.

The two hundred lines of *Lycidas* are among the most precious treasures of English poetry. Their pastoral dress is out of date and they abound in mythological allusions. There is religious satire in them, as in Spenser's eclogues; and they are not eminent for simple pathos. They have a very powerful but a special fragrance which cannot be appreciated without some initiation.

It is not King but Milton who should be sought in them. The death of this friend who was so young, and whose future promised so much, led Milton to reflect on his own life. Lycidas, or King, had been wont "to scorn delights and live laborious days," devoting himself wholeheartedly to the Muse without ambition of worldly success. To what end, Milton asks. Nowhere else has he so poetically uttered the haunting thought:

> Alas! what boots it with incessant care
> To tend the homely slighted shepherd's trade,
> And strictly meditate the thankless Muse?
> Were it not better done as others use,
> To sport with Amaryllis in the shade,
> Or with the tangles of Neæra's hair?

Yet he does not hesitate in his choice. Phœbus tells him that the guerdon is not fame, "that last infirmity of noble mind," but that he must "in heaven expect thy meed," and as he thinks of this distant and austere reward he sighs no longer.

His train of thought is interrupted when the Church is suggested, for, like all the more ardent Reformers, those who became Puritans, he was irked by Laud's tyranny and by the Romanising tendency of some churchmen. He inserts an invective which presages the part he was to play in controversy. But it is isolated. *Lycidas* remains the poem of a refined humanist, an example of supreme perfection of style, imagery and versification. A spell is woven as Milton laments that he must sing before his genius is ripe—

> I come to pluck your berries harsh and crude,
> And with forced fingers rude
> Shatter your leaves before the mellowing year—

and also by the lines in which he strews the hearse of Lycidas with flowers, then remembers that he has no tomb but the waters, then stays his tears at the vision of his friend rapt to heaven. Art in this poem rebels against strictness, in such wise that the most spiritual poetry constitutes a feast for the most fastidious ear. Milton mastered his instrument to such a point that he could write free verse, obeying no law but his own. The heroic line gives place from time to time to a short line; rhymes follow no fixed order; there are neither couplets nor stanzas, but rhymes variously and flexibly interlaced and occasional unrhymed lines. The only rule is that of the poet's exquisite ear. The echoing sounds cross each other capriciously, now widely separated, now suppressed, now, in obedience to the poet's melodic sense, repeated as often as six times, like the sound *ear* in the opening lines. The result is a marvel of liquid, blended harmony, whence monotony has been expelled.

At thirty years old Milton was still, more than anything else, a child of the Renascence. Although about to play a passionate part in the civil and ecclesiastical struggle, he had not yet abandoned the ambition to devote himself to pure poetry and write a great epic. He dreamt by preference of the legendary Arthur and the battles between the Britons and the Saxons. To accomplish his great work he must complete his poetic education, and to this end he travelled to the classical land, and spent sixteen months in Italy, not suffering the revolt of the Scottish Presbyterians against Laud to detain him. To stay where the abhorred popes had their seat was also to dwell in the land of literary glory, both ancient and modern. He was in Florence, Rome and Naples, not hiding his faith, but giving himself up to enjoyment of art, taking part in academic discussions, writing fine Latin and Italian verses which caused the men of letters to marvel at the culture of this Northerner. In Naples he became the friend of Manso, Marquis of Villa, who had been the patron first of Tasso and then of Marini. In Rome, the singing of Leonora Baroni awoke his enthusiasm; it seemed to him that in her harmonious notes he heard the voice of God—"Nam tua præsentem vox sonat ipsa Deum"—that God, who was everywhere, spoke only through her:

> Quod, si cuncta quidem Deus est, per cunctaque fusus,
> In te una loquitur, cætera mutus habet.

Returning home by way of Lucca, he fell in love with an Italian whose praises he sang in five Italian sonnets. On all sides the voices of the Renascence were whispering their precious memories in his ear, telling him of beauty and love.

2. The Period of Political Strife. The Sonnets.—Meanwhile, in England, the struggle between the king and the Parliament had begun, and he says that it hastened his return. Certainly it awoke his dormant religious ardour. For twenty years the realisation of all his great poet's dreams was suspended, at the cost of a sacrifice which cannot be exaggerated and which should be the measure of the nobility of his soul. He did indeed try for some years to reconcile his newly awakened religious fervour with his poetic ambitions. His dream of an Arthurian epic was succeeded by a plan for a religious tragedy on the fall of the angels, the creation and the fall of man. But this, too, was abandoned for the duties which he held to be more immediate. Henceforth, until the Restoration, he wrote only prose, "wherein," he said to himself, ". . . I have the use, as I may account, but of my left hand." He obliged himself "to embark on a troubled sea of noises and hoarse disputes, from beholding the bright countenance of truth in the quiet and still air of delightful studies," and

to club quotations with men whose learning and belief lies in marginal stuffings, who, when they have, like good sumpters, laid ye down their horseload of citations and fathers at your door, . . . ye may take off their packsaddles, their day's work is done. . . . Let any gentle apprehension, that can distinguish learned pains from unlearned drudgery, imagine what pleasure or profoundness can be in this, or what honour to deal against such adversaries.

Never did a poet torn from his Muse express his impatience more angrily. Yet he did not flinch, and until the Restoration silenced him as a polemist, he wrote no verse beyond some dozen occasional sonnets, of which four or five are, in their own genre, the most memorable in the language. They have nothing in common with the sonnet-series on love dear to the Elizabethans. As Wordsworth has well said of Milton's use of the sonnet:

> in his hand
> The thing became a trumpet.

Some of his sonnets are personal effusions, others allude to his polemical writings, or they are fragments of the great living epic in which he played a part—addressed to Fairfax, Cromwell and Sir Harry Vane. Many are deliberately rude and harsh, witnesses to his refusal to cultivate the slighter graces in this tragic time. But Milton was visited by Beauty even though he received her coldly. Try as he might, he could not shut out beauty and feeling. When in 1652 he had gone blind as a consequence of his controversy with Saumaise, and mourned the extinction of his "one talent" before he had had time to serve his Maker as he would,

> . . . Patience, to prevent
> That murmur, soon replies, God doth not heed
> Either man's work or his own gifts; who best
> Bear his mild yoke, they serve him best; his state
> Is kingly; thousands at his biddings speed,
> And post o'er land and ocean without rest:
> They also serve who only stand and wait.

There is powerful pathos in the sonnet he wrote to his second wife, Catherine Woodcock, who died in childbed in 1658, fifteen months after their marriage. Milton had never seen her in life; his first sight of her was in his dream, after her death, when she

> Came vested all in white, pure as her mind:
> Her face was veiled, yet to my fancied sight
> Love, sweetness, goodness, in her person shined
> So clear, as in no face with more delight.
> But O, as to embrace me she inclined,
> I waked, she fled, and day brought back my night.

The most marvellous of his sonnets is, however, that on the massacre of the Waldensians by the Piedmontese. The Waldensians were dear to Protestants because they were supposed to have preserved primitive Christianity, and in England their massacre was greeted with horror which Milton interpreted. Here we see what his genius made of the sonnet. He returned to the Italian form at its strictest, the two quatrains followed by the two tercets, each with their two rhymes. But he makes no division in the idea. The fourteen lines follow a single uninterrupted train of thought; a phrase is continued from one line to another, even from one quatrain to another. The effect is surprising: sentences seem to be cut short, not by art but by indignation. But the most striking feature of the sonnet is the rhymes—on *ones*, *old*, *ay*, and the long *o*. They ring out like a knell or an alarm-bell, or like the groans of the poor unfortunates slaughtered on cold Alpine slopes. These fourteen lines are at once the explosion of a wrath as genuine as it was deep and an inexhaustible lesson on art.

3. The Great Works of Milton's Maturity.—In 1660 the Restoration forced Milton to return to private life. Both his life and liberty were at first in some danger, but he finally enjoyed security in his retreat, whither some friends penetrated and where he was able to return to the poetic projects of his youth. They resulted in his three capital works, *Paradise Lost*, published in 1667, *Paradise Regained* and *Samson Agonistes*, published in 1671. The Milton they reveal is new. His private misfortunes and the anguish of the nation had darkened his thought, and his long and vehement participation in controversy had implanted in him an ineradicable dialectical habit. He felt something like contempt for the exquisite productions of his youth, blushed that he had so loved rhyme. He felt the need of a severer harmony based only on rhythm and articulate only as was his thought. Henceforward he wrote none but blank verse. He had done with pastorals, lyrics of determined form and songs, and also with slight subjects and with the fine analysis of subtle spiritual states. The blind poet rejected the themes of the Renascence and found inspiration and matter only in the Bible. He sang the creation, the fall of the angels, the fall of man and Christ's reconquest of Paradise, and he told of the sacrifice of Samson, who died willingly because his death entailed that of the enemies of his country.

(*a*) "PARADISE LOST."—*Paradise Lost*, Milton's principal work, is the most Hebraic of great English poems. It is the fruit of a Puritan's prolonged meditations on the Bible: it paints the visions the Bible has given him. He let nothing intervene between the Bible and himself; he allowed himself complete liberty in interpreting it, but he gave it entire faith. He accepts the whole of Biblical history as authentic and sacred. But he retells it as one who bears all the burden of contemporary knowledge, whose personality is intense and self-centred, and who has little dramatic sense. He projects himself, his feelings, knowledge and aspirations, into the characters of his epic, both the primitive human creatures and the superhuman beings, whether celestial or infernal.

The strange result is a perpetual conflict between his faith and his nature which deflects the poem from its purpose and distributes sympathy in despite of the poet's intentions. The moral thesis of Genesis is submission to the Almighty which makes disobedience into sin. But Milton, who wished to emphasise this moral, had an independent spirit and had lived independently. He had acclaimed and advocated the rebellion against the prelates and even the king, and celebrated the glories of regicide. In spite of himself, he was in deep sympathy with Satan, the great rebel of heaven and the enemy of God. The pride and indomitable courage of the revolted angel rekindled the emotion of the intensest hours of his life, and, do what he would, he saw God as the king of England, surrounded by submissive and docile angels, as by courtiers, who spent their lives feasting, singing and fighting in glorious wars. Devoutly, but mechanically, he paid lip-service to the duty of obedience, but in his heart he was chanting a hymn to freedom and rebellion. It is in Satan that he has put most of himself, his pride and his temperament. As a sincere believer, he intended to "justify the ways of God to men." But he could not do it on the impulse of confident love. He attempted it in speeches and arguments, often subtle and sometimes sophistical, and these are the least personal part of the epic, the work of a pupil of the theologians. An immense place in the poem is given up to arguments by which it is encumbered and chilled. Academic arguing in favour of divine foreknowledge and human free-will leaves even the pious reader in doubt and ill at ease.

When the dialectics are voiced by Adam or Eve, the surprise is considerable that primitive beings, who might be expected to have direct and simple sensations, to be guided by impulse and pure instinct, should habitually utter so many syllogisms. Thus facts which belong to history in Milton's time and his own mental habits constantly find their way into the ancient legend, which he transforms while he accepts it and falsifies while he professedly respects it. Hence result the limitations of *Paradise Lost*, and the element of the ridiculous which this noble poem includes and of which Taine made so much.

The imagination by which a man can get outside himself and his own time and evoke strange and far-away beings was not among Milton's gifts. His conceptions could, however, be vast: he could present the universe with a sense of its immensity which leaves far behind the curious, grotesque and complicated conceptions of Dante. The two Hells have often been compared—Dante's various and fragmentary, divided into innumerable compartments; Milton's immense and indeterminate, and producing an incomparable total effect with its "darkness visible," and with the gigantic forms of the angels changed into demons who sprawled on the burning marl. The picture of the creation of the world is no less great. A powerful imagination vivifies the Biblical text and the Creator's act, when he drew space out of chaos and made it fruitful, is described with marvellous force.

The picture of Eden has been derided as too much like an English park. Each man's ideal garden is indeed made of the most beautiful spot he has seen. It is none the less true that Milton has diffused the richest poetry over his, yet never let his descriptions fade to vagueness. About his lawns and groves he has caused a sun to revolve, marking the hours, a sun and stars in their earliest perfect splendour. This painter drew accurately, but his total effects are none the less great and splendid. His Paradise remains one of the most beautiful dreams of the men who have been in love with Nature.

He transported into it, as his subject required, the eternal drama of conscience, man hesitating between good and evil, exposed to temptation and prone to fall. The Bible supplied him with the elements of this drama as he had himself experienced it. Love had set the snare in which his own life had all but been destroyed: at thirty-five years old he had married a Royalist girl who had left him, and in his anger he had clamoured for the legalisation of divorce. Two subsequent and happy marriages had not appeased his resentment. For him, the danger to a man's soul lay in woman, a danger which was great in proportion to his susceptibility to love. His own experience, as much as his meditations on the Bible, and doubtless on Roman virtues also, had led him to revise the conception of love and of woman which, ever since the introduction of the chivalrous ideal, had governed poetry. In the lyrics of the Middle Ages and the Renascence, inspired by the chivalrous tradition or the cult of the Virgin Mary, woman was the star, the queen of beauty and virtue. A knight must live prostrated before her; her least need was sacred. She was so high, pure and ethereal that natural love was too coarse for her and marriage too material. True love was platonic and bound a lover who had overcome his carnal desires to an inaccessible mistress. Therefore the marriage tie was despised. The ideal was, in the last analysis, still monastic: it was virginity.

To Milton, woman was man's inferior, an imperfect creature, dangerous if she were not mastered. His view was supported by his memories as by the story of Eve. His Eve is charming and capricious, coquettish and wayward, incapable of sound reasoning and an easy prey to sophistry. Man's duty is not to humble himself before her, but to feel and proclaim himself master. If passion blind him too much, he is blamed by the angel Raphael or by Christ Himself. Adam's crime consists in his chivalrous behaviour on the day on which he sinned, and for this he is doomed to share the punishment of his criminal wife.

Milton also rebels against the doctrine of the superiority of virginity to marriage. In the complete union of husband and wife, in which the husband is the chief and the wife his obedient companion, Milton sees supreme morality and true felicity. His famous apostrophe, "Hail, wedded love," sounded the dirge of the old conception, and restored true and perfect love, equally distinct from lust and from asceticism or Platonism, to its place in the centre of human life.

Milton so constantly returns to himself in his epic that he limits its objective value, but this very self-centredness imparts to it a continuous emotion and eloquence and a lyrical ardour which culminate when, on the threshold of his great subject, he invokes the Holy Ghost, or when he utters the complaint of his blindness, but which are present as often as the sacred legend touches a chord in his memory. His absorbent personality is the central force of the poem, while his art, more austere than in his youth but still sovereign, makes its beauty.

It is still a humanist's art. His superb rejection of rhyme is in the spirit of the humanists of the Renascence who were most in communion with the ancients. The very form of the epic, replete with Hebraic matter, is derived from ancient models. Its aspect, its divisions, and its style are those of the Æneid or the Iliad. A unique event, the fall of man, is depicted. It is enhanced by episodes closely connected with it—the fall of the angels, the creation and a vison of future times, which are inserted in the form of narrations by one of the characters, like Æneas's story of the destruction of Troy in the Æneid. Christian miracles are substituted for pagan marvels. Classical mythology supplies only terms of comparison, but in a way which betrays acute consciousness of the relations between the myths of various religions.

The style is more Latin than that of any other English poem. The meaning of the words, the syntax, the division of sentences and the use of the ablative absolute, constantly remind the scholarly reader of classical authors. The periodic style and the unrhymed line, with its beauty dependent only on its cadence, and its inversions, have a severe solemnity, an unbending energy. The work is more full of meaning, denser, more uninterruptedly distinguished and more constantly lifted above the level of prose than any other in English poetry. When *Paradise Lost* is compared with the *Faerie Queene*, the gain and loss which it represents can be computed. The joy of free and adventurous curiosity and of fancy, the bold enjoyment of whatever charms the senses, the prodigious variety and the voluptuous music of stanzas and rhymes: all these Milton had lost. He had gained constructive force, unity of design, concentration of effort, moral seriousness, and the restraint which enables effect to be produced by quality rather than quantity. Spenser multiplied his monsters, but his description of Error, and of the Dragon who lays·waste the lands of Una's father, is superficial, childish ornament, beside the terrifying visions of Sin and Death in the second book of *Paradise Lost*. This comparison gives the measure of the difference between the imaginations and natures of the two poets.

(*b*) "PARADISE REGAINED."—*Paradise Regained* completes and answers *Paradise Lost*. Its theme is taken from the first verses of the fourth chapter of St. Luke's Gospel—Christ withstanding Satan's temptations after forty days of fasting in the wilderness. Milton traces the Redemption back to this triumph, which Giles Fletcher had already sung in *Christ's Victory and Triumph*. Paradise was lost by Eve when she yielded to Satan's temptation, regained by Christ when He got the better of the same tempter, and thereby ended the reign of Satan upon earth.

Our first impression as we pass from *Paradise Lost* to *Paradise Regained* is of brilliancy dulled, a greyer atmosphere and lowered tones. By comparison, the second poem even seems to drag, to move sadly. Imaginative greatness, Heaven and Hell are gone, or nearly gone. Satan has shrunk in stature and his fire is quenched. Instead of indomitable energy he has tortuous slyness and hypocrisy. Instead of a marvellous epic we have a morality. The poem is entirely human, its interest concentrated on the temptation of a single soul. Milton, the great heretic, did not see God in Christ, but only superior humanity. It is only metaphorically that he calls Him the Son of God. He describes the efforts, the meditations and the interior struggles through which Christ determined and accomplished His mission. We are struck by the resemblance between Milton's Christ and the poet himself (I. 195–207). This Christ has rejected the idea of an heroic war as Milton did that of an Arthurian epic. Like Milton, He has searched His soul in order to know His mission on earth. His temptations are Milton's own, save that Christ is proof against the love of women, which Milton was not. To the offer of kingly dominion or of untold gold, Christ answers like an ascete and a republican. The tempter thereupon offers Him Greece, her art, literature and philosophy and her eloquence, which to Milton would certainly have been the supreme temptation. He praises the wisdom of the ancients and describes Athens, mother of art and oratory. But the Saviour retorts by throwing contempt on knowledge which does not come of the fountain of light, and on wise men and their endless and vain disputing:

> Alas, what can they teach, and not mislead,
> Ignorant of themselves, of God much more,
> And how the world began, and how man fell,
> Degraded by himself, on grace depending?

Knowledge without true wisdom is vain. Even Greek poetry is inferior to Hebrew poetry; Greek mythology is a tissue of absurdities; Greek orators are far beneath the Hebrew prophets.

This poem has not the greatness, the vigour or the brilliancy of its predecessor, but it arrests and holds our interest by its revelations of Milton, his soul, and the change which had gradually come over him since the days of his passionate devotion to classical authors and the poets of the Renascence.

(c) "SAMSON AGONISTES."—*Samson Agonistes*, Milton's final work, is as personal as *Paradise Regained* and more beautiful. Even more than in *Paradise Lost*, the despiser of the Greeks shows himself their disciple. In form, the poem is a completely regular tragedy after Sophocles. It has choruses made of lines of unequal length which constitute long and free lyrical strophes and are interpolated in the dialogue, and the verse is rhymed only in the choruses, and there only exceptionally. The action of the drama passes in one place and during a single day. The conformity with Greek tragedies is outwardly greater than in any of the so-called classical modern tragedies. We must add, however, that the essential part of tragedy —progress and action—is wanting. Milton, lacking the dramatic sense, succeeded, after all, in producing only one more powerful lyrical poem. Not until the end of the tragedy, line 1300—when the total number of lines is 1750—can we discern a plot or perceive that the action is progressing and a future is indicated. Until then no issue is in prospect. There are only Samson's eloquent and pathetic laments and memories of the past. The play is almost entirely retrospective; in that it fails to arouse curiosity and uneasiness about the future, it neglects a fundamental element of tragedy.

But apart from this, the various scenes have a pathos, sufficient for a poem not intended for the stage, which derives from the old blind Puritan fighter's instinctive identification of himself with the Hebrew champion who was Dalila's victim, and who suffered the yoke of the Philistines. He too had survived the triumph of adversaries he despised for their mean souls and vile pleasures, and in his heart the memory still rankled of the betrayal of his faith by a wife from the enemy camp. The drama is all Samson—the sadness of his lot, his remorse for his errors, his grief that his cause and his nation have been laid low, his impotence in a world in which he has become the slave of those whom he conquered and whom he despises. The scene is superb in which Dalila approaches him. " Like a stately ship" "with all her bravery on, and tackle trim," she hypocritically implores his pardon, advancing every pretext to excuse her betrayal—love, for she wanted him all to herself, and religion, for she claims to have acted in the name of her gods. He replies to all her advances by overwhelming her with his disdain, will not let her even touch his hand, and finally flings her an insulting pardon—

> At distance I forgive thee; go with that—

and the chorus thereupon descant bitterly on the mystery of woman, whose love is not to be won by merit, whose nature is deceit.

After enlarging on woman's inferiority to man, they end with Milton's own conclusion:

> Therefore God's universal law
> Gave to the man despotic power
> Over his female in due awe.

This drama, with its strong, naked language, worthy of the poet of *Paradise Lost*, although it discovers him in another aspect, was a noble conclusion to Milton's poetic career. It confirms what was evident from the first, that his work proceeded from a pride which reached sublimity and from an heroic egoism. It proceeded also from his incomparable art, shown equally, although diversely, in the delicate rhymed poetry of his youth and in the powerful blank verse of his maturity.

The appearance of these later poems in a dissolute, cynical time, incapable of feeling either poetic sublimity or religious exaltation, was strange. Milton was the last survivor of the great age.

A gulf, perhaps deeper than that between the English Middle Ages and the Renascence, separates the Renascence from modern times. But what a marvellous transformation was accomplished in the century which intervened between the appearance of the first works of Spenser and Sidney, in 1579, and the last works of Milton, in 1671! The country which hitherto had always received the impulse to literature from abroad had become proudly conscious of her strength and originality. She had given birth not only to a multitude of men of varied talents, but also to a line of geniuses truly her own, in whom she henceforth admired herself and who were gradually admitted throughout Europe to a place in the very first rank of artists. Such was their prestige that even the revolution of taste and the appearance of new doctrines could not long or deeply modify their sovereignty. After the Restoration period, during which they were, it is true, unknown or despised with few exceptions, their memory prepared the way, throughout the eighteenth century, for the imaginative renewal which led finally to Romanticism. Distance increased their stature and they came to dominate English literature. Rich though this literature be in admirable writers, it has never produced any to surpass Bacon or Spenser, to attain to the same height as Milton, or to approach, even from afar, the place whence the light of Shakespeare shines on all the world.

END OF VOL. I

INDEX

INDEX

This index contains the names of the writers referred to in the text. It does not include the critics, commentators and editors who figure in the notes, nor (with a few exceptions) the historical personages mentioned in the course of the work.

Titles of anonymous works, of works of doubtful authorship and of works written in collaboration will be found printed in italics. For all others, the reference is to the name of the author.

Principal references are denoted by figures in heavy type.

MADE AT THE
TEMPLE PRESS LETCHWORTH
IN GREAT BRITAIN